Liberty, Slavery, and Conquest:
A History of the American People

Volume I ∞ to 1877

8/e

Project Development Manager: Brae Buhnerkemper

Project Development Assistant: Brandi Cornwell

Managing Editor: Joyce Bianchini

Photo Researcher: Michelle Hipkins

Design and Illustrations: Rachel Weathersbee

Typesetter: Suzanne Schmidt

Text and Cover Printing: Quad Graphics

Sales Manager: Robert Rappeport

Marketing Manager: Richard Schofield

Permissions Coordinator: Della Brackett

Art Director: Esther Scannell

ISBN: 978-1-60229-956-6

Liberty, Slavery, and Conquest: A History of the American People

Volume I ⌘ to 1877

8E

CARL N. DEGLER
Stanford University

VINCENT P. DE SANTIS
University of Notre Dame

BRIAN FARMER
Amarillo College

HEATHER E. BARRY
St. Joseph's College

BVT
PUBLISHING

Custom Publishing Division

iStockphoto

Brief Contents

Table of Contents

AP Wide World Photo

3 Resistance, Revolution and Independence, 1763–1783   85

Wikipedia photo

iStockphoto (frame)

4 Establishing the Republic, 1781–1800   133

5 The Jeffersonian Era, 1800–1824

Library of Congress

8 Westward Expansion, 1824–1854   305

9 The Nation at Mid-Century   333

iStockphoto (frame)

Wikipedia photo

Library of Congress

iStockphoto (frame)

10 The Sectional Crisis, 1848–1861   371

11 The War Between the States, 1861–1865   421

iStockphoto (frame)

Wikipedia photo

12 Reconstruction, 1863–1877 469

Appendix 502

Index 520

MAP OF

NORTH AMERICA,

INCLUDING PART OF THE

WEST INDIA ISLANDS.

LONDON:
Published by C. SMITH, Mapseller, No. 172, Strand.
1849.

List of
Maps & Charts

List of Maps & Charts (cont'd)

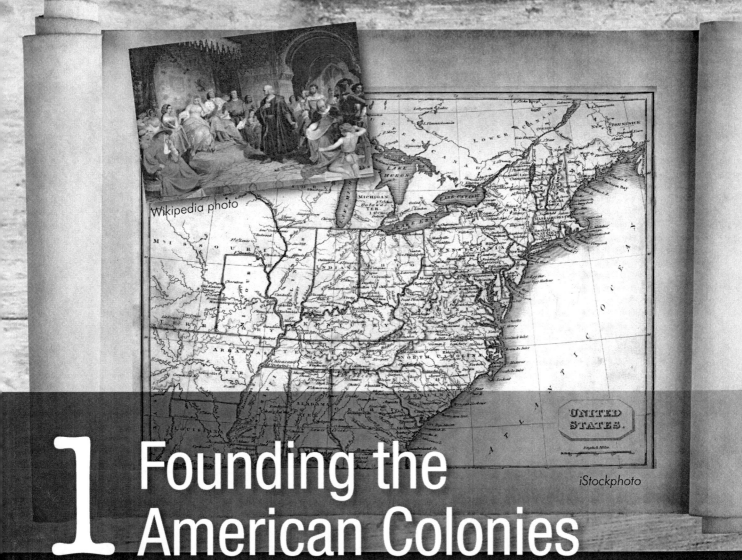
Wikipedia photo

iStockphoto

1 Founding the American Colonies

Outline

iStockphoto

Wikipedia photo

shutterstock

iStockphoto

iStockphoto

       3. Puritan Child-rearing practices

       4. Witchcraft in Puritan society

       5. Early Quakers

       6. Mature Quakers

  K. Puritan Society

  L. Puritan Success

  M. The Spreading Colonies of New England

  N. Puritanism

  O. Puritans and Human Nature

  P. Puritan View of the Bible

  Q. Puritans and Free Thought

  R. Hutchinson Heresy

  S. Puritans and Quaker Persecution

  T. Puritans and Witches

  U. Witches of Salem Village

  V. Puritans and the Natives

  W. The Capture of New York

  X. The Jerseys

  Y. "The Holy Experiment"

  Z. Quakers

  AA. Quaker Laws

  BB. Pennsylvania Economy and Growth

  CC. Settlement of the Carolinas

  DD. Carolina Economy

  EE. The Division of Carolina

  FF. Georgia

IV. Colonial Economy

  A. New England

  B. The Southern Colonies

  C. The Mid-Atlantic Colonies

  D. English Regulatory Acts

  E. Conflict with the Native Americans

Those Who Came First

Before the officially documented arrival of Christopher Columbus in 1492, there were approximately four million indigenous people organized into a multiplicity of tribes and speaking hundreds of discrete languages in what would become the United States. Clearly, humans had inhabited the Western Hemisphere thousands of years before Columbus. The exact date of the arrival of the first Americans is in dispute, but historians generally believe that they arrived somewhere between 15,000 and 20,000 years ago. Although prior to the twentieth century, historians believed that the earliest humans had only arrived in North America 3,000–4,000 years ago, a discovery was made in 1908 proved that humans had arrived in North America thousands of years earlier. The artifacts that were found from these early Americans were nineteen flint spear points discovered near Folsom, New Mexico, amid the bones of a giant bison, a species that had already been extinct for 10,000 years when the remains were found. One of the spear points was still stuck between the ribs of this extinct giant bison, thus proving that the spear points had not been dropped on the site at a later date. These "Folsom Points" provided evidence that the first Americans had migrated to the Western Hemisphere at least 10,000 years ago.

The Anasazi

When they arrived in the Southwest in the fifteenth century, the Navajos called the people who had inhabited the region earlier the Anasazi—or "ancient ones." Ancestors of the modern Pueblos, the Anasazi lived in the Four Corners region where the states of Arizona, New Mexico, Utah, and Colorado come together. They learned how to grow their crops of corn, beans, and squash in this arid region in such a way as to take advantage of virtually every precious drop of rainfall. They built irrigation devices to improve their chances of watering the crops adequately. Moreover, archeologists have discovered parrot feathers among their remains, items that could only have originated some 1,500 miles to the south in Mesoamerica. This evidence suggests that the Anasazi traded with those who were a long way away. Further, there is compelling evidence that the Anasazi knew how to keep track of key dates, such as the solstices, because various ruins contain spirals pierced by a dagger of sunlight at noon on the day in question. And finally, some four hundred miles of roads in one of the most important Anasazi regions, Chaco Canyon in New Mexico, attest to a complex web of interconnectedness within the region itself. The Anasazi road system connected Chaco Canyon to more than seventy outlying villages. Several of the Anasazi roads were almost one hundred miles long.

But it is their buildings that have captivated the succeeding generations since the first Euro-Americans discovered those structures in the late nineteenth century. Some were built into hillsides, hence the term "cliff-dweller" that has been used to characterize the Anasazi. Others were free-standing and built on a scale that suggests a people with a sophisticated social structure. The largest complex is called Pueblo Bonito, and it is located in Chaco Culture National Historical Park. With at least 650 rooms and stretching up to

▶ The Cliff Palace is the largest cliff dwelling in North America. The structure was built by the Ancient Pueblo Peoples in Colorado, in the Southwestern United States. *Wikipedia photo*

four stories, Pueblo Bonito poses many mysteries: Was it an apartment complex? A ceremonial center? A storehouse for supplies? What is certain is that the people who built it included master architects and skilled masons.

Beginning around 300 B.C.E., the Anasazi culture flourished for more than a millennium. But then, for reasons still unknown, the Anasazi abandoned their carefully constructed dwellings around 1150 C.E. and moved on. Generations of archeologists have wrestled with explanations, which include environmental stress, conflict, and soil exhaustion.

The Mound-Builders

In contrast to the Anasazi, the people who lived in the Mississippi watershed enjoyed an environment that was lush, with abundant water and a temperate climate. What the two groups had in common, however, was their ambitious building projects, developed around the same time, 900–1100. At the largest Mound-builder settlement—at Cahokia, located in Illinois just across the Mississippi from St. Louis—there were more than one hundred earthen mounds used for ceremonial purposes. The principal one, Monks Mound, is the largest prehistoric earthen construction in the Western Hemisphere, rising one hundred feet with a base spreading over fourteen acres. It is believed that these Native Americans were sun worshipers and the purpose of the mounds was to elevate elites nearer to the divine power of the sun. Sun calendars have been unearthed at this site, too, as well as many other evidences of a complex social organization with powerful chiefs. In one mound, a man, presumably the chief, was buried with the bodies of more than sixty people who were evidently executed at the time of the chief's burial. Several bodies, thought to be either servants or enemies, were buried with their hands cut off. Also in the mound are the bodies of fifty young women, presumably wives, who evidently had been strangled. The entire Cahokia site encompasses almost twenty acres and it is estimated that it was once home to 20,000 people, easily the largest settlement in North America prior to Columbus.

Also known as the "Mississippians," these people had a well-developed agricultural system, once again based on corn, beans, and squash. They were able to supplement this diet with animal protein, because of abundant game and fish, and consequently had a good enough food supply that they could construct cities, with houses built around plazas. They, too, engaged in extensive trade, and they abandoned their sites—circa 1500—for reasons which are not fully known. The contributing factors may have been some combination of war, disease, and depletion of natural resources.

The Iroquois

The Iroquois, a group who came into intense contact with Europeans, was comprised of the Seneca, Cayuga, Oneida, Onondaga, and Mohawk people. They lived in large villages in the woodlands of what is now New York and Ontario, Canada. Their success in the cultivation of corn and other crops allowed them to build permanent settlements of bark-covered longhouses, some up to one hundred feet in length that housed as many as ten families. Women were the primary agriculturalists, while male jobs centered on hunting and on frequent warfare. Iroquoian societies were also matrilineal, with property of all sorts, not limited to, but including land, children, and inheritance, belonging to women. Women were considered the heads of households and family clans and selected the male chiefs that governed tribes. Jesuit priests who lived among them in New France were much struck by their culture, including the close attention they paid to dreams, and by child-rearing practices that seemed overly permissive to Europeans.

But it was their breakthrough in political organization for which they are best-known. One hundred or so years before the Europeans arrived, there was apparently a substantial enough population increase among the Iroquois that they began to put pressure on the hunting grounds of neighboring groups such as the Algonquian. Not surprisingly, this led to even more frequent warfare. Scholars believe that it was this increase that led the Iro-

▶ Pictured are deer-like creatures which were totem symbols of the Iroquois, a confederacy of Five Nations. *iStockphoto*

quois to form a confederacy for mutual defense. In the early sixteenth century a prophet by the name of Deganawida appeared among them. He and his chief disciple, Hiawatha, preached the benefits of unity and peace, and this persuaded the Iroquois to form a Great League of Peace and Power.

Background to Colonization
The Beginnings of European Expansion

America had been "discovered" by Europeans as early as 1000 C.E., when the Vikings dominated northern Europe and the northern Atlantic. Yet their adventures did not stimulate European expansion into the Americas. Obviously, a significant change had taken place in Western Europe by the time of Columbus's voyage in 1492, not only making overseas expansion possible but also instilling an adventurous spirit among Europeans so that they were eager to explore different lands and new opportunities.

Wikipedia photo

Portugal was the first nation bordering the Atlantic to engage in wide-scale exploration, especially along the western coast of Africa. This primacy was not accidental. Portugal was the first of the Atlantic nations to be unified, giving its leaders an opportunity to look outward rather than to be preoccupied with internal disorder. Portugal in the fifteenth century enjoyed internal peace and reasonably efficient government at a time that most of Europe was beset by war and internal upheaval. Portugal's location at the intersection of the Mediterranean and Atlantic also made the Portuguese look outward to the maritime possibilities. The Portuguese were aware that Arab caravans crossed the Sahara to bring back gold, slaves, and ivory from sub-Saharan Africa. Arab traders also spoke of how the Mandingo King Musa of Mali controlled more gold than anyone in Europe. The Portuguese believed that an Atlantic voyage to points on the West African coast south of the Sahara could tap into Africa's riches and undercut the Arab traders.

Among the most forward-looking of the Portuguese leaders was Prince Henry the Navigator (1394–1460), who established a center for the study of cartography and astronomy and for the improvement of ships and seamanship. The Portuguese studied the Arab ships and borrowed from the Arab designs and improved upon them. The Portuguese increased the ratio of length to width from a standard 2:1 ratio to 3:1, borrowed the lateen (triangular) sail from the Arabs, and created a new kind of ship called the *Caravel,* of which the *Nina,* used on Columbus' first voyage, was one. The Portuguese also learned how to mount heavy cannon on their ships, made full use of the compass, and borrowed the astrolabe from the Arabs, a device that permitted calculation of latitude from looking at the stars. Prince Henry sponsored some fifteen voyages along the African coast and launched Portugal's era of expansion.

The Portuguese began colonization efforts when they took possession of the uninhabited Madeira Islands off the northwest coast of Africa in 1418, the Azores due west of Portugal in 1427, and the Cape Verde Islands off of Africa's west coast in 1450.

Beginning in the 1440s, the Portuguese colonists began using African slave labor on sugar plantations and in vineyards on their new colonial possessions. The Portuguese would purchase their slaves from African traders who often sold their captured enemies that they had gained through tribal warfare. The Portuguese were thus able to build a profitable slave trade by exploiting rivalries between the tribes on the West African coast. Slavery, and the agricultural products that were profitably produced through the use of slave labor, became a major impetus to overseas exploration. For the first three hundred years after Columbus, the majority of persons that came to the Western Hemisphere were not Europeans, but African slaves brought to the Americas to provide the labor for sugar, rice, indigo, tobacco, and later cotton plantations.

Because of the profits afforded from slavery, along with African gold, Portuguese exploration could continue to expand throughout the fifteenth century so that by the 1480s Portugal sought a water route to Asia around the tip of Africa. Portugal was eventually rewarded when Bartholomew Diaz rounded Africa's southernmost Cape of Good Hope in 1488 and when Vasco da Gama reached India by way of the Cape of Good Hope in 1498. Da Gama's voyage lasted over two years but resulted in large profits for the spices that Da Gama eventually brought back to Portugal from India. Subsequent Portuguese sailors would eventually trade in both Japan and Indonesia.

Settlement of the lands where the Portuguese traded, however, was not a major Portuguese goal. Only when Pedro Alvares Cabral accidentally discovered Brazil in 1500 (he was blown off course while trying to round the Cape of Good Hope) did the Portuguese attempt to settle a far away land where their mariners traded.

Successful overseas expansion required the support of a stable government and a unified nation-state. The significance of national unity was underscored when Columbus' voyage in 1492 coincided with the expulsion of the Islamic Moors from Spain by the capture of Granada by Spanish soldiers. For the first time in centuries, the entire Iberian Peninsula was united under Christian rulers. Columbus' voyage, sailing west to reach the fabulous riches of the East, marked the great historical divide which eventually made the Atlantic rather than the Mediterranean the principal artery of trade and communication.

Catastrophe and Conquest

European contact with the indigenous population in the late fifteenth century caused a demographic catastrophe. Millions of Native Americans died as a result of European diseases. The culprit was microbes carrying the deadly diseases of smallpox, measles, and influenza. Europeans unintentionally brought these diseases with them to the Americas, which resulted in a demographic catastrophe. The implications of this catastrophe were vast and infiltrated the entire Native American society. The death by disease was a tragic beginning for America and the next stage involved conquest and slavery. These diseases ameliorated European conquest of the Americas.

MAP 1.1 Columbus' Voyage in 1492

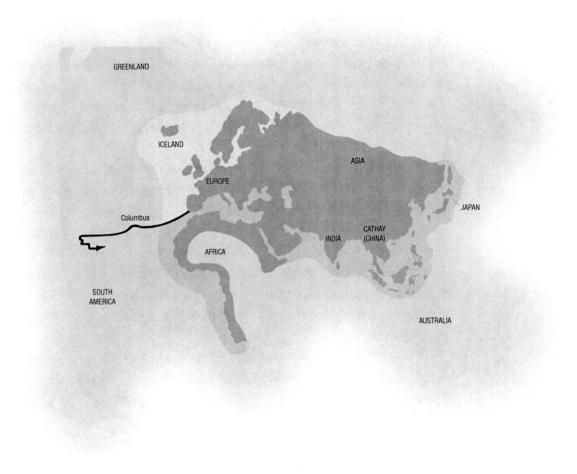

Cultural Misunderstanding

WAR   Contact that occurred between Europeans and Native Americans caused many points of cultural misunderstanding. How and why both groups fought wars was one such point of misunderstanding. North American Native Americans fought wars to replenish their numbers by adopting conquered peoples. Therefore, the war strategies that Native Americans used involved killing as few people as possible. Native American battles involved only adult male fighters and saved the women and children so they could be adopted into the group. The captured warriors, however, were tortured to death by their captives. Native American acts of torture appalled Europeans and led them to believe the Native Americans were "uncivilized" and "barbaric."

European warfare also appalled Native Americans. European warfare occurred on an open battlefield and the objective was to kill as many people as possible. Native Americans considered this tactic a waste of lives and they believed the gods would be sure to punish Europeans for wasting so many souls. In addition, Europeans introduced the tactic of killing women and children to instill fear in Native Americans. native Americans did not understand this form of warfare. Warfare was a major point of cultural misunderstanding between these groups.

GENDER   Another point of cultural misunderstanding between Native Americans and Europeans involved gender. Women in Native American society owned most moveable property, cultivated the land, and held considerable power. Women in European societies owned very limited property, rarely farmed the land, and held limited political power. Because men were responsible for cultivating the land in European society, Native Americans considered European men to be "feminine." On the contrary, Europeans considered Native American men lazy since they "let" their women farm the land. Both sides misunderstood each other's cultural practices.

Factors in English Expansion

Although John Cabot, representing the English crown, explored the eastern coast of North America within a decade of Columbus' voyage, (1497) successful English settlement was delayed for a century. Cabot landed on the North American coast, perhaps at Newfoundland or Labrador, but did not journey further than the range of a crossbow from the shore line. The English would not attempt to establish a settlement in North America until 1583 when Henry Gilbert led an expedition to Newfoundland. Though Gilbert was successful in at least landing on the coast of Newfoundland, he proceeded along the coast of the Island in search of a good place for a military outpost when he became caught in a storm and was lost at sea, thus leaving England without a North American colony.

▶ Sir Walter Raleigh dispatched two groups to the island of Roanoke. The first expedition experienced irreconcilable difficulties with the natives, and the second disappeared mysteriously. *Corbis Images*

The Lost Colony of Roanoke

Undeterred by Gilbert's failure, in 1585 Sir Walter Raleigh dispatched a group under the command of Richard Grenville to an island called Roanoke off the coast of North Carolina. The English experienced problems with the Natives almost immediately as the English accused the Natives of theft of a silver cup. In retaliation, the English destroyed a Native village, leading to enmity with the Natives. When Sir Francis Drake arrived on Roanoke in the spring of 1586, the colonists boarded his ship and abandoned the colony. The next year (1587), Raleigh dispatched another expedition of ninety-one men, seventeen women, and nine children that he hoped would begin a successful plantation. Shortly after arrival, one of the women gave birth to a daughter, Virginia

Dare, the first person born in North America to English parents. Dare's grandfather, John White, returned to England a few weeks after her birth to recruit more settlers and bring more supplies. When he returned to Roanoke in 1590, he found the island deserted and no clues to the fate of the settlers other than the inscription "Croatoan" carved on a post.

Theories abound as to what happened to the settlers. Some argue that they were all killed in a war with the Native Americans. Others argue that they were adopted by the Natives and then taken off the island. Perhaps segments of both theories are correct, but no conclusive evidence has ever been found to prove either. In any case, it would be twenty years before another English group would attempt to establish a colony in North America.

In spite of the failure at Roanoke, other factors would lead to further English colonial attempts in North America. The economic, religious, and political factors that led to the establishment of the English colonies were entirely different from those that had influenced the Spanish colonies. Two significant economic changes were in trade and agriculture. Whereas few trading companies flourished before 1500, over two hundred English trading companies operated aggressively by 1600, including the Muscovy Company (1553), the Levant Company (1592), and the famous East India Company (1600). In 1500 German and Italian merchants dominated English trade. By 1600 this domination had been eliminated and a strong group of English merchants had emerged. In 1500 most of the raw wool raised in England was shipped to Flanders to be made into cloth. By 1600 an English textile industry in England absorbed much of the wool produced in England.

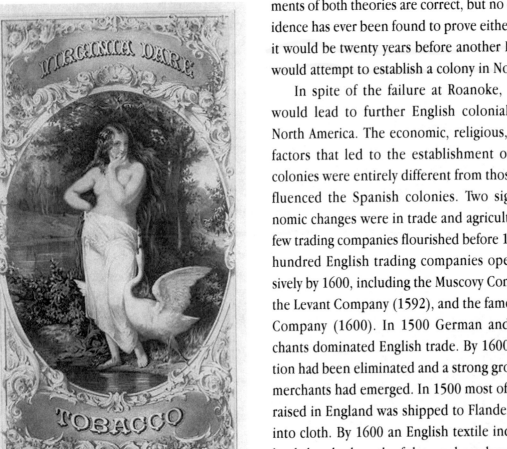

▶ A tobacco brand was named for Virginia Dare, the first person born in North America to English parents. *Wikipedia photo*

These economic changes had a direct effect upon the development of the English colonies. The first three successful English colonies in America—Virginia, Plymouth, and Massachusetts Bay—were planted by cooperatively owned joint-stock companies, precursors of modern corporations, in which a number of investors pooled their capital. Many of those engaged in the American enterprises had gained their experience in trading companies elsewhere, and they continued to participate in trading enterprises throughout the world.

The experience in trade influenced mercantilist thought in England. Mercantilism embodied a set of economic ideas held throughout Western Europe from 1500 to 1800, though the precise measures taken differed from country to country. The mercantilist advocated that the economic affairs of the nation should be regulated to encourage the development of a strong state. A number of propositions were

MAP 1.2 Voyage of Exploration

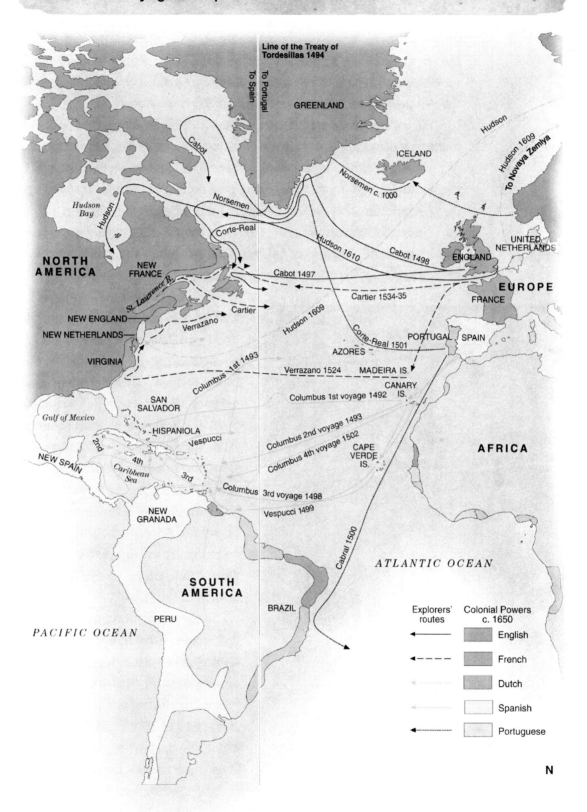

Line of the Treaty of Tordesillas 1494

To Spain
To Portugal

GREENLAND

ICELAND

Hudson
Hudson 1609
To Novaya Zemlya

Norsemen c. 1000

Cabot

Hudson
Bay

Hudson

Norsemen

Corte-Real

Hudson 1610

Cabot 1498

UNITED
NETHERLANDS

ENGLAND

NORTH
AMERICA

NEW
FRANCE

Cabot 1497

EUROPE

Cartier 1534-35

FRANCE

St. Lawrence R.

Cartier

Corte-Real 1501

PORTUGAL   SPAIN

NEW ENGLAND

Verrazano

Hudson 1609

AZORES

NEW NETHERLANDS

Verrazano 1524   MADEIRA IS.

VIRGINIA

Columbus 1st 1493

CANARY
IS.

Columbus 1st voyage 1492

SAN
SALVADOR

Gulf of Mexico

HISPANIOLA

Columbus 2nd voyage 1493

2nd

Vespucci

Columbus 4th voyage 1502

CAPE
VERDE
IS.

AFRICA

NEW SPAIN

4th
Caribbean
Sea

3rd

Columbus 3rd voyage 1498

NEW
GRANADA

Vespucci 1499

Cabral 1500

ATLANTIC OCEAN

SOUTH
AMERICA

BRAZIL

PERU

PACIFIC OCEAN

Explorers' routes	Colonial Powers c. 1650	
←		English
◄ - - -		French
◄ ······		Dutch
◄ -------		Spanish
◄ ·········		Portuguese

N

customarily included in this policy. A nation could become stronger by exporting more than it imported, resulting in a "favorable balance of trade." National self-sufficiency should be encouraged by subsidy of domestic manufactures. A nation's wealth was to be measured by the amount of precious metals it could obtain (thus the emphasis on the accumulation of bullion). Labor should be regulated for the wellbeing and benefit of the state. And colonies should be established to provide the nation with raw materials that it was unable to produce.

Although this does not exhaust the list of propositions supported by mercantilist thinkers, it does show that trade was considered one of the most important measures of a nation's wealth and that colonies were valued because they contributed to that wealth. In England the mercantile emphasis between 1500 and 1600 was upon internal regulation. After 1600 the emphasis was on external regulation, particularly the commercial relationship of England to its colonies. The phenomenal increase in English mercantile activity not only provided an agency—the joint-stock company—to create colonies but also provided a national purpose for doing so.

▶ With Parliament's help, King Henry VIII of England broke with the Roman Catholic Church and established the Church of England, which made him the ecclesiastical sovereign of England. *Wikipedia photo*

A second significant economic change took place in agriculture. Between 1500 and 1600 an enclosure movement gained strength in Britain. Essentially, "enclosure" meant that smaller landholdings in certain areas of England were incorporated into larger holdings, forcing some people off the land. The result was a dislocation of population that caused many political thinkers to conclude that England was overpopulated and that, therefore, almost anyone should be permitted to go to the Americas to reduce "overpopulation." Spain, by contrast, had restricted immigration to selected individuals favored by the crown.

In the sixteenth century the Protestant Reformation swept through Europe and profoundly affected the religious and political development of England, which in turn placed an enduring stamp upon its colonies in America. In 1500 England was within the fold of the Roman Catholic Church. Mostly for political reasons in the 1530s, the King of England, Henry VIII, believed it was necessary to create a state church, the Church of England, and forsake the Roman Catholic Church. For political reasons, Henry VIII enlisted the aid of Parliament. Parliament passed a series of enactments creating a national church, culminating in the Act of Supremacy (1534), which made Henry, instead of the pope, the ecclesiastical sovereign of England. Eventually, by means of parliamentary acts, lands in England belonging to the Roman Catholic Church were taken over by the king, greatly enhancing his wealth.

The ramifications of these actions infiltrated almost every sphere of English life, but two had the most effect on the colonies: (1) The king, by utilizing the support of Parliament, demonstrated that in practice the authority of the crown was limited, a concept carried to the English colonies in America and a concept in direct contrast to Spanish doctrine, which held the power of the sovereign to be without restriction; and (2) the break with the Roman Catholic Church opened the way for a wide diversity of religious groups in England but more so in the colonies.

Some people, believing that separation from the Roman Catholic Church should never have taken place, remained Roman Catholics. Others believed that Henry VIII and, later, Elizabeth I had not gone far enough. Puritans, an ardent and vocal minority, believed that the Reformation in England had stopped short of its goal, that ritual should be further simplified, and that the authority of crown-appointed bishops should be lessened. However, they resolved to stay within the Church of England and attempt to achieve their goals—that is, "purify" the church—without a division. Another group formed and they were Separatists, a small minority, who believed that each congregation should become its own judge of religious orthodoxy. They were no more willing to give allegiance to the crown than they had been to give it to the pope.

This religious factionalism was transferred to the American colonies. Of the first four settlements, Virginia was Anglican, Plymouth was Separatist, Massachusetts Bay was Puritan, and Maryland was Roman Catholic.

Early in the seventeenth century, a number of English "dissenters"—men and women who were dissatisfied with political, economic, or religious conditions in England—were ready to migrate to the Americas and English trading companies provided an agency for settlement.

The English Settlements

One hundred fifteen years after Columbus, the English had not established a single permanent foothold in the Western Hemisphere. As late as 1600, although they had made several voyages and two attempts at settlement, they had not one colony to show for their efforts. By 1700, however, some twenty colonies, with some 350,000 inhabitants, stretched all the way from Newfoundland on the North Atlantic to the island of Barbados in the southern Caribbean. Heavy losses originally deterred growth, but promoters and settlers learned to adjust to the new environment.

iStockphoto

Founding Virginia

The first permanent English colony in America was Virginia, begun at Jamestown in 1607. In 1606, King James I granted a group of London merchants the privilege of establishing colonies in "the part of America commonly called Virginia." Securing a charter, this Virginia Company of London raised sufficient funds by the sale of shares to outfit three ships. The *Godspeed*, *Discovery*, and *Susan Constant* sailed with 144 men to Virginia, where on May 24, 1607, the 104 men and boys that survived the voyage established a settlement, Jamestown—a peninsula extending from the banks of the James River. Unfortunately, the colonists did not choose their site wisely. The peninsula was low and swampy, in addition to being hot and humid in the summer, resulting in an abundance of mosquitoes that caused malaria outbreaks among the colonists. The site was chosen, however, because it appeared to be a good place to build a defensible fort, and the colonists wanted to avoid the Native American attacks that were believed to have destroyed the ill-fated colony at Roanoke.

The early Jamestown settlers had no experience in colonization. Many of them had come for adventure rather than from any desire to become permanent residents in the wilderness. They knew nothing of subsistence farming and displayed little ingenuity. Approximately a third of the original colonists were "gentlemen" who were, in the words of John Smith, "averse to work." Another third of the colonists were criminals who had been given a second chance in the New World.

MAP 1.3 Migrations from England Before 1640

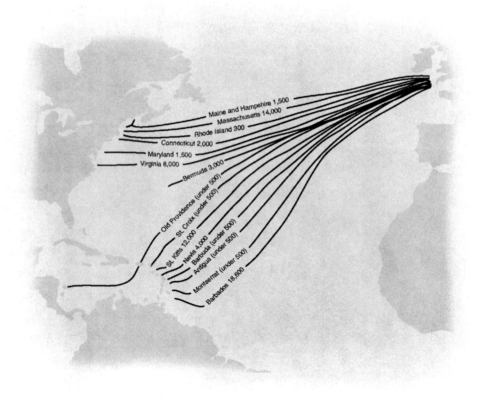

They too, according to Smith, were averse to work. Although the James River teemed with fish, they nearly perished for want of food. Instead of fishing and engaging in agricultural pursuits, the colonists spent their time on fruitless hunts for gold. Of the 104 that had landed in Jamestown in May, only thirty-eight survived until a ship full of supplies arrived in January, and even that many might not have survived if it were not for the Native Americans offering to barter food for English goods in the fall of 1607. This pattern of failure and death would continue over the next several years as new colonists arrived. Of the first five thousand people who migrated to Virginia, fewer than one thousand survived. The winter of 1609–1610 was particularly harsh and became known as the "starving time." John Smith had alienated the natives by raiding their food supplies, and the natives retaliated by killing off the livestock in the woods and keeping the colonists barricaded within their settlement. The English lived by eating dogs, cats, rats, snakes, toadstools, horsehides, and even cannibalizing the bodies of the dead. One man reportedly sat and watched his wife die and then quickly chopped up her body and salted down the pieces. The man was executed for eating what Smith referred to as "powdered wife." The English imposed draconian laws for stealing food, including the death penalty for stealing a bunch of grapes. One man was nailed to a tree by the tongue for stealing three pints of oatmeal.

Reorganization

Upon their arrival in Jamestown, leadership of the colony had been divided between several members of an ineffective ruling council. In the fall of 1608, however, John Smith became the council president and imposed his will on the community. Smith traded with the Native Americans for food when he could, but organized raids to steal their food at other times. He also kidnapped natives and forced them to explain to the English how to plant corn. In 1609, Smith returned to England after suffering a severe powder burn. Smith's successors, Sir Thomas Dale and Sir Thomas Gates, imposed harsh discipline, organizing settlers into work gangs and sentencing offenders to flogging, hanging, or being broken on the wheel. The Virginia Company raised money by selling stock and encouraged immigrants by providing free passage to the New World for people who would serve the Company for seven years. Eventually, Dale decided that colonists would work harder if he permitted private ownership of land. Still, life in Virginia was harsh, and mortality rates remained high. Over nine thousand people immigrated between 1610 and 1622, but the population was only two thousand in 1622.

Gradually, the Jamestown colonists devised ways of making a livelihood. John Rolfe developed the skill of growing tobacco prof-

► Tobacco was a profitable crop in the New World and was in high demand in Europe. By 1700, thirty-five million pounds of tobacco had been exported from Chesapeake Bay. *iStockphoto*

itably and planted the first tobacco crop in 1612. Rolfe's contribution ensured Virginia's prosperity, for tobacco was a commodity much in demand in Europe after its introduction from the New World. The first commercial shipment of tobacco reached England in 1617. In 1620, the colony with fewer than a thousand residents sent sixty thousand pounds of tobacco across the waters. By 1700, there were approximately one hundred thousand colonists in Chesapeake Bay, and they exported thirty-five million pounds of tobacco. The Virginia colony was finally an economic success, but one built on smoke. Even King James I denounced tobacco as "loathsome to the eye, hateful to the nose, harmful to the brain, and dangerous to the lungs" but it failed to slow the expansion of tobacco exports.

Indentured Servitude

Tobacco is a labor-intensive crop and successful cultivation required Virginia planters to find a reliable supply of low-cost labor. To fill this need, Virginia tobacco growers turned to indentured servants, who willingly sold themselves into a form of temporary slavery for a set number of years (normally four years) in exchange for passage to the New World. In the seventeenth century 80 percent of the immigrants to the Chesapeake colonies came as indentured servants. Approximately 75 percent were single males under the age of twenty-five.

Life for indentured servants in the seventeenth century Chesapeake colonies was harsh. Approximately half of the indentured servants died before fulfilling their indenture contract and securing their freedom. The harsh working conditions of the tobacco plantations, along with tropical diseases, decimated the indentured workforce. Masters often cared only if their servants survived the years of their contracts and thus worked them from "can" (can see or sunrise) to "can't" (can't see or sundown). Indentured servants could also be sold for the remainders of the contracts, and therefore had no control over whom they might work for. Masters were even known to gamble away indentured servants in card games. Women could also be sold into indenture, and therefore often endured sexual abuse from mas-

▶ In the seventeenth century, 80 percent of immigrants came to the New World as indentured servants. Servants willingly sold themselves into slavery, (by signing a contract, such as the above example) in exchange for passage to the New World. *Wikipedia photo*

ters. To make matters worse, women had time added to their indenture contracts (two years) for pregnancy and childbirth. Time was also added for both men and women for attempting to run away or committing crimes, such as stealing food or livestock. Women could be released from indenture through marriage if prospective grooms had the resources with which to purchase their indenture contracts; hence, many indentured women actively sought husbands. Both women and men received compensation at the end of their indenture contracts in the form of one suit of clothing and one barrel of corn. The more important benefit, of course, was the freedom to seek one's own economic prosperity in the New World.

Pocahontas

Pocahontas was the daughter of the Native American chief Powhatan, who became famous both for saving the life of John Smith and for marrying the English tobacco planter John Rolfe and thus securing a temporary peace between the English and the Native Americans. Shortly after arriving in Jamestown, in December 1607, John Smith wrote that he was "feasted by the Indians according to their best, barbarous manner" and then taken and held down upon a rock where a native with a large rock threatened to "beat out his braines." Right before the native was to crush his skull, Pocahontas, whom Smith described as a "well featured, but wanton young girl," probably eleven years old, placed her own head on the rock next to Smith's so as to save him from certain death. Smith wrote that Pocahontas "hazarded the beating out of her own braines" to save his. Instead of a story of romance, however, historians generally interpret the story as part of a staged ceremony that signified Powhatan's power over the life and death of Smith. Instead of a love story, it was most likely a staged ceremony of subordination.

In a raid on Powhatan's camp, the English eventually captured Pocahontas in 1613. When Powhatan refused English ransom demands, Pocahontas remained with the English, converted to Christianity, and married the English tobacco planter, John Rolfe. After giving birth to a son, Thomas Rolfe, Pocahontas accompanied Rolfe back to England in 1616 and became known as a gracious woman in English society. Unfortunately, her life in England was short-lived as Pocahontas died of European diseases in 1617, probably at the age of twenty-one.

Religion in Jamestown

Jamestown's Charter declared that the Anglican Church would be the official state religion of the colony and that bringing Christianity to the Natives was the true purpose of the colony. John Smith, however, debunked this facade by stating, "it was absurd to cloak under the guise of religion the true intentions of profit." Smith added that what quickened

▶ Instead of a romance, historians generally interpret the story of Pocahontas and John Smith as part of a staged ceremony that signified Powhatan's power over the life and death of Smith; a ceremony of subordination. *Wikipedia photo*

the heart of most Chesapeake folk was "a close horse race, a bloody cock fight, or a fine tobacco crop." The religion of Jamestown was officially Anglican, but the passion of the people was most certainly tobacco, which was not only the primary source of income but smoked constantly by virtually all inhabitants. Still, most of the colonists of Jamestown were nominally Anglican and attendance at Sunday services and conformity to Anglican doctrines were required of all Virginia colonists. The Anglicans officially did not allow religious dissent; and Baptists, Presbyterians, Catholics, Quakers, and other "heretics" were persecuted, whipped, fined, imprisoned, and forced to financially support the Anglican Church through a church tax. Anglican Church Courts punished fornicators, blasphemers, and served notice on those who spent Sundays "goeing a fishing." Fines were imposed for fornication, and in 1662, a law was passed making the fine double if one were caught fornicating with a Negro.

Governing Virginia

In governing the colony, the Virginia Company at first adopted a policy of having severe laws administered by a strong-armed governor. After this failed, it made the momentous decision to let the settlers share in their own government. When Governor George Yeardley arrived in Virginia in 1619, he carried instructions to call annually an assembly to consist of two members, or burgesses, from the various local units in the colony. These burgesses were to be elected by property owning citizens. This assembly, which met in the church at Jamestown in the summer of 1619, was the first representative law-making body in English America. Even in 1624, when the Virginia Company at last succumbed to bankruptcy and lost its charter, with the result that Virginia became a royal colony, the company's greatest contribution was preserved intact: the Virginia House of Burgesses continued to meet.

Life in the Chesapeake region revolved around tobacco. Tobacco governed the economy, the trade, immigration, patterns of settlement, standards of living, and government policy. Male indentured servants dominated immigration and the labor force until decades surrounding 1700. An estimated average ratio of men to women in the seventeenth-century Chesapeake was 5:1. Most people in the region were single, men, indentured servants, born in England, married late in life, and died early. The environment in the region led to the development of a very different type of society than life in England.

Few seventeenth-century women emigrated to the Chesapeake region. Women who did were on average 20 years old and indentured to a master for 4–5 years. Their work as indentured servants depended on the master's position and could range from household duties to working in tobacco fields. Women went to the region for husbands, most likely because their prospects in England were limited. The experience women had varied but many died of diseases, such as dysentery, influenza, and malaria. There were also stiff penalties for women who became pregnant before completing their term of service. Punishments ranged from heavy fines, whippings, and years added to their contract. If a woman survived her term of service, she became a planter's wife and bore an average of 4–5 children, but only about 2 children lived to adulthood.

A LAW
OF
MARYLAND
Concerning
RELIGION.

Oraſ much as io a well-governed and Chriſtian Commonwealth, Matters concerning Religion and the Honour of God ought to be in the firſt pla e to be taken into ſerious conſideration, and endeavoured to be ſettled. Be it therefore Ordained and Enacted by the Right Honourable CÆCILIUS Lord Baron of *Baltemore*, abſolute Lord and Proprietary of this Province, with the Advice and Conſent of the Upper and Lower Houſe of this General Aſſembly, That whatſoever perſon or perſons within this Province and the Iſlands thereunto belonging, ſhall fro n henceforth blaſpheme GOD, that is curſe him ; or ſhall deny our Saviour JESUS CHRIST to be the Son of God ; or ſhall deny the Holy Trinity, the Father, Son, & Holy Ghoſt, or the Godhead of any of the ſaid Three Perſons of the Trinity, or the Unity of the Godhead, or ſhall uſe or utter any reproachful ſpeeches, words, or language, concerning the Holy Trinity, or any of the ſaid three Perſons thereof, ſhall be puniſhed with death, and confiſcation or forfeiture of all his or her Lands and Goods to the Lord Proprietary and his Heirs.

▶ In 1649 Lord Baltimore sponsored the Maryland Toleration Act to guarantee freedom of worship to Christians. The act marked an advance in the direction of full religious freedom in the New World. *http://teachpol.tcnj.edu/amer_pol_hist/*

Roman Catholic Maryland

While Virginia was gradually gaining vitality, a neighboring colony developed on its northern flank. In 1632, Sir George Calvert, First Lord Baltimore, received a charter from Charles I for the tract of land extending from the fortieth degree of north latitude to the south bank of the Potomac River. Calvert, a Roman Catholic, intended to make Maryland a refuge for oppressed Catholics. He died before he could settle his grant, but his son Cecilius became lord proprietor and sent his brother Leonard to take possession of Maryland. The first group of Catholic settlers landed on March 25, 1634.

A "proprietary colony" such as the Calverts obtained was a return to a feudal and baronial system which in the seventeenth century was becoming outmoded. The manorial system of land tenure, which made the inhabitants of Maryland tenants of the Calverts instead of landowners, was the source of much unrest and would never have lasted at all had the Calverts not made tenancy similar to ownership. Calvert planned an aristocratic society ruled from the top, but those who immigrated to Maryland created their own democratic structures and often ignored rule from above.

From the outset, in order to attract settlers and procure a profit, the Calverts encouraged Protestants, as well as Catholics, to go to Maryland. Though most of the manorial families were Catholic, Catholics never constituted a majority of the general population. Calvert attracted settlers with low cost land, with the result that the vast majority of immigrants came to Maryland for economic opportunity rather than freedom from religious persecution. Nevertheless, unlike Virginia, Catholics and Anglicans in Maryland held separate worship, and Lord Baltimore refused to allow the Jesuits in the colony to place any restrictions upon Protestants. In 1649 he sponsored the famous Maryland Toleration Act, which guaranteed freedom of worship to all Christians.

Proprietary Colonies

Except for Maryland, the original colonies were established by joint-stock companies, but after 1660, almost all the newly founded colonies were proprietaries. Joint-stock companies as a whole did not make a profit, and business enterprisers became less interested in investing in colonial establishments. After 1660, King Charles II began to grant large segments of American

These two documents are from two people who lived in the seventeenth-century Chesapeake region. They give two different perspectives on indentured servitude. Indentured servitude was an institution that involved a contract between two people. One person agreed to pay for the passage of the other to travel to North America. In exchange the person wanting passage agreed to work a certain amount of time for the person paying their passage. The time varied but most contracts involved a 4 or 5 year commitment.

Letter from Richard Frethorne, an indentured servant, 1623

Loving and kind father and mother, my most humble duty remembered to you hoping in God of your good health, as I my self am at the making hereof, this is to let you understand that I your Child am in a most heavy Case by reason of the nature of the Country is such that it Causeth much sickness, as the scurvy and the bloody flux [dysentery], and diverse other diseases, which maketh the body very poor, the Weak, and when we are sick there is nothing to Comfort us; for since I came out of the ship, I never ate any thing but peas and loblollie (that is water gruel) as for deer or venison I never saw any since I came into this land, there is indeed some fowl, but We are not allowed to go and get it, but must Work hard both early and late for a mess of water gruel, and a mouthful of bread, and beef, a mouthful of bread for a penny loaf must serve for 4 men which is most pitiful if you did know as much as I, when people cry out day, and night, Oh that they were in England without their limbs and would not care to lose any limb to be in England again. … But I have nothing at all, no not a shirt to my backe, but two Rags nor no Clothes, but one poor suit, nor but one pair of shoes, but one pair of Stockings, but one Cap, but two bands, my Cloak is stolen by one of my own fellows. … I am not half a quarter so strong as I was in England, and all is for want of victuals, for I do protest unto you, that I have eaten more in a day at home than I have allowed me here for a Week. You have given more than my day's allowance to a beggar at the door. … If you love me you will redeem me suddenly, for which I do entreat and beg, and if you cannot get the merchants to redeem me for some little money then for God's sake get a gathering or entreat some good folks to lay out some little sum of money, in meat, and Cheese and butter, and beef, any eating meat will yield great profit, … and look whatsoever you send me be it never so much, look what I make of it. I will deal truly with you. …

A statement made by George Alsop, a resident of Maryland, 1666

There is no truer Emblem of Confusion either in Monarchy or Domestick Governments, then when either the Subject, or the Servant, strives for the upper hand of his Prince, or Master, and to be equal with him, from whom he receives his present subsistence: Why then, if Servitude be so necessary that no place can be governed in order, nor people live without it, this may serve to tell those which prick up their east and bray against it, That they are none but Asses, and deserve the Bridle of a strict commanding power to rein them in: For I'me certainly confident, that there are several Thousands in most Kingdoms of Christendom, that could not at all live and subsist, unless they had served some prefixed time, to learn either some Trade, Art, or Science, and by either of them to extract their present livelihood.

Then methinks this may stop the mouths of those that will undiscreetly compassionate them that dwell under necessary Servitudes. …

... Let such, where Providence hath ordained to life as Servants, either in England or beyond Sea, endure the pre-fixed yoak of their limited time with patience, and then in a small computation of years, by an industrious endeavour, they may become Masters and Mistresses of Families themselves. And let this by spoke to the deserved praise of Mary-Land. That the four years I served there were not to me so slavish, as a two years Servitude of a Handicraft Apprenticeship was here in London. ...

They whose abilities cannot extend to purchase their own transportation over in to Mary-Land, (and surely he that cannot command so small a sum for so great a matter, his life must needs be mighty low and dejected) I say they may for the debarment of a four years sordid liberty, go over into this Province and there live plentiously well. And what's a four years Servitude to advantage a man all the remainder of his days, making his predecessors happy in his sufficient abilities, which he attained to partly by the restrainment of so small a time? ...

The Merchant commonly before they go aboard the Ship, or set themselves in any forwardness for their Voyage, has Conditions of Agreements drawn between him and those that by a voluntary consent become his Servants, to serve him, his Heirs or Assigns, according as they in their primitive acquaintance have made their bargain, some two, some three, some four years; and whatever the Master or Servant tyes himself up here in England by Condition, the Laws of the Province will force a performance of when they come there: Yet here is this Priviledge in it when they arrive. ...

He that lives in the nature of a Servant in this Province, must serve but four years by the Custom of the Country; and when the expiration of his time speaks him a Freeman, there's a law in the Province, that enjoyns his Master whom he hath served to give him Fifty Acres of Land, Corn to serve him a whole year, three Sutes of Apparel, with things necessary to them, and Tools to work withall; so that they are no sooner free, but they are ready to set up for themselves, and when once entered, they live passingly well.

The Women that go over into this Province as Servants, have the best luck here as in any place of the world besides; for they are no sooner on shoar, but they are courted into a Copulative Matrimony, which some of them (for aught I know) had they not come to such a Market with their Virginity might have kept it by them until it had been mouldy. ...

In short, touching the Servants of this Province, they live well in the time of their Service, and by their restrainment in that time, they are made capable of living much better when they come to be free; which in several other parts of the world I have observed, That after some servants have brought their indented and limited time to a just and legal period by Servitude, they have been much more incapable of supporting themselves from sinking into the Gulf of a slavish, poor, fettered, and intangled life, then all the fastness of their pre-fixed time did involve them in before.

Source: *The Records of the Virginia Company,* ed. Susan M. Kingsbury, IV Washington, DC: U.S. Government Printing Offices 1935.

land to those who had supported the Stuart claim to the throne during the English Interregnum (1642–1660). Proprietors had been unsuccessful in the late sixteenth century because they could neither command sufficient capital nor sustain a colonizing effort over an extended period of time. With the successful founding of Virginia, Maryland, Plymouth, and Massachusetts Bay in the early seventeenth century, the risk of founding proprietary colonies appeared greatly reduced. As a result, the territory of the Carolinas was given to a number of proprietors in 1663, and Pennsylvania was founded as a proprietary colony in 1682. New Jersey began as a proprietorship but eventually was made a crown or royal colony, in which affairs were directed by crown officials. New York also began as a proprietary colony under the Duke of York, after its capture from the Dutch. It became a royal colony when York ascended the throne as James II.

▶ By the early seventeenth century, Virginia, Maryland, Plymouth, and Massachusetts Bay were established as colonies. The risk of founding new colonies was reduced, and territories in Pennsylvania, the Carolinas, New Jersey, and New York were soon claimed by the crown or other European groups. *Wikipedia photo*

The English and the Native Americans

The relationship between the English in North America and the Native Americans was different from that between indigenous peoples and any other European group. A small number of Spanish conquistadors under Hernán Cortés, for example, were able to dominate Mexico by conquering the Aztecs, who held lesser tribes in subordination. The English in North America, however, faced a different situation that produced a decidedly different result. Powerful tribes blocked the westward expansion of the English settlers. In the triangular area between Lakes Ontario, Erie, and Huron, were the Hurons. Along the spine of the Appalachians, it was the Iroquois in New York and Pennsylvania, the Susquehannas in Pennsylvania and Virginia, and the Cherokees in the Carolinas. In the Mississippi Valley below the Ohio River, the Chickasaws and, farther south, the Choctaws interfered with English settlers. There were many other tribes interspersed throughout; however, no single nation had achieved ascendancy. Defeat for one tribe did not mean defeat for all.

Since the most powerful groups of Native Americans in English America did not dwell along the Atlantic seacoast, the first white settlers from England frequently faced tribes that were friendly or, if warlike, easily defeated. If the Native Americans had joined forces to drive the English from North America at any time during the first half century of colonization, they could have succeeded. Lack of will—of unity of purpose—not an absence of power, explains their failure to do so.

From the beginning, the English treated Native Americans as members of separate nations or separate tribes, never as subjects of the crown. Warfare and negotiation involved two nations: England and the particular tribe or nation in question. In contrast to the fusion of cultures that

▶ The relationship between the English and the Native Americans was different from that between indigenous peoples and any other European group. In the Southern Mississippi Valley, Choctaws, such as those depicted in this painting, conflicted with English settlers.
Wikipedia photo

took place under the Spanish colonial system, the white and Native American cultures remained separate in English America.

The Pilgrims in Plymouth

On November 11, 1620, colonists arrived off Cape Cod at Plymouth Rock, in the Mayflower, and made the first permanent settlement in New England. They had been granted permission to settle farther south, but their ship had been blown off course. The core of the group of about one hundred settlers was a small, devoted band of Separatists, part of a larger number of religious dissenters who had left England for Holland in 1608. The Separatists viewed the Anglican Church as corrupt and beyond correction; thus, proper service to God required that they separate themselves from the Anglican Church and establish their own separate society. The Separatists first moved to rural England; but finding it impossible to escape Anglican decadence in England, moved to the Netherlands in 1608. The Separatists would find constructing a pure society of uncorrupted Christians in the Netherlands to be futile as well. In the words of Separatist leader, William Bradford, "many of their children, by the great licentiousness of youth in Holland, and the manifold temptations of the place, were drawn away by evil examples." Unsuccessful in the Netherlands, the Separatists obtained permission to settle in the New World in the lands granted to the Virginia Company. In August 1620, 102 Pilgrims boarded the *Mayflower* to emigrate to the Americas. The expedition, which put out from Plymouth, England, was financed by a joint-stock company in which the Separatists, their fellow passengers, and outside investors participated.

The story of these Separatists, who now called themselves Pilgrims, has become a part of the American legend: the hardships of the first winter, the friendship of the Native Americans Samoset and Squanto, who taught the settlers to plant corn, and the first harvest and thanksgiving festival.

During their eleven-week voyage, the Pilgrims were blown off course and ended up far north of the Virginia Company lands. Realizing that they had no legal authority to settle at Ply-

►Protestant pilgrims, such as those that sailed to the New World on the *Mayflower*, are led in prayer prior to their departure from England for their new home. Women and children are shown perhaps to emphasize the importance of family in the community, and a rainbow is depicted symbolizing hope and divine protection. *Wikipedia photo*

mouth, the Pilgrims drew up the Mayflower Compact the day they arrived as a document that would provide a claim to legitimacy and provide security and order. In the document, the Pilgrims agreed to "covenant and combine ourselves together into a civil Body Politick, for our better Ordering and Preservation." The signatories also agreed to enact and obey just laws. William Bradford was quickly elected Governor.

Unfortunately, the Pilgrims got off to a difficult beginning in the New World. William Bradford's wife jumped overboard and committed suicide by drowning in Plymouth Harbor before ever setting foot in North America. For the rest of the Separatists arriving on the *Mayflower* that November, the weather was harsh and food was scarce. As a result, half of the Pilgrims died the first winter, and they were only able to build seven houses. More might have died of starvation had the Pilgrims not stolen native corn while the natives were away from their houses toiling in the fields. Bradford credited God with sending the natives away so that the Pilgrims could steal the natives' food. The Pilgrims at first attempted a communal lifestyle with no private property, but Bradford disappointedly explained that this early attempt at communism was abandoned in 1623 because it apparently sapped the work ethic.

Squanto, the legendary helpful Native American, arrived in the Pilgrims' camp in March of 1621, with the simple greeting, "Welcome Englishmen." Obviously, this meant that Squanto had had previous experience with Englishmen, but Bradford interpreted Squanto as a "special instrument sent from God for the Pilgrims' good." Historians believe that Squanto had been sold into slavery in Virginia in 1614; and he had been transported to Spain, France, and then England, where he convinced the Newfoundland Company that he could be a useful guide and trade broker. Consequently, the English Newfoundland Company evidently returned Squanto to North America.

Bradford writes that Squanto taught the Pilgrims the "Indian way" of planting corn, directing that the Pilgrims place four fish in each corn mound and that the corn mounds be 1.5 feet apart.

▶ The legendary Squanto, historically described as the great helper to the settlers, actually may have been a slave, traded several times throughout France and Europe and then returned to North America. Squanto may have helped the settlers but with his primary motive was likely personal gain through trade. *Wikipedia photo*

Unfortunately, historians doubt that either the Pilgrims or the Native Americans could have followed such a method since it would have meant using 27,844 fish per acre or 2,784,400 fish per one hundred acres. Furthermore, there is no evidence of any other Native Americans in North America using fish for fertilizer in the manner and quantity prescribed by Squanto. Instead, there is evidence that fish waste was used for fertilizer in coastal Spain and France in the seventeenth century. It is therefore suggested that Squanto, in actuality, gained the fish-for-fertilizer idea during his time as a slave in Europe. Squanto also evidently often kept portions of goods traded between the English and natives for his own personal profit. Historians believe that he coerced Native Americans into trading with the English by telling them that the English kept the plague in the ground, and they would release it on the Native Americans if they refused to trade. Instead of an instrument from God, it appears that Squanto was primarily a salesman and an opportunist.

Puritans in the Massachusetts Bay Colony

THE "GREAT MIGRATION"   Although the character and heroism of the Pilgrims bequeathed a poetic heritage to the American people, the larger colony of Massachusetts Bay contributed more to New England's civilization. The main body of Puritan settlers, under the leadership of John Winthrop, arrived in the summer of 1630 on the *Arbella*. This was one of four ships that carried the first wave of the "Great Migration" that between 1630 and 1640 brought some twenty thousand people into Massachusetts. The Pilgrims of Plymouth would be essentially overwhelmed and absorbed by the larger Puritan society. The Puritans, like the Pilgrims before them, were a splinter group from the Anglican Church who viewed the Anglican Church as corrupt. In contrast to the Pilgrims, who viewed the Anglican Church as beyond reform, the Puritans sought to reform or "purify" the Anglican Church from within.

Puritans who settled in the Massachusetts Bay Colony came for religious reasons. Most Puritans came in family units, left considerable land and security in England, and were similar ages to those who stayed in England. These characteristics have led historians to argue that Puritans had no other reason for moving to the Massachusetts Bay Colony during the early years except for religion.

Leaders of the Massachusetts Bay Colony, such as John Winthrop, reveal the deeply imbedded religious belief of the Puritan elite. The Puritans wanted to create a godly society that would serve as a "city upon a hill." Puritans settled in Massachusetts for religious liberty, which they defined as the right to practice the true religion. They did not, however, move to Massachusetts to escape religious persecution. Many Puritans in England were politically connected citizens who were Members of Parliament, land holders, and business owners. The Puritans who decided to leave England were against changes implemented by King Charles's Archbishop of Canterbury, William Laud, which was scarcely persecution.

The Winthrop group had managed to obtain a royal charter for the Massachusetts Bay Company. Unlike other colonial enterprises, this company vested control, not in a board of governors in England but rather in the members of the company, who themselves were emigrating. They came bringing their charter with them and were self-governing, subject only to the English crown. Voting privileges were granted to those who were members of the Puritan Church of the colony, and during the early years of settlement a close relationship between church and state was the key to authority and lifestyle. In all cases, however, the civil magistrates, not the clergy, held preeminence.

Puritans were followers of John Calvin's Protestant reforms. They emphasized conversion experiences, predestination, sermons, and covenant theology. The Puritan conversion experience was an ambiguous element to their beliefs. In order to be considered a "saint" one had to experience a conversion, which was witnessed before a group of confirmed saints or elders. The panel of elders decided whether or not the person's conversion was legitimate. If yes, then the person became a full member of the church. Puritans were firm believers in the Calvinistic belief of predestination. Predestination meant God held absolute power over salvation. Nothing a person did could save them. Sermons became the center of worship for Puritans. On average Puritans attended two sermons on Sunday, each two hours long. Sermons were lessons derived from the *Bible*. The *Bible* was the center of Puritan worship. Consequently, Puritans held the highest literacy rates in all the British North American colonies.

WOMEN IN PURITAN SOCIETY Inequality among the sexes was the norm in Puritan society. Women needed to be protected and sheltered from the evils of the world. This inequality was tempered by the belief that women were capable of full church membership, receiving grace, and reaching salvation. In addition, the law protected women against spousal abuse and they could own property and sign contracts.

PURITAN CHILD-REARING PRACTICES Puritan religious beliefs in predestination led to strict child-rearing practices, mainly a practice called "the breaking of the will." Puritan parents believed that it was their responsibility to break the sinful will of their children. Puritans focused on mental will breaking, however, physical discipline was used when all else failed.

WITCHCRAFT IN PURITAN SOCIETY Puritans had a preoccupation with witchcraft for a few reasons. Puritans believed in Satan and feared his power. Puritans also believed that it was their duty to protect their godly society from the power of Satan. In seventeenth-century New England the majority of accused witches were women primarily because they were viewed as weaker and highly susceptible to Satan's power. In addition, the accused tended to be Puritans of middle-age (40-60 years old), married, of low social position, and used abrasive speech. Contrary to popular belief, most of the accused were found innocent after standing for trial. The accused, however, were highly suspicious if another case of witchcraft arose in the same area.

The infamous Salem Witch trials resulted in an atypical experience. This case was an aberrant series of events that led to 20 people sentenced to death. The reasons why the Salem trials resulted in a peculiar experience is unknown. Some historians argue social and political reasons and others assert economic issues led to the accusations during the Salem trials. Perhaps it was a combination of all.

EARLY QUAKERS A group of "friends" began to arise in England during the English Civil War (1642–1660). These people later called themselves the "Society of Friends" and became known as the Quakers. During the 1640s and 1650s Quakers became the bane of existence for Puritans in England and after they arrived in New England in the mid-1650s. Early Quakers were a revolutionary sect that was radical, enthusiastic, unorganized, and millennial. Quakers asserted that an "inner light" resided in everyone and if one listened to it, they could be saved. Quakers rejected most Puritan religious beliefs and practices such as predestination, clergy, tithes, ceremonies, and churches. Quakers rejected religious and social hierarchies; they refused to uphold customary dress and speech customs of England. Quakers refused to doff their hat to social superiors, they declined to pay taxes to the state church and they shunned oaths. The early Quakers were mostly poor, uneducated, female, and they went to great lengths to disrupt the English in general but primarily they focused on infuriating the Puritans. Early on Quakers believed their "inner light" called them to witness to Puritans about their incorrect religious beliefs. Quakers did this by interrupting Puritan meetings, witnessing to them in the streets, and overtly denying Puritan values of harmony and order. Anti-Quaker pamphlets proliferated in England and stated how "dangerous" these Quakers were to social order. These pamphlets were also transported to the Massachusetts Bay Colony so when the first couple of Quakers arrived, the Puritans were ready for them. The Puritans in Massachusetts called the Quakers "invaders" and went to great lengths to "protect" their godly society from them.

In 1656 two female Quakers arrived in Boston and they were immediately jailed, strip searched, and held until the captain of the ship who brought them left the colony. The actions of the Puritans only encouraged Quakers to continue to protest to Massachusetts Puritans. Soon Quakers were able to infiltrate the colony and they attempted to disrupt the harmonious environment Puritans tried to create. The Quakers attended Puritan sermons solely to interrupt them. One Quaker woman ran naked through a church during a sermon while yelling that the Puritan teachings were all wrong. Other Quakers broke bottles during Puritan gathering. The Massachusetts General Court passed a series of law against Quakers that supported strict penalties for disrupting the colony. Quakers were fined, whipped, imprisoned, and even hanged but they kept coming to New England.

MATURE QUAKERS By the 1670s Quakers began to develop into a more organized, moderate, and rational group. These mature Quakers left behind their early practices of radical protest and developed into an established group. They no longer lived to solely protest against Puritans. People of the middling and upper echelons of society became Quakers. They began to be more educated and family oriented. Quakers held firm to their beliefs in the inner light, rejection of hierarchy, pacifism, and spiritual equality for men and women. A large group settled in Pennsylvania as a part of William Penn's "holy experiment." In Pennsylvania the Quakers created a society centered on nurturing childrearing, family, and community.

Puritan Society

From the very beginning, Puritan society was very Democratic in form for Puritan men, and the Puritan society stressed religion, work, family, and education. Leaders in the Puritan community were university trained ministers and Harvard University was begun in 1636 as a theological seminary for Puritans. In 1647, all towns with fifty families were ordered to establish elementary schools and towns of one hundred families were required to establish secondary schools, making the Puritan colonies of New England the most educated of the American colonies.

New England Puritans expressed themselves in prose and poetry. Sometimes their tone was harsh, but it was always unmistakably clear. Sermons were cultivated as a literary form and were published by the press founded in Massachusetts Bay in 1639, the first printing press in the New World. This press became the voice of Puritanism in America. Its productivity was fabulous. Its output exceeded that of the presses of Cambridge and Oxford in England.

The Puritans began democratic self-government almost immediately. Male church members elected a governor and colonial legislature as well as local selectmen that handled most political matters. Annually, all townspeople would meet at a town meeting to decide local political matters

▶ Present day Harvard University; leaders in the Puritan community were university trained ministers, and Harvard University was begun in 1636 as a theological seminary for Puritans. *iStockphoto*

(a practice that continues in small New England towns through the present). Puritans had a multiplicity of municipal offices including surveyors of deer, town criers, measurers, and purchasers of grain. Ten percent of all adult males held some sort of municipal office.

Each Puritan town was founded by a grant from the Massachusetts Colony General Court in Boston. Settlement grants were given only to groups of Puritans that signed a compact signifying the unity of their purpose. "We shall live by all means, labor to keep off from us such as are contrary minded, and receive only such unto us as may be probably of one heart with us." After receiving a charter from Boston, Puritan communities enjoyed much local autonomy.

The New England Puritans turned to congregationalism as a form of church government. But they attempted informally to establish close ties among the individual congregations by means of synods, or assemblies of delegates, for discussion and decision on ecclesiastical affairs. Theoretically, each congregation could select its own course of action, but in practice a consensus of the Puritan leaders usually determined the course.

It would be a mistake, however, to think that the Puritan clergy were all-powerful; indeed, civil authority enforced conformity to Puritan beliefs. Lay leaders like John Winthrop, not the leading ministers, were primarily responsible for the banishment of colonials who protested against the Puritan doctrines.

The premises of New England Puritanism affected every sphere of life—political, economic, cultural, social, and intellectual. For example, land was distributed to church congregations so that a social-religious community could be created and sustained. Settlements by towns enabled the Puritans to center their lives and activities around the church, and designated practice could easily be enforced. With the Puritans in political control, and thus able to determine those groups who were to receive land grants, the objective of creating a Bible Commonwealth could be achieved.

Puritan Success

Puritans had astounding success in terms of survival as compared to the Chesapeake colonies. Ordinary settlers came as family units with men and women almost equal in numbers. Very few were indentured servants. The Puritans' economy was a mix of agriculture, fishing, timber, and fur trade. Puritans farmed in open fields shared by all and grazed livestock in open meadows. Firewood was cut from communal woodlands. Life expectancy was sixty years by 1700, exceeding life expectancy in England; and 90 percent survived childhood to marry (only 50 percent survived childhood in the U.S. in 1900). The Puritan population doubled every twenty-seven years to reach one hundred thousand by 1700. Furthermore, most of the population increase is accounted for by natural increase since only twenty-five thousand immigrated to New England in the seventeenth century. Large scale Puritan immigration ended after 1642, due to an English Civil War that ended their persecution.

In contrast to the Puritans' success, seventy-five thousand immigrants to Chesapeake in the seventeenth century yielded a population of only seventy thousand by 1700. By 1680, the average Massachusetts household had a kitchen, parlor, and sleeping loft instead of just one room as in Chesapeake; Puritan living standards were equal to those in England.

The Spreading Colonies of New England

Occasionally colonists left Massachusetts Bay because they had offended the ruling authorities or because they were discontented with a thoroughgoing Puritan commonwealth that punished nonconformists severely and tried to impose its religious tenets upon all comers. Freedom of conscience or religion was not a virtue of Massachusetts Bay. Roger Williams, pastor of the church at Salem, was banished from the colony in 1635, because he had complained publicly that interference of the clergy in politics threatened the freedom of individual congregations, and because he questioned the right of the settlers to take land from the Native Americans. Williams fled in the dead of winter to the Narragansett Native Americans, and in January 1636, he arranged to purchase land from them for a little settlement that he called Providence. Before long, other fugitives from the persecution of the Puritan clergy in Massachusetts Bay found their way to Williams's colony, including a group led by the religious dissenter, Anne Hutchinson.

The Providence settlers made a compact that provided for the separation of church and state. Other groups came to the area and settled at Portsmouth, Newport, and Warwick; and in 1644, Parliament granted Williams a charter that united the various groups into one civil government, which is now Rhode Island. A royal charter, in 1663 once more reiterated the liberties established earlier. This charter remained the basis of Rhode Island's laws until 1842. Rhode Island was far ahead of its time in its legal provisions. As early as 1647, for example, it outlawed trials for witchcraft and imprisonment for debt. The Rhode Island Constitution did not, however, provide for complete religious freedom. In particular, the Rhode Island Constitution of 1644 denounced Catholics and Quakers for "Belching out fire from Hell."

Massachusetts Bay emigrants settled a colony at New Haven under conservative Puritan leadership. As in Massachusetts, only church members were permitted to vote, a policy that in effect gave the church political control over the affairs of the colony. Since the Scriptures made no mention of jury trials, New Haven—in contrast to other New England colonies—forbade such trials and left the dispensation of justice in the hands of the magistrates.

In 1662, Connecticut received a royal charter that confirmed the rights of self-government and provided for the Fundamental Orders, a platform of government extending the franchise to nonchurch members. New Haven, to its distress, was absorbed into Connecticut, and its citizens thereby gained the guarantees of Connecticut's charter.

Other Massachusetts Bay residents moved into New Hampshire and Maine, where settlers had already established in small fishing villages. Massachusetts laid claim to both regions, but after many disputes New Hampshire in 1679, gained a royal charter and freed itself from the domination of Massachusetts. Maine was not separated until 1820.

Puritanism

Puritanism is representative of a religious and political movement to return society to a "better, vanished time," in this case, the time of the Christian Church in the days of the Acts of the Apostles. The Puritans viewed the first century as an uncorrupted golden age of Christianity that had become corrupted over the centuries, first by the Catholic Church, and then the Anglican Church, complete with defiling and unnecessary traditions, rules, and decorations. Human history, in the Puritan view, was a history of religious (and therefore human) decline and increasing human depravity.

The Puritans were heavily influenced by John Calvin and believed Calvin's doctrine of predestination, which holds that before the creation of the world, God exercised his divine grace and chose a few human beings to receive eternal life. Only God, however, could know who the elect are, and nothing could change God's choice. Yet if one were among the elect, one would be expected to act like it and the saintly behavior would be visible to all.

An obvious problem with the Puritan predestination doctrine, however, is that if one is predestined to eternal bliss, and nothing could change God's mind, why worry about sin? In another apparent contradiction with Calvin's predestination doctrine, the Puritans stressed the conversion of "those who could not find God's truth in their hearts." If the decision were predestined by God before the beginning of the world and had nothing to do with humans, why evangelize?

The Puritans rarely saw the contradictions in their logic. Even when they were forced to do so, they continued to believe that their position was sound because it came from God. The Puritans were confident that they knew the truth from God in its entirety; consequently, their logic was necessarily infallible regardless of any problems that seemed to be obvious contradictions on the surface. Puritan logic was not a method of discovery or of learning the truths in science and nature. Instead, Puritan logic was a rhetorical means of communicating the logic received from God to others. Since the Puritans already knew the truth, there was little need for inductive reasoning.

Nevertheless, the Puritans viewed the salvation of themselves, as well as the salvation of others within the congregation, as the concern of everyone in the Puritan community; each Puritan was responsible for helping others achieve their spiritual goals. To further this purpose, the Puritans engaged in "Holy Watching," or moral surveillance of each other to ensure that they did not sin. Puritan houses were built in close proximity so that Puritans could hear their neighbors and know what they were doing. Curtains on the windows were forbidden so that one could see inside of the house of one's neighbor and ensure that no one inside was engaging in sin. The physical layout of the towns was such that houses faced inward toward their neighbors so as to allow Puritans to keep better watch on one another and guard against ungodly behavior.

Puritans and Human Nature

Puritans espoused the negative view of human nature, believing that humans are naturally bad and untrustworthy. Consequently, single men and women were prevented from living alone because, left to their own devices, it was expected that people would sin. In the words of Thomas Hooker, "Every natural man and woman is born as full of sin as a toad is of poison." In order to compensate for the depravity of human nature, Puritans believed that coercion was necessary to ensure proper behavior, and civil and religious transgressions, therefore, were severely punished. Puritans also believed that people were naturally slothful, but work was godly and therefore, work was stressed as the primary method of serving God. To ensure that Puritans served God faithfully through work, the Puritans meted out punishment for slothfulness. Puritans purged themselves of all luxuries to focus on God's work. Physical beauty and aesthetics were disparaged. In 1634, the General Court forbade garments with any lace, silver or gold thread, all cutworks, embroidered or needlework caps, bands and rails, all gold and silver girdles, hatbands, belts, ruffs, and beaver hats, and all clothing whereby the nakedness of the arm may be discovered. The court also forbade long hair, and neither Christmas nor Easter was celebrated. In addition, religious wedding ceremonies were outlawed, and a magistrate married couples in a civil ceremony.

Laws were also passed ensuring that one was not entertained. Prohibited entertainment included: sledding, swimming, music, and dancing. According to Puritan leader Increase Mather, "Mixt or Promiscuous Dancing of Men and Women could not be tolerated since the unchaste Touches and Gesticulations used by Dancers have a palpable tendency to that which is evil." Also prohibited were cards, dice, shuffleboard, and other games of chance. To make sure that Puritans did not waste time entertaining themselves, the Court specifically forbade enjoyment when one might be better employed, enjoyment on the Sabbath, Sunday walks, and visits to the harbor. In 1670, John Lewis and Sarah Chapman were convicted of "engaging in things tending much to the dishonor of God, the reproach of religion, and the prophanation of the holy Sabbath." Lewis and Chapman specifically were "sitting together on the Lord's Day, under an apple tree in Goodman Chapman's orchard." Perhaps the most notorious case of all, however, was the case of Thomas Granger, who was executed in 1642 for having sex with a mare, two cows, five calves, two goats, five sheep, and a turkey. All of the animals were also put to death according to the instructions of Leviticus 20:15—their carcasses were thrown in a pit and all persons were ordered to make no use of them.

Puritan View of the Bible

The Puritans viewed the Bible as a complete guide to societal organization and "God's laws," as outlined in their Holy book, also should be civil laws. In the Puritan mindset, everything that occurred in their world was somehow analogous to some event in the Bible, and therefore, a reproduction of divine will. The fact that the Bible was "complete" meant anything that could not be justified by a passage found somewhere in the Bible was forbidden. In the minds of the Puritans, they spoke when the Bible spoke and were silent when the Bible was silent. The Puritans were extremely legalistic in their approach to the Bible and paid great attention to Biblical details, so much so that they were often open to the criticism that they were paying more attention to the Biblical "trees" than to the forest. In the words of historian Kai Erikson,

> "The Scriptures not only supplied rules for the broader issues of church polity
> but for the tiniest details of everyday life as well, and many Puritans were
> fully capable of demanding that a clergyman remove some emblem from his

▶ The Puritans conceived of themselves as a covenanted people. In essence, the "covenant theology" held that God had made a contract with humans setting down the terms of salvation. *iStockphoto*

vestments unless he could justify the extravagance by producing a warrant for it from the pages of the Bible."

The Puritans conceived of themselves as a covenanted people. In essence, the "covenant theology" held that God had made a contract with humans setting down the terms of salvation. God had pledged Himself to abide by these terms. This covenant in no way changed the doctrine that God elected the saints, but it did explain why certain people were elected and others were not. Individuals knew that they were numbered among the elect by experiencing God's grace and reflecting this regeneration—spiritual rebirth—before their peers.

Because the terms of the covenant were to be found in the Bible, the Bible was the source of the rules of conduct and was constantly searched for meaning and interpretation. Because of the covenant, each law, each act, each policy demanded literal Biblical support. They firmly opposed all religious enthusiasms or any evidence of self-revelation (the doctrine that God revealed Himself directly to an individual).

Puritans and Free Thought

Like the seventeenth century Anglicans and the Catholics whom they disparaged with unrestrained zeal, the Puritans refused to tolerate those that thought differently than themselves in religious matters and such heretics were therefore vigorously persecuted. The Puritans not only believed in the literal interpretation of the inerrant Bible but also believed that the teachings of the Bible were moral absolutes that transcended time and place. Furthermore, they believed that they had possessed the correct interpretation of the Bible to the exclusion of all other groups with whom they disagreed. As a consequence, if anyone offered a persuasive argument that shook the Puritans' certainty, or if someone developed a clever line of reasoning that could confuse the Puritan or cause him to question his beliefs, the Puritans suspected that Satan must somehow be involved. In order to prevent such confusion, settlement grants in the Puritan colony were granted only to groups of Puritans that signed a compact signifying the unity of their purpose. The compact stated that,

> "We shall live by all means, labor to keep off from us such as are contrary minded, and receive only such unto us as may be probably of one heart with us."

Hutchinson Heresy

In 1636, the Puritan community of Boston became divided between the male clergy and the theological teachings of Anne Hutchinson. Hutchinson considered herself a devout Puritan, but she challenged the Puritan view of women as subservient. In I Timothy 2:10–11, the writer states that women should be submissive to men, silent in Church, and not teach men. Hutchinson essentially violated all three, teaching her own version of the gospel, and built up a major following at her home after church services. Hutchinson had no official church training or standing, but she gained a wide respect from converts within the community with her teachings. Hutchinson preached that salvation was through grace, which she viewed as more important than works, thus violating the premium placed on works in orthodox Puritan theology. Hutchinson also stated that the "Holy Spirit was absent in the Preaching of some Ministers," thus challenging the spirituality and legitimacy of the Puritan leadership.

▶ Anne Hutchinson considered herself a devout Puritan but taught the gospel differently, preaching that one was granted salvation through grace, not works. Hutchinson also challenged the legitimacy of many Puritan leaders. Hutchinson was banished for her radical views on faith. Today, her statue stands outside the State House in Boston, MA. *AP Wide World Photo*

Hutchinson was, therefore, placed on trial by male clergy and judges in 1637, convicted of sedition and contempt, and banished as a "woman not fit for our society, cast out and delivered to Satan to become a heathen and a leper." Hutchinson was also convicted of the heresy of prophecy, the "erroneous" claim that God revealed his will directly to a believer instead of exclusively through the Bible. On the stand in her trial, Hutchinson claimed, "the Lord hath let me see which was the clear ministry and which was wrong by the Voice of God's own Spirit into my Soul." In claiming that God had spoken to her directly, Hutchinson committed heresy before the Puritans' very eyes. In all, Hutchinson was convicted of preaching eighty-two heresies and banished from the Massachusetts colony, only to help found the colony of dissenters in Rhode Island.

Puritans and the Natives

Natives in Massachusetts Bay were estimated to number around 125,000 in 1600. However, English fishermen brought smallpox to the area and an epidemic wiped out over half the population by 1610, twenty years prior to arrival of the Puritans. In 1633, three years after the Puritans' arrival, a second smallpox epidemic hit the natives and again wiped out over half the population. The Puritans believed the epidemic was proof that God had given them Native American land, just like God gave Canaan to the Israelites by allowing the Israelites to kill all of the inhabitants of the land of Canaan. In this case, God had wiped out the indigenous inhabitants himself through pestilence. After the plagues, the remaining Native Americans welcomed the Puritans because they now had surplus land, and they lacked the manpower to tend all the land they had cleared. Untended land in New England will very quickly return to forest. The natives also needed trade with the Puritans, who had many things the natives could use, including steel blades, axes, guns, and steel kettles for boiling water and cooking food. The remaining Massachusetts Bay natives also recognized the value of English protection from tribal enemies to the north and, thus, hoped that the Puritans could be an aid to their own security.

Puritans sought to Christianize the Native Americans and succeeded in converting over one thousand natives by 1640. The Puritan Charter claimed that the Puritans' "Principal end is to convert the natives to Christianity." Some natives resisted Christianization, leading to a war in 1637, won by the Puritans. In typical Puritan fashion, William Bradford credits God for giving the Puritans the victory over the Native Americans in the Pequot war, recounting how the Puritans massacred four hundred Native Americans in a raid on the Native American village, with most of the Native Americans dying in a fire set by the Puritans that burned the natives out of their homes. In the words of Bradford,

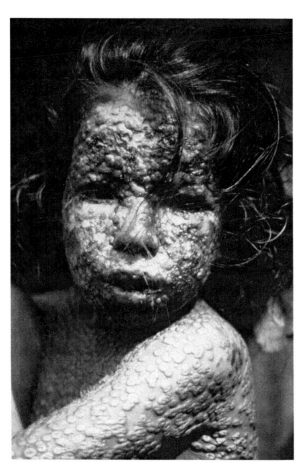

▶Pictured here is a young child with Smallpox, which was brought to the New World by English fishermen. A Smallpox epidemic killed off approximately half of the native population. Puritans took this as a sign that God had given them the Native Americans' land. *Wikipedia photo*

"It was a fearful sight to see them thus frying in the fire and the streams of blood quenching the same, and horrible was the stink and scent thereof; but the victory seemed a sweet sacrifice, and they gave the praise thereof to God, who had wrought so wonderfully for them, thus to enclose their enemies in their hands and give them so speedy a victory over so proud and insulting an enemy."

At the close of the war, all the Native Americans in eastern Massachusetts were essentially under Puritan control. In order to aid in the conversion of the natives and avoid security threats from them in the future, however, it was decreed that all Puritan men were to be trained in the use of firearms.

The Capture of New York

In 1609, Henry Hudson, an Englishman in the employ of the Dutch East India Company, sailed the Hudson River as far as the present town of Albany while in search of a "Northwest Passage" to Asia. In 1623, after the monopoly of a private Dutch company in the area had run out, the Dutch West India Company was formed to develop trade in the region along the river that Hudson had discovered. In 1626, Dutch West India Company director, Peter Minuit, purchased Manhattan Island from the natives for trade goods equal to a dozen beaver pelts. A settlement was begun on Manhattan known as "New Amsterdam," which became the trading center for the new Dutch colony that was named New Netherlands.

Despite incompetent governors, quarreling inhabitants, and frequent wars with the Native Americans the colony made progress and New Amsterdam (New York City) became an important shipping point for furs and farm products. By the 1660s, with a population of 2,500, it was second only to Boston as a trading port. The colony as a whole had about eight thousand settlers, many of whom were not Dutch.

Since the citizens of Holland were largely content, the new company had trouble finding colonists, so the early settlers included French Protestant refugees and non-Dutch emigrants from Holland. From the earliest times, New Netherlands (later New York) was a polyglot region. The Dutch tried to attract settlers by granting patroonships—allotments of eighteen miles of land along the Hudson River—to wealthy stockholders who would bring fifty families to the colony. Only one patroonship succeeded, and the settlers that were attracted were diverse peoples from Sweden, Holland, France, and Germany. The Dutch sent a minister of the Dutch Reformed Church to oversee religion in the new colony, and the minister wrote back and complained that the colonists were unreceptive. In his words, "Several groups of Jews have recently arrived, adding to the religious mixture of Papists, Mennonites, and Lutherans among the Dutch, and many Puritans and many other atheists who conceal themselves under the name of Christians." Due to the diversity, the Dutch West India Company imposed religious freedom on the Colony in 1664, declaring, "The consciences of men should be free and unshackled."

The English had never admitted the right of the Dutch to the territory they had occupied. In 1664, Charles II named his brother James, Duke of York, proprietor over lands oc-

▶ In 1681, King Charles II granted to William Penn, a Quaker, land that stretched between New Jersey and Maryland, naming him and his heirs forever owners of the soil of Pennsylvania, as the domain was called. Penn established Pennsylvania as a colony that would refuge persecuted Christians from all lands. *Wikipedia photo*

cupied by the Dutch in the Americas. York sent out an expedition to take over New Netherlands with the English claiming that this was not an act of war but merely an action to regain from the Dutch West India Company territory that which was rightfully English. With an English fleet in the harbor of New Amsterdam, the Dutch governor, Peter Stuyvesant, surrendered on September 9, 1664. The town and territory were both rechristened New York in honor of the royal proprietor.

The Jerseys

Soon after the Duke of York took over New Netherland in 1664, he granted the land between the Hudson and the Delaware to John Lord Berkeley and Sir George Carteret, royalists who had defended the island of Jersey against the Parliamentarians during the Puritan Revolution in England. Berkeley sold his proprietary right to two Quakers, and in 1676, the province was divided into East Jersey (belonging to Carteret) and West Jersey (which became a Quaker colony). The later division of the two portions of New Jersey among many heirs of the proprietors bequeathed a land problem so complex that it vexes holders of real estate in that state to the present day.

"The Holy Experiment"

In 1681, King Charles II granted to William Penn, a Quaker, a charter to the land between New Jersey and Maryland, naming him and his heirs forever owners of the soil of Pennsylvania, as the domain was called. Penn set about establishing a colony that served as a refuge for persecuted Christians from all lands. He drew up his celebrated first Frame of Government and made various concessions and laws to govern the colony, which already had a conglomerate group of English, Dutch, Swedish, and Finnish settlers. After his own arrival in Pennsylvania, he provided for the calling of a popular assembly on December 4, 1682, which passed the "Great Law," guaranteeing, among other things, the rights of all Christians to liberty of conscience. Penn's colony is generally considered the most democratic and free anywhere in the New World to that point. Legislative power was vested in a directly elected assembly and suffrage was granted to all free males, not just Church members. In addition, trial by jury was guaranteed to all citizens.

Penn, determined to keep peace with the Native Americans, was careful to purchase the land that his settlers occupied. The tradition of a single "Great Treaty" signed under an ancient elm at Kensington is probably a myth, but Penn held many "powwows" with the Native Americans and negotiated treaties of peace and amity after purchasing needed land. To the credit of Penn and the Quakers, these agree-

▶ Penn's colony, assembled by way of treaty with the Native Americans, became the only colony where land from the Native Americans was purchased, rather than taken. *Wikipedia photo*

ments with the Native Americans were, for the most part, conscientiously kept. Penn's colony became the only colony where land from the Native Americans was purchased, rather than taken. In the words of Voltaire, "This was the only league between the Indians and Christians that was never sworn to and never broken."

Quakers

Like Puritans and Pilgrims, Quakers were a fundamentalist Protestant sect that regarded the Anglican Church as corrupt and renounced its formalities and rituals. Based on their reading of Hebrews, Chapters 4–8, Quakers rejected all church officials and institutions, instead claiming that every individual could claim salvation on an individual basis. Quakers were persecuted in England after the 1650s, since they challenged the legitimacy of the existing church (and therefore the political hierarchy since Anglican Clergymen sat in the upper house of Parliament).

Quakers were despised by English nobles for their failure to observe customary deference (for instance, the tipping of one's hat to noblemen). The Quakers refused such deference because they believed that all men were equal before God; consequently, no one should be tipping one's hat in deference to anyone else based on birthright. Quakers also refused to pay church taxes that went to the Anglican Church, and refused to sign witness oaths on the Bible (Jesus said "swear not"). Quakers also refused violence, including military service, taking Jesus' admonition to "turn the other cheek" literally. All of these beliefs and practices set them at odds with the Anglican Church and the political authority in England.

Quaker Laws

Though persecuted by others both in England and in the New World, the Quakers, like Anglicans and Puritans, also used civil government to enforce religious morality. One of Pennsylvania's first laws provided severe punishment for "all offenses against God: lying, profane talking, drunkenness, drinking of healths, obscene words, all prizes, stage plays, cards, dice, May games, gamesters, masques, revels, bull-baitings, cock-fightings, bear baitings, and the like, which excite the people to rudeness, cruelty, looseness, and irreligion."

Pennsylvania Economy and Growth

Pennsylvania's growth from the first was phenomenal. Penn's success was largely due to his own skill as a promoter. He wrote enticing tracts, and on preaching journeys he described the opportunities offered by his colony. Mennonites from Switzerland and Germany—especially Pietists from the Rhineland, which had so often been overrun by invading armies—soon were coming to Pennsylvania in large numbers. Dutch sectarians, French Huguenots, Presbyterian Scots from Ulster, Baptists from Wales, and distressed English Quakers also came. Somewhat after the Mennonites, Lutheran emigrants from Germany swarmed into Pennsylvania's backcountry, where they cleared the forests and developed fertile farms. From the beginning Pennsylvania was prosperous. Pennsylvania avoided the starvation periods that beset the other colonies due to fertile ground and a longer growing season than in the northeast, and it escaped the tropical diseases that plagued the South. Philadelphia became a major international port due to its excellent harbor on the Delaware River, and the city was larger than New York City by 1700.

Settlement of the Carolinas

Among the later proprietorship colonies to be settled was Carolina. In 1660, the Monarchy was restored to the throne in England. King Charles II rewarded those who helped him regain the throne, including a Barbadian planter named John Colleton and seven other men, with a charter to establish a colony south of Chesapeake and North of Spanish Florida. The proprietors drew up an instrument of government called the Fundamental Constitutions. This document provided for a hierarchy of colonial nobility and set up a platform of government with a curious mixture of feudal and liberal elements. Eventually, it had to be abandoned in favor of a more workable plan of government. For the short term, however, Colleton and the small group of nobles officially monopolized political power in the new colony, but they also followed the Chesapeake example of settlement by enticing immigration through the promise of 150 acres of free land and free religion. In 1670, the first settlement was founded just across from present day Charleston.

Most of the early settlers were Englishmen from the English Caribbean colony of Barbados. Carolina was the only seventeenth century English colony to be settled principally by colonists from other colonies rather than from England. The colonists were a diverse mix of Swiss, Scotts, Irish, French, English, and African slaves (who made up one-fourth of the first settlers). Religious

▶ From the beginning, Pennsylvania was prosperous. The city of Philadelphia, which was larger than New York City by 1700, became a major international port because of its excellent harbor on the Delaware River. *Wikipedia photo*

diversity prevented any group from creating a Church/State relationship. The new settlers, however, generally ignored the political rule of the nobles and opted instead for local self-rule.

Carolina Economy

The leaders of Carolina sought to exploit the Native Americans in Carolina for deerskin trade. In the words of Colleton, "All of Carolina is one continuous deer park." Settlers, however, found greater profit in the trade of natives as slaves for sale in New England or the West Indies. Local planters would arm and reward one tribe for helping them bring in enemy tribes, and then would capture and sell the tribe that helped them into slavery as well. By 1700, the native population of Carolina was essentially wiped out. The end of the native population caused the British to begin the importation of African slaves to South Carolina since white Europeans refused to work in the swamps of the Carolina rice and indigo plantations. In 1680, South Carolina was 80 percent white. In 1720, South Carolina was 70 percent African American. Like Virginia and Maryland, the climate of South Carolina was conducive to malaria and high mortality rates, and African slaves were more resistant to malaria. John Colleton described it thusly, "Carolina is in the Spring Paradise, the Summer Hell, and in the Autumn, a Hospital."

The Division of Carolina

The division of Carolina into two distinct colonies came about gradually. English settlers were already occupying land around Albermarle Sound when the proprietors received their charter, and Albermarle continued to attract a scattering of settlers. It was geographically remote from the other settlement on the Ashley and Cooper rivers to the south. As the two separate sections gained population, they set up separate legislative assemblies, approved by the proprietors. In 1710, the proprietors appointed a governor of North Carolina, "independent of the governor of Carolina," thus recognizing the separation of North from South Carolina. In 1721, South

Carolina was declared a royal province, and eight years later North Carolina also became a crown colony. North and South Carolina also had different economies and different demographics. North Carolina's economy was a mix of livestock, tobacco, and naval stores. Naval stores provided lumber, rope, and pine tar for sailing ships. Those that worked in the pine tar industry gained the name "tar heels." In terms of population, while South Carolina was 70 percent African slaves by 1700, North Carolina remained 80 percent white.

Georgia

Twenty trustees in England administered Georgia, founded in 1733, for two decades. Georgia was established to serve many purposes: as an extension of the southern provincial frontier; as a buffer or a first line of defense between the Spanish colony of Florida and the English settlements; as a planned Utopia where the trustees hoped to establish a model society; as a refuge for persecuted Protestants from Europe; as a new opportunity for men who had been released from debtor's prisons in England; as an Enlightenment project to make productive use of England's "deserving poor" and as a model "colony" that would produce commodities that England wanted, notably silk and citrus fruits.

In its inception, Georgia was governed strictly by its Board of Noble Trustees and had no popularly elected assembly. The Trustees brought in silkworms from China and grapes from France for their planned economy of silk and wine. Alcohol was prohibited in Georgia so as to dissuade the laziness of poor people and "second chance" criminals. Slavery was prohibited for the same reasons.

The "model colony" that was envisioned by the Board of Trustees never materialized due to multiple problems. The wine business failed in Georgia due to grape-eating bugs and birds. The silk business also failed because silkworms needed the trees from China and Georgia birds feasted on the imported silkworms. As a consequence, the population of Georgia was only 2,800 in 1750; hence, Parliament passed the legalization of slavery and alcohol in Georgia. Georgia then developed into a rice and indigo plantation economy based on slave labor like South Carolina.

Colonial Economy

New England

The rise of capitalism throughout Western Europe, which coincided with the founding of the English colonies, determined that the American provincial economy would be capitalistic in orientation with an emphasis on trade, production for market, and eventual regional specialization. Each colony's economy at the outset was rather primitive—merely an appendage of the economy of the mother country. However, shortly after the mid-eighteenth century an indigenous, well-developed capitalism emerged.

The economic development of New England was strongly influenced by the systems of land distribution and of trade. In the seventeenth century, land was granted by the legislature to groups—usually church congregations—that, in turn, distributed the land among their members.

The result was the encouragement of the famous New England township system, whose principal aim was to maintain an effective social-religious community. After provision for the church, sometimes a school and a village green had been made, each family was customarily granted a town lot. Plots of land outside the town were then distributed among members of the group, with common land retained for grazing purposes and a specified number of acres reserved for latecomers.

Distributing the land in this fashion meant that all members of the group were in proximity to the church, the heart of the Puritan community. It also meant that sending youngsters to school raised no serious problems and that towns became the basis for representative government with town meetings providing the political structure to resolve local issues.

In the eighteenth century the New England land system changed. It was no longer so important to plant a concentrated social-religious community, and therefore settlement along western frontier lands was seldom made by church groups. Instead, people of influence and means began to buy large blocks of land for speculative purposes, selling off smaller parcels to individual farmers.

Even in the older towns conditions changed. Original settlers or descendants of original settlers moved out, often selling their land to newcomers. Absentee ownership of town lots and township lands was common. Whereas in the seventeenth century town proprietors were nearly always residents of the town, this was less often the case in eighteenth-century communities.

Although farming was the predominant occupation in New England up to 1640, trade gained increasing importance thereafter. From 1640 to 1660, the English were preoccupied with civil war and political upheaval at home, and colonials began to replace the English merchants as the trading enterprisers. It was at this time that the developing resources of New England fisheries encouraged trade between the Puritans of New England and Puritans who had settled in the West Indies.

New England merchants gradually gained a position of economic and political primacy. By the end of the seventeenth century they had already begun to replace the Puritan magistrates as the source of economic and political power. By the 1760s, they constituted the single strongest voice in New England.

It is important to remember that merchants were not alone in their dependence on trade for prosperity. The artisans who repaired canvas and built vessels and the farmers who exported meat products—in fact, the entire population in one way or another—were partly dependent upon prosperous commercial relations. Meat, fish, and lumber, which were the principal articles of export, found their major market in the West Indies. New England was also dependent on its role as a carrier of exports from other provinces and of imports from England.

For labor, New Englanders depended largely on members of their own families, though they sometimes hired local servants and imported indentured servants. New England, in contrast to some of the other regions, was attractive to skilled workers because they could find a ready market for their talent in an area dominated by a town system. Each town needed a carpenter and a blacksmith, for example. Slavery, though never as important to the northern economy as it was further south, was fully legal in all of the New England colonies.

▶ Skilled workers, such as blacksmiths, found ready markets in New England towns. *Corbis Images*

The Southern Colonies

Three significant factors affected the economic development of the Southern colonies: the distribution of land, the evolution of the plantation system, and the tremendous production of staples for market. In the seventeenth-century Chesapeake colonies, Virginia and Maryland, land was distributed directly to individuals, in contrast to the practice in early New England. Moreover, colonists scattered up and down the rivers of the Chesapeake area instead of settling in groups. Each planter tried to have his own landing where an ocean-going vessel could readily load the tobacco he produced and unload the goods he had ordered from England. This method of settlement made the county the basis of local government, discouraged the establishment of a school system because of the distances involved, and noticeably influenced the transplantation of the Anglican Church.

In the seventeenth century the average landholding was relatively small, since labor to cultivate extensive landholdings was lacking. The headright system, whereby a planter could obtain fifty acres of land for each dependent or servant brought to the colonies, allowed the first accumulations of land to occur. It was not until the eighteenth century, when American colonists obtained control of the machinery to distribute land, that large grants became fairly common.

Although slaves were imported into the Chesapeake colonies and into South Carolina in the seventeenth century, the principal labor force was composed of indentured servants, including convicts and paupers who were sentenced to labor in America. Over 1,500 indentures were imported annually into Virginia alone in the 1670s and the 1680s.

In the following years the plantation system became larger and African slaves became the predominant source of labor. The Mid-Atlantic colonies—New York, the Jerseys, Pennsylvania, and Delaware—expanded to compete for indentured servants. At the same time, the supply of English indentures decreased because the demand for labor in England increased. As a result, the institution of slavery became fastened upon the eighteenth-century Southern colonies. The planter elite, whose power was based on slaves, now dominated a society that had been made up largely of yeomen.

▶Tobacco was a staple product in the development of the Southern colonies. *iStockphoto*

Tobacco continued to be the main staple in the Chesapeake colonies; however, rice became prominent in South Carolina; and the indigo introduced by Elizabeth Pinckney became an important crop. Naval stores became a major export of North Carolina. Deerskins were the important goods obtained through trade with the Native Americans.

In the seventeenth century, no merchant group developed in these colonies because planters sold directly to English merchants. In the eighteenth century, an important merchant group developed in strategically located Charleston, South Carolina, trade center for a vast hinterland. However, no major tensions developed between merchants and planters in the South because the prosperity of one was directly related to the wellbeing of the other. In fact, the same individual might belong to both groups, since many merchants bought land and planters sometimes became merchants.

The Mid-Atlantic Colonies

During the eighteenth century English migration decreased because demand for laborers and opportunities for advancement greatly increased at home as Britain expanded its trade and manufactures. However, a tremendous influx of non-English peoples—Germans, Scotch-Irish, Irish, Swiss, and French Huguenots—into the mid-Atlantic colonies resulted in expansion of that region at a rate exceeding that of New England or the Southern colonies.

The reasons for the migration of non-English peoples were fundamentally economic, although religious intolerance and fear of destructive wars at home sometimes played a part. Opportunities for the Scotch-Irish in Ireland were limited, whereas opportunities in the British colonies appeared much more attractive. German Pietists came to Pennsylvania in large numbers because that colony offered an attractive land policy as well as religious toleration.

Land policies in Pennsylvania, the Jerseys, and New York varied greatly. In New York land was granted to royal favorites, who established extensive manors. An ordinary settler was often forced to accept leasehold and become a renter instead of obtaining a clear title to the land. The distribution of lands in Pennsylvania was much more favorable. Small grants could be obtained by outright purchase. Scotch-Irish settlers on the frontier of Pennsylvania frequently assumed title to the land by right of settlement and refused to pay the proprietors.

New York and Philadelphia developed into major ports in the eighteenth century, with Philadelphia becoming the second largest city within the British Empire. Both cities developed a strong mercantile class and attracted skilled artisans—cabinetmakers, silversmiths, gunsmiths, and the like. Both exported grain. Grain was the principal commodity of the mid-Atlantic colonies, which became the "breadbasket" of colonial America.

Pennsylvania's rapid growth and early economic maturity reflected the astonishing general growth of the colonies. The handful of English settlers had become 250,000 strong by 1700. By 1760, the colonies provided a good livelihood for a population of approximately two million—almost half the population of England. No wonder, then, that trade quadrupled, banking and currency became important issues, tradesmen and merchants carried on sophisticated economic practices, and that a relatively stable society was formed.

English Regulatory Acts

As the economy of the American provinces matured, imperial regulations were enlarged to prevent foreign and colonial commercial competition with the mother country. Although restrictions were placed on the tobacco trade as early as the 1620s, a series of enactments passed from 1651 to 1700 laid the framework for the English imperial system.

The Navigation Act of 1651 was designed primarily to reduce competition from foreign shipping. It provided that non-European goods brought to England or its possessions could be transported only in English (including colonial) ships, and that goods from the Continent could be brought into England or its possessions only in vessels belonging to the country that had produced the goods. A second Navigation Act (often called the Enumeration Act), passed in 1660, closed the loophole that had permitted colonials to import directly from Europe. It provided that all goods, regardless of origin, could be imported into or exported from any English colony only in English ships. "Enumerated" goods—including sugar, cotton, indigo, dye goods, and tobacco—of colonial origin were to be shipped only to England or its colonies; they could not be exported directly to other European countries.

The Enumeration Act was particularly hard on Virginia and Maryland, for it meant that colonial tobacco—which the English market could not absorb—had to be shipped to England and then reexported to Continental markets. Reexportation costs—including handling charges, storage charges, and the costs of frequent loss of tobacco stored in English warehouses—were extremely high. The enumeration of tobacco produced an economic depression in Virginia and Maryland in the late seventeenth century and was responsible for the later concentration of land ownership, since only the large-scale producer could meet the disadvantages of the market.

In 1663, a third Navigation Act—the Staple Act—required that most commodities (excluding salt, servants, and wine) imported into the colonies from Europe had to be shipped from England in English-built ships. However, the colonists found a loophole. Often ships stopped at several colonial ports before returning to Europe; therefore, colonial merchants loaded enumerated goods at one port supposedly designated for a later colonial port. In actuality, the goods remained on the ship and went directly to Europe.

To close this loophole, a fourth Navigation Act was passed in 1673. It provided that whenever the vessel carried enumerated commodities, a plantation duty—that is, a bond—had to be paid before a ship could clear a colonial port. A final enactment in 1696 provided for the creation of vice-admiralty courts in America, to place the enforcement of the navigation laws in the hands of men appointed directly by the crown. Research indicates that the burden of the Navigation Acts was greater at the end of the seventeenth century than at any other time during the colonial period, and that the acts were seldom evaded.

Whereas in the seventeenth century the English regulations were directed principally at commerce, in the eighteenth century—with the maturing of the American economy—the regulations were directed principally at manufactures. The Woolen Act of 1699, which forbade colonial export of wool products, had little impact upon the American colonies because their exportation of textiles was limited anyway. However, the Hat Act of 1732—which prohibited exportation of hats from one colony to another and severely restricted the colonial hat industry—adversely affected New York and New England that had been usurping a vital European market. The act eliminated this colonial enterprise, greatly benefitting London hatters that had exerted pressure in Parliament to pass the bill.

The Molasses Act of 1733 placed a heavy duty upon sugar, rum, molasses, and other commodities imported into the colonies from the non-British West Indies. This enactment seriously hampered the trade of the American colonies. They had been importing these commodities—molasses in particular—in quantity from Spanish and French colonies at a price cheaper than could be obtained in the British West Indies. The Molasses Act was evaded by extensive smuggling because the act seriously encroached upon this customary channel of trade.

The Iron Act of 1750 encouraged the colonial production of pig and bar iron for use by the English iron and steel industry but prohibited the building of slitting mills, forges, and other iron-finishing equipment in the colonies. Certain colonies, notably Pennsylvania, defied the prohibition; and when war broke out between France and England in 1752, the home authorities were unable to enforce the act with vigor. After 1763, of course, the continual crises between the mother country and the colonies prevented effective enforcement.

Conflict with the Native Americans

Throughout the seventeenth century, there was conflict with the Native Americans, who saw themselves being dispossessed of their land and their way of life. In 1622, for example, the Powhatans under Opechancanough nearly succeeded in wiping out the new settlement of Jamestown in Virginia. After the English murdered the Powhatan war captain and religious leader Nemattanew, Chief Opechancanough and the Powhatans waged a war on the white population of Virginia that led to the death of approximately 25 percent of the English population. By the time the Native Americans were finally subdued, the Virginia Colony was bankrupt.

After Opechancanough's revolt, the English adopted a policy of "perpetual enmity" toward the natives in Virginia and only viewed them as obstacles to English progress that must be eradicated. John Smith was given orders from England to "root out the Indians from being any longer a people." John Smith wrote that many believed that the orders would be good for the plantation because "now we have just cause to destroy them by all means possible." In 1623, the Eng-

► From 1636–1637, the Puritans fought a bitter war of annihilation against the Pequots. The English burned villages full of unarmed women and children, trying to eradicate the race of those who lived on this land first. *Wikipedia photo*

lish invited the Native Americans to a feast in celebration of peace; and then at he feast served the natives poisoned wine, thus leading to the death of approximately two hundred natives.

During 1636–1637, the Puritans fought a bitter war of annihilation against the Pequots. In the Pequot war, William Bradford wrote that the Puritans burned a native village full of unarmed women and children. Bradford noted that it was "frightful to see the Indians frying in the fire and their blood quenching the same." He also noted the stench from burning flesh, but credited God with the victory.

The next big war between whites and Native Americans in New England occurred in 1675–1676. Known as King Philip's War, the war entailed fierce fighting along the frontier. In 1671, the Plymouth colonists had forced Native American leader Metacomet (referred to as King Philip by the colonists) to surrender the Native Americans' stock of guns and accept a treaty of submission acknowledging English rule. In 1675, other Native Americans murdered a Native American informant, and the Puritans retaliated by executing three natives that were accused in the murder. The executions sparked a war of retaliation led by Metacomet. The native tribes banded together and launched an offensive against their white oppressors, who now had superior numbers and greater technology.

At first, the natives scored resounding victories. In all, the Native Americans under King Philip attacked fifty-two of the ninety Puritan towns and completely destroyed thirteen. In reaction, New England passed the first military draft law in American history in 1676. Helped by the infusion of new draftees, the native offensive had been thwarted, and the colonists had nearly exterminated the Narragansetts, Wampanoags, and Nipmucks by the spring of 1676. King Philip was killed in battle, and his head was put on public display in Plymouth for twenty-five years. However, the conflict left so strong a legacy that one scholar, Mary Beth Norton, has argued that it was a contributing factor in the hysteria about witches that erupted in Salem in 1692. The estimated cost of the war was greater than all the personal property held in New England. Fear of evoking another war with the Native Americans prevented the New England colonists from extending their boundaries any further into Native American territory for forty years.

MAP 1.4 King Philip's War (1675–1676)

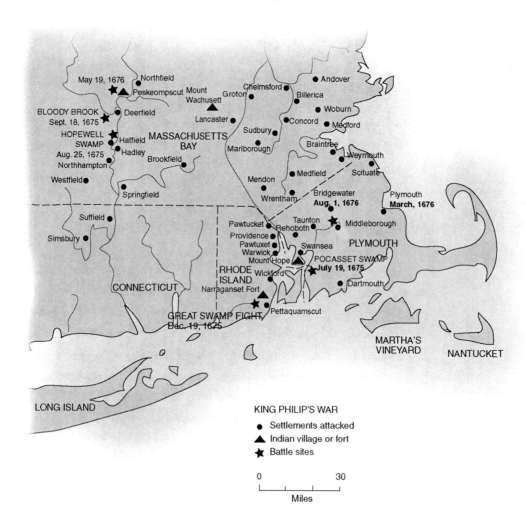

In need of labor, English settlers sometimes tried to make slaves of the Native Americans captured in skirmishes. But it did not work. The captives could too easily slip off and return to their own people. In some colonies—South Carolina, for instance—captured Native Americans were shipped off to the West Indies as slaves around 1700.

Efforts were also made to convert Native Americans to English ways. Schools were established for them in several colonies; but once the Native Americans returned to their own people, they took up their traditional ways and customs.

On occasion, the practice of treating Native Americans as a foreign power had gratifying results for the English. When Iroquois and Cherokee leaders were brought to London to sign treaties of friendship, the crown made these occasions festive and special. Both Indian nations remained invaluable allies of England for a century.

In the colonial period powerful nations of Native Americans blocked English access to the interior of the continent. These Native Americans controlled the interior trade by their defensive position along the Appalachian range and were strengthened by their ability to play off the European rivals, France and England, against each other. They held the balance of power in America for a century (1660–1760). Not until the French had been eliminated as a major participant in colonizing the continent were the English finally able to penetrate the Appalachian barrier in any great numbers.

Trade represented one of the most important contacts between the settlers and the Native Americans and accounted for the founding of many of the first modest provincial fortunes. In South Carolina, for example, the early road to riches was gained not by raising rice but by trading in deerskins, one of the most valuable exports from the Carolinas until well into the eighteenth century. In Pennsylvania James Logan's emergence as the first citizen of that colony was made possible through what he called the "stinking" fur trade. In New York the trade brought a fortune and a title to Sir William Johnson.

During the eighteenth century the locus of the fur trade shifted. By 1730 New England's share was limited, if not negligible. The mid-Atlantic colonies, the area of greatest expansion, had become the center of the trade, with New York and Pennsylvania well in the lead. In the South, Virginia had controlled the principal trade with the Cherokees and the Chickasaws in the late seventeenth century, but early in the eighteenth century South Carolina developed into a serious rival. Then Georgia moved into contention. By the mid-eighteenth century, New York and Georgia were perhaps the two colonies most deeply engaged in the trade with the natives.

Chapter Review ▶ ▶ ▶

Summary

The first Americans migrated to the Western Hemisphere during the last ice age over a land bridge from Asia some 15,000 years ago. Eventually, the descendants of these hunting and gathering societies would develop agriculture, including irrigated agriculture, 3,000 years before the arrival of Columbus. Advanced societies developed in the Andes, Yucatan, and Central Valley of Mexico with the Incas, Mayas, and Aztecs, who built pyramids, produced advanced mathematics, and accurate calendars. The journeys of Marco Polo overland to Asia prompted Europeans to seek an easier route to Asia via the sea to exploit Asian wealth in gold and spices. Norse explorers under Leif Erikson began a colony in North America in 1001, but abandoned it the next year and the Western Hemisphere remained unknown to the Europeans. Portugal pioneered navigation and exploration under Prince Henry the Navigator in the fifteenth Century culminating in Vasco da Gama's successful voyage to Asia around the Horn of Africa in 1498. Meanwhile, Columbus, seeking a Western water route to Asia for Spain, landed in the New World in 1492 touching off an age of European exploration and colonization. The Spanish conquered the Native American societies with horses, swords, guns, and European diseases. Meanwhile, the English and French, who were later to the colonization game, would plant colonies in North America. The first permanent Spanish settlement in the U.S. was at St. Augustine, Florida, in 1565, while the French planted colonies in 1608 in what is now Montreal and Nova Scotia. The first successful English colony was at Jamestown, Virginia, in 1607 (after a failed English attempt at Roanoke 1585–1588) and the success of the colony was largely due to the commercial success of tobacco.

Beginning with the colonization of Jamestown by the Virginia company in 1607 and proceeding through the establishment of Georgia as a colony for the "deserving poor" in 1732, the English successfully colonized the East Coast of what is now the United States with thirteen colonies from Georgia to New Hampshire. The colonies were diverse, though most were proprietary colonies where profit was the motive and the lure of economic advancement was the primary motive for immigration. Outside of New England, in the 17th century most immigrants from Europe arrived as indentured servants seeking economic opportunity and most came as single males. In New England, immigrants arrived as family units fleeing persecution between 1630 and 1642. African slaves were brought to North America as early as 1619 in Virginia and composed 80 percent of the population of South Carolina by the early 18th century. Though all English, the colonies were diverse both economically and culturally with Puritan dominance in New England and others nominally Anglican, but with religious diversity dominating in most colonies. Pennsylvania was unique as a planned refuge for Quakers and peace with Native American tribes due to land purchases rather than seizures. Maryland was unique as a "planned refuge for Catholics" that never had a Catholic majority, but enjoyed religious tolerance until 1789 when an Anglican revolt removed the Calverts as Catholic proprietors.

Religious tolerance prevailed in New York and other areas where religious diversity precluded dominance by any one group, but Puritanism dominated in New England where charters called for the rejection of all that were "contrary-minded." The Calvinist-influenced Puritans arrived in America to practice their religion freely, but denied religious freedom to those in their midst, persecuting, banishing, and even executing

Summary (cont'd)

heretics or those that thought differently. Quakers in particular bore the brunt of the Puritan persecution. Consequently, Rhode Island was founded by persons banished from the Puritan community and William Penn founded Pennsylvania as a refuge for Quakers.

Native Americans were generally viewed as obstacles to colonial progress in spite of sometimes profitable trade and cases where European colonists were saved from starvation by Native Americans, such as at Plymouth in 1620. Land was purchased from the Natives rather than taken in Pennsylvania, but armed struggles between whites and Natives began almost the moment the English arrived at Jamestown and continued intermittently throughout the seventeenth century.

English administration of its colonies in North America was slow to develop, beginning with the King's Privy Council and progressing through the Lords of Trade in 1675 and culminating with the rule by Parliament after the Glorious Revolution of 1688. The Colonies themselves in North America had their own governing structures that included Royal Governors that were representatives of the King, Colonial Councils which served as the upper houses of the legislatures as well as the high courts in the colonies, and Colonial Assemblies that were elected by freemen, but there were normally property requirements for voting. The members of the Colonial Councils were members of the elite class and often appointed by the King, while members of the Assemblies represented the common people in the colonies.

The American provincial economy emerged from its agricultural base with an emphasis on trade, production for market, and eventual regional specialization. In New England, shipping merchants gradually gained a position of economic and political primacy, but artisans who repaired canvas and built vessels and the farmers who exported meat products were also important. For labor, New Englanders depended largely on members of their own families, though they sometimes hired local servants and imported indentured servants. In the Southern Colonies, Plantation agriculture developed using primarily African slave labor and indentured servants. In the Middle Colonies, grain agriculture developed along with artisanship and international shipping. Philadelphia became the second largest city in the British Empire.

A series of English Regulatory Acts or Navigation Acts between 1651 and 1700 were designed to prevent foreign commercial competition and the competition of colonial manufactures with those of the mother country.

Throughout the seventeenth century, there was bloody conflict between the colonists and the Native Americans. In Virginia, Opechancanough's revolt in 1622 resulted in "perpetual enmity" between the English and the Native Americans, while five decades later, land pressures in Virginia led to Bacon's rebellion in 1675 and another Native American defeat. Meanwhile, in New England, Puritans burned entire Native American villages in the Pequot War of 1637 and put down the bloody Native American revolt led by Metacomet in King Philip's War in 1675–76. The English, however, were not the only Europeans that found themselves in disputes with the Native Americans as the Spanish suffered heavy losses and found themselves expelled from territory they claimed in the Southwest during the Pueblo Rebellion in 1680.

Chapter Review (cont'd) ▶ ▶ ▶

Chronological Time Line

20,000–12,000 B.C. Asian peoples migrate to North America across the Bering Strait

9000 B.C.   Global warming leads to the extinction of mammoths and other large game animals

1500 B.C.   Agriculture develops in North America

300 B.C.   Beginning of Anasazi culture

900–1100 C.E. Mississippian culture

982 C.E.   Erik the Red reaches North America

1001 C.E.   Leif Erikson establishes a Norse settlement in North America

1095 C.E.   Crusades begin

1150 C.E.   Anasazi culture vanishes

1418   Portugal takes the Madeira Islands and begins colonization.

1477   Marco Polo's travels published in Europe

1492   Columbus lands in the New World

1497   John Cabot is first English explorer to North America

1498   Vasco Da Gama reaches India via Cape of Good Hope

1493–1555   Spanish savagery and European diseases decimate Native populations in the Caribbean and Central America

1519–1522   Magellan's expedition sails around the world

1512–1565   Spain explores the Southern portion of North America

1519–1521   Cortez conquers the Aztecs

1532–1535   Pizarro conquers the Incas

1565   Spain founds a colony at St. Augustine, FL

1585–1588   The first English colonization attempt fails at Roanoke

Time Line (cont'd)

1607	Jamestown founded by England's Virginia Company
1608	Champlain plants French colonies at Quebec and Acadia
1612	John Rolfe plants the first English tobacco crop
1607	Jamestown is founded at Virginia
1619	First Africans are brought to Virginia
1620	Pilgrims land at Plymouth Rock on the Mayflower
1622	Opechancanough's revolt
1626	Peter Minuit purchases Manhattan from the Natives for goods equal to twelve beaver pelts.
1630	Puritans arrive in Massachusetts Bay
1632	Maryland is founded by George Calvert as a planned refuge for Catholics
1636	Harvard is founded as a Puritan theological seminary
1637	Pequot War in New England
1640–1660	Political unrest and Civil War in England
1642	Puritans gain control in England and end persecution of Puritans
1649	Maryland Toleration Act
1651	Navigation Act
1660	Second Navigation Act (Enumeration Act)
1660	Execution of Mary Dyer
1663	Carolina is founded as a proprietary colony
1663	Third Navigation Act (Staple Act)

Chapter Review (cont'd) ▶ ▶ ▶

Time Line (cont'd)

1670	Settlement is started near present-day Charleston, S.C.
1673	Fourth Navigation Act
1675	England defeats the Netherlands in a war and gains permanent control of the colony on the Hudson, renamed New York
1675	Lords of Trade is created
1675–1676	Bacon's Rebellion in Virginia
1675–1676	King Philip's War in New England
1680	Pueblo Revolt
1681	King Charles II grants a charter for a colony to William Penn
1686	Lords of Trade creates the Dominion of New England
1688	Glorious Revolution elevates the power of Parliament in England
1688–1691	Glorious Revolution in England installs Protestant William of Orange to the throne and England passes religious toleration while Maryland deposes the Calverts and ends religious toleration.
1689–1697	King William's War (1689–1697)
1692	Witch Trials in Salem Village
1696	Lords of Trade is replaced by the Board of Trade
1696	Creation of vice-admiralty courts in America to place enforcement of navigation laws in the hands of men appointed directly by the crown.
1699	The Woolen Act, which forbade colonial export of wool products
1702	Queen Anne's War (1702–1713)
1713	Peace of Utrecht 1713
1732	Hat Act prohibited exportation of hats from one colony to another

Time Line (cont'd)

1733	Georgia is founded as a colony for the deserving poor
1733	Molasses Act placed a heavy duty upon sugar, rum, molasses, and other commodities imported into the colonies from the non-British West Indies
1738	Mose founded by the Spanish in Florida as a community of runaway English slaves
1739	Stono Rebellion
1740–1748	King George's War.
1741	New York Conspiracy Trials
1750	The Iron Act encouraged the colonial production of pig and bar iron for use by the English iron and steel industry
1754	Acadians leave Nova Scotia for New Orleans.
1754	George Washington is defeated by the French at Fort Necessity.
1754–1763	Seven Years War or French and Indian War
1755	George Washington and General James Braddock are defeated near Fort Duquesne by the French.
1756	William Pitt becomes Prime Minister 1758–1759
1758–1759	British take Forts Duquesne, Niagara, and Ticonderoga
1759	British capture Quebec
1760	British capture Montreal
1763	Peace of Paris: France cedes French possessions in North America to England
1763	Proclamation of 1763 orders white settlers to return east of the Appalachians.

Chapter Review (cont'd) ▶ ▶ ▶

Sources Consulted

Virginia DeJohn Anderson, "Migrants and Motives: Religion and the Settlement of New England," *New England Quarterly*, LVIII (1985), 339–383.

Bernard Bailyn, *Voyages to the West: A Passage in the Peopling of America on the Eve of the Revolution* (1986).

Kathleen M. Brown, *Goodwives, Nasty Wenches, and Anxious Patriarchs: Gender, Race and Power in Colonial Virginia* (1996).

Lois Green Carr and Lorena Walsh, "The Planter's Wife: The Experience of Women in Seventeenth-Century Maryland," *William and Mary Quarterly*, 3d ser., XXXIV (1977), 542–565.

Alfred W. Crosby, *The Columbian Exchange: Biological and Cultural Consequences of 1492* (1972).

David Hackett Fischer, *Albion's Seed: Four British Folkways in America* (1989).

James Horn, *Adapting to a New World: English Society in the Seventeenth-Century Chesapeake* (1994).

Karen O. Kupperman, *Indians and English: Facing Off in Early America* (2000).

Barry J. Levy, *Quakers and the American Family: British Settlement in the Delaware Valley* (1988).

Mary Beth Norton, *In the Devil's Snare: The Salem Witchcraft Crisis of 1692* (2002).

Carla G. Pestana, *Quakers and Baptists in Colonial Massachusetts* (1991).

Alan Taylor, *American Colonies* (2002).

Laurel Thatcher Ulrich, *Good Wives: Images and Reality in the Lives of Women in Northern New England* (1982).

2 The British Atlantic World

Outline

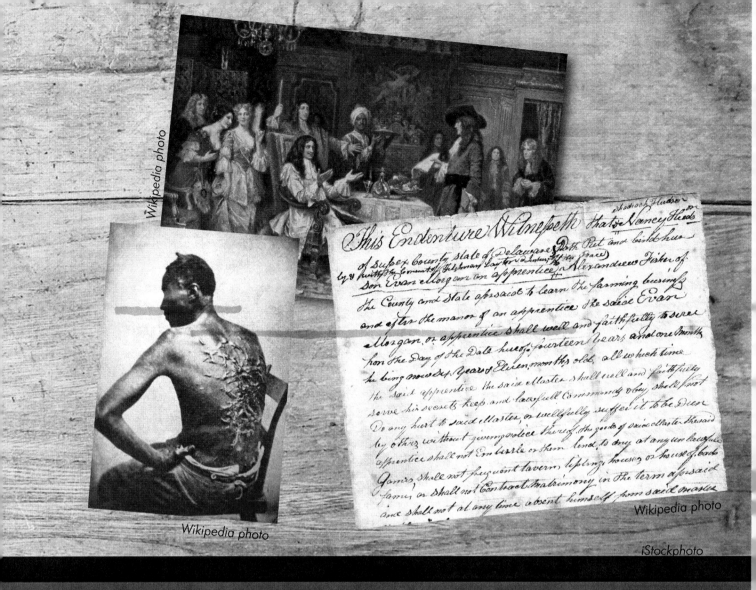

Wikipedia photo

Wikipedia photo

Wikipedia photo

iStockphoto

Slavery

The British Caribbean

The Caribbean, or British West Indies, was the richest part of the British colonies in America. The British West Indies included Bermuda (1612), Barbados (1627), Leeward Islands (St. Kitts, Antigua, Nevis, and Montserrat), and Jamaica (1655). The main objective for settlement in these areas was profit. The environment was very different from England and disease such as malaria killed many so only people willing to take the risk settled in the Caribbean. Mostly young sons of the English gentry or merchant families came to make a fortune in hopes to return home wealthy men. Many also moved to this area as indentured servants. Tobacco was the first crop of the area but was soon replaced with sugar, which turned a significant profit. Since sugar production required large investment capital, the wealthiest inhabitants began to consolidate power and indentured servants no longer saw opportunity in these colonies. As a result, indentured servants went elsewhere and large plantation owners began to import slaves from Africa as the main labor force. As slaves became the majority of the population, a very strict slave code was established and the slave system became the most horrendous out of all the British colonies.

The Caribbean was where most slaves arrived before arriving in the British mainland colonies. Because of ocean currents and trade winds, the ships from Africa readily arrived in the Caribbean first. It became a practice to "season" slaves in the Caribbean, which meant slaves were beaten into submission and punished harshly to "break their will" and then when they arrived in the mainland colonies, they were more submissive. Moreover, once a slave was "seasoned" they were worth more money.

The Caribbean influenced the mainland colonies in several ways. First, the mid-Atlantic colonies developed an important market for their foodstuffs. Since every parcel of land in the West Indies went toward sugar production because of the vast profit margins involved with the crop, plantation owners needed to import food. Second, many people who made their fortunes in Barbados moved to South Carolina to escape the harsh environment of the island. With them they brought their strong materialistic and commercial mentality including the harsh slave system they developed.

The Atlantic Slave Trade

The first Africans to arrive in the British mainland colonies came to Virginia in 1619 as part of what became a vast and very profitable Atlantic trade in humans, a trade that had begun about 100 years earlier with the slaves sent to the West Indies. The records do not reveal whether the Africans brought to Virginia in 1619 came as indentured servants or slaves, but it is known that by 1650 Virginia had both black freemen and black slaves. African immigration grew slowly during the seventeenth century.

The human cargo arrived in colonial America from Africa under particularly cruel conditions. Having purchased captured Africans from African middlemen, the traders loaded them onto ships for the infamous "Middle Passage." Two competing goals were in play for the traders. On the one hand, it was in their economic interest to deliver their goods alive and in good enough health to be sold into slavery. On the other, they wanted to cram as many people in as they could, once again to maximize their profits. Typically, the captives made the long voyage to America below decks and in shackles.

Once put on shore and sold, the captives found themselves the property of people speaking an unfamiliar language and with unfamiliar customs and laws. Scholars debate the extent to which slaves were able to reconstitute their own culture, family life—which was centered more on extended kin networks than was the European model—and religious traditions, given such unfavorable circumstances. What is clear is that much of American culture, jazz being the prime example, has been profoundly influenced by the African legacy. Hence we know that despite all of the suffering, the Africans were not stripped of their culture, as had been thought formerly.

Late in the seventeenth century the pace of importation of African slaves quickened. Most were brought to the Southern colonies of Maryland, Virginia, North Carolina, South Carolina, and eventually Georgia. By the beginning of the American Revolution people from Africa comprised 20 percent of the population. Given the size of this group, it is hardly surprising that the unwilling immigrants from Africa had an enduring impact on life in what was to become the United States of America.

The proportion of slaves in the population of Virginia rose to 25 percent in 1720, and to 41 percent in 1750. Slavery became the labor base upon which the large-scale plantation system in Virginia, Maryland, and North and South Carolina was founded. Virginia, Maryland, and South Carolina were desperately in need of workers. In the seventeenth century, indentured servants had been the primary labor force in Virginia and Maryland; and indentures in modest numbers were introduced into New England, where family labor predominated. Beginning in the late seventeenth century, however, and accelerating in the eighteenth century, indentured servants were increasingly attracted to the mid-Atlantic colonies. As a result, the Southern colonies were correspondingly desperate for labor as large landholdings became more numerous.

By 1775, 20 percent of the population of the English colonies in North America was composed of African Americans, most of them slaves. More than four hundred thousand lived in the colonies of Maryland, Virginia, North Carolina, South Carolina, and Georgia—a number almost equal to the total population of New England.

Although it has often been asserted that the British Royal African Company brought most of the slaves to America, free traders were the principal conveyors of slaves. New Englanders, infrequently the Dutch, and later Southern merchants or planters, imported slaves from the Caribbean as well as from Africa. Some of the colonies tried to end by law the increasing importation of slaves, but the British Board of Trade rejected each act adopted by the individual colonial legislatures. Because of the profitability of the slave

MAP 2.1 Georgia and the Carolinas

The following two documents are from the eighteenth-century. The first is a portrait of Olaudah Equiano who first published his autobiography, *The Interesting Narrative of the Life of Olaudah Equiano or, Gustavus Vassa, The African,* in London in 1789. Equiano commissioned this portrait to use as the frontispiece for his narrative. The second document is an excerpt from his work. There is some debate about Equiano's birth place but Equiano claims that he was born in Africa in current-day Nigeria around 1745, then kidnapped around 1755/56 and sold to European slave traders. He endured the middle passage and experienced slavery in the Caribbean, the North American mainland colonies, and in Britain during his life. Predominantly, Equiano's slave experience was spent on the Atlantic while serving his master on merchant ships. He became a skilled sailor, learned how to read and write and his skills eventually allowed him to save enough money to buy his freedom by 1766. As a result of his experiences he wrote his story and published it primarily as an anti-slavery edict.

TO THE LORDS SPIRITUAL AND TEMPORAL, AND
THE COMMONS OF THE PARLIAMENT
OF GREAT BRITAIN.

My Lords and Gentlemen,

Permit me, with the greatest deference and respect, to lay at your feet the following genuine Narrative; the chief design of which is to excite in your august assemblies a sense of compassion for the miseries which the Slave-Trade has entailed on my unfortunate countrymen. By the horrors of that trade was I first torn away from all the tender connexions that were naturally dear to my heart; but these, through the mysterious ways of Providence, I ought to regard as infinitely more than compensated by the introduction I have thence obtained to the knowledge of the Christian religion, and of a nation which, by its liberal sentiments, its humanity, the glorious freedom of its government, and its proficiency in arts and sciences, has exalted the dignity of human nature.

I am sensible I ought to entreat your pardon for addressing to you a work so wholly devoid of literary merit; but, as the production of an unlettered African, who is actuated by the hope of becoming an instrument towards the relief of his suffering countrymen, I trust that such a man, pleading in such a cause, will be acquitted of boldness and presumption.

May the God of heaven inspire your hearts with peculiar benevolence on that important day when the question of Abolition is to be discussed, when thousands, in consequence of your Determination, are to look for Happiness or Misery!

I am,

MY LORDS AND GENTLEMEN,
Your most obedient,
And devoted humble servant,
OLAUDAH EQUIANO,
OR
GUSTAVUS VASSA.
Union-Street,
Mary-le-bone,
March 24, 1789.

Olaudah Equiano
or
GUSTAVUS VASSA,
the African

Source: www.gutenburg.net.

MAP 2.2 African Origins of the Slave Trade

trade, Britain considered it to be the basis for its entire trading structure.

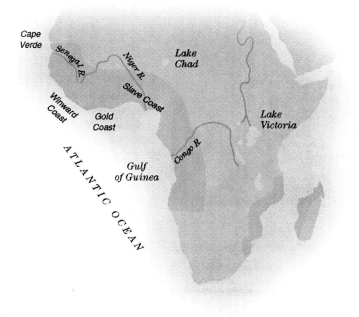

Slavery in the British Colonies

That the slaves came to the English colonies with no skills and that the culture of Africa was vastly inferior to that of the Western World were myths. Most slaves came with skills equal to those of an ordinary laboring Englishman. For example, the original source of the rice that became a successful crop in South Carolina was Madagascar, where Africans had been cultivating it for centuries. When Eliza Pinckney of South Carolina was unsuccessful in making the commercial dye indigo with a white overseer, she imported an African American slave whose knowledge, together with her own perseverance, culminated in an important marketable staple.

The agricultural tools of the African farmer and the English leaseholder did not vary greatly. In time, the transplanted African became the skilled worker in the Southern colonies—the cook, cooper, cobbler, and blacksmith. Sometimes a planter to put in a request for a slave from a special region of Africa because of the particular skills of its inhabitants.

The slave experience in the colonial period was varied and depended on where the slave lived and when. There were four distinctive slave experiences including slaves who lived in the North, the Chesapeake, the Lower South and the Caribbean. In addition, there were differences in the slave experience depending on if they lived in urban areas or rural areas. Slavery developed differently in each area due to the environment, ratio of slaves to free people in the regions, and the crop that was grown. Some were able to maintain various cultural traits from Africa while others were more likely to assimilate into white society.

Slave Life

Life for slaves varied across the American colonies depending on the colony in which they lived and the type of work in which they were engaged. Approximately 75 percent of slaves were involved in agriculture and most of the rest were involved in domestic servitude; consequently, slavery was primarily a way of organizing agricultural work so as to produce the greatest profits for landowners. A number of agricultural crops, including rice, tobacco, and cotton, were very labor intensive, and in the case of rice, required work in mosquito-infested swamps that few laborers for hire were inclined to do. African slaves with their greater resistance to tropical diseases provided the solution.

► A number of agricultural crops, including rice, tobacco, and cotton, were very labor intensive and, in the case of rice, required work in mosquito-infested swamps. African slaves with their greater resistance to tropical diseases provided the solution at low cost for farmers and plantation owners. *iStockphoto*

Most of the African slaves in the colonies, an estimated 80 percent, lived and worked on large plantations with two hundred slaves or more; and by far, most slaves lived in the Southern colonies, with South Carolina having the most slaves in the seventeenth century. Most southerners, however, did not own slaves. Only one in five southerners owned slaves, and 80 percent of slave owners owned fewer than five slaves.

Once on the plantation in America, slaves lived as family units in rustic small, crowded, slave cottages. Marriage between slaves was illegal, but informally encouraged and practiced as slave owners understood that slave men with wives and children were less likely to rebel. Slave owners could then use the threat of the sale of family members as a way to ensure discipline, hard work, and other preferred behavior. In spite of this, most slaves would experience the loss of family members through sale as slave reproduction often exceeded plantation labor demands and sales of excess laborers therefore became economically expedient for the masters.

Slave breeding was also common since slave owners desired to increase their slaveholdings through reproduction. Women who resisted the forced breeding would be subjected to the whip. Some women were also forced to satisfy the sexual desires of the master or other male members of the master's family. These relations often produced children, causing difficulties in the slave cottages as slave patriarchs raised the master's slave children in their cottages.

Not all slave/master sexual relations were forced, however. Some slave women sought sexual relations with the master as a way to improve their lives and the lives of their children. Slave mistresses of the master were more likely to have jobs in the house on the plantation rather than in the field, were more likely to have nicer clothing, and were more likely to have more frequent baths. Furthermore, the children of the master and the slave woman often received special treatment and preferred jobs on the plantation.

Slave Resistance and Rebellion

The devastating social consequences of slavery pervaded every aspect of colonial life. Conflict between African Americans and whites led to the enactment of elaborate codes for the conduct of slaves. Runaway slaves were normally caught, and the consequences for runaways were dire. That being the case, the most common forms of slave revolt were covert resistance such as faking illness, slacking work, breaking tools, and moving as slowly as masters would allow while staying ahead of the whip.

Mose

Beginning in the 1680s, Spain offered freedom to slaves from the English colonies that could make their way to Florida and accept Catholicism. In 1738, the Spanish Governor in Florida established a town north of St. Augustine for escaped slaves from the British colonies. The town, Gracia Real de Santa Teresa de Mose (Mose for short), was administered by an African-American Catholic convert named Francisco Menendez, a name he took at his Catholic baptism. Menendez was an escaped slave from Carolina who learned not only to speak but also to read and write Spanish. Menendez was given charge of Mose in 1738, and Mose became the first community of free African Americans in an area that is now the United States.

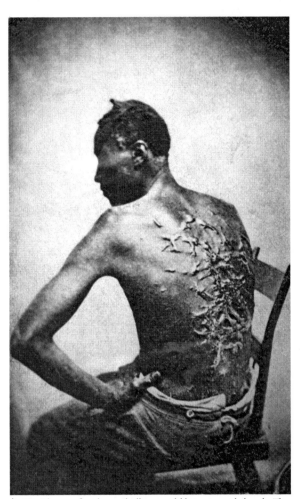

▶ Punishment for slave rebellion could be extremely harsh. The whip was commonly used to keeps slaves working throughout the day or to give lashings in retaliation for resistance.
Wikipedia photo

Stono Rebellion

In 1739, the Spanish Governor of Florida offered freedom to any slaves that could make their way to Florida from Carolina (there were no slaves in Georgia at the time). This announcement, along with word about a free settlement for African Americans in Mose, ignited the Stono Rebellion in South Carolina—the largest slave revolt in American history. On a Sunday morning before dawn, a group of some twenty slaves attacked a country store and killed the store's two shopkeepers while confiscating the store's guns and ammunition. The slave rebels placed the severed heads of their victims on the store's front steps and then journeyed toward Spanish Florida—attacking Southern plantations along the way and enticing other slaves to join their rebellion. The slave rebels burned and plundered over a half-dozen plantations and killed over twenty white men, women, and children. A force of whites was quickly assembled to put down the revolt and over sixty rebels were killed and their heads placed atop mileposts along the road as reminders to other slaves of the consequences of rebellion.

The fate of the rebels illustrated the fact that slaves had no chance of overturning slavery, and that rebellion would lead to certain death for the rebels. The Stono Rebellion stunned the white population, however, and fear of future revolts prompted defensive measures. Laws were passed to restrict the importation of slaves and to encourage the importation of white indentured servants. White settlements were promoted on the frontier as protection for older slave-centered communities.

▶ Phillis Wheatley: Black Poet

▶ Phillis Wheatley *Library of Congress*

There are few enslaved Africans brought to the British colonies in North America whose lives are as well documented as that of Phillis Wheatley. Part of the explanation lies in the Wheatley family history. More importantly, Phillis Wheatley left a living, written record in her verses.

In both respects, her life was very different from those of the great majority of Africans brought to America. Yet, her story represents the importance of the forced migration from Africa, not only because the numbers of people involved exceeded the migration of peoples from Western Europe in the colonial eighteenth century, but also because of the many talents brought to America by Africans. Unlike many other blacks, Phillis Wheatley was encouraged to develop her talents and was accepted into white society.

Phillis Wheatley was first seen in America as a delicate little girl, about eight years old, aboard a slave ship from Senegal that reached Boston in 1761. Susannah Wheatley, wife of tailor John Wheatley, wished to have a special personal servant. John purchased the young slave, brought her home, and named her Phillis.

At the time Phillis entered the Wheatley household, it included, in addition to the husband and wife, a son, Nathaniel, and a daughter, Mary. Three other children had died in their early years.

Susannah Wheatley and her daughter Mary, who was eighteen, observed that Phillis absorbed her lessons quickly. As a result, they began to instruct her, giving preference to biblical teachings. Within about sixteen months Phillis could read difficult passages in the Bible with ease. Encouraged, Mary taught Phillis a smattering of astronomy, ancient and modern geography, ancient history, and even a few of the Latin classics. Homer became Phillis's favorite author, and soon she began to write verse. In the household, she was increasingly considered a daughter rather than a slave, and it became a familiar treat among the Wheatley friends to have Phillis recite the poetry of others or verses of her own. Her first poem, entitled "A Poem, by Phillis, a Negro Girl, in Boston, On Death of the Reverend George Whitefield," appeared in print in 1770.

In 1771, Mary Wheatley married the pastor of the Second Church in Boston, the Reverend John Lathrop. In that same year, Phillis became a member of the congregation of the Old South Meeting house, a significant departure for that faith. Because Phillis's health appeared to fail, the Wheatley family physician recommended sea air. Nathaniel was about to leave for England on business, and so it was decided that Phillis would sail under protection of her foster brother. She was made a freed person before she left in May 1773.

The Countess of Huntingdon, for whom Whitefield had served as chaplain, welcomed Phillis in England. She attracted wide attention not only because of her writing talent but also because of her unusual gift of conversation. Brook Watson, the Lord Mayor of London, was sufficiently impressed to present Phillis with a 1720, Glasgow edition of *Paradise Lost*.

Phillis was urged to stay in London, but word reached her that Susannah Wheatley was seriously ill and longed for her return. Turning aside all entreaties to remain in London, Phillis left for Boston. However, before departing she arranged to have her collection of poems published under the title *Poems on Various Subjects, Religious and Moral.*

Nothing but despair greeted her upon returning to Boston. Susannah Wheatley died in March 1774. Four years later Susannah's husband John died, followed by the death of Mary Wheatley Lathrop. Nathaniel, the only remaining member of the family, was living abroad.

In April 1778, Phillis became the wife of John Peters. In her letters she wrote of him as an agreeable man, but she quickly discovered that he lacked qualities to which she had become accustomed in the Wheatley household, among them diligence and industry. Pursued by poverty, deeply affected by the war that cut her off from friends in England, Phillis finally earned her living by doing daily chores in a lodging house. She died December 1784, preceded in death by two of her three children.

Phillis Wheatley was a tragic figure; a victim of slavery who was rescued by a loving and talented family, a victim of a war that turned minds to politics rather than to poetry; yet her verses live on. First editions of her poems appeared in 1793. Since then, her verses and her life have been the subject of continuous study.

Her piety and upbringing in the Wheatley family are revealed in these lines from "On the Death of the Reverend Mr. George Whitefield."

> Thou, moon, hast seen, and all the stars of light,
> How he was wrestled with his God by night.
> He prayed that grace in ev'ry heart might dwell;
> He longed to see America excel;
> He charged its youth that ev'ry grace divine
> Should with full luster in their conduct shine.

Somewhat surprisingly, Phillis's references to slavery are limited. When it surfaces, as in her dedicatory verses to the Earl of Dartmouth, she links it to a larger context of freedom, a commentary on her extraordinary perception, well in advance of her time and place, and a fitting epitaph.

> Should you, my lord, while you peruse my song,
> Wonder from whence my love of Freedom sprung,
> Whence flow these wishes for the common good,
> By feeling hearts alone best understood,
> I, young in life, by seeming cruel fate
> Was snatched from Afric's fancied happy seat:
> What pangs excruciating must molest,
> What sorrows labor in my parent's breast!
> Steeled was that soul, and by no misery moved,
> That from a father seized his babe beloved:
> Such, such my case. And can I then but pray
> Others may never feel tyrannic sway?

The next year, Georgia's Governor James Oglethorpe retaliated against the Spanish for inciting the Stono Rebellion. He led an invasion of Florida and an attack on Mose, where he dispersed the free African Americans living there, before being forced to retreat by the Spanish. Oglethorpe reported, however, that Spanish priests were living in disguise among the free African Americans at Mose and that the Spanish were instigating slave revolts in the British colonies.

Oglethorpe's report spread panic and fear of slave revolt throughout the British colonies and in particular a panic gripped New York City, where over two thousand slaves were located. The largest concentration of slaves in North America at the time was in New York City, and a slave revolt there in 1712 had led to the execution of twenty-one slaves. In the summer of 1741, a series of fires in the city were blamed on a white tavern owner and a number of slaves. In the conspiracy trials that lasted the summer of 1741, one witness in the trials, sixteen-year-old Mary Burton, who had been granted immunity for her testimony, caused a sensation when she testified that the tavern of John Hughson where she worked was the center of a plot by the Pope to murder the city's white population and install white tavern owner John Hughson as king of the Africans. By the time the courts were finished, four whites and eighteen slaves were hanged, thirteen slaves were burned alive, while seventy were banished to the West Indies. One man, John Uty, who was a clergyman and Latin teacher that had just arrived in New York, was hanged as a likely Spanish Priest. The New York conspiracy trials of 1741 have been often compared with the Salem witch trials in terms of their irrationality and panic, but more people were executed in New York in 1741 (thirty-five) than in Salem Village (twenty).

Anglicizing the British North American Colonies

The Enlightenment

During the seventeenth century, English intellectual life underwent a transformation triggered by the momentous advance of science and the application of the theoretical framework of science to all phases of human experience. The writings of the father of scientific reasoning, Francis Bacon, marked the beginning of a movement called the Enlightenment. This movement was consummated by the great scientific discoveries of Sir Isaac Newton, whose *Mathematical Principles of Natural Philosophy* (1697) set forth, by precise demonstration, the laws of motion and gravitation.

The Enlightenment also affected religious thinking. Newton had used reasoning to discover laws in the physical universe. Many reasoned that laws must govern the relationship

▶ Sir Isaac Newton, 1642–1727 *Library of Congress*

between the human race and the spiritual universe too. In this view, God created the universe with a perfectly operating, harmonious system of unchangeable laws—the laws of nature. Once the universe had been created, so the reasoning went, God no longer took an active part in ruling it; and the natural laws set the requirements for human behavior.

Fortunately, these laws could be discovered; and once they were known, people had only to adjust their lives and their political and educational systems accordingly—in conformity with the requirements set by natural law. The closer to alignment between human activity and the laws of nature, the closer human institutions would be to perfection. In this view, people were perfectible and progress was inevitable. The deists believed that there was a God or supreme being that created the Universe; but they viewed him essentially as a "great watchmaker" who sets all of the laws of nature in motion, but does not intervene in human affairs. The deists did not accept Jesus of Nazareth as the "Son of God," instead viewing him as a "cynic sage" endowed with great wisdom. As for the human existence, the deists believed that life is what humans make of it and little, if anything, is left to fate or some Divine plan. Prominent deists included Ben Franklin, who described himself as a "thorough deist" in his autobiography, Thomas Paine, Ethan Allen, and perhaps Thomas Jefferson, though Jefferson stated, "I never told anyone my own religion."

iStockphoto

In spite of the influence of deism on some prominent Americans, it should be emphasized that the ideas of the Enlightenment affected only a small minority of the English and far fewer colonials in the seventeenth century. Most people went about their daily lives unaware of intellectual trends. Enlightenment ideas did not gain strong advocates in America until the mid-eighteenth century, and even then their influence was sharply restricted. In England, Enlightenment ideas permeated literature as well as political thought, whereas in America, they found expression chiefly in political thought. The *Declaration of Independence* appeals to the "laws of nature and nature's God."

The Enlightenment constituted only one current in the mainstream of intellectual life in eighteenth-century America. Whereas the English Age of Faith had dominated seventeenth-century colonial America, the widespread immigration of non-English groups brought a diversity of cultures. By the eighteenth century the colonies reflected what was to become a characteristic of the American mind—a wide diversity of intellectual streams.

The Enlightenment in America

The greatest influence of the Enlightenment in America was the encouragement it gave to scientific inquiry. Cotton Mather, the most prominent New England clergyman in the late seventeenth and early eighteenth centuries, was attracted to scientific investigation. He was an advocate of smallpox inoculations when others greeted this medical advance with uncertainty or fear. William Byrd II of Virginia, along with other colonials, belonged to England's Royal Society and frequently sent observations of colonial phenomena to his friends in England.

The contribution of most colonials was to that aspect of science called "natural history." Almost every botanical specimen collected in America constituted a contribution to knowledge because it added to the storehouse of scientific information. Carolus Linnaeus of Sweden, the foremost botanist in Europe, called John Bartram, who collected specimens throughout the provinces and cultivated rare species in his garden at Philadelphia, the finest contemporary "natural botanist." A celebrated work was Mark Catesby's extraordinary *Natural History of Carolina*.

Benjamin Franklin epitomized the Enlightenment in America. His profession was a printer and he used his position to expose people to Enlightenment thought. He readily published the works of John Locke and Baron de Montesquieu along with popular works by John Trenchard and Thomas Gordon in his various newspapers. Franklin's publications encouraged middling people to ponder Enlightenment ideas.

Franklin established the *Junto* in 1727 in Philadelphia for people to meet and discuss ideas that could improve society. In 1743 he established a more formal organization called the American Philosophical Society. This society established an extensive library, published journals, and held regular meetings for people to come and discuss various issues in the humanities and sciences. Early members of this society included George Washington, John Adams, Thomas Jefferson, Alexander Hamilton, Benjamin Rush, James Madison and many others.

Franklin contributed to theoretical science, although many of his provincial contemporaries pursued allied investigations with vigor and persistence. Fortunately for Franklin, he entered a field of physics in which relatively little work had been done; and thus he was not disadvantaged by his lack of background, particularly his limited knowledge of mathematics. His identification of lightning as electricity (though it was his son William, not Ben, who dangerously flew the kite in the lightning storm), his observations concerning the flow of electricity, and the equalization that took place between highly charged particles and those less highly charged—all were contributions that won him a reputation throughout Europe.

Endowed with an active and inventive mind, as well as quick wit, Franklin famously invented bifocals, the lightning rod (which greatly reduced the incidents of barn fires in America), and the Franklin Stove, an invention that proved to be a much more energy-efficient way of burning wood than a brick fireplace.

Franklin is also representative of the fact that although science became increasingly important in the colleges, those outside the institutions of learning pursued it most fervently. As proper eighteenth-century generalists, they were interested in politics, science, writing, and other broad-gauged, stimulating activities.

In vital ways, Enlightenment ideas affected the whole society. For one thing, provincial America—it represented a new, formative society—appeared in the eyes of some European and American observers to be the laboratory of the Enlightenment. American society, free from the embedded traditions of Europe, could presumably adjust to the new found ideas about the laws of nature more readily than Europeans.

Influences on Cultural Development

In intellectual and social life, as in political and economic life, the first English settlers in America shared the attitudes, ambitions, and habits of thought of their peers in the home country.

During the colonial period, however, these characteristics were modified. In part this was because of the changing intellectual life in England, which affected the colonies in a variety of ways. In part it was because the men and women born and educated in America knew firsthand only the ways of their colonial neighbors. They experienced English culture and English intellectual currents second-hand.

Furthermore, the immigration of non-English peoples brought added diversity and dimension to the social and intellectual scene. An evaluation of the degree of distinctiveness of American culture depends on the relative weight placed upon these elements—English, American, and non-English. Because individual historians have placed different emphasis upon these factors, their judgments have differed. But all agree that conditions in the British colonies influenced social and intellectual development.

Influence of English Society

In Elizabethan England, the social rank of a family was determined strictly by the status of the male head of the household. The top level of this patriarchal and paternalistic society consisted of noble families, whose position depended upon extensive landholdings and the favors that accrued to a privileged segment of society. The nobility was not quite a closed circle. Younger sons who did not inherit a substantial estate or title generally sought their fortunes through the life of the gentry, through commercial connections, or through such professions as the army and the church. It was possible for a highly successful entrepreneur to penetrate the nobility, though full-fledged acceptance was often delayed for several generations.

Below the nobility ranked the gentry, the country gentlemen. The life of the gentry centered around the land. The country gentleman knew his tenants and their problems, and he experienced at first hand the uncertainties, as well as the blessings, of farming. The gentry served as the backbone of governing authority, in part because the sovereign encouraged their participation as a shield against ambitious nobles. The gentry formed the largest group in Parliament, and they held those local offices which were mainly responsible for enforcing the statutes of the state. Marriage alliances between gentry and families engaged in trade were fairly frequent, and gentry families often contributed younger sons to trade, to adventure, to the military, to the church, and sometimes to the universities.

Below the gentry ranked the yeomen, who could be leaseholders or owners of small estates. A yeoman was a small scale farmer, a man attached to the soil who lived a simple life and farmed with frugality. The laborers and servant classes of Elizabethan England ranked below the yeomen. A laborer might be an apprentice who in time would enter a trade and make a good living, or he might be a man who worked for daily wages and whose chances of rising to a better social and economic position were remote. In the same fashion, to be a servant could mean to serve with a gentry family in the expectation that by means of a good marriage or hard work an elevation of status could be secured, or it could involve the meanest kind of position, from which no escalation of status seemed possible.

The English social structure was not transplanted intact to America. Members of the English aristocracy did not come to America. They were relatively content and well off at home, so they had no incentive to migrate to a primitive colonial wilderness. Occasionally, younger sons of noble families came to America to try their fortune, but even this element was rare.

Liberty & Equality

Liberty was one of the most important terms in the eighteenth-century British Empire. Neither Puritans nor Virginians came to the colonies looking for liberty because they believed they already had it under the British system of governance. Both carried to the region many of the distinctions of the British social system.

But Calvinism also pointed in another direction: It rejected much of the church hierarchy, believed in the priesthood of all believers, and introduced elective methods into portions of church policy. Later, philosophers of the Enlightenment included the principle of equality within their listings of "natural rights," and John Locke and Jean Jacques Rousseau added wider dimensions to the term's meaning.

More important, however, the idea of equality had a strong practical basis in the American colonial experience. The wilderness stripped away the distinctions of civilization and tended to put white men on an equal footing. Native Americans, disease, starvation, and other hazards of frontier life killed an earl's or a tinker's child with equal disregard. The lack of fixed organization in a new society made it possible for Americans to be both free and equal in an actual, visible sense. Social mobility allowed them to change their status, within limits, rather rapidly. The rough equality forced on American society by the frontier was the most compelling fact about it.

Colonial and republican society, like England's, was built on stratifications that few questioned. Everyone recognized, a Virginian wrote in 1760, that there were "differences of capacity, disposition, and virtue" among people, which divided them into classes. Yet these strata were broader and more vague than England's. Colonial society possessed the whole range of criteria for class distinctions, including wealth and property, dress, manners, speech, and education, but these carried less weight than they did abroad. There was not so much doffing of caps, bowing or curtseying, and pulling of forelocks; British General Carleton complained that it was difficult to uphold "the dignity of the throne and peerage" in American society. Few foreign travelers failed to remark on the fluidity of American classes, much of it the result of broad economic opportunities offered by an expanding society.

Eighteenth-Century Political Culture

By the mid-eighteenth-century, many of the colonial governments mirrored the English government. Most colonial governments had governors, councils, and assemblies that emulated the King and Parliament. Most the colonies were royal, which meant the King of England appointed the governors. The councils were usually appointed by the governor of the colony and the assemblies were popularly elected by white, property-owning men. In many of the colonies throughout the eighteenth century the assemblies grew stronger.

Newspapers proliferated in the eighteenth-century British North American colonies and many of the Enlightenment ideas of John Locke, Algernon Sidney, James Harrington, Thomas Hobbes, and Baron Montesquieu were prevalent. Most of the ideas of these Enlightenment

The following excerpt is from a collection of essays called *Cato's Letters*. The authors, John Trenchard and Thomas Gordon, were both political writers who published in London during the early eighteenth century and almost immediately attracted British colonial printers. This excerpt was one of the most popular essays in the colonies.

The Right and Capacity of the People to judge of Government.

What is government, but a trust committed by all, or the most, to one, or a few, who are to attend upon the affairs of all, that everyone may, with the more security, attend upon his own? A great and honourable trust; but too seldom honourably executed; those who possess it having it often more at heart to increase their power, than to make it useful; and to be terrible, rather than beneficent. … Honesty, diligence, and plain sense, are the only talents necessary for the executing of this trust; and the public good is its only end. … Publick truths ought never to be kept secrets; and they who do it, are guilty of a solecism, and a contradiction: Every man ought to know what it concerns all to know. Now, nothing upon earth is of a more universal nature than government; and every private man upon earth has a concern in it, because in it is concerned, and nearly and immediately concerned, his virtue, his property, and the security of his person: And where all these are best preserved and advanced, the government is best administered; and where they are not, the government is impotent, wicked, or unfortunate; and where the government is so, the people will be so, there being always and every where a certain sympathy and analogy between the nature of the government and the nature of the people.

Source: *American Weekly Mercury,* 13 February 1722, 20 September 1733, 27 April 1738; *New York Weekly Journal,* 10 December 1733, 21 July 1735; *Pennsylvania Gazette,* 1 December 1737, 10 November 1737, 11 May 1738; *South Carolina Gazette,* 1 August 1748; *Boston Gazette,* 12 May 1755, 19 May 1755.

writers were popularized by London writers such as John Trenchard and Thomas Gordon, Joseph Addison, and Viscount Bolingbroke. The popularized versions of these Enlightenment writers were then printed in various colonial newspapers increasing the role of citizens in many of the urban areas in the colonies. In particular, Trenchard and Gordon's works reinforced a political culture that encouraged the participation of lower and middling groups and lessened deferential society especially in Pennsylvania, New York, and Massachusetts. It could be argued that unintentionally political writers gave colonists the language needed to oppose British politics during the 1760s and 1770s.

The Great Awakening

The Great Awakening was a transatlantic movement that resulted in a series of religious revivals preached by itinerant preachers. The Great Awakening affected England, Scotland, Ulster, New England, and the mid-Atlantic colonies.

George Whitefield was one of the most prominent itinerant preachers during the Great Awakening and began his career in England. He then decided to travel to the British North American colonies to raise money for an orphanage he wanted to have built in Georgia. He made sure to encourage newspaper printers to announce his arrival, which brought many people to his open-field sermons. In 1740 he preached in Middletown, Connecticut and a resident there, Nathan Cole, heard Whitefield preach and wrote: "I felt the Spirit of God drawing me by conviction." Whitefield preached in George, South Carolina, Delaware, Pennsylvania and many areas in the New England area.

Another preacher who encouraged revivals was Jonathan Edwards of the Northampton Church in Massachusetts. He used Enlightenment reasoning to construct a theological contradiction to Enlightenment ideas. Beginning in the 1720s, many New England ministers were influenced by a theology basing salvation on human moral effort as well as divine grace. Edwards opposed this tendency and reasserted the absolute justice of God's power to elect or to condemn as He chose, defending with exceptional skill the basic Calvinistic position that God was omnipotent and that, before God, humans were impotent.

The Great Awakening caused divisions within existing church organizations. Church members attracted to the evangelical group were called "new lights," and they attempted to wrest control of the church from the conservative members who held power, the "old lights." The Awakening fervor also was responsible for the founding of four colleges by separate religious denominations: Dartmouth (Congregationalist), Princeton (Presbyterian), Brown (Baptist), and Rutgers (Dutch Reformed). The premise in each case was that the existing institutions of higher learning—Yale, for instance, which had been founded in 1701—were unsuitable for training acceptable "new light" ministers.

The Awakening, because it was a transatlantic movement, created another Anglicizing episode. Many historians have advanced the idea that colonists believed these religious revivals were part of a greater British experience. Since colonists wanted to be Britons, revival preachers—especially from England, attracted them to the movement. In so doing the movement aroused a democratic spirit that influenced the revolutionary generation. This generalization cannot be proved or disproved, but it seems fair to suggest that in reviewing traditional institutions the Awakening encouraged a climate of freedom. It also offered women the choice of whether to stay with an Old Light congregation or affiliate with the New Lights, which was an important choice in a period when women lacked a political voice.

Britain Wins Supremacy in North America
New France

France had originally claimed land in America because of the voyages of Giovanni da Verrazano in 1523 and of Jacques Cartier in 1534, but not until 1608 was the permanent settlement of Quebec established by Samuel de Champlain. New France, as the French settlements on the North American continent were called, was slow to grow, being virtually all male. Trading in furs was the most lucrative enterprise, and it flourished in a wilderness setting. Settlers in farms and villages intruded upon the wilderness and its inhabitants.

In the 1660s the French became more determined in expanding their hold on North America. As a consequence, families were encouraged to settle in New France. They were provided with land, livestock, seed, and tools. Women were sent to become wives of unmarried men. Those who elected to remain unmarried were required to pay special taxes and were excluded from some of the subsidies provided to married settlers. In five years the population in New France doubled.

The French, much like the Spanish, encouraged exploration of the interior, sending Jesuit priests along with specially selected explorers. In 1673 Father Jacques Marquette, whose personal goal was to establish missions among the Illinois Native Americans, was ordered by his superior in Quebec to accompany Louis Jolliet, picked by the governor of New France, to explore the "Great River," the Mississippi. Accompanied by five trappers, Marquette and Jolliet followed the Wisconsin River down to the Mississippi River, which awed them with its grandeur.

Marquette kept a lively journal describing the buffalo, the Native Americans along the route, the heat—it was mid-July—and their experiences and encounters along the route. After feasting on dog meat and other delicacies with the Native Americans on the Arkansas River, the explorers decided to return to Canada, in part because they feared being captured by the Spanish.

Robert de La Salle launched a less successful expedition in 1683, although he did reach the mouth of the Mississippi. Both explorations not only gave New France a strong claim to the interior of the territory of mid-America but also encouraged the French to fortify the Mississippi and Ohio rivers, laying the background for a clash of interests between the British and French colonies on the North American continent.

Early Border Conflicts

The shifting balance of power in eighteenth-century Europe, brought about in part by the emergence of France and Britain as the major nations of the Western world, produced a ceaseless contest for position in both Europe and the colonies. To the English colonials, the strength of New France was a particular danger. French fur traders in the wilderness were capable of stirring up the Native Americans to hostility against English traders and settlers who began to penetrate the region, and French control over the interior threatened to curb the westward expansion of the English colonies in America.

The War of the Spanish Succession (1702–1713), or Queen Anne's War, saw a conflict of the colonists with both Spanish and French forces. In 1739 Great Britain attacked Spain in a conflict that soon merged into the War of the Austrian Succession, or King George's War (1740–1748). Believing that the time was ripe to neutralize French power in Canada, the governor of Massachusetts organized a force of militia. On June 17, 1745, the Americans, in one of the most audacious—and lucky—episodes in the colonial wars, captured Louisbourg, a fort on Cape Breton Island. In 1748, however, the British returned the fortress to the French in exchange for Madras in India.

The Great War for Empire

The French now showed a greater determination than ever to hold Canada and the Ohio and Mississippi valleys. In 1755 they erected blockhouses to fortify the Ohio and Appalachian river valleys against the British.

In the meantime, planters from Virginia and Maryland had organized the Ohio Company to exploit new lands as far west as the present site of Louisville, Kentucky. To prevent these western lands from falling into possession of the French, the governor of Virginia in 1753 sent George Washington, a young surveyor, into the Ohio valley to remonstrate with the French commander. The mission accomplished nothing, and when Washington was sent the next year with a force of men, his little army was surrounded, captured, and sent home. This began the conflict that was to develop into the French and Indian War and explode in Europe as the Seven Years' War (1756–1763), allying England and Prussia against France, Austria, and Spain.

With the danger of a Native American war threatening the frontier, the colonies were particularly concerned with counterbalancing the Native American allies of the French. To conciliate the powerful Iroquois, who had given invaluable support to the English in the past, the British government called a conference in Albany of commissioners from seven Northern and Middle colonies. This "Albany Congress" was more important for its political proposals than for its few accomplishments in dealing with the disaffected Iroquois. Because the delegates realized that a closer union of the colonies was needed to provide better collective defense and control of Native American affairs, they listened attentively to the "Plan of Union" put forward by one of Pennsylvania's leading citizens, Benjamin Franklin. Franklin's proposals would have brought all of the colonies under "one general government" with an executive and legislature, but with each colony retaining its separate existence and government. No colony gave the plan serious consideration and the British government disregarded it altogether.

To protect the colonies, the British government sent two regiments of regulars and a British fleet. In an attempt to dislodge the French from Fort Duquesne, a strategic position that controlled the upper Ohio valley, a detachment of regulars and colonial militia under British General Edward Braddock marched toward the fort, but it was ambushed and routed by French

▶In the Great War for Empire, 1754–1763, the English defeated the French and led to their abandonment of North America. This caused the Native Americans to lose their strategic position in fending off the English from assuming more land to the West. *Wikipedia photo*

and Indian forces. After Braddock's defeat, George Washington was given the responsibility of protecting more than three hundred miles of the Virginia frontier against incursions of Native Americans and French marauders.

The year 1755 was a period of almost unrelieved misfortune for the British, and for the next two or three years the war raged intermittently and disastrously along the frontier, with the French under Marquis de Montcalm winning a succession of victories in the north.

The Capture of Quebec

William Pitt, who had become British Secretary of State for War in 1757, realized that part of the trouble in America resided in the incompetence of Britain's officers. To remedy this, he ordered to America fresh troops under a new command. He also won more substantial cooperation from the American provincials by promising that Britain would reimburse the individual colonies for their war expenditures.

The campaign against the French soon began to show favorable results. The victory that finally decided the issue in Canada came on September 13, 1759, when General Wolfe led a successful attack on Quebec, which had been under siege since late June. The capture of Quebec sealed the fate of France in North America. Elsewhere—in Europe and India—British arms were also victorious, and France could do nothing but capitulate. In 1762 France ceded Louisiana to Spain in recompense for aid in the war and a year later, by the Treaty of Paris, ceded to Great Britain all of Canada except the tiny islands of St. Pierre and Miquelon. Paradoxically, the very magnitude of the British victory paved the way for the disintegration of the British Empire in America.

Chapter Review ▶ ▶ ▶

Summary

The first African slaves were brought to Virginia in 1619 and increased greatly in number, especially in the Southern colonies. Slaves increased in the Southern colonies with the decline of indenture and the rise of England as a naval power. Southern colonies, especially South Carolina, grew into rice, indigo, and tobacco-based export economies built on African slave labor by the end of the seventeenth century.

Though the thirteen English colonies founded in what is now the United States over a 126 year period from 1607 were diverse in terms of culture and economics, they shared an English heritage and English colonial experience that would bind them together eventually to form one nation before the eighteenth century would come to a close.

Colonial culture in the eighteenth century very much reflected English heritage, from language, to social and intellectual life, to politics, though the colonies were developing diversity due to the diverse ethnic mix of the immigrants arriving from Europe and the unique features of the colonial frontier life in contrast to England.

African slaves provided a solution to the immense labor demands in the colonies and hostile Native American tribes to the West forced most colonists to remain near the eastern seaboard where thriving urban coastal centers, such as Philadelphia, developed. Nevertheless, the colonists developed a thriving fur trade with the Native Americans as well as trade with Europe. Meanwhile France developed a trading empire on the Mississippi River and St. Lawrence Seaway that hindered English expansion in the North, while the Spanish established a series of Missions and Presidios in the South from Florida along the coastal bend and through Texas and the Southwest all the way to California. The French barrier to English expansion would finally be eliminated in the Great War for Empire from 1754–1763.

The eighteenth century in Colonial America was both an age of faith and the age of reason. Led by the writings of Isaac Newton, the European Enlightenment spread to the American colonies, with American icon Benjamin Franklin being the most noteworthy American contributor. Enlightenment thinkers believed that humans could progress through reason and scientific inquiry. Coterminous with the Enlightenment was the rise of deism, the adherents of which held that there was a supreme being or creator, but that creator does not interfere in human affairs or the laws of nature.

While the Enlightenment spread, the colonies simultaneously experienced a Great Awakening or religious revival. The shift from a single male dominated society to one dominated by families, the arrival of gifted evangelists, a focus on emotion and the conversion experience, and the idea that anyone with "inspiration" could preach the Gospel, all contributed to the Awakening. The Awakening also left lasting effects as education reflected the new religious diversity with the emergence of new Universities affiliated with New Light religious organizations. The older established Churches divided into "New Light" and "Old Light" factions, sometimes within individual congregations themselves. The focus on emotion and the idea that anyone with "inspiration" can preach the Gospel has remained prevalent in the American religious culture ever since.

Summary (cont'd)

Finally, the religious diversity that accompanied the Awakening eventually forced a movement to separate Church and State. The idea that one could challenge authority that arose during the Awakening would surface again in the 1770s, but this time the authority challenged would be political rather than religious.

In the Eighteenth Century, the British found themselves involved in Wars for empire with France in Queen Anne's War, King George's War, and the Seven Years War. Finally, in 1763, the French were expelled from North America by the British and would never again be a colonial force in North America, but the British were left in debt and the colonists would not be inclined to pay their part of the English debt with France no longer a threat in North America.

Chronological Time Line

1607	Jamestown is founded at Virginia
1608	French established their first settlement in North America at Quebec, Canada
1619	First Africans are brought to Virginia
1620	Pilgrims land at Plymouth Rock on the Mayflower
1626	Peter Minuit purchases Manhattan from the Natives for goods equal to twelve beaver pelts.
1630	Puritans arrive in Massachusetts Bay
1632	Maryland is founded by George Calvert as a planned refuge for Catholics
1636	Harvard is founded as a Puritan theological seminary
1636	Roger Williams Founds Rhode Island.
1642	Puritans gain control in England and end persecution of Puritans
1649	Maryland Toleration Act
1660	Execution of Mary Dyer
1660	Restoration of the Stuart Monarchy

Chapter Review (cont'd) ▶ ▶ ▶

Time Line (cont'd)

1662	Adoption of the Half-Way Covenant in Massachusetts
1663	Carolina is founded as a proprietary colony
1670	Settlement is started near present-day Charleston, S.C.
1675	England defeats the Netherlands in a war and gains permanent control of the colony on the Hudson, renamed New York
1681	King Charles II grants a charter for a colony to William Penn
1683	Francis Daniel Pastorious leads the first German settlers into Pennsylvania
1688–1691	Glorious Revolution in England installs Protestant William of Orange to the throne and England passes religious toleration while Maryland deposes the Calverts and ends religious toleration.
1690–1742	Boston, Newport, New York, Philadelphia, and Charleston tripled their populations
1691	Property ownership is established as the basis for the franchise in Massachusetts
1692	Witch Trials in Salem Village
1697	Isaac Newton's Mathematical Principles of Natural Philosophy demonstrates the laws of motion and gravitation
1704	First Newspaper in the colonies published in Boston
1710–1770	Wave of 225,000 German Settlers to North America
1730–1760	The Great Awakening spreads across America
1732–1758	Ben Franklin is Editor of Poor Richard's Almanac
1733	Georgia is founded as a colony for the deserving poor
1738	Mose founded by the Spanish in Florida as a community of runaway English slaves
1739	Stono Rebellion
1739	George Whitefield arrives in Boston

Time Line (cont'd)

1741	New York Conspiracy Trials
1754–1763	Great War for Empire
1776	Philadelphia is the second largest city in the British Empire
1786	Thomas Jefferson's Virginia Statute on Religious Liberty

Sources Consulted

Bernard Bailyn, *The Origins of American Politics* (1968).

Bernard Bailyn, *Voyages to the West: A Passage in the Peopling of America on the Eve of the Revolution* (1986).

Heather E. Barry, *A "Dress Rehearsal" For Revolution: John Trenchard and Thomas Gordon's Works Eighteenth-Century in British America* (2007).

Edmund Berkeley and Dorothy S. Berkeley, *The Life and Travels of John Bartram: From Lake Ontario to the River St. John* (1990).

Ira Berlin, *Many Thousands Gone: The First Two Centuries of Slavery in North America* (1998).

Charles E. Clark, *The Public Prints: The Newspaper in Anglo-American Culture, 1665–1740* (1994).

Richard Dunn, *Sugar and Slaves: The Rise of the Planter class in the English West Indies, 1624–1713* (1972).

A. Roger Ekirch, *Bound for America: The Transportation of British Convicts to the Colonies* (1987).

Ned Landsman, *From Colonials to Provincials: Thought and Culture in America, 1680–1760* (1998).

Lawrence W. Levine, *Black Culture and Black Consciousness: Afro-American Folk Thought from Slavery to Freedom* (1977).

Henrietta Mcburney, *Mark Catesby's Natural History of America* (1997).

Russell R. Menard, "From Servants to Slaves: The Transformation of the Chesapeake Labor System," *Southern Studies,* 16 (1977).

Edmund S. Morgan, *American Slavery, American Freedom: The Ordeal of Colonial* Virginia (1975).

Mark A. Noll, *The Rise of Evangelical Religion: The Age of Edwards, Whitefield, and the Wesleys* (2003).

Chapter Review (cont'd) ▶ ▶ ▶

Sources (cont'd)

David S. Shields, *Civil Tongues and Political Letters in British America* (1997).

Ian K. Steele, *The English Atlantic, 1675–1740: An Exploration of Communication and Community* (1986).

John Thornton, *Africa and Africans in the Making of the Modern World, 1400–1800* (1998).

Peter H. Wood, *Black Majority: Negroes in Colonial South Carolina from 1670 through the Stono Rebellion* (1974).

3 Resistance, Revolution and Independence, 1763–1783

Outline

II. Resistance to Revolution

    A. Tea Act Crisis

    B. The First Continental Congress

    C. Lexington and Concord

    D. Second Continental Congress and Revolt

    E. Bunker Hill

    F. Declaration of Causes and the Olive Branch Petition

    G. Momentum Toward the Declaration

    H. The *Declaration of Independence*

    I. The Internal Revolution

    J. The Loyalists

III. Executing the War
    A. Revolutionary Finances
    B. Military Strategy
    C. Slavery and the Revolution
    D. The War in the North
    E. The French Alliance
    F. New Campaigns in the North
    G. The War in the South
    H. Battle of Yorktown
    I. The War in Retrospect
    J. The Peace of Paris, 1783
IV. Effects of the War
    A. The King's Friends
    B. "Our Old Home"
    C. "Go to Hell or Halifax"
    D. Unrestricted Trade
    E. The Westward Movement
    F. Modifications of American Society
    G. American Nationalism
    H. The *Articles of Confederation*

Reform and Resistance

The Character of the Revolution

The American Revolution was multifaceted. It began as a revolt and eventually became a war for independence in which colonists fought to be separated from the strongest nation in the world, Great Britain. It was a civil war in which Englishmen fought Englishmen and, occasionally, colonials fought colonials. It was part of a world war fought in two hemispheres involving not only the British North American colonies and England but also France and Spain. It involved a struggle for power within each colony between patriots and loyalists and between elites and commoners. Although the purpose of the Revolution was not to establish democracy any more than it was to establish a union, one of the results of the struggle within certain states was to give the average property-owning white male American a greater voice in government.

Finally, it should be remembered that the first revolt by colonials against the homeland in modern times—the American colonies against Britain—occurred under the most enlightened and least burdensome imperial system of contemporary Europe. Europeans who lived in the English colonies enjoyed far more privileges in every sphere of life than did their counterparts in the French and Spanish colonies.

Why were the least restricted colonials the first to revolt? The American colonials had enjoyed what they thought of as their liberties for a century or more, and they had no intention of seeing these liberties restricted, even if, comparatively, they were better off than colonials elsewhere. They also did not want to pay taxes to a government far away in which they believed they were inadequately represented. Any action to limit existing privileges automatically produced friction. How deep the friction was to become depended upon the course of events and the response to these events by American colonials and by the authorities in Britain.

Reform and Protest

The crises within the empire from 1763 to 1776 were provoked by a series of specific enactments, but to review the prelude to revolution in such narrow terms is to misconstrue the essential issues that were in dispute. An adjustment in the relationship between Britain and its colonies was made inevitable by several sweeping changes that had been occurring during the eighteenth century.

The colonial and commercial systems of Britain had been established in the seventeenth century, based on the mercantilist theory—already several centuries old. That theory had seen colonies as important, primarily, for the wealth that could be extracted from them. During the course of the eighteenth century, colonies began to be important primarily for the role they played in British commerce. Moreover, when the system was inaugurated, England possessed only a few colonies. After the Peace of 1763, Britain had more than thirty colonies scattered throughout the world, each with its individual characteristics. Did the policies initiated in the 1660s suit conditions in the colonies in the 1760s? Should the same system apply to India and Massachusetts?

Even before the specific crises that occurred between 1763 and 1776, the British-colonial relationships required adjustment to meet the new realities. Three major changes were clearly evident. First, the American colonies had matured from the early days of Jamestown to become bustling commercial and agricultural successes.

MAP 3.1 North America after the Treaty of Paris (1763)

UNEXPLORED

PACIFIC OCEAN

HUDSON BAY

OREGON
Disputed by Russia and Spain

INDIAN RESERVE

NEW FOUNDLAND

ST. PIERRE & MIQUELON (FRANCE)

NOVA SCOTIA

NEW ENGLAND THE THIRTEEN COLONIES

VIRGINIA

CAROLINAS

EAST FLORIDA

ATLANTIC OCEAN

GULF OF MEXICO

CUBA

BRITISH HONDURAS

HISPANIOLA

HAITI (FRANCE)

CARIBBEAN SEA

NEW GRANADA

English
Spanish
Russian
French
Settled Areas

Proclamation line of 1763

Second, the political transition in England by which Parliament had steadily gained power at the expense of the crown required a redefinition of relationships within the empire. Third, the colonies in the New World had become a critical factor in the European balance of power.

By 1760, the British colonies in America were no longer infants dependent solely upon the protection of the mother country. From limited self-government to mature self-government, from inexperience to experience with authority, from a primitive to a complex, well-developed indigenous economy—this had been the course of the American colonies. Any imperial system that failed to recognize these realities was doomed. As it existed, the imperial system had become, in some of its parts, an anachronism. The American provinces had become an insatiable market for British goods, but the British system failed to adjust to this fact. The American colonies required more enlightened monetary and banking policies, but the British tried to continue outworn theories.

The political transition in England required a rethinking of the constitutional structure of the empire. The colonies had been established under the auspices of royal charters. They had been administered through the king, the executive authority. As Parliament assumed greater authority, fundamental questions arose. Did Parliament have unlimited legislative supremacy over the colonies? Did Parliament gain the executive power previously exercised by the crown? The home authorities said yes, but American colonials said no. Moreover, the Industrial Revolution of the eighteenth century in England introduced new problems with regard to mercantile theories that were never resolved—notably the importance of colonies as a market.

During the eighteenth century, the Spanish, French, and British colonies in the Americas had become increasingly critical factors in the European balance of power. Beginning particularly with the Peace of Utrecht in 1713, the European powers attempted to establish equilibrium in that balance. It was clearly tipped in England's favor by the Peace of Paris in 1763, when Britain acquired New France in North America as well as French possessions elsewhere in the world.

These British acquisitions created uneasiness and uncertainty throughout Western Europe, and France began to explore avenues to redress the balance of power. Soon after 1763, the French recognized the possibility of doing so, not by recapturing its lost colonies or by capturing British colonies, but by encouraging a separation between Britain and its colonies in America. This reasoning was responsible for French intervention in 1778 on behalf of the Americans.

MAP 3.2 Map of Territorial Growth 1775

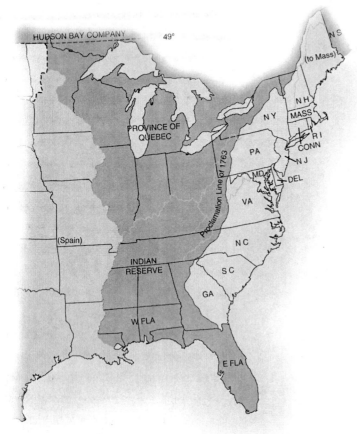

Boundary between Mississippi River and
49th parallel uncertain due to misconception that
source of Mississippi River lay further north

1775

Any one of these major changes in the eighteenth century—the maturation of the colonies, the political and economic transition in Britain, and the diplomatic evolution—was destined to produce problems in the relationship between England and the colonies. Together, they helped to produce a revolution.

The Constitutional Issue

The British and the American colonials had different concepts of the constitutional structure of the empire. The British assumed that the self-government practiced by the separate colonies was a favor granted by the mother country—a favor that could be enlarged, curtailed, or even eliminated. The ultimate authority rested in Britain. The colonies possessed no power except that granted by the home authorities. The colonials, on the other hand, held that self-government rested upon the consent of the governed (the colonial electorate), not upon royal grace and favor. The Americans believed they possessed rights (at first called the Rights of Englishmen, later called American Rights) that Britain could in no way curtail. Each colonial assembly viewed itself as struggling against a royal governor (and thus against the king), much like the House of Commons, in its struggle to gain power at the king's expense.

During the Seven Years' War, the colonial assemblies gained power in juxtaposition with the colonial governors as a result of their roles in extracting taxation from the colonists. Governors were unable to collect the necessary taxes without assistance from the colonial assemblies. The assemblies provided that assistance, but they extracted concessions of power from the governors in return for their role in revenue extraction.

iStockphoto

The rising power of Parliament, along with the rising power of the colonial assemblies, posed an additional question: What were the limits to the legislative power of Parliament over the colonies? Conflict on this point was inevitable, and it became a critical issue in the revolutionary crisis that developed.

Constitutional Confrontations

During the Great War for Empire several British policies annoyed the American provincials. In 1759, the Privy Council instructed the governor of Virginia to refuse to sign any bill that failed to include a "suspending clause"—that is, a clause preventing the act from becoming effective until it had been approved by the home authorities. In 1761, general writs of assistance empowered officers of the British customs service to break into and search homes and stores for smuggled goods. This provoked strong opposition from the provincials, who claimed that the writs were contrary to law and to the natural rights of men. In that same year the Privy Council prohibited the issuance in New York and New Jersey of judicial commissions with unlimited tenure, specifying that such commissions must always be subject to revocation by the king, even though in England, judges no longer held their posts at the king's discretion. In 1764, the Currency Act extended to all colonies the restrictions on the issuance of paper money that previously had applied only to Massachusetts. All colonists would now have to pay British merchants in gold or silver, thus severely diminishing colonial buying power in an economy that was already in recession following the Seven Years War.

Problems of Defense and Western Lands

The Peace of Paris of 1763 eliminated the French threat to English expansion on the North American continent and made available to English colonials opportunities in the West (West of the Appalachians, primarily the Ohio Valley) that had been denied them for a quarter of a century. However, the Peace of Paris raised problems with regard to the administration and distribution of this land. It also raised the issue of how to raise the necessary revenue to pay the cost of administering the empire. Most important, the Peace of Paris, by eliminating the French threat, made the American provincials bolder in stating their views since they no longer viewed themselves as in need of English protection against the French. Once they had adopted a position, the colonists became more tenacious in clinging to it.

Among the principal problems faced by the British was the settlement of the territory west of the Appalachians. The issue was complicated by the revolt in 1763 of the Native Americans in the west under the leadership of Pontiac, chief of the Ottawa tribe. Farms and villages along the colonial frontier from Canada to Virginia were laid waste. The uprising was put down largely by British troops, but the problem of future defense assumed great importance. This incident—together with a previous policy of appointing a commander in chief for America, the fact that the British now controlled French Canada with a population that did not desire British rule, and the fact that the British viewed the American colonies as unruly—produced the major decision on the part of the British to send 10,000 British regulars on the American mainland and in the West Indies.

This action, however well intentioned, was met with stern provincial opposition. Americans who had faced the French competition at close quarters for a century could not understand why British troops were needed now that the French menace had been eliminated. Animosity between the British Redcoats and the colonials increased the tension, especially in New York (after 1765), and in Boston (after 1768) where the troops were stationed. Moreover, the colonials were not accustomed to the accepted British practice of expecting the people who were being "de-

▶ In 1763, the Native Americans in the west, under the leadership of Pontiac, revolted. This caused problems for the British who wished to settle the territory west of the Alleghenies.
Corbis Images

fended" to quarter the troops. The Quartering Act of 1765, which required New York colonials to house the soldiers and to make supplies available, was bitterly resented. The British did not actually intend for the colonists to quarter the British army in private homes, though that was a possibility under the Quartering Act as a last resort. Instead, the British intended for the colonists to fund and build barracks for the British troops, and the threat of quartering the soldiers in private homes would serve as a motivation for the colonists to build housing for the troops. Instead, the Quartering Act provided colonial revolutionaries with a symbol of British oppression.

The solution to the problem of western lands beyond the Appalachians was equally irritating. If the colonies in proximity to the western lands—such as Pennsylvania, New York, Virginia, and the Carolinas—were permitted to extend their boundaries westward, colonies without a hinterland—Connecticut, Rhode Island, New Jersey, and Maryland—would be placed at a disadvantage. Should new colonies, therefore, be formed in the territory beyond the Appalachians?

The solution formulated by the British government was the Royal Proclamation Line of 1763, which established a line along the crest of the Appalachian Mountains west of which colonials could not take up land. This policy of delay seemed sensible in London, but the colonials were impatient to take advantage of the new territory. Virginians had fought in the Great War for Empire specifically to open this area to settlement. Not only were frontiersmen eager to exploit these opportunities, but the land companies in Pennsylvania, Virginia, and New England, whose membership included affluent colonials and Englishmen, also wished to act. For these men the Proclamation Line was a disappointment—an unexpected barrier to enterprise and opportunity.

The Proclamation Line, intended originally as a temporary measure to gain time for a permanent policy, was not revoked before the Revolution. Meanwhile, the Quebec Act of 1774 further annoyed the provincials by annexing the western lands north of the Ohio River to the Province of Quebec. The former French colony, viewed by the colonials as the enemy, was to be rewarded while the faithful colonists that had fought to free that territory from French control were denied the fruits of their sacrifices.

The problems of western lands and defense did not bring on the Revolution, but they caused a lingering grievance. When added to the other irritations of British rule, they decreased the probability of compromise and increased the chances of hostility.

Aftermath of the Seven Years War

The Seven Years War effectively redrew the map of North America and eliminated France as a major colonial power in North America. In addition, it also had immense and lasting political and economic impact on the British colonies of North America. The war had produced an economic boom in the colonies as American merchants were awarded British military contracts to outfit the British military with ships, arms, uniforms, shoes, and food. When some thirty thousand British troops departed from North America, however, an economic recession and unemployment followed as the war orders ceased.

During the war, colonial governments licensed American privateers (legally commissioned pirates) to attack and seize French shipping, often at great profits to the privateers. For example, in 1758, one noted privateer, John MacPherson, seized eighteen French ships and profited enough that he purchased an estate near Philadelphia for fourteen thousand pounds. With the close of the war, this lucrative but dangerous business would cease. All colonists who served in the war, however, had not been so fortunate. For example, the 1764 census of Boston counted 3,612 adult females and only 2,941 adult males. This sex imbalance, created by war deaths, contributed to severe poverty in New England due to a severe widow and orphan problem.

Finally, the Seven Years' War left England with massive financial obligations. The forward placement of troops in the colonies would be costly, but England was saddled with 145 million pounds in debt from the War. In order to service the debt and finance the forward placement of troops, British Prime Minister, George Grenville would propose new taxation both in England and the colonies. Without the threat of the French, the colonists would view the forward placement of troops, as well as the new taxation, as unnecessary; and the contentment among the colonists with being British subjects, which appears to be widespread as late as 1762, would come to an abrupt end.

The Stamp Act

British Prime Minister George Grenville was perhaps neither an imaginative nor a clever man, but he was a determined one. Coming into office just at the close of the Great War for Empire, and believing as most of his countrymen did that the American colonists would be the greatest beneficiaries of the vast territory bordering the Ohio and Mississippi rivers that had been won from the French, he was determined that the colonists should pay at least part of the costs of defending and pacifying this territory. Currently no revenue was coming from the colonists to aid in imperial defense. Smugglers were evading duties imposed by the Molasses Act of 1733. In fact, the American customs service was costing more to operate than it was collecting in fees.

In an attempt to remedy the situation, in 1764, Grenville led Parliament to adopt the Revenue Act or Sugar Act, an act intended to produce revenue—a purpose clearly stated in its preface—by enforcing the payment of customs duties on sugar, wine, coffee, silk, and other goods. The act declared that a number of colonial commodities could only be imported from England, and it required tighter control over ships' cargo. American shippers would have to post bonds guaranteeing observance of the Revenue Act before loading their cargoes. The act also strengthened the admiralty courts where the violators of British customs laws were prosecuted. Although the act reduced the duty on molasses bought from non-British sources from six pence to four pence per gallon—on the surface, an attractive reduction—provincials actually had been smuggling in molasses for no more than a pence and a half per gallon as a bribe to customs officials. Now Grenville intended to enforce the trade laws by stricter administrative procedures. The crux of the issue, however, was the British intention to tax the colonists for purposes of revenue. Before this, duties had been imposed merely as a means of regulating the trade of the empire. The New York legislature protested that any tax by Parliament solely for the purpose of raising revenue, rather than to control trade, violated the rights of overseas English subjects who were taxed without representation in Parliament.

The Stamp Act of 1765, which provoked spontaneous opposition throughout the colonies, brought the issue of taxation, raised by the Sugar Act, to a crisis. Grenville announced his intention to extend to America stamp duties that he had already imposed in England. Grenville gave the colonies one year to propose an alternative way to raise the same

MAP 3.3 Proclamation of 1763

Proclamation line of 1763

amount of revenue before the act would go into effect. Instead of coming up with a plan, the colonists spent the next year denouncing the idea of the Stamp Act, but the year elapsed with the colonists offering no revenue-raising plan of their own. As a consequence, in November 1765, the Stamp Act went into effect, placing a stamp fee on all legal documents, deeds and diplomas, custom papers, and newspapers, liquor licenses, playing cards, and dice. It directly influenced every articulate element in the community, including lawyers, merchants, preachers, and printers. Moreover, the act raised not only the question of who had the right to tax but also more significant questions: Who had what power? Could Parliament legislate for the colonials in all matters? Was Parliament's authority without limit or were there bounds beyond which it could not reach—bounds based upon certain rights inherent in all Englishmen?

Reaction to the Stamp Act

The conflict was contested on two levels—that of action and that of constitutional debate— and the massive American reaction to the Stamp Act shocked the British government. In every colony British Stamp Act collectors were forced to resign, sometimes under the threat of force. Newspapers defied the act by printing skulls and crossbones in the space where the stamps belonged. Sons of Liberty were organized in key colonies to enforce a colonially self-imposed prohibition on the use of stamps.

Occasionally mob spirit carried opposition to extremes, as it did in Boston, Massachusetts, when a band of provincials rioted in what is known as the Stamp Act Riot. On August 14, 1765, Bostonians hanged an effigy of Boston Stamp Distributor Andrew Oliver from a tree on the south end of town. That evening, a crowd of several thousand people paraded the effigy through town and held a mock trial before beheading and burning the effigy. The crowd then destroyed the new stamp distribution office at the wharf. Stamp Distributor Oliver resigned the next day out of fear for his life; and twelve days later, another angry mob ransacked the home of Lieutenant Governor Thomas Hutchinson, whom the Bostonians mistakenly believed to be in support of the Stamp Act. A reward of three hundred pounds was offered for the arrest and conviction of the riot organizers, but not a single person came forward with a lead. The courts and the ports, which could not operate legally without using the stamps, continued after a momentary lull to carry out their regular functions in defiance of the act.

▶ In the Virginia House of Burgesses, Patrick Henry introduced resolutions, declaring that only the general assembly of a colony has the right to tax the residents of the colony. *Wikipedia photo*

Boston's riots sparked similar actions by other Sons of Liberty in almost fifty towns throughout the colonies, and Stamp Distributors resigned throughout the colonies. Each colonial legislature met to decide on a course of action. The most famous incident occurred in the Virginia House of Burgesses, where Patrick Henry introduced resolutions declaring that the "General Assembly of this Colony have the only and *sole exclusive* Right and Power to lay Taxes and Impositions upon the Inhabitants of This Colony." Any other course, said Henry, would tend "to destroy British as well as American Freedom." One of Henry's resolutions, which did not pass because the Virginia House of Burgesses feared it might be treasonous, declared it "illegal, unconstitutional, and unjust" for anyone outside of Virginia to tax Virginians. Henry also resolved that Virginians did not have to obey any externally imposed tax and labeled anyone who denied Virginia's exclusive right to tax as "an enemy of the colony." Though Henry's radical resolutions failed to pass, they were widely circulated throughout the colonies creating a furor. Massachusetts governor Francis Bernard termed the Virginia resolves as "an alarm bell for the disaffected."

At the invitation of Massachusetts, nine colonies sent delegates to New York in October 1765 to form the Stamp Act Congress, in which a set of resolutions was adopted denying the authority of Parliament to tax the colonials. A boycott of British goods by the colonists—the use of economic coercion to achieve political ends—was introduced on the theory that the colonial market was so necessary to Britain that it would abandon the act to regain the market. It should be noted that scholars of women's history have argued that the use of the boycott following the Stamp Act began to bring women into the political process, since consumer choices about what to buy had typically been part of women's domain. Moreover, in many instances, women were required to produce the goods no longer being purchased from England.

On the second level, that of defining constitutional theory, the respective arguments of the colonials and the authorities in England developed differently. Colonials argued that they could not be free without being secure in their property and that they could not be secure in their property if, without their consent, others could take it away through taxation. This argument revealed the close tie between property and liberty in the minds of the eighteenth-century Anglo-Americans.

In response, the British asserted that the Americans were not being taxed without their consent because they were "virtually," if not directly, represented in Parliament. They argued that many areas in Britain—notably Manchester and other substantial communities—were not directly represented in Parliament (the British did not require members of Parliament to live in their districts), but that no one denied that an act of Parliament had authority over those communities. The same concept of "virtual representation," asserted the British leaders, applied to the colonies. Just as a Member of Parliament that represented Manchester might live in London, a Member of Parliament that represented Virginia might live in London.

Colonists vigorously opposed this interpretation of representation. Most of the colonial legislatures echoed Maryland's argument "that it cannot, with any Truth or Propriety, be said, that the Freemen of this Province of Maryland are Represented in the British Parliament." Daniel Dulaney, a Maryland attorney, in his *Considerations on the Propriety of Imposing Taxes in the British Colonies*, argued that even those people in Britain who did not have the right to vote were allied in interest with their contemporaries.

"But who," he asked, "are the Representatives of the Colonies?" Who could speak for them?

> The Right of Exemption from all Taxes without their consent, the Colonies claim as *British* Subjects. They derive this Right from the Common Law, which their Charters have declared and confirmed … A Right to impose an internal Tax on the Colonies, without their Consent *for the single Purpose of Revenue,* is denied; a Right to regulate their Trade without their Consent is admitted.

In brief, the colonists argued that Parliament had power, but not unlimited power. It could *legislate* and impose external duties to regulate trade, but it could not *levy a tax* for revenue. In time, as the revolutionary crisis deepened, the colonial position was modified to deny Parliament's authority to legislate for or tax the colonists for any purpose whatsoever.

George Mason of Virginia, who implicitly denied the indefinite subordination of the colonies, expressed a view much closer to the eventual stand taken by the colonists. "We rarely see anything from your [the English] side of the water free from the authoritative style of a master to a school boy: 'We have with infinite difficulty and fatigue got you excused this one time; pray be a good boy for the future, do what your papa and mama bid you.'" He warned the British, "Such another experiment as the stamp-act would produce a general revolt in America."

Parliament backed down—not on the principle at issue, but on the act itself. The Stamp Act was repealed in 1766. At the same time, however, the Declaratory Act was passed, stating that Parliament possessed the authority to make laws binding the American colonists. "in all cases whatsoever." The Americans mistakenly believed not only that their arguments were persuasive but also that the economic pressure brought on by the boycott of English goods had been effective.

The boycott, however, only delayed British reaction; but the Americans, unaware of its failure, were to employ the boycott as a standard weapon against the British at each time of crisis.

The Townshend Duties

The next major crisis arose in 1767. Misinformed by Benjamin Franklin, who in February 1766 had told the House of Commons that the provincials objected only to internal taxes, not to taxes on trade, the British Parliament enacted the Townshend Duties on glass, lead, paper, paints, and tea in 1767. These import or "external" taxes were designed to exploit the distinction between internal taxes and external duties that Parliament mistakenly supposed the Americans were making. At the same time, Parliament reorganized the customs service by appointing a Board of Customs Commissioners to be located at Boston. The Townshend Act also designated that customs officials were to be paid directly from the duties collected (an incentive for customs officials to be diligent collectors).

The Massachusetts House of Representatives responded to the Townshend Acts by sending a circular letter written by Sam Adams, denouncing the Townshend duties to all the other colonies. Adams declared that the payment of customs officials from duties collected was unconstitutional. Parliament quickly demanded that Massachusetts rescind the circular; and when they refused, Parliament declared the Massachusetts legislature to be dissolved.

Liberty Incident

In the summer of 1768, tension mounted in Boston when customs officials seized the *Liberty*, a ship owned by John Hancock, for evading customs duties. An angry mob of Bostonians reacted by attacking the customs officials, who fled to the safety of a British warship in Boston Harbor. In response, the British sent two regiments of troops to Boston, in part at least because

▶ A 1776 illustration representing the repeal of the Stamp Act. George Grenville is depicted carrying the tiny coffin, followed by British Dukes and two bishops. *Wikipedia photo*

of the urging of customs commissioners. By the time all the British troops were in place, there were four thousand British soldiers in Boston, which only had a population of sixteen thousand. Such numbers were, perhaps, a formula for disorder without any other accompanying political stimulants because the British troops competed with Boston men for part-time employment and the attention of Boston women.

Though the Townshend Duties failed to awaken the spontaneous reaction of the Stamp Act, they tested once again the colonial versus British theory of the empire and posed anew the question: What were the limits to the power of Parliament? Again the American colonists resorted to a boycott, although no intercolonial congress was called. John Dickinson, in his *Letters from a Farmer in Pennsylvania*, reaffirmed the position of the colonials that duties, even "external" duties, could not be levied primarily to obtain revenue, though measures enacted to regulate trade were admitted as a proper prerogative of Parliament. Dickinson's essays were not revolutionary in tone or in spirit. Neither, however, did they back away from the fundamental position taken by the colonists—that they alone could levy a tax upon themselves.

▶ John Hancock *Wikipedia photo*

As for the British, the Board of Customs' Commissioners who came to enforce the Navigation Acts, the Sugar Act of 1764, and the Townshend Duties carried out its responsibility in such a perfidious way that the commissioners were properly accused of customs racketeering, although the real significance of the board was the breadth of opposition it aroused. Not only those colonists most vulnerable to its activity—particularly New England merchants—were disposed to stand against the British, a consensus of opposition pervaded all the colonies, many of which experienced no serious problem with customs officials. This consensus was made possible because of the more profound issue: Where did the regulatory power of Parliament end and that of the colonials begin?

The Townshend Duties disappointed their advocates, for they did not produce the revenue expected due to colonial boycotts that caused imports of British goods to decline as much as 40 percent. In 1770, therefore, the British repealed the Townshend Duties (except the duty on tea, which was retained as a symbol of Parliament's right to tax). The Americans relaxed their opposition and reopened their ports to British goods, though they condemned tea drinking as unpatriotic.

Boston Massacre

In February 1770, violence erupted as colonists surrounded the house of Ebenezer Richardson, a low-level British customs official. As colonists smeared a batch of "Hillsboro Paint" (a mixture of feces and urine) on the building, Richardson fired his gun into the crowd in an attempt to get them to disperse and accidentally killed a seventeen-year-old boy. Though the boy's death was an accident, some view it as the first death of the American Revolution.

H ere is an excerpt that was printed in the *Boston Gazette and Country Journal* on Monday, March 12, 1770.

A few minutes after nine o'clock four youths, named Edward Archbald, William Merchant, Francis Archbald, and John Leech, jun., came down Cornhill together, and separating at Doctor Loring's corner, the two former were passing the narrow alley leading Mr. Murray's barrack in which was a soldier brandishing a broad sword of an uncommon size against the walls, out of which he struck fire plentifully.... On hearing the noise, one Samuel Atwood came up to see what was the matter; and entering the alley from dock square, heard the latter part of the combat; and when the boys had dispersed he met the ten or twelve soldiers aforesaid rushing down the alley towards the square and asked them if they intended to murder people? They answered Yes, by G-d, root and branch! With that one of them struck Mr. Atwood with a club which was repeated by another; and being unarmed, he turned to go off and received a wound on the left shoulder which reached the bone and gave him much pain. Retreating a few steps, Mr. Atwood met two officers and said, gentlemen, what is the matter They answered, you'll see by and by. Immediately after, those heroes appeared in the square, asking where were the boogers? where were the cowards? But notwithstanding their fierceness to naked men, one of them advanced towards a youth who had a split of a raw stave in his hand and said, damn them, here is one of them. But the young man seeing a person near him with a drawn sword and good cane ready to support him, held up his stave in defiance; and they quietly passed by him up the little alley by Mr. Silsby's to King Street where they attacked single and unarmed persons till they raised much clamour, and then turned down Cornhill Street, insulting all they met in like manner and pursuing some to their very doors. Thirty or forty persons, mostly lads, being by this means gathered in King Street, Capt. Preston with a party of men with charged bayonets, came from the main guard to the commissioner's house, the soldiers pushing their bayonets, crying, make way! They took place by the custom house and, continuing to push to drive the people off pricked some in several places, on which they were clamorous and, it is said, threw snow balls. On this, the Captain commanded them to fire; and more snow balls coming, he again said, damn you, fire, be the consequence what it will! One soldier then fired, and a townsman with a cudgel struck him over the hands with such force that he dropped his firelock; and, rushing forward, aimed a blow at the Captain's head which grazed his hat and fell pretty heavy upon his arm. However, the soldiers continued the fire successively till seven or eight or, as some say, eleven guns were discharged.

Source: *Boston Gazette and Country Journal* on Monday, March 12, 1770.

Violence would be greater on March 5, 1770, when what would be called the "Boston Massacre" occurred—by coincidence the same day the Townshend Duties were repealed. A small group of townspeople, described by the Boston lawyer John Adams as a "motley rabble of saucy boys, negroes, and mulattoes, Irish teagues and outlandish Jack Tars," shouted catcalls and insults while hurling snowballs and rocks at British troops on duty. The crowd referred to the British soldiers as "Lobsterbacks" due to their red coats and referred to a British soldier as a "damned rascally scoundrel lobster son of a bitch." A scuffle erupted, and the Redcoats opened fire, killing five persons and wounding six more. Among the slain was Crispus Attucks, who was a man of African descent.

The accused soldiers stood trial and were defended by John Adams. Only two soldiers were convicted and sentenced to thumb brandings and released. This was hardly a massacre but some colonists wanted the incident to seem like it was. Some colonists used this incident as propaganda to encourage anti-British sentiment.

The acting governor, Thomas Hutchinson, ordered the removal of British regiments in Boston to an island in the harbor so as to prevent further bloodshed. Hutchinson then jailed eight British soldiers until they could stand trial. John Adams and Josiah Quincy defended the British soldiers in the colonial court. Adams defended the British soldiers so as to show the British that even unpopular suspects in America could receive a fair trial. All but two of the British soldiers were acquitted; and the remaining two were convicted of manslaughter, but given the "benefit of clergy" and merely branded on their thumbs as punishment.

▶ The bloody Boston Massacre occurred on March 5th, 1770, when a mob of angry townspeople began taunting British soldiers on duty, throwing rocks and snowballs. The soldiers opened fire and killed five people and injured six more. *Wikipedia photo*

Following the trial, a form of informal truce developed between the colonists and the British. Imports of British goods again increased, and the American boycotts essentially collapsed. The colonists continued to boycott tea since the British had symbolically retained the small Townshend duty on tea. It appeared, at the end of 1771, that revolt might be averted after all.

Resistance to Revolution

The Boston Tea Party and the Coercive Acts

Beginning in 1772, the informal truce collapsed and new unrest erupted. In June 1772, a British patrol boat, the *Gaspee,* ran aground in Narragansett Bay south of Providence. The *Gaspee's* commander, Lieutenant Dudingston, was detested by the colonists for what they viewed as overzealous prosecution of smugglers and illegally seizing ships' cargo. Colonists, therefore, seized the opportunity for revenge and burned the *Gaspee* to the water level as it sat helplessly in Narragansett Bay. To make matters worse, the colonists arrested Lieutenant Dudingston and convicted him of illegally seizing what he contended was smuggled rum and sugar. The British attempted to try the colonial culprits for the arson, but no witnesses to the events could be found. Shortly thereafter, Governor Thomas Hutchinson announced that the British Crown rather than the local legislature would now pay the governor and colonial judges. The colonists viewed the action as an attempt by the British to bias the courts and government against them. In reaction, a Committee of Correspondence was established in Massachusetts at the urging of Sam Adams, John Adams's cousin. By the end of 1772, eighty Massachusetts towns had such committees. Furthermore, all but three of the other colonies followed the Massachusetts pattern and formed such committees by the end of 1773 in order to keep one another informed of possible British action.

Tea Act Crisis

In 1773 and 1774, with the Boston Tea party and the passage of the Coercive Acts, the conflict between Great Britain and its colonies entered a new and conclusive phase. In the early 1770s, colonists had been drinking moderate amounts of English tea (from India) and paying moderate duties on the tea without major objections. However, they were also smuggling large quantities of Dutch tea, thus cutting into the tea sales of Britain's East India Company and also cutting into the British government revenues gained by taxes on tea. With the Tea Act of May 1773, the British government permitted the British East India Company, which was near bankruptcy but had built up an excess stock of tea in England (an estimated seventeen million pounds in English warehouses), to market—"dump" would perhaps be a better term—the tea in America. The East India Company's overstock had been caused partially by colonial boycotts and partially by competition from Dutch tea smuggled into the colonies. Normally, the East India Company sold its tea to British wholesalers, who in turn sold to American wholesalers that then distributed the tea to local colonial merchants for sale to the public. By eliminating English middlemen and British import taxes, the Tea Act would allow the colonists to purchase less expensive tea and the East India

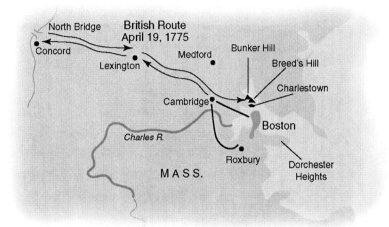

MAP 3.4 Boston and Vicinity (1775)

Company could undersell smuggled Dutch tea. The British government would get modest revenue from the small Townshend duty that remained on tea and the East India Company would be saved from bankruptcy.

With this act the British reawakened the latent hostility of the American colonists. Some Americans objected to what they viewed as a British attempt to control American trade. Colonial merchants denounced the "monopoly" given to the East India Company and predicted that other monopolies would follow and colonial middlemen of all types would be eliminated. Others viewed the Tea Act as a British plot to induce Americans into buying more tea. Many colonists believed that the real goal of the act was to increase British revenue, which in turn would be used to pay royal governors and judges. The Tea Act was, therefore, viewed by many as an insidious example of Parliament's claim to the power to tax and legislate for the colonies "in all cases whatsoever," a principle that many colonists rejected. When Americans drank the tea, they would also be "swallowing" the British right to tax Americans and control their trade.

Before any of the East India Company's tea arrived in Boston, the Sons of Liberty had already pressured British tea agents to resign and vowed that the "obnoxious" tea would be stopped at the water's edge. When the ships carrying the tea arrived, they were met with opposition. In some ports, the ships were forced to return to England without unloading; in other cases the tea was placed in a warehouse to prevent its distribution. In Boston, five thousand persons gathered at the Old South Church on December 16, 1773. The colonists resolved that Governor Thomas Hutchinson must clear the ships for a return to England, but he refused. At nightfall, a band of one hundred to one hundred fifty colonists, disguised as Native Americans, dumped the 342 chests of tea valued at eleven thousand pounds (approximately one million dollars in 2010) into the harbor.

The reaction in England was prompt and decisive: The prevailing mood in Parliament was that punitive legislation must be passed to punish the people responsible for the damage to private property. Even members of Parliament previously well disposed to the Americans endorsed this position. In quick succession, three coercive acts (denounced as "Intolerable Acts" by the colonists) were passed. First, the Boston Port Act (March 31, 1774) closed that port to commerce until the colonists paid for all of the destroyed tea. Next, the Massachusetts Government Act (May 30, 1774) altered the manner of choosing the Governor's Council from election by the lower house to appointment by the governor, authorized the governor to prohibit all but annual town meetings, installed General Thomas Gage as governor of Massachusetts, and, more significantly, indicated to the Americans that parliamentary power knew no limits. Finally, the Administration of Justice Act (May 30, 1774) removed certain cases involving crown officials from the jurisdiction of Massachusetts courts. British officials were declared immune from local court trials for acts committed while suppressing civil disturbances in the colonies.

The other colonies immediately rallied to the support of Massachusetts in opposing these "Intolerable Acts"—much to the surprise of the British authorities, who had expected the support rather than the condemnation of the colonies outside Massachusetts. After all, had not property been destroyed? No action on the part of the Americans revealed the basic issue so clearly. Essentially, the issue was not customs racketeering, the presence of Redcoats, the problem of western lands, or even taxes. The issue was: Who had what power?

The colonials at this stage were not calling for independence. Such a step was too frightening. The Americans had lived within the British Empire for more than a century. They had been content being British as late as 1763. The British government, with all of its flaws, was still the most enlightened government of its time, where rule of law was a fact and liberty was a word that meant something. It was not a step to be taken, as the revolutionary fathers later declared in the *Declaration of Independence,* for light and transient causes.

▶ In protest of the Tea Act, the Sons of Liberty had vowed that the East India Company's tea would be refused at the water's edge. At nightfall, a band of over one hundred colonists, haphazardly disguised as Native Americans, dumped 342 chests of tea, valued at eleven thousand pounds (approximately one million dollars in 2010), into the harbor. *Wikipedia photo*

The First Continental Congress

Events proceeded once again on two levels—that of action and that of theory. The First Continental Congress was called to meet in Philadelphia in September 1774. A number of important decisions made early in the deliberations set the tone of the meeting. Carpenters Hall, instead of the legislative chambers of Pennsylvania, was selected as the meeting hall—a victory for Sam Adams of Massachusetts and those who wished to take firm action against Britain. A more important show of strength came when resolutions proposing a union of colonies were offered, resolutions regarded as conciliatory. They were tabled by a close vote; and the Suffolk Resolves were adopted, asserting that the colonies should make no concessions until Britain first repealed the Coercive Acts. The burden of conciliation was thus upon the home authorities.

In addition, the First Continental Congress adopted a series of resolutions embodying its position and sent them to the king. The colonists claimed that they were not represented in Parliament and claimed that each colonial government had the exclusive right to legislate and tax for its own people. The colonists acquiesced to British trade regulations so long as the regulations were not covert forms of raising revenue. At the same time a Continental Association was established to terminate trade with the British. Although Congress avowed its "allegiance to his majesty" and its "affection for our fellow subjects" in Great Britain, the position it took placed Britain on notice.

Lexington and Concord

When the First Continental Congress adjourned, its members agreed to meet again in the spring of 1775, if no action was forthcoming from Britain. Conditions failed to improve; they became worse. In Massachusetts minutemen were training to guard against possible actions by British Redcoats stationed in Boston. Guns, powder, and other military stores were being collected at Concord.

On April 18, 1775, the British military governor sent out from Boston about seven hundred British regulars to destroy the colonists' military stores at Concord. As the British marched from Boston toward Concord, Paul Revere and William Dawes mounted their horses and rode out to warn the minutemen of the British advance. When the British reached Lexington between Boston and Concord, about seventy-five colonial minutemen met them. The British demanded that the colonists lay down their weapons and disperse; but someone—no one knows who—fired a shot, and in the next two minutes more of both the Americans and British fired their weapons. By the time the firing stopped, the Americans dispersed; however, eight Americans were killed and ten were wounded. The first shots of the Revolution, termed by the Americans as the "shots heard round the world," had been fired. The British then continued their march toward Concord, some fifteen miles west of Lexington, while colonists gathered to defend Concord. When the British arrived at Concord, they were unable to find the bulk of the American ammunition because the Americans had quickly removed most of it. However, the British burned what little they did find. The minutemen engaged the British at Concord's Old North Bridge, where two Americans and three British soldiers were killed. The British retreated to Boston; and the colonists, hiding in the trees, attacked them along the way. Before their day was spent, the British had suffered nearly three hundred casualties and had only escaped total destruction because reinforcements came from Boston. Dogging the regulars all the way, the minutemen encamped on the land approaches to Boston

Wikipedia photo

and began a siege. However, the colonial effort had not come without a cost: ninety-five Americans were killed by the time the British reached Boston. With the confrontations at Lexington and Concord, the American Revolution had begun.

Second Continental Congress and Revolt

The Second Continental Congress met in May 1775 and appointed Virginian George Washington as commander-in-chief of the provincial forces surrounding Boston. His nomination by John Adams, a Massachusetts man, revealed the determined effort of the Americans to present a united front. Congress also authorized the outfitting of a navy under the command of Commodore Esek Hopkins of Rhode Island. In order to finance the war effort, Congress authorized a paper currency issue of $2,000,000. Meanwhile, on May 10, New England forces led by Benedict Arnold and Ethan Allen captured Fort Ticonderoga on Lake Champlain. Subsequently, they moved northward to seize points along the Canadian border.

Bunker Hill

In June, colonists seized Breed's Hill and Bunker Hill in Boston with the intention of shelling the British positions on the peninsula of Boston. The colonists set up defenses on Breed's Hill, and General William Howe and 2,500 British troops assaulted the hill on June 17, 1775, in an effort to drive them off. In what the colonists referred to as the battle of Bunker Hill (though it was actually fought on Breed's Hill), the colonists twice turned the British back before the British were able to take the hill when the colonists ran out of ammunition. It was for this reason that the famous order, "don't fire until you see the whites of their eyes" was issued—as the colonists, short on ammunition, needed to make sure that every shot counted. The battle lasted only two hours, but the British suffered one thousand casualties along with four hundred American deaths. Though the British accomplished their objective, the battle proved to the colonists that they were capable of competing with the British army. In the words of British General Henry Clinton, "It was a dear bought victory; another such would have ruined us."

The heavy casualties on both sides also reduced any chance for a negotiated settlement, and the spilling of so much blood only caused each side to become more determined to force the other to submit militarily. General Howe perhaps erred at Bunker Hill in failing to pursue the Americans as they fled the battlefield. If Howe had pushed westward after the battle, many military historians suggest that he might have decisively defeated the Continental army. Instead, Howe held his army in Boston and abandoned the town without a fight nine months later.

Declaration of Causes and the Olive Branch Petition

In July of 1775, Congress adopted the "Declaration of the Causes and Necessity of taking up Arms," in essence, a declaration of war, in an attempt to assure fellow Britons that dissolution of the union was not intended, but also that Americans refused to capitulate. "Our cause is just. Our union is perfect. Our internal resources are great, and, if necessary, foreign assistance is undoubtedly attainable." The "Declaration" stated that the British government had left the American people with only two alternatives: "unconditional submission to the tyranny of irritated ministers or resistance by force." Congress simultaneously pursued war and peace, however, as they also drafted and sent to the king an "Olive Branch Petition" that humbly begged the king to remove obstacles to reconciliation. Congress also moved to secure the neutrality of the Native American tribes, erect a post office, and approve plans for a military hospital.

In August 1775, the king declared that his subjects were in rebellion, effectively rejecting the Olive Branch Petition, and began to recruit foreign mercenaries and prepare the British regulars. Twenty thousand British troops were sent to the colonies to quell the rebellion. Parliament also passed the "Prohibitory Act," which closed the colonies to all overseas trade and made no concessions to American demands. The British enforced the Prohibitory Act with a naval blockade of colonial ports.

During the remainder of 1775, the Americans under Benedict Arnold and Richard Montgomery attempted the conquest of Canada, chiefly in order to deprive Britain of a base of attack before British reinforcements could arrive. After capturing Montreal, Montgomery pushed northeastward to Quebec while Arnold pushed north to Quebec from the territory of Maine. Arnold's contingent was decimated by smallpox and freezing rain, and more colonists died in the campaign from disease than from battle with the British. Nevertheless, Arnold and the colonists heroically reached Quebec and jointly attacked the British with Montgomery. However, the American attack was repulsed, and the Americans were forced to withdraw.

Momentum Toward the Declaration

Beginning in January 1776, the movement for independence gained ground. On January 1, 1776, the British gave the Americans a military shove by shelling Norfolk, Virginia, an act that was viewed as barbaric by the colonists. The same month, Thomas Paine published his *Common Sense*, asserting "'tis time to part." Up until this point, few Americans had questioned the legitimacy of the king; but in this pamphlet, Paine condemned the monarchy as a form of government in bold language, stating that "nature disapproves it; otherwise she would not so frequently turn it to ridicule by giving mankind an ass for a lion." Paine not only denounced the monarchy in general but also King George in particular, referring to him as a "Royal Brute" and the "hardened sullen-tempered Pharaoh of England." To replace the monarchy, Paine advocated republican government based on the consent of the people. Appreciatively read by thousands of people, *Common Sense* helped to crystallize opinion. The denunciation of the king as an "ass" helped to break down the traditional British deference that most Americans still had for the monarchy. The British also gave the independence movement a boost when news that the British were using Hessian mercenaries reached the colonies. The use of mercenaries, who had a reputation for rape and pillage, was considered ungentlemanly—an improper thing for the British to do in a dispute with their American brothers. By late spring, a number of colonies instructed their delegates to the Continental Congress to advocate independence.

On June 7, 1776, Richard Henry Lee of Virginia, once again reflecting the unity of the colonials regardless of region, introduced a resolution calling for independence. Thomas Jef-

Thomas Paine's *Common Sense* convinced many British colonists to support independence. One way Paine did this was by explaining how the Americans mistakenly thought they had liberty under the British system of government.

I draw my idea of the form of government from a principle in nature which no art can overturn, viz. that the more simple any thing is, the less liable it is to be disordered, and the easier repaired when disordered; and with this maxim in view I offer a few remarks on the so much boasted constitution of England. That it was noble for the dark and slavish times in which it was erected, is granted. When the world was overrun with tyranny the least remove therefrom was a glorious rescue. But that it is imperfect, subject to convulsions, and incapable of producing what it seems to promise is easily demonstrated.

Absolute governments, (tho' the disgrace of human nature) have this advantage with them, they are simple; if the people suffer, they know the head from which their suffering springs; know likewise the remedy; and are not bewildered by a variety of causes and cures. But the constitution of England is so exceedingly complex, that the nation may suffer for years together without being able to discover in which part the fault lies; some will say in one and some in another, and every political physician will advise a different medicine.

I know it is difficult to get over local or long standing prejudices, yet if we will suffer ourselves to examine the component parts of the English Constitution, we shall find them to be the base remains of two ancient tyrannies, compounded with some new Republican materials.

First. — The remains of Monarchical tyranny in the person of the King.

Secondly. — The remains of Aristocratical tyranny in the persons of the Peers.

Thirdly. — The new Republican materials, in the persons of the Commons, on whose virtue depends the freedom of England.

The two first, by being hereditary, are independent of the People; wherefore in a CONSTITUTIONAL SENSE they contribute nothing towards the freedom of the State.

To say that the constitution of England is an UNION of three powers, reciprocally CHECKING each other, is farcical; either the words have no meaning, or they are flat contradictions.

First. — That the King it not to be trusted without being looked after; or in other words, that a thirst for absolute power is the natural disease of monarchy.

Secondly. — That the Commons, by being appointed for that purpose, are either wiser or more worthy of confidence than the Crown.

Source: Thomas Paine, *Common Sense and the Rights of Man* (New York: Penguin), 1969.

ferson was appointed chair of a committee to draft the document that was presented to Congress on June 28. Congress debated the document on July 1. Although many delegates were apprehensive, the resolution was adopted on July 2 by a unanimous vote with twelve colonies voting for independence and New York abstaining so that the vote could be unanimous. On July 4, 1776, the document went to the printer and became public knowledge.

The *Declaration of Independence*

Action and theory were moving together. In 1774, James Wilson, later a Supreme Court justice, had published *Considerations on the Authority of Parliament*, which posed a series of questions. "And have those, whom we have hitherto been accustomed to consider as our fellow-subjects, an absolute and unlimited power over us? Have they a natural right to make laws, by which we may be deprived of our properties, of our liberties, of our lives? By what title do they claim to be our masters? … Do those, who embark freemen in Great Britain, disembark slaves in America?" Wilson answered by affirming, without qualification, that Parliament had no authority over the colonies. Their dependence upon Britain was exclusively through the crown. The colonies were "different members of the British Empire …, independent of each other, but connected together under the same sovereign."

Wilson's assumption underlay the philosophy of the *Declaration of Independence*. The colonists directed the entire document against the king. Nowhere is Parliament mentioned.

The Continental Congress could have separated from Britain by means of a simple declarative resolution. An elaborate document to explain the reason for revolution was unnecessary. That such a document was written is in itself an insight into the nature of the Revolution, for it did not feature tattered flags, starved and desperate people, or lawlessness. Its leadership included some of the most substantial and prominent individuals in America. Because of their influential position and their regard for law, they and their associates felt a deep need to explain to a "candid world" why they took such a drastic step.

Five delegates of the Continental Congress, among them John Adams and Benjamin Franklin, were assigned the task of writing the Declaration; the draft, however, was composed primarily by Thomas Jefferson of Virginia. The members of the committee made modest changes; and the document was then debated in Congress where more changes were made.

The Declaration included a list of specific charges that add up to a devastating indictment, too often treated by historians as an excuse or a rationalization for an act already taken. The list of grievances was meant to show that the Declaration was not based on transient causes but rather upon a long pattern of abuse. With the acceptance of the Declaration by the Continental Congress, the British view that the rights of the colonies depended on the sufferance of the royal grace and favor was forever demolished. Ben Franklin added some gallows humor that reflected the grave nature of the situation when he stated to John Hancock that "we must all hang together, or surely we will all hang separately" when signing the *Declaration of Independence.*

With the Declaration, the character of the conflict changed, also. Whereas the colonials had been secretly soliciting aid from France since 1775, the Continental Congress, representing an independent people, now established ministries throughout Europe to obtain recognition and help for the independent colonies, soon to become the United States. Washington,

▶ The *Declaration of Independence iStockphoto*

who had been leading a militia force to obtain recognition of the rights of colonials, now headed an army fighting for American independence. Thirteen colonies became thirteen states with the problem of working out appropriate constitutions.

Facing the experience of union, the Americans also had to work out an acceptable constitutional structure for the national government. With the Declaration, the Continental Congress was no longer an extralegal body of rebels but, rather, the symbol of a sovereign nation.

The Internal Revolution

Emphasis has been placed on the principal issue—what were the limits of the power of Parliament? Yet historians have investigated a second question: Within each colony, who was to possess authority? Their point of view has ranged widely on this question. Some have insisted that the issue of who was going to rule at home was preeminent, that the break with Britain was brought about by radical dissenters within each colony who were so anxious to overthrow the power structure in their colony that they worked for revolution to accomplish this purpose. Other historians contend that those who held power in the late colonial period were willing to fight to maintain it.

The present consensus among historians is perhaps best expressed as follows: Conflicts within individual colonies contributed to the coming of the Revolution because some people hoped to correct grievances under a new regime. Nonetheless, this internal struggle for control was not the decisive or preeminent force. The principal issue was the conflict over the constitutional framework of the empire. Even without an internal struggle, the Revolution would have occurred. The internal grievances were related, however, to later developments in the revolutionary and post-revolutionary periods as Americans set about to resolve their own problems.

The Loyalists

The *Declaration of Independence* was a divisive rather than a unifying document. It had an impact upon every colony, county, and town and almost every family. With its adoption, people had a decision to make: Would they remain loyal to Britain and its government? Or would they join those who advocated independence and be called rebels?

Regardless of their political views or associations, the present generation of Americans claims the American Revolution as its rightful heritage and consequently regards this decision as a foregone conclusion. The literal "patriots" of 1776 were those who upheld the existing British government. The word *patriotism* derives from *patrios*, meaning "established by forefathers."

In discussing the division between those who supported separation from Britain and those who opposed it, historians have customarily used rather gross figures, holding that one-third of the revolutionary generation remained loyal to Britain, one-third remained uncommitted, and one-third supported independence. Closer examination reveals that the percentage varied substantially among colonies as well as among localities within colonies.

Furthermore, the percentage of loyalists versus patriots was fluid and changed over time.

Wikipedia photo

Figures indicate that 20 percent, about five hundred thousand of the white population became Loyalists. During and after the Revolution, as many as one hundred thousand persons left the colonies for Canada, England, the West Indies, and other places of exile. Historian Robert R. Palmer has calculated that twenty-four persons per thousand of the population left the colonies compared with five persons per thousand of the population of France during the French Revolution, a startling fact that raises the issue of Loyalists to a new level of importance.

These divisions were reflected among families and friends. Governor Morris of New York took up the cause of independence. His mother and many other members of his family remained loyal to Britain. Benjamin Franklin's son William, who was governor of New Jersey, became a Loyalist, causing Franklin to write that his son caused him more personal grief by this act than he had experienced in a lifetime. Close friends and trading associates Thomas Willing and Robert Morris of Philadelphia took opposite sides: Willing remained a supporter of the crown, while Morris became a principal leader of the Revolution.

Some of the most distinguished and honored leaders in these and other provinces left. Daniel Dulaney of Maryland, who wrote so convincingly about the evils of the Stamp Act, could not bring himself to accept independence. Neither could Joseph Galloway, Speaker of the House in Pennsylvania. Chief Justice William Smith of New York finally decided to migrate to Canada after refusing to take a loyalty oath to the revolutionary government in New York.

To list these names tends to imply that only the upper social strata became Loyalists, but the total of five hundred thousand—20 percent of the population—demonstrates that people from every social class became Loyalists. Slaves left plantations to follow the British in the hope of gaining freedom, but servants and artisans also sought the protection of the British government and army.

During the course of the War for Independence, it is estimated that as many as thirty thousand Loyalists served in the British army. As many as eight thousand Loyalists served in the British forces in 1780. Washington's forces at that time numbered no more than nine thousand.

What is more difficult to ascertain is the number of Loyalists who remained in the colonies, trying not to offend the supporters of the Revolution but assisting the British troops when they came. The colonies of Georgia, New York, and South Carolina were the staunchest Loyalist strongholds, followed by New Jersey and Massachusetts. Indeed, the British planned military campaigns in these provinces in the expectation that Loyalists would flock to their standard. The decision to concentrate on New York in 1776 and again in 1777 was based, at least in part, on this assumption. The decision in 1779–1780 to redirect the military effort to Georgia and South Carolina was also prompted by the expectation of winning support throughout the countryside.

Loyalists who did not wish to speak out had good reason to retain a low profile. To leave was to abandon their homes and land, for few Loyalists were able to convert their possessions into cash. Revolutionary governments confiscated Loyalists' property to be resold to the highest bidders. For this and many other reasons, few Loyalists, with the critical exception of those who migrated to Canada, left an imprint upon their adopted homelands.

Those who left for England were probably the ones that had become most disenchanted with England. The nation and the government they had held in such high esteem seemed unrecognizable at close range. The rampant corruption, the flagrant bidding for position and favor, even the lifestyle of eighteenth-century England—all seemed alien to provincial leaders. Persons accustomed to leadership in the colonies became, for the most part, inconsequential in England. On the whole, the Loyalists, because they chose the losing side, became lost among their contemporaries and, in many respects, to history.

Executing the War

The Continental Congress

To make independence a reality, the war had to be won. Though the Continental Congress had neither a specific grant of authority nor a fixed constitutional basis until 1781, it resolved financial, military, diplomatic, and constitutional questions during this critical period. Occasionally, action lagged and arguments centered upon trivialities, but the Continental Congress should be remembered for its major achievements rather than for its minor failures. It unified the American war effort and fashioned an instrument of national government without violating individual liberty and without producing dissension so divisive as to splinter the Revolution. Most of America's greatest leaders of the Revolutionary generation served at one time or another in the Congress, gaining their first political experience at the national rather than at the colony-state level.

Revolutionary Finances

One of the early problems facing Congress was how to finance the war. Four major methods were used: Loan Office Certificates, the equivalent of present-day government bonds; requisitions, that is, requests for money and later supplies from individual states; foreign loans, which were *insignificant* until 1781; and paper currency.

Congress made the first issues of paper money before the *Declaration of Independence*. This avenue of revenue was one that had been used by many colonies during the colonial period. At first the paper money circulated at its face value; but as more money was issued, its value declined (although intermittently the value of the currency increased when successful military operations revived hopes for a quick victory). By the spring of 1781, the value had declined so precipitously that paper currency cost more to print than it was worth once it was printed. Up to that point, however, paper money paid for no less than 75 percent of the cost of the war.

After 1781, foreign loans became especially important because these loans provided capital for the establishment of a national bank, the Bank of North America. From that bank the government borrowed money in excess of the bank's capitalization. After 1781, Morris Notes—a form of paper currency backed by the word of Robert Morris, the Superintendent of Finance—helped to restore the public credit. At the conclusion of the war the national government, as well as the various states, had incurred a substantial debt that was to figure in the movement to write the federal Constitution of 1787.

Military Strategy

The British did not take advantage of their most promising military strategy until 1782, when, too late, they managed to blockade all the American ports. An intensive blockade, if it had been coordinated with swift, devastating land campaigns to lay waste the resources of the Americans, might have brought success, because in order to win the British had to demand unconditional surrender. The Americans, to be successful, needed an army in the field as a symbol of resistance. Any negotiations automatically recognized the United States as an independent nation because a sovereign power does not negotiate with rebels.

After leaving Boston in the spring of 1776, British were concentrated in the mid-Atlantic states in an attempt to divide the United States physically between North and South, thus crippling its unity and exploiting the possibility of support from American Loyalists, which was much stronger in New York than in Massachusetts. Control of New York, with its excellent harbor and river connections to the interior, was also viewed as crucial to the strangulation of American trade. The British believed that control of the Hudson River system would allow them to isolate New England, which they viewed as the center of the rebellion. British armies could then descend on New England from Canada while simultaneously pushing northward from New York and strangling New England trade with the blockade. The British believed that once New England was subdued, Loyalists in the middle colonies would force New York, Pennsylvania, and New Jersey to fall in line. When the New York strategy failed to sufficiently divide the colonists and end the war, the British emphasis shifted to the Southern theater of operations, beginning in 1780 with the intention of exploiting Loyalist sentiments in the South so as to subdue troublesome rebels in Virginia.

Slavery and the Revolution

The policy on enlisting African Americans in the Continental forces changed throughout the course of the war. At the beginning of the fighting, the Continental army and most state militias accepted

▶ A 1779 fifty-five dollar bill of Continental currency. An example of some of our country's first paper money, developed for use by Benjamin Franklin.
Wikipedia photo

African American enlistments, both slaves and freemen. Prince Estabrook, an African American, fought at Lexington, for example, and Peter Salem fought at Lexington, Concord, and Bunker Hill. One Rhode Island regiment included 125 African Americans, thirty of which were freemen.

Early attitudes changed. The Council of War convened by General Washington in Massachusetts in October 1775 decided not to accept further enlistment of African Americans because other troops, especially those from the South, refused to accept them as equals. Free African Americans protested to Washington, and in December 1775 he ordered the reopening of enlistments to free African Americans. Meanwhile, he requested the Continental Congress to review the issue. In January 1776 Congress ruled that free African Americans who had already served could reenlist; but other African Americans, whether slave or free, were excluded. State militias followed this pattern set by the Continental army.

The British attitude fluctuated as much as that of the American provincials. The British recognized that recruiting slaves could cripple the planter colonies, so they promised freedom in exchange for service. They offered indentured servants the same promise. When planters found their slaves leaving to answer the British call, they became alarmed and angry. In Virginia, slave patrols were doubled to catch runaways.

Toward the end of 1776 and early in 1777, manpower shortages caused Continental policy to change once again and African Americans were recruited for the Continental and state navies. The state of Maryland enlisted African Americans in its militia, and even the Virginia militia was willing to accept them. By 1779, the Continental Congress recommended that South Carolina and Georgia raise a military force of five thousand African American soldiers. Owners of slaves who enlisted were to be compensated, and the slaves, in return, would receive freedom and $50 cash. The two states rejected the recommendation, but enlistment of African Americans did grow in the North. In 1781, Baron Von Closen found that one-fourth of the encampment of soldiers at White Plains was composed of African Americans.

Although slavery would continue after the Revolution, a few faltering steps were taken toward emancipation during the war years. In 1780, Pennsylvania provided for the gradual abolition of slavery. In 1784, Connecticut and Rhode Island followed Pennsylvania's lead; soon thereafter New York and New Jersey followed suit. In 1783, the Supreme Court of Massachusetts ruled that the phrase "men are created free and equal" meant what it said, thereby freeing slaves in that state. Massachusetts was the only state where slaves were freed by the state against the will of their masters. In contrast, a proposal in the Maryland legislature to free slaves lost by a vote of 32 to 22. Significantly, no grand plan of emancipation was adopted anywhere in the new nation.

The reason for the continuation of slavery was largely the attitude of the whites toward the African Americans. Jefferson, in a public statement called *The Summary View*, acknowledged that slaves should be freed; but he also declared that African Americans were inferior human beings. The fear of living with African Americans as equals, the loss of property, and the social consequences—all paralyzed the movement to free the slaves. Consequently, the possibility that slavery could be ended during the Revolution faded. The movement was taken up again by a later generation that resolved the issue on the battlefield.

The War in the North

In March 1776, Washington forced the British under General Sir William Howe to abandon Boston by capturing Dorchester Heights, from which they could shell British positions from the high ground. Howe then loaded his troops on transports and sailed to Nova Scotia to prepare for an attack on New York. Howe took with him more than a thousand Loyalists who preferred residence in Canada to independence from Great Britain, thus demonstrating the divisiveness among the American colonists even in the revolutionary hotbed of Boston.

In an effort to prevent Howe's taking New York, Washington moved south and occupied Brooklyn Heights on Long Island. There, on August 27, 1776, Howe, with an army of thirty-three thousand, attacked and defeated Washington, who withdrew to Manhattan Island under the cover of night and fog after suffering some fifteen hundred casualties. Washington then attempted to hold his ground against the British by occupying forts with Washington and Lee on either side of the Hudson River. In November, Howe attacked the forts, forcing Washington to retreat across New Jersey into Pennsylvania. Howe pursued Washington across New Jersey and at one point was only one hour behind the fleeing Continental army; but Howe decided to rest his men for a day and allowed Washington to escape. The Continental Congress, however, meeting in Philadelphia, fled to Baltimore as the British army approached.

▶ General George Washington *Wikipedia photo*

Military historians tend to argue that Howe failed to press his advantage while he had Washington on the run. They contend that had Howe attacked Washington's army at Philadelphia, Howe would have taken the city and crushed the Continental army. Instead, Howe decided to winter his Hessian troops in quarters along the Delaware River and delay his advance until spring, confident that the colonists would be unable to mount an attack. As fate would have it, however, on December 25, 1776, in a freezing rainstorm Washington moved his army across the Delaware River in the dead of night and attacked the unsuspecting Hessians early in the morning, taking nine hundred prisoners. Washington read to the troops a selection from a Thomas Paine pamphlet entitled "American Crisis" the famous words, "These are the times that try men's souls ... The summer soldier and the sunshine patriot will, in this crisis shrink from the service of their country, but he that stands it now deserves ... love and thanks." A week later on January 3, Washington continued his surprise attacks with an assault on Princeton before moving his army to winter quarters at Morristown. The colonial victories in New Jersey were important less for their strategic significance than for their boost to morale. The victories convinced many Americans that they should continue the fight though the strategic prize, New York City, would be occupied by British troops for the duration of the Revolution.

In 1777, British General Howe sent an army, by sea, against Philadelphia while Washington proceeded overland south of Philadelphia. Washington's army met units of Howe's army at Brandywine Creek on September 11, 1777, and suffered defeat after being badly outmaneuvered. Howe entered Philadelphia with ease, but British units were severely tested when Washington launched an unexpected counterattack at Germantown on October 4. Just when it appeared that the American army would prevail, Washington's troops suddenly retreated in confusion. Though the American army was defeated, its offensive spirit aided the cause of independence at home and in France. Washington then withdrew his army to Valley Forge, Pennsylvania, where a combination of freezing weather, bad food, shortages of blankets and shoes, and disease cost twenty-five hundred American lives. Washington complained to Congress that nearly three thousand of his men were "unfit for duty because they are bare foot and otherwise naked." Food and clothing were available elsewhere in the different states; however, states were reluctant to send their supplies of blankets, shoes, and food for use by soldiers outside of their home states. To make matters worse, the American supply lines were fraught with corruption. Teamsters that hauled barrels of salt pork drained out the brine to lighten their load, thus allowing the meat to rot in transit. Blankets were delivered to Washington's army that proved to be only one-fourth of the normal size, and gunpowder purchased by the Continental army often turned out to be defective.

In the meantime, the British had planned a three-pronged attack to capture the Hudson Valley and thus isolate New England from the colonies to the south. From Canada, General Sir John Burgoyne was to push southward down Lake Champlain and the upper Hudson with the expectation of joining General Howe, who would be up the Hudson from New York City. General Burgoyne would then join Howe in an attack on Philadelphia and the occupation of other rebel territory to the south. However, Howe had received conflicting orders and decided that the immediate capture of Philadelphia was more urgent than cooperating with Burgoyne, thus delaying his scheduled rendezvous with Burgoyne's army descending from the north.

Burgoyne had also expected to converge with a third British force under General Barry St. Leger (mostly Loyalists and Native Americans) moving eastward from Lake Ontario along the Mohawk Valley; but this force was beaten back by American troops, many of whom were German in ethnicity, and Native Americans at the Battle of Oriskany. The Americans suffered heavy losses. Five hundred of the eight hundred Americans were killed, but the British forces were forced to retreat and would not rendezvous at Albany with Burgoyne. Nevertheless, throughout the summer of 1777, Burgoyne pressed southward toward Albany. Burgoyne captured Fort Ticonderoga in July after three thousand American defenders, low on food and supplies, fled when they saw the coming British army. Burgoyne, however, was slowed in his march by the accompaniment of his troops by some one thousand laundresses, cooks, and musicians, as well as four hundred Native American warriors and scouts. Burgoyne required four hundred horses to pull his heavy artillery, and he also carried thirty trunks of personal belongings, including his wardrobe and fine wines. At last, failing to receive aid from either Howe or the force from Lake Ontario, he suffered complete defeat to American forces under Horatio Gates and Benedict Arnold in two battles fought near Saratoga. On October 17, 1777, with food supplies running out, he surrendered his entire army of 5,800 men to American General Horatio Gates. Burgoyne's defeat signaled the end of the British hope of isolating New England by occupying the Hudson Valley.

MAP 3.5 Central Campaigns (1776–1778)

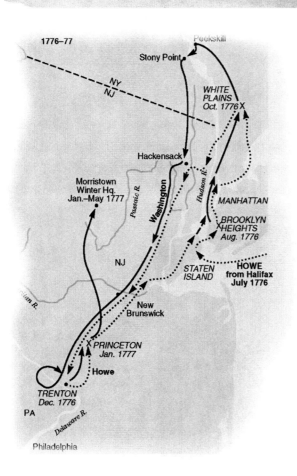

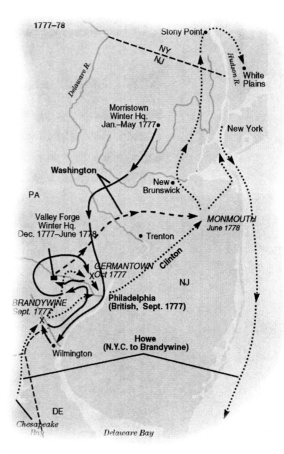

The French Alliance

The victory over Burgoyne at Saratoga and the Battle of Germantown had significant political results. They indicated to European politicians that the Americans could win independence. France, of course, was anxious for revenge upon its ancient enemy, and the efforts of American diplomats in Paris began to bear fruit. Meanwhile, Benjamin Franklin proved a most effective ambassador to France. Wearing a fur cap as the symbol of republican and frontier simplicity, he soon became the toast of Paris and made friends with those politicians best able to help the American cause. Recent research in French archives has revealed how very skilled a diplomat he was.

On February 6, 1778, Franklin consummated an alliance and a Treaty of Amity and Commerce with France. France recognized American independence, thus granting America status as an independent nation under international law. France promised to the United States full military support until U.S. independence was recognized by England, and both France and the United States agreed that neither would sign a separate peace with England. Finally, the United States was to be militarily allied with France indefinitely. France immediately supplied limited funds to aid the American cause and, in 1780, dispatched troops and ships. French ports were opened to such war vessels as the Americans had, and privateers could attack British vessels and stand a better chance of getting away to a safe haven. The French navy provided sea power that the colonies had previously lacked.

Eager to gain access to American markets that Great Britain had long prevented, Holland also provided aid, largely in the form of loans underwritten by the French. Thus European aid, prompted by self-interest, contributed to the American victory. Since Spain was at the time closely allied to France, America expected aid from Spain also; however, Spanish actions never fulfilled American expectations.

New Campaigns in the North

General William Howe was relieved in 1778 by Sir Henry Clinton, who evacuated Philadelphia and returned to New York for a new campaign in the North. Washington, without the power to inflict defeat, could only hang on the flanks of the British army. He established a base at White Plains, New York, and saw to it that West Point on the Hudson was fortified. The arrival of the French naval force

▶ Washington moved his army arcoss the Delaware river during the night to spring an attack on the unsuspecting Hessians the following morning.
Wikipedia photo

▶ General Washington and his army at Valley Forge. Here, freezing weather, poor quality food, shortages of blankets and shoes, and plights of disease took twenty-five hundred soldiers' lives. *Wikipedia photo*

off the coast of New York, however, did little to help the American cause because it soon sailed away to the West Indies. Only from the western frontier was the news encouraging. American George Rogers Clark, leading a group of colonial frontiersmen, helped to hold the West against the British.

The War in the South

In 1778, the British adopted a new strategy designed to take advantage of Loyalist sentiments in the South and play on the destabilizing factor of the presence of thousands of slaves who could be freed by a British victory. The British hoped to reestablish British rule in the southern colonies one by one, beginning with lightly defended Georgia and then moving north up the southern colonial coast. The British captured Savannah in December 1778, and subsequently installed a Loyalist government. Fourteen hundred Georgia militiamen then signed an oath of allegiance to the king and would fight for the British against American rebels. In April and May 1780, the British laid siege to Charleston where 3,300 Americans were forced to surrender after five weeks of fighting. As in Georgia, pardons were offered to Carolinians who swore loyalty oaths to the king and then proved their loyalty by taking up arms for the British. When the Continental army under Horatio Gates attempted a counterattack in August at Camden, South Carolina, American militiamen dropped their weapons and ran when they saw the approaching British cavalry. By the second day of the battle when the Americans tried to regroup, only seven hundred of the three thousand American troops showed up; the remaining were killed, captured, or deserted.

The British victories in the South were aided by information that the British gained from America's most famous traitor, Benedict Arnold. Arnold had been a hero at Saratoga but had been denied the command of the Southern army that was given to Horatio Gates, whom both Arnold and many military historians viewed as Arnold's inferior on the battlefield. Instead

Arnold was given command of a fort at West Point, a post he did not want. This combined with a romantic relationship with a pro-British lover evidently pushed Arnold to espionage. Arnold's treason was discovered when a man was caught carrying plans of West Point's defense from Benedict Arnold to British General Henry Clinton.

In South Carolina, Washington replaced Horatio Gates after the defeat at Camden with General Nathanael Greene, who divided his army into small guerrilla bands and launched a series of hit and run attacks on the British. Some six thousand men engaged in twenty-six battles with the British and Loyalists, and the guerrilla war spread into Georgia and North Carolina. Both patriots and Loyalists committed murders and atrocities and ravaged their opponents' property, and the southern backcountry slipped into near anarchy. In the worst of these fratricidal skirmishes, on October 7, 1780, patriots massacred fourteen hundred Loyalists at King's Mountain in western South Carolina. In January 1781, the patriots followed with a brilliant victory involving Daniel Morgan and his farmer-cavalrymen at the Battle of Cowpens, South Carolina, where local militia units backed by the Continental army defeated the British army. These successes turned the tide in the Carolinas. By autumn those British that had not moved north to Virginia with Cornwallis were pocketed in a small area around Charleston, South Carolina.

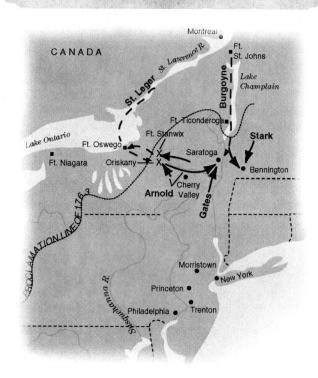

MAP 3.6 Northern Campaigns (1777)

Battle of Yorktown

Meanwhile, in 1780, the French dispatched an army of 5,500 men under an able soldier, the Count de Rochambeau, to aid Washington. These troops encamped at Newport while Rochambeau and Washington waited to see what success collaborative effort would bring. The Count de Grasse, a brilliant French naval commander with a well-equipped squadron, had arrived in the West Indies.

After an exchange of correspondence, de Grasse decided that his squadron could attack more successfully in the Chesapeake than in the harbor of New York. A decision was made for a coordinated land and sea attack in Virginia. Cornwallis and his army, supplemented by troops under the turncoat Benedict Arnold, were being engaged by forces led by French general Lafayette. Washington and Rochambeau began to move their armies south, a maneuver that the British believed was a ploy to catch them off guard in New York, where they expected the main attack to take place.

With de Grasse controlling the Chesapeake Bay area and with a French and American force of fifteen thousand men surrounding Cornwallis's camp on the York peninsula, Cornwallis was trapped; he surrendered on October 19, 1781. When the news of Yorktown reached Britain, the king's ministers agreed that peace must be made with the rebellious colonies.

▶ On October 17, 1777, General Sir John Burgoyne surrendered his entire army of 5,800 men to American General Horatio Gates. The British could no longer isolate New England for themselves by occupying the Hudson Valley. *Wikipedia photo*

Though the nation of Great Britain still had resources with which to continue the fight, the war had been too costly both in terms of economic damage and in human casualties; and the British people lacked the will to continue the unpopular fight.

The War in Retrospect

The war had been a strange, and at times, hopeless one for the Americans. Yet Washington had emerged as a persistent, determined leader. He may have lacked brilliance as a military tactician, but he had the courage, integrity, and character essential to successful command. Despite the demoralization of his forces by lack of supplies, by desertions, and occasionally by mutinies, he held on until the Americans, with French help, achieved victory.

British incompetence played a part in the eventual outcome of the war. Without the assistance that British commanders—Howe and Clinton, particularly—unwittingly gave the patriots, the end might have been different. It was the good fortune of America that Great Britain had been engaged in a world war and that some of its best troops and more competent commanders were in India, Africa, the West Indies, and elsewhere.

Although a few young Frenchmen such as Lafayette came to America to fight for the patriots out of sheer idealism, the alliance of the Bourbon powers, France and Spain, against Great Britain was not motivated by love of liberty or of the republican principles so nobly stated in the *Declaration of Independence*. By a ruse of fate, however, these very principles of liberty eventually exercised an enormous influence in France within a few years and overturned the French monarchy. In the conflict between the American colonies and Great Britain, however, France was merely playing the game of power politics. It sought to avenge an ancient enemy and perhaps to regain some of the American territory it had lost.

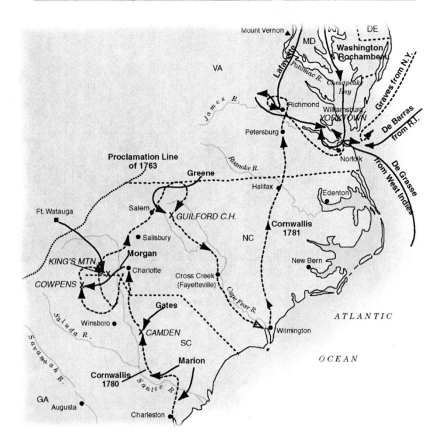

MAP 3.7 Southern Campaigns (1780–1781)

Spain also had an interest in territory west of the British possessions in North America. To weaken Great Britain's strength in the New World would provide possible opportunities for later aggrandizement there for both France and Spain. A weak and struggling republic without money and friends would be easy to dominate and perhaps to devour.

France had promised Spain that it would help extort Gibraltar from the British, but had attacked Gibraltar in vain. Now France proposed to appease Spain with territory west of the Appalachians. In the peace negotiations, which had begun even before Yorktown, the disposition of western territories was a critical consideration.

The Peace of Paris, 1783

To negotiate a peace with England, Congress appointed five commissioners: Benjamin Franklin, envoy in France; John Jay, American agent in Spain; John Adams, envoy in Holland; Henry Laurens; and Thomas Jefferson. Only the first three, assembled at Paris, took an active part in the discussions. At the outset, Jay was suspicious of the motives of the Count de Vergennes, the French foreign minister, and of the British agent, Richard Oswald. Oswald had come with instructions to treat the commissioners as if they represented rebellious colonies.

Although the commissioners had received from Congress full power to negotiate the best treaty possible, Congress had specifically instructed them to take no steps that France rejected. Since Jay was convinced that France was determined to sacrifice American interests to satisfy Spain, he persuaded Adams and Franklin to deal secretly with England and to make a preliminary treaty that promised favorable terms.

The news leaked out and Vergennes was incensed. Franklin, a great favorite of the French, managed to placate him by admitting that their action was merely an "indiscretion." Nevertheless, the preliminary treaty had established the pattern for the final treaty, which was signed on September 3, 1783.

Great Britain, partly to propagate dissension between the Bourbon allies and partly to win the friendship of the late colonies and keep them from becoming satellites of France, offered such favorable terms that Vergennes, in anger, declared that the English were ready to "buy peace rather than make it." Instead of letting Spain have the trans-Appalachian region, Great Britain agreed that the Mississippi should be the western boundary of the United States. Although Franklin had tried to obtain all of Canada "to insure peace," it was agreed that the Great Lakes should determine the northern border. In the end, Great Britain gave Florida back to Spain, and the treaty set the southern border of the United States at 31 degrees north latitude. The provisions of the treaty seemed clear, but in some areas the boundary lines were not stated precisely. In Maine (at that time still part of Massachusetts) the border remained in dispute for years.

The treaty also provided that American citizens were to enjoy the same fishing rights in Canadian waters as British subjects. The two countries agreed that the Mississippi River should be forever open to navigation by both American and British shipping. The British demanded restitution of Loyalist property confiscated during the war, but all Congress could do was to recommend that this be done. The treaty also stipulated that the United States would not impede the payment of debts to the British, but Congress had no means by which to force any American debtors to pay their British creditors. Since Congress also had no authority over the states, it was agreed that suits might be brought by British subjects in the state courts for the recovery of debts. Congress ratified the Treaty of Paris on January 14, 1784.

Effects of the War

Wars traditionally result in social and financial upheavals, and the American Revolution was no exception. Within the twenty years of controversy and war, old and settled traditions were altered; and the patterns of a new society emerged. Obviously, among the most important changes was the fact that the colonists were no longer English. Consequently, as soon the Revolutionary War ended, the new government faced a number of problems, not the least of which was what to do about those who had remained loyal to George III.

The King's Friends

The Treaty of Paris of 1783 contained two clauses concerning the American Loyalists. One recommended that they be restored their "estates, rights, and properties." The other stated that refugees be allowed to return for a year, without persecution or prosecution, to settle their affairs. The States, however, did not always follow these recommendations. The bitter war that "set Nabor against Nabor" had left fierce antagonisms. Loyalists who had served with the British—there were twenty-one Loyalist regiments in the British army—faced beatings, tar and feathers, and possibly hanging. As a consequence, most Loyalists who fled did not return.

There were two waves of Loyalist migration: one in the early years of the war, the other near the end. Refugees in the first wave went chiefly north to Canada. In 1781–1784, those in the second wave of "late Loyalists" were probably motivated as much by the promise of cheap land as by loyalty to the King.

Estimates are hard to substantiate, but about sixty thousand Loyalists total left the United States. Of these, forty thousand went to Canada, ten thousand to England, and most of the rest (including over one thousand free African Americans and slaves) to the West Indies and Africa.

"Our Old Home"

The Loyalists who went to England, chiefly to London and Bristol, were first glorified and then neglected. Governor Hutchinson of Massachusetts, who on arrival was offered a baronetcy (which he could not afford) and an honorary Oxford degree, wrote two years later, "We Americans are plenty here, and cheap. Few, if any of us, are much consulted or inquired after."

Some liked London, of course, but others found that they did not like the British and that the British, with their prejudice against colonials, did not particularly like them. Britain's tightly woven, hierarchical society had few openings for them in the usual vocations—church, military, law, politics—and not many had the capital or connections needed for business.

Then too, the Loyalists were not British, but British-American; and England was not home. "I would rather die in a little country farmhouse in New England," said Hutchinson, "than in the best nobleman's seat in Old England." Nevertheless, a parliamentary commission, appointed in 1783 to deal with Loyalist war claims, eventually paid out three million pounds to about two-thirds of the claimants.

MAP 3.8 North America 1783

"Go to Hell or Halifax"

Loyalists who went to Canada did much better. The British promised half-pay to ex-officers as well as land, lumber, seeds, stock, tools, and clothing, and kept most of their promises. A larger number went to Nova Scotia—to the great port city of Halifax or to the fertile St. John Valley. Others went to the St. Lawrence area. Since the Maritime provinces of Canada were a geographical and economic extension of New England, and central Upper Canada, north of the St. Lawrence River, was a similar extension of New York State, the Loyalists easily fit into Canadian society. In fact, in 1784, the British created the Province of New Brunswick to separate the Loyalists from the more conservative society of Nova Scotia.

The arrival of the Loyalists had significant impact on subsequent Canadian history. It placed thriving English-speaking settlements where none had been before, thus reinforcing Canada's Britishness at a crucial point in its development. Without the arrival of the Loyalists, Upper Canada might have gravitated toward New York State, the Maritimes toward New England, and present-day Canada might not exist. Refugees from one North American nation, in a sense, became the founders of another. "By Heaven," wrote Loyalist Edward Winslow from New Brunswick, "we will be the envy of the American States. I am in the midst of as cheerful a society as any in the world." One Loyalist wife wrote, however, as she saw the last ships depart for Massachusetts, "Such a feeling of loneliness came over me that though I had not shed a tear through the entire war, I took my baby in my lap and sat down on the moss and wept."

Unrestricted Trade

No longer were the American colonies the source of raw materials supplied exclusively to Great Britain. Dutch, French, Spanish, and Portuguese ships could slip into American ports and load tobacco, wheat, corn, meat, rice, and other products needed in Europe. Despite the war—even as a result of it—some American merchants made more money than ever before; and some European commodities, received in exchange for produce, were more abundant during the war than previously.

War profiteers made a few fortunes. More importantly, however, a network of colonial merchants experienced the challenges and problems of unrestricted trade on an international scale. Patriotism did not keep some dealers from making 200 or 300 percent profit on clothing and supplies needed by the Continental soldiers. New industries that focused on war products developed. Iron foundries multiplied. Gunsmiths flourished, and factories for the manufacture of muskets, gunpowder, and cannon were built, particularly in New England and in Pennsylvania. Since the usual trade in English woolens and other fabrics was cut off, cloth making was encouraged.

The Westward Movement

With the elimination of the prohibition against movement into the trans-Appalachian region that the British had tried to enforce after 1763, new migrations began. Frontiersmen were soon filtering into valleys and clearings beyond the mountains. In 1776, Virginia had organized into a county a portion of what later became the state of Kentucky. Before the Revolution, frontiersmen from Virginia had settled on the Watauga River, in what later became

Tennessee. After the Revolution, uprooted citizens and restless souls all along the frontier began a trek west that continued until one day the American continent as far west as the Pacific was occupied. Land companies were organized, and within a few years speculation in western lands became an obsession. As a result Native Americans lost their land, culture, and lives. The group who lost the most as a result of the American Revolution was the Native Americans.

Modifications of American Society

Socially, the Revolution brought changes, also. The most immediate result was the elimination of royal governors, other British officials, and the cliques of socially elite who gathered about them. Even in colonies that had no royal officials, those who were subservient to the mother country were swept out and new leaders took their places.

Yet as important as these changes were, the United States nowhere experienced the kind of social revolution that swept France a few years later. The structure of American society was modified rather than radically altered. In Virginia, for example, the influence of the tidewater aristocrats diminished somewhat, and backcountry politicians of the type represented by Patrick Henry gained power. The families who had produced leaders before the Revolution, however, still continued to supply many of the leaders in the new nation.

One reason the new republic moved with relative ease from the status of a colony to that of a self-governing nation was the tradition of local responsibility established in all of the colonies early in the development of the British settlements. This inheritance from the British tradition of local self-government ensured an array of leaders from which individuals could be drawn for any level of responsibility required. Though lacking a French-style social revolution, it must still be said that within a generation or so after the Treaty of Paris, American society had undergone extraordinarily rapid change.

▶The British promised Loyalists who went to Canada better opportunities. They would grant half-pay to ex-officers as well as land, lumber, seeds, stock, tools, and clothing, and kept most of their promises. The larger number went to Nova Scotia—to the great port city of Halifax. *iStockphoto*

The *Articles of Confederation*

Soon after the *Declaration of Independence,* a committee was appointed to draw up the *Articles of Confederation* to bind the thirteen states together into a union. It took more than a year to draft the Articles, and they then had to be submitted to the states for ratification. This took until the spring of 1781.

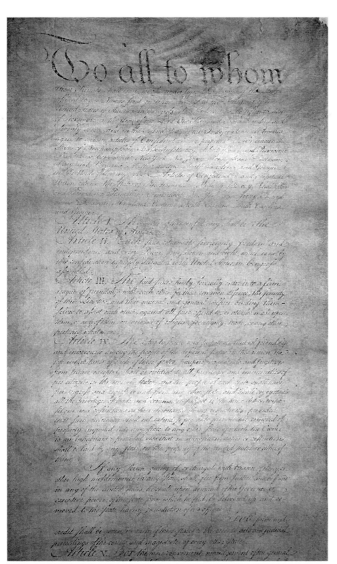

▶ The *Articles of Confederation,* ratified by all thirteen colonies in 1781, was the basis for the United States government until the Constitution was drafted. *Wikipedia photo*

In the meantime—during almost the entire war—the colonies operated under the authority of the extralegal Continental Congress. Among the most important contributions of the Articles were their preservation of the union and their definition of powers to be granted to the state governments as opposed to a central government. The delay in ratifying the *Articles of Confederation* was due chiefly to a conflict of land interests. Massachusetts, Connecticut, New York, Virginia, Georgia, and the Carolinas—under the terms of colonial charters, royal grants, Native American treaties, or proprietary claims—asserted ownership of tremendous grants of lands in the West. To be able to retain these western lands would be a great economic asset since the sale of the back regions would provide the state governments with a steady income and make it unnecessary for them to tax their citizens at all.

Naturally, the advantage that would come to states with western land claims was resented by the states with fixed boundaries. For example, Rhode Island could claim no land west of Rhode Island since the state of Connecticut is immediately west of Rhode Island. Conversely, Virginia claimed all land west of Virginia in its latitude as far as it could claim land across the continent. The "landless" states such as Rhode Island protested that the War for Independence was being fought for the benefit of all and that every state should share in the rewards to be found in western territory. Thus, these landless states were reluctant to sign the *Articles of Confederation* until the westward limits of the existing states were set and until Congress was given authority to grant lands and to create new states beyond these limits.

The debate was not motivated entirely by the question of the equality of the states. Land speculators had formed companies in Maryland and Pennsylvania, for example, and had made purchases from the Native Americans in the Ohio valley. Now they wished governmental validation of their titles. How could they secure clear title to land claimed by Virginia and New York when such states were inclined not to recognize the purchases made by out-of-state residents?

Eventually, after considerable political maneuvering and propagandizing, both sides gave in. Between 1777 and 1781, the land companies vacated their claims to western territory purchased from the Native Americans; and upon recommendation of a congressional committee in 1780, the landed states, led by Virginia, New York, and Connecticut, gave up claim to most of the trans-Appalachian country, making the western lands the territory of the nation. In February 1781, the last of the landless states, Maryland, ratified the Articles; and on March 1, the Confederation was formally proclaimed.

When the war was over, many thoughtful citizens throughout the country feared that the *Articles of Confederation* would not permit the evolution of a nation strong enough to survive. For example, in foreign policy much depended upon the power of a centralized authority. Furthermore, a central authority was required to establish the financial stability of the nation and to deal with problems of credit, the issuance of money, and the maintenance of national defense. These problems and their solution formed an important chapter in constitution making.

Chapter Review

Summary

At the close of the Seven Years War in 1763, Americans were generally content to continue being British, but a number of changes brought about by the War itself would lead to an American revolt against England in less than a generation. The Seven Years War left England deeply in debt and also with new, unruly territory to control with the acquisition of French Canada. The British viewed the American colonies as unruly as well, as evidenced by incidents such as the Boston Impressment riot a generation earlier. Consequently, the British determined that forward placement of troops in the American colonies, as well as in the newly-acquired former French colonies, was necessary to ensure order.

Forward placement of troops, however, was expensive, and that coupled with the debt incurred from the Seven Years War induced the British to impose taxes on the colonists to extract from them what the British viewed as their share of the burden. In the British view, the British troops had not only provided security for the colonists in the Seven Years War, but were continuing to provide security from which the colonists benefited.

In the view of the colonists, however, forward placement of troops in the American colonies was unnecessary since the French effectively had been removed from North America as a threat. Consequently, the colonists rejected both the new British taxes and the new British restrictions on trade, engaging in boycotts of British goods, riots, and eventually dumping a large shipment of tea in Boston Harbor.

When the British had finally had enough and sent troops to "quell the rebellion," most Americans favored resistance, though whether or not it would result in American independence remained unclear. British use of Hessian mercenaries combined with Thomas Paine's *Common Sense* to produce enough sentiment for a *Declaration of Independence* in July 1776 and the war became a war for independence. Though Americans lost most of the battles, the superior British army was never able to completely squelch the rebellion. The shocking American victory at Saratoga resulted in French assistance and a Treaty of Alliance with France. The British moved the War south in an attempt to exploit stronger Loyalist sentiments in the South and scored major victories at Savannah and Charleston, but when the French arrived at Yorktown to trap General Cornwallis and 7500 British troops between the Americans and the French, the British decided that it was time to negotiate an end to the costly war.

The Revolution brought a number of changes to American society in addition to self-rule. The former colonists now had a new American identity, language and culture as they attempted to forge a new Republic and deal with the social and economic problems left over from the War. Slavery had been abolished in Massachusetts and was in the process of being abolished in other Northern states. Questions remained over the weakness of the Confederation, however, as contentious issues over Western lands had delayed ratification of the *Articles of Confederation* until 1781. Nevertheless, the principles of the American Revolution of freedom and self-rule would be a guiding beacon of ideals to the world for centuries to come.

Chapter Review (cont'd) ▶ ▶ ▶

Chronological Time Line

1759	The Privy Council instructed the governor of Virginia to refuse to sign any bill that failed to include a "suspending clause"
1761	General writs of assistance empowered officers of the British customs service to break into and search homes and stores for smuggled goods
1763	Pontiac's Rebellion
1763	Peace of Paris concludes Seven Years War
1764	Currency Act restrictions on the issuance of paper money forces colonists to pay British merchants in gold or silver
1764	Revenue Act or Sugar Act declares that a number of commodities could be imported only from England.
1765	Quartering Act requires colonists to provide Housing for British troops
1765	Stamp Act Riots
1766	Declaratory Act declares that Parliament can legislate in all matters "whatsoever," but Stamp Act repealed
1767	Townshend Act imposes new duties on a number of commodities
1768	Liberty Incident
1770	Repeal of Townshend duties except for a symbolic duty on tea
1770	Boston Massacre, March 5.
1772	*Gaspee* Incident: Colonists burn a British ship in Providence Harbor
1773	Tea Act and Boston Tea Party
1774	Quebec Act annexes lands in the northwest to Quebec
1774	Coercive Acts or "Intolerable Acts."
1774	First Continental Congress meets at Carpenter's Hall in Philadelphia
1775	First Shots of the Revolution fired at Lexington, April 18

Time Line (cont'd)

1775	Second Continental Congress appoints George Washington as commander of troops around Boston
1775	Battle of Bunker Hill on June 17 reduces chances for negotiations
1775	Olive Branch Petition is rejected by England
1776	News arrives that England is using Hessian Mercenaries in January
1776	Thomas Paine publishes Common Sense
1776	British withdraw from Boston in March
1776	George Washington is defeated at Long Island in April
1776	Richard Henry Lee proposes a *Declaration of Independence* in June
1776	*Declaration of Independence* goes to the printer on July 4.
1776	Washington is defeated at Manhattan in November
1776	Washington crosses the Delaware River and defeats Hessian Mercenaries at Trenton on December 25.
1777	Washington suffers defeat at Brandywine Creek on September 11
1777	Washington is defeated at Germantown on October 4
1777	Washington withdraws to winter his army at Valley Forge, PA
1777	Saratoga: 5800 British surrender to Horatio Gates on October 17
1778	Treaty of Alliance with France on February 6
1778	British capture Savannah in December
1780	Pennsylvania provides for gradual abolition of slavery
1780	British capture Charleston in May
1780	Patriots massacre 1,400 Loyalists at King's Mountain on October 7

Chapter Review (cont'd) ▶ ▶ ▶

Time Line (cont'd)

1781	British defeated at Cowpens, South Carolina in January
1781	Yorktown, British General Cornwallis surrenders on October 1, trapped between American and French troops.
1783	Massachusetts Supreme Court abolishes slavery
1783	Treaty of Paris officially concludes Revolutionary War September 3

Sources Consulted

David Ammerman, *In the Common Cause: American Response to the Coercive Acts of 1774* (1974).

Bernard Bailyn, *The Ideological Origins of the American Revolution* (1967).

Richard M. Brown, *The South Carolina Regulators* (1963).

Stephen Conway, *The War of American Independence, 1775–1783* (1995).

David Hackett Fischer, *Washington's Crossings* (2004).

Sylvia R. Frey, *Water from the Rock: Black Resistance in the Revolutionary Age* (1991).

Ronald Hoffman and Peter J. Albert, eds., *Women in the Age of the American Revolution* (1989).

Woody Holton, *Forced Founders: Indians, Debtors, Slaves, and the Making of the American Revolution in Virginia* (1999).

Pauline Maier, *American Scripture: Making the Declaration of Independence* (1997).

Pauline Maier, *From Resistance to Revolution: Colonial Radicals and the Development of Opposition to Britain, 1765–1776* (1972).

Gary B. Nash, *The Urban Crucible: Social Change, Political Consciousness, and the Origins of the American Revolution* (1979).

Charles Royster, *A Revolutionary People at War: The Continental Army and American Character, 1775–1783* (1979).

John Shy, *A People Numerous and Armed: Reflections on the Military Struggle for American Independence* (1990).

Stanley Weintraub, *Iron Tears: America's Battle for Freedom, Britain's Quagmire: 1775–1783* (2005).

4 Establishing the Republic, 1781–1800

Outline

iStockphoto

Wikipedia photo

Wikipedia photo

Wikipedia photo

Wikipedia photo

The Search for Stability

Balancing Federal with Local Authority

Of prime importance in the political life of the United States throughout its history has been the problem of federalism—the division of power between the states and the federal government—or, more simply, the issue of local control or "states' rights" versus national power or central authority. The origins of this problem stemmed from the British imperial system of the mid-eighteenth century. At the center of this system stood Great Britain, whose government had directed foreign affairs and intercolonial relations with the goal of keeping the machinery and policies of the empire working in harmony. At the extremities of this system had been the colonies themselves, each of which had attained the right to govern its internal affairs.

In practice, however, the dividing line between imperial and local affairs was variously interpreted, and out of the conflict of interpretations came the American Revolution. With the *Declaration of Independence,* the American colonies rejected the government in London altogether and, under the pressures of war, united sufficiently to create a limited central authority of their own making—the Confederation.

When Richard Henry Lee, on June 7, 1776, offered a resolution to the Continental Congress declaring American independence, he also proposed that "a plan of confederation be prepared and transmitted to the respective colonies for their consideration and approbation." A little over a month later, on July 12, a committee headed by John Dickinson of Pennsylvania presented such a plan to the Continental Congress. On November 15, 1777, after more than a year of debate, the *Articles of Confederation* were approved and sent to the states for ratification—a process that took four years and the *Articles of Confederation* would not be ratified until 1781. During almost the entire Revolutionary War, therefore, the country operated under the authority of the Continental Congress without a formal central government.

▶ Richard Henry Lee *Wikipedia photo*

The loyalty of individual Americans was strongly attached to their states; therefore, it was readily agreed that the states should hold the sovereign powers of government. The Articles were designed to create an assembly of equal states, each of which retained its "sovereignty, freedom, and independence, and every Power, Jurisdiction, and right." The *Articles of Confederation*, therefore, created a loose confederation of states with a new Congress almost exactly like the wartime Continental Congress then in existence, in which each state—regardless of size, population, or wealth—had an equal vote. The Articles delegated to Congress the power to declare war, make peace, conclude treaties, raise and maintain armies, maintain a navy, establish a postal system, regulate Native American affairs, borrow money, issue bills of credit, and regulate the value of the coinage of the United States and the several states. However, nine of the thirteen states had to give their consent before any legislation of importance could be enacted, and enforcement of the decisions of Congress depended upon the cooperation of all the states. Ultimately, all power rested in the states rather than in the national government. For example, Congress could make treaties, but could not force the states to live up to their stipulations. It could authorize an army, but could not fill its ranks without the cooperation of each state. It could borrow money, but had to depend on requisitions from the states to repay its debts. Nor did the Articles provide standing agencies of enforcement. Congress could pass laws, but there was no formal executive or judicial branch to execute and adjudicate them. The day-to-day operations of government were handled rather precariously by officials or committees appointed by Congress.

Because of their recent quarrels with Parliament over questions of taxation and commercial regulation, the states also withheld two key powers from their new central government: the power to levy taxes (Congress could merely request contributions from the state legislatures) and the power to regulate commerce. This proved to be problematic during the Revolution as states actually fulfilled only 10 percent of Congressional requisitions. Without the powers to tax and regulate commerce the Confederation government could not depend upon a regular

▶ John Trumbull's famous depiction of the drafting committee presenting its work to the Congress on July 12, 1776, though the articles were not ratified until 1781. *Wikipedia photo*

and adequate supply of revenue to sustain its own functions, nor could it attempt to foster a national economy, a factor essential to the political unity of America.

The central government, therefore, was what the Articles called it—nothing more than "a firm league of friendship." Sharing a common cause of facing common danger, such as an invading British army on American soil, its members could work together with some measure of effectiveness. Any suspicion that Congress would infringe upon the states' rights of independent actions, however, would throw the states on their guard; and once imminent danger passed, the states tended to work independently rather than together.

The State Governments

In 1776, the *Declaration of Independence* had made necessary the creation of two kinds of government: central and local. While only tentative motions were made toward centralization, the people were quick to make the transition from colonial government to state government. Actually, the process was one of revision and adaptation, since each of the former colonies already possessed a government with its own methods of operation. Indeed, two states (Connecticut and Rhode Island) continued to operate under their colonial charters by simply deleting all references to the British crown. Ten other states completed new constitutions within a year after the *Declaration*, and the last (Massachusetts) by 1780. The state constitutions, though varying in detail, reflected both the colonial experience and the current revolutionary controversy.

The framers of these constitutions placed the center of political authority in the legislative branch, where it would be especially responsive to popular and local control. As a Massachusetts town meeting bluntly resolved in 1778, "The oftener power Returns to the

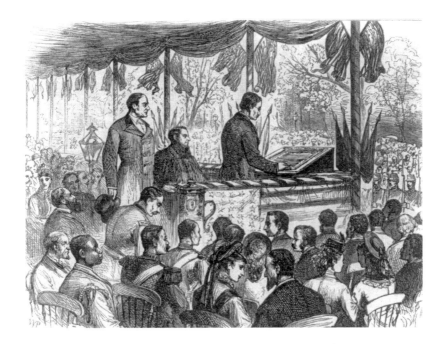

▶ Richard Henry Lee reading the *Declaration of Independence* at Philadelphia
Library of Congress

hands of the people, the Better … Where can the power be lodged so Safe as in the Hands of the people?" Members of the legislature, if they wished to be reelected, had to keep in mind their people "back home." Legislators were held accountable by being restricted to brief terms: in ten states the lower house, which originated tax legislation, was newly elected every year; in Connecticut and Rhode Island it was every six months; in South Carolina, every two years.

Framers of the constitutions, remembering their recent troubles with royal governors and magistrates, restricted the powers of governors and justices almost to the vanishing point. The average governor, contemporary jokesters claimed, had just about enough authority to collect his salary. Opposition to a single strong executive was so strong that in Pennsylvania, the position of the governor was abolished and replaced with a council of twelve.

The imbalance of power among the branches of government often severely hampered the states' abilities to meet and solve the political and economic problems that faced them during and after the war. Yet whatever their shortcomings, these constitutions were the first attempts form governments. They were constructed on the premise, novel to the eighteenth century, that a government should be formed under a *written* document, thus recognizing the first time in modern political life the difference between fundamental and statute law, and between rule of law and rule of men. The introduction of such precisely formed instruments of governmental law, on such a grand scale, was a major contribution to the science of government.

The state constitutions reaffirmed the powerful colonial tradition of individual freedom in their bills of rights, which guaranteed each citizen freedom of religion, speech, and assembly, trial by jury, the right of habeas corpus, and other natural and civil rights. In general, they extended the voting franchise to the majority of white male citizens. In all states, a man had to own some property to vote. In many, he had to own a more substantial amount to hold office. Since property formed the basis for voting qualifications, and since the states quickly increased opportunities to own land, many white males could probably meet the requirements. New

Jersey even gave the vote to women, only to withdraw it in 1807. Over the years, gradual abolition of property qualifications further widened the suffrage until all property requirements were eliminated, on a state-by-state basis, by 1852.

The popular fear of governmental power tended to render the state governments politically and financially impotent. Afraid to antagonize the voters, who could quickly run them out of office, legislators had difficulty, for example, in passing effective measures of taxation. Even when they did so, revenue men found it difficult to extract them from the people.

The Confederation Period

Historians have come to believe that the years of the Confederation were more creative and constructive than once was supposed. During those years a peace was won on terms highly favorable to the United States. An orderly policy for western territorial expansion was established. A postwar recession was overcome and replaced by economic prosperity and the population increased. Finally, at the end of the "critical period," the Constitution was born. In general, the achievements of the period were due largely to the efforts of particular individuals and groups, and to some of the more foresighted state governments.

Establishing a Western Policy

The solution to the western land problem that had kept the last state, Maryland, from ratifying the Articles until 1781, was of paramount importance to the new government. It represented a first step toward nationalization and made certain that the nation, as it moved west, would gradually evolve as a unit rather than as thirteen colonies with a set of permanent dependent territories. It also meant that since Congress now controlled all the western lands, it could determine a central policy for the development of this vast unpopulated territory.

During and after the Revolution a surge of people migrated west, creating an urgent need for a systematic plan of land sale and territorial government. A land ordinance passed by Congress in 1785 provided for a government survey to divide the land of the Northwest Territory (north of the Ohio River, west of Pennsylvania, and east of the Mississippi River) into townships of thirty-six square miles. Each township was to be split into thirty-six sections of one square mile (640 acres) each and every section into quarter sections. Four sections in every township were reserved as bounties for soldiers of the Continental Army, and another section was set aside for the use of public schools. The remainder of the land was to be sold at public auction for at least one dollar an acre, in minimum lots of 640 acres.

The Ordinance of 1785 proved advantageous to wealthy land speculators, who bought up whole townships and resold them at handsome profits. Sensing even greater returns, a group of speculators (including some congressmen and government officials) pressed for further legislation to provide a form of government for the Northwest. The result was the Northwest Ordinance of 1787, based largely on a similar ordinance drafted by Jefferson in 1784, but never put into effect.

MAP 4.1 Western Lands Ceded by the States (1782–1802)

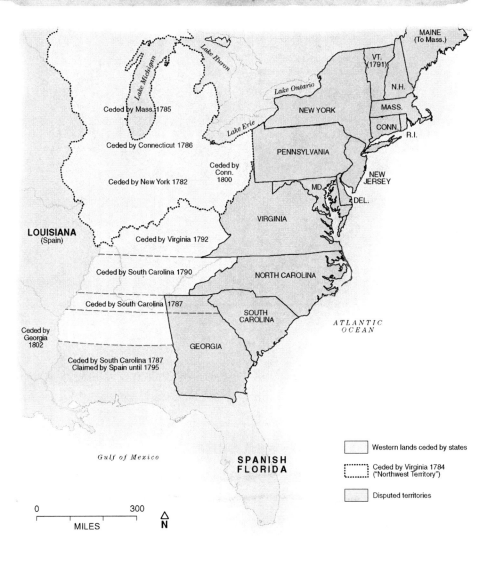

Though it favored the wealthy land speculator over the impoverished farmer, the Northwest Ordinance did provide an orderly process for translating the unsettled Northwest, by orderly political procedures, from frontier to statehood. It provided that Congress should appoint from among the landholders of the region a governor, a secretary, and three judges. When the territory reached a population of five thousand free adult males, a bicameral legislature was to be established. When there were sixty thousand free inhabitants (the population of the smallest state at the time), the voters might adopt a constitution, elect their own officers, and enter the Union on equal terms with the original thirteen states. From three to five states were to be formed from the territory. Slavery was forbidden in the area, and freedom of worship and trial by jury were guaranteed.

So successfully did the Northwest Ordinance accomplish its political aims that it set the pattern for the absorption of the entire West into the Union (as well as Alaska and Hawaii some-

MAP 4.2 Map of Trans-Allegheny Settlements (1790)

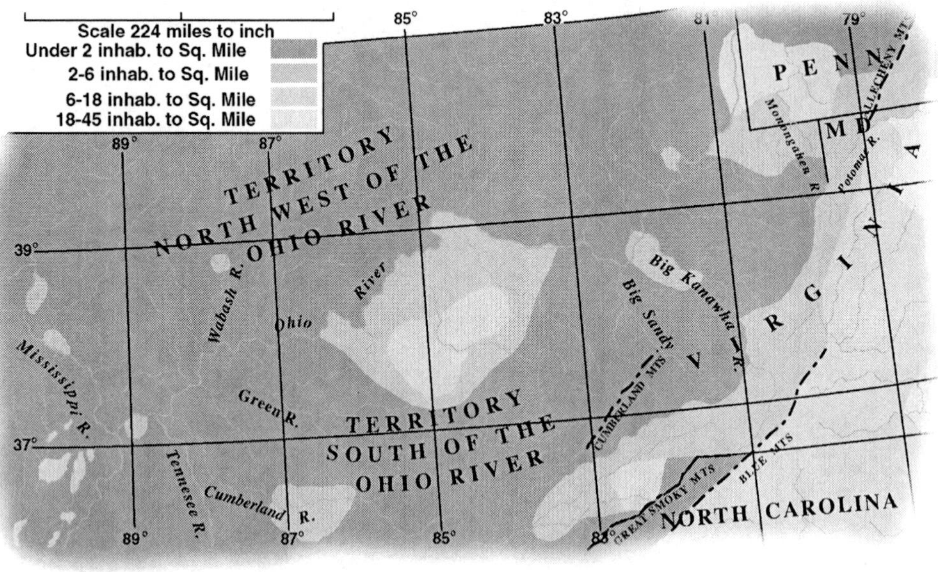
Scale 224 miles to inch
Under 2 inhab. to Sq. Mile
2-6 inhab. to Sq. Mile
6-18 inhab. to Sq. Mile
18-45 inhab. to Sq. Mile
TERRITORY NORTH WEST OF THE OHIO RIVER
TERRITORY SOUTH OF THE OHIO RIVER
Wabash R.
Ohio River
Mississippi R.
Green R.
Tennessee R.
Cumberland R.
Big Sandy
Big Kanawha R.
Monongahela R.
Potomac R.
CUMBERLAND MTS
GREAT SMOKY MTS
BLUE MTS
PENN
MD
VIRGINIA
NORTH CAROLINA
89°
87°
85°
83°
79°
39°
37°

what later). Settlers flooded into the Northwest Territory as soon as the ordinance went into effect. The great drive westward had begun, not to cease for another one hundred years.

Relations with Europe

Perhaps the most serious problems facing Congress under the Articles arose from its lack of a unified, coherent foreign policy and its lack of authority to evolve one. The core of diplomatic power resided equally among the states, each of which possessed the right to arrange its own foreign affairs, with the national government virtually helpless to operate independently. At one point England withdrew its foreign minister to the United States. John Adams protested and demanded an explanation, to which the English replied that they did not know whether they should send one representative or thirteen.

The United States was in a most delicate position in regard to England, France, and Spain. There was no reason to suppose that Britain intended to allow America to remain independent without interference if Britain's interests dictated otherwise. The United States, for its part, desperately needed trade agreements with Europe and especially with England, its largest market.

America's foreign challenges also involved a border dispute with Spain over Florida; and when the Spanish, who controlled the lower Mississippi and New Orleans, closed them to American trade in 1784, the nation was in trouble. The closing of the Mississippi effectively shut down vital trade to the American interior, and the livelihood of the nation was in peril. If Congress could not open the Mississippi to trade, a number of Western leaders favored either taking New Orleans by force or joining a British protectorate that might help them to do so. Washington believed that the West in 1784 was so near to secession that "the touch of a feather" might divide it from the country.

The Spanish, who needed American trade, seemed willing to negotiate; and in 1785, the Spanish minister Diego de Gardoqui discussed terms with Secretary of Foreign Affairs, John Jay. Both diplomats were bound by specific instructions, which led to a stalemate; but eventually, in 1786, Jay agreed to a commercial treaty. This treaty would have allowed the United States to trade with Spain but not with its colonies—if the Americans would "forbear" navigation of the Mississippi River though not the *right* to use it.

Such a roar of protest went up from the West that Jay let the negotiations lapse. The Spanish helped matters in 1788 by opening the river under restrictions with which the West could live, though not happily, until the Pinckney Treaty of 1795 settled the issue. These negotiations with Spain not only pointed up the impotence of the Articles in foreign affairs but also left behind in the West a lingering suspicion of the East.

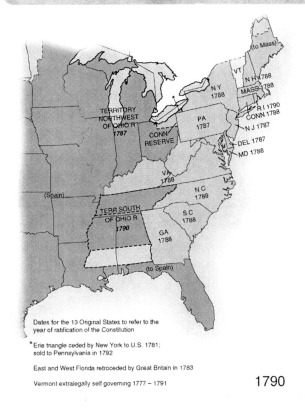

MAP 4.3 Map of Territorial Growth 1790

Dates for the 13 Original States to refer to the year of ratification of the Constitution

*Erie triangle ceded by New York to U.S. 1781; sold to Pennsylvania in 1792

East and West Florida retroceded by Great Britain in 1783

Vermont extralegally self governing 1777 – 1791

1790

The Difficulties of Trade

When the colonies left the imperial system, thus giving up their favored economic position, American merchants and shippers found themselves in cutthroat competition with the British, Dutch, and French for world markets. John Adams tried unsuccessfully for three years to make some kind of trade agreement with England; but as Lord Sheffield commented, putting his finger squarely on the commercial weaknesses of the *Articles of Confederation*, "America cannot retaliate. It will not be an easy matter to bring the Americans to act as a nation. They are not to be feared by such as us."

Sheffield proved to be correct, for when Congress asked the states in 1784 for exclusive authority to regulate foreign trade over a fifteen-year period, the states immediately refused. Under the *Articles of Confederation*, Congress was powerless to do more than protest.

Domestic commerce as well as foreign trade suffered from interstate rivalries. The states used their power to levy tariffs against each other, creating barriers that seriously hampered domestic commerce and caused further dissatisfaction with the central government. At the same time, American industry was struggling to survive. The war and blockade had stimulated American manufacturing by cutting off imports from Britain and the Continent. Some of the states, in fact, had offered premiums and subsidies for the production of domestically manufactured goods. With the return of peace, however, much of the artificial stimulation that had encouraged American industry was withdrawn, and the inevitable postwar slump set in. Capital was short, the currency disordered, transportation deficient, and investments risky.

Frenzied Finances

▶ Secretary of Foreign Affairs John Jay *Wikipedia photo*

The *Articles of Confederation* gave the national government no power to tax. If the states refused to pay their levies in full or on time, Congress simply was forced to accumulate ever-larger foreign and domestic debts. The states responded erratically to the requests from Congress for revenue, so that while Congress occasionally had money, it never had enough at the right time. Although Congress repudiated most of its war debts by simply canceling out millions of dollars in the currency issued under the Continental Congress in 1785, the country still owed about $35 million in domestic debts and had a growing foreign debt. The fledgling government owed money to its soldiers that had fought the Revolution, but could not pay them. Congress had sold war bonds in an effort to finance the Revolution; but those bonds were now coming due, and Congress had no means with which to meet its obligations. As the government defaulted on its obligations, bondholders sold their bonds to speculators for as little as 10 cents on the dollar. The states, meanwhile, had war debts of their own, which they increased after the war by taking on the amounts of the congressional debt that were owed to their citizens.

In addition to the problem of these debts, both national and state governments lacked a uniform, stable, sound currency. There was no trustworthy federal currency. Both the states and the central government issued over $200 million in paper currency during the Revolution with the predictable result that currency inflation reached 12,000 percent at one point during the 1780s. The inflation had the effect of essentially rendering the savings of Americans as worthless. The Americans that refused to tax themselves sufficiently to pay for the Revolution essentially paid for the Revolution through the depletion of their savings caused by the massive inflation. The postwar slump, which hit the country in 1783, plunged to its nadir in mid-1786 and affected farmers and small debtors most of all. In states where these groups controlled the legislatures, the solution seemed easy: Seven state legislatures simply approved the issue of paper money in larger quantities. In addition, to help distressed farmers, these states passed "stay laws" to prevent creditors from foreclosing on mortgages.

Crisis and Rebellion

At the depth of the depression in 1786, there was a severe hard-money shortage. Farmers, especially, were in dire situations. The problems were most acute in Massachusetts where the debt situation led to a decree by the state government that all debt must be repaid at face value, and new taxes were levied by the state to pay the state's debts. The citizens of Massachusetts, however, lacked the resources with which to pay the new taxes. Twenty-nine Massachusetts towns declared their inability to meet their obligations. Tax collector Peter Wood of Marlborough, Massachusetts, reported that "there was not … the money in possession or at command among the people" to meet their obligations. Protest meetings in several states won some concessions from the legislatures; however, in Massachusetts, a Hampshire County convention of fifty towns met and passed resolutions condemning the state legislature, lawyers, court fees, and of course, the taxation. The Massachusetts county courts became the targets of the citizens' wrath when the courts issued writs of foreclosure on farmers that had been demanded by creditors and the state taxing authorities. When a group of men forced the closure of the courts at Northampton, Worcester, and Springfield, thus preventing farm foreclosures and prosecutions for debt, Governor James Bowdoin sent in the militia to scatter them.

In reply to Bowdoin, Daniel Shays, a veteran of the American Revolution and Bunker Hill, began organized resistance to the Massachusetts' government. Shays issued a set of demands—including a demand for new paper money issues, tax relief, a moratorium on debts, and the abolition of imprisonment for debt. Shays organized a band of some 1,200 farmers in the winter of 1786 for an attack on the Springfield Arsenal, from which he hoped to obtain arms. The governor sent a militia force of some three thousand men (paid for by contributions from Boston businessmen) to protect the arsenal; and the Shaysites' poorly mounted attack in February 1787 by outnumbered farmers failed miserably. Four of Shays's men were shot and killed by the Massachusetts militia and twenty were wounded, sending Shays's rebels into retreat. Shays fled toward Canada, but he was caught and subsequently arrested and imprisoned. Over one thousand of his followers were also arrested and jailed. Samuel Adams, who only a decade earlier had led a revolt against the taxation policies of the British government, denounced Shays and the rebels for treason. Two of the rebels were executed; sixteen more were sentenced to death, but later granted reprieves. Four thousand gained leniency by confessing their misconduct and swearing a loyalty oath to the state. The Massachusetts legislature passed a Disqualification Act that prohibited the rebels from voting, holding public office, serving on juries, working as schoolmasters, or operating taverns for a period of up to three years.

Shays's Rebellion had swift consequences in Massachusetts. Governor Bowdoin was defeated in the next election by John Hancock, and the legislature prudently decided to grant the farmers some measure of relief. Debtor laws in Massachusetts were reformed, and Shays and his followers were released. The effect on the country at large was equally swift and much greater, as the rebel-

▶ A monument stands at the place of the final battle of Shays's Rebellion, in Sheffield, Massachusetts. *Wikipedia photo*

lion shook the confidence of elites in the ability of the confederation to maintain order. Abigail Adams exemplified the attitudes of the elites in a letter to Thomas Jefferson where she wrote that when "ignorant, restless desperadoes, without conscience or principles" could persuade "a deluded multitude to follow their standards ..." who could be safe, anywhere in the land? "There are combustibles," wrote Washington, "in every state which a spark might set fire to."

Framing a New Constitution

The Drift Toward a New Government

Even the most earnest states' rights advocates were willing to admit the existence of imperfections in the *Articles of Confederation*. Proposals for conventions to discuss amending them had already appeared in the New York legislature in 1782 and in Massachusetts in 1785. In 1786, under the cloud of Shays's Rebellion, Congress agreed that the Articles needed revision, although as James Monroe told Jefferson, "Some gentlemen have inveterate prejudices against all attempts to increase the powers of Congress, others see the necessity but fear the consequences."

In 1786, James Madison called for a meeting of delegates at Annapolis, Maryland to discuss needed changes in the *Articles of Confederation* and hopefully reach agreement on a uniform tariff. The lack of a uniform tariff had seriously hindered American trade and rendered the confederation impotent in its efforts to retaliate against high British tariffs on American goods. New York, with its busy harbor, opposed high tariffs and preferred more open trade policies in an attempt to boost trade in the port of New York. No agreement was reached in the convention of 1786, and only five states even participated; but it provided the opportunity for Alexander Hamilton of New York to seize the initiative. When James Madison of Virginia invited representatives from the states to meet at Annapolis in 1785 for a discussion of problems of interstate commerce, only a few responded. Hamilton called upon the states to appoint delegates to a meeting to be held in May 1787 at Philadelphia, to discuss ways "to render the Constitution of the Federal Government adequate to the exigencies of the Union." Since at almost the same time Daniel Shays's men, pursued by Boston militia, were providing an example of the kind of "exigency" Hamilton referred to, his call found receptive audiences in the states. Congress adopted his suggestion and authorized a convention "for the sole and express purpose of revising the *Articles of Confederation* and reporting to Congress and the several legislatures such alterations and provisions therein."

While there were those who believed that the Articles could be amended and reworked into an effective and efficient government, a number of determined political leaders—among them Alexander Hamilton, James Madison, John Jay, and Henry Knox—were convinced that the country's interests demanded a much stronger central government. They believed in executive and judicial control rather than legislative and did not fully trust the decentralized, mass-dominated state governments. There was a general belief among the mercantile and financial classes that, as Madison wrote, the United States needed the kind of government that would "support a due supremacy of the national authority, and leave in force the local authorities so far as they can be subordinately useful."

The Question of Federalism

The meetings at Philadelphia began on May 25, 1787, but conspicuously absent were many of the popular leaders of the pre-revolutionary era. These men such as Samuel Adams and Patrick Henry, became known as "antifederalists" due to their opposition to a federal form of government that would place more power in the national government at the expense of the states. These men had involved themselves in the Revolution when it still comprised a scattering of colonial protests and then state revolts, rather loosely guided by the Continental Congress. Deeply devoted to winning independence for their own states, most of them continued to believe that the states should be governed without the interference of a strong central government. Some antifederalists, such as George Clinton of New York, had a vital stake in local state politics, which the enlargement of the powers of a continental government might endanger. Others saw the need to strengthen the Confederation, but insisted that the supremacy of the states should not be basically altered. Others feared a strong executive due to what they viewed as abuses of executive power under the English monarch. All of the antifederalists were passionately convinced that a republican system could survive only on the local level, under their watchful eyes. A republic on a continental scale was beyond their imagination.

The fifty-five delegates who made their appearance in the Philadelphia State House held generally broader views. George Washington (chosen presiding officer of the convention) and Benjamin Franklin were distinguished representatives of an older generation, long experienced in guiding the military and diplomatic affairs of the colonies as a whole. Although Washington, in particular, contributed little to the proceedings at the convention, his presence gave the convention legitimacy in the eyes of the public. Most of the delegates, however, were in their thirties or forties. Their careers had only begun when the Revolution broke out, and their public reputations had been achieved as a result of their identification with the continental war effort. With the coming of peace, these "nationalists" had been disquieted by the ease with which the states slid back

▶ Samuel Adams, among others, became known as "antifederalists." These men were committed to winning independence for their own states, and believed that the states should be governed without the interference of a strong central government. *Wikipedia photo*

into their old provincial ways. In vainly advocating revenue and commercial powers for the Confederation Congress, Robert Morris, James Wilson, James Madison, Alexander Hamilton,

Charles Pinckney, and others began to see the futility of trying to govern a large country with thirteen states following diverse policies. These men who favored placing more power in the national government became known as "federalists."

These federalists distrusted unchecked power in government as much as their opponents did, and they favored retaining state autonomy as much as possible. They believed, however, that under the current system, power *was* being exercised in one quarter without effective restraints. There was no way to appeal the decisions of the state legislators. The state executive and judicial branches, and even the central Confederation, were powerless to overrule the legislative branches in the thirteen states. In addition, nations abroad were beginning to look with contempt upon the disunited states, and there were even dangerous signs of territorial encroachments—from Britain in the Northwest and Spain in the South and Southwest. The English had not withdrawn all of their troops from American soil in the Ohio Valley as Americans had expected after the Peace of Paris. The British remained on American soil in an effort to exploit trade with Native American tribes in the Ohio Valley, but also to induce the Americans to pay their British debts. Spain controlled the mouth of the Mississippi River and could, therefore, cut off trade to the American interior by closing the Mississippi to American trade at their discretion. The U.S. had no standing army and was too weak militarily to do anything about either the Spanish or the British situation. National survival, commerce, and prestige, the federalists insisted, demanded that a stronger central government be created.

The Philosophy of the Constitution

The feeling of urgency that permeated the minds of the delegates goes far toward explaining their eagerness to reach compromises on matters in dispute. Whenever the debates became deadlocked, speakers rose and warned the delegates of the consequences should the Convention fail. Elbridge Gerry said at mid-session: "Something must be done or we shall disappoint not only America, but the whole world.... We must make concessions on both sides." Caleb Strong also warned, "It is agreed, on all hands, that Congress is nearly at an end. If no accommodation takes place, the Union itself must soon be dissolved."

Such warnings climaxed a series of heated arguments during the meetings. There were 569 votes taken at the convention, sixty just to decide on one executive in the form of the president. Of the fifty-five persons that attended the convention, only thirty-nine signed the document and four voted against it. Of the three New York delegates that attended, only Alexander Hamilton remained at the end, as the other two left in disgust. In the end, the document that emerged is best viewed as a political compromise since the founders were not in agreement on many details.

The delegates generally believed that the central government must be empowered to act without the mediation of the states and to exercise its will directly upon individual citizens. It must have its own administrative agencies, with the ability to enforce its own laws and treaties, to collect its own revenues, and to regulate commerce and other matters of welfare affecting the states generally.

Second, they believed that power in government, although imperative, must somehow be held in check. Like most enlightened people of the eighteenth century, they recognized that human nature was not perfect. "Men are ambitious, vindictive, and rapacious," said Alexander Hamilton; while his language was strong, his colleagues generally shared his appraisal of human nature. They agreed with the French political philosopher Montesquieu that "men entrusted with power tend to abuse it." The system advocated by Montesquieu to prevent this evil was to distribute the functions of government among three coequal branches of government, each of which would hold a veto or check on the power of the others. John Adams had earlier outlined this doctrine of "separation of powers":

> A legislative, an executive, and a judicial power comprehend the whole of what is meant and understood by government. It is by balancing each of these powers against the other two, that the efforts in human nature toward tyranny can alone be checked and restrained, and any degree of freedom preserved in the constitution.[1]

That a three-branch system had failed in the state governments did not shake the delegates' faith in the *principle* of separation of powers. For the most part, the states had only gone through the motions of creating three branches. In actuality, they had not given the executive and judicial branches sufficient checks on the legislatures.

Finally, most of the delegates were committed to some form of federalism, the political system that eventually united the states under an independently operating central government while permitting them to retain some portion of their former power and identity. Few agreed with George Read of Delaware that the states "must be done away." Even Alexander Hamilton, who formally introduced such a scheme, acknowledged that the Convention might "shock the public opinion by proposing such a measure." It was generally agreed that the states must remain. The argument arose over how, in operating terms, power could be properly distributed between the states and the national government.

The Convention at Work

Four days after the Convention commenced, Edmund Randolph of Virginia proposed fifteen resolutions, drafted by his colleague James Madison. The general intent was clear at once: to proceed beyond mere revision of the *Articles of Confederation* in favor of forming a new national government. The founders held essentially conflicting goals since they desired to both increase national government power, yet retain state sovereignty. In order to solve this dilemma, Randolph's plan called for a national government sufficient for security, powerful enough to prevent dissension among the states, and strong enough to provide for national development. This "Virginia Plan" proposed a national executive, a national judiciary, and a national legislature consisting of two houses, both representing the states proportionally according to either population or tax contributions and with the lower house popularly elected and the upper house chosen by members of the lower one. Although William Paterson proposed a rival "New Jersey Plan," which in substance would merely have enlarged the taxation and commerce powers of the Con-

[1]*Papers of John Adams* April 1776.

federation Congress, it was never seriously considered. After four months of debate, amendment, and considerable enlargement, the Virginia Plan became the United States Constitution.

Although the delegates agreed upon the main features of the new government, discord over the details almost ended the Convention. That a breakup was avoided is attributable, in part, to the delegates' recognition of the undeniable need for a new form of government, thus forcing the delegates into compromise and concession. They were pressed to balance special interest against special interest, the large states against the small, and section against section, in order to work out a constitution that the majority could accept. No state could be perfectly satisfied with the result, but each had to believe they were more contented than before.

Major opposition to the original Virginia Plan came from the small states. In the existing Congress each of their votes was equal to that of any large state, but under the proposed system of proportional representation in the national legislature they would be consistently outvoted by the larger, more populous states. Delegates from the large states retorted that government should represent people, not geography. "Is [a government] for *men*," asked James Wilson, "or for the imaginary beings called *States*?" The issue came down to the question of how federal the federal government should be. In acknowledging the permanence of the states, were the delegates obligated to go further and introduce the concept of the states into the very structure and representation of the new central government?

The final answer to this question was "Yes." In the end, the large states gave in. After the New Jersey Plan was rejected and the principle of a bicameral (two-house) legislature established, the small states, while hesitating to object to proportional representation in the lower house, persisted in claiming the right of equal representation for states in the Senate, or upper house. By threatening to walk out of the Convention, they won. In essence, this "Great Compromise," as it came to be called, was hardly a compromise at all. The major issue concerned representation in the Senate; and when the large states conceded on this point, they received no concession in return. However, the major crisis

▶ This "Virginia Plan" proposed a national executive, a national judiciary, and a national legislature consisting of two houses, both representing the states proportionally. This Virginia plan became the United States Constitution. The United States Constitution is the oldest written constitution still in use by any nation in the world. *iStockphoto*

of the Convention had been resolved.

In the process of accepting this two-house legislature, the delegates acknowledged not only a balance between large and small states but also a balance between the common people and the propertied interests. Many delegates had argued against giving the people a direct voice in government. "The people," said Roger Sherman, "should have as little to do as may be about the government. They want information, and are constantly liable to be misled." Elbridge Gerry pointed to the "evils" that "flow from the excess of democracy." Other delegates agreed, however, with James Madison who stated "that the great fabric to be raised would be more stable and durable, if it should rest on the solid foundation of the people themselves." Thus the basis of representation in the lower house was set at one representative for every forty thousand persons—each representative to be elected by voters eligible to elect "the most numerous branch of [their] State legislature." On the other hand, the senators of the upper houses—two from each state—were to be chosen by the state legislatures, putting them at a second remove from popular control. As a result, the Senate was expected to represent the more conservative interests, "to consist," as John Dickinson noted, "of the most distinguished characters, distinguished for their rank in life and their weight of property." In sum, the two houses of Congress were to balance the rights of the lower and higher ranks of society, but with the edge given to the higher.

Another issue arose over the manner of choosing the president—the head of the executive branch of the new government. To have the national legislature appoint him, as the original Virginia Plan proposed, might mean, it was argued, that a candidate to that high office would be "a mere creature of the legislature." A second plan, championed by James Wilson, called for popular election of the president, but the delegates had too great a distrust of unchecked democracy to find this plan fully acceptable. Other proposals sought to bring the states into the elective process by having either the state legislatures or the governors combine to elect the nation's chief executive.

The final compromise embodied elements from all these plans. Each state legislature was to appoint a number of presidential "electors" equal to the total number of senators and representatives to which the state was entitled in Congress. The electors would meet in their own states and vote for two presidential candidates, and the candidate receiving the majority of votes from all the states would become President. It should be noted that the method of choosing the electors was left to the decision of the state legislatures. Thus, the legislatures might decide to keep the power of appointment in their own hands, as most of them did; or they could submit the appointment to popular vote, a method that became widespread only much later. In either case, the electoral system was intended to minimize popular influence in the choice of the president.

Few of the delegates, however, believed that the election would end in the Electoral College. It was believed that each state would try to advance a native son, and thus no candidate would receive a majority vote. In that event, the election would be referred to the House of Representatives, where votes would be taken by state delegations with each state having one vote. In effect, this presidential compromise echoed the earlier issue over proportional representation. In the first phase of the election, votes would be drawn on the basis of population. In the second phase (the Electoral College), voting would be on the basis of statehood.

The conflict between North and South was not as serious in the Convention as it was later to become, but the differing sectional economies did arouse specific issues of governmental structure and powers. The South, being an agricultural region dependent on a world market for its staple exports like tobacco and rice, wanted commercial regulation—tariffs and export duties—eliminated or minimized. Southerners were also committed to slavery, not necessarily through moral conviction of its justice but because of their inescapably large investment in slave labor. Finally, the Southern states, six in number and comparatively less populous than the Northern states, were aware that in Congress the North would outnumber them. They thus felt compelled to secure constitutional guarantees for their sectional interests before launching a new government in which they could be consistently outvoted.

In the North, on the other hand, agricultural products such as grain and livestock had, for the most part, a ready domestic market. Many Northerners were more interested in having the government promote shipping and foster manufacturing by means of protective tariffs. Some also vigorously condemned slavery and demanded an end to the "nefarious" slave trade. Their attitude, however, was not entirely without self-interest. The Convention had already agreed that direct taxes were to be assessed on the basis of population. The North was quite willing to have slaves counted as part of the population in apportioning such taxes, hence upping the South's assessments. However, Northerners objected to counting slaves in apportioning representation in the House of Representatives, a plan that would enlarge the Southern delegations.

The Convention resolved these differences by negotiating compromises. In regard to commerce, the South won a ban on export taxes and a provision requiring a two-thirds vote in the Senate for ratification of treaties. In return, the North secured a provision that a simple congressional majority was sufficient to pass all other acts of commercial regulation. The slave trade could not be prohibited before the year 1808, but a tax up to ten dollars might be imposed on each slave imported. The so-called three-fifths compromise specified that five slaves would equal three free men for purposes of both taxation and representation.

The influence of the states in the framework of the new constitution was greater than some nationalists would have liked. One of the most important factors shaping the delegates' decisions were their practical recognition that they had to offer a constitution that the people would approve. Popular loyalty to the respective states was too strong to be ignored.

New powers granted to the national government under the Constitution were designed to remedy the primary concerns of the time. The Constitution empowered Congress to construct a standing army and navy to provide for the security of the United States. In addition, Congress was granted the power to impose tariffs, both to raise revenue for the American government and to aid American commerce in competition with overseas competitors. Congress was empowered not only to raise revenue but also to pay the debts of the United States. Furthermore, Congress was empowered to establish uniform laws of bankruptcy in an effort to help resolve some of the contentious debt problems present in the states. Congress also was given the power to regulate interstate commerce, a power that has grown immensely since its inception, and the power to coin money and regulate its value. Moreover, Congress was given exclusive authority over foreign policy. Two vague clauses, the power to "provide for the common defense and the general welfare" and the power to make all laws "necessary and proper" for the carrying out of its powers, provided the potential for great expansion of national government powers if the clauses were interpreted broadly.

Referral to the States

By the close of the summer, the Constitution was slowly taking shape; and on September 17, 1787, twelve state delegations voted approval of the final draft. Edmund Randolph and George Mason of Virginia, along with Elbridge Gerry of Massachusetts, refused to sign it, asserting that it went too far toward consolidation and lacked a bill of rights. (Randolph, however, later decided to support it.) The remaining thirty-nine delegates affixed their signatures and sent the document to Congress with two recommendations: that it be submitted to state ratifying conventions especially called for the purpose, rather than directly to the voters; and that it be declared officially operative when nine (not thirteen) states accepted it, since there was real doubt that any document so evolved could ever obtain unanimous approval. Some of the delegates feared that they had far exceeded their instructions to *revise* the Articles, for the document they sent to Congress certainly represented much more than revision.

Federalists and Antifederalists

The new Constitution met with great favor and equally great opposition in the states. Its strongest supporters, who adopted the name "Federalists," were drawn from the ranks of bankers, lawyers, businessmen, merchants, planters, and men of property in the urban areas. Hamilton and Jay favored it in New York. Madison, Randolph, and John Marshall argued for it in Virginia. Furthermore, the fact that Washington and Franklin, the two most honored Americans, supported it was much in its favor. Opposition to its ratification came from the small farmers, laborers, and the debtor, agrarian classes. It is misleading, however, to arrange the argument over ratification on lines of economic interest alone. Obviously, there were businessmen and merchants who voted for the document because they thought it would mean expanded markets, better regulation of commerce, greater credit stability, and less control of trade by the states. Just as obviously, there were farmers and debtors who voted against it for equally self-interested economic reasons. The lines of delineation between rich and poor, or mercantile and agrarian interests, however, were by no means so clear in the voting as one might expect. Claiming that the nation could obtain progress and prosperity under the Articles if they were revised, the anti-federalists accused the Convention of creating a government that eventually, as George Mason of Virginia thought, might "produce either a monarchy or a corrupt aristocracy." There was "apprehension," Rufus King of New York told Madison, "that the liberties of the people are in danger." In Massachusetts, the pioneering woman historian Mercy Otis Warren, who belonged to an elite family, was also in opposition to the Constitution on these grounds.

Happily for the fate of the Constitution, the federalists, who might more accurately have been called nationalists, possessed a group of leaders of great drive and organizing skill. It was not easy to out argue or outmaneuver men such as Hamilton, Jay, Madison, James Wilson, or Henry Knox. Furthermore, they had the initiative and kept it, giving their opposition little time to temporize or organize. The federalists immediately began an energetic campaign for ratification in their own states. In New York, where opposition was strong, the Constitution was brilliantly defended in a series of eighty-five newspaper articles written by Hamilton, Madison, and Jay. The essays later were collected in a single volume called *The Federalist Papers*.

The anti-federalists had only a few such talented leaders. George Clinton, Patrick Henry, Elbridge Gerry, Luther Martin, and James Warren were able men; but none, for example, was capable of producing the brilliant *Federalist Papers* or of handling the New York campaign as Hamilton did. The anti-federalists tried to fight the battle piecemeal, without a positive program, and showed a curious reluctance to match the aggressive, shrewd campaigning of the federalists.

It has sometimes been fashionable among historians, particularly in the early twenty-first century, to consider the struggle over ratification as a contest between "conservatives" and "liberals." If the *Declaration of Independence* represented "radical" or revolutionary thought, the Constitution, it was assumed, therefore, represented a conservative counterrevolution that undid some of the Revolution's work. On reexamination, however, it becomes less clear which side deserves which label. It was the federalists, after all, who proposed the bold, decisive change to complete the powerful nationalism engendered by the revolutionary effort. This was a daring step—to create from a bundle of disparate states a single, unified nation bound together by common consent and national pride. The anti-federalists, fearful of any power not under their direct restraint, preferred the status quo. To them, apparently, the great experiment in federalism suggested by the Constitution seemed too new as well as dangerous. They could not conceive of a nationalized government that did not threaten republican principles.

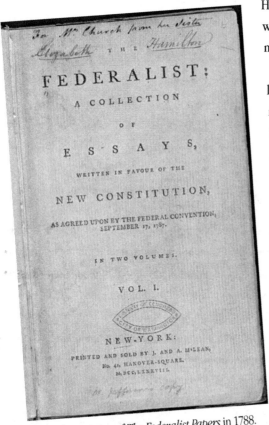

▶ The first printing of *The Federalist Papers* in 1788. These were a collection of eighty-five essays written by Alexander Hamilton, James Madison, and John Jay, defending the Constitution. *Wikipedia photo*

Ratification of the Constitution

The ratification of the document proceeded smoothly in most of the smaller states, which were generally satisfied with the compromises created to protect them. By January 1788, five states (Delaware, New Jersey, Georgia, Connecticut, and Pennsylvania) had accepted it, with stalwart opposition recorded only in Pennsylvania. The Massachusetts state convention ratified the Constitution by a vote of 187 to 168 after a long dispute, and then only after attaching a strong recommendation for a bill of rights. Maryland and South Carolina ratified, while New Hampshire, the ninth state, took two conventions (the second by a margin of nine votes) to accept it in June 1788. Legally the Constitution could now go into effect, yet most people understood that without New York and Virginia it could not function successfully.

In Virginia, the federalists won a narrow victory, eighty-nine to seventy-nine, on June 25. Like Massachusetts, Virginia attached proposals for twenty changes and a recommendation for a specific bill of rights. In New York, Hamilton and the federalists pulled the document through on July 26, by the breathtakingly small margin of thirty to twenty-seven. North Carolina refused

The framers of the Constitution made one major blunder. They thought that the large size of the republic would prevent any powerful political parties or factions, as they referred to them, to dominate politics. James Madison asserted in essay Number 10 of the *Federalist Papers*:

The other point of difference is, the greater number of citizens and extent of territory which may be brought within the compass of republican than of democratic government; and it is this circumstance principally which renders factious combinations less to be dreaded in the former than in the latter. The smaller the society, the fewer probably will be the distinct parties and interests composing it; the fewer the distinct parties and interests, the more frequently will a majority be found of the same party; and the smaller the number of individuals composing a majority, and the smaller the compass within which they are placed, the more easily will they concert and execute their plans of oppression. Extend the sphere, and you take in a greater variety of parties and interests; you make it less probable that a majority of the whole will have a common motive to invade the rights of other citizens; or if such a common motive exists, it will be more difficult for all who feel it to discover their own strength, and to act in unison with each other. Besides other impediments, it may be remarked that, where there is a consciousness of unjust or dishonorable purposes, communication is always checked by distrust in proportion to the number whose concurrence is necessary.

Source: *The New York Packet,* 23 November 1787.

to ratify the Constitution until a bill of rights was actually attached to it and finally approved it in late 1789. Rhode Island held out until 1790.

The debates over the ratification indicated that the chief issue was the Constitution's lack of a bill of rights, so in 1789, the First Congress proposed ten amendments (ratified in 1791). Of the ten amendments, the First prohibited Congress from interfering with freedom of speech, press, religion, and assembly. The Fifth placed the citizen under "due process" of law, and the Sixth and Seventh guaranteed trial by jury. The Tenth reserved to the people and to the states all powers not delegated to the federal government, thereby providing a guarantee of decentralized political power.

The ideas expressed in the Constitution were implicit in the *Articles of Confederation,* the *Declaration of Independence,* and the revolutionary arguments. The Constitution merely gave those ideas an explicit, final form. The idea that government should protect life, liberty, and property was already accepted. The idea that government should be powerful enough to

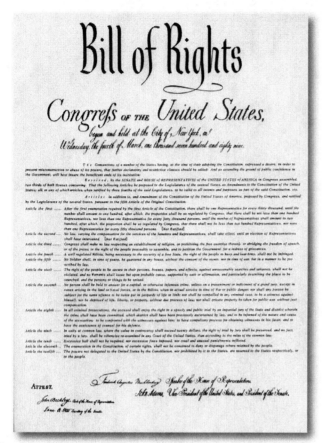

► The Bill of Rights is the name for the first ten Amendments, proposed by James Madison, to the United States Constitution. The Constitutional Amendments came into effect on December 15, 1791. *iStockphoto*

perform its functions was already recognized, even in the Articles—though there were sharp differences of opinion over how powerful that need be.

Launching the Government

George Washington

After the balloting for president and for Congress in January 1789, under the terms of the new Constitution, the presidential electors met in February to choose George Washington as the first President of the United States. John Adams, who had received the smaller number of electoral ballots, was installed as vice-president in mid-April. On April 30 Washington, standing on the balcony of the Federal Building at Broad and Wall Streets in New York, was inaugurated as President of the United States.

For the first few months of the new administration, Congress and the president moved carefully. Congress created the three executive departments of State, Treasury, and War; and Washington chose Thomas Jefferson, Alexander Hamilton, and Henry Knox to serve as the respective secretaries. Congress then passed a tariff on imports and a tonnage duty on foreign vessels, both intended to raise revenue and to protect American trade. The Judiciary Act of 1789 created the office of attorney general, a Supreme Court, three circuit courts, and thirteen district courts, filling in the outlines of the federal legal system.

The Issue of Finance

Washington left the most critical problem of his first term to Alexander Hamilton, his confident young Secretary of the Treasury. Hamilton believed that the government should play an active, even decisive role in economic affairs; the nation might then achieve a self-sufficient, expanding economy, balanced among agriculture, manufacturing, and trade. To this end he proposed, in his *Report on the Public Credit* (1790), *Second Report on the Public Credit* (1791), and *Report on Manufactures* (1791), a firm, unified policy enforced by a strong federal authority.

Hamilton's economic program also had clear political aims. He was convinced that the new government could not last unless the Constitution were strengthened by interpretation and made responsive to changing needs, and unless the forces of wealth and property supported it. As a result he hoped to win business and financial groups to the support of the

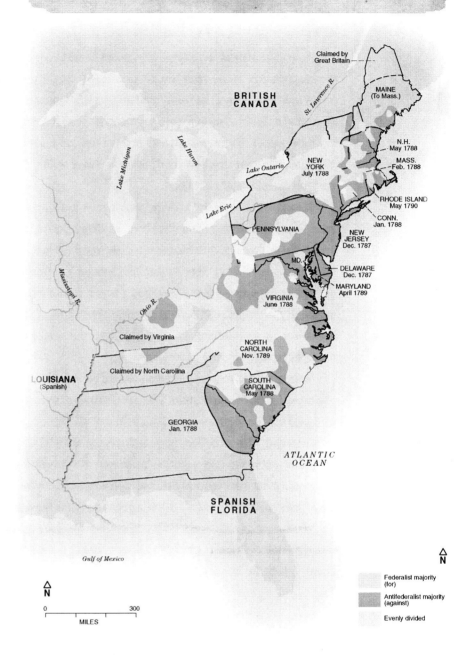

MAP 4.4 Vote on Ratification of the Constitution

federal government, and to bind these groups to the national interest. Hamilton fashioned his program from three basic components including the assumption of state revolutionary war debts, a national bank, and an excise tax on whiskey.

He first set the foundation for the Hamiltonian system. Under the previous regimes—that is, the Continental and Confederation congresses—the general government had accumulated a foreign debt of about $12 million, owed chiefly to France and Holland, and a domestic debt of about $40 million, owed to American nationals. The separate states owed a total of about $22 million more. Hamilton proposed that the federal government promise full payment of all these debts at par value, thus taking over, or *assuming*, the unpaid debts of the states. Since the federal government did not possess the money to pay this debt, totaling about $74 million, Hamilton recommended *funding* the entire debt. That is, in exchange for their old Continental and Confederation bonds, creditors would be issued new interest-bearing bonds that would be the direct obligation of the new federal government.

No opposition was voiced against payment of the foreign debt in full, but full payment of the domestic debt at face value was another matter. On the open market, these old domestic bonds had been selling at far below their original face value. Because the previous central governments had failed to meet interest payments or provide for retirement of the debt, the original owners of the bonds had lost faith in them and had sold them for a fraction of face value. The purchasers were usually men of means who were willing to buy cheap on the chance that the government would make good.

Hamilton did succeed in convincing Congress to make the old bonds good at face value (many congressmen were themselves bond holders); in so doing, he aroused charges from his opponents that the new government was being operated in the interest of the wealthy. Hamilton's intentions, however, were actually both honorable and farsighted. In his plan, he believed, the middle and upper classes would find a strong motive for sustaining the national government; and their confidence in the solvency and good faith of the government would stimulate business activity. In addition, creditors could use the funded debt, in the form of negotiable bonds, as capital to finance new enterprises.

Vehement opposition to the assumption of the state debts by the federal government was also evoked in the Southern states, which had already paid off most of their debts. Southerners protested the use of national funds to help pay off the obligations of states with large outstanding debts, such as the New England states. Hamilton's assumption program was defeated on its first vote in the House, but he finally won in a bargain with Jefferson. In exchange for an agreement to locate the new national capital in the South (on the Potomac across from Virginia), Jefferson's congressional forces agreed to assume the debts of the states.

The second part of Hamilton's program called for the creation of a central bank, modeled after the Bank of England, which would serve as a depository for federal funds, issue paper money (which the Treasury by law could not do), provide commercial interests with a steady and dependable credit institution, and serve the government with short-term loans. Some leaders in and out of Congress objected to this proposal on two grounds. First, four-fifths of the bank's funds were to come from private sources, which might then control the bank's (and the nation's) fiscal policies and, more importantly, opponents of the bank argued that it was unconstitutional. Jefferson and Madison, among others, argued that since the federal government was not specifically authorized by the Constitution to create a national bank, it would be unconstitutional for Congress to do so.

Hamilton, aware that the bank bill might set an important precedent, argued that Congress was authorized by the Constitution to do what was "necessary and proper" for the national good. If the proposed bank was necessary, then the Constitution gave Congress "implied powers" to act in ways not precisely defined in the document. He took the position "that every power vested in a government is in its nature *sovereign* and includes, by *force* of the *term*, a

► Part of Hamilton's program called for the creation of a central bank. Such a bank would act as a depository for federal funds, issue paper currency, provide commercial interests with a dependable credit institution. It would also issue the government short-term loans. The First Bank was chartered by the United States Congress on February 25, 1791, and still stands in Philadelphia, Pennsylvania. *Wikipedia photo*

right to employ all the *means* requisite and fairly applicable to the attainment of the *ends* of such power...."

Jefferson, on the contrary, argued that the federal government possessed only those powers explicitly granted to it in the Constitution, and that all others, as the Tenth Amendment said, were reserved to the states. Jefferson argued that the language of the Constitution must be strictly construed. "To take a single step beyond the boundaries thus especially drawn around the powers of Congress," he wrote, "is to take possession of a boundless field of power, no longer susceptible of any definition." Neither the "general welfare" nor the "necessary and proper" clause of the Constitution, he maintained, could be so broadly interpreted. Washington and Congress, however, accepted Hamilton's argument and in 1791 created the Bank of the United States with a charter for twenty years.

The Whiskey Rebellion

In order to help finance the new national government's obligations, Hamilton proposed to levy an excise tax on a number of commodities to supply money to the federal Treasury for, he wrote, "...the creation of debt should always be accompanied by the means of its extinguishment." Among the items included in the bill, passed in 1791, was a 25 percent excise tax on whiskey to be paid by farmers when they brought their grain to the distillery. The cost would be then passed on to consumers in the form of higher prices for whiskey. In western Pennsylvania and North Carolina, conversion into whiskey was an efficient way of getting grain to market and avoiding the high transportation costs of shipping their excess bulk grain over the mountains to the market in the east, Hamilton's excise tax was, therefore, a tax on the farmers' most valuable cash crop. Farmers viewed the tax as especially oppressive since they already paid half the value of their crop to the distillery to distill their grain; and after the tax was taken out of the farmers' remaining half, less than a third remained. Hamilton exacerbated the farmers' anger by his flippant comment that "farmers drink too much anyway."

Farmers in Western Pennsylvania gathered in meetings in the summer of 1792, and a convention at Pittsburgh denounced the tax and declared that the people would prevent its collection. Collections almost ceased in this area of Pennsylvania in 1792, and irritated Pennsylvania farmers manhandled a few tax collectors in 1793. Some were even tarred and feathered. One tax collector in particular, John Neville, in July 1794 had his house burned to the ground by an angry agrarian crowd estimated at five hundred. Neville escaped, but one man in the crowd that attacked Neville's house was killed and several were wounded as a dozen soldiers inside Neville's house fired into the crowd. This violent incident, however, appeared to be only the beginning of a larger revolt. The next year a sizable force of as many as seven thousand angry whiskey makers vowed to march on Pittsburgh to challenge federal authority at its nearest point.

Memories of Daniel Shays were still fresh in Congress, and President Washington acted quickly. He issued a proclamation ordering the Pennsylvanians to return to their homes and declared western Pennsylvania in a state of rebellion. President Washington then mounted his horse and led Alexander Hamilton and Henry Lee with a force of fifteen thousand militiamen, more troops than the average strength of the Continental Army during the American Revolution, to Pennsylvania. Upon the arrival of federal troops, the farmers promptly scattered. Hamilton, determined to teach the unruly frontiersmen a lesson in federal authority, saw to it that a score of the ringleaders were arrested and tried; and two were sentenced to death. Washington wisely pardoned the rebels, but neither Hamilton nor federalism was ever again popular in that region of Pennsylvania.

Hamilton viewed the government's action in the Whiskey Rebellion as a smashing success, preventing another Shays's Rebellion. Others, including Thomas Jefferson and ardent federalist Fisher Ames, opposed the use of federal troops on its own citizens as an abuse of power and viewed the actions of Washington and Hamilton as proof that the national government had been granted too much power under the Constitution.

The Perils of Neutrality

The French Revolution

The outbreak of the French Revolution forced the Washington administration into the first real test of its foreign policy. In 1789, a number of Americans welcomed the news of the French uprisings as the logical outcome of their own revolution. "In no part of the world," wrote John Marshall, "was the Revolution hailed with more joy than in America." The overthrow of the French monarchy and its replacement with a "Republic" based on the ideals of "liberty, equality, and fraternity" seemed in concert with American Revolutionary ideals. The execution of King Louis XVI and the Reign of Terror that followed, during which France devolved into fratricidal chaos, however, led many to sober second thoughts. The French declaration of war against England, Holland, and Spain in February 1793 introduced the difficult question of neutrality directly into American foreign policy.

One segment of opinion, holding that Britain was still the United States' major enemy, favored the French cause. Furthermore, technically, the United States was still obligated under the Treaty of Alliance, signed in 1778 during the American Revolution, to defend France when it was attacked. France had aided the U.S. against Britain during America's time of need; therefore, some argued that the U.S. must aid France during theirs. Others argued that British trade was so essential to American prosperity that the United States, whatever its sympathies with revolution, could not afford to offend the world's greatest naval and economic power. Still others, observing the chaos of Jacobin Paris, saw France as a threat to the security and order of society everywhere—even to Christianity itself. Up to a third of the population of western France died in the chaos of the French Revolution, and some twenty thousand were guillotined as "enemies of the Republic." Regardless of the slogans of "Liberty, Equality, and Fraternity," many Americans viewed this carnage as nothing worthy of support.

When Washington received news of the outbreak of war between France and Britain in April 1973, he declared a "fair and impartial policy." Although avoiding the word "neutrality" because Washington believed that since Congress declared war, Congress must also declare neutrality—Washington's proclamation guaranteed the belligerents the "friendly and impartial conduct" of the United States. America, he believed, needed peace—the opportunity to build up its strength—more than anything else. "If this country is preserved in tranquility twenty years longer," he wrote, "it may bid defiance in a just cause to any power whatever...." His proclamation, which was to influence American foreign policy for the next half-century, derived from his firm conviction that the United States should avoid, at all reasonable costs, the "brawlings of Europe." The following year Congress passed a Neutrality Act that made Washington's position the official American policy.

Genet Affair

Official neutrality aside, many Americans continued to support France both in spirit and in deeds. The supporters of the French Republic noted that the American Republic had been born in blood as well and concluded that the shedding of blood was, therefore, sometimes necessary for the establishment of liberty. In the words of John Bradford of the *Kentucky Gazette:*

> Instead of reviling the French republicans as monsters, the friends of royalty in this country should rather admire their patience in so long deferring the fate of their perjured monarch, whose blood is ... atonement for the safety of many guilty thousands that are still suffered to remain in the bosom of France.

Citizens' associations in support of the French Revolution, known as Democratic Republican societies, formed throughout the American states. In 1793, these associations received a boost with the arrival of Edmund Genet, an envoy dispatched from France to the United States for the purpose of garnering support for the French Republic in its war with England. Instead of meeting with the president or other members of Washington's administration, however, Genet landed in Charleston, South Carolina, where pro-French senti-

ments were much stronger. Upon his arrival in the U.S., Genet began commissioning American privateers to seize British shipping, a clear violation of American neutrality. Genet even publicly urged Congress to reject Washington's "friendly and impartial policy" and support Republican France. Washington reacted by demanding that Genet be recalled to France under the premise that his conduct could lead to "war abroad and anarchy at home." Before Genet could return to France, however, the political situation changed in the tumultuous political atmosphere of revolutionary France; and Genet was charged with treason, for which the penalty was death. President Washington granted Genet political asylum under the condition that he withdraw from public life. In doing so Washington began the American tradition of political asylum that has continued through the present.

▶ President Washington's decision to grant political asylum to Edmund Genet, who was charged with treason, began the powerful American policy still used today. *Wikipedia photo*

Strained Relations with Britain

The British navy was large, the French navy small, and the British blockade of France very effective. When the French, desperate for trade, opened up their West Indian ports to American ships, the British immediately declared that any trade with France was a military act and that ships caught at it were subject to seizure. Not only did British men-of-war confiscate American cargoes, but also, claiming that some American sailors were really deserters from the British navy (as, indeed, a few were), they forcibly "impressed" a number of American seamen into naval service. Still, though American ships were in danger wherever they went in Atlantic waters, wartime trade was so lucrative that many American merchants asserted that the profit was worth the risk; and incidents multiplied.

Jay's Treaty

Hoping to reduce tensions, Congress passed an embargo act in 1794 that forbade British ships to call at American ports and forbade American ships to sail in areas where they might be subject to British seizure. Since this weakened American trade more than it hindered the British navy, the embargo lasted less than two months. American protests, however, induced the British to relax some of their rules; and in 1794, Washington requested Chief Justice John Jay to sail for London to discuss a treaty to settle outstanding differences.

Jay's arguments were no doubt good ones, but perhaps more important, French military successes persuaded the British that it was unwise to unduly antagonize the United States unduly. Under the terms of Jay's Treaty (the Treaty of London, signed in 1794) the British agreed

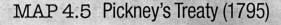

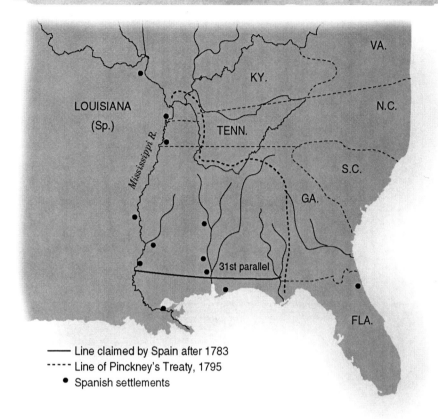

MAP 4.5 Pickney's Treaty (1795)

——— Line claimed by Spain after 1783
----- Line of Pinckney's Treaty, 1795
• Spanish settlements

to evacuate the frontier posts by 1796; to open the British West Indies to American trade under certain conditions; to admit American ships to East Indian ports on a nondiscriminatory basis; and to refer to a joint commission the payment of pre-Revolutionary War debts and settlement of the northwest boundary dispute.

The British simply refused to discuss other important points at issue, however, including impressments and the "Indian question"; and they made far fewer concessions than Jay had been instructed to acquire. Washington reluctantly submitted the treaty to the Senate, which ratified it by only one vote. Not only was the Washington administration severely criticized for the settlement, but also Jay himself was burned in effigy in various cities. Alexander Hamilton suffered bombardment of eggs and tomatoes when he attempted to speak in support of the treaty. Americans opposed to the Jay's Treaty began a campaign of graffiti where they painted on fences the slogan, "Damn John Jay, and Damn everyone who won't Damn John Jay."

Not all the news was bad, however. The Jay Treaty allowed the U.S. to avoid what could have been a disastrous war with England and resume normal trade, thus boosting American well being both in terms of security and economic well being. Spain, badly mauled by France in the land war, had signed a separate peace in 1795; and, fearing British retaliation for its defection, Spain needed American friendship. In the Pinckney Treaty (the Treaty of San Lorenzo), signed on October 27, 1795, Spain recognized the line of 31-degree latitude as the southern boundary of the United States and granted free navigation of the Mississippi with a three-year right of deposit at New Orleans.

Early Political Parties

The Emergence of Party Politics

The dispute over Jay's Treaty revealed a deep division in Washington's administration, as well as growing public opposition to a number of Hamilton's financial policies. The French Revolution, the Franco-British War, and subsequent problems in foreign relations created further political differences in Congress. By 1792, opposing factions had begun to coalesce around the two strong men of Washington's cabinet, Hamilton and Jefferson. The Hamiltonians wanted a broad construction of the Constitution and an emphasis placed on the "necessary and proper" clause. The Jeffersonians wanted a strict construction of the Constitution and a limited use of the elastic clause. Reluctantly, these two groups acquired official party names and the two-party system emerged in the United States. Both sides were hesitant to create a political party because they viewed them as corrupt and interest based; however, both groups realized they needed to organize in order to further their interpretation of the Constitution. They eventually become known as the Federalists (Hamiltonians) and the Democratic-Republicans (Jeffersonians). The dream of a republic free from the corruption of factions, as Madison proclaimed in Federalist No. 10, had disintegrated.

The Republicans opposed the administration's program chiefly because of what they believed was its tendency to concentrate wealth and influence in a relatively small class. They also opposed the expansion of national power at the expense of the states and the broad construction of the Constitution that created the doctrine of implied powers. Certainly neither Jefferson nor his followers objected to sound currency and credit or to economic stability and prosperity. Rather, they opposed the Hamiltonian methods of obtaining them—the Bank, tariffs, excise taxes (but not the assumption of state debts)—because these measures expanded national power at the expense of the states and might serve to create a permanently privileged class whose interests could well become inimical to the opportunities and welfare of the greater number of people.

Through Washington's first term the rivalry between the two factions increased. Despite these internal tensions, however, the Federalists easily reelected Washington for a second term in 1792 against token opposition, with John Adams as his vice-president.

The Election of 1796

Democratic Republicans formed around the commanding figure of Thomas Jefferson and men such as James Monroe and James Madison of Virginia, George Clinton and Aaron Burr of New York, Albert Gallatin and Alexander Dallas from Pennsylvania, Willie Jones, the North

Carolina back-country leader, and others from the Middle and Southern states joined. Among the Federalists were Hamilton, Philip Schuyler, and John Jay of New York, Timothy Pickering and John Adams of Massachusetts, Thomas Pinckney of South Carolina, and John Marshall of Virginia, President Washington is conspicuously absent from this list because he refused to surrender to the party system. He was determined not to concede to factions. Nonetheless, his actions of supporting Hamilton's financial programs and foreign policy, made him a Federalist in all but name.

When Jefferson, convinced that he could no longer work with Hamilton and the administration, resigned as secretary of state in 1793, Republican partisan politics began in earnest. Hamilton resigned from the Treasury in 1795, partly because he could not afford to neglect his law and business interests; but he still remained the most powerful Federalist leader since Washington decided not to run again in 1796.

Washington's achievements as president have been overshadowed by his image as "The Father of His Country" and by the dramatic contest during his second term between Hamilton and Jefferson. Washington was not the scholar or thinker that Jefferson, Hamilton, Adams, and Madison were; nor is he remembered for his talents as an orator. On a personal level, Washington was notoriously aloof and addicted to appearances, writing more letters as president concerning his plantation at Mount Vernon than concerning the policies of the nation. Moreover, when Washington solicited advice from his advisors, he was more likely to ask how he should appear in any given situation than what policies should be pursued. Generally, his greatest accomplishments as president are often listed as stepping down after two terms and reducing the fear that the presidency would grow into a monarchy by his unassertiveness in his official capacities. Washington's unassertiveness, in turn, stemmed from his goal of being a "disinterested gentleman." Washington believed that becoming involved in political bickering was not becoming of a gentleman and believed that he, himself, should appear to be above the fray. Presidents typically do not go down in history as great leaders if they avoid assuming policy leadership or publicly taking a stand on issues of substance. More recently, however, historians have acknowledged Washington's real skill as an administrator: his guiding hand held the fledgling nation together and the importance of his contributions to the efficiency of the newly created government. Since Washington set several important precedents during his presidency, he did more than anyone else to establish the tone of the presidential office and to establish a set of delicate relationships among the executive, the cabinet, the Congress, and the judiciary. Moreover, he imbued the fledgling nation with his immense dignity.

Washington was a towering figure at over six feet, three inches tall, a born leader of men, and in possession of great wealth as the heir of one large estate who married the wealthiest woman in Virginia. Washington's carriage was drawn by six white horses, his leopard skin saddle fringed in gold. A staff of slaves attended his every need at the White House where Washington held nightly social affairs and allowed the liquor to run freely. The parties were all over at 9:30, however, so "His High Mightiness the President," as Washington preferred to be called, could turn in for bed.

When Washington decided in September 1796 not to seek a third term as President, thus establishing an American two-term precedent, he submitted to the press a "Farewell Address"

MAP 4.6 Elections of 1796 and 1800

Election of 1796

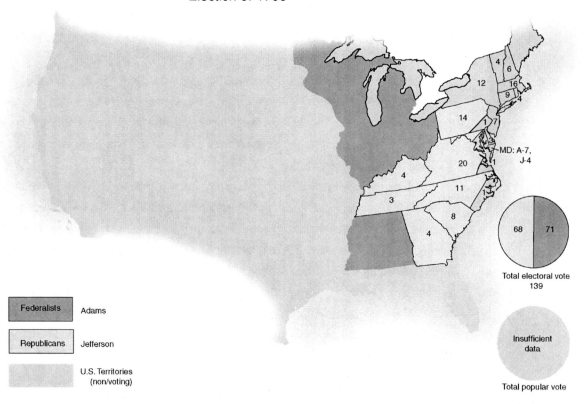

Federalists   Adams

Republicans   Jefferson

U.S. Territories
(non/voting)

Election of 1800

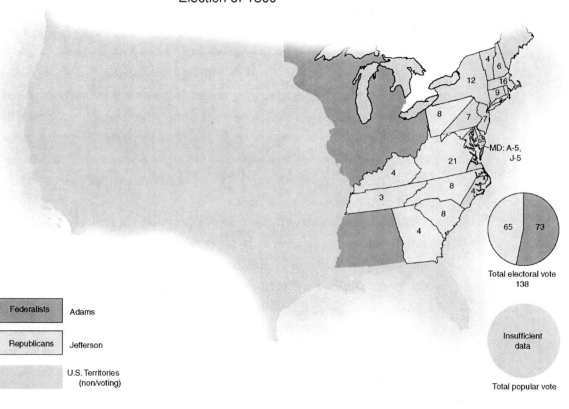

Federalists   Adams

Republicans   Jefferson

U.S. Territories
(non/voting)

which he had written with the aid of Madison and Hamilton. In his valedictory, published in newspapers throughout the nation, Washington explained his reasons for declining to seek a third term. He stressed the necessity of preserving the Union, the "main prop" of individual liberty, and pointed out the obligation of all Americans to obey the Constitution and the established government, " 'till changed by an explicit and authentic act of the whole People." He warned of the dangers of a party system, particularly one based on a division along geographical lines; urged that the public credit be cherished; and admonished Americans to observe "good faith and justice toward all Nations."

The most enduring passages of the Farewell Address, however, are those in which Washington counseled Americans to steer clear of permanent alliances with the foreign world. Isolationists consistently quoted Washington's admonitions for a foreign policy of neutrality over the succeeding century and a half to justify a long-dominant American policy of avoiding involvement in international politics:

> ... The great rule of conduct for us, in regard to foreign Nations, is, in extending our commercial relations, to have with them as little Political connection as possible.... Europe has a set of primary interests, which to us have none, or a very remote relation.—Hence she must be engaged in frequent controversies, the causes of which are essentially foreign to our concerns.—Hence therefore it must be unwise in us to implicate ourselves, by artificial ties in the ordinary vicissitudes of her politics.... Taking care always to keep ourselves ... on a respectably defensive posture, we may safely trust to temporary alliances for extraordinary emergencies.[2]

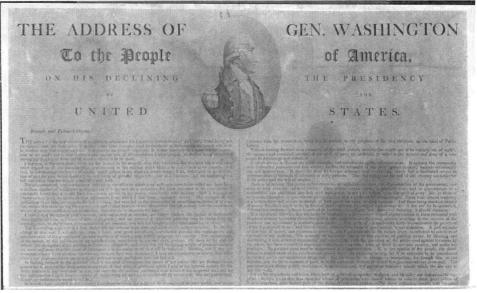

▶ General Washington decided in 1796 not to seek a third term as President, thus establishing the presidential two-term precedent. In his address, Washington stressed perseveration of the Union, individual liberty, and the obligation of all Americans to obey the Constitution and established government. *Wikipedia photo*

After eight years in office, Washington left behind a government that possessed a reasonably good civil service, a workable committee system, an economic program, a foreign policy, and the seeds of a body of constitutional theory. He also left behind a party beginning to divide. The election of 1796 gave clear indication of the mounting strength of the Republican opposition. Thomas Jefferson and Aaron Burr campaigned for the Republicans, John Adams and Thomas Pinckney for the Federalists. The margin of Federalist victory was slim: Adams had seventy-one electoral votes, Jefferson sixty-eight. Since Jefferson had more votes than Pinckney, he became vice-president.

Federalists and Republicans

It is too broad a generalization to say that the Federalists represented the conservative, commercial, nationalistic interests of the Northeast and mid-Atlantic States and the Republicans the more radical, agrarian, debtor, states' rights interests of the South and West, though there is more than a germ of truth in the generalization. In actuality, the two parties drew support from all kinds of people in different parts of the country.

The differences in the parties reflected many factors—personalities, religious and educational backgrounds, ideologies, economic interests, political necessities, and the like. It would be more accurate to say that these parties were loose combinations of certain economic, social, and intellectual groupings, held together by a set of common attitudes and interests.

Fundamentally, they reflected two different opinions about the qualities of human nature. Hamiltonians were acutely aware of the "imperfections, weaknesses, and evils of human nature." They believed that if people were fit to govern themselves at all, it must only be under rigid controls imposed upon them by society and government. Jeffersonians, on the other hand, believed that people were by inclination rational and good. If freed from the bonds of ignorance, error, and repression, they might achieve real progress toward an ideal society. Others, of course, took positions between these two extremes.

These contrasting concepts of human fallibility were reflected in contemporary political opinions about the structure and aim of government. The Federalists emphasized the need for political machinery to restrain the majority. They believed in a strong central government and a strong executive, with the active participation of that government in manufacturing, commerce, and finance. They believed that leadership in society belonged to a trained, responsible, and (very likely) wealthy class who could be trusted to protect property as well as human rights.

The Jeffersonian Republicans distrusted centralized authority and a powerful executive, preferring instead a less autonomous, more decentralized government modeled more on confederation than on federalism. They believed in the leadership of what Jefferson called "a natural aristocracy," founded on talent and intelligence rather than on birth, wealth, or station. Most Republicans believed that human nature in the aggregate was naturally trustworthy and that it could be improved through freedom and education—and therefore that wise self-government, under proper conditions, would be possible.

[2]George Washington's Farewell Address, September 17, 1796.

The Trial of John Adams

The XYZ Affair

John Adams took office at a difficult time, for the Federalist Party that had elected him was showing strain at the seams. Hamilton still dictated a large share of party policy from private life. He did not like Adams and had maneuvered before the election in an attempt to defeat him. Adams was a stubbornly honest man, a keen student of government and law, but blunt, a trifle haughty, sometimes tactless. (Indeed, many of his most amiable qualities were reflected in his relationship with his remarkable wife, Abigail, rather than in his conduct as a public figure.)

The Adams administration promptly found itself in trouble. Within his party there was a violently anti-French group, including Adams' Secretary of State, Thomas Pickering, who virtually demanded a declaration of war against France. The French minister to the United States, Pierre Adet, had openly tried to influence the 1796 election in favor of Jefferson and the Democratic Republicans. The French, angry at Jay's Treaty and at American neutrality that appeared to favor Britain, began seizure of American ships at sea carrying British goods. By March 1797, three hundred American ships had been seized by French privateers. France also refused to receive Adams' new minister to France, Charles Cotesworth Pinckney. Adams, who did not want war, sent John Marshall, C. C. Pinckney, and Elbridge Gerry to Paris in 1797 to try to find some way out.

The French foreign minister Talleyrand, dealing with the American commission through three intermediaries called (for purposes of anonymity) X, Y, and Z, demanded not only a loan of $12 million to the French government but also a bribe of $240,000, and an apology for negative comments that John Adams had made about France. The Americans indignantly refused the demand with Pinckney's retort of "no, not a sixpence." When the news of the "XYZ Affair" leaked out, the ringing slogan "Millions for defense, but not one cent for tribute!" became popular. Adams asked Congress to prepare for war, and the French accelerated the seizure of American ships at sea. The U.S. Navy was sent to the Caribbean to repel the French navy; and, with powder and shot provided by the British, it captured over one hundred French privateers in what historians refer to as the "Quasi-War" with France since plenty of shots had been fired on the open sea, but war was not declared.

The Treaty of 1800

Capitalizing on the war fever, Congress created a Department of the Navy, built a number of new ships, armed American merchantmen, and authorized an army of ten thousand men. Though his own party leaders (Hamilton among them) argued that war with France was inevitable, Adams refused to listen; and as it turned out, the French did not want war either. Adams received scathing reviews from Republican newspapers and even endured abuse from members of his own party. After nearly a year of undeclared naval war, the French government suggested that if an American mission were to be sent to Paris it would be respectfully received.

By the time the American commissioners arrived in France in March 1800, the country was in the hands of Napoleon Bonaparte, who quietly agreed to a settlement of differences. The Treaty of

This is an excerpt from the infamous 1798 Sedition Acts that were passed by Congress while John Adams was president.

SEC. 2.

And be it further enacted, That if any person shall write, print, utter or publish, or shall cause or procure to be written, printed, uttered or publishing, or shall knowingly and willingly assist or aid in writing, printing, uttering or publishing any false, scandalous and malicious writing or writings against the government of the United States, or either house of the Congress of the United States, or the President of the United States, with intent to defame the said government, or either house of the said Congress, or the said President, or to bring them, or either of them, into contempt or disrepute; or to excite against them, or either or any of them, the hatred of the good people of the United States, or to excite any unlawful combinations therein, for opposing or resisting any law of the United States, or any act of the President of the United States, done in pursuance of any such law, or of the powers in him vested by the constitution of the United States, or to resist, oppose, or defeat any such law or act, or to aid, encourage or abet any hostile designs of any for-eign nation against the United States, their people or government, then such person, being thereof convicted before any court of the United States having jurisdiction thereof, shall be punished by a fine not exceeding two thousand dollars, and by imprisonment not exceeding two years.

Source: *The Laws of the United States of America,* printed by Richard Folwell, Philadelphia, 1796–1798.

1800 was not popular with the Federalists or Congress, but it was ratified. It avoided a war and also dissolved the French-American alliance forged during the Revolution. "The end of war is peace," said Adams, "and peace was offered me." John Adams acquired peace, but probably at the expense of victory in the coming elections for himself and his party.

The Alien and Sedition Acts

The popular outcry against France, and the near-war that carried through 1797–1799, gave the Federalists a good chance, they believed, to cripple their Republican political opponents under cover of protecting internal security. The country had been infiltrated, so the Federalist press claimed, with French agents and propagandists who were secretly at work undermining the national will and subverting public opinion. Since most immigrants were inclined to vote Republican, the Federalist Congress capitalized on anti-foreign sentiments in 1798 by passing a series of Alien Acts which lengthened the naturalization period from five to fourteen years, em-powered the President to deport undesirable aliens, and authorized him to imprison such aliens as he chose in time of war. Though he signed the bill, Adams did not like the acts and never seriously tried to enforce them.

▶ In the year 1800 control of France was in the hands of Napoleon Bonaparte. *Wikipedia photo*

As the second step in its anti-Republican campaign, Congress passed the Sedition Act, also in 1798. Under this act, a citizen could be fined or imprisoned or both for "writing, printing, uttering, or publishing" false statements or any statements which might bring the president or Congress "into contempt or disrepute." Since this last clause covered almost anything Republicans might say about Federalists, its purpose was quite plainly to muzzle the opposition and its primary targets were newspaper editors that opposed the Adams administration. Under the Sedition Act twenty-five editors and printers were prosecuted and twelve were convicted for criticizing the Adams Administration—though they were later pardoned and their fines returned by the Jeffersonians.

With the Alien and Sedition laws, the Federalists went too far. Republicans opposed the acts on the grounds that they were in violation of the free speech and free press protections of the Bill of Rights. Federalist judges who would not rule against the Federalist Congress or the Adams administration, however, dominated the judiciary branch. Public opinion sided with the Republicans. The legislatures of Kentucky and Virginia (home to Republican leaders Jefferson and Madison) passed resolutions in 1798 and 1799 (Jefferson drafted Kentucky's; Madison, Virginia's) condemning the laws and asking the states to join in nullifying them as violations of civil rights. Actually none did, but the Kentucky and Virginia resolutions furnished the Jeffersonians with excellent ammunition for the approaching presidential campaign. The Kentucky and Virginia resolutions also put forth the idea that states could nullify federal laws that they found to be unconstitutional.

The Election of 1800

Washington's death in December 1799 from a throat and upper respiratory infection along with the detrimental medical treatment of bloodletting, symbolized the passing of the Federalist dynasty. The party that he had led was in dire distress and divided into wrangling factions. The Republicans were in an excellent position to capitalize on a long string of political moves which had alienated a significant number of voters—the handling of the Whiskey Rebellion, Hamilton's financial policies, the Jay Treaty and Jay's negotiations with Spain in 1786, the Alien and Sedition Acts—as well as conflict and resentment within the Federalist party.

In effect, the Federalists had been unable to maintain a balance between the nationalist business interests that formed the core of their support and the rapidly growing influence of the middle and lower urban and agrarian classes of the South, the West, and the mid-Atlantic states. After

Washington, who had held the party together by the force of his example, no Federalist leader found a way to absorb and control the elements of society that, after 1796, began to look to Jefferson for leadership. The clash of personalities within the Federalist camp, of course, damaged the party further.

John Adams, who through his entire term had to face the internal opposition of the Hamiltonians as well as the Republicans from without, deserves more credit than he is often given. Except for Adams's stubborn desire to keep the peace, the United States might well have entered into a disastrous war with France, and without him the Federalist Party under Hamilton's control would probably have killed itself ten years sooner than it did. Adams's decision to stay out of war, made against the bitter opposition of his own party, was not only an act of courage but also very likely his greatest service to the nation.

Although Hamilton circulated a pamphlet violently attacking the President, the Party had no other satisfactory candidate for the election of 1800 and decided to nominate Adams again, choosing Charles Cotesworth Pinckney to run with him. The Republicans picked Jefferson and Burr once more, hoping thus to unite the powerful Virginia and New York wings of the party. The campaign was one of the most bitter in American history. In the end, the Republicans, who won the mid-Atlantic States and the South, emerged with a small edge in total electoral votes.

Under the Constitution, the candidate with the most votes was president and the next votegetter, vice-president; but when the Republican electors all voted for Jefferson and Burr, they created a tie. This threw the election into the House of Representatives, still controlled by lame-duck Federalists. The Federalists' hatred of Jefferson was so intense that many of them preferred Burr. At the same time, Burr's own party wanted Jefferson, but Burr refused to step aside. Hamilton, much as he disagreed with Jefferson's principles, considered Burr a political adventurer and deeply distrusted him—as well he might have, given that Burr killed him in a duel a few years later. He therefore threw his influence in Congress behind Jefferson, who was declared president by the House of Representatives on February 17, 1801. Subsequent historians have seen this election as particularly significant because it was the first one in American history in which the party in power lost and then turned that power over to its victorious opponents peacefully and in legal, democratic fashion.

Developing a Native American Policy

At the close of the Revolution the issue between Native Americans and white Americans remained as insoluble as ever. It seemed impossible to divert or delay the American drive westward, where the groups possessed undeveloped lands of great value.

Of the losers in the Revolution, the Native Americans—most of whom had fought with the British—lost the most. The Peace Treaty simply left them out. Britain ceded the lands west to the Mississippi to the Americans without mentioning the natives who lived there, while the Americans considered them a conquered people whose lands were subject to confiscation.

"With respect to the Indians," wrote one of the negotiators, "we claim the right of preemption; with respect to all other nations, we claim the sovereignty over the territory." Though tribal leaders protested to the British negotiators that they had no right to give away Native American lands, and to the Americans that they had no right to abrogate previous treaties, neither side listened.

"Noble Red Man" or "Barbaric Savage?"

Federal and state policy toward the Indians was greatly influenced by the white Americans' perception of them. Whites found Indians difficult to negotiate with, for few Americans understood much of Indian psychology, politics, or culture. Both Indians and whites were heirs of two hundred years of constant and vicious warfare. White explorers and settlers, almost from their first contacts with the Indians, had developed contrasting images of the "noble red man" on the one hand, and the "barbaric savage" on the other. These images persisted in the minds of later Americans.

Some Americans, particularly the educated minority, viewed the various Native American cultures with respect and sympathized with the plight of the natives. These Americans hoped the tribes could be assimilated into American society. Both President Washington and his secretary of war, Henry Knox, who had charge of Native American affairs, believed in assimilation. Knox reaffirmed Native American land claims in a series of reports in early 1789. "Instead of exterminating part of the human race," he wrote, Americans should instead take pride in having "imparted knowledge of cultivation and the arts to the aboriginals of the country...."

Others tended to see the native as irredeemably—though tragically—savage, incapable ever of learning the ways of civilization. Frontiersmen, too, had vivid recollections of Native American attacks during the Great War for Empire and bitter, still-fresh memories of Loyalist-native raids in New York and Pennsylvania during the Revolution. Meanwhile, the possibility of an alliance between the western tribes and the British army, still in Canada, posed a threat to the Ohio-Indiana frontier.

Moreover, although the British had promised at the Peace of Paris to give up their posts in the Northwest, they apparently intended to hold them as long as possible. Orders from the Colonial office to the governor-general of Canada, one day before the proclamation of the Treaty in 1784, instructed British commanders to do exactly that. So many Americans were convinced that the only sound policy toward the Native Americans was removal.

Assimilation or Removal

Relations with the Native Americans developed over two phases in the years before 1812. From the end of the war until the election of Washington in 1789, Congress assumed that all native lands belonged to the United States and that all tribes were under government control. Congress appointed commissioners to handle Native American affairs, but most direct dealings with the tribes were carried out by the states.

Land was the issue. Both federal and state policy was to move Native Americans off lands that settlers wanted, but this required more military power and money than either federal or state governments possessed. The removal policy also raised questions among those who saw this as a moral problem as well as a military and political one.

By 1786, both state and federal governments realized that establishing an effective, acceptable native policy involved a large set of complex issues. The central problem was how to establish white settlements in "Indian country" and still treat the natives with humanity and justice. The lure of open, fertile land, a growing nationalism, and the need for strategic defenses

▶Delaware Indians hunting buffalo across the plains. If land and game disappeared, tribes would be pushed ever farther west by treaty and expansion. If this continued, the race in its entirety might have disappeared. *Wikipedia photo*

against France, Spain, and British Canada all had to be balanced against the new nation's desire to act in accordance with the principles of its revolution and a Christian conscience.

American leaders therefore reactivated the British colonial policy of recognizing Native American land rights and acquiring the necessary acres by treaties and purchases, meanwhile establishing strict boundaries to control the advance of white settlers. The Northwest Ordinance of 1787, which had officially opened the West to settlement, stated that "Indians" should be dealt with in "utmost good faith," their "property, rights and liberty" protected, their lands "never to be taken from them without their consent."

This new policy did not fully satisfy the national conscience, however. At best, it was a temporary solution. If land and game disappeared and the tribes were pushed ever farther west by treaty and expansion, the whole group might soon disappear.

Plenty of Americans, particularly on the frontier, did not care. But many others did not want their country, which they believed to be a new and better experiment in enlightened government, held responsible for the destruction of an entire people.

In the view of the Enlightenment, Native Americans were as much part of the human race as were white men. Such differences as existed between them were seen as the results of education and environment. The solution, then, was to "civilize" them by giving them education, religious training, and the means of making a living, thus bringing them into the mainstream of American society. "In leading them to agriculture, to manufacture, and civilization," said Jefferson, "I trust and believe we are acting for their greatest good."

Westward expansion was therefore given a moral basis by being seen as an extension of the advantages of a "higher" social order to a "lower" group. The concept was neither new

▶ General Arthur St. Clair's defeat was the most costly defeat for the U.S. in the history of the Indian wars. President Washington denounced St. Clair as "worse than a murderer" and demanded his resignation. *Wikipedia photo*

nor American. It was a common principle in European thought and continued to be, whether the subjected people were Gauls, or Aztecs, or Maoris.

Clashes on the Frontier

Treaties negotiated with the tribes of the Northwest brought only temporary peace, while in the South the Spanish encouraged the Creeks' harassment of frontier settlements. In response, the Americans took military action.

In 1790 General Josiah Harmar's expedition against the Native Americans in the Ohio country was ambushed and scattered. In 1791 General Arthur St. Clair's larger force did no better. In 1793–1794 Tennessee militia temporarily stabilized the Southwestern frontier in a series of small, sharp engagements.

Washington then gave command to General "Mad Anthony" Wayne, who took 4000 men into northwestern Ohio, where the British had authorized the construction of a fort inside American boundaries. Wayne defeated the native forces at the Battle of Fallen Timbers in the late summer of 1794. The next year the twelve strongest tribes ceded most of the Ohio country to the United States by the Treaty of Greenville.

Chapter Review ▶ ▶ ▶

Summary

When the colonists declared their independence in July of 1776, they were left with the difficult task of forming a government and governing the nation while at war with England. The thirteen states were united for their defense against England, but very diverse in their interests otherwise, spread from Georgia to New Hampshire along the Eastern seaboard. When Richard Henry Lee of Virginia proposed a *Declaration of Independence* in June, 1776, the Continental Congress also began work on forging the *Articles of Confederation*, America's first Constitution. Divisions among the states, however, especially a dispute over Western lands, delayed the ratification of the *Articles of Confederation* until 1781. Furthermore, the governmental structure created under the *Articles of Confederation* quickly proved to be insufficient.

With no standing army, America suffered from a lack of security as British troops remained on American soil after the Revolution, there were problems with Native Americans on the frontier, and Spain closed the Mississippi River to American shipping. The national government was in debt, but did not have the power to tax, and states would not send the money requisitioned by Congress to pay the debts. Both the national government and the states issued paper money, with the result that inflation reached 12,000 percent. Foreign trade remained confused as the states could not agree on a uniform tariff. Finally, when farmers in Massachusetts under Daniel Shays rebelled against taxation and farm foreclosures, many felt that the *Articles of Confederation* had to be revised.

The Constitutional Convention was held in the summer of 1787 attended by 55 delegates from throughout the U.S. Though the authors of the Constitution disagreed on numerous issues, they eventually settled on a federal form of government with one executive and a bicameral legislature with one house apportioned by population and the other apportioned equally among the states with two Senators per state. The authors of the Constitution created a government with both separation of powers and checks and balances in an attempt to prevent concentration of power and ensure liberty.

Two-thirds of the states had to ratify the Constitution and those opposed to its ratification, known as anti-federalists, argued that the national government and the President would grow too powerful under the Constitution. Federalists, led by Alexander Hamilton, James Madison, and John Jay, argued that federalism, separation of powers, and checks and balances would prevent the national government from growing too powerful and destroying state sovereignty. The Constitution was ratified in 1789, and a Bill of Rights was added to the Constitution in 1790 to help guard against arbitrary government power.

In 1794 when a group of Pennsylvania farmers rebelled against a federal excise tax on Whiskey, both federalists and anti-federalists felt vindicated. George Washington led the U.S. army to Pennsylvania to quell the rebellion, an action that proved to anti-federalists that the national government was too powerful under the Constitution. Conversely, federalists were satisfied that the government had been able to restore order.

By 1796, opposition to the policies of the federalists began to coalesce around Thomas Jefferson and the first democratic opposition political party, the Democratic Republicans, was born. The Democratic Re-

(cont'd)

publicans became the first opposition party to win an election in 1800 when Thomas Jefferson defeated the incumbent John Adams in spite of the underhanded machinations of Jefferson's running mate, Aaron Burr, who attempted to hijack the election from Jefferson in the House of Representatives.

During the same time period, the young Republic was faced with major challenges from abroad as the French Revolution of 1789 quickly led to war between the great monarchical powers of Europe and Revolutionary France. President George Washington proclaimed "a fair and impartial policy," essentially meaning American neutrality in 1793, but neutrality would prove difficult as France seized American merchant ships at sea. In what is known as the "Quasi-War" with France, Americans retaliated by seizing French merchant ships.

The Quasi-War produced a domestic backlash as Congress passed the Alien and Sedition Acts authorizing the President to deport or imprison aliens deemed to be dangerous and criticism of the Adams administration was prohibited. Antagonisms with France would finally come to an end with the Convention of 1800 that normalized relations, but not quickly enough to save the unpopular Adams administration. With the election of Jefferson, America would move into a new era as the 18th century came to a close.

Chronological Time Line

1776	Richard Henry Lee proposes a *Declaration of Independence* and "Confederation" on June 12
1777	*Articles of Confederation* are approved by the Continental Congress on November 15 and sent to States for ratification.
1781	*Articles of confederation* is ratified by the States
1784	Spain closes the Mississippi River to American trade
1784	Congress asks the States for the exclusive power to regulate trade, but States refuse.
1785	A Land Ordinance passed by Congress provided for a government survey to divide the land of the Northwest Territory into townships.
1786	Annapolis Convention fails to settle on a uniform tariff or revise *Articles of Confederation*
1787	Shays's Rebellion against taxation and farm foreclosures in February
1787	Northwest Ordinance provided an orderly process for translating the unsettled Northwest from frontier to statehood.

Chapter Review (cont'd) ▶ ▶ ▶

Time Line (cont'd)

1787	Constitutional Convention held in Philadelphia
1788	Spain opens restricted Mississippi River trade to the U.S.
1788	Constitution is ratified by the required nine states
1789	Bill of Rights is added to the Constitution
1789	Constitution goes into effect
1789	New Congress is elected in January and George Washington is elected President by the electors in the Electoral College.
1789	*Articles of confederation* is Ratified by the States
1789	Judiciary Act of 1789 creates the office of Attorney General, a Supreme Court, three circuit courts, and thirteen district courts
1789	Outbreak of the French Revolution in July
1790	Rhode Island ratifies the Constitution, the last state to do so.
1791	Congress creates the Bank of the United States
1793	Revolutionary France declares War against England, Holland, and Spain
1793	Washington's Proclamation of Neutrality
1793	Genet Affair
1790–94	War with Natives in the Ohio Valley results in a White victory in the Battle of the Fallen Timbers in 1794
1794	Whiskey Rebellion in Pennsylvania is put down by U.S. army troops under the command of President George Washington.
1794	Jay Treaty preserves peace with England in spite of unpopularity in America
1795	Pinckney Treaty sets border with Spain and opens the Mississippi to U.S. trade.
1796	John Adams is elected President

Time Line (cont'd)

1797	XYZ Affair
1797–1800	Quasi War with France
1798	Alien and Sedition Acts
1798–1799	Kentucky and Virginia Resolutions
1800	Treaty of 1800 secures peace with France and end of Alliance of 1778
1800	Thomas Jefferson is elected President in the House of Representatives after his running mate, Aaron Burr, attempts to steal the election.

Key Terms

Federalism: A way of organizing government where there is division of powers between the central government (the U.S. government) and the political subunit governments (the states)

Articles of Confederation: America's first Constitution proposed in 1776 and ratified in 1781 that created a Confederal form of government with all of the power in the states and a weak national government

Northwest Ordinances of 1785 and 1787: Surveyed and divided the Western lands into townships in 1785 and provided an orderly process for governing and the eventual transition to statehood in 1787.

Daniel Shays: Led a rebellion of Massachusetts farmers against taxation and foreclosures on farms in 1786. Shays's Rebellion convinced many that a stronger national government was needed.

Checks-and-balances: Constitutional measures that recombine some of the powers in the American system of separation of powers. The Executive has some legislative powers, such as the veto, as a check on Congress and Congress has some Executive powers, such as the power to confirm Presidential appointees, as a check on the Executive.

Separation-of-powers: The American structure that separates Legislative, Executive, and Judicial powers into three separate bodies, Congress, the President, and the Courts.

Virginia Plan: Also known as the "large state plan" that called for apportionment in Congress by population.

New Jersey Plan: The "small state" plan that called for each state to be represented equally in Congress.

Great Compromise: The compromise over apportionment that created a bicameral Congress with a lower house apportioned by population and an upper house apportioned equally among the states at two Senators per state.

The Electoral College: The Constitutional system of electing the President where each state chooses electors based on its representation in Congress to cast the actual vote for the Presidency.

Chapter Review (cont'd) ▶ ▶ ▶

Key Terms (cont'd)

Three-fifths Compromise: The compromise between North and South over apportionment in the House of Representatives where slaves would count as 3/5 of a person for purposes of representation.

Antifederalists: The faction that opposed the Constitution largely because they believed that the National government and the President would be too powerful under the Constitution.

The Federalist: A series of eighty-five essays written by Alexander Hamilton, James Madison, and John Jay that explained the Constitution and advocated its ratification.

Bill of Rights: The first ten Amendments to the U.S. Constitution in 1790 that guaranteed individual rights.

Hamilton's Assumption Plan: The U.S. government would assume all of its debts incurred under the *Articles of Confederation* at face value.

The Whiskey Rebellion: A revolt by Pennsylvania farmers in 1793–94 against a federal excise tax on Whiskey that was put down by George Washington and the U.S. Army.

Little Turtle: Native American Chief in the Ohio Valley that rebelled against white encroachment from 1790–1794

Battle of Fallen Timbers: Battle where Little Turtle was finally defeated by the U.S. Army in 1794.

Jay's Treaty: Treaty of London in 1794 with England that preserved peace with England and resumed normal trade, but was unpopular in the U.S.

Pinckney's Treaty 1795: Set the border with Spain at thirty-one degrees north latitude and opened the Mississippi River to American trade.

Democratic—Republicans: The first democratic opposition political party that coalesced around Thomas Jefferson

Edmund Charles Genet: French diplomat that came to America seeking American aid to France in their War with England and Holland, but was forced to seek political asylum in the U.S. when the political situation changed in France.

XYZ Affair: Three French Diplomats that demanded bribes from American diplomats prior to negotiations.

Quasi War with France: Period of agitation between France and the U.S. 1797–1800 where both France and the U.S. seized merchant ships at sea

Alien and Sedition Acts: Acts of Congress under the Adams administration that allowed the President to imprison or deport aliens he considered dangerous and made it a federal crime to utter malicious statements against the Adams administration.

Virginia and Kentucky Resolutions: Nullification laws passed by Virginia and Kentucky condemning the Alien and Sedition Acts.

Sources Consulted

Saul Cornell, *The Other Founders: Anti-Federalism and the Dissenting Tradition in America* (1999).

Stanley Elkins and Eric McKitrick, *The Age of Federalism: The Early American Republic, 1788–1800* (1993).

Joseph J. Ellis, *Founding Brothers: The Revolutionary Generation* (2000).

Stuart Leibiger, *Founding Friendship: George Washington, James Madison, and the Creation of the American Republic* (1999).

Jack N. Rakove, *Original Meanings: Politics and Ideas in the Making of the Constitution* (1996).

Thomas G. Slaughter, *The Whiskey Rebellion: Frontier Epilogue to the American Revolution* (1986).

Richard White, *The Middle Ground: Indians, Empires, and Republics in the Great Lakes Region, 1650–1815* (1991).

Gordon S. Wood, *The Creation of the American Republic, 1776–1787* (1969)

iStockphotos

5 The Jeffersonian Era, 1800–1824

Outline

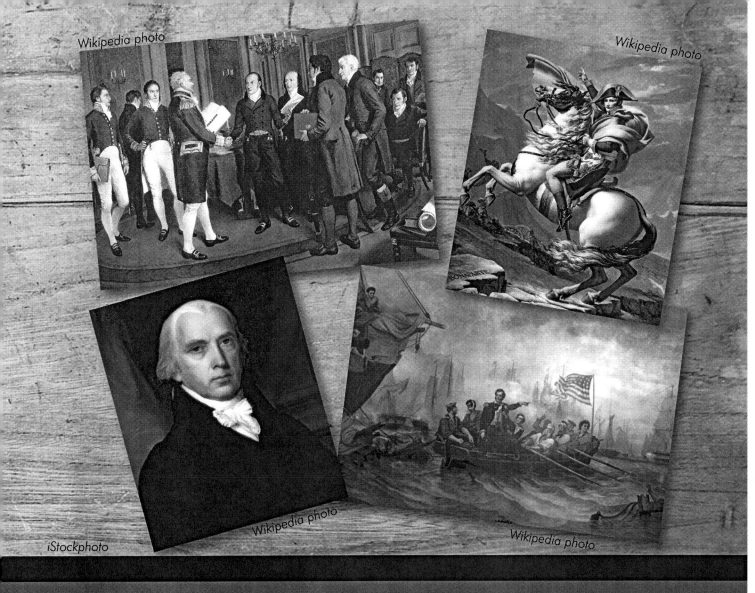

IV. America Makes a New Start
   A. A Confident Nation
   B. The Aftermath of War
   C. A Protective Tariff
   D. Renewing the Bank of the United States
   E. Building Better Connecting Links
V. America Moves West
   A. Land Hunger Versus Native American Rights
   B. Resistance to Federal Policy
VI. Growing Pains
   A. The Election of 1816
   B. The "Era of Good Feelings"
   C. Prosperity and Panic
VII. "Fire Bell in the Night"
   A. Sectionalism and Slavery
   B. The Missouri Compromise
VIII. Evolving a Foreign Policy
   A. Catching Up on Old Problems
   B. The Monroe Doctrine
   C. The Triumph of Isolation

Jefferson in Power

"The Revolution of 1800"

Thomas Jefferson usually referred to his presidential election victory as "the revolution of 1800." Although it was hardly a "revolution" in the usual sense, it was, nonetheless, an important election, for it shifted national political authority toward the South and West and introduced a new emphasis on decentralized power and state sovereignty. In actual practice, however, Jefferson did surprisingly little to erase what his predecessors had done, and there was much greater continuity from the Federalist decade into his own than there appeared at first glance. Indeed, in his inaugural address he proclaimed, "We are all Republicans; we are all Federalists."

Thomas Jefferson

Thomas Jefferson, the third President of the United States and first secretary of state, is viewed by historians as a bit of an enigma and a man of contradictions. Jefferson owned a tobacco plantation but did not smoke. Jefferson drank little alcohol but planted a vineyard and made wine at his Monticello plantation. In a time where the rugged frontiersmen of Virginia tended to be familiar with guns and game, Jefferson did not hunt, ate little meat, and was concerned with protection of the environment. Jefferson was a large plantation owner and a member of Virginia's elite class; but he showed no respect of persons by spending entire days in his housecoat, serving guests himself, and accepting visitors in the order that they arrived rather than in the order of importance. Jefferson was also a slave owner who viewed African Americans as inferior and opposed inter-racial "mixing," yet he also favored the return of African Americans to Africa and had sexual relations and children with at least one of his slaves, Sally Hemmings. Jefferson favored a balanced budget for the nation and a small military; yet he was generally known as a spendthrift in his personal life, and for most of his life his personal debts exceeded his financial resources. He also violated his balanced budget principles when he borrowed $15 million from English bankers to purchase Louisiana. Jefferson believed the nation would be best served if it did not build great cities and remained a nation of small farmers, yet he built a nail factory on his own plantation where he put slave children to work making nails for profit.

Jefferson is considered one of America's "scholar-presidents," and few would doubt that he had an active and inquisitive mind. Jefferson wrote over thirty thousand personal letters in his lifetime, was very well-read, and his personal library became a major contribution to the beginnings of the Library of Congress after his death. Jefferson is also generally credited with founding the University of Virginia. Jefferson wrote not only the *Declaration of Independence* but also the Virginia Statute on Religious Liberty in 1786 that essentially separated Church and State in Virginia. Jefferson's religious views appear to lean toward Deism, as evidenced by his letter to his nephew Peter Carr where Jefferson argues that one should "read the Bible as you would Livy or Tacitus." In addition, Jefferson wrote his own gospel where he essentially assembled the sayings of Jesus absent the miraculous deeds depicted in the New Testament.

▶ The construction of the Jefferson Building and the Library of Congress took almost seven years, spanning from July 8, 1888, until May 15, 1894. *Wikipedia photo*

▶ Lieutenant Stephen Decatur reclaimed the USS *Philadelphia* from the Tripoli pirates and burned her in the harbor. Decatur became an American hero, famous for his unrestrained patriotism. *Wikipedia photo*

Jefferson is known as an advocate of states' rights and less government, stemming from his negative view of human nature. Jefferson believed that government was a necessary evil that, by its very nature, limits freedom. In spite of these beliefs, however, Jefferson also expanded the power of the national government with his purchase of Louisiana. Jefferson also espoused strict construction of the Constitution and therefore opposed the Bank of the United States because the Constitution mentions nothing specifically about a bank. In contrast, purchasing territory, such as his acquisition of the Louisiana Purchase, also is not mentioned in the Constitution.

Finally, although Jefferson himself denounced political parties, he is credited with forming the first democratic opposition political party, the Democratic Republicans, in opposition to the policies of John Adams and Alexander Hamilton. Jefferson's party would be so successful that it would dominate American politics for decades and eventually morph into the Democratic Party as it exists in the twenty-first century.

Settling the Barbary Corsairs

Jefferson's administration had hardly caught its breath before it was plunged into a vortex of swift-moving foreign affairs. The president's first problem involved the depredations of pirates from the Barbary States of North Africa (Tunis, Algiers, Morocco, and Tripoli), who had preyed on Mediterranean commerce for a quarter century, enslaving seamen and levying tribute on shipping. During the previous administrations, Washington and Adams paid out more than $2 million in ransom and bribes to the Barbary potentates. Jefferson was determined to end the affair when the pirates announced an increase in the bounty. Jefferson refused to pay the increase, and Tripoli responded by declaring war on the United States. Tripoli captured an American ship, the USS *Philadelphia*. In response, the United States sent to the Mediterranean four naval squadrons led by Stephen Decatur, who reclaimed the USS *Philadelphia* and in a series of brilliant actions finally forced some of the pirate states to sue for peace. Decatur quickly became an American hero and was famous for his unrestrained patriotism, exemplified by his statement, "My country right or wrong, but may she always be right."

Under a treaty signed in 1805, the United States agreed that it would continue to pay a bounty to the pirates but at the previous lower price. The U.S. also agreed to pay a ransom for the return of some captured U.S. seamen, and the pirates agreed to allow unmolested passage in the Mediterranean to the U.S. However, the U.S. navy remained in the Mediterranean to protect American shipping. In 1807, President Jefferson recalled the navy due to a conflict with Britain. All of the bounties were not ended until 1815, when Algiers declared war on the U.S. and resumed disruption of American shipping. The U.S. navy returned to the Mediterranean and with help from European navies finally defeated the pirates and ended the payment of tributes and piracy.

The Louisiana Purchase

In 1801, Napoleon Bonaparte recovered the territory of Louisiana, lost by France to Spain in 1763. Jefferson recognized the potential danger to the United States due to this sudden shift in ownership of half the American continent from an impotent Spain to an imperial France. The United States could not afford to have New Orleans, he wrote, possessed by "our natural and habitual enemy," Napoleon. Jefferson was a believer in Manifest Destiny and favored the expansion of the United States across the continent. Therefore, French control of Louisiana was counter to Jefferson's long-term goals. Jefferson reacted to the news of French ownership of Louisiana by securing the authorization for fifteen gunboats to patrol the Mississippi and the federalization of eighty thousand state militiamen for duty along the Mississippi. Jefferson also declared, "The day that France takes possession of New Orleans, we must marry ourselves to the British Navy." Jefferson's actions were in actuality little more than "saber rattling," but the French well understood that they could not control the vast territory that was Louisiana; and they might also be unable to prevent the United States from taking the territory by force.

In March 1801, Napoleon resumed war against England and could ill-afford to spare troops for the defense of Louisiana in North America. Napoleon had amassed an army for the defense of Louisiana; but his army never made it to the New World because it was iced-in at port in the Netherlands in the winter of 1802–1803. Moreover, Napoleon had tried to reconquer Haiti (then called Saint Domingue), which had been lost to France after a rebellion of African American slaves led by Touissaint L'Ouverture in 1793. The venture had not been a success, and Napoleon was eager to cut his losses on the western side of the Atlantic. In 1802, a slave rebellion in Saint Domingue cost Napoleon twenty-four thousand French soldiers, most of whom died from yellow fever. Despite the presence of fifty thousand French troops in Saint Domingue, Napoleon's General Victor Leclerc suggested that seventy thousand more troops were needed and that every slave over twelve years of age must be killed in order to quell the rebellion. Napoleon, therefore, gave up Saint Domingue for lost in 1803, proclaiming, "Damn sugar, damn coffee, damn colonies."

▶ In 1801, Napoleon Bonaparte recovered the territory of Louisiana for France. Thomas Jefferson sent James Monroe to negotiate purchasing New Orleans. Monroe returned having purchased New Orleans and the Louisiana Territory for $15 million. *Wikipedia photo*

As Napoleon searched for solutions to his problems in the Western Hemisphere, Jefferson sent

MAP 5.1 American Explorations of the Far West

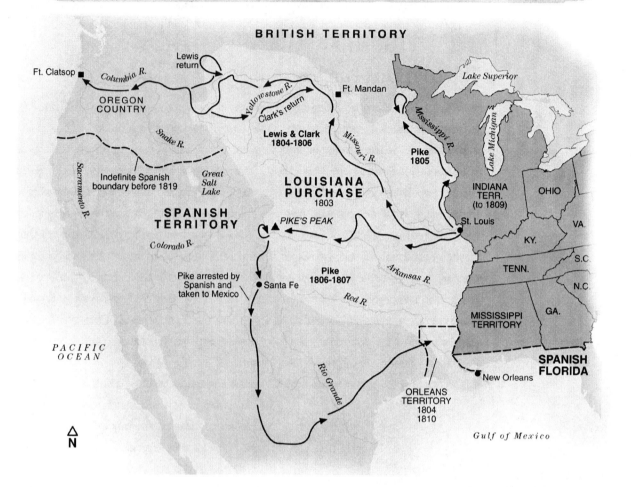

James Monroe to Paris to assist the American Minister to France, Robert Livingston, in discussing the possible purchase of New Orleans and East and West Florida (the coastal bend between Baton Rouge and Pensacola). It was either buy now, Jefferson said, or fight for it later. Jefferson privately authorized Monroe to offer as much as $10 million for New Orleans and the Floridas. If France should refuse to negotiate, Monroe was instructed to depart to England and negotiate an alliance with the British (the type of Anglo-American alliance against France that the French greatly feared). The French emperor, therefore, decided to sell; and in Paris the French Foreign Minister, Tallyrand, asked Livingston if the U.S. would like to own all of Louisiana rather than just New Orleans. Two days later, Monroe arrived in Paris, and Livingston and Monroe agreed that the U.S. should buy all of Louisiana even though they lacked the explicit authority to commit the U.S. to such an agreement. In April 1803, the United States offered to purchase the Louisiana Territory and West Florida for $15 million. France accepted the American offer, and the agreement was signed on May 2, 1803. Baring Brothers of London financed the purchase for America.

Jefferson, though overjoyed at the bargain, was also embarrassed by the fact that nowhere in the Constitution could he find presidential authority to purchase territory. He finally accepted Madison's view that the purchase could be made under a somewhat elastic interpretation of the treaty-making power, a view he had earlier rejected. Jefferson argued to the Senate, "Strict observance to higher law was one of the high duties of a good citizen, but not the highest. The laws of necessity and of self-preservation when a country is in danger are of a higher obligation." The brilliance of the maneuver obscured the Constitutional question involved, but the "strict constructionist" doctrine (that the government is limited to powers specifically stated in the Constitution) was never the same again since its most celebrated proponent had abandoned the principle when it became expedient.

The agreement was also problematic in that Spain claimed that under the provisions of an earlier treaty, Louisiana was rightfully Spain's because France had agreed that Louisiana could not fall to a third power when Spain transferred ownership of Louisiana to France. Furthermore, it was unclear whether or not the purchase included West Florida (Spain argued that it did not). Jefferson had also declared all of the inhabitants of Louisiana to be U.S. citizens, a power that is not granted to the president by the Constitution, once again contradicting Jefferson's own preference for strict construction of the Constitution. It was also unclear at the time if all of the residents of Louisiana, many of whom were of French heritage, would accept U.S. citizenship or control, placing the U.S. in a position similar to that of England when the British had taken control of French Canada.

Whatever its constitutionality, the Louisiana Purchase was one of the most important presidential decisions in American history. With one stroke the United States became a continental power, master of the continent's navigation system, and owner of vast new resources that promised greater (and perhaps final) economic independence from Europe. It also put an end to the likelihood that the West could ever be split from the East, which set a precedent for future territorial expansion.

The Problems of Political Patronage

In addition to the need for keeping a watchful eye on Europe and the Mediterranean, Jefferson had political problems at home. His cabinet, a particularly able group, included Secretary of State James Madison of Virginia and the brilliant Swiss from Pennsylvania, Secretary of the Treasury Albert Gallatin. Quite aware of the utility of patronage, Jefferson quietly replaced Federalist appointments with his own; and before the close of his first term, he had responsible Democratic Republicans in most positions of importance.

One of his thorniest problems, however, was that of the so-called "midnight judges" appointed by John Adams under the Judiciary Act of 1801. The act reduced the number of Supreme Court justices to five, created sixteen new circuit courts, and added a number of federal marshals and other officials. About a month before Jefferson's inauguration Adams had nominated Secretary of State John Marshall as Chief Justice of the Supreme Court. Then on the eve of the inauguration, Adams filled many of the new judicial posts with solid Federalist Party men. Under the Constitution (then as well as now), federal judges are appointed for life.

John Marshall was a stalwart Federalist, but beyond that he was a convinced nationalist who believed that the Constitution was the most sacred of all documents, "framed for ages to come…, designed to approach immortality as nearly as human institutions can approach it."

He did not trust the Jeffersonians, and he entered the Court determined that none should play fast and loose with the Constitution so long as he could prevent it.

Jefferson Versus Marshall

Jefferson was sure that Marshall, "that crafty chief judge," would set as many obstacles as he could in the administration's path, and that the "midnight judges" would undoubtedly follow his lead. In 1802, when Jefferson persuaded Congress to repeal the Judiciary Act of 1801, all of Adams's judges were left without salaries or duties. This, the Federalists claimed, was unconstitutional.

To test the constitutionality of Congress' repeal, William Marbury (one of the "midnight" appointments) asked Secretary of State Madison to give him his commission as justice of the peace of the District of Columbia. Madison refused so Marbury petitioned the Supreme Court for a writ of mandamus ordering Madison to do so. In what became the case of *Marbury v. Madison*, Chief Justice John Marshall was presented with a problem: Although Marshall desired to order Madison to deliver Marbury his commission as a federal judge, Marshall knew that Madison would not do so if he issued such a ruling. The Court would then lose respect if the president and secretary of state could ignore its rulings.

Marshall found a loophole in that the Constitution established very limited jurisdiction for the Supreme Court and under the Constitution alone, the Court would not have had jurisdiction in the case. The Judiciary Act of 1789, however, expanded the Court's jurisdiction to include cases such as the petition filed by William Marbury. Marshall therefore ruled that the Judiciary Act of 1789, which gave the Court jurisdiction, was unconstitutional since it conflicted with the jurisdiction of the Court spelled out in the Constitution. In doing so, Marshall removed himself from the case because the Court did not have jurisdiction. However, by declaring part of an Act of Congress to be unconstitutional, he had just established the power of Judicial Review (the power of the courts to determine the Constitutionality of statutes and actions). The Constitution, wrote Marshall, is "the *supreme* law of the land, superior to any ordinary act of the legislative." "A legislative act contrary to the Constitution is not law," Marshall went on, "and it is the province and duty of the judicial department to say what the law is." In saying so, Marshall had seized for the Court a power that had not been specifically granted to it in the Constitution, and thus elevated the judicial branch to coequal status with the legislative branch and the executive. William Marbury did not get his commission as a federal judge, but

▶ Chief Justice John Marshall's court opinions helped lay the basis for American constitutional law and grant the Court power to overrule Congress. Marshall was also the longest-serving Chief Justice of the United States. *Wikipedia photo*

that was beside the point. Jefferson may have successfully derailed the "midnight judges," but the Court had taken for itself a far more important power.

The Jefferson administration then launched an attack directly on the Federalist-dominated judiciary itself, at one point leading Congress to cut off funding for the Court, effectively closing it for a year. Jefferson and the Democratic Republican Congress then began using as its tool the constitutional power of impeachment for "high crimes and misdemeanors" against Federalist judges. The first target was John Pickering of the New Hampshire district court, who was apparently both insane and suffering from alcoholism. Pickering was impeached by the House, judged guilty by the Senate, and removed from office. Next, in 1804, the Democratic Republicans picked Associate Justice Samuel Chase of the Supreme Court, a violently partisan Federalist who had presided over several trials of Jeffersonian editors under the Sedition Act of 1798. In 1805, when the Senate decided it could not convict Chase, Jefferson conceded that impeachment was ineffective as a political weapon. Congress then gradually created a series of new judgeships and filled them with Democratic Republicans, a slower process but one that worked.

Marshall and Constitutional Law

Jefferson's differences with Marshall were temporarily settled, but Marshall's long tenure as Chief Justice was a most important influence on the rapid growth of the power of the federal government over the next three decades. Marshall served on the Court from 1801 to 1835, participated in more than one thousand opinions and decisions, and wrote some five hundred of them. Whenever opportunity presented itself, as it often did, Marshall strove to affirm two principles: that the Supreme Court possessed the power to nullify state laws that were in conflict with the Constitution, and that the Court alone had the right to interpret the Constitution, especially in regard to such broad grants of authority as might be contained in terms such as "commerce," "general welfare," "necessary and proper," and so on. His opinion did not always become the final version of constitutional issues, but the consistency of his attitudes, carried over a whole generation of legal interpretations, had much to do with the shaping of American constitutional law. Marshall's principles of Judicial Review and broad construction of the Necessary and Proper Clause of the Constitution, along with his affirmation of the supremacy of the Constitution and the national government in its sphere, remain cornerstones of Constitutional Law through the present.

Opening the West

After the Louisiana Purchase there was great anxiety to find out about what the nation had bought, more or less sight unseen. Jefferson, a respected scientist in addition to his many other achievements, had already made plans for the exploration of these newly acquired lands and persuaded Congress to finance an expedition up the Missouri River, across the Rocky Mountains, and if possible on to the Pacific. To lead this expedition, Jefferson chose his private secretary, a young Virginian named Meriwether Lewis, and William Clark, brother of George Rogers Clark, a frontier soldier. Congress appropriated $2,500 for an expedition that eventually cost $38,000. The mission itself was political, scientific, and commercial as Lewis and Clark were charged with making note of the landscape, finding natives with whom the United States could engage in profitable trade, and finding plants and animals that could be useful.

In the spring of 1804, Lewis and Clark's party of forty-eight, including several scientists, left St. Louis for the West. In one 55-foot keelboat and two pirogues (dugout canoes), Lewis and Clark went forth mapping, gathering specimens of plants and animals, collecting data on soil and weather, and observing every pertinent detail that they could of the new country. They journeyed up the Missouri River and wintered in the Dakotas with the Mandan Indians, who welcomed the expedition for their usefulness as a security measure against their rivals, the Sioux Indians. The expedition experienced tragedy when sergeant Charles Floyd perished at Council Bluffs from appendicitis, the only death on the expedition.

A French fur trader, Toussaint Charbonneau, and his Shoshone Indian wife, Sacajawea, aided Lewis and Clark on their journey. Charbonneau and Sacajawea served as language interpreters rather than guides since they did not know the way across the Rocky Mountains to the Pacific. Sacajawea was probably about fifteen-years-old at the time and had been kidnapped in her youth by another Native American tribe, kept as a slave, and then sold as a wife to Charbonneau. Sacajawea's presence with the expedition may have been most helpful in that other tribes viewed the presence of a woman as an indication that Lewis and Clark's group was not a war party. Sacajawea also may have saved the entire expedition from annihilation when Shoshone warriors aborted what appeared to be a staged attack when they recognized Sacajawea as a family member who had been kidnapped six years prior. Nevertheless, Lewis and Clark were unable to avoid problems with all native tribes along the way. On the return trip

MAP 5.2 Territorial Growth (1810)

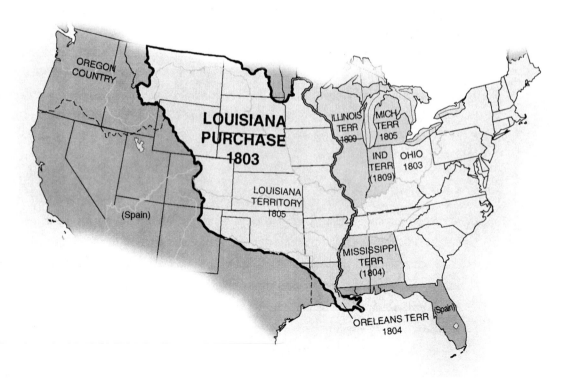

one Blackfoot Indian was stabbed while attempting to steal a gun, and Lewis shot another for stealing a horse. As a consequence, the expedition traveled sixty miles nonstop over the next three days to escape the pursuing Native Americans.

Lewis and Clark crossed the Rockies and followed the Columbia River to the Pacific, catching their first glimpse of the sea in November 1805. In the Columbia River valley, Lewis and Clark encountered the Clatsop and Chinook Indians, who were very poor tribes that made their existence by spear fishing in the river. The males in these tribes were all blind by age thirty, their retinas burned from the sun's reflection on the river. Lewis administered laudanum, an opiate, to the Native Americans. Although Lewis wrote that the Native Americans were not cured, he also stated that they "felt much better." Lewis himself would eventually become addicted to laudanum as a result of a wound he suffered on the expedition. It is recorded that Lewis and Peter Cruzatte went elk hunting wearing elkskin, and Cruzatte, whose vision was impaired by the fact that he had only one eye, accidentally mistook Lewis for an elk and shot him in the buttocks. Lewis took laudanum for the pain and as a result developed an addiction that would plague him the rest of his life.

By autumn of 1806, the expedition was back in St. Louis. They brought back both scientific data and vivid accounts that fed the imaginations of their fellow Americans. Lewis and Clark returned with dozens of plant and animal species, including two bear cubs that President Jefferson kept in a pit on the White House lawn. The explorers also made accurately detailed drawings of other wildlife as well as precise maps of the Missouri River. Lewis and Clark became national heroes, and Clark was appointed governor of Missouri. Clark died of natural causes in 1838 at the age of seventy-five.

Meriwether Lewis was appointed governor of Louisiana, but, addicted to alcohol and drugs, committed suicide in 1809 at age thirty-six. Lewis shot himself in the head and chest; and when servants arrived at his room, they found him cutting himself head to toe with a razor. Lewis stated to his servant, "I am so strong, it is hard to die."

At almost the same time, a party under Lieutenant Zebulon Pike was exploring the upper Mississippi and the mid-Rockies. Pike's expedition proved to be less successful than that of Lewis and Clark because he failed to keep accurate records. Nevertheless, Pike's Peak, perhaps the most famous mountain in Colorado, still bears his name. Other explorations followed, and the Louisiana Territory was soon organized on the pattern of the Northwest Ordinance of 1787. Its first state, Louisiana, entered the Union in 1812. The West was no longer a dream; it was a reality.

The "Essex Junto"

The prospect of more states being carved out of the wide new West greatly disturbed the Federalist Party leaders. Ohio entered the Union in 1803, a soundly Democratic Republican state; and the probability that all the new states from the Northwest Territory, plus all those to be developed from the Louisiana Purchase, might lean politically to the Jeffersonians was profoundly worrisome to Federalists. United only in their common hostility to the president, the Federalists had neither issue nor leader to counter his popularity and had little chance of finding either.

The gloom was especially prevalent in New England, so much so that a small number of Federalists (nicknamed the "Essex Junto") explored the possibilities of persuading the five

New England states, plus New York and New Jersey, to secede from the Union to form a separate Federalist republic—a "Northern Confederacy," said Senator Timothy Pickering of Massachusetts, "exempt from the corrupt and corrupting influence and oppression of the aristocratic democrats of the South."

Alexander Hamilton of New York showed no inclination to join them, so the New Englanders approached Aaron Burr. Since Burr believed it unlikely that he would be nominated for vice-president again, he consented to run for the governorship of New York, an office from which he might lead a secession movement.

Hamilton disliked Jeffersonians, also, but he considered Burr a dangerous man and campaigned against him. After Burr lost, he challenged Hamilton to a duel—on the basis of certain demeaning remarks reported in the press. (Hamilton accused Burr of incest with his daughter, while Burr accused Hamilton of adultery with his sister-in-law.) Burr killed Hamilton in July 1804, with the same gun that had been used to kill Hamilton's son Philip in a similar duel.

Alexander Hamilton died as he had lived, a controversial man who aroused strong feelings. His blunt distrust of "King Mob" and his frank preference for British-style constitutionalism had never endeared him to the public, but the leadership he provided for the country during the crucial postwar years had much to do with its successful transition from a provincial to a federal philosophy. Above all, he had a rare ability to think in large terms about what

MAP 5.3 Map of Presidential Election of 1804

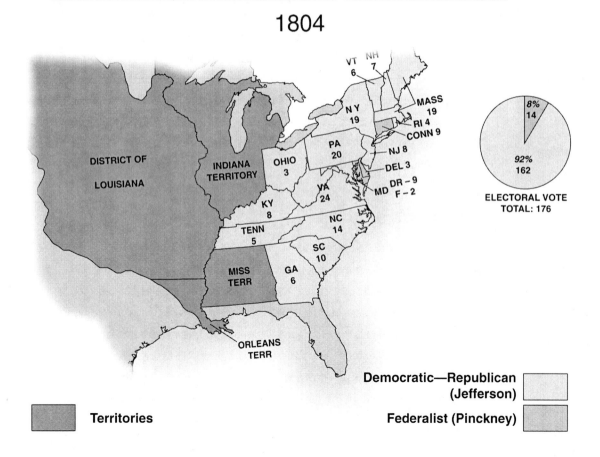

it took to create a powerful national economy. Accordingly, Hamilton made an invaluable contribution when it mattered most.

The duel ruined Burr's reputation and helped to begin the eclipse of the Federalist Party. Yet Burr himself was not quite finished. After the Democratic Republicans passed him over as their vice-presidential candidate in 1804 in favor of George Clinton of New York, he apparently entered into a scheme to carve a great empire of his own out of the American West. This conspiracy plot ended with his trial for treason in 1807. In 1806, Burr and General James Wilkinson, then governor of Louisiana, organized a force of about eighty men at Blennerhassett Island in the Ohio River for the purpose of taking New Orleans militarily from the United States. Wilkinson betrayed Burr to Jefferson, who issued a proclamation warning the nation and calling for Burr's arrest. Burr was brought to Richmond in Jefferson's home state. However, Jefferson's nemesis, John Marshall, tainted the trial with his instructions to the jury that were so narrow that Burr's attempt to militarily seize New Orleans from the U.S. did not fall under Marshall's definition of treason. Marshall stated to the jury, "organizing a military assemblage … is not a levying of war." Furthermore, Marshall stated that "to advise or procure treason, is not treason itself." Jefferson, however, also tainted the trial by offering a pardon to any Burr associate that would testify against him.

Although Burr was acquitted thanks to Marshall's narrow instructions to the jury, everyone drawn into his plan was ruined. Burr was forced to flee to England to escape further prosecution for Hamilton's death and additional charges of treason in six states. In his old age, Burr would eventually return to the U.S., where he fathered two illegitimate children in his seventies and was divorced by his wife, on the grounds of adultery, at age eighty. Meanwhile, the Federalist Party approached the election of 1804 with its brilliant leader dead, its reputation tarnished, and neither candidates nor issues of any public value.

The Election of 1804

The election of 1804 was barely a contest. The Democratic Republican caucus nominated Jefferson for a second time, with George Clinton of New York as his running mate. The Federalists ran the reliable Charles Cotesworth Pinckney and Rufus King of New York. Jefferson carried every state except Connecticut and Delaware, garnering 162 of the total 176 electoral votes and sweeping in an overwhelmingly Democratic Republican Congress with him.

Jefferson's first administration ended on a high note of success—as John Randolph said later, the United States was "in the 'full tide of successful experiment.' Taxes repealed; the public debt amply provided for, both principal and interest; sinecures abolished; Louisiana acquired; public confidence unbounded." Unfortunately, it did not last.

America and the Woes of Europe

Neutrality in a World at War

Napoleon Bonaparte loomed large in the future of both America and Europe. Jefferson did not like him; but to Jefferson and many other Americans, France was still the country of Lafayette,

▶ Emperor Napoleon Bonaparte at the Battle of Austerlitz in 1805. *Wikipedia photo*

Rochambeau, De Grasse, and the great French philosophers of the Enlightenment. Against Napoleon stood England, whose aim Jefferson believed was "the permanent domination of the ocean and the monopoly of the trade of the world." He did not want war either, nor did he wish to give aid to either in the war that flamed up between them in 1803.

It is an oversimplification to assume that American foreign policy of the period was governed primarily by a like or dislike of France or England. The objectives of Jefferson's foreign policy, like Washington's and Adams's, were to first protect American independence and second maintain as much diplomatic flexibility as possible without irrevocable commitment to any nation.

In the European power struggle between England and France that developed after 1790, Jefferson saw great advantages to the United States in playing one against the other without being drawn into the orbit of either. An American friendship with France would form a useful counterbalance against the influence of Britain and Spain, the chief colonial powers in North and South America. A British and Spanish defeat might well mean the end of their American empires.

At the same time Jefferson did not want to tie America's future to the fortunes of Napoleon, who might be an even greater threat to American freedom if he won. The wisest policy, therefore, resided in neutrality toward all and trade with anyone—or, as the British wryly put it, America's best hope was "to gain fortune from Europe's misfortune."

America's major gain during the European war stemmed from American misuse of a naval doctrine known as the "doctrine of the broken voyage." Under this doctrine, if merchant ships broke a voyage from French or Spanish islands in the Caribbean by paying duties in an American port, the status of the cargo changed to American. Given that the U.S. was neutral in the war, the cargo shipped under American flags was not legally subject to seizure by the warring nations. As a result, a "re-export" business boomed in the U.S. In 1806 alone, the U.S. exported 47 million pounds of coffee, none of which was grown in the U.S.

Maintaining neutrality was as difficult for Jefferson as it had been for Washington and Adams before him. The British navy ruled the seas; and Napoleon, after the Battle of Austerlitz in 1805, ruled Europe. The war remained a stalemate while the two countries engaged in a battle of proclamations over wartime naval commerce. Each side blockaded the other's ports, The British argued that the American re-export business was illegal because the U.S. often rebated 90 percent of the duties paid by a foreign power in its ports. As a consequence, the British argued that the voyages were not "broken" but "continuous" and, therefore, subject to seizure by the British. The British stationed their warships near U.S. ports, and then forced American ships carrying French and Spanish re-exports to Canada for trial in a British admiralty court, where the British would confiscate the cargo.

In 1803, the British also angered the Americans by returning to their policy of impressments in an effort to meet the demands for sailors caused by the war against France. The demand for sailors was caused not only by the war but also by a high desertion rate (2,500 per year) among British sailors. Many of the deserters found work on American merchant ships, as American merchants were pleased to hire professionally trained sailors. The British, therefore, began stopping American ships and impressing sailors who could not prove American citizenship. The British seized over ten thousand men from American ships between 1803 and 1812, although 3,800 were released after they proved their American citizenship.

To make matters worse, the British did not recognize American naturalized citizens. England claimed that all persons born in England were forever English citizens, even if they had become recognized as naturalized citizens by the United States. Americans exacerbated the situation by forging naturalization papers. In the words of Britain's Lord Vincent, "Every Englishman may be made an American for a dollar."

The British at Sea

In 1806, the British announced the first of a series of "Orders in Council" (orders from the King's privy council) that proclaimed a blockade of Europe. Napoleon retaliated with the Berlin Decree, which declared all British ports closed. The result was that the U.S. was caught between two warring nations and American vessels were liable to confiscation by either one if they obeyed the rules of the other.

Finally, in the summer of 1807, the British warship *Leopard* stopped the United States navy's *Chesapeake* (a warship, not a merchant vessel), killed or wounded twenty-one men, and impressed four sailors (three of whom were Americans). The British sailor Jenkin Ratford was hanged, and the three Americans languished in a British prison. The British action was an act of war under international law, as well as an insult to American honor; and America burst out in a great roar of rage. Had Congress been in session, it almost certainly would have declared war on the spot. However, Jefferson held his temper, demanded apologies and reparations, and ordered British ships out of American waters to prevent further incidents. Jefferson understood America's naval inferiority at the time and viewed nonmilitary options as preferable. Though the British apologized, they also reaffirmed their right to search American ships and seize deserters. The *Leopard-Chesapeake* affair rankled in American minds for years and had much to do with the drift toward war with Britain in 1812.

The "Obnoxious Embargo"

Jefferson and Secretary of State Madison bent every effort to avoid provocation that might lead to war. There were only two choices—war or some kind of economic substitute. The easier choice would have been war, for which Jefferson could have obtained public and congressional support. Instead he chose peace, pinning his hopes on "peaceful coercion," as he called it, by means of a boycott of British goods and a set of nonimportation acts that Congress passed in 1806 and 1807.

Neither was sufficiently effective to do much good, however. As the situation between the two nations steadily deteriorated, Jefferson asked Congress for a full-scale embargo—a logical move since Britain needed American trade, especially foodstuffs, in increasing quantities as the war in Europe progressed. In late 1807, Congress passed the Embargo Act, which forbade American ships to leave the United States for any foreign port or even to engage in the American coastal trade without posting a heavy bond. Jefferson hoped that the Embargo Act of 1807 would do two things: first, that it would discourage the British from seizing American ships and sailors and force them to greater regard for American rights; and, second, that it would encourage the growth of American industry by cutting off British imports.

England suffered shortages, but not enough to matter. France approved of the embargo since it helped, second hand, to enforce Napoleon's own blockade of England. Meanwhile, American ships rotted at anchor along the Eastern seaboard. Shipping merchants went bankrupt, and American farm surpluses piled up. In New York, one traveler wrote, "The streets near the waterside were almost deserted. The grass had begun to grow upon the wharves." American exports dropped 80 percent in 1808, and British exports to the U.S. dropped 50 percent. The negative impact of the Embargo Act on the American economy was exacerbated by the fact that the export business was the fastest growing segment of the American economy.

▶ James Madison, who also wrote several of "The Federalist Papers," won the election of 1808 by a landslide.
Wikipedia photo

While the shipping interests suffered, however, New England and the mid-Atlantic port states did begin a transition to manufacturing that was soon to change their economic complexion. With foreign competition removed, capital previously invested in overseas trade was available for new factories and mills, which sprang up in profusion along the seaboard. These economic benefits, however, were difficult to see in the midst of the paralyzing effects of the embargo.

American merchants in New England circumvented the Embargo Act by smuggling goods into Canada and then "re-exporting" the goods to England. Some New Englanders even talked of secession; and New England jurors, sympathetic to the smugglers, often found violators of the Embargo Act not guilty. Jefferson's policy was violently attacked in the taverns and counting houses, and finally Congress repealed the Embargo Act. On March 1, 1809, three days before his successor Madison took office, Jefferson reluctantly signed the bill.

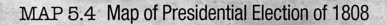

MAP 5.4 Map of Presidential Election of 1808

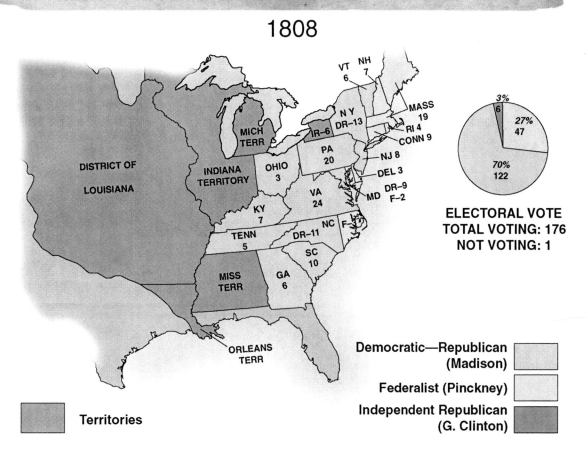

ELECTORAL VOTE
TOTAL VOTING: 176
NOT VOTING: 1

Democratic—Republican (Madison)
Federalist (Pinckney)
Independent Republican (G. Clinton)

Territories

The end of Jefferson's second term came during the pungent disputes over the embargo; and Jefferson, who had wished for some time to retire to his beloved Monticello, was relieved to accept Washington's two-term precedent and announce his retirement. His eight years in the presidency, begun in such high confidence, ended on a much more equivocal note. Ironically, Jefferson, the believer in decentralized government, found himself under the Embargo Act wielding more power over American life than any Federalist would have dreamed of. Though a believer in states' rights, he had coerced the New England states into an economic boycott that impaired their commerce.

The Election of 1808

Jefferson trusted and admired James Madison and easily secured the Democratic Republican nomination for him. The Federalists nominated the tireless Charles Cotesworth Pinckney again. However, in spite of the embargo and divided Democratic Republican sentiment, Madison won by 122 to 47 electoral votes.

James Madison, far from being a mere graceful shadow of Jefferson, was very much his own man. His role in the formation of the Democratic Republican Party was a decisive one, and the political philosophy of the Jeffersonian group owed much to his thinking. Madison wrote a number of the *Federalist Papers*; and without his persuasive arguments, the Constitution might never

▶ The battle of The *President*, an American ship, and *Little Belt*, a British ship, took place off the Virginian coast. The *Little Belt* incident was one of the many incidents and events that led to the War of 1812. *Wikipedia photo*

have been ratified. Madison also took notes at the Constitutional Convention so that future generations would know what actually went on in Philadelphia that summer, although the proceedings at the time were kept secret so as to foster free and open debate. Madison is also considered to be the principal author of the Bill of Rights, and the Constitution may reflect Madison's ideas as much as anyone's. In fact, the American system of government with federalism, separation of powers, checks and balances, and multiple restrictions on concentrated power is often referred to as the "Madisonian model." Madison, however, did not view the Constitution as sacred or perfect, and instead termed it as a political compromise that reflected the best that the men at the convention could forge together at the time. If changes to the Constitution would be expedient in the future to ensure better governance, Madison would expect the Constitution to be changed.

The Drift to War

Madison was a profound student and an astute practitioner of politics. However, when he succeeded Jefferson, he inherited a large bundle of thorny problems. Madison replaced the Embargo Act in 1809 with the Non-Intercourse Act, which allowed American ships to trade with any nations except France and England. The act also provided that the U.S. would resume trade with Britain or France if either would respect freedom of the seas. The Non-Intercourse Act was ineffective at remedying the economic problems, however, because the vast majority of American trade had been with England and France. Furthermore, the Non-Intercourse Act was unenforceable in that no one could prevent ships from actually sailing to France or England once they had left American ports. When France began confiscating American cargo and seizing and imprisoning American sailors, Congress followed the Non-Intercourse Act with Macon's Bill No. 2 (named after the chairman of the House Foreign Affairs Committee), which relieved American shipping from all restrictions while ordering British and French naval vessels out of American waters. The bill stipulated, however, that if either Britain or France would recognize American rights at sea, the U.S. would reinstate the Non-Intercourse Act against the other.

Napoleon announced that his government would lift restrictions on U.S. shipping, thus forcing Madison to invoke the Non-Intercourse Act against England in February 1811. Three months later tensions heightened when an American ship, the *President*, fired on the smaller British ship, *Little Belt*, off the Virginia coast. Nine British sailors were killed and twenty-three were wounded in the exchange. This failed to influence British policy, but "peaceable coercion" was beginning to impair England more than the British admitted and more than Madison realized. Parliament was preparing to relax some of its restrictions even as Congress moved toward a declaration of war. In the summer of 1811, the British returned two of the impressed Americans from the USS *Chesapeake* (the third had died in prison) and made reparations to the United States for the incident. It simply did not happen soon enough to change the course of events.

The War Hawks

Jefferson's "peaceful coercion" policy was probably the best that could have been pursued under the circumstances, and except for some exceedingly clumsy diplomacy abroad and mounting pressures for war at home, it might have worked. Much of the pressure came from a group of aggressive young congressmen (the first of the postrevolutionary generation of Western politicians)—Henry Clay of Kentucky, John C. Calhoun and Langdon Cheves of western South Carolina, Peter B. Porter of western New York, Felix Grundy of Tennessee, and other so-called "buckskin boys." Intensely nationalist and violently anti-British, this group of "War Hawks," as John Randolph of Roanoke called them, clamored loudly for an attack on Britain via Canada and on the seas.

"War Hawks" believed that they had special reasons to dislike England. The West had fallen on hard times in the years from 1805 to 1809, and it blamed the British navy rather than the Embargo Act. More serious, however, was the charge that the British, from their Canadian posts, were stirring up the Native Americans and arming them for pillaging raids across the American frontier. In 1811, there was a Native American uprising in the Ohio Valley led by Chief Tecumseh and his brother "The Prophet." The Native Americans were defeated at the Battle of Tippecanoe by General William Henry Harrison, but the Americans discovered that the weapons used by the Natives in the uprising were purchased from the British.

"Mr. Madison's War"

The origins of war are normally complex, and the War of 1812, especially, seems to have developed from a bewildering complexity of causes. Historians have advanced a number of explanations as to why the United States, after seven months of somewhat disordered debate in Congress, decided on June 18, 1812, to declare war on Great Britain. The vote was close in the Senate—19 to 13—and not overwhelming in the House—79 to 49. Simultaneously, Congress narrowly defeated a proposal for a Declaration of War against France as well.

Nineteenth-century historians tended to agree on the causes of the war; first, to "vindicate the national character" (as the House Foreign Affairs Committee said) and second, to retaliate against British violations of America's maritime rights. The largest vote for war came from the South and West, however, where sea trade was less important. New England, the center of American sea trade, opposed the war. At the news, flags flew at half-mast in New England, and there were minor riots in some port cities.

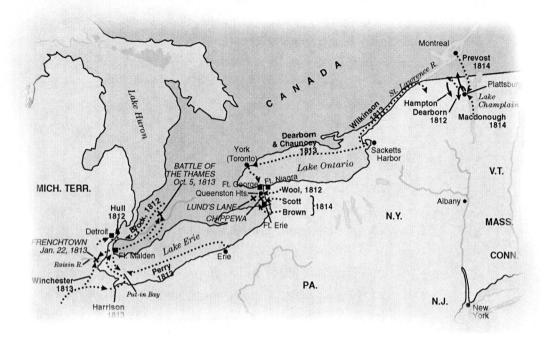

MAP 5.5 Northern Campaigns (1812–1814)

The Eastern Federalist press dubbed it "Mr. Madison's War," and so it remained. Some, too, regarded it as a stab in Britain's back when that nation stood alone against Napoleon, who in 1812 was on his way to Moscow for what seemed likely to be his last great conquest.

Later historians, noting the rhetoric of the Congressional debates and the distribution of the vote, concluded that the South and West hoped by the war to annex Canada and Florida as room for expansion, an expression of what later became known as America's "manifest destiny" to occupy the continent. Some still favor this expansionist interpretation; however, other historians have suggested that fear of Britain's economic dominance—a reassertion of England's old imperial power over her former colony—also played an important role. Whatever the motivations, it was a brief, confused, and, except for a few instances, not very heroic war that, nonetheless had a crucial role in the national development.

The War of 1812

War on the Land: First Phase

Many Americans believed that Canada not only ought rightfully to join the United States but that it wanted to. The *Articles of Confederation* had provided for Canada's admission to the Union, while the first Congress called itself "Continental" by design. Some Americans believed that the only way to end their problems with the British in North America was to militarily expel them from Canada. Other Americans simply desired land in Canada and believed that Canada would be an easy military conquest. Henry Clay, for instance, argued that taking

Canada was "a mere matter of marching." Secretary of War William Eustis wrote in 1812, "We have only to send officers into the Provinces and the people, already disaffected toward their own government, will rally to our standard."

There was, indeed, a good deal of pro-American sympathy in the Western St. Lawrence region—then called Upper Canada and later Ontario; but American Loyalists controlled both the Assembly and the Governor's Executive Council. As the Anglican Bishop of Upper Canada wrote, they and the British Canadians wanted no part of that "degenerate government ... equally destitute of national honor and virtue," that lay to the south. French Quebec, with vivid memories of Revolutionary anti-Catholic propaganda, feared the loss of its language and its religion under American rule; while neither British nor French merchants in Montreal could see any advantage in a change.

In April 1812, Congress imposed a ninety-day embargo on all ships in port—an action generally regarded as preparatory to war. That same month in England, disruption of trade and economic recession had spurred enough political unrest that the government announced that it would repeal the Orders in Council under which the British had been seizing American shipping if the Americans resumed normal trade and the French rescinded their restrictions on trade. Two months later on June 16, the British announced that they would suspend the Orders in Council on the condition that the U.S. resume normal trade relations. Congress declared war two days later on June 18, not knowing that England had agreed to suspend the Orders in Council.

Upon hearing of the American War Declaration, the British expected Madison to suspend the American War Declaration as soon as he learned of the British suspension of the Orders in Council. Madison did not do so, however, because the British had not agreed to end impressments, which he viewed as an affront to American honor and sovereignty.

The War of 1812 was very unpopular in New England from the outset. New Englanders talked of secession, loaned money to the British, aided British soldiers moving through the country, and traded with Canada and England while the U.S. was at war. In return, the British allowed New England merchant ships to trade with England.

The United States was totally unprepared for war. Its defenses were outmoded, and its army, reduced to about seven thousand badly equipped men, was scattered across the frontier and poorly led. Madison called for one hundred thousand state militiamen, but only ten thousand reported for duty (even though state militia rolls contained seven hundred thousand names). The British situation was no better. Canada had a thousand miles of border, with six thousand scattered British regulars and a militia pool of perhaps sixty thousand to defend it. John C. Calhoun figured that a complete conquest of Canada might take a month. Henry Clay thought one company of Kentucky militia could do it. Both turned out to be overly optimistic.

The American strategy was threefold: first, take Montreal and seal off the St. Lawrence route to the interior; second, invade the Niagara region and secure control of the central St. Lawrence Valley; third, invade western Canada from Detroit, securing the Great Lakes and the Northwest.

None of it worked. The expedition into Quebec failed at Crysler's Farm and at Châteauguay, due chiefly to the stubborn defense of the French-Canadian militia and the fact that some of the American militiamen refused to fight outside of their home states. General William Hull, the American commander at Detroit, crossed into Canada in July of 1812, lost

▶ Oliver Hazard Perry transferring from US Brig *Lawrence* to US Brig *Niagara* during the battle. The United States' victory ensured American control of the Lake for the rest of the war. Lake Erie was considered one of the most savage naval actions of the era. *Wikipedia photo*

his courage, and quickly returned. British General Isaac Brock, with a smaller force, bluffed Hull (who was later court-martialed and sentenced to death, but pardoned by the president) into surrendering Detroit on August 14, with a fictitious report about the size of the Native American army allied with the British. Hull surrendered, without a shot, to a Native American army half the size of his American force. When Fort Michilimackinac in upper Michigan and Fort Dearborn in Illinois fell soon after, the British controlled the Northwest. Brock then rushed his army toward Niagara in 1813, where he defeated an American invasion at Queenston Heights in mid-October. Brock was killed in the battle, but he had saved western Canada for the British.

The British proclaimed a blockade of the entire United States, and the U.S. lacked the naval power to do anything about it. At the outset of the war the U.S. had only sixteen seaworthy ships and a fleet of 170 small gunboats that were fit only for harbor or river patrol.

In the middle of these military failures, Madison was nominated for another term. An Eastern antiwar wing of the Democratic Republicans, however, nominated De Witt Clinton of New York against him, and the Federalists added their support for Clinton. Madison won, 128 to 89 electoral votes; however, Clinton carried, significantly, all of New England and the mid-Atlantic states except Vermont and Pennsylvania. At the same time, the Federalists doubled their delegation in Congress.

War on the Land: Second Phase

Despite its early disasters, the army kept trying to conquer Canada. In the winter of 1812–1813, American sailors commanded by Captain Oliver Hazard Perry built a small fleet; and in September 1813, it met and smashed the British lake squadron at the Battle of Lake Erie, near Sandusky, Ohio. Lake Erie was one of the most savage naval actions of the era (Perry's flagship suffered 80 percent casualties). After three hours of fighting, Perry dispatched his message to General William Henry Harrison commanding the forces near Detroit: "We have met the enemy and they are ours." Without control of Lake Erie, the British evacuated Detroit and fell back to-

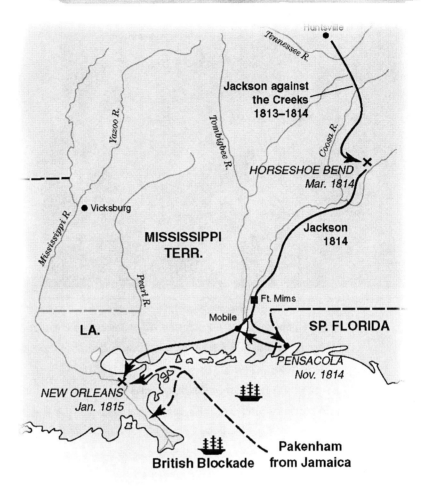

MAP 5.6 Southwest Campaigns (1813–1815)

ward Niagara, but Harrison's swiftly advancing force caught and defeated them at the Battle of the Thames on October 5, 1813.

By reason of Perry and Harrison's victories, the United States now commanded the Northwestern frontier. London, however, was sending more British regulars, and the Canadian militia was gaining experience. Two American invasions were turned back at Stoney Creek and Beaver Dam; and on July 25, 1814, a bitter battle at Lundy's Lane near Niagara Falls stopped a third attempt. The British then struck back at Buffalo, capturing and then burning the town. Later that year they took Fort Niagara.

War at Sea

The American navy entered the War of 1812 with sixteen ships. The British had ninety-seven in American waters alone. The out-numbered Americans, therefore, limited themselves to single-ship actions, in which they did surprisingly well. The *Constitution* ("Old Ironsides"), a forty-four-gun frigate commanded by Yankee Isaac Hull, defeated the British frigate *Guerriere* on August 19, 1812, in one of the most famous sea fights in history. The *Constitution's* victory proved that the American ships and sailors could compete with the British when their ships

▶ The *Constitution,* a forty-four-gun frigate commanded by Yankee Isaac Hull, defeated the British frigate *Guerriere* in one of the most famous sea fights in history. *Wikipedia photo*

were of a similar class. The frigate *United States*, commanded by Captain Stephen Decatur, captured the British *Macedonian* a few weeks later; but the American *Chesapeake* lost a bitter fight to the British *Shannon* in 1813.

American privateers contributed most to the success of the war at sea. These swift ships sailed circles around the British, captured or destroyed thirteen hundred British merchantmen, and even had the impudence to sack British shipping in the English Channel in full sight of the shore. They gave the American public something to boast about now and then, though the overall effect on the outcome of the conflict was negligible. The British naval blockade was quite effective, and by 1813 the majority of American ports were securely blockaded. British naval captains even forced American cities to pay tribute in order to avoid bombardment.

War on the Land: Final Phase

Napoleon abdicated in April 1814 and was exiled to the isle of Elba in the Mediterranean. With Bonaparte gone and the French war finished, England turned its massive army of fourteen thousand veterans toward American shores. The strategy of the British general staff was to make three coordinated attacks: one from the north, from Canada down Lake Champlain into New York State; a second on the coast, through Chesapeake Bay, aimed at Baltimore, Washington, and Philadelphia; a third up from the south, at New Orleans. The end was in sight, wrote the *London Times*, for this "ill-organized association" of states. Indeed, it appeared that way.

The northern campaign began in July 1814. Since Lake Champlain in upstate New York was the vital link in the invasion route, British General Sir George Prevost wanted it cleared of American ships; but in September 1814, the American lake squadron under Captain Thomas Macdonough decisively defeated the British. Without control of the lake the British drive stalled and eventually dissolved at Plattsburgh, New York, where the British army retreated from an American force it outnumbered eleven thousand to thirty-three hundred.

▶ The signing of the Treaty of Ghent was the peace treaty that ended the War of 1812 between the United States and Great Britain. Though celebration was quickly widespread among Americans, "Mr. Madison's War" had actually accomplished very little in the military or political sense. *Wikipedia photo*

The British were more successful at Chesapeake Bay, where in August 1814 General Robert Ross landed a strong force that marched on Washington. The American government fled into Virginia; and the British, in retaliation for the American burning of York (Toronto) in 1813, set fire to the White House and the Capitol before moving toward Baltimore. Here they were stopped at Fort McHenry, where a spirited defense inspired Francis Scott Key to write "The Star-Spangled Banner," by putting patriotic words to an old English drinking song. Unable to crack the Baltimore defenses, the British set sail for the West Indies.

The third British offensive, aimed at New Orleans and commanded by General Edward Pakenham, sailed from Jamaica in November 1814, with seventy-five hundred seasoned veterans. To oppose Pakenham, Andrew Jackson took his frontier army on a forced march in December. Though neither Jackson nor Pakenham knew it, American and British representatives were already at work in Belgium on a treaty of peace. Two weeks after the Treaty of Ghent was signed on December 24, 1814, Jackson's Western riflemen almost annihilated Pakenham's army. The British lost two thousand men (including Pakenham), while Jackson's loss totaled eight dead and thirteen wounded in a battle—The Battle of New Orleans. There is controversy over the significance of this battle among historians. Since it occurred two weeks after the peace treaty ending the War of 1812, some historians argue it did not really change the war or the peace. Others, however, disagree and assert that the battle not only made Andrew Jackson a national hero and increased the spirit of nation; it secured the west for the United States. If the Battle of New Orleans was not won by the Americans, it was a good possibility that the British would have stayed in the area and tried to dominate it after the war. Moreover, the Treaty of Ghent was signed two weeks before the battle, however, the British Parliament and United States Congress still had to approve it.

The Hartford Convention

In 1814, when American prospects seemed darkest, the Federalist Massachusetts legislature called a convention at Hartford, Connecticut, to discuss "public grievances and concerns"—that is, the Democratic Republican conduct of the war. The delegates, who came primarily from the Massachusetts, Connecticut, and Rhode Island legislatures, had a great deal to discuss. Some advised amending the Constitution to clip Congress' war-making powers. Others suggested negotiating a separate peace with England.

Curiously enough, the delegates, all Federalists, appealed to the doctrine of states' rights—the same doctrine that the Jeffersonians had used against Federalist centralization during Adams's administration. They argued that since the Democratic Republican Congress had violated the Constitution by declaring an unwanted war, those states that did not approve had the right to override congressional action. At the conclusion of the meeting, Massachusetts and Connecticut sent commissioners to Washington to place their protests before Congress. When the commissioners arrived, the war was over; and whatever they had to say was forgotten. Probably, the biggest accomplishment of the Hartford Convention was to weaken the Federalist Party even further.

A Welcomed Peace

Early in 1813, Czar Alexander I of Russia had offered to mediate between the United States and Britain, since he wanted the British free to concentrate their full military force on Napoleon. Madison sent commissioners to Russia, but Lord Castlereagh, the British foreign minister, refused to accept the czar's suggestion. Late that same year, however, Castlereagh notified Secretary of State James Monroe that he was willing to discuss differences between the two nations; and in August 1814, American and British representatives met in Ghent, Belgium.

As the meetings dragged on, it became plain that the British could not successfully invade the United States—nor could the United States successfully take Canada. The defeat at Plattsburgh convinced the British that the Americans were determined to hold on to their land and continue fighting. Public opposition in Britain to the "worthless" war in the Americas, coupled with fears that Napoleon could return to power, pushed the British to genuinely seek a negotiated settlement. Both British and Americans were war weary and wanted to finish it, and on December 24, 1814, the commissioners signed a peace treaty. The British had originally demanded American land in the area of the Great Lakes, and the U.S. had demanded the cession of Canada to the U.S. Both sides reduced their demands to "*status quo ante bellum*," or a return to how things were before the war. Based on this principle, both sides signed the Treaty of Ghent. Interestingly, the treaty did not mention impressment, Madison's reason for not rescinding the Declaration of War after Britain rescinded the Orders in Council; nor did it mention the British blockades, seizures at sea, or any of the major disputes that seemed to have precipitated the war.

The Results of the War

The reaction of war-weary Americans to the news of the Treaty of Ghent, which arrived in the United States in February 1815, was swift and spontaneous. Bells rang, parades formed, newspapers broke out in headlines to proclaim the "passage from gloom to glory." Yet "Mr. Madison's War" had accomplished very little in a military or political sense. The treaty realized few if any of the aims for which the war had presumably been fought; and most notably, it did not end impressment, which had been Madison's reason for not rescinding the Declaration of War after hearing of British suspension of the Orders in Council. In short, Madison had fought the war to end impressment and did not achieve his goal.

The most that can be said is that the treaty opened the way for future settlements to be worked out over the next decade with Britain, Spain, and France. The war dislocated business and foreign trade, deranged currency values, and exposed glaring cracks in the national political organization.

To the American people the outcome, ambiguous as it was, marked a turning point in patriotic self-esteem. True, the war might have been avoided by better statesmanship, and it might even have been fought with France on equally reasonable grounds. Yet from the American point of view, the War of 1812 gave notice to the rest of the world that the United States had arrived as a nation. Henceforth, the powers of Europe would tread on American sovereignty only at a price. "Who would not be an American?" crowed *Niles' Register*. "Long live the Republic! All Hail!"

Madison had also used the war to seize both East and West Florida for the United States. Madison had Congress officially annex West Florida (the Gulf Coast from Pensacola to Baton Rouge) in the spring of 1812 and sent troops into West Florida to defend American control of the area. American troops under General James Wilkinson took Mobile from the Spanish in 1813; and Americans under Andrew Jackson took Pensacola from the Spanish in 1814, though the U.S. returned East Florida (current day Florida) to Spain at the conclusion of the war.

The War and Canada

The War of 1812 marked the first step in the creation of the nation of Canada, which was to emerge a half-century later as a sovereign nation. In the conflict between England and the United States, British and French Canadians were caught in the middle, as they had been in the American Revolution. For England to strike at the United States, the route lay through Canada. For the United States to strike at England, the only vulnerable point was Canada.

To the average Canadians, however, whether British or French, the war's causes meant little; and they had a small stake in it. Canada's problem was simply survival, and it survived. Whatever their differences, French, British, and Loyalists joined in common cause to outlast a war and preserve their part of the British Empire.

America's attempted invasions intensified already strong anti-American feelings, while Canada's repulse of them was understandably a source of growing national pride. Opposition to the United States and wariness of its motives thus became continuing factors in subsequent Canadian-American relations. The war strengthened Canada's "Britishness" and at the same time gave Canada the beginnings of its own sense of identity.

America Makes a New Start

A Confident Nation

The War of 1812 marked the end of America's lingering sense of colonial inferiority. Some have called it a, "second war of independence," because a new spirit of national consciousness resulted. Albert Gallatin wrote, "It has renewed and reinstated the national feeling and character which the Revolution had given, and which were daily lessening. The people now have more general objects of attachment.... They are more Americans: they feel and act more as a nation."

After the Treaty of Ghent, the United States turned toward the great hazy West, where half a continent lay virtually empty. America could now concentrate on its domestic problems with less concern for European standards, ideals, and entanglements. Indifference to foreign affairs after 1814 was so great that even Napoleon's escape from Elba, his return to France, and his final defeat at Waterloo in June 1815, excited little attention in the American press. American indifference to foreign affairs, however, was in part made possible by the conclusion of the Napoleonic wars and the Congress of Vienna in 1815 that brought peace to the great powers of Europe. With Europe at peace and the United States no longer caught between the warring powers, the interest of the United States centered on perfecting and expanding the nation it had constructed out of two wars and a generation of experiment. In other words, its chief task lay in developing modern America.

The Aftermath of War

The most persistent postwar American problems were economic. Finances during the war had been handled almost as ineptly as military affairs, and banks had multiplied profusely and without proper control. As a result, the country was flooded with depreciating paper money, and prices were at the most inflated level in America's brief history. Furthermore, the shipping industry had been badly hurt by war and blockade. On the other hand, the value of manufacturing had increased tremendously—the total capital investment in American industry in 1816 was estimated to be more than $100 million. The West, now producing foodstuffs and raw materials in abundance, balanced on the verge of a tremendous boom. As soon as peace was established, the Democratic Republican Congress began to consider a three-point program for economic expansion: a tariff to protect infant American industry; a second Bank of the United States, since the charter of Hamilton's original Bank had expired in 1811; and a system of roads, waterways, and canals to provide internal routes of communication and trade.

A Protective Tariff

The protection of America's infant industries was a matter of first priority. New factories, encouraged by the war, had grown in great numbers, especially in the textile industry, where for the first time, the workforce was comprised of young women. As soon as the wartime blockade ended, British-made products streamed toward the United States; and young industries that had flourished under conditions of embargo and war found it quite another matter to compete in an open peacetime market. Whereas the total value of United States imports in 1813 had been $13 million, by 1816 it had leaped to $147 million. American manufacturers begged for protection.

Congress in 1816 passed a tariff to protect the new factories—the first United States tariff passed not to raise revenue but to encourage and support home industry. The argument over this protective tariff exposed some potentially serious sectional economic conflicts and marked the first appearance of a perennial political issue. Southern producers and New England shippers opposed the tariff; however, the growing factory towns of New England supported it, as did some of the younger Southern cotton politicians, who hoped to encourage industrial development in the South. The mid-Atlantic States and the West favored it, and the Southwest divided on the issue.

Renewing the Bank of the United States

In 1816, Congress turned its attention to the National Bank. The charter of the first Bank of the United States had been allowed to expire because the Democratic Republicans believed that, as Jefferson originally claimed, banking powers properly belonged to the states and Hamilton's centralized bank was therefore unconstitutional. The new Western Congressmen, however, were much less interested in the bank's constitutionality than in its usefulness. Henry Clay, who had opposed the first bank in 1811 on constitutional grounds, now supported the second bank, he explained, because it was necessary for the national (especially Western) interest to have a stable, uniform currency and sound national credit. Therefore, in 1816 Congress gave the second bank a twenty-year charter, on much the same terms as before but with about three and a half times more capital than the first and substantially greater control over state banks.

Building Better Connecting Links

The British wartime blockade and the westward movement had exposed a critical need for roads, improved waterways, and canals. When coastal shipping was reduced to a trickle by British offshore naval patrols, forcing American goods to move over inland routes, the roads and rivers were soon choked with traffic. The Democratic Republican program of improved internal communications was especially popular in the West; but more conservative Easterners, including President Madison, doubted the constitutionality of federal assistance for roads and canals—unless an amendment to the Constitution was adopted for the purpose.

John C. Calhoun of South Carolina introduced a "bonus bill" into Congress in 1816, empowering the use of federal funds for internal improvements. It cited the "General Welfare" clause of the Constitution as providing authority for such action. The bill was passed, but Madison vetoed it on his last day of office in 1817. Many of the states began digging canals and building roads themselves. Madison's successor, President James Monroe later agreed that the federal government did have the authority to fund such internal improvements, thus inaugurating the great canal and turnpike era of the 1820s.

MAP 5.7 New Boundaries Established by Treaties

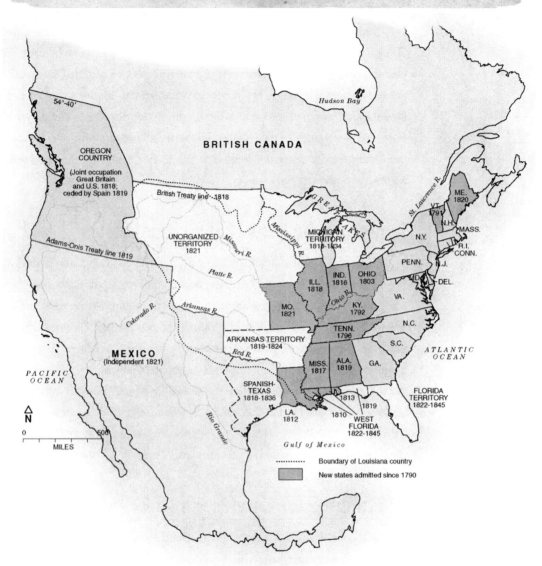

America Moves West

The Treaty of Ghent released a pent-up flood of migration toward the West. In 1790, a little more than 2 percent of the population lived west of the Appalachian mountain chain. In 1810, it was 14 percent; and in 1820, 23 percent, with the proportion still rising. The stream of migration moved west in two branches following the east-west roads and rivers—one from the South through Cumberland Gap into the Southwest, the other from the northeastern states through the Hudson River system into the Northwest Territory (Ohio River valley and Great Lakes area).

There were a number of reasons for this great westerly movement. One was America's soaring population, which almost doubled in the first two decades of the nineteenth century (5.3 million in 1800 to over 9.6 million in 1820). Another was the discharge of war veterans, accompanied by a rush of immigrants from Europe, who moved west to look for new opportunities. Still another was improved transportation. Whereas there had been few good routes to the West, the number of roads and turnpikes grew, while the Great Lakes-Ohio River water-way provided an excellent route for settlers to move into the Northwest.

The most compelling force behind the westward migration, however, was land—the rich, black bottomlands of the Southwest and the fertile forest and prairie lands of the Northwest. Governor William Henry Harrison of Indiana Territory persuaded Congress in 1800 to reduce the minimum requirement for the sale of land to a half section at two dollars an acre, with four years to pay. In 1804, Congress reduced the minimum to a quarter section, and in 1820 to eighty acres at a base price of $1.25 an acre. As prices were reduced, more people could afford cheap land in the West. This was the great magnet that drew settlers to move west.

▶ Shawnee Chief Tecumseh gathered followers of united Native Americans to resist and reject the white man and his ways. His alliance gathered strength up until his death at the Battle of Thames. With the death of their leader, so also died the united Natives' resistance. *Wikipedia photo*

Land Hunger Versus Native American Rights

In 1789, Congress had assured the Native Americans that their "land and property shall never be taken from them without their consent." In appropriating funds to pay certain tribes for land claims, Congress had tacitly recognized Native American ownership of certain lands in the west. At the time, however, George Washington had remarked that despite the government's good intentions, he doubted that "anything short of a Chinese wall" would ever keep land-hungry settlers out of Native American lands.

Washington would prove to be correct. The Native Americans, reported Thomas Forsyth from frontier country in 1818, "complain about the sale of their lands more than anything else." "The settler," he wrote, "tells the Indian that that land, with all that is on it, is his," and, treaty or not, "to go away or he will kill him etc." Such constant clashes between Native Americans and settlers had forced the natives to surrender much of their land; yet Congress' Native American policy was neither sufficiently definite nor amply aggressive to satisfy impatient settlers, traders, land speculators, or the Native Americans.

Resistance to Federal Policy

The possibility that the two groups might live together in "perpetual peace and affectionate attachment," as Jefferson had hoped, quickly faded. Particularly in the South, state governments resisted federal Native American policy, while on the frontier few paid attention to boundaries or treaties.

Conflicts between settlers and Native Americans became increasingly violent and frequent; and the emergence of a remarkable Native American leader, the Shawnee Chief Tecumseh, crystallized Native American resistance. Tecumseh was born in Ohio in 1768 during a period of conflict over land between Native Americans and white men. Tecumseh's childhood was marred by repeated violence between whites and natives, and five times between 1774 and 1782, young Tecumseh experienced raids by American soldiers that destroyed his homes and villages. Tecumseh's father and two brothers were killed in battles, and Tecumseh's mother left him in the care of an aunt at age ten and subsequently left Ohio for the South.

As an adult, Tecumseh rejected all American claims to Native American lands; and along with his medicine man brother, Tenskwatawa, who renamed himself "the Prophet" after having a near death experience accompanied by a "vision" in 1805, sought to unite all Native Americans against white encroachment. The Prophet urged natives to return to traditional ways and preached that white men were the children of the Evil Spirit and destined to be destroyed. Tecumseh and the Prophet organized a village along Tippecanoe Creek (Indiana), they called Prophetstown. They attracted thousands of followers to their message of spiritual regeneration, unity of the red man, and resistance to the white men. Tecumseh and the Prophet began to organize the tribes of the Northwest into a loose and effective alliance beginning as early as 1800. Tecumseh traveled throughout the Great Lakes area encouraging tribes to join a pan-Indian confederacy. In 1811, Tecumseh also traveled to the South, visiting tribes in Mississippi and Georgia and encouraging them to join his Native American confederacy and to resist white encroachment on their lands.

MAP 5.8 Map of Presidential Election of 1816

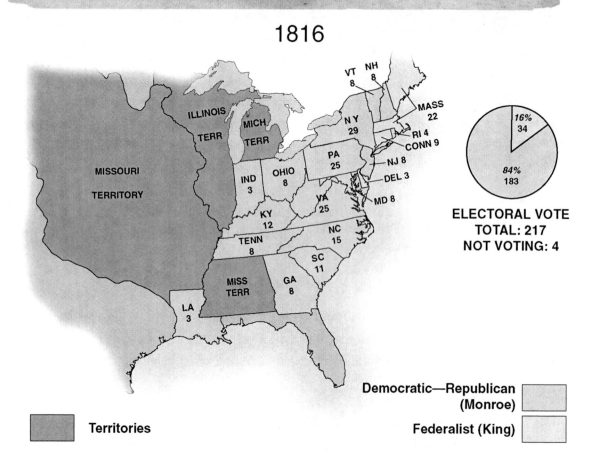

1816

ELECTORAL VOTE
TOTAL: 217
NOT VOTING: 4

Territories

Democratic—Republican
(Monroe)

Federalist (King)

This alliance was finally broken by General William Henry Harrison, governor of Indiana Territory, at the Battle of Tippecanoe in November 1811, while Tecumseh was absent. Tecumseh then joined the British army in Canada and reappeared with eight hundred of his allies in the War of 1812. He was killed at the Battle of the Thames in 1813, and with him died the efforts to organize and resist.

At the close of the War of 1812, with the British threat removed from the Northwest and the French from the Southwest, the federal government could at last proceed with its policy of assimilation or removal. After 1815 the political power of those who, such as Andrew Jackson, wanted to clear the Native American lands immediately. In 1817, the Senate Committee of Public Lands recommended exchanging public lands in the trans-Mississippi region for the Native American lands east of the Mississippi, but only with the consent of the tribes.

Very soon it became clear that the tribes were not willing to consent. The only remedy, John C. Calhoun wrote in 1820, was to place them "gradually under our authority and laws." "Our opinions, and not theirs," he continued, "ought to prevail, in measures intended for their civilization and happiness." In 1825, Secretary of War Calhoun and President Monroe presented Congress with a plan to remove the eastern tribes into the region beyond Missouri and Arkansas—a plan opposed by those who felt such an act to be a betrayal of the national honor. The opposition was inadequate, however; and by the 1830s, the tribes were removed—many to present-day Oklahoma and Kansas. By 1848, twelve new states had been created from what had once been Native Americans country.

Growing Pains

The Election of 1816

Madison selected James Monroe of Virginia for his successor in the presidential election of 1816; and although some Democratic Republicans favored William H. Crawford of Georgia, the party caucus agreed to choose the third Virginian in succession for the presidency. The Federalists, disheartened by the Hartford Convention, failed to nominate an official candidate, although in some states they supported Rufus King of New York. King received only the votes of Massachusetts, Connecticut, and Delaware; and Monroe won easily by 183 to 34 electoral votes.

A tall, distinguished, quiet man, James Monroe had studied law with Jefferson and was the older statesman's close friend and disciple. He drew his advisers impartially from different sections of the country, choosing John Quincy Adams (son of John and Abigail Adams) of Massachusetts as secretary of state, William H. Crawford of Georgia as secretary of the treasury, John C. Calhoun of South Carolina as secretary of war, and William Wirt of Maryland as attorney general. Henry Clay of Kentucky, the Speaker of the House, and others of the Western group dominated Congress, with Daniel Webster of New Hampshire and other New Englanders furnishing the opposition.

The "Era of Good Feelings"

Due to the virtually unchallenged Democratic Republican control of political life until 1824 and a robust economy following the war of 1812, these years were labeled "The Era of

Good Feelings." The Federalist Party was dead, and it seemed for a time that the two-party system itself was ending. There were no European wars of consequence during the period to involve the United States, nor any crucial issues in foreign affairs. President Monroe contributed to the "good feelings" in that he possessed a personality that seemed to bring people together. Monroe toured New England, the area that had been fraught with secessionist discontent during the War of 1812, and espoused a position of nationalism to enthusiastic crowds. Unfortunately, like most labels for any particular time period, the "Era of Good Feelings" is an oversimplification. Feelings were "good," but subterranean conflicts were soon to destroy the political peace.

Underneath the "good feelings," sectional interests and aspirations were growing and changing. The new Northwest, as it gained stature and stability, demanded greater influence in national policy. The South was increasingly tied to cotton, and New England, changing from an agricultural to a manufacturing economy, were both undergoing inner stresses that took outward political form. Specifically, these sectionalized rivalries were shortly to appear in the form of two issues—tariffs and slavery—that terminated the good feelings and produced new bad divisions.

Prosperity and Panic

After 1815, the national economy flourished with the resumption of normal trade that followed the War of 1812. The wartime boom continued, industry grew strong behind its tariff wall, and American ships carried goods and raw materials over the entire world. In spite of these economic positives, there were some economic problems lurking beneath the surface. American agricultural exports had been abnormally high due to the devastation in Europe caused by the Napoleonic Wars. As Europe recovered after 1815, American agricultural exports to Europe would be in decline by 1819. Furthermore, revolutions in Latin America had disrupted the flow of precious metals, the basis of the international money supply, from the mines of Latin America. American bankers attempted to remedy the currency crisis by issuing paper bank notes that were essentially used as currency. Many small Southern and Western banks had issued far too much paper money in excess of their capital reserves; and in 1818, the second Bank of the United States (which suffered from mismanagement itself) began to close out some of these "wildcat" banks by collecting their notes and demanding payment.

The purpose was fiscally sound—to force stricter control of banking practices—but the effect was disastrous. By early 1819, a number of shaky banks had already collapsed, and others were about to follow. In fact, the entire national banking system, which had not been sound for several years, was nearly ready to topple. In the Panic of 1819, the new nation experienced its first failure of the market economy. In 1819, more and more banks crashed, businesses failed, and a wave of losses and foreclosures swept over the nation, especially through the West. In Philadelphia, it is estimated that unemployment reached 75 percent and eighteen hundred people were imprisoned for debt. Other cities experienced similar problems, and the economy was no better in rural areas. Not understanding their plight, the Bank of the United States then became the nation's scapegoat. The consequences of the 1819 crisis continued to be felt until 1832, when President Andrew Jackson would do away with the Bank.

"Fire Bell in the Night"

Sectionalism and Slavery

As the tariff issue of 1816 had exposed some of the sectional economic tensions beneath the surface of "good feelings," so the Panic of 1819 revealed more. The second great issue, the question of the existence and extension of the institution of slavery, was also projected onto the national stage in 1819, coming before Congress that year because of Missouri's impending statehood.

Slavery had been a submerged issue in national politics since Washington's time. In 1793, during Washington's administration, Congress had passed a fugitive slave law and later forbade the further importation of slaves, beginning in 1808, without unduly arousing sen-

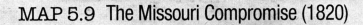

MAP 5.9 The Missouri Compromise (1820)

timent in North or South. Furthermore, there were many in both sections who hoped that the 1808 act might lead to the eventual extinction of the entire system. In the North, where slavery was unprofitable and unnecessary, all the states had legally abolished it by 1804 (as the Ordinance of 1787 already had abolished it from the Northwest Territory). Even in the South, antislavery societies actively campaigned against it. Still, after 1816 there was growing harshness in Northern and Southern discussions of the slavery question.

The most important area of disagreement over slavery concerned its economic relationship to Southern cotton culture. Eli Whitney's invention of the cotton gin (1793), the introduction of new strains of cotton, the expanding postwar textile market at home and abroad, and the opening to production of the rich "Black Belt" lands of the Southwest—all combined to make cotton an extremely profitable cash crop. Cotton was on the way to becoming "King" in the South and it required a large, steady supply of cheap, unskilled labor. Many believed that slaves best filled this need. At the same time, it was found that the delta lands of Louisiana and Mississippi were ideal for sugar cane, while tobacco culture moved from the coastal South into Kentucky and Tennessee. These too required much hand labor and were viewed as conducive to slavery.

In 1800, there were about 894,000 African Americans in the United States, almost wholly concentrated in the eastern South. In 1808, when the importation of slaves ceased, the figure stood at over one million; and by 1820, the South's investment in slaves was estimated to be nearly $500 million. It was perfectly clear that slavery and cotton provided the foundation of Southern society and would continue to do so.

The Missouri Compromise

Early in 1819, Missouri, carved out of the territory acquired in the Louisiana Purchase, counted sixty thousand persons and applied for entry to the Union as a slave state. The application probably would have passed but James Tallmadge, Jr., of New York introduced in the House an amendment requiring the gradual abolition of slavery in the new state as a condition of its admission. This amendment immediately exposed the heart of the issue.

As the nation moved west, the tendency had been to maintain a rough balance of power between slave- and free-state blocs in Washington. The North and Northwest, however, had gained a million more persons than the South and Southwest since the 1790 census, thereby proportionately increasing their congressional representation. The slave states were already outvoted in the House; only in the Senate were the sections equally represented, a situation that might not continue for long.

Of the original thirteen colonies, seven became free states and six slave states. Between 1791 and 1819, four more free states were admitted and five slave. Thus, when Missouri applied for entrance to the Union in 1819, the balance was even, and Tallmadge's amendment involved far more than Missouri's admission alone.

Slavery was already barred from the Northwest Territory but not from those lands acquired through the Louisiana Purchase. If Missouri and all other states subsequently admitted from the Louisiana Purchase lands were admitted as slave states, the balance of federal political power would be tipped toward the South and slavery. If they were to be free states, their entry favored the North and emancipation.

At stake lay political control, present and future, of the Union. "It is political power that the northern folk are in pursuit of," Judge Charles Tait of Alabama wrote to a friend concerning the Missouri question, "and if they succeed, the management of the Gen'l Gov't will pass into their hands with all its power and patronage." Most Northerners were not at this time opposed to slavery on moral grounds; but they believed that the Three-fifths Compromise gave southern states disproportionate strength in Congress since they could count three out of five of their growing slave population for purposes of representation in the U.S. House of Representatives. Thus, Northerners opposed the admittance of Missouri as a slave state for the advantage it would give to Southerners in Congress.

Nevertheless, Tallmadge's bill finally passed the House in February, after hot and protracted debate. Congress adjourned, however, until December; and during the interval Maine, long attached to Massachusetts, applied for statehood. Sensing compromise, the Senate originated a bill accepting Maine as a free state and Missouri as slave, thereby preserving the balance. The House accepted it, but added a proviso that slavery be banned forever from the Louisiana Purchase lands above the line of 36° 30' or Missouri's Southern border.

The bill was passed and signed in March 1820; but this so-called Missouri Compromise merely delayed the ultimate confrontation of the problem of slavery. The "momentous question," wrote Jefferson from Monticello, "like a fire-bell in the night, awakened me and filled me with terror." The debates over Missouri sparked the first protracted public discussion of the contradiction between the ideals expressed in the *Declaration of Independence* and the institution of slavery—thus foreshadowing the decades of sectional conflict to come, and hence, the reason for the alarm of the aging Jefferson.

Evolving a Foreign Policy

Catching Up on Old Problems

Following the Treaty of Ghent, the United States and Britain gradually worked out their differences one by one. In 1815, the U.S. and England signed a commercial convention that established a reciprocity agreement in trade. Nevertheless, the U.S. and England still distrusted each other, and each began fortifying its possessions on the Great Lakes. The Rush-Bagehot Agreement of 1817 demilitarized the Great Lakes; however, both countries retained land fortifications, and the U.S.-Canadian border remained a guarded border until 1871. The next year, the Convention of 1818 gave U.S. nationals fishing rights off the coasts of Labrador and Newfoundland, established the northern boundary of the Louisiana Purchase at the forty-ninth parallel, and left the Oregon country, which both claimed, under joint occupation for ten years.

America and Spain, too, settled some old disputes. The United States took one section of Florida (West Florida) from Spain during the War of 1812, and Secretary of State John Quincy Adams continued negotiations for the rest of the territory. His diplomacy faltered, however, due to Florida's Seminoles, who kept up raids (with Spanish and British assistance) on the Georgia border. In 1818 General Andrew Jackson raised an army and marched into Florida, claiming that he had received a letter from President Monroe authorizing the invasion. Mon-

MAP 5.10 Population Density (1820)

Under 2 inhabitants per square mile

2 to 18 inhabitants per square mile

18 to 45 inhabitants per square mile

45 and over inhabitants per square mile

roe denied that he had given his approval. Jackson claimed that he burned the letter, so any evidence that Monroe ordered the invasion was destroyed, if it existed. Jackson led three thousand Americans and two thousand Native American allies into Florida, captured two Spanish forts, and executed two suspected British agents in what is known as the First Seminole War.

Americans were divided over Jackson's actions. Secretary of War John C. Calhoun called for Jackson's court martial since Jackson had acted without authority from Calhoun's War Department. Congressman Henry Clay introduced a motion of Censure in Congress, which failed to pass. Meanwhile, local governments in New York and Philadelphia praised Jackson's actions.

Britain viewed Jackson's invasion as a violation of international law and demanded an explanation for the execution of two British citizens. Jackson replied that "the execution of these two unprincipled villains will prove an awful example to the world and convince the government of Great Britain that certain though slow retribution awaits those unchristian wretches who, by false promises, delude and excite a Native American tribe to all the horrid deeds of savage war." The British were particularly unimpressed with Jackson's explanation. Yet they decided not to press the issue because they believed Jackson's principle that a sovereign nation could invade its neighbor if that neighbor could not control its border. That principle could become useful to them in the future should they experience border problems with the United States from Canada.

John Quincy Adams argued that Jackson's invasion was an act of self-defense against the chaos that Spain had been unable to control and unable to prevent from spilling over into the U.S. Adams announced an ultimatum to Spanish minister Luis de Onís in October, 1818: Maintain order in the Floridas or cede them to the U.S.

▶ John Quincy Adams *Wikipedia photo*

The Spanish posts captured by Jackson were quickly returned to Spain; but Jackson's action helped precipitate a treaty, signed by Adams and Spanish minister Luis de Onís in February 1819, by which Spain renounced its claims to West Florida and ceded East Florida to the United States. Spain, at the time, had greater problems than Florida, with insurrections erupting all over Latin America. It lacked the military resources to force the U.S. to back away from its ambitions in Florida. That being the case, the Spanish opted to give up Florida in exchange for favorable boundaries in the West and a secure claim to Texas. In the Adams-Onís Treaty, the Spanish also agreed to a boundary line stretching across the continent to the Pacific, redefining the Louisiana Purchase line, and dividing the old Southwest from Spanish Mexico. In addition, the Spanish gave up their somewhat vague claims to Oregon in return for a clear title to Texas, where the U.S. relinquished any claims. The U.S. also assumed $5 million worth of claims by U.S. citizens against Spain.

The Monroe Doctrine

Reduced to a third-rate power and racked by internal dissension, Spain was losing its empire in Central and South America. Beginning in 1807, its colonies revolted one after another until, by 1821, nearly all had declared themselves independent republics. By 1830, all of Latin America except Cuba and Puerto Rico had gained independence. Sympathetic to such revolutions and alert to opportunities for new markets, the United States waited until its treaty with Spain was accepted and then recognized these republics early in 1822.

Spain, of course, continued to consider the new Latin American nations simply as Spanish colonies in rebellion. In Europe, meanwhile, Austria, Prussia, Russia, and France had formed an alliance and "congress system" for the purpose of crushing popular revolutions wherever they occurred. The United States feared that the alliance would decide to send an army to restore Spain's lost colonies, making royal Catholic Spain once more a power in the New World. The alliance was not the only threat to the Americas. Russia had already established trading posts in California, and in 1821, Czar Alexander's edict claimed part of the Oregon country for Alaska and barred foreign ships from a large area of the northwest Pacific.

The British, who had no desire to see Spain regain its empire or Russia expand its colonial holdings, offered to join with the United States in a declaration against any interference in the Americas on the part of the alliance; but Secretary of State John Quincy Adams convinced President Monroe and the cabinet that the United States should handle the problem alone. For one thing, Adams did not want his country, he said, to "come in as a cockboat in the wake of the British man-of-war." Furthermore, Adams and others recognized the potential value of the new Latin American republics as markets. Lastly, no one wanted to write off the possibility of American expansion southward if one or more of the new republics asked to be annexed to the United States.

President Monroe, in his annual message to Congress on December 2, 1823, therefore stated the official attitude of the United States on the issue. The Monroe Doctrine, as it came to be called, rested on two main principles—non-colonization and non-intervention.

Concerning the first, Monroe stated that any portions of the Americas were "henceforth not to be considered as subjects for future colonization by any European power." In regard to the second, he drew a sharp line of political demarcation between Europe and America. "The political system of the allied powers is essentially different ... from that of America," he said. "We should consider any attempt to extend their system to any portion of this hemisphere as dangerous to our peace and safety." At the same time, Monroe promised that the United States would not attempt to interfere with the internal affairs of European nations or with any of their existing colonies such as Cuba.

These ideas had been implicit in all American foreign policy since Washington's Farewell Address, but Monroe's message restated, in precise terms, the classic American principles of hemispheric separation and avoidance of foreign entanglements that had motivated the diplomacy of his predecessors. His enunciation of American domination over half the globe appeared "arrogant" and "haughty" to European statesmen. Nor were the Latin American republics particularly pleased with such doubtful protection. What both knew, however, whether Monroe or the American public cared to admit it, was that it was the British navy and not the Monroe Doctrine that barred European expansion into the Americas.

The Triumph of Isolation

The Monroe Doctrine simply articulated what Americans had believed since the beginnings of their foreign policy—that there were two worlds, old and new, contrasted and separate. The

Old World of England and Europe seemed to Americans regressive, corrupted, and plagued by wars and ancient hatreds. The New World was thought to be democratic, free, progressive, and hopeful. The objective of the United States, reflecting these attitudes, was to keep these worlds apart, lest the "taint" of the old besmirch the "fresh future" of the new.

The first generation of American statesmen, from Washington to Monroe, unanimously insisted that the United States should, whenever possible, avoid entanglements in Old World politics or problems. At the same time, it was perfectly clear to them that the United States could not exist without European trade. In addition, since the major European powers still held territorial possessions in the New World, it would be extremely difficult to avoid some sort of implication in their almost continuous wars. The foreign policy of every president from Washington to John Quincy Adams was shaped by this constant tension between the dream of isolation and the reality of involvement. Still, there were certain accepted positions on foreign affairs that the United States, throughout the period, believed it must maintain—freedom of the seas, freedom of trade, neutrality in European disputes, national integrity, and, above all others, the promotion of the cause of liberty throughout the world. In practice, American diplomats found it difficult to work out solutions within this somewhat rigid framework. Did maintenance of freedom of the seas, for example, justify involvement in a European war? Would American assistance to other nations' revolutions justify entanglement in European affairs, even for the best of motives? Should American policy, when it coincided with that of a European power, be pursued jointly? Ought the United States to assume responsibility for internal affairs of democracy in other American republics?

In attempting to answer these and similar questions, the makers of American foreign policy during the early years of the Republic followed rather closely the principles laid down by Washington and the first generation. Fortunately for them, Europe was so preoccupied with its own power conflicts that American diplomacy had the time to temporize and the room to make a few mistakes. Still, every statement about foreign affairs in the early decades of the nineteenth century derived from the American assumption that the United States was detached from Europe and must remain so; always free to pursue its special ends.

Chapter Review ▶ ▶ ▶

Summary

In 1800 Thomas Jefferson was elected President, representing a shift from the Northern and urban based Federalists to Jefferson's more Southern and agrarian Democratic Republicans. Jefferson also represented the expansion of Democracy to common men and a shift to a more states' rights orientation, though he would also expand the power of the national government as President, one of Jefferson's many contradictions.

Almost immediately, Jefferson was confronted with a foreign policy challenge from the Barbary Pirates, who increased the bounty they charged merchant ships to operate in the Mediterranean. Jefferson, who had opposed a large military, sent the U.S. Navy to the Mediterranean to defeat the Pirates, but the U.S. would continue paying bounties until 1815. Simultaneously, Jefferson, who had opposed a national debt, borrowed $15 million from Baring Brothers of London to purchase Louisiana from France. Jefferson had also argued for a strict interpretation of the Constitution that would not allow the government to do things not specifically stated in the Constitution, yet the Constitution did not authorize the President to purchase territory.

Jefferson then commissioned the Lewis and Clark expedition to explore Louisiana, departing from Missouri in 1804, and the successful expedition reached the Pacific coast at Oregon and then returned to Missouri with samples of exotic flora and fauna in 1806.

Domestically, Jefferson did battle with the federalist Supreme Court under Chief Justice John Marshall with the result that the Court claimed for itself the power of Judicial Review in *Marbury v. Madison* in 1803. Jefferson attempted to rid the Courts of federalist judges through closing the Court and impeaching judges, but Marshall would stay on the Court until 1835, exerting great influence on American Constitutional Law.

The Napoleonic Wars in Europe beginning in 1803 resulted in disruption of American trade by both England and France and eventually in the War of 1812 with England over American sovereignty rights and freedom of the Seas. President James Madison, elected in 1808, waged the War with the British primarily to end the British practice of impressments after embargoes against the English had not achieved the desired results. The war itself resulted in a British invasion of America and the burning of the American Capitol, but a decisive victory by the Americans at Plattsburgh caused the British to seek a negotiated peace to the costly war. The Treaty of Ghent ended the war on the principle of "status quo antebellum" and the British did not end impressments, but America had proven that Europeans could tread on American sovereignty only at a price.

The War of 1812 was followed by an "Era of Good Feelings" where America was at peace and the economy was robust under popular President James Monroe. The "good feelings" would be shattered, however, by a major economic panic in 1819 followed by a slavery dispute the next year. In the Compromise of 1820, viewed as the "final solution" to slavery, Missouri was admitted as a slave state, but slavery was to be prohibited west of Missouri and north of Missouri's southern border. Meanwhile, Native Americans in the Southeastern United States were slated for removal to Indian Territory in the West (Oklahoma).

Summary (cont'd)

Finally, all of Latin America would revolt against Spain in the second decade of the nineteenth century. Spain ceded Florida to the U.S. in 1819 a year after an Andrew Jackson invasion with the stipulation that the U.S. would give up any future claims to Texas. By 1823, all of Latin America would achieve independence from Spain, prompting James Monroe to declare that the Western Hemisphere was now closed to European colonization and that European interference in the Western Hemisphere would be viewed as unfriendly toward the U.S. In return, the U.S. would stay out of European affairs.

Chronological Time Line

1800	Thomas Jefferson is elected President in what he called the "Revolution of 1800"
1801	France regains possession of Louisiana
1802	Slave revolt on Saint Dominique leads to the death of 24,000 French troops.
1803	Jefferson sends the U.S. Navy to confront the Barbary Pirates.
1803	The U.S. purchases Louisiana from France for $15 million
1803	The U.S. Supreme Court claims Judicial Review in *Marbury v. Madison.*
1803	A group of federalists known as the Essex Junto attempt to persuade New England states to secede.
1803	War between England and France under Napoleon causes England to renew impressments of American sailors
1804	Aaron Burr kills Alexander Hamilton in a duel.
1804	Thomas Jefferson is reelected President
1804–1805	House Impeaches Supreme Court Justice Samuel Chase, but the Senate does not convict.
1804–1806	Lewis and Clark expedition reaches the Pacific and returns to Missouri
1805	Treaty with Barbary Pirates ends hostilities and returns bounties paid to Pirates to the previous lower level.
1806	Aaron Burr's failed attempt to conquer New Orleans.

Chapter Review (cont'd) ▶ ▶ ▶

Time Line (cont'd)

1806	British Orders in Council effectively blockade Europe
1807	Jefferson recalls the navy from the Mediterranean due to antagonism with Britain
1807	*USS Chesapeake* is fired upon by *HMS Leopard.*
1807	Embargo Act
1808	James Madison elected President
1809	Embargo Act lifted
1809	Non-Intercourse Act and Macon's Bill #2
1811	Chief Tecumseh is defeated at the Battle of Tippecanoe
1812	Congress declares war on England on June 18 and War of 1812 begins.
1814	British burn Washington D.C.
1814	Francis Scott Key pens National Anthem based on events at Fort McHenry
1814	Treaty of Ghent signed December 24 officially ends War of 1812
1815	Americans under Andrew Jackson defeat the British in the Battle of New Orleans in January after the signing of the Treaty of Ghent.
1815	U.S. Navy with help from European navies defeats Barbary Pirates and ends bounties.
1815	Napoleon's final defeat at Waterloo.
1815	Congress of Vienna
1815–1819	Era of Good Feelings
1816	James Monroe elected President
1818	Andrew Jackson invades Florida in First Seminole War
1819	Transcontinental Treaty with Spain
1819	Panic of 1819

Time Line (cont'd)

1820   Missouri Compromise

1823   James Monroe enunciates the Monroe Doctrine

Key Terms

Jeffersonian Democracy: Democracy expanded to common men

Sally Hemmings: Jefferson's slave mistress with whom he fathered children.

Virginia Statute on Religious Liberty: 1786 Statute written by Thomas Jefferson that separated Church and State in Virginia

The Barbary Wars: Wars between the U.S. and Arab-Muslim Pirates on the Mediterranean in the early nineteenth century.

Stephen Decatur: America's patriotic hero of the War with the Barbary Pirates.

The Louisiana Purchase: The land between the Mississippi River and the Rocky Mountains purchased by the United States from France in 1803.

Lewis and Clark Expedition: Expedition from Missouri to the Pacific led by Meriwether Lewis and William Clark 1804-1806

Charbonneau and Sacajawea: French Trader and his Native American wife that acted as interpreters for Lewis and Clark.

The "war on the judiciary": Jefferson's conflict with the Federalist Supreme Court of John Marshall.

Marbury v. Madison: Case where the Supreme Court asserted its right to Judicial Review

Chief Justice John Marshall: Chief Justice of the United States from 1801-1835

The "Essex Junto": A group of federalists that attempted to persuade the New England states to secede

Aaron Burr: Running mate of Thomas Jefferson in 1800, slayer of Alexander Hamilton in 1804, and leader of insurrection conspiracy in New Orleans in 1806

Twelfth Amendment: Required that the Vice President would be the top vote recipient for Vice President.

Doctrine of the Broken Voyage: If ships paid a duty in the port of a third country, the ship's cargo changed its status to that of the third country.

Re-Export Business: Goods brought into an American port from a foreign port, and then "re-exported" from the American port to a different foreign port after paying a duty.

Orders in Council: Orders of the English King's Privy Council proclaiming a blockade of Europe.

U.S.S. Chesapeake: Navy ship fired upon by the *HMS Leopard.*

The Embargo of 1807-08: An Act of Congress placing an embargo on Europe

Chapter Review (cont'd) ▶ ▶ ▶

Key Terms (cont'd)

Non-Intercourse Act 1809: Act of Congress opening trade to all countries except England and France, but providing that trade would be open with either if they would recognize American rights at sea.

Impressment: The British practice of forcing British citizens into service in the Royal Navy.

James Madison: Secretary of State under Thomas Jefferson and Fourth President of the United States.

The War of 1812: War with England 1812-1815 essentially over American sovereignty rights and freedom of the seas.

General William Hull: Tricked by the British at Detroit, surrendered without a shot.

Captain Oliver Perry: American ship Captain that defeated the British navy on the Great Lakes.

U.S.S. Constitution: American frigate known as "Old Ironsides" that defeated the British frigate *Guerriere*.

Plattsburgh: Battle in the Lake Champlain Valley won by the Americans that induced the British into a negotiated settlement to the War of 1812

Francis Scott Key: Author of the National Anthem.

The Treaty of Ghent: Treaty with England in Ghent, Belgium that officially ended the War of 1812.

The Hartford Convention: Meeting of New England federalists opposed to the War of 1812, citing states' rights

The Congress of Vienna: Meeting of European Countries at the conclusion of the Napoleonic Wars that brought lasting peace in Europe.

James Monroe: Fifth President of the United States elected in 1816

Tecumseh: Native American Chief that led a rebellion in the Ohio Valley in 1811.

Tippecanoe: Battle where Native Americans are defeated in the Ohio Valley

"Indian removal": The U.S. policy of removing Native American tribes from the Southeastern United States to Indian Territory (Oklahoma)

The "Era of Good Feelings": The period following the War of 1812 between 1815 and 1819 where the country experienced robust economic growth and peace at home and abroad.

Panic of 1819: Economic Depression and financial collapse.

The Missouri Compromise: Viewed as the "final solution" to the slavery dispute, Missouri was admitted as a slave state, but no slavery would be permitted west of Missouri and North of Missouri's southern border.

The Convention of 1818: Treaty with England granted U.S. nationals fishing rights off the coasts of Labrador and Newfoundland, established the northern boundary of the Louisiana Purchase at the 49th parallel, and left the Oregon country, which both claimed, under joint occupation for ten years.

The Adams-Onis Treaty: Also known as the Transcontinental Treaty with Spain, the U.S. gained East and West Florida in exchange for renunciation of any claims to Texas

The Monroe Doctrine: Enunciated by James Monroe, the U.S. would view any European interference in the Western Hemisphere as unfriendly to the U.S. and the U.S. would stay out of European affairs.

Sources Consulted

John Ashworth, *'Agrarians and Aristocrats': Party Political Ideology in the United States, 1837–1846* (1983).

Lance Banning, *The Jeffersonian Persuasion: Evolution of a Party Ideology* (1980).

Donald R. Hickey, *The War of 1812: A Forgotten Conflict* (1989).

Daniel Walker Howe, *The Political Culture of the American Whigs* (1979).

Lawrence Kaplan, *"Entangling Alliances with None": American Foreign Policy in the Age of Jefferson* (1987).

Drew R. McCoy, *The Elusive Republic: Political Economy in Jeffersonian America* (1980).

Peter Onuf, *Jefferson's Empire: The Language of American Nationhood* (2001).

Robert V. Remini, *The Battle of New Orleans: Andrew Jackson and America's First Military Victory* (2001).

6 American Culture Comes of Age

Outline

Technology

The Excitement of Progress

In the half-century preceding 1830, the United States had made great progress in establishing itself as a viable nation. The victory at Yorktown, the Constitution, the Bill of Rights, the Louisiana Purchase, the Battle of New Orleans, the Missouri Compromise, and the Monroe Doctrine were landmarks passed within the memory of many citizens living in 1830. The increase in the population, the growth of the national domain, and the development of cities and industries were only a few of the reasons for Americans' sense of gratification.

At the close of the Jacksonian Era, only about six decades had elapsed since the eventful months of ratification of the Constitution. Yet distinctive intellectual, artistic, and scientific progress had been made, especially during the most recent twenty years. Authors, artists, and scientists already were giving eloquent and sustained evidence of the richness of thought and variety of American life. Ordinary Americans were participating in the growth of their fledgling country, and they and their descendants reaped the benefits.

Technological Change and Economic Development

Such heady developments should not obscure the fact that the majority of Americans lived simple lives. In the decades before the Civil War, most of them still were farmers and most farms were small. What happened to them from dawn to dusk was changing.

Since the arrival of Europeans in the New World, the amount of physical labor that had been required to convert unimproved land to cultivated fields had limited agricultural productivity. The agriculturalists of the eastern United States had spent countless hours swinging axes against trees, removing stumps, and digging rocks out of their fields. In 1813, Richard B. Chenaworth developed a cast iron plow made in three separate pieces, which made possible the replacement of broken parts. The plow was used with great success in the east. As Americans opened land further west geographical changes were dramatic. There was less rainfall, fewer trees, and the soil was more demanding. The heavy western soils would stick to the cast-iron plow, which then proved too brittle to break the ground of the western prairies. In 1837, John Deere patented a steel plow that provided the solution to breaking the western land.

In 1834, Cyrus McCormick patented the mechanical reaper, which greatly reduced the labor involved in harvesting grain. Prior to McCormick's invention, farmers still cut grain by hand—swinging cradles that cut swathes through the grain. The cut grain then was gathered in sheaves and hauled away for threshing. McCormick's mechanized reaper greatly increased agricultural production. More food and fiber could be produced by the same amount of land with the combination of the cast-iron plow, the steel plow, and the mechanical reaper. This led many farmers to acquire and cultivate more soil. It also meant that increasing numbers of the small farmers, no longer agriculturally essential, would be free to move to cities where— mainly in the Northeast—mills and factories were springing up.

No invention wrought more changes in everyday living than the steam engine, invented by Oliver Evans in 1802. Prior to the steam engine, it was virtually impossible for anyone to build a factory away from a river because factories were powered by water wheels and an interconnected system of wheels and belts, all connected to the water wheel. The steam engine provided a power source that allowed the construction of factories in locations never before possible. Machines found their way into diverse settings, most importantly the new factories that were located in towns and small cities in the Eastern United States, thereby transforming once-rural people into urbanized workers with year-around income. Steam-propelled riverboats provided cheap, smooth transportation. They speeded up the expansion of river cities like Cincinnati and St. Louis. Railways, from the 1830s and 1840s on, were to have a similar impact on inland communities. One of the most amazing changes was the coming together of ship and rail traffic, notably at a spot where the small village of Chicago was incorporated in 1837.

In 1830, the first steam locomotive (a European invention) built in America was that of Peter Cooper. By 1850, nine thousand miles of rail had been laid, most of it on the eastern

▶ In 1830, the first steam locomotive was built in America. By 1860, thirty thousand miles of rail had been laid— more miles of track than in all the rest of the world combined. *Wikipedia photo*

seaboard. By 1860, thirty thousand miles of rail had been laid—more miles of track than in all the rest of the world combined.

Railroads had tremendous spin-offs into the American economy at large. Trains traveling at twenty miles per hour allowed farmers in far-flung locations to get their produce to market before it spoiled. This allowed true agricultural specialization as different areas of the country could import their agricultural products rather than grow their own. In addition, railroads stimulated western movement and the development of frontier towns as water stops for the trains. The production of iron, steel, coal, and timber began to increase in order to meet the needs of the trains. Railroads also aided in the development of the telegraph industry. Telegraph lines were built alongside railroad tracks so that the railroad men could relay problems with the tracks or anything else from any location.

The railroads were essentially financed by federal land grants to private railroad corporations. The federal government granted the railroads up to six square miles of land for every mile of track laid by the railroad corporation. The railroads then sold their land to settlers for profits, thus both financing the railroad operation and spurring settlement of the American West. By 1860, Congress had granted the railroads twenty million acres of federal land, thus providing great wealth to the railroads that would last for decades.

The railroads also stimulated the American banking system since the building of the railroads required large amounts of capital. The number of state chartered banks in the U.S. at the close of the War of 1812 was less than one hundred, but by 1830 there were over three hundred. Banks stimulated the economy by making loans to railroads, manufacturers, and merchants—thus expanding the money supply and enabling the expansion of America's rail, manufacturing, and commerce.

▶ The invention of the telegraph (a replica of the first telegraph is shown here) enabled instantaneous communication over long distances for the first time in human history. *AP Wide World Photo*

Other scientific thought and technological innovation had similar economic and social impacts. Samuel F. B. Morse, an admirable portrait painter, invented the telegraph and sent his first message in 1844. For the first time in human history, communication over long distances became instantaneous. Charles Goodyear discovered the process known as the vulcanization of rubber, which made rubber much more useful by preventing it from sticking and melting in hot weather. Goodyear's process made possible the manufacture of a wide array of rubber products, most notably the overshoe. From the mind and skill of Samuel Colt came the first practical firearm with a revolving chamber, and Elias Howe is given credit for the first sewing machine. Indeed, the sewing machine reminds us that during this period there were countless other inventions of a more humble nature that changed the nature of housework, such as the first appearance of the cast iron stove for cooking, which replaced cooking over an open hearth.

In Georgia and New England, a medical breakthrough with the discovery of anesthesia would ease the suffering of countless medical and dental patients. Crawford Long, in 1842, was the first to administer ether during surgery. Ether reduced both pain and the risk of patients going into shock during surgery. William Beaumont, an American army doctor on the Michigan frontier, was the first student of gastric digestion. Oliver Wendell Holmes, the Massachusetts poet-physician, saved the lives of countless mothers and babies by demonstrating that antiseptics could prevent puerperal ("child-bed") fever.

With the combination of technological change, growth of industrial production, and improved transportation, more and more goods that previously had been produced at home began to be commercially available, including soap, textiles, and clothing. This, in turn, meant that the women who had traditionally produced such products could now fill their days with other activities: they had more time to read, for example, and more time for needlework of an aesthetic nature. They also had more time to join a variety of new organizations—in some cases church-affiliated organizations, and in other cases associations of an explicitly reformist nature.

The Role of Reformers

American Women

Most women spent their lives at tedious, repetitive labor, whether in frontier cabins, isolated farmhouses, or urban dwellings—although their work was becoming somewhat lightened by the availability of new products. Some left farms and villages to tend machines in such new "mill towns" as Lowell and Lawrence, Massachusetts, where the primary employment in the towns consisted of textile mills. Recently arrived immigrant girls took menial jobs—often as domestic servants—in Atlantic seaboard cities and interior communities.

Certain legal restrictions on women carried over from earlier periods into the Jacksonian Era and even into the twentieth century. Women could not vote, and property rights for married women were circumscribed at best. Laws often prevented wives from controlling their own inheritances. With rare exceptions, women, no matter how talented or ambitious, found themselves excluded from most professions. Yet in these years, amid the legal and social limitations, women began to lay the groundwork for considerable change.

The 1820s, 1830s, and 1840s marked the start of major reforms, many of them spearheaded by women. Fundamental to these efforts was the improved education being extended to girls in hundreds of private female academies that emerged all over the United States. Beginning in the 1930s, states began to open teacher-training academies known as "normal schools," exclusively for female students. Many of the noteworthy female reformers—women's rights advocate Elizabeth Cady Stanton being the prime example—had attended one of the new academies.

Oberlin College in Ohio began admitting white women and African American men in 1851 and graduated its first women in 1855. No other colleges admitted women until after the Civil War. However, there were several private "female seminaries" established to provide college-equivalent education to women. Emma Willard, who founded Troy Seminary in New York in 1821, and Mary Lyon, who founded Mount Holyoke in Massachusetts in 1837, were the two most well-known pioneer educators. Mention should also be made of Catherine Beecher, sister of the novelist Harriet Beecher Stowe, who founded the Harford Seminary in Connecticut. Harriet Beecher Stowe, who taught at the Hartford Seminary, argued that women are better teachers than men. In the words of Stowe, "If men have more knowledge, they have less talent at communicating it. Nor have they the patience, the long-suffering, and gentleness necessary to superintend the formation of character."

Women also became involved in the abolitionist movement. Sarah and Angelina Grimké, sisters from a prominent South Carolina family, were among the many that crusaded in the North for the abolition of slavery—thereby challenging the taboo against respectable women speaking in public. The Grimkés were among the first, but many other courageous women, African American and white, soon followed. Dorothea Dix was another earnest friend of the unfortunates. Many women were widely known as writers and editors. It was an augury of the future when Elizabeth Blackwell entered medical school in the 1840s, becoming the first woman to receive an M.D. degree in 1849.

Above all, these years were distinguished by the first appearance of a women's suffrage movement, launched at a gathering in Seneca Falls, New York in 1848. The two women who called the meeting, Elizabeth Cady Stanton and Lucretia Mott, had first met in 1840 at an anti-slavery convention in London. There they had been denied the right of full participation on account of their sex. This slight infuriated both women and many others. When they met again in the upstate New York town, they decided to call a meeting for a week in Seneca Falls where they inaugurated what became a revolution in gender mores. Stanton drew up a document, modeled on the *Declaration of Independence,* to present to the approximately three hundred people who attended the meeting. In this "Declaration of Sentiments" she announced that "All men *and women* are created equal" and cited eighteen specific injuries that women suffered at the hands of men (as Jefferson had adduced evidence against George III), including the denial of access to the professions and to higher education. Stanton stated, "The history of mankind is a history of repeated injuries and usurpations on the part of man toward woman, having in direct object the establishment of an absolute tyranny over her." Stanton added that through the doctrine of male supremacy men had "endeavored in every way they could to destroy her confidence in her own powers, to lessen her self-respect, and to make her willing to lead a dependent and abject life." Stanton demanded that women be granted all the rights and privileges that men have as U.S. citizens, including—most radical of all—the vote, an act which was then seen as belonging entirely to "the male sphere."

The great abolitionist, Frederick Douglass, was in attendance and spoke on behalf of women's suffrage, which the delegates voted to support after a lively debate. Many decades passed before suffrage was attained, but a few of the other items on the list, such as a married woman's right to control her own property, began to be redressed in that era. From 1848 forward, through the perseverance of many, a network of women's rights advocates emerged. Over twenty other women's rights conventions would be assembled before the Civil War, each also calling for the franchise. It was not yet a social movement, and its progress would be interrupted by the Civil War. However, it was the beginning.

Fighting Ills, Woes, and Evils

That so much humanitarian reform was taking place in mid-nineteenth century owed much to religious changes. In brief, the older emphasis on original sin and human depravity was giving way to a more optimistic set of beliefs in human possibility, doctrines that began appearing in many sectors of American Protestantism. The theory and practice of democracy, when carried to their logical conclusions, likewise led humanitarians to devote days, years, and even lifetimes to helping unfortunates. Numerous reformers were motivated also by the desire to impose order on the fast-changing society of which they were a part. Finally, we should consider the influence of the Romantic Movement, with its emphasis on the individual's insights, intuitions, and personal responsibilities.

Just as not everyone was politically active, the number of steadfast participants in some of these reforms was small; however, enough Americans believed in human perfectibility to make reform a key characteristic of this period.

The zeal of reformers, both men and women, found many targets in the very nation where so many opportunities for improvement and advancement beckoned. The number of people arriving from Europe, particularly from the 1840s on, was larger than America could neatly accommodate. Many poor and uneducated immigrants crowded into port cities where they received low wages for long hours and lived in squalor in what came to be known as slums.

In 1824–1854, the attempts to cope with such social problems were limited and, on the whole, were unsuccessful. Most of the effort to improve the lot of urban workers came from the relatively weak labor unions, but the unions consisted mainly of skilled artisans. They were interested principally in bettering their own lot, not that of the unskilled newcomers. In general, the chief gain for both groups stemmed from workers' demands for free public schools, which were established in New York in 1832. Philadelphia followed two years later.

Wikipedia photo

Both urban and rural Americans ate too much fat meat, too many fried foods, and too few fruits and vegetables. Reformers such as Sylvester Graham, for whom Graham bread and Graham crackers were named, did their best to promote dietary change. In the 1830s, Graham argued that the keys to better health could be found through proper diet, exercise, and hygiene.

▶ Dorothea Lynde Dix: Humanitarian

by James M. McPherson

▶ Dorothea Lynde Dix *Library of Congress*

The remarkable career of Dorothea Lynda Dix illustrates several important themes in early and mid-nineteenth century America: the upswelling of humanitarian reform; the changing role of women; the development of modern institutions for deviant members of society; the growth of more humane and scientific concepts of "insanity." She is known primarily as a pioneer in the field of mental health. Although her achievements were built on the foundation of earlier reforms, her single-minded dedication to improving conditions for people suffering from mental illness or retardation was the most important agency of progress in this field.

Dorothea Dix was born on April 4, 1802, in the frontier village of Hampden, Maine (then part of Massachusetts). From her Puritan forebears she gained an intense commitment to education, duty, hard work, and self-discipline. But these Protestant Ethic values seem to have skipped her improvident father from whose chaotic household Dorothea escaped at the age of twelve to live in Boston with her stern but supportive grandmother, the widow of a successful physician and businessman.

At the age of nineteen, Dorothea opened a grammar school for girls in Boston, the type of school then known as a "dame school." For the next twenty years she alternated between teaching and periods of recovery from incipient tuberculosis. Much influenced by the great Unitarian clergyman William Ellery Channing, Dorothea became a Unitarian and published several undistinguished books of a devotional and poetic nature.

Approaching her fortieth year, Dix seemed headed for a typically genteel but sterile existence as a New England spinster. However, an incident in March 1841 changed her life and launched her career as a reformer. Visiting an East Cambridge jail to teach a Sunday school class for women inmates, she found female "lunatics" freezing in filthy, unheated cells. Shocked by such cruelty, she publicized the conditions and won public support for improving them.

From this experience, Dix went on to make an eighteen-month study of jails, almshouses, and other public institutions in Massachusetts. In 1843 she presented to the legislature a hair-raising report of "helpless, forgotten, insane and idiotic men and women" confined "in *cages, closets, cellars, stalls, pens: Chained, naked, beaten with rods,* and lashed into obedience!" Five years later, after traveling thirty thousand miles to make similar investigations in more than a dozen states, she presented a petition to Congress: "I have myself seen *more than nine thousand idiots, epileptics, and insane in these United States, destitute of appropriate care and protection* ... bound with galling chains, bowed beneath fetters and heavy iron balls attached to drag chains, lacerated with ropes, scourged with rods, and terrified beneath storms of profane execrations and cruel blows."

In truth, the treatment of the mentally ill was not everywhere this bad. There had been much progress beyond the medieval practice of treating insanity as a form of possession by demons, to be cured or punished by exorcism or scourging. The Quakers, in particular, had in the eighteenth century influenced the establishment of "lunatic asylums" where the mentally ill received humane treatment. About a dozen such asylums existed in the United States at the time Dix began her crusade.

But these hospitals reached only a small percentage of the mentally ill. Most persons believed to be insane were either locked up at home by embarrassed relatives or incarcerated as lunatic paupers in jails and poorhouses, where conditions were often as bad as Dix portrayed them.

Dix's tireless, selfless work in state after state, all the more heroic because of personal shyness and chronic ill health, paid off with extraordinary victories. Her first success was the enlargement of the state insane asylum at Worcester, Massachusetts, in 1843. From there she went on to persuade the New Jersey legislature in 1845 to establish the state's first mental hospital, which Dix called "my firstborn child."

During the next thirty years she was directly responsible for the founding of thirty-two mental hospitals at home and abroad, and indirectly responsible for the establishment of many more. From 1854 to 1856, she visited several European countries and inspired the same kinds of reforms in the care and treatment of the insane there, as she had done in the United States. Wherever Dix went, a network of voluntary associations was created to aid her cause and sustain her initiatives after she moved on. By 1880, when she retired from active work, the dozen American mental hospitals of 1840 had increased tenfold to 123.

Dix's observations of jails and penitentiaries led her into the cause of prison reform, a subject on which she produced influential writings. She also sympathized with other reform movements, especially the movements for temperance, women's rights, and education. However, she focused her active efforts on the plight of the mentally ill, except during the Civil War when she served as Superintendent of Female Nurses for the Union army.

Single-minded in her ideas of how things should be done and no longer shy about expressing herself, Dix sometimes clashed with army surgeons and intimidated inefficient nurses, who called her "Dragon Dix." She also won the commendation of the secretary of war for her services. Dix's wartime activities were part of a broader development in which nursing was evolving from a menial occupation into a genuine profession. This in turn opened up new career opportunities for women.

(Continued)

Dorothea Lynde Dix: Humanitarian (Continued)

After the war Dix resumed her work for better institutional treatment of the insane. Although she favored therapeutic rather than merely custodial care, she contributed little directly to the development of psychiatry or to the psychology of mental illness. However, her institutional achievements did create a framework for future advances in psychiatry. In 1881, old and infirm, she retired to live with her "firstborn child," the Trenton *state mental hospital,* where she died on July 18, 1887.

However, Graham also argued that celibacy was essential to proper health and that women should have intercourse only for procreation. A medical doctor and associate of Graham's added that women ought not to be educated because the blood needed for the women and procreation would be diverted to the head, thus breeding "puny men." As for men, Graham's associate argued that semen was not to be expelled, but should be saved for reproductive purposes and should not be used for pleasure either in masturbation or in intercourse. Such use of semen, the doctor contended, would lead to "enervation, disease, insanity, and death." Furthermore, the doctor argued that expenditure of sperm would mean a loss of needed energy from the economy and that such a drain of energy from business to sex was wasteful and a contributor to social disorder.

Reformers similarly progressed substantially in many other areas. One such area was the struggle to eliminate imprisonment for debt. Headway was also made in the movement to end the traditional flogging of wayward sailors. Thomas H. Gallaudet labored ably on behalf of the deaf; and Samuel G. Howe, with equal dedication, educated the deaf and the blind. Horace Mann was an effective crusader for public education in Massachusetts.

Progress in Education

Among the most striking reforms of the Jacksonian period were those in the field of education. If some citizens objected to paying for the instruction of other people's children (public education), most people agreed—at least in the Northeast—to endorse the drive for public schools below the college level. The impetus came from sources as contrasting as Harvard graduates and New York union members. Parents wanted sons and daughters to have the educational exposure they themselves had lacked.

As a member of the Massachusetts legislature in the 1830s, Horace Mann persuaded the legislature to provide support for the schools in the form of taxation. In turn, he supported the establishment of a state board of education, of which he became the head. Mann argued that private property was actually held in trust for the good of the community and, therefore, "is pledged for the education of all its youth up to such a point as will save them from poverty and vice, and prepare them for the adequate performance of their social and civil duties." Mann framed the argument for public education as a means to teach not only the basics but also to teach morality, discipline, and order to potential ruffians and revolutionaries. This belief converted the middle and upper classes to support the funding of education with tax money. As a result, the public schools of the nineteenth century taught math, English, and science; but they also included the Protestant values of industry, punctuality, sobriety, and frugality stressed in *McGuffey's Eclectic Readers* (1836)—written by William Holmes McGuffey. Therefore, millions of American children learned to read while also learning of the terrible consequences of sloth, drunkenness, or wastefulness as illustrated in McGuffey's parables. More and more children grew familiar with Noah Webster's excellent grammar and speller; and as young Americans read and memorized the offerings of McGuffey, some of the finest literature of the ages became part of their consciousness. However, critical thinking was largely ignored.

Public education did not spread evenly across the country. Primary and secondary education in rural regions was limited by the long distances separating farm families, with the resultant problem of assembling students under one roof. As there were more situations of this sort in the South and West than in the Northeast, it was southern and western girls and boys living outside towns and cities who were most frequently deprived of the advantages of public education. Wealthy families in these areas hired private tutors but this eliminated most children from receiving an education.

In higher education, prestige continued to be identified with Harvard, Yale, and Princeton. The University of Virginia admitted its first students in 1825. Generally, however, small denominational colleges were more typical, making Latin, Greek, and mathe-

MAP 6.1 Territorial Growth (1830)

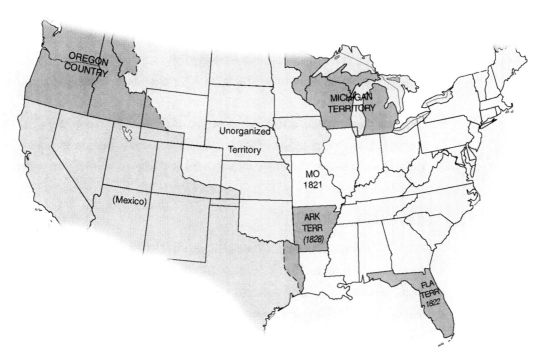

1830

matics available in out-of-the-way places. Such institutions received marginal support from their respective churches.

There were few medical schools, and fewer still for engineering. Most young lawyers acquired their training in established attorneys' offices. Nevertheless, sons of farm and village families had more opportunities than their fathers—even though few state universities thrived. The era also provided a beginning for the higher education of women when coeducation was inaugurated at Ohio's Oberlin College in the 1830s.

Communitarians

For some idealists, devotion to reforms *within* established society could not suffice. A small minority of American men and women were disillusioned with the current social order. They felt the majority toiled and suffered many privations and indignities. To them, the society had become utterly harsh and materialistic, and therefore should be forsaken in favor of communitarian living. The communitarians' idea was for a limited number of people to live together in a small community, wholly or mainly self-sufficient and more or less separately from the general society surrounding it.

These communities could be either religious or secular. Among the Christian communitarians were the Shakers, who believed in separation from the cruel and wicked world, in simplicity of language, and in celibacy.

Secular communities resembled the Christian communities in that the purpose was to join people together so as to face collectively the challenge of the frontier or to confront collectively the trends toward industrialization. Many secular communities had their philosophical bases in the social contract theories of the eighteenth century. Among the secular experiments were New Harmony in Indiana, the North American Phalanx in New Jersey, and Fruitlands in Massachusetts.

A number of free thinkers inaugurated a Massachusetts community named Brook Farm, known for its intellectually talented members that included George and Sophia Ripley. Although Brook Farm was a communitarian working farm where women and men were all paid equally, Sophia Ripley opened a private school that became so successful that it became the community's most important source of income. One Brook Farm resident, a French theorist named Charles Fourier, published a journal—the *Harbinger*—where he expounded on his socialist ideas. Unfortunately, Brook Farm was devastated by a fire in 1847 and forced to close.

Oneida Community

One of the longest-lived religious communities was Oneida, founded in upstate New York by John Humphrey Noyes. Deeply religious, Noyes also believed in a system of "complex marriage," which was a rejection of monogamy. Noyes argued that the root of evil was in marriage and in "men's conviction that women are their private property." Noyes also argued that when the will of God is done on earth as it is in heaven, there will be no marriage on earth because Jesus stated that in heaven people do not marry. In order to reproduce this vision of heaven on earth, Noyes advocated complete sharing in family relationships as a step toward what he called "perfect cooperation." That being the case, Noyes and his fifty-one followers shared everything, both economic and sexual. Child rearing was the responsibility of the entire community, and there was no differentiation of gender roles in work. All private property was relinquished to the community.

In Noyes' complex marriage, every "saved" man was married to every "saved" woman. All who were "saved" were considered to be without sin. Although Noyes preached complete sharing of everything, he also decreed that only certain "spiritually advanced" males were allowed to have sex and father children. Noyes also taught that women could become "spiritually advanced" through sex with "spiritually advanced" males and he considered himself to be "first husband," helping many women to "spiritual advancement." One Oneida community woman, Mary Cragin, appears to have been one of Noyes' favorite. She described her sexual experiences with Noyes as spiritual experiences as well. In the words of Cragin,

"In view of God's goodness to me and of his desire that I should let him fill me with himself, I yield and offer myself, to be penetrated by his spirit, and desire that love and gratitude may inspire my heart so that I shall sympathize with his pleasure in the thing, before my personal pleasure begins, knowing that it will increase my capability for happiness."

Noyes also argued that sex should be a public act that could be performed in public to the pleasure of all, much like music or dancing. Noyes even argued that watching such public sex would give pleasure to "older people who have nothing to do in the matter." In addition to these oddities, to his credit, Noyes also tried a number of expedients to give women more freedom, such as communal nurseries. Oneida lasted from 1848 to 1879. Then Noyes fled to Canada to avoid prosecution for adultery. After that, his followers abandoned complex marriage and set up manufacturing enterprises—animal traps, silverware, and kitchenware—that survived into the twenty-first century.

▶ John Humphrey Noyes founded the Oneida colony, which rejected traditional Christian beliefs—including monogamy—and lived as a community that shared everything, both economic and sexual. Noyes and his followers believed that sharing in family relationships was a step toward "perfect cooperation." *Wikipedia photo*

The Oneida community was consistent with other religious and secular communitarianism in that it shared such features as vegetarianism, prohibition of alcoholic beverages, equitable division of labor, and community ownership and control of property.

Most secular experiments did not last long, perhaps owing to an absence of the Christian zeal that, in the case of the Mormons and the Shakers, proved a reliable source of community strength. In all, only a few thousand people committed themselves to communitarianism. Such communities, however, received much attention then and since because they embodied visionary goals of social justice, perhaps inspired by Charles Fourier at Brook Farm, or in the case of New Harmony, by the ideas of the British thinker, Robert Owen.

Religion and the People

Religion played an important part in the lives of average Americans. The Baptist and Methodist churches had more members than any others. They were successful in developing African American congregations. The Presbyterian, Congregational, Episcopal, and other denominations also appealed to substantial segments of the population. The establishment of Sunday schools constituted a standard medium for indoctrinating the young.

Religious diversity also increased in America. With the influx of Irish and German immigrants by the hundreds of thousands during the 1840s and 1850s, growing numbers of Americans adhered to the Roman Catholic and Lutheran faiths. Supplementing churches with European origins were indigenous ones like the Disciples of Christ, Mormons, and Seventh Day Adventists.

Widespread evangelistic endeavors also characterized the era. Especially in the South and West, the example of Bishop Francis Asbury inspired his Methodist successors to "ride the circuit" and present in graphic language the punishments for sin and the rewards of salvation. In the East and then in Ohio and Indiana, Lyman Beecher and his sons preached powerful Calvinistic sermons and attacked such social ills as dueling and alcoholic indulgence.

More popular than any other evangelist in the West and North, Charles Grandison Finney in countless revival meetings emphasized the individual's ability to repent. Salvation, Finney believed, represented only the start of a useful life: The person saved should then save others. Finney's theology, lacking the orthodox Calvinistic tenet of predestination, won converts by the tens of thousands.

No longer were clergymen as apt as in the past to bewail a "low state" of American Protestantism. No longer did religion—as in the 1790s—appear to be removed from the masses in mid-Atlantic and other communities, with church memberships declining and the dissensions and arguments of ministers severely damaging their sects. If—as the French traveler Alexis de Tocqueville thought in the 1830s—religion was the foremost American institution, there were solid reasons for its number one rank. The "Second

▶ Charles Grandison Finney was a Presbyterian evangelist and the most popular preacher in the West and North. Finney emphasized a sinner's ability to repent, and won tens of thousands of converts. *Wikipedia photo*

Great Awakening," which had begun with the turn of the century, continued into the time of de Tocqueville's visit and its spiritual force was felt long after that.

The evangelists of the Second Great Awakening did much of their preaching and exhorting outside the doors of churches. They reached the people at massive camp meetings in the countryside or at medium-sized revivals. The significant part of their ultimate effect was to lead zealous converts into Baptist and other church folds where continuing inspiration, strength, and comfort could be found.

There was also a close relationship between the assailing and reforming of social sins and the Protestant Ethic concept of hard work as a glorification of God. The excitement of economic progress and the challenge of technology had an undeniable identification with thrift, industry, and self-discipline. So it was not accidental that Christianity was far from being a Sunday-only affair in the Jacksonian period. Both rural and urban faithful attended prayer meetings on weeknights. Grace was said before meals in innumerable homes, and devotional services were held in family circles with parents and children devoutly kneeling.

William Miller and the Millerites

A preoccupation with the expected return of Christ also experienced a boost in the mid-nineteenth century. William Miller, a farmer from upstate New York, claimed in 1842 that he had mathematically calculated the exact time of the second coming of Christ as March 21, 1843. According to Miller, the correct meaning of Daniel 8:14 that states "the sanctuary will be cleansed after 2,300 days" was that the earth would be destroyed by fire 2,300 years after the prophecy, thus mandating Christ's return in 1843. Miller also concluded that the earth would be six thousand years old on that date.

Miller published his conclusions in the 1830s and began preaching at churches and camp meetings, rapidly building a following. It is estimated that by 1843, some fifty thousand Americans believed Miller's predictions and an estimated million more expected "something" to happen. Miller and his followers gave away their worldly belongings in March of 1843, donned white robes, and flocked to the hills and tops of buildings to wait for Jesus' return. March 21 passed without incident, however, causing Miller to recalculate several times. Christ failed each time to return.

Miller died in 1848 as a discredited prophet in terms of the date of his prediction. His followers continued to adhere to his teaching that Christians must still "Remember the Sabbath and Keep it Holy." Therefore, they must worship on Saturday (instead of Sunday) and perform no work on that day. Miller's followers eventually became known as the Seventh Day Adventists who continue to honor the Sabbath in the twenty-first century as Miller instructed.

Mormons

Perhaps no new religious group of the early nineteenth century has placed a greater stamp on America than the Mormons. In the 1820s, Joseph Smith of Palmyra, New York claimed to have been visited by the Angel Moroni, who along with his horoscope led Smith to dig on a particular day for some golden plates buried in the ground near his home. Written on the plates in an indecipherable language, which Smith described as "reformed Egyptian," were more than five hundred pages of the *Book of the Mormon*. Smith also uncovered two sacred stones, Urim and Thummim, that enabled him to interpret the plates.

Smith then went about the business of interpreting the plates and dictated the *Book of Mormon* to a scribe who wrote down what Smith interpreted from behind a curtain. Some witnesses were amazed that Smith could interpret the plates using the Sacred Stones while the plates themselves remained under a sheet. At least eight other people testified, however, that they had personally seen the plates before Smith returned them to the Angel Moroni.

The plates described the one true church and a "lost tribe of Israel" that had been missing for centuries. The Book of Mormon essentially provided an explanation as to how the Native

▶William Miller's prophetic time chart from 1843 about the prophecies of Daniel and Revelation. Miller claimed in 1842 that he had mathematically calculated the exact time of the second coming of Christ as March 21, 1843. Miller began the movement that developed into the religious denomination of Seventh-day Adventists. *Wikipedia photo*

▶Joseph Smith founded the Latter Day Saints movement. Smith published what he said was an English translation of the Book of Mormon from gold plates he found buried near his home.
Wikipedia photo

Americans had come to be in the Western Hemisphere—a fact that had bewildered Christians everywhere for centuries. The Native Americans were explained in the *Book of Mormon* to be the lost tribe of Israel, and it was further explained that Jesus Christ had come to America after his Resurrection and preached to the Native Americans. The original site of the Garden of Eden was identified as a place near Independence, Missouri. The *Book of Mormon* also contained the prediction of the appearance of a prophet in America who would establish a new pure kingdom of Christ in the United States. Furthermore, the Book contained the prediction of the coming of the Civil War, proof later to many that Smith was a true prophet of God, and that the *Book of Mormon* was God's Word.

Skeptics point out, however, that the Book also mentions the presence of horses, steel, and wheat in the Western Hemisphere prior to the arrival of Columbus. Furthermore, in 1835 Smith purchased and translated Egyptian Papyruses that he claimed were written by Abraham. Twentieth century Egyptologists, however, contend that Abraham did not write Smith's papyruses, but that they are copies of the Egyptian *Book of the Dead.*

Theologically speaking, Smith's Mormonism is a Christian religion. The teachings of Smith's Mormonism include not only belief in the one true God of Christianity, but in Jesus Christ as the Son of God and savior of all humanity. Smith's Mormonism also taught that human life on earth is part of the human progress toward eventual status in heaven essentially equivalent to that of God in the Old Testament. The logic, in essence, is that if humans are God's children, then when humans "grow up" in the afterlife, they will be "Gods" residing on a distant planet, orbiting the star Kolob. While in heaven, human males will be sexually active with the heavenly mother and other wives in a paradise of jewels and gold. In Mormonism, marriage is eternal, and people will be reunited in the afterlife.

While on earth, Mormons avoided strong drink, including alcohol, coffee, and tea. Mormonism also taught that prosperity is a path to godliness; and, thus, the Mormons stressed work. Mormonism is also hierarchical—a "First President" and twelve Apostles head the church. At first, Mormonism taught that converts must give all their property to the Church; but Joseph Smith found that the wealthy rebelled against the practice. Therefore, he changed the requirement from "all property" to a tithe. This alteration is an early example of the doctrine of "continuous Revelation," which allows doctrine to evolve with changing times. Famously, Mormonism also allowed polygamy and Joseph Smith himself had twenty-eight wives; however, the Mormon Church abandoned the practice in 1890 after it was struck down as unconstitutional by the United States Supreme Court.

Polygamy, of course, was controversial and caused the Mormons to be persecuted by the larger communities around them. Mormonism also requires evangelism, which aids in the growth of Mormonism, but also alienates those who do not care to be evangelized. Thus, Smith and his followers were forced to migrate from Palmyra, New York, to Kirtland, Ohio, then Missouri, and then to Nauvoo, Illinois. In spite of the migrations, Nauvoo had a Mormon population of fifteen thousand by 1844, and Smith petitioned Congress for separate territorial status and even ran for President. The entire Mormon population at the time of Smith's untimely death at the hands of an angry mob in 1844 was estimated at twenty-six thousand.

The persecution of Mormons by the larger community was undoubtedly severe, thus leading to the multiple migrations. However, Smith's (and later Brigham Young's) Mormonism was not entirely pacific, and the Mormons at times lashed back at their persecutors. Smith's Mormonism contained the idea of "blood atonement," whereby Mormon believers could justify killing enemies of the Church or those that had fallen away from the Church. For those who had fallen away and desired to return to the Church, they could regain their salvation by killing the enemies of the Church. To do so, the throats of the victims were slit, and it was required that their blood be spilled on the ground. In 1838, at Haun's Mill near Kirtland, Ohio, seventeen people were killed in this manner when they refused to migrate with the rest of the Mormon community. Even more tragic, in 1857 at Mountain Meadows, Utah, Mormons slaughtered 140 men, women, and children from Arkansas who were in the process of crossing Utah in a wagon train. Twenty children, age seven and under, were spared as "innocents" and adopted by the Mormons. Later, as adults, they recounted the truth of the massacre. If it were not for the coming of the Civil War, the U.S. government might have invaded Utah and arrested Brigham Young for his responsibility in the Mountain Meadows massacre. Due to the magnitude of the sectional crisis in the U.S. at the time, the U.S. government directed its energy elsewhere.

▶Smith's Mormonism contained the idea of "blood atonement," whereby Mormon believers could justify killing enemies of the Church or those that had fallen away from the Church, such as was demonstrated in 1857 at Mountain Meadows, Utah. Mormons slaughtered 140 men, women, and children from Arkansas who were in the process of crossing Utah in a wagon train. *Wikipedia photo*

The Unitarian Influence

For the Christians whose ardor and faith have just been depicted, God the Son and God the Holy Ghost were as integral to the Deity as God the Father. Concurrently, however, spreading in New England was the influence of Unitarians. They rejected the doctrine of the Trinity, believing that God exists in only one person.

Unitarians accepted Christian revelation, but only so far as it accorded with what they conceived to be human reason. The Calvinistic belief in the doctrine of election was not for them because it implied an arbitrary God. Instead, Unitarians underscored the Deity's benevolence and declared that Jesus was divine in the sense that all people are divine. To a degree, they were reacting against both the creed and the formalism of Congregationalists and the fire-and-brimstone evangelism of the Great Awakenings, although one also finds links between the latter and Unitarian individualism. To Unitarians, the life of Jesus represented an example to be emulated by persons who already were innately good and spiritually free.

A spokesman for Unitarian thought and action was the Boston clergyman, William Ellery Channing. Implicit in his ideas was the prominence of the individual—independent, yet spiritually obliged to "transcend" individualistic self by intimate identification with the Deity. Though Channing had been reared in the creed of Calvinism, he came to deny the doctrine of original sin and to believe firmly in the freedom of the will. Many of the era's reformers and intellectuals were Unitarian in their beliefs.

Romanticism Revisited

It is not difficult to understand why Channing and other Unitarian thinkers appealed to young scholars and writers who had been impressed by the ideas of Romanticism because the belief in human possibility was congruent with Romanticism. Romanticism had already had an important influence on the thinking of people during the early years of the republic. In 1824–1854, Romanticism's influence was, if anything, even more pervasive.

Romantic writers and artists had as their goal the "liberation" of the individual—the full realization of the human potential. To accomplish this, they asserted that individuals should give free rein to imagination and emotion, experimenting with new ways and innovative ideas. The emphasis was on informality, the picturesque, the exotic, and the sensuous as ways of appreciating external nature and capturing the transient aspects of life. They shunned tradition, beliefs that human intuition and poetic sensibility were best qualified to lead people to truth.

The growth of democratic government during the Jacksonian period also reflected this new emphasis on the value of the individual and faith in the ability of the common person. This individualism was not necessarily "nonconformist." Most Americans still took their cue for behavior from the majority. They tended, however, to admire the rugged individualists among them, whether in life or in literature, such as the heroes of James Fenimore Cooper (*The Last of the Mohicans*).

The ultimate liberated men were those who invaded the wilderness, drove the Native Americans out, and established settlements in the West. These men saw themselves as economically self-reliant and capable of almost any achievement. They developed versatility, robustness, and resilience, along with physical courage.

The Romantics believed that society was a growing organism that could be changed and improved. Thus, Romanticism as well as Christianity nourished the reform movements of the period. Most American Romanticists, however, thought their country already had the political foundations it needed and so concerned themselves largely with social and humanitarian reforms.

The Golden Age of Literature

Emerson and Transcendentalism

The period from the triumph of Jacksonian democracy to the Civil War was one of the greatest eras in American literary history. It has been called "The Golden Day," "The New England Renaissance," and "The Flowering of New England." Ralph Waldo Emerson, Margaret Fuller, and Henry David Thoreau were among the leading proponents of the Boston-based transcendentalist movement— into which the two intellectual streams of Unitarianism and Romanticism flowed.

Transcendentalism has been defined philosophically as "recognition in man of the capacity of knowing truth intuitively, or attaining knowledge transcending the reach of the senses." Transcendentalists believed that the power of the solitary individual was limitless and that people should not conform to the materialistic world. Instead, people should look within themselves and to the natural world for guidance.

In his first little book, *Nature*, published in 1836, Emerson asked penetrating questions:

> Foregoing generations beheld God and nature face to face; we, through their eyes. Why should not we also enjoy an original relation to the universe? Why should not we have a poetry and philosophy of insight and not of tradition, and a religion by revelation to us, and not the history of theirs?

Emerson pointed out that Jesus "spoke of miracles," for Jesus believed "man's life was a miracle" and man's "daily miracle shines, as the character ascends," but the churches' interpretation of the word miracle, Emerson added, gave a false impression and was "not one with the blowing clover and the falling rain."

The allusion to clover and rain as miracles symbolized the transcendentalists' search for revelations of divinity in external nature as well as in the individual's own nature. Emerson viewed the different aspects of the

▶Ralph Waldo Emerson believed that the human being could reach a direct, exalted relationship with the universal spirit. *Wikipedia photo*

▶Margaret Fuller was America's first recognized female intellectual and a close friend of Ralph Waldo Emerson. Unable to attend Harvard University due to her gender, Fuller read extensively and was able to hold her own with any and all of the other transcendentalists. *Wikipedia photo*

universe as diverse manifestations of a central spirit, which he called the Over-Soul. Man and woman, according to Emerson, could be channels for the higher truths of the Over-Soul by developing their intuitive powers to the fullest. Emerson's doctrine of the Over-Soul also implied a belief in self-reliance, as expounded in his famous essay of that name. When he wrote about self-reliance, Emerson's meaning was that the human being could reach a direct, exalted relationship with the universal spirit.

Emerson's philosophy was essentially a variety of philosophical idealism, as distinct from materialism. Broadly speaking, an idealist is one who sees basic reality as spiritual; the materialist is one who sees it as physical or material. Emerson's idealism was concerned ultimately with the conduct of life. For this he asserted that men and women have the capacity to draw upon a power greater than their own.

One of Emerson's chief allies in the transcendentalist project was Margaret Fuller, one of America's greatest female intellectuals. A few years younger than Emerson, Fuller was unable to attend Harvard as so many of the men did, but she pursued a ferociously ambitious program of reading. Therefore, she was able to hold her own with any and all of the other transcendentalists. In the fall of 1836 a number of these Boston intellectuals began meeting informally in what evolved into the Transcendentalist Club. For a brief period they published a journal, the *Dial*, of which Fuller was the editor. A brilliant conversationalist, Fuller visited the Emerson household in Concord, where she and her host talked for hours. After her untimely death in 1850, Emerson wrote a memoir about her.

Thoreau

Although Emerson published many volumes of poetry and essays, he was more widely known in his lifetime as the most popular lecturer of his day, while Fuller was known for her journalism. In contrast, Henry David Thoreau's contacts with his contemporary Americans were minimal. Very few bought or read his *A Week on the Concord and Merrimack Rivers* (1849) or even his now-celebrated *Walden* (1854), both of which related his experience and thinking in the 1840s.

Today Thoreau is considered one of the major American writers of all time. Emerson comprehended the younger man's greatness as a stylist, testifying that "Thoreau illustrates with excellent images that which I convey in a sleepy generality." An erstwhile schoolteacher and local handyman, Thoreau spent the years 1845–1847 in a shack on the edge of Walden Pond near Concord. Here he dwelt among the birds and beasts, reading and writing with few distractions. "I went to the woods because I wished to live deliberately," he explained, "to front only the essential facts of life."

Independence and self-reliance dominated Thoreau's life. He actively helped the "underground railroad" to convey runaway slaves to the freedom of Canada. He spent a night in jail rather than pay a tiny tax to support a government then prosecuting what he considered an unjust war against Mexico.

Out of the latter experience came *Civil Disobedience*, a highly influential political essay that the modern author and critic Henry S. Canby referred to as "Gandhi's textbook in his campaign of passive resistance" against the British in twentieth-century India. It was the writings of Thoreau and Mahatma Gandhi that later greatly influenced the nonviolent resistance of Martin Luther King, Jr. Thoreau declared it the duty of citizens to deny allegiance to a government they believe is wrong.

Such an attitude is essential to the health of a democracy. It is the opposite of that apathy which prevents citizens from taking a stand, allowing important contests to go by default. Thoreau was not antisocial. He merely took his duties as a citizen more seriously than most Americans.

The Boston Brahmins

In his own day, Thoreau was not nearly so well known as Henry Wadsworth Longfellow, James Russell Lowell, or Oliver Wendell Holmes. Each of these was an admired poet (and Holmes, somewhat later, the author of well-regarded prose). Although Lowell and Longfellow attacked slavery in verse, all three were primarily literary aristocrats. Holmes applied the label "Brahmin caste of New England" to the cultivated, exclusive class he typified.

These "Brahmins" were inclined to view literature as something lofty and ennobling. Much of the time in writing, they erected barriers against unpleasant or perplexing social and philosophic questions. The dreamy utopias of Emerson and the back-to-nature living of Thoreau were not for them in the 1830s and 1840s—nor were the portrayals of evil that characterized the books of Nathaniel Hawthorne and Herman Melville. Benevolent toward others, the "Brahmins" were usually satisfied to savor the pleasant intellectual life of Boston and Harvard—where all three were professors. Although (or perhaps because) he had a sense of humor, Holmes considered Boston "the thinking center of the continent, and therefore of the planet."

Hawthorne

The writer who most brilliantly opposed transcendentalist tendencies was Nathaniel Hawthorne of Salem, Massachusetts. He was the chief literary inheritor of the old Puritan tradition, and his works—particularly his novel *The Scarlet Letter* (1850)—embodied Puritan ideas. His ancestors had been Puritan magistrates charged with persecuting Quakers and condemning "witches" at Salem court. While disapproving of their bigotry and cruelty, he recognized the ancestral tie: "Strong traits of their nature," he said, "have intertwined themselves with mine.

Hawthorne rejected both the optimism inherent in transcendentalism and the reform movements abetted by it. He held the Puritan belief that people are innately sinful, that

CHAPTER 6 ● American Culture Comes of Age   **252**

evil is an ever-present reality (not an illusion to be brushed aside), and that self-reliant individualism alone cannot save a person from destruction. In Hawthorne, the persistence of the Puritan point of view is evident into the Jacksonian Era.

Unlike Emerson, who denied that evil existed in an ultimate form, Hawthorne made evil central in his stories and novels. *The Scarlet Letter* deals with secret guilt, the effects of crime on man and woman, and the need for penance through confession or love. In *The House of the Seven Gables* (1851), evil appears as a hereditary taint visiting the sins of the fathers on the children in a study of degeneration and decay. *The Blithedale Romance* (1852) is, in part, a satire on the secular community Brook Farm—the villain showing how a reformer's zealotry can mesh with unconscionable ambition and thus serve evil rather than good.

▶Nathaniel Hawthorne, author of the famous 1850 novel *The Scarlet Letter. Wikipedia photo*

Melville

A writer close to Hawthorne, both in his concern with the "deep mystery of sin" and in his revulsion against Emersonian currents of optimism, was Herman Melville. Born in New York, reared there and in the Berkshires of Massachusetts, Melville as a youth shipped as a sailor on a merchantman plying the Atlantic and later on a whaler bound for the South Seas. On these voyages he saw first hand, a world of violence, crime, and misery.

Such early Melville books as *Typee* and *Omoo* were popular, but his increased pessimism caused the novelist to be neglected after the 1840s. He was "rediscovered" in the 1920s by post-World War I readers, to whose mood of disillusionment propagated the powerful appeal of Melville's *Moby Dick* (1851).

Although Melville, like Hawthorne, was a philosophical pessimist, he arrived at his pessimism along intellectual avenues differing from Hawthorne's in three ways. First, Hawthorne still cherished Calvinist values though critical of them and all others, whereas Melville rebelled against the religious conservatism he had known as a boy. Second, in Liverpool and in the South Seas, Melville was shocked by the roughness and cruelty of "civilized" men—brutalities that neither Hawthorne nor Emerson experienced. Finally, just as he lacked Emerson's optimism, he lacked Hawthorne's resignation.

James Fenimore Cooper

The disparity between the dream of a peaceful, democratic society in the virgin wilderness and the reality of frontier life was frequently reflected in the thought and literature of this period. The real Western frontier posed many problems of adjustment for its settlers. Land speculation, political corruption, and immorality were common in the poorly organized towns. In short,

"Both jaws, like enormous shears, bit the craft completely in twain."

—*Page 510.*

▶Herman Melville wrote the great American classic *Moby Dick. Wikipedia photo*

the real frontier bore little resemblance to the literary legend or to the popular tall tale.

The first major writer of fiction to exploit the literary potential of the frontier was James Fenimore Cooper. His series of "Leatherstocking Tales" both romanticized the wilderness and conveyed the loss many Americans felt when they became aware of the crude fashion in which the frontier was being settled. For instance, Cooper convincingly expressed the tragedy of the Native Americans, pushed out of ancestral lands by the advancing white settlers.

Although it is easy to lampoon his didacticism, stock characters, and strained and starchy dialogue, at his best Cooper was a captivating storyteller with a talent for both description and perceptive social criticism. "The Leatherstocking Tales" represents a romantic view of the West, just as Sir Walter Scott's novels and ballads romanticized with charm and skill the people and places of a lost Europe. Cooper's West, however, was confined mainly to upper New York State before 1800. He never saw the prairie, never neared the Rocky Mountains—in fact, never even crossed the Mississippi River.

Southern Romanticism

The South produced numerous authors before the Civil War, yet there were few direct literary connections with New England. Sectional interests influenced literature, just as they influenced politics. With many Southerners convinced that slavery must be maintained and allowed to spread, Southerners liked to idealize their plantations as happy feudal domains where slaves benefited from the most humane treatment. Southern writers praised Greek democracy, where *inequality,* rather than *equality,* had prevailed. There and in the American South, they held, competent individuals directed and cared for the less competent—acting in the interest of all.

Because of the feudal emphasis in his work, the dominant influence on romantic southern literature in these years was the British author Sir Walter Scott. Scott's fictional recreation of the Middle Ages, his knights in shining armor, his defenders of glamorous ladies in distress, and his heroes' exemplary characters fitted in with notions of Southern chivalry—as opposed to Northern commercialism and reformism.

A number of American writers attempted to romanticize the "feudal" South in works of fiction. One of the best of those novels was John P. Kennedy's *Swallow Barn* (1832), which depicted rural Virginia in the 1820s. A resident of Baltimore, Kennedy strung together sketches of idealized plantation aristocracy with a minimal plot. In it the master of the estate of Swallow Barn is genial and generous, his relatives and friends are virtuous, their hospitality is bountiful, and the African Americans are cheerful.

▶ James Fenimore Cooper *Wikipedia photo*

Edgar Allan Poe

Reared as a foster child in Virginia, Edgar Allan Poe nevertheless can be treated only partly as a Southerner. In his personal life he was—or wanted to be—a conservative Southerner. Although he supported the works of other Southern authors and praised the Southern defense of slavery, Poe's writings rarely reveal a Southern tone or setting. In his tales he was more influenced by the "Gothic" tradition in English fiction—the kind of fiction that used certain stock properties such as old castles, decayed houses, dungeons, secret passages, ancient wrongs, and supernatural phenomena.

Poe was not concerned with portraying contemporary scenes or providing moral reflections on life. He believed that poetry, for example, should exist for its own sake, never as an instrument of instruction. It may be that no other American has maintained more consistently that literature exists primarily and perhaps solely to entertain. However, Poe did not take this function lightly. In his own poetry and prose, he applied the theories of literary technique that he expounded in his critical writings. There was a great deal of originality in Poe's writing, particularly in his short stories and detective stories. Both his poetry and his prose were enormously admired abroad, especially in France.

Journalism and Popular Culture

Writing for the People

Americans of the time read newspapers more avidly than even the most exciting fiction. New York City produced some of the best journalism in Horace Greeley's *Tribune* and poet-editor William Cullen Bryant's *Post*. James Gordon Bennett's *New York Herald*, a pioneer in the "penny press" field, presented national and world news alongside lurid accounts of murders and sex scandals. Nowhere else had there ever been so many newspapers as in America at this time. While quality varied from town to town, Americans knew more about what was going on than any other general population anywhere.

After stereotyping began in 1811 and electrotyping in 1841, the influence of technology on popular culture was evident. Printers used steam presses to mass-produce books which, cheaply bound and extensively distributed, sold for as little as 25 cents. Intellectuals read such magazines as the *North American Review* and the *Southern Literary Messenger*. Tillers of the soil preferred the *American Farmer*, the *American Agriculturist*, and the *Southern Cultivator*. In addition to agricultural articles, these offered fiction and verse to farm families.

Religious periodicals abounded—notably the *Biblical Repertory* (Presbyterian), the *Biblical Repository* (Congregationalist), the *Christian Review* (Baptist), the *Christian Examiner* (Unitarian), the *Methodist Magazine,* and the *United States Catholic Magazine.* Carrying theological arguments and sectarian messages, many of them also disseminated miscellaneous culture. "Of all the reading of the people," a commentator observed in 1840, "three-fourths is purely religious." In 1848, fifty-two religious journals were published in New York City alone.

Magazines and Books for Women

Discerning innovators discovered that women comprised one of the most dependable magazine markets. From 1830 on, a Philadelphia periodical called *Godey's Lady's Book* enjoyed an enviable circulation, helped along by the efforts of its gifted editor, Sarah Josepha Hale. By the 1850s, its subscription list reached one hundred fifty thousand. Eventually, its publisher amassed a million-dollar fortune. *Graham's Magazine,* which made its bow in 1841, instantly appealed to both women and men. Soon it had forty thousand subscribers and an annual profit of

▶ Edgar Allan Poe
Wikipedia photo

$50,000. It included short stories, essays, poetry, colored fashion plates, book reviews, and a department on fine arts. Bryant, Cooper, Lowell, and Longfellow contributed to *Graham's.* For a time Poe was literary editor, and some of his best work graced its pages. Combining the insipid and sentimental important topics, *Graham's* and *Godey's* provided exactly what their readers wanted.

Women writers were widely published during the period. Authorship lent opportunity to women when most other vocational doors were shut. Ann Stephens, co-editor of the *Ladies' National Magazine,* sent florid but thrilling tales to the *Lady's Wreath* and similar media. Poems and articles by Lydia Sigourney won acceptance in countless journals. Among women authors with large followings were Catharine M. Sedgwick and Anna Mowatt. Caroline Lee Hentz and E.D.E.N. Southworth, popular novelists of the 1850s, in the previous decade. Margaret Fuller edited the *Dial* in Boston, and later, in New York on Greeley's *Tribune,* gained more admirers of her astute criticism. Her volume, *Women in the Nineteenth Century,* drawn from her writings for the *Tribune,* projected advanced views on women's rights.

Slavery and Democracy

Garrison and Abolition

For all the change and all the pride in the Americans of these years—for all the artistry of the gifted, the technology of the inventive, and the fun and frolic and misery and strivings and achievements of the masses of people—the dark cloud of slavery deeply troubled first the few and then the many.

In the 1820s the ranks of abolitionists tended to be filled by Quakers, such as the Philadelphian, Benjamin Lundy. Then in Boston in 1831, a journeyman printer named William Lloyd Garrison founded *The Liberator*, a new kind of abolitionist paper. It was new because it carried an unprecedented tone of moral urgency. Garrison could see no good in the legal sanctions protecting slavery in half the country. Constitutionalism meant far less to him than securing freedom for his fellow human beings. It was no coincidence that Garrison's insistence on this reform occurred at the very time when other movers and shakers were spurring other reforms—both religious and secular.

According to Garrison's concept of Christianity, slavery was sinful. As *The Liberator's* editor, he was motivated primarily by this sinfulness. Fervent in his conviction, he attacked the Constitution as "a covenant with death and an agreement with hell" and called for an immediate end to slavery. It was hardly surprising that most "respectable" northerners would not subscribe to what was seen as extremism in a day when John Quincy Adams, himself against slavery but no Garrisonian, described the abolitionist faction as small and shallow.

Garrison was persistent, however. In 1843, he began the first of twenty-two terms as president of the American Anti-Slavery Society. The seed nourished by Garrison and fellow abolitionists eventually flowered in the emancipation of slaves from bondage. Long depicted in historical writing as a fanatic, Garrison is now regarded as one of the era's most influential reformers, primarily but not exclusively for his abolitionism. He also espoused women's rights and pacifism.

Yet, it must be stated that the possibility of slavery's westward extension—rather than the existence of slavery in states where it was legal—was what millions of Northerners strenuously objected to from the outbreak of the Mexican War forward. The approach to the slavery issue of Abraham Lincoln and other political leaders was anything but that of Garrison.

Second only to Garrison in national fame among abolitionists, perhaps, was Frederick Douglass, an African American who had escaped from slavery and become an agent of the Massachusetts Anti-Slavery Society. With his commanding appearance and gift as an orator, Douglass established an antislavery paper—the *North Star*—and was well received by both American and British audiences. Another well-known African American abolitionist was the eloquent Charles L. Remond, born free, who for a time rivaled Douglass on abolitionist platforms. African American clergymen also played significant parts in the antislavery cause. Two, the Presbyterian Henry H. Garnet and the Congregationalist Samuel R. Ward, held pastorates in upstate New York but were known chiefly as abolition spokesmen. Finally, there were a number of clubs composed of African American women abolitionists; and two women, Frances Watkins Harper and the former slave Sojourner Truth, were touring anti-slavery lecturers.

▶ Harriet Beecher Stowe authored *Uncle Tom's Cabin*, which depicted the separation of families, maternal loss, and other evils inherent in slavery. It turned out to be the greatest work of propaganda ever written by an American. *Wikipedia photo*

The Literary Antecedents to Civil War

From 1833 on, the New England Quaker, John Greenleaf Whittier, contributed poems and prose to the abolitionists' campaign. In 1842, Longfellow published a few antislavery poems but never became a Garrison adherent. James Russell Lowell wrote for the *National Anti-Slavery Standard*. Other younger authors—Thoreau, Melville, and Walt Whitman—were repelled by slavery and so commented. Then, while Holmes and Hawthorne continued to abstain from the agitation, Emerson swung around in the 1850s to laud the abolitionist crusader John Brown and to compare Brown's gallows—Brown was executed after being captured in the attempt to lead a slave revolt in 1859—to the cross of Jesus.

It was a powerful novel, however, that proved to be the most effective tool deployed by any of those who opposed slavery. Written by Harriet Beecher Stowe—daughter, wife, and sister of Calvinist ministers and a woman abundantly aware of her own New England conscience—*Uncle Tom's Cabin* (1852) provided a searing indictment of "the peculiar institution." Stowe contended that God inspired the book, which depicted the separation of families, maternal loss, and other evils inherent in slavery. Inspired or not, it turned out to be one of the greatest work of propaganda ever written by an American. It sold hundreds of thousands of copies and imbued the anti-slavery crusade with a moral fervor that captured Northern attention as well as sympathy in an unprecedented manner. It changed the nature of the discourse Stowe's depiction of slavery caused many Americans to view African Americans as human and face the inhumanity of slavery. Southern fiction, produced by way of reply, had no comparable punch, although it is noteworthy that the sectional conflict was fought with words before it was first fought with bullets.

The ablest Southern arguments were in essay form and came mostly from politicians and educators. Many slaveholders agreed with John C. Calhoun and William Harper of South Carolina and Thomas R. Dew of Virginia that far from being harmful, slavery was a positive good. Other Southerners merely saw—or thought they saw—a practical necessity for retaining the slave labor system.

When *The Impending Crisis of the South*, a book attacking slavery on economic grounds, was published in 1857, its author, Hinton R. Helper of North Carolina, was bitterly assailed by Southerners. On the other hand, those who denounced Helper warmly praised the writings of a Virginian, George Fitzhugh, in the 1850s. In *Sociology for the South*, Fitzhugh said slavery was a social, political, and economic blessing—and avowed that people trying to eliminate it were blind to Southern realities.

Alexis de Tocqueville's America

Alexis de Tocqueville, the young French magistrate who spent nine months in the United States between 1831 and 1832, has been mentioned previously for his views on life in America. His noteworthy contribution to political science, sociology, and history was *Democracy in America*

(1835). He concluded that American democracy was functioning successfully; that its success depended chiefly on separation of church and state and on the absence of centralization; that American political morality was important; and that American democracy was not for export to Europe until such time as Europeans elevated their standards of governmental morality.

The Frenchman was particularly struck by what he saw as an American tendency toward the practical, an avoidance of traditions, and an optimistic hope that in the new social system people would be able to progress rapidly toward perfection. One of his principal theses was that the American system of government derived from a dominant principle—the will of the people—that had been felt all during the nation's history.

The French magistrate, who stayed long enough to look around thoroughly and to reflect on what he saw and heard, was by no means oblivious to problems involved in the questions of slavery and race. "The most formidable of all the ills which threaten the future existence of the Union," he wrote, "arises from the presence of a African American population upon its territory; and in contemplating the cause of the present embarrassments or of the future dangers of the United States, the observer is invariably led to consider this as a primary fact."

Social mobility was a feature of American life that intrigued de Tocqueville. He believed that, with one exception, such mobility would prevent both class stratification and extreme social conflict resulting from it. This exception he found in black-white relationships. If and when Southern African Americans "are raised to the level of freemen," he predicted, "they will soon revolt at being deprived of almost all their civil rights; and as they cannot become the equals of the whites, they will speedily show themselves as enemies." Northern whites, he observed, "avoided the Negroes with increasing care in proportion as the legal barriers of separation are removed."

The French observer was not without other doubts concerning the American experiment. He saw a potential danger to freedom of the individual in the possibility that majorities would crush minorities or nibble away at minority rights. He also thought he discerned a trend toward mediocrity in popular leaders and in American culture—this in a country where Emerson, Fuller, Thoreau, Hawthorne, Melville, Stowe, and Lincoln were all living when de Tocqueville's book went to press. Still, while the French visitor guessed wrong at times, he was remarkably correct in the aggregate.

▶ Alexis de Tocqueville, a young French magistrate, spent nine months in the United States between 1831 and 1832. De Tocqueville reported back about the nature of the new country's democracy, morality, and revolutionary ideas regarding separation of church and state. *Wikipedia photo*

This is an excerpt from Alexis de Tocqueville's Democracy in America:

Chapter XVIII

THE PRESENT AND PROBABLE FUTURE CONDITION OF THE THREE RACES THAT INHABIT THE TERRITORY OF THE UNITED STATES

THE principal task that I had imposed upon myself is now performed: I have shown, as far as I was able, the laws and the customs of the American democracy. Here I might stop; but the reader would perhaps feel that I had not satisfied his expectations.

An absolute and immense democracy is not all that we find in America; the inhabitants of the New World may be considered from more than one point of view. In the course of this work my subject has often led me to speak of the Indians and the Negroes, but I have never had time to stop in order to show what place these two races occupy in the midst of the democratic people whom I was engaged in describing. I have shown in what spirit and according to what laws the Anglo-American Union was formed; but I could give only a hurried and imperfect glance at the dangers which menace that confederation and could not furnish a detailed account of its chances of survival independently of its laws and manners. When speaking of the united republics, I hazarded no conjectures upon the permanence of republican forms in the New World; and when making frequent allusions to the commercial activity that reigns in the Union, I was unable to inquire into the future of the Americans as a commercial people....

Among these widely differing families of men, the first that attracts attention, the superior in intelligence, in power, and in enjoyment, is the white, or European, the MAN pre-eminently so called, below him appear the Negro and the Indian. These two unhappy races have nothing in common, neither birth, nor features, nor language, nor habits. Their only resemblance lies in their misfortunes. Both of them occupy an equally inferior position in the country they inhabit; both suffer from tyranny; and if their wrongs are not the same, they originate from the same authors.

If we reason from what passes in the world, we should almost say that the European is to the other races of mankind what man himself is to the lower animals: he makes them subservient to his use, and when he cannot subdue he destroys them. Oppression has, at one stroke, deprived the descendants of the Africans of almost all the privileges of humanity. The Negro of the United States has lost even the remembrance of his country; the language which his forefathers spoke is never heard around him; he abjured their religion and forgot their customs when he ceased to belong to Africa, without acquiring any claim to European privileges. But he remains half-way between the two communities, isolated between two races; sold by the one, repulsed by the other; finding not a spot in the universe to call by the name of country, except the faint image of a home which the shelter of his master's roof affords.

The Negro has no family: woman is merely the temporary companion of his pleasures, and his children are on an equality with himself from the moment of their birth. Am I to call it a proof of God's mercy, or a visitation of his wrath, that man, in certain states, appears to be insensible to his extreme wretchedness and almost obtains a depraved taste for the cause of his misfortunes? The

Negro, plunged in this abyss of evils, scarcely feels his own calamitous situation. Violence made him a slave, and the habit of servitude gives him the thoughts and desires of a slave, he admires his tyrants more than he hates them, and finds his joy and his pride in the servile imitation of those who oppress him. His understanding is degraded to the level of his soul.

The Negro enters upon slavery as soon as he is born, nay, he may have been purchased in the womb, and have begun his slavery before he began his existence. Equally devoid of wants and of enjoyment, and useless to himself, he learns, with his first notions of existence, that he is the property of another, who has an interest in preserving his life, and that the care of it does not devolve upon himself; even the power of thought appears to him a useless gift of Providence, and he quietly enjoys all the privileges of his debasement.

If he becomes free, independence is often felt by him to be a heavier burden than slavery; for, having learned in the course of his life to submit to everything except reason, he is too unacquainted with her dictates to obey them. A thousand new desires beset him, and he has not the knowledge and energy necessary to resist them: these are masters which it is necessary to contend with, and he has learned only to submit and obey. In short, he is sunk to such a depth of wretchedness that while servitude brutalizes, liberty destroys him.

Oppression has been no less fatal to the Indian than to the Negro race, but its effects are different. Before the arrival of white men in the New World, the inhabitants of North America lived quietly in their woods, enduring the vicissitudes and practicing the virtues and vices common to savage nations. The Europeans having dispersed the Indian tribes and driven them into the deserts, condemned them to a wandering life, full of inexpressible sufferings.

Savage nations are only controlled by opinion and custom. When the North American Indians had lost the sentiment of attachment to their country; when their families were dispersed, their traditions obscured, and the chain of their recollections broken; when all their habits were changed, and their wants in- creased beyond measure, European tyranny rendered them more disorderly and less civilized than they were before. The moral and physical condition of these tribes continually grew worse, and they became more barbarous as they became more wretched. Nevertheless, the Europeans have not been able to change the character of the Indians; and though they have had power to destroy, they have never been able to subdue and civilize them.

The lot of the Negro is placed on the extreme limit of servitude, while that of the Indian lies on the uttermost verge of liberty; and slavery does not produce more fatal effects upon the first than independence upon the second. The Negro has lost all property in his own person, and he cannot dispose of his existence without committing a sort of fraud. But the savage is his own master as soon as he is able to act; parental authority is scarcely known to him; he has never bent his will to that of any of his kind, nor learned the difference between voluntary obedience and a shameful subjection; and the very name of law is unknown to him. To be free, with him, signifies to escape from all the shackles of society. As he delights in this barbarous independence and would rather perish than sacrifice the least part of it, civilization has little hold over him.

Source: Alexis de Tocqueville, translated by Henry Reeve, *Democracy in America,*(New York: Addison-Wesley Educational Publishers, 1997).

Chapter Review ▶ ▶ ▶

Summary

The first half of the nineteenth century was a time of great advancement in terms of economic growth and invention as well as in the growth of American democracy, but it was also a time that witnessed the flowering of American culture in literature, magazines, and architecture. The period was also one of social experimentation with utopian societies and the founding of new religions. It was also a time of social progress as temperance, women's suffrage, and abolitionist movements all gained strength.

The economic growth was boosted by the opening of the west, which was made possible by the steam locomotive, John Deere's steel plow, and Cyrus McCormick's reaper. Samuel Morse's telegraph allowed Americans to build a communication network that would eventually connect the entire nation.

While these men's inventions would transform the nation, women worked to reform the nation so that they could have full participation in it. The first Convention on women's suffrage was held in Seneca Falls in 1848. Simultaneously, women's seminaries were founded to educate women and Oberlin College in Ohio first accepted women in 1851.

Education in general received a boost when Horace Mann led the fight for the first publicly supported schools in Massachusetts. Others would follow and the first free public schools in New York opened in 1832.

The more educated society would quickly become a more well-read society and great American authors, including Nathaniel Hawthorne, Herman Melville, and James Fenimore Cooper turned out masterpieces of literature that remain classics in the twenty-first century. Americans were also treated, however, to literature with a purpose such as Harriet Beecher Stowe's *Uncle Tom's Cabin* and William Lloyd Garrison's abolitionist Newspaper, *The Liberator*. Ralph Waldo Emerson and Henry David Thoreau wrote transcendentalist essays, while Joseph Smith of Palmyra New York dictated the Book of Mormon and founded the Mormon religion. After Smith's death at the hands of an angry mob in 1844, Brigham Young would lead Smith's followers to Utah where Mormonism remains the largest religion to date.

As Alexander de Tocqueville observed, American democracy flourished in the first half of the nineteenth century based on social mobility, decentralization, an optimistic vision, and the will of the people. Tocqueville did see a danger, however, in that there was the possibility that the majority could crush minority rights. In fact, since slavery remained, the rights of a significant minority were already crushed. Tocqueville, however, warned that if the slaves were freed, they would be likely to revolt because they would still be denied full citizenship rights and therefore remain without social mobility and unhappy with their plight. Although Tocqueville was not always right, in this case it appears that he accurately foresaw the American future.

Chronological Time Line

1802	Oliver Evans invents the steam engine.
1813	Richard B. Chenaworth developed a cast iron plow made in three separate pieces that made possible the replacement of broken parts.
1821	Emma Willard founds Troy Seminary, a private female seminary in New York.
1826	Josiah Holbrook organized a series of public lectures that were to form the basis of the National American Lyceum movement.
1830	Benjamin Silliman, professor at Yale, published *Elements of Chemistry*
1830	Peter Cooper builds the first American locomotive.
1830	Joseph Smith publishes the *Book of Mormon*
1831	William Lloyd Garrison founded *The Liberator*
1832	Free public schools established in New York
1832	John P. Kennedy publishes *Swallow Barn.*
1834	Cyrus McCormick patented the mechanical reaper, which greatly reduced the labor involved in harvesting grain.
1835	Alexis de Toqueville publishes *Democracy in America*
1836	Ralph Waldo Emerson publishes *Nature.*
1837	John Deere patented a steel plow that provided the solution to breaking the western land.
1837	Chicago becomes an incorporated municipality
1837	Mary Lyons founds Mount Holyoke, a private women's seminary, in Massachusetts.
1842	Crawford Long administers ether in surgery
1842	William Miller predicts that Jesus will return on March 21, 1843
1844	Samuel Morse sends his first telegraph message.

Chapter Review (cont'd) ▶ ▶ ▶

Time Line (cont'd)

1844	Joseph Smith is murdered by an angry mob
1847	Brook Farm is destroyed by fire.
1848	Elizabeth Cady Stanton and Lucretia Mott begin the women's suffrage movement at Seneca Falls, NY.
1848	John Noyes founds the Oneida Community.
1849	Elizabeth Blackwell becomes the first woman to be granted an M.D.
1850	Nathaniel Hawthorne publishes *The Scarlet Letter*
1851	Oberlin College begins admitting white women and African American men.
1851	Herman Melville publishes *Moby Dick*.
1852	Harriet Beecher Stowe publishes *Uncle Tom's Cabin*
1854	Henry David Thoreau publishes *Walden*.
1857	140 persons from an Arkansas wagon train are massacred by Mormons at Mountain Meadows, Utah

Key Terms

Richard B. Chenaworth: Invented a cast iron plow that could break the land in the West in 1813

John Deere: Invented a steel plow that was better for breaking land in the West than the iron plow in 1837

Cyrus McCormick: Invented the mechanical reaper in 1834

Oliver Evans: Invented the Steam Engine in 1802

Peter Cooper: Constructed the first Steam Locomotive in America in 1830

Charles Goodyear: Discovered the process known as vulcanization of rubber

Vulcanization: Makes rubber more useful by preventing it from becoming too sticky in hot weather

Samuel F. B. Morse: Invented the telegraph

Samuel Colt: Invented the pistol revolver

Key Terms (cont'd)

Seneca Falls Conference: First conference on women's suffrage

Normal Schools: Colleges constructed primarily to train teachers.

Dorothea Dix: Founded facilities to help the mentally ill.

Elizabeth Cady Stanton: A founder of the women's suffrage movement

Sylvester Graham: Inventor of the Graham Cracker who favored better living through better diet, hygiene, exercise, and celibacy.

Horace Mann: Instrumental in founding public education in America in Massachusetts.

Communitarians: Those that believed in the sharing of income and property.

John Noyes: Founded a community in Oneida New York based on "complete sharing" and "complex marriage."

William Miller: Founder of the Seventh Day Adventists who predicted that Jesus would return on March 21, 1843

Joseph Smith: Founder of the Mormon Church who dictated the *Book of the Mormon*

Brigham Young: Mormon leader that led the Mormons to Utah

Blood Atonement: A way for excommunicated Mormons to return to the Mormon Church by killing the enemies of the Church

Mountain Meadows Massacre: 140 members of an Arkansas wagon train were massacred by Mormons in 1857 in apparent blood atonement murders

Second Great Awakening: Religious Revival in the early to mid nineteenth century

Ralph Waldo Emerson: Leading Transcendentalist and author of *Nature*.

Henry David Thoreau: Leading Transcendentalist and author of *Walden*

Transcendentalism: The idea that humans should look within themselves for guidance

Nathaniel Hawthorne: Author of *The House of Seven Gables* and *The Scarlet Letter*

Herman Melville: Author of *Moby Dick*

James Fenimore Cooper: Author of *The Last of the Mohicans*

Edgar Allan Poe: Author of The Raven and numerous other classic and sometimes chilling tales.

Minstrel show: Featured white men wearing blackface make-up, and it was both a racist spectacle deriding African Americans and a vehicle for calling attention to aspects of African American folk culture

William Lloyd Garrison: Founder of *The Liberator,* an abolitionist Newspaper

Frederick Douglass: African American abolitionist and advocate of women's suffrage

Harriet Beecher Stowe: Author of *Uncle Tom's Cabin*

Alexis de Tocqueville: Frenchman who toured America and published his observations in *Democracy in America* in 1835

Chapter Review (cont'd) ▶ ▶ ▶

Sources Consulted

Elizabeth Fox-Genovese and Eugene Genovese, *The Mind of the Master Class: History and Faith in the Southern Slaveholders' Worldview* (2005).

Nathan O. Hatch, *The Democratization of American Christianity* (1989).

Walter Johnson, *Soul by Soul: Life Inside the Antebellum Slave Market* (1999).

David S. Reynolds, *Beneath the American Renaissance: The Subversive Imagination in the Age of Emerson and Melville* (1988).

Jane Tompkins, *Sensational Designs: The Cultural Work of American Fiction, 1790–1860* (1985).

Bertram Wyatt-Brown, *Southern Honor: Ethics and Behavior in the Old South* (1982).

7 The Growth of Democratic Government, 1824–1844

iStockphotos

Outline

Wikipedia photo

iStockphoto

Wikipedia photo

Wikipedia photo

The Election of 1824— "The Corrupt Bargain"

Four Political Factions

▶Henry Clay, Speaker of the House of Representatives, chose to support Adams in his presidential campaign. Once Adams was elected, Clay was appointed his Secretary of State.
Wikipedia photo

The sands of political allegiance never shifted more swiftly than in the last year and a half of James Monroe's administration when the "Good Feelings" in the immediate aftermath of the War of 1812 degenerated into feuding so intense that historian Sean Wilentz labeled the period "The Era of Bad Feelings." There was still, for all practical purposes, only one political party. Although the Federalist Party continued to exist for a while in enclaves, most citizens called themselves Democratic Republicans, including the four leading candidates for the presidency in 1824.

Before 1824, the congressional caucus of the Democratic Republican majority had chosen the party's presidential candidates; however, during Monroe's second administration, the caucus—as a means of choosing Presidential candidates—met with increasing opposition. The public considered the caucus as undemocratic and sought reforms that would be more democratic in process.

There was also growing conviction that it was not in the country's best interest for a newly elected president to think that he owed his office to Congress. This provides an excellent example of the evolution of the American party system, for criticism of the caucus eventually led to establishment of national party conventions in the 1830s.

Politicians, impressed by the strenuous objections against the caucus, moved to distance themselves from it. In a number of states, either the legislature or state conventions nominated their own favorite sons, and a full three quarters of the states elected candidates by popular vote. The result was that when the Democratic Republican caucus was held in February 1824 only 66 of the 216 Democratic Republican congressmen even attended.

The caucus chose Secretary of the Treasury William H. Crawford, a Georgian, as their candidate. Most of Crawford's strength was in the Southeast, and his rivals and their many followers scorned his selection. New England supported John Quincy Adams of Massachusetts, son of John Adams and secretary of state in Monroe's cabinet. Kentucky, Missouri, and Ohio looked to Speaker of the House Henry Clay of Kentucky. Meanwhile, Pennsylvania, most of the West, and some of the Southeast rallied behind "Old Hickory," General Andrew Jackson of Tennessee, the famous hero from the War of 1812.

MAP 7.1 The Presidential Election of 1824

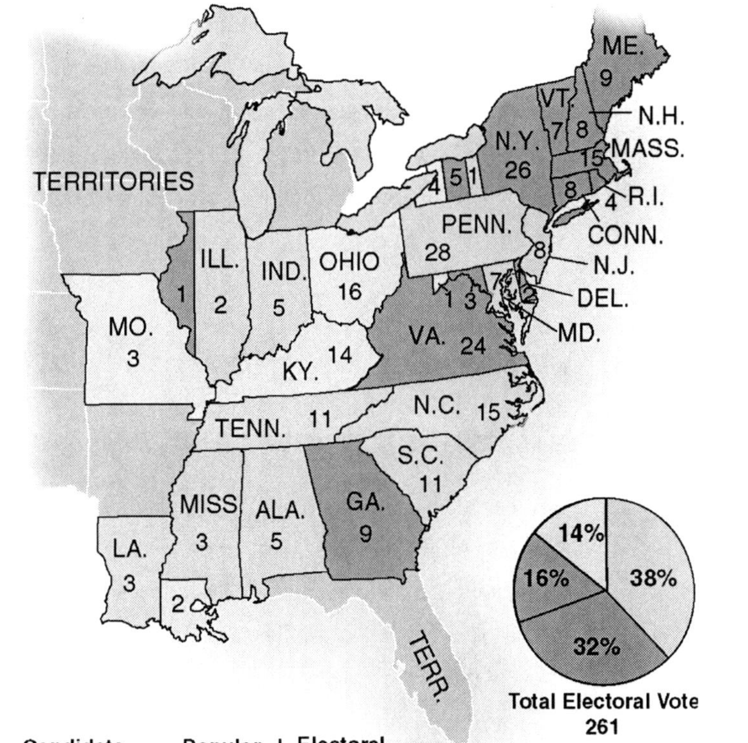

Candidate (No. Parties)	Popular Vote	Electoral Vote
Adams	108,740	84
Jackson	153,544	99
Crawford	46,618	41
Clay	47,136	37

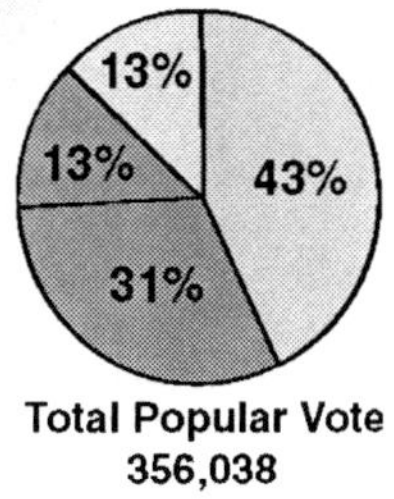

Adams Defeats Jackson

The real contest in the presidential election of 1824 was between Adams and Jackson. Jackson received approximately 153,000 popular votes to Adams's 108,000 and ninety-nine electoral votes to Adams's eighty-four. However, Crawford and Clay, with forty-one and thirty-seven electoral votes respectively, split the total sufficiently that neither Jackson nor Adams received a majority of the electoral vote.

Constitutional procedure, in such cases, called for the decision to be referred to the House of Representatives. Here each state had one vote, and the three candidates with the most electoral votes—Jackson, Adams, and Crawford—remained in the running.

House Speaker Clay, no longer a presidential candidate, held the balance of power in the House decision. Although he earlier had instigated an anti-Adams campaign in the West, Clay personally disliked Jackson more than Adams and feared him as a future Western rival. As a consequence, Clay made amends with his former adversary and decided to support Adams.

With Clay's support in the House, Adams was elected on the first ballot on February 9, 1825. The new President promptly appointed Clay his secretary of state. Just as promptly, Jacksonians angrily charged that a "corrupt bargain" accounted for both Adams's election and Clay's appointment. There probably was an implicit—if not explicit—understanding between Adams and Clay that the latter would receive the Cabinet post in exchange for his support, but no evidence exists to demonstrate corruption. In fact, whether or not such a bargain is corrupt at all, or just good Democratic politics remains a matter of debate. The appointment of Clay was, however, an enormous political problem for the Adams administration; it saddled both men with tarnished reputations and ensured that the new administration commenced under a cloud. To Jackson supporters, the idea that the man who had won a plurality of both the popular vote and the electoral vote would not be president violated their sense of justice.

The J. Q. Adams Interlude

Adams in the White House

President Adams projected a bold domestic program. An intellectual like his father before him, in his first annual message he called for laws creating a national university (first proposed by Washington), a naval academy, and a national astronomical observatory. Adams likewise advocated a consistent national militia law, a uniform bankruptcy law, an orderly, federally financed system of internal improvements, and a Department of the Interior to manage America's vast public land holdings.

Such accomplishments, however, simply were not forthcoming. From the outset Adams made little effort to push his policies once he had enunciated them. A principal cause of this failure was his view that the executive should abstain from what he considered undue interference in the legislative branch. As a consequence, numerous White House proposals, made year after year, were never introduced in Congress as legislative bills or resolutions. This is in spite of the fact that Adams was endowed with a sharp mind and a Puritan work ethic that had him awake and working at 4:00 A.M. daily. Adams wrote so much as President that he learned to write with both hands so as to alleviate writer's cramp.

Despite his work ethic and intellectual prowess, Adams had personal defects that prevented his being a natural leader. A man of determined character and a high degree of moral integrity, Adams was aloof and unpleasant toward many associates and disliked public contact. Though a man with his diplomatic background should have overcome such traits, he could appear ungracious and petty in the most minor human relations.

Compounding such personal handicaps were continuing complexities as to what was constitutional and what was not. Politicians had conflicting ideas on what the federal government's role in the economy should be and how much authority the federal government should have over the states. While these problems were not peculiar to the period 1825–1829, the White House provided no strong directing force toward helping to solve them.

Disagreements among senators and representatives over the construction of the Constitution, coupled with their local interests, contributed to the refusal by Congress to develop a systematic national public works program. This was one of Adams's greatest disappointments. Furthermore, Congressional appropriations followed no logical pattern; and thus legislative logrolling—the exchange of favors among lawmakers—left undone some of the most necessary projects.

Despite this haphazard approach, however, internal improvements during Adams' tenure were significant. Rivers were dredged and harbors made more serviceable with increased federal appropriations voted for those purposes than in the previous thirty years. Lack of funds had halted work on the National Road in 1818, but new federal money permitted construction to resume in 1825. By mid-century this important highway stretched from Cumberland, Maryland, to Vandalia, Illinois.

Democratic Republicans, National Republicans

Off to an inauspicious start in the first half of his term, Adams was hopelessly beset after 1826 by a congressional coalition fighting him at every turn. Increasingly, Jackson people were known as Democratic Republicans, and Adams-Clay people as National Republicans. Jacksonians did not forget that a "deal" had made Adams President despite the electorate's clear preference for Jackson. Sectional hostilities were increasing, and states' rights adherents opposed Adams's bold plans to expand federal authority. Political idealists might praise Adams for being one of the least dominating of all our chief executives, but his effectiveness suffered for this very reason. His opponents played politics to the hilt, especially after they came to control Congress.

Sectionalism and partisanship in the 1820s were most flagrant in the area of tariff debates and tariff votes. One reason for the passage of the tariff of 1824, enacted while President Monroe was still in office, had been its inclusion of duties on raw wool and other farm products. These tariffs were attractive to the West, but Eastern manufacturers of woolen textiles complained that their profits diminished because raw materials were so expensive. Yet in 1827, a bill containing a compromise that was supposedly acceptable to both Northeasterners and Northwesterners was defeated in the Senate by Vice-President Calhoun's tie-breaking vote.

The next year a tariff crisis occurred that led to further tariff disputes. In drafting the tariff bill of that year, Jacksonians in Congress gave top priorities to the protectionist features desired by the mid-Atlantic States, where Jackson hoped for strong support in the next presidential election. His congressional friends virtually ignored New England interests, assuming that Adams's fellow New Englanders could not avoid voting for a high tariff in any case. The measure was offensive to a wide variety of individuals and regions, however, especially the Southeast.

Painted into a corner by the shrewd strategy, Adams loathingly signed the bill. Then, because of his signature, he—not the Jacksonians—bore most of the blame for it. Thereafter his name was associated with what critics labeled the "Tariff of Abominations."

Foreign Relations

Adams's background in diplomacy had led his supporters to believe he would leave a memorable record in foreign affairs. Yet he achieved nothing as president on a par with his earlier success as secretary of state. During Adams' presidency, the United States failed to obtain from England the right of free navigation of the St. Lawrence River. Furthermore, American shippers had to resort to a roundabout trade when the ports of the British West Indies were closed to Yankee merchantmen as tightly as they had ever been in 1826. Adams retaliated by closing American ports to England. The result was that American trade with England diminished precipitously, and the American economy sagged.

Other diplomatic problems also went unsolved during the Adams years. Old claims against France for damages arising out of the wars of the French Revolution were no nearer settlement in 1829 than in 1825. Additionally, though delegates were sent to the Congress of Panama in 1826—called for the purpose of establishing cooperation among the republics of the Western Hemisphere—one died en route to Panama and the other arrived too late. The mission accomplished nothing.

In the entire field of foreign relations, Adams could point with pride only to an unprecedented number of minor treaties and to the renewal in 1827 of the Anglo-American agreement covering joint occupation of Oregon. With these exceptions, his administration was a negative interlude in diplomatic history.

Jackson Triumphant

The Election of 1828

The election of 1828 has long been seen as a watershed in American political history, owing partially to the vastly increased voter turnout that year; but it also marked the beginning of a new era. It was the first presidential election after two momentous deaths that had occurred on July 4, 1826. On that day—exactly fifty years since the *Declaration of Independence*—both Thomas Jefferson and John Adams died. Since Washington had died in 1799, therefore the country had lost its first three presidents—its most important living links with the Revolution. Moreover, his awe-inspiring father would no longer be around to challenge—and sometimes torment—John Quincy Adams.

Even if Adams's personality had been more attractive, his attitude more gracious, and his leadership more compelling, he would have had trouble in any contest with the forces arrayed against him. As early as 1825, the general assembly of Tennessee placed Andrew Jackson on the track for the 1828 presidential race. Moreover, except in New England, enthusiasm for Jackson appeared everywhere. From New York to Illinois and from Pennsylvania to Louisiana, acclaim for Jackson resonated. Furthermore, Jackson had impressive allies. Vice-President Calhoun, an outstanding South Carolinian who had been Monroe's secretary of war, did little to conceal his antipathy toward Adams. Another important addition to the Jackson high command was Senator Martin Van Buren of New York. Formerly a Crawford lieutenant, the ingratiating Van Buren worked dexterously with Calhoun and others to weld a powerful combination of Southerners and Northerners opposing Adams and favoring Jackson. The combination was especially powerful in that it included both established men and those representing popular democratic movements.

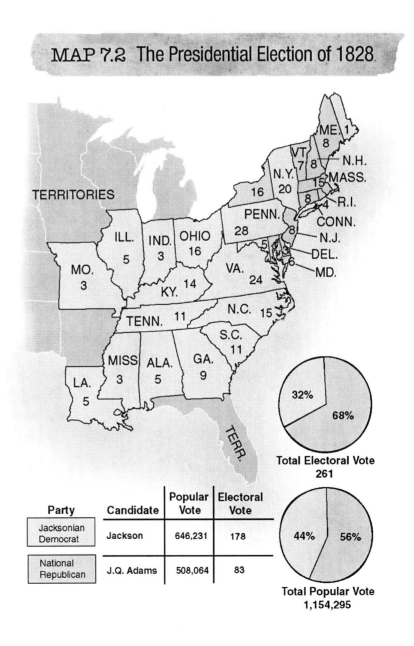

MAP 7.2 The Presidential Election of 1828

Total Electoral Vote
261

Total Popular Vote
1,154,295

Party	Candidate	Popular Vote	Electoral Vote
Jacksonian Democrat	Jackson	646,231	178
National Republican	J.Q. Adams	508,064	83

The election of 1828 is also noteworthy for the fact that during the campaign, backers of both Adams and Jackson indulged in disreputable tactics. Pro-Adams journalists made much of Jackson's reputation for military highhandedness. They dragged the name of Jackon's wife Rachel through the gutters of partisan filth by reminding voters that her divorce from another man had not been final in the 1790s when she became Jackson's wife. Furthermore, Jackson's detractors pointed out that there was no record of Jackson's actual marriage to Rachel and argued, therefore, that he was "living in sin." This infuriated Jackson and he "remarried" Rachel during the campaign so as to satisfy the critics. The underhanded publicity and criticism may have had something to do with Rachel Jackson's death from a heart attack soon after the election. Pro-Jackson editors, however, were no innocent bystanders when the mud was slung; and Adams was pilloried as a billiards-playing aristocrat who was out of touch with the common people. That Jackson was a wealthy plantation owner was beside the point.

Substantive issues, however, were not entirely ignored. Since the country had not reached the period of national conventions and platforms, there was no formal enunciation of principles. Jackson in some minds was linked with proposals for tariff reform; and Adams—fairly or unfairly—was linked with the Tariff of Abominations. Critics of the Second Bank of the United States hoped that Jackson, as President, would oppose it. However, some advocates of the federally funded construction of roads and canals and the dredging of rivers and harbors preferred Adams because he had spoken out in favor of federal appropriations for these purposes. Nevertheless, there was no unanimity on the issue, as others believed that Jackson would support federal funding for internal improvements more heartily than Adams.

"Hurrah for Jackson!" was the rallying cry that appealed to most Americans. About three times as many people voted in 1828 as had voted four years before, and the results were recorded with more care. Jackson, the Democratic-Republican candidate, scored a clear triumph with approximately 647,000 popular votes to 508,000 for Adams. In the Electoral College the margin was two to one, with 178 votes for Jackson and 83 for Adams. This growth in the size of the electorate reflected three things: population growth, an increased turnout of eligible voters, *and* a growth in voting eligibility due to property ownership qualifications that had been more or less eliminated by this time in a number of states.

"King Mob"

Jackson's inauguration in March 1829 was accompanied by a demonstration unparalleled in American history. The thousands of people assembled in Washington behaved well outside the Capitol while Jackson read his in-

▶During the election of 1828, pro-Adams journalists made a scandal of Andrew Jackson's marriage to Rachel Jackson, claiming she had not been legally divorced when Jackson married her in the 1790s. An angry Jackson remarried his wife during the campaign to satisfy the public's concern. *Wikipedia photo*

augural address. When the time came for the White House reception, however, "King Mob" took over. In muddy boots and shoes men, women, and children crashed, trampled, and crushed their way into and through the White House. Only when someone thought of placing refreshments on the White House lawn did the crowd move outdoors.

Jackson's political enemies were shocked by this public demonstration and talked darkly of a reenactment of French Revolution excesses on American soil. Actually, the scene had been more a matter of bad manners and an explosion of pent-up energy than anything else. The base of governmental support had broadened appreciably in the several years preceding the election, but no excesses other than social ones upset the evolutionary development of an increasingly democratic state. Nevertheless, when the multitude faded away shortly after inauguration day, the symbol of "King Mob" remained as a counterweight to "King Caucus" of old.

Andrew Jackson: Man of the People

Andrew Jackson resonated so well with the common people partially because of his humble roots. Though Jackson was a wealthy planter at the time of his election, he had been born in a log cabin in North Carolina and had made his reputation as the hero of the Battle of New Orleans and one of the country's greatest Native American fighters. Jackson also connected with the common people through his speech, which was laden with incorrect grammar like that of the uneducated masses. Jackson had little formal education, was a poor writer, and an atrocious speller. Like the common people that loved him, Jackson also chewed tobacco incessantly and spit tobacco juice into spittoons while entertaining guests at the White House.

Jackson had a deserved reputation as a real-life tough guy. In the words of one of Jackson's fellow law students, he was the "most roaring, rollicking, game-cocking, horse racing, card playing, mischievous fellow." His nickname was "Old Hickory" because hickory was such

▶ The "King Mob" incident occurred at the reception for Andrew Jackson's inaugurational speech. In muddy boots and shoes, men, women, and children crashed, trampled, and crushed their way into and through the White House. The drunken mob left the White House a great mess, with several thousand dollars worth of damage. *Wikipedia photo*

▶Americans identified with their new president; Jackson came from humble beginnings, had little formal education, chewed tobacco like the common people, was a real-life tough guy, and he had a very Southern sense of honor, which he attributed to his mother. *Wikipedia photo*

a hard wood, and Jackson was such a hard man. In addition, Jackson had a very Southern sense of honor, which he said that he got from his mother, who instructed him to "never lie, cheat, steal, or sue anyone at law for insults. Handle insults to one's honor yourself." As a consequence, Jackson was twice wounded by gunshot defending his honor: once in the shoulder in a bar fight and once in the chest from a duel in 1806. Jackson had allowed his opponent to shoot first. The bullet lodged in Jackson's ribs, which caused Jackson pain the rest of his life.

Reorganization of the Cabinet

The Democratic Party of sixty-two-year-old President Jackson charted its administrative course in an atmosphere of confusion. Though Jackson's close associate Martin Van Buren became secretary of state, several cabinet members were more closely identified with Vice-President John C. Calhoun than with either Jackson or Van Buren.

Almost at once there erupted one of those odd controversies that occasionally have influenced American political history, a controversy whose ramifications played themselves out over a course of two years. Secretary of War John H. Eaton, a Jackson appointee who had long been on intimate terms with the new president, had recently married a young widow whose comeliness was said to have attracted him before her first husband's death. The story was that Calhoun's wife and the wives of Calhoun's cabinet friends took the lead in snubbing Peggy Eaton. Jackson resented the social chill, associating it with the shameful treatment of his own late wife during the campaign.

Van Buren, who endeared himself to Jackson by siding with the Eatons (and who, being a widower, had no wife to consult about the matter), offered to resign from his cabinet post because he knew that a cabinet reorganization would enable Jackson to be rid of the problem. Eaton followed Van Buren's example, and in the spring of 1831 Jackson requested resignations from all the remaining cabinet members except one. Calhoun's supporters were excluded from the succeeding cabinet while Van Buren retained the confidence of Jackson, who promptly named him minister to Britain. John Eaton eventually resigned from the Cabinet in an attempt to put an end to the affair as Washington women continued to snub his wife, Peggy. Happiness, however, did not come to the Eaton household with John's resignation. Peggy, age fifty-nine, subsequently left her husband for a nineteen-year-old dance instructor.

Changing Problems, Changing Arguments

Meanwhile, a more fundamental division between Jackson and Vice-President Calhoun developed over two other issues. First, the President was greatly disturbed to discover that years before Calhoun had recommended Jackson be court-martialed for his conduct during the Seminole War of 1818. More significantly, Jackson hotly disapproved of Calhoun's contention that a state had the right, within its borders, to nullify a federal statute. It was concerning this "nullification" question that the smoldering antipathies of the two ranking officials of the country flared into the open.

The nullification stand of Vice-President Calhoun and his fellow South Carolinian, Senator Robert Y. Hayne, resulted from their state's opposition to the tariff policies of the United States—especially the Tariff of Abominations. They believed that while the industrial Northeast benefited from the higher tariffs, the agricultural South was damaged by the rising customs duties.

Economic conditions in the Southeast in the early 1830s were steadily worsening. The extension of cotton planting to the rich bottomland of Alabama, Mississippi, and Louisiana (then the Southwest) had expanded production of the staple; cotton prices consequently dropped. Many planters in the Southeast, threatened with ruin by their inability to compete on relatively poor soil, pulled stakes and took their slaves to the Southwest for a fresh start. The consequent loss of population compounded the Southeast's financial difficulties. There were also political reverberations, since fewer people meant smaller representation in Congress for South Carolina and similarly affected states.

Calhoun joined Hayne and other South Carolina politicians in the conviction that most of their state's troubles could be traced to the tariff. In 1828, while running for reelection to the vice-presidency as a Jackson adherent, Calhoun had secretly written the "South Carolina Exposition." This document, published without his name, declared protective tariffs unconstitutional. It went on to assert the right of any state to "nullify" or prevent the enforcement within its boundaries of what it deemed to be an unconstitutional act of Congress. Calhoun's authorship of the "Exposition" was not generally known in 1830, but his new position was becoming clear in some minds, including Jackson's.

In 1830, Vice-President Calhoun carefully coached the less brilliant Hayne when the latter eloquently defended the extreme states' rights position in a dramatic Senate debate with Senator Daniel Webster of Massachusetts. As Massachusetts had become more industrialized and accordingly adopted a high tariff policy, Webster had abandoned his low-tariff convictions (he opposed the Tariff of 1824); and by 1830, he was a high-tariff advocate. Moreover, Webster identified the changed economic attitude with a political nationalism that contrasted with the growing sectionalism of South Carolina. In so doing, he sought to equate the North's economic interest with patriotic virtue.

The famous Senate debate of 1830 arose as the result of a resolution by Connecticut Senator Samuel A. Foot, which had as one aim a restriction of the sale of public land. The land question was a vital matter to congressmen from the West. Current land laws, in effect since the early 1820s, provided key components: a minimum purchase of eighty acres; a minimum price of $1.25 an acre; no credit system; and exceptions that recognized, but did not wholly satisfy, Western insistence on lower land prices and on the preemption principle by which genuine settlers would have the first chance to buy at the minimum price. Already in the air were proposals for liberalizing land policies. Eastern laborers joined western farmers in favoring such liberalization, and Southerners saw an advantage in linking western land desires to

Southern low-tariff hopes. Thus, the opposition to Foot's restrictive resolution was not limited to any single section.

Senator Thomas H. Benton of Missouri resoundingly assailed Foot's resolution. Benton saw it as a scheme of New England manufacturers—fearful of losing factory operatives to the lure of the West—to make cheap land inaccessible and so keep their workers in the East. Hayne took the issue to Benton's supporters, but he took a different approach. If Foot's proposition were put into effect, he said, future prices of western land would be high. The income would then constitute "a fund for corruption," adding to the power of the federal government and endangering the independence of the states. Thereupon, Webster launched his first reply to Hayne. Denying that the East was illiberal toward the West, the erstwhile sectionalist from Boston proclaimed his nationalism.

Hayne again spoke, reminding his hearers of New England's anti-Union attitude during the War of 1812. Where, he asked, were New England nationalists then? Had not residents of Webster's section, plotters of the Hartford Convention, favored the same constitutional arguments contained in the "South Carolina Exposition"? The Northeastern sectionalists of old, Hayne insisted, currently championed theories that they formerly had decried. Their sincerity, he implied, was open to grave doubts and their past words and tactics hovered as reminders of appalling inconsistencies.

Webster's "Second Reply to Hayne"

After Hayne spiritedly elaborated on the extreme states' rights point of view, Webster answered him in what is widely regarded as one of the greatest speeches ever delivered in Congress. In New England, he said, what Hayne had discussed was consigned to a previous time. New Englanders were thinking not of the past, but of the present and the future. Vital now was the wellbeing of America as a whole. Nothing could be more preposterous than the idea that twenty-four states could interpret the Constitution as each of them saw fit. The Union should not be "dissevered, discordant, belligerent." The country should not be "rent with civil feuds, or drenched ... in fraternal blood." It was delusion and folly to think of "Liberty first, and Union afterwards." Instead, "dear to every true American heart" was that blazing sentiment—"Liberty *and* Union, now and forever, one and inseparable!"

In subsequent years, countless young Americans memorized the peroration of Webster's "Second Reply to Hayne," regarded at the time and subsequently in the nineteenth century as a particularly eloquent statement of democratic nationalism. Calhoun, the idea man for Hayne, had morphed from an ardent defender of a strong central government to a defender of states rights in order to protect his key constituency, the South Carolina planters, while Webster had gone in the other direction.

Calhoun and Jackson succeeded Hayne and Webster in the public spotlight during the spring of the same year (1830) when a Jefferson birthday banquet was held in Washington's Indian Queen Hotel. Jackson offered fellow Democrats a toast: "The Federal Union, it must be preserved!" Calhoun countered with a toast of his own: "The Union, next to our liberty, most dear!" The disparate sentiments were not lost upon the diners. President Jackson had hurled down the gauntlet, and Vice-President Calhoun had picked it up. After that, their relations became ever more strained; and before Jackson's first term ended, Calhoun had resigned the vice-presidency.

Two Controversial Vetoes

Jackson sternly opposed the Bank of the United States and objected to most proposals to use federal funds for internal improvements. The improvements question loomed large in 1830, when Congress passed a bill authorizing subscription of stock in a private company constructing a road between Maysville and Lexington, Kentucky. Jackson vetoed the proposition on the ground that the Maysville Road lay wholly in one state and therefore was not entitled to financial support from Washington.

Jackson's controversial veto seemed tyrannical to many, and enemies dubbed him "King Andrew." Henry Clay and other transportation-minded Americans charged the President with being an impediment in the march of progress. Clay, it should be noted, was the prime advocate of the so-called "American System," a plan that encompassed a national bank, protective tariffs, and federal aid for internal improvements. The veto, however, was well received by Southern strict constructionists and by others resentful of what they deemed undue interference by the federal government in purely state affairs. Moreover, Jackson's selection of a Western road as a target of his disapproval pleased those in New York and Pennsylvania who had financed their own projects locally and saw no reason why people in other regions should get government money.

Jackson was hostile to the Bank of the United States for at least four reasons. First, he held the Jeffersonian strict-construction view. He maintained that Congress was not empowered by the Constitution to incorporate a bank outside the District of Columbia (in spite of the fact that the Supreme Court had ruled the Bank constitutional in 1819, along with the doctrine of Implied Powers from the Necessary and Proper Clause in *McCulloch v. Maryland*). Secondly, Jackson also doubted that the Bank served the nation's welfare and accused it of not having established a sound and uniform currency. Old Hickory had an ingrained suspicion of the note issues of all banks (trusting only gold and silver)—with the Bank of the United States the most notorious offender because it was above all the most powerful. His third objection was that the Bank played politics in election campaigns and influenced congressmen by lending them money or placing them on its payroll. Finally, Jackson erroneously argued that the bank was controlled by foreigners though 80 percent of the bank's stock was held by domestic entities.

Moreover, it should be noted that there was a political payoff to the anti-bank stance. One of the key proponents of the Jacksonian constituency, the urban workingmen, tended to see the Bank as an undemocratic monopoly; and these workers were organizing into parties in cities such as New York and Philadelphia.

Jackson's charge against the Bank of political activity and legislative influence was for the most part warranted. Jackson came to consider the Bank a monopoly. Although government deposits were exclusively entrusted to it, the Bank was not a monopolistic enterprise in the customary sense of the term. Instead, there were many competing private banks. To be fair, under Nicholas Biddle's leadership, the Bank of the United States had made important contributions to American economic stability. Regardless of what Jackson said, it did provide a sound currency. Moreover, its monetary standards and the financial power it wielded often exerted a salutary effect on the fluctuating currencies of state banks—many of which were dangerously weak.

In 1832, the Bank of the United States' charter had four years to run. However, Clay, at that time a United States senator, was in full accord with bank president Biddle's desire to see the institution re-chartered long in advance of the legal deadline. Consequently, Clay pushed a Bank Bill through both houses of Congress. Then, chosen by the National Republicans as their standard bearer in opposition to Jackson, he strove to make the bank the main issue in the campaign of 1832. Jackson lost no time in vetoing the re-chartering act in July 1832.

The Election of 1832

It can be argued that Clay was disadvantaged in his presidential race by the existence of an Anti-Masonic third party that considered the Masonic fraternity an aristocratic threat to democratic institutions. There was opposition to both Jackson and Clay because they were Masons.

The Anti-Masons nominated William Wirt of Maryland, who had served for twelve years as attorney general under Monroe and Adams. Ironically, Wirt was also a Mason. They chose their candidate by a party convention, foreshadowing the method soon to be adopted by all the parties. The choice of National Republicans was Clay, while the Democrats supported Jackson, with Van Buren as his running mate. In most states, the anti-Jackson following was concentrated behind either Clay or Wirt, with the other man staying out of the contest. Even with

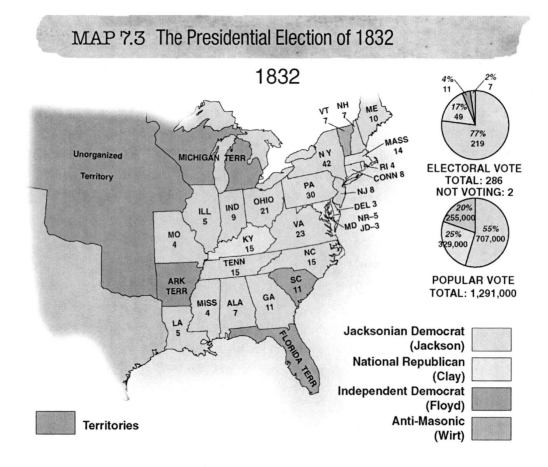

MAP 7.3 The Presidential Election of 1832

this tactical advantage, however, neither Clay nor Wirt had a very good chance to oust the popular Jackson. Furthermore, the bank issue did not aid Clay as he had anticipated it might.

Not all historians agree on the exact size of the popular vote. It is clear, however, that Jackson won easily; his popular vote was approximately 687,500 against 530,000 for Clay and Wirt combined. Jackson was victorious in nearly the entire South and West, plus the "big" states of New York and Pennsylvania. In the Electoral College, Jackson scored 219 to Clay's 49 and Wirt's 7. South Carolina, still voting through its legislature, refused to back any of the regular candidates and cast eleven protest ballots for John Floyd of Virginia.

"King Andrew"
Crisis Over Nullification

No sooner was the 1832 election decided than South Carolina brought the nullification controversy to the forefront. The issue immediately in question was the Tariff of 1832, which lowered customs duties, but not enough to satisfy critics in the state. The newly elected state legislature, composed predominantly of "nullifiers," ordered a special state convention to deal with the problem. The convention met in Columbia in November and took three major steps: It declared the tariffs of 1828 and 1832 null and void within South Carolina, called on the state legislature to prohibit collection of duties in the state after February 1, 1833, and warned that South Carolina would secede if the federal government used force to collect duties.

Jackson responded to South Carolina's saber rattling by dispatching naval and military units to that state and issuing a stirring Nullification Proclamation, which declared in part:

> I consider, then, the power to annul a law of the United States, assumed by one State, incompatible with the existence of the Union, contradicted expressly by the letter of the Constitution, unauthorized by its spirit, inconsistent with every principle on which it was founded, and destructive of the great object for which it was formed.

Possible bloodshed was averted when Senator Clay of Kentucky sponsored a compromise tariff bill providing for a gradual reduction of duties year by year until 1842. Though the protectionist New England and Middle Atlantic states bitterly opposed such a tariff reduction, Congress passed the compromise bill and Jackson signed it on March 2, 1833. On the same day, a Force Bill—giving Jackson congressional authority to use arms to enforce collection of customs—became law. Jackson threatened to send two hundred thousand federal troops to South Carolina, if necessary, to enforce the tariff.

The Compromise Tariff of 1833 was much more reasonable by South Carolina's standards than preceding tariffs had been. The Columbia convention met once again and withdrew its nullification ordinance, but as a face-saving gesture the convention nullified Jackson's Force

Bill. The President regarded this last defiant act as of little practical significance. Both sides now considered the issue closed, and both claimed victory.

The United States Bank

Jackson, interpreting his success in the 1832 election as a mandate from the voters to continue action against the Bank of the United States, decided to remove federal deposits from the Bank gradually and deposit them in selected state banks. An order to this effect was issued on September 26, 1833. When Secretary of the Treasury Duane refused to enforce it, Jackson replaced him with Attorney General Roger B. Taney. By the end of the year twenty-three state banks—dubbed "pet banks" by anti-Jacksonians—had been selected as depositories.

Jackson's move against the Bank met with considerable political opposition, and his policy was attacked in Congress. In December 1833, Henry Clay introduced Senate resolutions to censure both the Treasury action and President Jackson for having "assumed upon himself authority and power not conferred by the constitution and laws, but in derogation of both." By the spring of 1834, President Jackson's opponents even had a new name: the Whig Party. This name played off of the idea that Jackson was acting as if he were "King Andrew," and it was the Whig Party in Britain that espoused the limiting of royal power.

When the Senate resolutions were adopted, Jackson formally protested that it had charged him with an impeachable offense but had denied him an opportunity to defend himself. The Senate, however, rejected Jackson's protest and, as a further measure of defiance, did not approve Taney's nomination as secretary of the treasury. Only after a three-year Senate battle did Jackson's supporters succeed in having the resolution of censure expunged from the Senate record. Nevertheless, in eliminating the Bank of the United States, Jackson had eliminated a security measure against a banking crisis and rendered the entire American banking system more volatile.

Hard Money and Land

Jackson's bank policy contributed to a series of severe nationwide economic reverses. Even though the administration withdrew federal funds from the United States Bank gradually, using them to meet current expenses while depositing new revenue in "pet banks," the Bank's decline was sharp enough to instigate an economic recession in 1833–1834. Nicholas Biddle's actions aggravated the situation: To make up for the lost federal deposits and to force congressional reconsideration of the Bank's charter, Biddle took the unnecessarily harsh step of calling in all outstanding loans, thus creating demands for credit from state banks which they could not meet. Only under strong pressure from businessmen and from the governor of Pennsylvania did Biddle at last reverse his policy.

The country quickly pulled out of the economic doldrums by the end of 1834 and almost immediately headed into a dangerous inflationary spiral. States chartered hundreds of new private banks, each issuing its own banknotes and setting its own interest rates, typically much higher than prior to Jackson's bank veto. These factors, along with an influx of silver from Mexican mines, caused prices to rise 50 percent between 1834 and 1837. State banks also used their newly acquired federal funds for speculative purposes. At the same time, the federal government greatly increased its sale of public land, inadvertently encouraging the most reckless speculators.

Although political leaders were divided in their reaction to the inflationary trend, Jackson agreed with Senator Benton's prediction that "the present bloat in the paper system" could foreshadow another depression. On July 11, 1836, Jackson chose to issue a Specie Circular, which provided that after August 15 all public lands purchased from the federal government were to be paid for only in gold or silver, with one exception: until December 15, people actually settling on the land were permitted to use state bank notes to purchase parcels of land up to 320 acres. The impact of Jackson's action was to greatly diminish the value of the money supply since paper banknotes could not be used to purchase federal land. Jackson's sudden policy reversal sharply curtailed western land sales and weakened public confidence in the state banks. It also encouraged the hoarding of specie (hard money) and was a factor in bringing on the Panic of 1837, a severe economic recession that would last through 1843.

The western land problem figured repeatedly in congressional debates from Jackson's day to Lincoln's and beyond. Benton and other Westerners favored the policy of "graduation," by which prices for the less desirable portions of the public domain would be reduced from $1.25 an acre to $1.00, 50¢, or less, depending on the length of time they had been on sale. Westerners also wanted the policy of preemption, which favored squatters that lived on the land, rather than speculators that bought the land for the purpose of resale at a profit.

Although Congress passed no graduation bill until 1854, a temporary Preemption Act in 1830 authorized settlers to buy up to 160 acres of public land at a minimum price of $1.25 an acre. The Act was renewed regularly and remained in force until 1842.

Not to be confused with preemption was Henry Clay's advocacy of "distribution." In 1833, the Kentuckian drove through both the House and Senate a bill stipulating that most of the revenue derived from public-land sales be distributed among all the states, with a smaller fraction earmarked for states where the sales took place. That was a typical example of Clay's desire to appeal politically to two sections at once. Jackson, however, pocket-vetoed the bill, thwarting his adversary and identifying himself further with the actual settlers of the Northwest and Southwest. Jackson was the first president to use the pocket veto, whereby any bill passed by Congress during the last ten days of a session does not pass without the president's signature. Since Clay's distribution bill was passed during the last ten days of a Congressional session, Jackson did not have to formally veto the bill to kill it; he merely did not sign the bill and thus accomplished the same result.

Jackson's Foreign Policy

Jackson's handling of foreign affairs was at times headstrong and unconventional. The only real diplomatic crisis during his two terms was the claim of seizures of American ships during the Napoleonic wars against France. Adams and preceding presidents had failed to collect; however, at Jackson's urging, France agreed to pay $5 million in a series of indemnity installments. The first $1 million was due in 1833. When the French made no payment then or the following year, but instead made payment to England that they also owed, Jackson viewed it as an insult to American honor and favored war with France. Jackson was poised to take coercive action, uttering, "I know them French—They won't pay unless they're made to." In December 1834, Jackson requested Congressional support for an ultimatum to France in demand of payment. Jackson also urged Congress to authorize reprisals on French property unless the money was speedily sent. The French responded with a demand for a "satisfactory explanation" of Jackson's ultimatum, which they viewed as an insult to French honor. For a few months there appeared to be danger of war, but the British offered mediation of the dispute and persuaded the French to accept Jackson's address to Congress asking for an ultimatum as an "explanation." The French desired to avoid war and accepted the British solution. French payment of the debt began in 1836.

Jackson also faced the problem of whether to recognize the independence of Texas, established in 1836. Texas was a potential slave state, and therefore Jackson was careful not to inflame the American people over the slavery issue and possibly jeopardize Van Buren's presidential hopes in the election of 1836. Jackson was fearful of angering Mexico, which insisted that Texas was still a Mexican State in rebellion. Jackson feared that any American interference with Texas could mean a war with Mexico, which he sought to avoid. Though there was no question about Jackson's personal sentiment—his sympathy for the Texan revolutionists was strong—he withheld recognition from the Texas republic until the very day he left office in 1837.

▶ Supreme Court Justice Roger B. Taney, appointed by Andrew Jackson, was in favor of slavery. In the famous *Dred Scott* decision, Taney declared that slaves had no rights and that they were no more than property. *Wikipedia photo*

The Supreme Court

Andrew Jackson's most enduring influence on the Supreme Court came indirectly through the justices he elevated to the bench. When he retired, five of the sitting judges were his appointees. That number included slavery advocate Roger B. Taney, who had succeeded John Marshall as Chief Justice on the latter's death in 1835.

Among the principal early decisions under Taney was *Briscoe v. The Bank of Kentucky* (1837), which reduced the application of constitutional limitations on state banking and currency matters. This decision held that it was not unconstitutional for a state that owned stock to issue bank notes. More famous is *Charles River Bridge v. Warren Bridge* (1837), which stressed community responsibilities of private property and modified the contract doctrines of Marshall. In *Bank of Augusta v. Earle* (1839), the Chief Justice denied that corporations had all legal rights of natural persons. He also held that while corporations could take part in interstate commerce, any state had the right to exclude another state's corporations.

This is traceable, in part, to the Court's changing personnel after Jackson's presidency, and in part to the alterations in Taney's own ideas.

For many years, it was the fashion among historians to be hypercritical of Taney's Supreme Court record. Continuing on the tribunal until he died during the Civil War, Taney became very unpopular in the North because of his position in favor of states' rights and because of the infamous Dred Scott decision in 1857, where he declared slaves to be property and without rights, including standing to sue. Actually, the judicial philosophies and influences of Marshall and Taney had many similarities. Taney and most of his associates believed that the growing power of corporations needed supervision by states in the public interest, but they were not unsympathetic toward property rights as such. Thus, modern authorities on judicial history see no sharp break between most constitutional interpretations of the two justices.

Jacksonian Democracy

The Influence of Economic Factors

In Jackson's time, as now, political changes were often tied to economic changes and alliances formed and reformed over economic issues. What had been the Democratic Republican Party had, by 1836, split into two parties known as the Democrats and the Whigs, with opposing views on government and its proper role in the economy. To find consistency in the political actions of Democrats and Whigs is difficult, chiefly because of shifts brought about by economic factors. Daniel Webster, for example, had begun his career as a champion of New England shipping interests and free trade. However, after the War of 1812 domestic manufacturing was growing, and Webster caught the spirit of industrial progress. He and other Whigs argued that the fledgling industries needed all the government protection they could acquire. Consequently, by the late 1820s, Webster had become an aggressive advocate of protective tariffs that fostered American industry. Besides a protected market, he and his fellow Whigs believed that industry also needed a sound banking system, which would provide a stable currency and ample credit.

Henry Clay, too, had changed his political convictions with changing times. Reared in the Virginia of Jeffersonian agrarianism, he migrated to Kentucky and was awakened to new Western economic ambitions. A spokesman for Western Whigs, Clay believed in a nationalistic program—his American System. Through federally funded internal improvements—a liberal policy of public-land sales, a central bank, and tariffs—the aim of this system was to reduce American dependence on foreign trade and provide a home market for the exchange of the North's manufactured goods and the West's agricultural products.

The Whigs asserted that government aid to business would promote the economic progress and well-being of all Americans. The Whig Party, however, also contained prominent Southern planters, although their reliance on cotton exports and low-cost imports caused them to oppose the protective tariffs advocated by the Northern Whigs. Like the leaders in other sections, those in the South took anguished turns in their search for adjustment. John

C. Calhoun of South Carolina began as a "War Hawk" nationalist during the days of Jefferson and Madison. Later, he became a defender of states' rights in defiance of federal "authoritarianism." Politically, he shifted from the Democrats to the Whigs and back to the Democrats.

Jackson was able to cope with these shifting factions. With a military hero reputation that aided him in politics, he was looked upon as a champion of the plain people and an enemy of "privilege" to any one class or section. Often arbitrary in method, Jackson was at times headstrong and uncompromising, such as in the case of the Bank Veto of 1832. He did, however, at times try to find a middle ground, favoring a "judicious" tariff and avoiding the annexation of Texas so as to prevent a heightening of sectional tensions. He approved or opposed federal funding for internal improvements on the merits of each individual case, and he and his Democrat followers were more aware than the Whigs of the potential dangers of "monopolies."

Characteristics of Jacksonian Democracy

The policies identified with Jacksonian democracy have been associated with five major trends. First, Jacksonian democracy represented a trend toward equality and expansion of democracy, with more men participating in the political process. While Jackson drew support from persons in many walks of life, common people were most inclined to identify themselves with Jackson and his policies. Second, Jacksonian democracy marked a departure from the domination of bankers and merchants, even though some bankers and merchants were steadfast Jacksonians. Third, Jacksonians were expansionists, committed to making room for white settlers on what had been Native American lands. Fourth, as seen in the South Carolina controversy, Jacksonian Democrats resolutely opposed weakening the Federal union. Finally, Jackson's followers approved Jackson's exercise of federal authority over the American economy.

To understand Jackson's influence, it is essential to understand why Jackson was so popular and what caused him to retain his popularity. The War of 1812 involved no other military victory on a par with Jackson's brilliant victory at the Battle of New Orleans. Fervidly admired because of his achievement, he intrigued fellow-Americans who found in him no mere child of luck but a man of iron will and ingenious battlefield prowess. Also, and this was nearly as important, Jackson seemed to symbolize the "outs" or non-establishment people in contrast with the "ins" of Washington. He had succeeded in the world on his own and was a leader of forcefulness and determination—the very sort of dynamic figure who makes enemies and yet attracts hosts of followers and friends. No understanding of Jacksonian democracy can be complete without the awareness of the charismatic Jackson image.

Evaluation of Jackson's Administration

As president, the active and dominant Jackson continued both to arouse strong adverse criticism and to inspire praise bordering on idolatry. The Tennessean's enemies did not hesitate to call him every unpleasant name in the book. They depicted him as "King Andrew," a would-be tyrant with slight regard for the ways of free people and with a ruthless intent to impose his will on the country. On the other hand, Jackson's friends loved him personally and held his political talents in the highest esteem.

In the perspective of the years, Jackson's record shows marked differences from issue to issue. Although moderation is not traditionally considered a trait of Jackson's, he was essentially a moderate on the tariff, and his attitude toward land policy was generally temperate. Though he did not block all internal improvements financed with federal funds, he was apt to be conservative or reactionary (depending on one's point of view) on projects in that category.

Many scholars have argued that Jackson's greatest mistake was his hostility to the bank, and that his Specie Circular reflected a miscalculation in timing if not in principle. On the other hand, Jackson's foreign policy was successful, and his nationalism was tellingly asserted in opposition to the nullifiers.

A slaveholder with the manners and tastes of a Southern planter, Jackson had, nonetheless, an acute awareness of public preferences and the public interest. He also had an instinct for reaching the "common" people and for identifying their desires with his own. A simple man with a fighting heart, Jackson lived in constant pain, owing to injuries he had received in the duels he had fought. The pain contributed to an irascibility of temper. That said, it could still be concluded that Jackson judged each issue on its merits—as he understood them—and contributed vigorous leadership to every cause he championed.

Democrats and Whigs

The Election of 1836

As Jackson's second term neared its end, Vice-President Martin Van Buren was the Democratic presidential nominee and received the endorsement of Jackson. The Whig opposition, tried to throw the contest into the House of Representatives by sponsoring several candidates on a regional basis. Van Buren faced Daniel Webster in the Northeast, Ohio's William Henry Harrison in the Northwest, and Tennessee's Hugh L. White in the South. These three Whigs won 14, 73, and 26 electoral votes respectively. South Carolina gave its 11 votes to the anti-Jacksonian Willie P. Mangum of North Carolina. Their combined total of 124 was well under Van Buren's figure of 170, and the Whig popular vote of 739,000 failed to match Van Buren's 765,000. So while the Whigs made gains, the 1836 regional scheme fell apart. Again the Democrats were victors.

The Panic of 1837

The "Little Magician" or "Red Fox of Kinderhook," as Van Buren was nicknamed, proved to be an unlucky president. Van Buren was a skilled attorney and adroit politician, but he found himself confronted by an economic disaster beyond his control. In May 1837, only two months after his inauguration, a New York bank panic signaled the start of one of America's deepest depressions. In part, the trouble stemmed from an English financial crisis during which many British creditors canceled their American investments. Yet Jackson and Van Buren drew much of the blame because the panic began shortly after Jackson's Specie Circular caused a rapid decline in land sales, and some of Jackson's "pet banks" were among those that failed. Furthermore, while the Specie Circular checked speculation

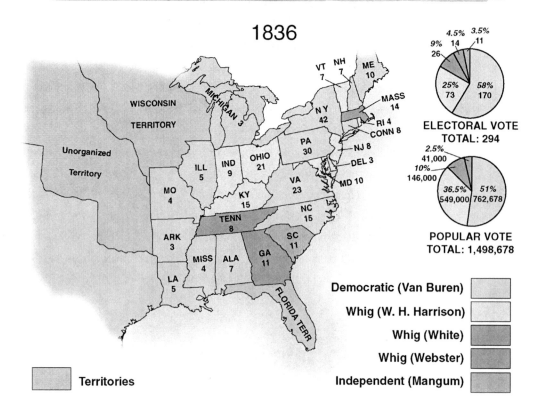

MAP 7.4 The Presidential Election of 1836

1836

ELECTORAL VOTE
TOTAL: 294

POPULAR VOTE
TOTAL: 1,498,678

Democratic (Van Buren)
Whig (W. H. Harrison)
Whig (White)
Whig (Webster)
Independent (Mangum)

Territories

in western lands, it curtailed the activities of financiers who had been supplying funds to speculators. Jackson's bank veto proved to make the banking system more fragile by eliminating the possibility of loans from the Bank of the United States to other banks that were capital short.

The depression affected the lives and fortunes of people in every part of the country. Widespread unemployment developed in seaboard cities of the Northeast, spread into interior communities, and fanned out to the South and West. Bread lines and soup kitchens relieved the hunger of poor families, including thousands of recent immigrants. Farmers received low prices for their crops, factories closed, and laborers walked the streets. Canal and railroad projects were halted as capital for investment evaporated. In 1839, the worst of the depression seemed to be over, but another decline occurred later that same year due to cotton overproduction and falling agricultural prices. Good times did not return to America as a whole until 1843.

In the meantime, Van Buren's fine display of statesmanship belied his reputation as a crafty politician. Beginning in 1837, he induced Congress to agree to a temporary issue of short-term treasury notes. These amounted to $47 million in the next six years and enabled the government to meet its obligations. He also advocated an independent treasury, where federal funds could be safely retained without either running state bank style risks or resorting to another Bank of the United States.

Most Whigs and some Democrats opposed the banking bill on the grounds that removal of federal funds from the state banks where they were deposited would restrict credit at a time when credit was sorely needed. The Independent Treasury Act finally was passed in 1840, but Van Buren's victory was short-lived. The next year, under the Tyler administration, the Act was repealed; for the next five years the Whig majority in Congress defeated Democratic efforts to reestablish this "subtreasury system."

"Indian Removal"

In 1830, the nation's land and water area covered more than 1.78 million square miles. In addition, more than twelve thousand square miles in the far Northeast and approximately half a million square miles in the far Northwest (Oregon Territory) were claimed by both Washington and London. Substantial numbers of Americans had spilled over into Texas, which then was still part of Mexico, on land that the Mexican government had granted to Moses Austin and his son, Stephen F. Austin.

Most pioneers, however, were less concerned with Mexican Texas or with Anglo-American boundary differences than with the nearby Native Americans. From the natives' points of view, it was utterly wrong for them to be forced off of their ancestral lands in order to make places for white settlers. Most whites had a very different attitude, considering Native Americans to be inferior and viewing them as in the way of "progress."

During this period, the pressure of frontiersmen and their families pushed tens of thousands of Native Americans west of the Mississippi River. In ninety treaties signed during Jackson's presidency—some less honorable than others—Native Americans reluctantly accepted new western lands in lieu of their old homes.

North of the Ohio River there was relatively little trouble for the white Americans when what was left of the Shawnees, Wyandots, Delawares, and Miamis were moved to western reservations. Although the move was a difficult one, the Northern tribes were to suffer less in the process of relocation than the tribes of the South.

The most dramatic example of resistance by Northern Native Americans in the 1830s was an exception to the rule. This involved a resolute Sauk, Black Hawk by name, who believed that a treaty ceding the Rock River region of southern Wisconsin and northwestern Illinois to the whites had been signed under conditions of trickery. Black Hawk reluctantly moved his people to the west bank of the Mississippi, but in 1832 he led them back to southern Wisconsin in search of fertile farm land. The ensuing Black Hawk War, won by the whites that summer, marked the end of organized Native American resistance in the Old Northwest. Westward migration of Sauk, Fox, Winnebago, and other tribes

▶ Martin Van Buren was elected president in the election of 1836. Unfortunately, two months after his inauguration the country fell victim to one of its deepest financial depressions and Van Buren was blamed. *Wikipedia photo*

increased. Within six years both Wisconsin and Iowa became territories; within sixteen years they became states, as settlers from the East populated the country of Native Americans, they were again dispossessed.

Beginning in 1819, Congress began an assimilation policy under which they granted $10,000 annually to a number of missionary associations for the purpose of "civilizing" Native Americans by converting them to Christianity. The program included teaching the English language and English literacy to Native Americans, as well as the teaching of traditional gender roles favored by whites. Not everyone agreed with the assimilation policy. Andrew Jackson, for instance, stated to Congress in his 1833 address that the Native Americans had "neither the intelligence, the industry, the moral habits, nor the desire of improvement which are essential."

In the judgment of many whites, however, southern Native Americans generally were making more "progress" toward assimilation than those being prodded westward north of the Ohio. Sequoya, inventor of a set of characters for Cherokee syllables, enabled thousands of Cherokee adults and children to read and write. By white standards, they were more advanced than other Native Americans. The Cherokees, Chickasaws, Choctaws, Creeks, and Seminoles were referred to as the "Five Civilized Tribes." Some of them, notably the Seminoles and the Creeks, did not always prove civilized if placidity is a criterion; but there is small wonder that enlightened leaders could not invariably remain placid in light of the whites' tricks and treachery.

The Native American Springs Treaty of 1825, involving Creek land in southern Georgia, was so unfair to the Creeks that the U.S. Senate rejected it. Often treaties were said to be the result of corrupt deals in which Native American "leaders" sold out to the whites in return for handsome rewards. In any case, the treaties secured the land for the whites. The Treaty of Dancing Rabbit (1830) relinquished nearly eight million Choctaw acres in Alabama and Mississippi, and in the next decade other substantial acreage was added. Many Cherokees and other Native Americans in the Southeast were forced to move west. Thousands died along the way on what has been called the "Trail of Tears," between their traditional homes in the Southeast and "Indian Territory" (present-day Oklahoma). Suffering not only indignities but also agonies on the twelve hundred mile trek, an estimated four thousand of the fifteen thousand Cherokees, Choctaws, and Chickasaws perished from the elements before they could reach their new homes. Andrew Jackson was president during the period in which the legal basis for removal was enacted; therefore, it is he, more than any other political leader, who is held responsible for this dark page in American history. In Jackson's first annual message to Congress in 1829, Jackson declared that moving the Native Americans to territory west of the Mississippi River was the only way to "save" them from extinction. Jackson repeated this message in his next seven annual addresses to Congress. It was also under Jackson in 1830 that Congress passed the Indian Removal Act of 1830 that appropriated $500,000 to relocate Native American tribes living on over one hundred million acres in the east to land west of the Mississippi, as Jackson had suggested the previous year.

Not all Southern tribes submitted passively to the intrusions on whites. Osceola, a Florida Seminole sub-chief, so resented the Treaty of Payne's Landing, which authorized removal of the Seminoles to west of the Mississippi, that he is said to have plunged his knife into the document when he was expected to sign it with his "X."

Resistance on the part of Micanopy, Alligator, Osceola, and other Native Americans—supported by some runaway slaves—culminated in the Second Seminole War. In 1835, the Seminoles ambushed and killed 107 of the 110 officers and men of Major Francis L. Dade. Taking full advantage of Florida's maze of inland rivers and swamps to hide their women and children, they harassed United States troops and then rushed back to cover. Osceola was seized and imprisoned when, under a flag of truce, he came for an interview with an American general. He died in a military prison; but the war—the bloodiest and most expensive of all our conflicts with Native Americans—continued until 1842. Although there are Seminoles in Florida in our own time, most of the original members were forced to surrender or were tricked into capture by the whites. Usually they settled in Native American Territory.

The Cherokee tribe of Georgia mounted a legal challenge to their removal. The Cherokees, perhaps more than any other tribe, had attempted to pacify whites through assimilation policies, adopted their own written constitution based on the American model, and adopted white ways in terms of clothing, housing, and cotton plantation agriculture—including the ownership of one thousand slaves. In 1832, in *Worcester v. Georgia,* the U.S. Supreme Court recognized the Cherokee nation as a sovereign entity with its own territory within which the laws of Georgia had no force. Andrew Jackson, understanding that it was the Executive branch, not the Judiciary that had enforcement powers, simply ignored the ruling and pressed the Cherokees to move west.

In 1835, Jackson's side received a break when a small, unrepresentative group of Cherokees signed a treaty ceding all tribal land in exchange for $5 million and equal acreage west of Arkansas. Cherokee Chief John Ross petitioned the U.S. to ignore the unrepresentative treaty, but Georgia rapidly sold the Cherokee's land to whites. Most Cherokees refused to vacate their land until President Martin Van Buren sent federal troops to Georgia to force their evacuation. Many Americans opposed the brutal treatment of Native Americans—including such prominent Northern Whigs as John Quincy Adams and Daniel Webster—but they were unable to prevail. One man whose bad conscience about Native Americans led him down the unusual path not of protest, but of artistic rendering of Native Americans, was the artist George Catlin. Giving up his career as a Philadelphia lawyer, he made five trips into the Great Plains during the 1830s, to paint the Plains Native Americans in the days before photography. Self-taught, Catlin was a man on a mission. When he completed his vast body of portraiture and scenes of daily life, he tried, unsuccessfully, to sell his paintings to Congress. In the end he had to travel to Europe and received the recognition he craved. Modern Americans are indebted to him because he left an invaluable record in some instances, such as the Mandans, of tribes that subsequently were wiped out by the white people's pathogens. Over time, the paintings found their way into American museums; and today hundreds of them are in the collection of the Smithsonian Institution in Washington, D.C., among other repositories.

The *Caroline* Affair

Another problem of the Van Buren regime concerned a quarrel with England along the Canadian border. In 1837, Canadian insurgents, dissatisfied with London's rule, fled to an island in the Niagara River, where American anglophobes reinforced them with recruits

▶ George Catlin gave up his career as a lawyer, and instead made five trips into the Great Plains during the 1830s to paint the Plains Indians. Though he received little fame in his day, today hundreds of them, such as the one above, are in the collection of the Smithsonian Institution. *Wikipedia photo*

and arms. The American steamer *Caroline* was employed in the supply service.

Canadian soldiers, crossing to the American side of the Niagara, set the *Caroline* afire and turned her adrift. Due to the high state of excitement, there was danger of mob invasions in either direction; and the slaying of an American citizen, Amos Durfee, on the night the vessel burned, further complicated the situation. The citizens of Buffalo placed Durfee's body, with a bullet hole in his forehead and blood still in his hair, on public display in the town square. New York newspapers called for war against England in the name of national honor and demanded an apology from Britain. However, no apology was forthcoming from Britain because, it argued, Durfee's death was an act of self-defense.

Three years later a Canadian deputy sheriff named Alexander McLeod was arrested in Lockport, New York, and indicted for murder and arson in connection with the *Caroline* affair after he had publicly boasted of killing Durfee in a Buffalo tavern. The British demanded the release of McLeod on the basis that if he had killed Durfee, it was a military action and he was acting under orders to defend a British territory (Canada) against insurgents. Furthermore, President Martin Van Buren had declared American neutrality in the Canadian rebellion. Consequently, it was illegal under international law for the United States to aid Canadian rebels in the conflict or the U.S. was violating its own neutrality. Although the Americans involved in aiding the Canadian rebels on the *Caroline* were doing so with private funds, the British pointed out that the U.S. had claimed the right to invade a country on its borders that did not sufficiently secure its own border via Andrew Jackson's invasion of Florida in 1818. The British threatened war if McLeod were not released and on both sides of the border additional sums were appropriated for the strengthening of boundary defenses. Even after McLeod was acquitted by a New York court in 1841 (his claim that he had killed Amos Durfee proved to be nothing more than drunken bravado), the case seemed an unpromising preliminary to the Webster-Ashburton negotiations on border disputes that took place the next year.

"Tippecanoe and Tyler Too"

During Van Buren's presidency, Webster and Clay continued to be prominent in the senatorial spotlight. Webster's oratorical ability was as outstanding as ever, and Clay distinguished himself as a parliamentary leader, thus helping to keep the Whig Party in the spotlight.

▶ In the *Caroline* incident, Canadian soliders seized the American Steamer *Caroline*, towed her into the current, set her on fire, and turned her adrift Niagara Falls. American citizen Amos Durfee was killed in the process, sparking more anger between the U.S. and Britain.
Wikipedia photo

Northern Whigs favored the creation of a new national bank and advocated a high tariff and federally financed internal improvements. If their anti-Jackson and anti-Van Buren advocates of the South did not agree about the tariff and the bank, the common bond linking all Whigs was the issue of "executive tyranny." Less domination by the president and more authority vested in Congress were aims that Southern and Northern Whigs shared. They also capitalized on the country's economic distress that had occurred under Van Buren's watch and were as one in their criticism of Van Buren as the 1840 election approached.

The Whigs played their cards cunningly in the 1840 test of skill. In the first place, their standard-bearer was neither Clay nor Webster—able men who had many friends, but also many enemies—but William Henry Harrison of Ohio. Harrison had run well as a regional Whig candidate in 1836 and had won a measure of military glory in the dim past at the Battle of Tippecanoe. Second, the Whigs turned to their own advantage a journalist's taunt that Harrison was unfit for the presidency. "Give him a barrel of hard cider, and settle a pension of two thousand a year on him," the newsman sneered," and [take] my word for it, he will sit the remainder of his days in his log cabin by the side of a 'sea coal' fire, and study moral philosophy."

Yes, the Whigs replied, their nominee was a man of the people who preferred a log cabin and hard cider to the dainty red-whiskered Van Buren. In reality, Harrison lived in a mansion near Cincinnati and was an aristocratic Virginian by birth and rearing. However, log cabins, barrels of cider, coonskin caps, and even live raccoons became Harrison symbols in the campaign.

For the vice-presidency the Whigs had chosen John Tyler of Virginia, a former states' rights Democrat who became a spokesman for the minority Southern element within the Whig party.

The Whigs were victorious in 1840. Harrison's Electoral College showing was impressive (234 to Van Buren's 60), and his popular vote was 1,274,000 to 1,127,000 for the Democrat.

Although the Whig margin was not vast in a number of critical states, it was large enough. North of the Mason-Dixon line Van Buren carried only New Hampshire and Illinois.

The 1840 election was not a "critical" or "realigning" one like those of 1800 and 1828, as no permanent party changes stemmed from it. Nevertheless, the Tippecanoe campaign did have importance as it showed how adroitly Whigs could play the Democrats' game and served as a model for presidential contests for more than a century.

President Without a Party

The sweet taste of triumph, however, soon turned bitter in Whig mouths. Inaugurated in March 1841, the sixty-eight-year-old Harrison gave his inaugural address on a cold day in Washington with no hat and no coat and died of pneumonia after a single month in office. Tyler, the first man to reach the presidency through the death of his predecessor, shared few of the ideas of the dominant Whig group in Congress. Twice he vetoed attempts to revive the Bank of the United States, and twice he vetoed Clay-sponsored tariffs. Several times he defeated distribution to the states of proceeds from public-land sales. All members of Harrison's cabinet, which Tyler inherited, resigned after six months, with the exception of Secretary of State Webster, who stayed on only long enough to complete ongoing negotiations over the border with Canada.

John Tyler found himself in the undesirable position of a president without a party. He did agree with Northern Whigs that the Independent Treasury law should be repealed, and this was accomplished in 1841; but his vetoes of Clay's tariff measures made him a deserter from their perspective. The Tariff of 1842, which Congress reluctantly passed and Tyler signed, was but mildly protective. Tyler also approved a General Preemption Act and

▶ For the presidential election of 1840, the Whigs chose William Henry Harrison of Ohio. Harrison had run well as a regional Whig candidate in 1836 and had won a measure of military glory in the dim past at the Indian Battle of Tippecanoe. *Library of Congress*

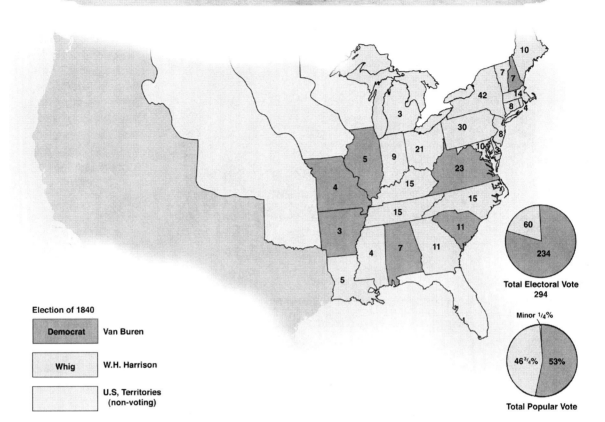

MAP 7.5 The Presidential Election of 1840

Election of 1840

Democrat	Van Buren
Whig	W.H. Harrison
	U.S, Territories (non-voting)

Total Electoral Vote
294

Minor ¼%

Total Popular Vote

cooperated more with Democrats than Whigs. Northern Whigs and border-states men such as Clay lamented the day when "Tyler too" had been asked to run with "Tippecanoe."

Features of American Democratic Growth

The years 1824–1844 were characterized by an increase in the number of elected officeholders, by a relative decrease in appointed officials at the state and local levels, and by some reflection of the popular will by the Supreme Court. There was far greater participation in government than had been the case in prior eras. By the time the period was well launched, all states except one chose presidential electors by popular vote. The popular vote itself steadily increased from campaign to campaign, not only because the population was greater but because such barriers as religious and property qualifications were gradually lowered on a state-by-state basis. Jacksonians regarded changes of these kinds as desirable reforms, whose democratizing purposes and spirit bore resemblances to the era's social reforms.

The development of democratic government was not without its growing pains. One of the most criticized aspects of the political scene was rotation in office, labeled by opponents as the "spoils system," by which governmental posts were allotted as "spoils" of victory to members of the party triumphant at the polls. Under Monroe and Adams a small number of federal clerks and minor administrators had held offices on what amounted to a lifetime good-conduct basis. Jackson removed a number of these perennials because

▶ Vice president John Tyler is depicted in this illustration as receiving news of President Harrison's death. Tyler was the first president to succeed to the presidency through the event of the elected president's death. *Wikipedia photo*

they had played the partisan game against him, because they were corrupt and inefficient, or because he wanted to create openings for partisans of his own. In 1832, Senator William L. Marcy, a Jackson supporter, had remarked, "To the victor belong the spoils of the enemy." Although the spoils system clearly leads to corruption and appointment of incompetent government officials, Jackson believed that most government jobs were so simple that they required little intellectual capacity and the damage was, therefore, mitigated.

Furthermore, during his entire presidency Jackson removed only a fifth of those holding office, but he did take a decisive step toward perpetuating rotation in office. Jacksonians defended the policy as the quickest and surest path to reform.

National party conventions, which came into being with the Anti-Masonic assembly held in 1831, were thoroughly established in the political structure by the end of Jackson's second term. Sometimes they have resulted in the choice of second-rate candidates for first-rate posts, but in the main the decisions of conventions have been sound. They were more directly representative and democratic than "King Caucus" ever was. After momentarily striking a pose of aloofness from Jacksonian electioneering tactics, Whigs imitated their rivals by adopting slogans and symbols similar to Democratic ones. For over a century styles of campaigning were patterned, to a substantial degree, on the 1840 ballyhoo techniques that promoted "Tippecanoe and Tyler Too!"

During Jackson's administration the personal advisers to the president relied to be known as the "Kitchen Cabinet"—because they ostensibly conferred with Jackson more intimately than did members of his official cabinet. Later, chief executives have followed Jackson's example by surrounding themselves with capable but unofficial counselors whose advice supplemented—or supplanted—that of department heads. It is doubtful that the

"Kitchen Cabinet" would have originated as and when it did if Jackson had not owed his election in part to Calhounite Deep South support, which at least two cabinet members personified but on which he chose not to rely once his administration was underway.

It would be a mistake to minimize the role of the West in the period 1824–1844. Public lands, the tariff, internal improvements, the United States Bank, and almost all other issues were of interest to Westerners. The West had its own viewpoint or viewpoints of a predominantly sectional variety, yet it also exerted a nationalizing influence. The Southwest had much in common with the Northwest; and Jackson proved to be a foremost nationalist who was supported as consistently in the Northwest as in any other portion of the country. Truly national political parties and affiliations had emerged and were here to stay.

Chapter Review ▶ ▶ ▶

Summary

A new era of politics began to take shape in 1824 as support coalesced around Andrew Jackson, who won the most electoral votes; however, no candidate won a majority of the electoral votes in 1824 and John Quincy Adams was able to win the White House by making a "corrupt bargain" with Henry Clay whereby Clay threw his support to Adams in return for being named Secretary of State. Though a brilliant man and a hard worker, Adams' would only serve one term as the American economy sagged due to trade restrictions with Britain and the masses would sweep General Andrew Jackson into the White House. Jackson's supporters, however, would be quickly denounced as "King Mob" when they vandalized the White House while celebrating after Jackson's inaugural.

Jackson was a poorly educated battle-hardened general that used poor grammar, tobacco, and alcohol, and related well with common Americans. Jackson would bring numerous innovations to American politics, including Party Conventions as a way of nominating candidates, more liberal use of the veto, the pocket veto, the spoils system, and the removal of Native American tribes from the Southeast to Indian Territory (Oklahoma). Jackson and his supporters were typically advocates of states' rights, but when South Carolina nullified the federal tariff in South Carolina in 1832, Jackson threatened to send 200,000 troops to South Carolina to enforce the tariff (though he simultaneously pushed Congress to lower the tariff).

In economic policy, Jackson would veto the renewal of the Charter for the Bank of the U.S. in 1832 and then in 1836 decree that federal land could only be purchased with specie (silver or gold). Jackson's actions led to a real estate and finance crash followed by bank failures, unemployment, and a severe economic recession that lasted into the 1840s and thus doomed the Presidency of his hand-picked successor, Martin Van Buren.

In foreign affairs, the impetuous Jackson almost caused war with France in 1834 over French nonpayment of debts. War was averted, essentially, because the French backed down and did not desire it. Meanwhile, Jackson delayed recognition of the Republic of Texas until his last day in office so as to avoid provoking a war with Mexico.

Shortly after Jackson left office, a Canadian rebellion against England almost dragged the U.S. into a war with England when the British attacked an American ship on the American side of the Canadian River and killed an American, Amos Durfee. When a British subject, Alexander McLeod, boasted of killing Durfee, Britain threatened War if he were not released. War was averted when McLeod was acquitted because his boast had been false.

In 1840, opponents of Jacksonian politics coalesced into the Whig Party and nominated 68 year-old hero of the Battle of Tippecanoe William Henry Harrison for President. Harrison and his running mate John Tyler defeated Martin Van Buren during the continued economic recession, but Harrison died of pneumonia one month after his inauguration after giving his inaugural speech with no coat and no hat on a cold day in Washington. John Tyler then assumed the Presidency, but the patterns of mass politics and the spoils system ushered in by Andrew Jackson were here to stay.

Chronological Time Line

1819	Supreme Court upholds the Constitutionality of the Bank of the U.S. in *McCulloch v. Maryland*.
1824	John Quincy Adams wins the Presidential election in the House of Representatives with the "Corrupt Bargain" of 1824.
1826	England closes the British West Indies to U.S. shipping.
1826	Both John Adams and Thomas Jefferson die on July 4.
1828	Andrew Jackson defeats John Quincy Adams in the Presidential election.
1828	John C. Calhoun writes the "South Carolina Exposition" claiming the right of states to nullify the federal tariff.
1829	"King Mob," a group of unruly Jackson supporters, vandalizes the White House in the rain after Jackson's inaugural in March.
1830	Webster-Hayne Debate
1830	Congress passes the Indian Removal Act
1831	Eaton Affair disrupts Andrew Jackson's Cabinet.
1832	Andrew Jackson vetoes the renewal of the Bank of the U.S.
1832	Andrew Jackson wins reelection
1832	South Carolina legislature nullifies the federal tariff.
1834	Jackson's opponents become the Whig Party.
1834	Jackson's ultimatum to France to pay debts to the U.S.
1835–1842	Second Seminole War in Florida
1836	Jackson's Specie Circular requires that all federal land be purchased with specie (gold or silver).
1836	Texas wins Independence from Mexico
1836	Martin Van Buren is elected President
1837	Andrew Jackson recognizes the Republic of Texas

Chapter Review (cont'd) ▶ ▶ ▶

Time Line (cont'd)

1837	Panic of 1837 follows the real estate crash caused by Jackson's Specie Circular and New York bank collapse.
1837	Caroline Affair and death of Amos Durfee
1840–41	William Henry Harrison defeats Martin Van Buren for the Presidency, but dies a month after his inauguration.
1841	John Tyler assumes the Presidency after the death of Harrison

Key Terms

The caucus system: The system of nominating Presidential candidates through informal votes in Congress

The "corrupt bargain": So-called by the supporters of Andrew Jackson, the political bargain between John Quincy Adams and Henry Clay where Clay was given the position of Secretary of State in return for his support of Adams as President.

The "American System": A plan supported by Henry Clay which encompassed a national bank, high tariffs, and federal aid for internal improvements.

National Republicans: The supporters of John Quincy Adams and Henry Clay

John Quincy Adams: Son of second President John Adams and the sixth President of the United States elected in 1824.

"Old Hickory": Nickname for Andrew Jackson because it was the "hardest wood."

"King Mob": A reference to unruly Jackson supporters that vandalized the White House after Jackson's inauguration in 1828.

Democratic Republicans: The political party spawned by Thomas Jefferson that also included James Madison, James Monroe, Andrew Jackson, and Martin Van Buren

John C. Calhoun: Ardent states' rights supporter and Vice President under Andrew Jackson

Andrew Jackson: Seventh President of the United States first elected in 1828 and credited with bringing mass politics and the spoils system to American politics.

Bank Veto: Jackson's veto of the renewal of the Charter of the Bank of the U.S.

Pocket Veto: A provision in the Constitution first exercised by Andrew Jackson whereby during the last ten days of a Congressional session, the President can kill a bill by not signing it.

Martin Van Buren: Andrew Jackson's hand-picked successor and eighth President of the U.S. elected in 1836.

Key Terms (cont'd)

Nullification: The idea advocated by John C. Calhoun that states could nullify federal laws within their borders.

Webster/Hayne Debate: Famous 1830 Congressional debate over nationalism verus sectionalism and states' rights.

Antimasonic party: Minor xenophobic political party that subscribed to a grand conspiracy theory that Masons were attempting to take over American politics.

Force Bill: Passed in 1833, gave Jackson congressional authority to use arms to enforce collection of customs.

"Pet banks": A reference by Jackson's opponents to the twenty-three banks that Jackson deposited federal funds into after he dissolved the Bank of the U.S.

Panic of 1837: Severe economic recession resulting from a real estate and financial collapse that followed Jackson's Specie Circular.

Assimilationist Policy: The U.S. government policy toward Native Americans that required them to adopt the language and culture of whites.

Indian Removal: The forced removal of Native American tribes from the Southeast to Indian Territory (Oklahoma).

Worcester v. Georgia: The U.S. Supreme Court recognized the Cherokee nation as a sovereign entity with its own territory in which the laws of Georgia had no force.

The Black Hawk War: War against Native Americans led by Black Hawk to expel the Natives from Southern Wisconsin and Northwestern Illinois in 1832.

The Trail of Tears: The trail from the Southeast to Indian Territory along which 4,000 Native Americans died.

The Seminole War: The revolt of the Seminole Indians against removal to Indian Territory from 1835-1842 that became the longest and bloodiest war against a Native American tribe in history.

George Catlin: A painter that produced a vast body of portraiture and scenes of daily life of Native Americans.

Roger B. Taney: Attorney General and then Secretary of the Treasury under Andrew Jackson and later Chief Justice of the Supreme Court that issued the Dred Scott decision in 1857

Whig Party: Opponents of Andrew Jackson that won the Presidency with William Henry Harrison and John Tyler in 1840

Jacksonian Democracy: Democracy built on mass politics and the spoils system.

Caroline Affair: During the Canadian revolt against England, the British attacked an American ship on the American side of the Niagara River that was carrying men and mercenaries for the Canadian rebellion.

Amos Durfee: American killed by the British in the attack on the Caroline.

Alexander McLeod: British subject who boasted of killing Amos Durfee in a Buffalo tavern and almost caused War between England and the U.S.

"Tippecanoe and Tyler Too": Whig campaign slogan in 1840.

Chapter Review (cont'd) ▶ ▶ ▶

Key Terms (cont'd)

William Henry Harrison: Hero of the battle of Tippecanoe in 1811, won the Presidency in 1840 only to die a month after giving his inaugural speech on a cold day with no coat and hat.

John Tyler: Vice President under William Henry Harrison who assumed the Presidency after Harrison's death.

Spoils System: System where government jobs and contract are awarded by elected politicians to the people that supported their electoral campaigns.

Sources Consulted

Richard E. Ellis, *The Union at Risk: Jacksonian Democracy, States' Rights and the Nullification Crisis* (1987).

William W. Freehling, *Prelude to Civil War: The Nullification Controversy in South Carolina, 1816–1836* (1965).

Edward Pessen, *Jacksonian America: Society, Personality, and Politics* (1985).

Robert V. Remini, *Andrew Jackson and His Indian Wars* (2001).

Robert V. Remini, *The Jacksonian Era* (1997).

Peter Temin, *The Jacksonian Economy* (1967).

Anthony F. C. Wallace, *The Long, Bitter Trail: Andrew Jackson and the Indians* (1993).

Harry L. Watson, *Liberty and Power: The Politics of Jacksonian America* (1990).

Sean Wilentz, *The Rise of American Democracy: Jefferson to Lincoln* (2006).

Sean Wilentz and Arthur M. Schlesinger Jr., *Andrew Jackson* (2005).

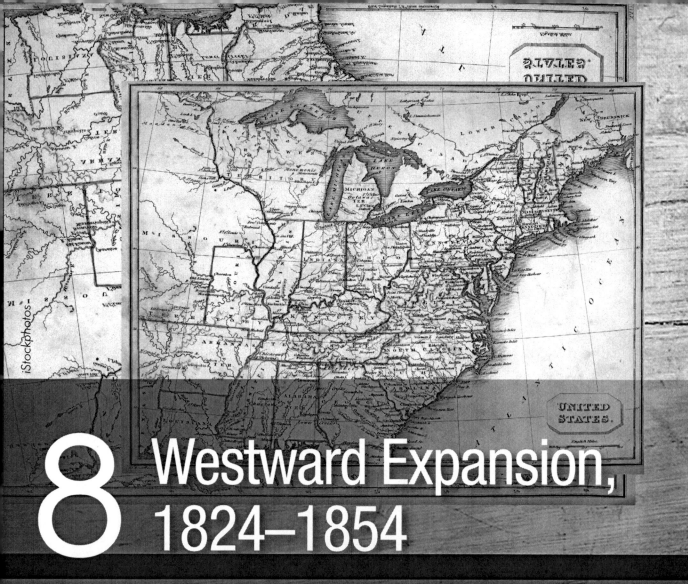

iStockphotos

8 Westward Expansion, 1824–1854

Chapter Objectives

Wikipedia photo

Wikipedia photo

iStockphoto

Wikipedia photo

Wikipedia photo

C.   Settlement of Texas

D.   War for Independence

E.   The Republic of Texas

F.   Annexation of Texas

G.   War with Mexico

H.   The Treaty of Guadalupe Hidalgo

I.   Gadsden Purchase

J.   California

K.   The Church of Jesus Christ of Latter-day Saints

L.   Growing Sectionalism

The Background of Expansion

Manifest Destiny

New York magazine editor John L. O'Sullivan proclaimed in 1845 that it was "the fulfill-ment of our manifest destiny to overspread the continent allotted by Providence for the free development of our yearly multiplying millions." O'Sullivan's exuberant words reflected the optimism of ardent nationalists who believed that the American banner soon would wave over all of North America and beyond. For the exponents of Manifest Destiny, even the addition of Texas, New Mexico, California, and the Oregon country to the nation would not be enough: God had destined the United States to extend its sovereignty over Canada, Alaska, Mexico, Cuba, other West Indian islands, and Hawaii. Millions of Americans firmly believed that God had singled out their country to play a special role in human history.

The dream of Manifest Destiny should be placed in the context of America's impressive achievements and realized dreams since 1776: nearly anything seemed possible in the next half century. In 1803 the Louisiana Purchase had doubled the area of the American republic, and later that year Lewis and Clark had left on their historic expedition. When they returned two and a half years afterward, they brought back not only data about the flora and fauna of the upper Missouri and the Columbia watersheds but also food for potent dreams about the West. By 1830, commerce with Europe was flourishing and trade with Asia was burgeoning, with adventurers extracting fortunes from China. Wealthy speculators were willing to invest in almost any feasible enterprise. Americans thus had a sense of themselves as a risk-taking people. Moreover, in 1840, the Bostonian Richard Henry Dana published a vivid description of the California coast in *Two Years Before the Mast*, thereby feeding the imagination of his fellow Americans about the region.

Wikipedia photo

Dreams of Manifest Destiny were both an indication of future hemi-spheric expansion and a concomitant of the westward expansion actually taking place between 1824 and 1848. During this period, Native Americans were moved out of the way of the conquering whites, and the immense areas of the new Southwest and the far West were added to the United States. It was a period that saw a rapid influx of European immigrants into the United States. Between 1830 and 1850 more than two million Euro-peans—most of them impoverished farmers or manual workers—crossed the Atlantic. Many were of the new German and Irish wave of immigrants. Between 1830 and 1850 the population of the United States as a whole almost doubled, from about 12.9 million to over 23 million.

Although much of the emphasis on the theme of expansion was ma-terialistic, and what would today be called racist, idealistic motives were also present. Protestant and Catholic missionaries, active in Oregon and elsewhere, hoped for numerous Native American converts, although it should also be noted that most of them were culturally insensitive. Many Americans took pride in the contrast between freedoms flourishing in their own country and oppressions evident in foreign lands—often flat-tering their own country by exaggerating the contrasts. There was also

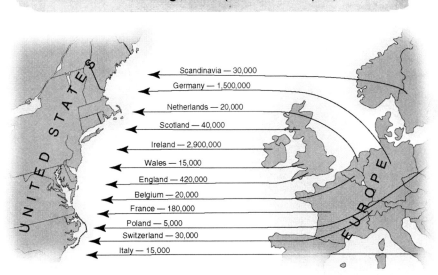

MAP 8.1 Immigration (1840–1860)

Scandinavia — 30,000
Germany — 1,500,000
Netherlands — 20,000
Scotland — 40,000
Ireland — 2,900,000
Wales — 15,000
England — 420,000
Belgium — 20,000
France — 180,000
Poland — 5,000
Switzerland — 30,000
Italy — 15,000

widespread concern that the intrigues of European imperialists would endanger the opportunities and liberties of ordinary Americans. Rumors spread that Britain and other powers were scheming to influence the internal and diplomatic policies of the Republic of Texas, to acquire Hawaii, and to control the Bays of San Francisco and San Diego as well as Puget Sound. (Some of the rumors had more substance than skeptics realized.) Would not encroachments of hostile courts and kings imperil the future of American democracy? Might they not also limit areas otherwise available for millions of oppressed Europeans, still hoping to come to American shores? Surely, it was God and America's way to counter and remove the threat through a constructive program of rapid expansion. This was the sincere conviction of idealistic believers in Manifest Destiny.

The Webster-Ashburton Treaty

Before Webster entered the State Department, the *Caroline* affair was not the only border incident fanning the flames of international misunderstanding. There was also the undeclared Aroostook War, caused by conflicting claims to the Aroostook River region on the undefined Maine-New Brunswick boundary. England and the U.S. had disputed the actual boundaries since the Peace of Paris in 1783 when it was discovered that the map used by the negotiators was flawed. In 1827, the King of the Netherlands mediated and formulated a compromise for the disputed border, which the English accepted and the U.S. rejected in 1831. Eight years later, the government of New Brunswick granted land titles to its subjects in areas north of the border that was drawn in 1831 but still claimed by the U.S. When Canadian lumberjacks moved into what Americans claimed was American territory in Maine, the Maine legislature authorized the Maine militia to expel the "Warriors of Waterloo." The Canadian lumberjacks clashed with the Maine militia and captured fifty American militiamen. In response, General Winfield Scott and 10,000 Maine troops were committed to the defense of the area subject to dispute in 1839. Instead of waging war with the Canadians, Scott arranged a truce that set the borders to be in the areas occupied by each side.

MAP 8.2 Webster-Ashburton Treaty and Treaty of Paris Boundaries

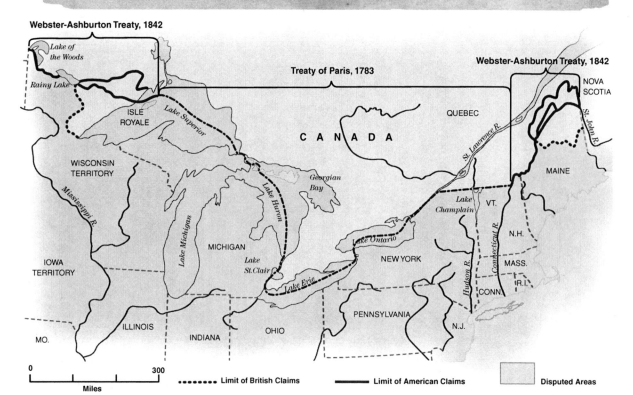

As the crisis eased, Secretary of State Daniel Webster met in a series of conferences with England's envoy, Lord Ashburton, to settle all items in dispute. In their treaty of 1842, Webster accepted a border very similar to the one drawn by the King of the Netherlands in 1831 after the British produced an old Ben Franklin map with the line drawn much further south than the 1831 border. New Brunswick received 5,000 square miles out of the 12,000 square miles in dispute, but the U.S. gained the area around Thunder Bay, Minnesota. In spite of the U.S. gains, the treaty was resented; and Webster's popularity was forever damaged in Maine, which considered itself shortchanged. Nevertheless, the Webster-Ashburton Treaty did help to achieve order and peace.

Return of the Democrats

Fresh issues exerted a vital impact on the election of 1844. Some had to do with the West, others with chattel slavery. Texans had won independence from Mexico in 1836, and now there was considerable sentiment for the annexation of the Republic of Texas by the United States. Southerners particularly favored such a step, while expansion-minded Northerners hoped that Americans would wholly occupy Oregon instead of it being divided between the United States and Britain.

Henry Clay's 1844 presidential nomination by the Whigs came as no surprise. Former President Martin Van Buren was shunted aside by the Democrats because he was thought to be anti-Texas, and little attention was paid to Tyler as a candidate since he was not a reliable party man. Instead, delegates to the Democratic National Convention nominated James K. Polk. As the former governor of Tennessee and Speaker of the House of Representatives, Polk seemed thoroughly at home on the Democratic platform and his western policy of "the rean-nexation of Texas" and "the reoccupation of Oregon" made that clear. Whigs made light of Polk's qualifications. "Who *is* James K. Polk?" they asked. Nonetheless, Polk's campaign strat-egy proved more effective than that of Clay, who tried to straddle the Texas dilemma and was accused of clear evasion of the issue.

Into the close contest came James G. Birney, heading the first partisan political expression of antislavery sentiment, the Liberty Party. Birney siphoned off Clay votes in New York and caused its electors to go to Polk, thus providing the winning difference for Polk. Polk received 170 elec-toral votes to Clay's 105. The popular outcome, however, favored the Tennessee man much more narrowly. Polk's 1,338,000 supporters outnumbered Clay's by only 38,000.

The Pathfinders

By the 1830s, with the removal of the Native Americans, the trans-Appalachian West was a great complex of newly admitted states, and already people were moving beyond the Missis-sippi River. Missouri had been admitted as a state as early as 1821, and Arkansas followed in 1836. The wilderness beyond the Mississippi provided attractive commercial opportunities for aggressive American frontiersmen. The lucrative fur trade in the Northwest, for example, had early drawn rugged trappers and traders to that area.

MAP 8.3 The Presidential Election of 1844

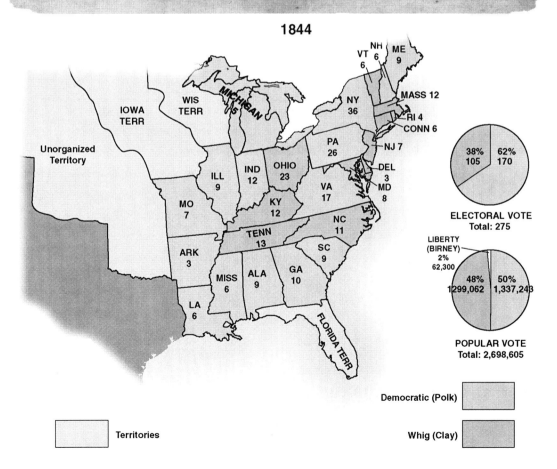

1844

ELECTORAL VOTE
Total: 275

POPULAR VOTE
Total: 2,698,605

Democratic (Polk)

Whig (Clay)

Territories

The most successful of the early fur traders was German-born John Jacob Astor, who organized the American Fur Company in 1808. His intention was to establish a monopoly of the fur trade throughout the West. Astor's acquisitiveness, ruthlessness, enormous capital, and efficient administration helped him take over trading posts in the Great Lakes and Mississippi areas that originally had belonged to other companies. In the 1820s he pushed west and northwest, absorbing the Columbia Fur Company in the Oregon Country and ruthlessly crushing rival trappers and traders.

Astor's business methods met with severe criticism on the frontier. An army officer wrote: "Take the American Fur Company in the aggregate, and they are the greatest scoundrels the world ever knew." Astor was undaunted by criticism and continued to prosper. In 1834 he withdrew from the fur business to concentrate on New York City real estate.

William Henry Ashley of St. Louis was another who made a fortune from furs in the Northwest. Ashley's Rocky Mountain Fur Company originated the revolutionary "rendezvous" method of fur trading, by which company agents, instead of trading with the Native Americans, bought furs directly from white trappers at an annual "rendezvous" in the mountains. From 1822 to 1826, Ashley and the rugged trappers on his payroll pushed north and west, penetrating the country of hostile tribes and continuing to trap beaver.

When Ashley retired, he sold his Rocky Mountain Fur Company to Jedediah S. Smith, the "Knight in Buckskin" whose explorations greatly fostered American interest in the far west. In the autumn of 1826, Smith led the first American overland expedition from Missouri to California. He carved an amazing career as "mountain man" and plainsman, accomplishing the daunting task of survival through self-reliance in the harsh elements of the Rocky Mountains. He used the methods and technology of Native Americans. Another fabulous character and "mountain man" was Jim Bridger, who may have been the first white man to see Salt Lake. Still another was Thomas Fitzpatrick, the noted guide and genuine friend of Native Americans.

Smith, Ashley, Bridger, Fitzpatrick, and the employees of the Astor interests were all experts with the knife, the rifle, and the trap; but more importantly, they contributed significantly to frontier expansion and marked the paths for others. They had much to do with the development of communities like St. Louis and of states and future states in what is now the western part of the Middle West. Accounts of their exploits as being men at one with nature while surviving the elements also turned easterners' eyes and imaginations out to the Rockies and beyond.

Perhaps the most famous explorer among his contemporaries—so famous that he was known as the "Pathfinder" and won the Republican nomination for President in 1856—was John C. Frémont. Son of a French émigré schoolteacher, Frémont early in life formed a strong taste for meeting and mastering wilderness challenges. It was in 1838–1839, when employed on a survey of the broad plateau between the upper Mississippi and upper Missouri Rivers, that this army officer acquired his real start as a geological observer, mapmaker, and scientific reporter. In the 1840s, he led several expeditions to the West exploring the Oregon Trail, the Sierra Nevada, California, the Colorado River, and the Rio Grande. His well-written reports, avidly read in the East, stimulated further emigration to the West.

The Santa Fe Trail

Santa Fe, in the Mexican territory of New Mexico, also provided attractive commercial opportunities for enterprising Americans. Though the volume of American trade in Santa Fe never was large, it was economically significant because American merchants were able to dispose of goods at handsome profit and because they also brought away silver in an era when silver was at a premium.

William Becknell of Arrow Rock, Missouri, initiated the Santa Fe trade in 1821, when he sold his goods for ten to twenty times what they would have brought on the banks of the Mississippi. Venturesome American merchants and farmers followed Becknell's example. They transported goods along the 800-mile Santa Fe Trail from Independence, Missouri to the great bend of the Arkansas to finally arrive in New Mexico, which was then a part of Mexico. Although the trip was arduous, and caravans were confronted with the dangers of rattlesnakes, heat, and storm, only eleven whites fell prey to Native Americans on the trail before 1843—a figure that illustrates that the Santa Fe Trail was less dangerous than it sometimes has been depicted.

MAP 8.4 Settlement of the Mississippi Valley

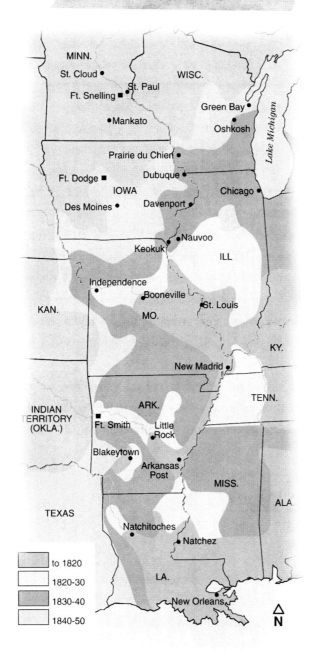

Legend:
- to 1820
- 1820-30
- 1830-40
- 1840-50

N

The Oregon Trail

Back in Jefferson's time, Lewis and Clark had traversed part of what was to become the celebrated route to the Pacific Northwest—the Oregon Trail. The mere mention of the Oregon Trail conjures up visions of wagon caravans moving west and carrying not merely merchants but also farmers and other permanent settlers. Other hardy spirits followed this route, adding discoveries of their own.

The Oregon idea was not difficult to sell to land hungry Americans even though Oregon at that time was jointly occupied by the United States and Britain. The Hudson's Bay Company, an English concern, had long been established on the Columbia River in the business of beaver pelts. Church interest heightened when such American Protestant missionaries as Jason Lee, Samuel Parker, and Dr. Marcus Whitman and his wife Narcissa went out to Oregon to convert Native Americans. National pride, missionary zeal, the lure of cheap land, and the favorable reputation of the region—all played a part in enticing thousands to Oregon.

As in the case of the Santa Fe Trail, Missouri towns such as Independence and St. Joseph were takeoff spots for the Oregon-bound. For a couple of days of travel, the two routes even coincided; then, as one went south, the other bent north. Out across various rivers including the Platte, and beyond to Fort Laramie, the covered wagons and pack trains of those seeking homes in the North-

▶John C. Frémont, known as the "Pathfinder" for his fame as an explorer, won the Republican nomination for president in 1856. *Wikipedia photo*

west made their way in the 1840s. On to Fort Bridger and along the Snake River they proceeded to the Whitmans' mission. At last they saw the storied Columbia River and reached Astoria on the Pacific Coast, or wherever they were going. The Oregon Trail stretched 2,000 miles—two and a half times the length of the Santa Fe journey.

Western Army Posts

The exploits of the mountain trappers, the Santa Fe traders, and the Oregon pioneers should not tempt us to overlook the role of the professional soldiers. From the 1820s well into the 1840s, the United States army never was large, but its role in aiding the settlement of the West can hardly be exaggerated. Speculators and homesteaders were more likely to bring their families to areas when the military was nearby. Army posts in time became villages, towns, and cities. It was not unusual for a retired officer to become a respected civilian in a new community. Soldiers brought steamboats to western rivers, constructed sawmills, and built their own forts. They farmed adjacent fields, introduced cattle, and disproved the widely credited legend that a "Great American Desert" existed between the Mississippi and the Rockies.

When it came to exploration, the army also played its part. In general, the information provided by military expeditions was more clearly documented and more useful than the stories from the mountain men. Although these military expeditions were not as colorful as the exploits of a Jim Bridger or of the famous trapper, Native American fighter, and scout Kit Carson, they were nevertheless essential in opening up the previously unknown West. Perhaps most important was the expedition of Stephen S. Long (1819–1820) who surveyed parts of the Great Plains and Rocky Mountains. Long, however, described the Great Plains as the "Great American Desert," fit only for the Indians and the buffalo, but not for cultivation or white settlement. As a consequence, for decades many maps of North America labeled the area between the Mississippi River and the Rocky Mountains as the "Great American Desert."

Conquering the West

A National Question

As long as the westward movement was confined to a few explorers and commercial adventurers, the United States government could act indecisively and put off any attempt to reach terms with London and Mexico City in connection with territorial disputes in the West. As American settlers poured into the Far West and the Southwest, setting up communities and then local governments, the United States government could no longer hesitate. The dispute with Britain over the boundaries of the Oregon country had to be settled, and the aspirations of fellow Americans living in Texas had to be heeded. What had been social and economic developments in the West had, by the 1840s, risen to the level of national political questions.

The Oregon Dispute

The "Oregon Country" was a great deal larger than the present state of Oregon, including what are now the states of Idaho, Oregon, and Washington as well as much of British Columbia. It was bounded roughly by the "Great Stony" Mountains on the east, the Pacific on the west, California on the south, and Alaska (then Russian) on the north. When informed men dis-

MAP 8.5 Trails of the Old West

cussed Oregon in the era after the War of 1812, they referred to a wondrously varied land with towering mountains and fertile valleys, swift-coursing rivers and magnificent forests. Details, however, eluded even the best informed of commentators because lack of surveys made it impossible to define its area precisely.

Early in the nineteenth century both Russia and Spain claimed sections of Oregon, but Spain relinquished its claim to the land in 1819. Russia in the next decade acknowledged 54°40′ as Alaska's southern line. Britain and the United States were left in contention over the Oregon Country between Russian Alaska and Spanish California.

The principal area in dispute was the territory between the Columbia River and the line of 49° latitude to the Pacific—the northwestern two-thirds of the present state of Washington. Britain based its claims on the exploration, discovery, and occupation of the region by British subjects and British fur trapping operations in the Columbia River Valley. American claims were also based on exploration and occupation, including Captain Gray's original discovery of the Columbia River in 1792, the Lewis and Clark expedition of 1804–1806, and the presence of American missionaries and settlers in the area in the 1830s and 1840s.

During Anglo-American negotiations in 1818, the United States proposed the boundary line of 49° to the Pacific Ocean. Britain agreed except for the part north and west of the Columbia River; it was unwilling to relinquish its claims to the Columbia River, the "St. Lawrence of the West," and home to British beaver trapping operations. Unable to reach a satisfactory agreement, in 1818 the two nations settled upon a treaty of ten-year joint occupation of the area "on the northwest coast of America, westward of the Stony Mountains." In 1827 the treaty was renewed for an indefinite period, with the provision that either party could terminate it on a year's notice.

Neither in 1818 nor at any other time until 1845 did the United States or Britain provide for civil government in Oregon. No marshal, no sheriff, no jury, no judge was empowered to carry out legal procedures. No laws could be executed because none had been enacted. As a consequence, men often took justice, or what they deemed was justice, into their own hands. A missionary, without the shadow of authority, might name a constable or a magistrate, and there were times when American traders and trappers tried alleged culprits for murder and other crimes; however, maintenance of order, while frequently successful, was unofficial at best. Native Americans in the Oregon territory did not become subject to American official authority until 1843, when President Tyler appointed Oregon's first Native American agent.

That was the year when the first large body of American immigrants arduously entered the Willamette Valley in western Oregon. It was also then that a committee, composed of American pioneers and their French-Canadian neighbors, met in Champoeg and formed a provisional government. Once the government came into being, it was almost immediately effective.

Soon the "Oregon fever" had hit the eastern United States, and British settlers in Oregon began to find themselves vastly outnumbered. This rapid influx of Americans prompted both Britain and the United States to try once again for a peaceful boundary settlement.

In 1844, one of James Polk campaign slogans was "fifty-four forty or fight," suggesting that Polk favored U.S. possession of Oregon all the way to the southern border of Alaska and anything less would mean war with England. Soon after the Democratic victory in the election of 1844, the newly elected President Polk, faced with the possibility of war with Mexico, once again proposed to Great Britain the boundary line of 49°. When the British minister in Washington peremptorily rejected the American offer, the United States on April 26, 1846, gave the required one-year notice to terminate the joint-occupation treaty of 1818. Later that year the British government decided to settle for the 49° line because the British had over-trapped in the Columbia River valley, and their business in beaver pelts was no longer profitable. Britain submitted a draft treaty to this effect to the United States; and Polk submitted the treaty to the Senate, which approved it on June 12 and formally ratified it a week later.

The Anglo-American settlement did not meet with unanimous approval in the United States. Northwestern exponents of Manifest Destiny and antislavery men charged that they had been betrayed by a South which, smugly complacent over the annexation of all of Texas, had been satisfied with less than all of Oregon. The Oregon Treaty, however, did have the important effect of preventing a possible third war between the United States and Great Britain at a time when the United States was involved in a war with Mexico over the question of Texas.

Settlement of Texas

In the 1820s and 1830s, a number of Americans—mostly Southerners—took advantage of Mexico's liberal colonization law offering cheap land to settlers and migrated to Texas. With the help of slaves and cotton gins, they farmed the fertile soil and conducted business under the aegis of Stephen Austin and other *empresarios* who had contracted with the Mexican government to settle a certain number of families in Texas in return for large grants of land.

In three centuries the Spanish government had brought only 4,000 subjects to Texas. Now the population of the Austin communities alone expanded from 2,000 in 1828 to more than 5,500 three years later. By 1836 more than 25,000 white men, women, and children were scattered between the Sabine River and San Antonio de Bexar. Colonists from the United States far outnumbered those of Spanish ancestry.

Friction between Mexicans and Americans in Texas was probably inevitable. Mexicans, long accustomed to Spanish procedures, naturally were unprepared for the expectations of Anglo-style administrative and legislative procedures by the immigrants. Blunt and self-assertive Americans in Texas were certain that their way of life was freer, healthier, happier, and in all ways superior to that of the Mexicans. They looked upon themselves individually and collectively as proper agents to impose reform and progress on what they deemed to be a benighted society, disadvantaged for generations by superstition and sloth. The average new-

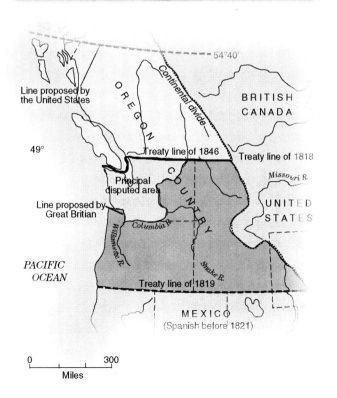

MAP 8.6 The Oregon Controversy

comer failed to recognize the spirituality and gentility of Spanish culture and criticized the Mexican peasants for being illiterate and ignorant. Americans also overlooked the equally pertinent truth that both Mexican peasants and their grandee overlords were sensitive and proud.

Americans in Texas were distressed by the changing Mexican policy and the uncertainty of their own status. The Mexican government appeared indifferent to educational needs and law enforcement; it did nothing to meet the Americans' request for the separation of Texas from the state of Coahuila, to which it had long been joined. This neglect, as well as the government's pressure to force the Roman Catholic religion on the settlers, impose taxes, impose centralized rule from Mexico City, and to abolish slavery, contributed to a drift that widened the gulf between the native Mexicans and the immigrants from the north.

▶ President James Polk, 1844. *Wikipedia photo*

War for Independence

In Mexico City, meanwhile, a growing trend toward dictatorial rule reduced the likelihood of conciliation. The master spirit of despotism was Antonio Lopez de Santa Anna, who became president of Mexico in 1833. Santa Anna, "the Napoleon of the West," was ambitious, adept at intrigue, and an able field commander as long as fate favored him. As president, he ruthlessly crushed every semblance of liberalism in Mexico's central government and then turned his attention to Texas, where Americans were vehemently protesting his abandonment of the eleven-year-old "enlightened" Mexican federal constitution of 1824. The Texans' protests culminated in a proclamation of independence from Mexico on March 2, 1836.

Four days later Santa Anna and his Mexican troops swept into Texas and massacred every one of the 188 Americans at the Alamo mission in San Antonio. Davy Crockett, Jim Bowie, and William B. Travis were among the Americans who died defending the Alamo. That same month, at Goliad on the south bank of the San Antonio River, the severely wounded James Walker Fannin surrendered his tiny command to Mexican General José Urrea, with the understanding that the Texans would be accorded the humane treatment normally extended to prisoners of war. Instead, acting under Santa Anna's orders, Urrea mercilessly executed most of the 300 prisoners in cold blood, with Colonel Fannin the last to go. As a result "Remember Goliad!" long served as rallying cries in Texas.

During the war for Texan independence, the young republic's forces were in the capable hands of General Sam Houston, who had fought under Andrew Jackson in the War of 1812 and had later settled in Texas. Not quite two months after the Texans' stunning defeats at the Alamo and Goliad, his troops surprised and defeated Santa Anna's forces at San Jacinto (near Houston) on April 21, 1836 and captured the Mexican dictator. Houston forced Santa Anna to sign the Treaty of Velasco, by which Mexico agreed to withdraw its forces from Texas and to recognize the Rio Grande as the southwestern boundary of the new Republic of Texas. Santa Anna also agreed to use his influence to induce Mexico to recognize Texas's independence.

MAP 8.7 The Texas Revolution

The Republic of Texas

The Texans' proposal for annexation was initially rejected by the United States because of fear that a serious sectional controversy might develop over extending slavery into the area—as, indeed, it did. Therefore the young republic, under the leadership of Presidents Sam Houston and Mirabeau B. Lamar, proceeded to develop its own foreign and domestic policies. One of its first problems was Mexico's refusal to recognize its independent status. Due to the fact that Santa Anna had signed the Treaty of Velasco under duress as a prisoner of war and Mexico had never ratified the treaty, the Mexicans denied its validity. Even though both Europe and the United States officially recognized Texas's independence, Mexico still withheld recognition and continued to consider Texas to be a Mexican state in rebellion.

Although the sizable volunteer army of the San Jacinto campaign was disbanded in 1837, Texas maintained armed troops against the danger of another military campaign by Mexico. The Texas Rangers, loosely organized until then, were developed to fight Native American raids and border incursions by Mexican cattle rustlers while the Texas navy made its presence known in the Gulf of Mexico. As late as 1843, Texan sailors fought against Mexican steam warships in the Gulf of Mexico.

Maintenance of a navy and defenses against Native Americans and Banditos, as well as maintaining the Mexican army that twice invaded Texas and took over the town of San Antonio in 1842, demanded more money than Texas had. Texan troops also unsuccessfully invaded the Mexican towns of Mier and Santa Fe in 1842, with the result that some 500 Texans were either dead or imprisoned in Mexico. The Republic's civil government desperately needed financial support. Bond issues were floated with varying degrees of success; however, the fiscal structure was never solid during the period of the Republic, which was experiencing inflation, currency devaluation, and massive debt.

Nevertheless, Texas prospered in that its population grew rapidly due to immigration, and most of the immigrants continued to be Americans. Large in territory and rich in untapped resources, Texas was regarded with desirous eyes by those American politicians who viewed it as a promising field for expansion, exploitation, and the extension of slavery.

Annexation of Texas

Presidents Jackson and Van Buren had been concerned about the North's opposition to the annexation of Texas due to the numerical balance between slave states and free states. Jackson favored annexation and was more outspoken about it after he retired from the presidency. In fact, Jackson had recognized Texas's independence on his last day in office in 1837. Hamstrung by the Panic of 1837, Van Buren marked time; but neither of his successors, Tyler nor Polk, had qualms about working toward annexation. Although both were slaveholders, neither seems to have been thinking primarily about considerations of slavery when pushing for Texas's annexation (Polk's diary gives abundant evidence to this effect). Instead, both couched their motives in terms of expansion: Would it be to the country's advantage to limit expansion of the federal

▶ In the infamous massacre at the Alamo, President Santa Anna and his Mexican troops swept into Texas and massacred every one of the 188 Americans at the mission in San Antonio. Among those who died defending the Alamo were Davy Crockett, Jim Bowie, and William B. Travis. *Wikipedia photo*

domain? This was substantially the same question Jefferson had asked himself in 1803 with reference to the Louisiana Purchase. Like Jefferson, Tyler and Polk answered with a ringing "No!"

Antislavery elements in the North, however, viewed the situation differently. Most Northerners—excluding the tiny minority of abolitionists—agreed with their Southern brothers that the Constitution protected slavery where slavery then existed. Extension of slavery into the West, however, they strongly disapproved. As a result, many citizens north of the Mason-Dixon line opposed the addition of Texas as a slave state.

Early in 1844 President Tyler, anticipating the presidential campaign of that year, sent to the Senate a treaty for the annexation of Texas. When the Senate rejected it by a vote of thirty-five to sixteen, Tyler recommended that Texas be annexed by joint resolution of both houses of Congress, since a joint resolution could be passed by a simple majority in both houses plus the President's signature, in contrast to the two-thirds Senate majority needed for treaty ratification. Congress adjourned before the measure could be brought to a vote; but when the second session convened on December 2, 1844, Tyler again urged a joint resolution to annex Texas.

Momentum gained for the measure in the fall of 1844. This was partially due to the election of James Polk, who campaigned for president on a Manifest Destiny platform that included the annexation of both Texas and Oregon. Many in Congress viewed Polk's election as a public mandate for expansion. Therefore, this time the resolution passed both House and Senate, and Tyler signed it on March 1, 1845. Under the terms of the resolution, Texas was offered statehood with the understanding that its territory might be subdivided into not more than four additional states. The Missouri Compromise line of 36° 30' was extended westward to permit slavery in Texas, but not in its territories north of the Missouri Compromise line. Texas was also allowed to retain its public lands so that it could sell the land and address the $10 million in public debt the state had incurred during its years as a republic.

Before the annexation resolution was passed, there had been hints and fears of British involvement in the fate of the Texas Republic. It was in England's interest, as well as that of Mexico, to see that Texas stayed out of the United States. A pending arrangement whereby Texas would ship cotton directly to Liverpool, for example, would mean the tightening of mutually advantageous Anglo-Texas economic ties.

The London government tried to induce Mexico to recognize Texas independence on the condition that the Lone Star republic would not become part of the United States. Mexico did assent to this proposal in May 1845, and Texans had a choice of being annexed to the United States or negotiating such a treaty with Mexico. The Mexican offer had come too late, however. Now that annexation to the United States was theirs for the taking, Texans, most of whom were recent immigrants from the United States, found this alternative the more desirable.

War with Mexico

Already irate over Texas's independence, the Mexican government became exceedingly resentful when, in 1845, its erstwhile possession was formally annexed by the United States. Mexico had threatened to declare war on the United States if Texas was annexed. Now it withdrew its minister to the United States and severed official relations with the American government.

Mexico and the United States also disputed the official border between Texas and Mexico. The United States claimed that the border was the Rio Grande, based on the Treaty of Velasco—signed by Santa Anna under duress and never ratified by Mexico. Mexico claimed that the border was the Nueces River (about 150 miles north of the Rio Grande) based on a border drawn by Spain in 1775 when Texas was part of New Spain prior to Mexican independence. In June 1845, President Polk ordered General Zachary Taylor and his troops into Texas to defend the territory. Taylor set up camp on the south bank of the Nueces River, about 150 miles from the Rio Grande. In November Polk dispatched John Slidell to Mexico on a special mission to discuss the outstanding issues between Mexico and the United States. Slidell was to propose that the United States assume the $2 million in claims of American citizens against the government of Mexico, in return for Mexico's recognition of the Rio Grande as the southwestern boundary of Texas. Polk also authorized Slidell to offer $5 million for New Mexico or $25 million for both New Mexico and California, whose port of San Francisco seemed highly desirable to a people now committed to trade with China.

The new Mexican government under President José Joaquín de Herrera refused to receive Slidell because public sentiment in Mexico was against the sale of territory to the United States. Slidell wrote to President Polk and argued, "nothing is to be done with these people until they have been chastised. War is desirable, and we can never get along with them until we have given them a good drubbing." Polk ordered Taylor to proceed to the Rio Grande, a movement of troops that was bound to be taken as provocative since Mexico claimed that the area was on Mexican soil. Polk also sent the U.S. navy to the coast of California so that the U.S. could easily take over the ports of California if Mexico attacked American troops in Texas.

On April 12, Mexico warned Taylor to withdraw to the Nueces River; but Taylor refused and instead instituted a blockade of the Port of Matamoros—an act of war under international law. On April 25, 1846, Taylor's troops were attacked by Mexican troops, and eleven men were killed. Congress declared war on the Republic of Mexico after Polk declared to Congress on May 11 that "blood has been shed on American soil" and that "war exists" between the United States and Mexico. One young Congressman from Illinois opposed the war declaration on the grounds that the spot where blood was shed might not have been American soil. For demanding to know the "spot" on which American blood had been shed, Congressman Abraham Lincoln gained the nickname "Spotty Lincoln."

President Polk aided the return of the exiled Santa Anna to power in Mexico, believing that Santa Anna would quickly negotiate peace in return. Instead, Santa Anna raised a 25,000-man army and moved north to meet Taylor's forces. The battles of Palo Alto and Resaca de la Palma followed: the first was an inconclusive artillery duel, the second a smashing American victory. These opening engagements of May 1846 were followed by the major encounters of Monterrey the next September and Buena Vista in February 1847. General Zachary Taylor, bearing battlefield and theater responsibility in the Monterrey area, displayed great gallantry and was popular with his men. However, he did not make much progress in the direction of Mexico City, partly because Polk transferred most of the seasoned soldiers from Taylor's command to that of Major General Winfield Scott on the southeastern Mexican coast.

It was Scott who, landing at Vera Cruz in March 1847, made that Gulf port his supply base and advanced inland to the mountain pass of Cerro Gordo, where he routed Mexican General Santa Anna. Other battles took place in 1847, and all were American victories. Scott entered Mexico City in September, but it was blood-soaked Buena Vista, more than half a year before, that made Taylor the next president. Before Scott entered Mexico City, he contacted the British minister in Mexico City to offer Santa Anna a peace settlement of $10,000 up front and $1 million to be paid later after a treaty was ratified. Scott made the $10,000 payment through a secret service fund, but Santa Anna then announced that the Mexican legislature opposed peace talks. On August 23, as Scott prepared for an assault on the capitol city, Santa Anna offered a cease-fire through the British embassy. Scott, however, distrusted Santa Anna due to the failed $10,000 bribe debacle and stormed the city anyway. Scott secured Mexico City on September 14, 1847, and Santa Anna resigned two days later.

Although the United States declared war on Mexico in May 1846, the news did not reach California for a number of weeks. Meanwhile, a group of California settlers, aided by explorer John C. Frémont and American naval officers, had revolted against Mexican rule and proclaimed California an independent republic. They raised a flag on which a grizzly bear, a red star, and the legend "Republic of California" were juxtaposed. However, when Americans received news that the United States had declared war against Mexico, the significance of the Bear Flag Revolt was greatly diminished.

In the summer of 1846 Colonel Stephen W. Kearny and a detachment of about 1,700 troops took possession of Santa Fe in the name of the United States. Polk subsequently ordered Kearny to take charge of American operations in California. The American elements previously led by Commodore R. F. Stockton were brought together under Kearny, and by the autumn of 1846 the conquest of California was complete.

The Treaty of Guadalupe Hidalgo

In April 1847 President Polk, eager to end the fighting as quickly as possible, delegated Nicholas P. Trist, chief clerk of the State Department, as peace commissioner to Mexico. Trist's instructions were to negotiate a treaty recognizing the Rio Grande as the southwest boundary of Texas and ceding to the United States, for $15 million, the Mexican states of Upper California and New Mexico. The United States also assumed the claims of United States citizens against Mexico up to $3.25 million.

Mexico's new government demanded a peace treaty that set the boundary at the Nueces River. Trist forwarded this demand to Polk, who was incensed over the demand. Polk immediately recalled Trist. Trist, believing that the time for peace talks was immediate because the moderates in power in Mexico could fall at any time and a less amiable government could take their place, sent a sixty-five-page letter to Polk explaining the situation and refused to return to Washington. With no official authority, Trist signed a treaty that incorporated all the provisions of his annulled instructions on February 2, 1848. Polk was furious at Trist's disobedience, declaring that Trist had acted "worse than any man in the public employ whom I have ever known," but Polk immediately sent the treaty to the Senate for ratification. Although two vocal minorities—those who had demanded the cession of all of Mexico and those who

MAP 8.8 Mexican War Campaigns

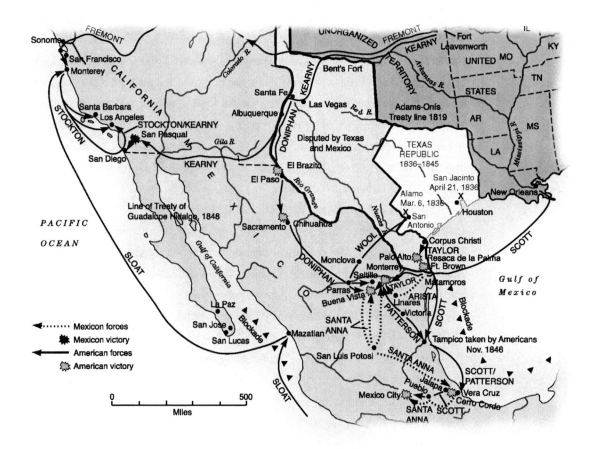

wanted none of the southwestern territory—denounced the Treaty of Guadalupe Hidalgo, the Senate ratified it on March 10, 1848. The United States now found itself in possession of the enormous region that includes the present states of California, Nevada, and Utah, most of Arizona and New Mexico, and parts of Colorado and Wyoming. It also found itself with a considerable number of Spanish-speaking residents, many who belonged to families who had lived there for generations. According to the treaty, they became United States citizens, and their property rights were entitled to respect.

The territory, however, had come at a great cost. The U.S. lost 13,000 men (11,550 from disease) from its army of 105,000, the highest death rate of any foreign war in U.S. history. The cost was even greater for Mexico, which lost 50,000 men and approximately half its territory. The war also created ill will toward the U.S. in Mexico, which lasted for generations.

Gadsden Purchase

Santa Anna returned to power in Mexico in the 1850s, and his government was desperate for money. Santa Anna knew that the United States coveted land in the Mexican Northwest for the construction of a railroad from Texas to California. Santa Anna, therefore, let President Franklin Pierce know that he would be willing to give up more borderlands in the

▶ The battle at Buena Vista was General Zachary Taylor's greatest battle of the war. His success at Buena Vista helped him win the presidential election in 1848. *Wikipedia photo*

desert Mexican Northwest in exchange for a generous offer. To avoid political dissent in Mexico, however, Santa Anna required that the U.S. amass its army near the Mexican border and appear to threaten another military incursion. President Pierce dutifully sent the U.S. military to the Rio Grande in a charade of force; and the U.S. Minister to Mexico, James Gadsden, secured 54,000 square miles of what is now southern Arizona and New Mexico for $10 million.

California

While settlement of Texas and the Oregon country was proceeding, other areas were luring pioneers westward in search of land or mineral wealth. Some who had started out on the Oregon Trail bound for the Northwest changed their destination to California. The path to California followed the Oregon Trail to the Continental Divide where, turning southwestward, it became the California Trail and led through the Sierra Nevada into California.

Before 1840, only fur traders penetrated into California, and occasionally whaling ships stopped there for supplies. In the early 1840s, some farmers began to move into the Pacific Coast valleys; but when war with Mexico broke out in 1846, there were only about 700 Americans in California. The discovery of gold at Sutter's Mill near Sacramento in 1848 started the "gold rush," which brought the total population of the area to 90,000 by 1850, when California became a state. The gold seekers came by sea around Cape Horn, by sea after an overland crossing of Mexico or Central America, or by various overland routes across the North American continent. The transcontinental journey was chosen by most immigrants—an estimated 40,000 using it in 1849. The California gold rush brought people—a disproportionate share of them male in the first years—from all over the world and left an imprint on the region that is arguably felt to this day, in that California is one of the most ethnically diverse regions of the country. As New Mexico continues to be regionally distinct because it was the most populous region in the Mexican domain before being sold to the United States in 1848, as New Orleans and Louisiana still show many traces of the French and Creole culture that preceded the

The following is the title page to the *Book of Mormon*.

*THE
BOOK OF MORMON
AN ACCOUNT WRITTEN BY*

THE HAND OF MORMON

UPON PLATES

TAKEN FROM THE PLATES OF NEPHI

Wherefore, it is an abridgment of the record of the people of Nephi, and also of the Lamanites—Written to the Lamanites, who are a remnant of the house of Israel; and also to Jew and Gentile—Written by way of commandment, and also by the spirit of prophecy and of revelation—Written and sealed up, and hid up unto the Lord, that they might not be destroyed—To come forth by the gift and power of God unto the interpretation thereof—Sealed by the hand of Moroni, and hid up unto the Lord, to come forth in due time by way of the Gentile—The interpretation thereof by the gift of God.

An abridgment taken from the Book of Ether also, which is a record of the people of Jared, who were scattered at the time the Lord confounded the language of the people, when they were building a tower to get to heaven—Which is to show unto the remnant of the House of Israel what great things the Lord hath done for their fathers; and that they may know the covenants of the Lord, that they are not cast off forever—And also to the convincing of the Jew and Gentile that JESUS is the CHRIST, the ETERNAL GOD, manifesting himself unto all nations—And now, if there are faults they are the mistakes of men; wherefore, condemn not the things of God, that ye may be found spotless at the judgment-seat of Christ.

*TRANSLATED BY JOSEPH SMITH, JUN.
First English edition published in 1830*

Source: *The Book of Mormon*, title page, 1830.

Louisiana Purchase, so too are San Francisco and northern California different today because "the world rushed in" in 1849. Two-thirds of the adult males in Oregon quickly immigrated to California in search of gold. Some 13,000 immigrants arrived in California from Mexico, South America, and Europe.

By the 1850s there were two frontiers in America, one moving westward beyond the Mississippi and the other moving eastward from California and Oregon into the Rocky Mountain area.

The Church of Jesus Christ of Latter-day Saints

The first settlement to fill the gap between the most Western territories and the mid-west was made by the Mormons, who moved to Utah in 1847. To escape persecution and under the leadership of Brigham Young, in 1846 the Mormons decided to move to a desert valley around the Great Salt Lake, where they hoped to find peace. The Mormons had chosen Utah because no one else wanted the barren territory, and they believed that they would be left alone. Thousands of Mormons migrated along the Mormon Trail, some 1,300 miles from Iowa to Utah, using handcarts. In one great exodus, 1,000 Mormons and their handcarts got stuck in the Rocky Mountain snow. Brigham Young sent an entourage of Mormons with mules to save the surviving 800 stranded pilgrims. They had some misfortunes and near disasters in the first few years but eventually became prosperous due to ingenious canal irrigation of the Rocky Mountain snowmelt. Moreover, they continued to practice polygamy. Brigham Young installed himself as President of the Mormon Church and considered Utah to be an independent country. Along with having twenty-three wives, however, Young was prone to self-aggrandizement and claimed his own death and resurrection.

With the close of the Mexican War the Mormons lost the nominal Mexican jurisdiction under which they had been free to do as they pleased. Congress organized the Mormon lands into Utah Territory in 1850, naming Brigham Young as territorial governor. For a few years after 1849, the Mormons profited substantially from the sale of supplies to gold seekers on the way to California. By 1860 there were 40,000 persons in Utah, but it was not admitted as a state until 1896 because the Mormon Church did not renounce the practice of polygamy until 1890.

Growing Sectionalism

While the economic bonds were tightening between Northeast and Northwest, the South depended increasingly on exporting cotton and other plantation products to the European market. Although there were notable exceptions, Southerners were basically pulling away from their earlier common interests with other parts of the country. The South's growing identification with an international market economy was natural for the specialized producer of seven-eighths of the world's cotton fiber.

Certain financial obstacles, however, prevented the South from completely freeing itself from dependence on the North. A growing demand for slaves meant continually rising prices for them. To buy land and slaves for the expansion of cultivation required new increments of capital, which the planter class—a leisure-loving economic aristocracy—simply could not provide for itself. The new capital, therefore, had to be acquired in the financial markets of the North and Europe in competition with an expanding and increasingly productive mechanized industry.

Likewise, the shipping and sale of cotton tended to be handled by mercantile agencies in the principal Northeastern seaports because the highly specialized shipping requirements of the Southern economy could not be met efficiently except in conjunction with the more general trade of the major ports. Southern ports did not offer such possibilities of pooling cargo and warehouse space. Southerners complained that Northern merchants who obtained the profits of the cotton trade and kept the Southern planters dependent upon them for mercantile credit took their own business away from them.

Nevertheless, the South continued to follow its policy of determined divergence from the economies of the other sections of the nation and continued to seek a free world market. Not all whites living in the South were in agreement on means and methods, but the most extreme elements believed that there was only one way in which their section could escape economic submission to the North and West. Only through secession from the Union, they were convinced, could the Southern states avoid being damaged by future economic policies that would destroy slavery and the plantation system. Ultimately the South indeed chose the path of secession, a path that led not only to the end of the institutions they had sought to save but also to the most destructive event in our national history—the Civil War.

Chapter Review ▶ ▶ ▶

Summary

Between 1824 and 1854 Americans spread across the North American continent subscribing to the belief in Manifest Destiny, or that American control of the continent was part of God's Divine plan. In 1803, Thomas Jefferson had purchased the vast area between the Rocky Mountains and the Mississippi River from France and in 1804 commissioned Lewis and Clark to explore it. Lewis and Clark made it all the way to the Pacific Ocean on the Columbia River, but England also claimed the area and America agreed to Joint Occupation of the Oregon Territory with the British in 1818.

In 1831, the King of the Netherlands drew a border between the U.S. and Canada in Northern Maine, but the U.S. rejected the new border. When Canada granted land to lumberjacks in an area south of the new border, an armed border clash followed between the Maine militia and the Canadian lumberjacks. Simultaneously, American support of Canadian rebels in Ontario resulted in a British attack on a U.S. ship, the *Caroline,* in U.S. waters and the death of an American, Amos Durfee. When British subject Alexander McLeod was arrested in Buffalo for his boast that he had killed Amos Durfee, the British threatened war. McLeod was found innocent, war was averted, and the Webster-Ashburton Treaty set the Maine Border at the James River and awarded upper Minnesota to the U.S.

In 1819-1820, Stephen S. Long explored the Great Plains and labeled it the Great American Desert; consequently, Americans would settle the Continent by bypassing the Desert and heading further west. 1821, the Santa Fe Trail opened a trade route from Independence Missouri to Santa Fe. In 1836, the Oregon Trail opened to wagon trains from Independence, Missouri to Oregon.

In 1844, James Polk won the Presidency on a Manifest Destiny Platform. Polk then waged war with Mexico to gain the Texas border at the Rio Grande and the Southwestern United States from Mexico. Polk then negotiated the division of Oregon with the British and the U.S./Canadian border was set at 49 degrees north latitude. In 1954, the U.S. would purchase 54,000 square miles of Southern Arizona and Southern New Mexico from Mexico in the Gadsden Purchase. Meanwhile, Brigham Young led his Mormon followers to Utah in 1846 and Gold was discovered at Sutter's Mill near Sacramento in 1848 leading to a rush of settlers west to California. Unfortunately, just as "Manifest Destiny" was coming together, sectionalism threatened to rip the country apart.

Chapter Review (cont'd) ▶ ▶ ▶

Chronological Time Line

1803	Louisiana Purchase adds land between the Mississippi River and Rocky Mountains
1808	Jacob Astor organizes American Fur Company
1818	U.S. and England agree on Joint Occupation of Oregon
1819	Stephen S. Long surveys Great Plains and declares it a "Great American Desert."
1821	William Becknell of Arrow Rock, Missouri, initiated the Santa Fe trade
1821	Missouri is admitted as a state
1826	Jedediah S. Smith led the first American overland expedition from Missouri to California.
1831	King of the Netherlands draws a border between Maine and New Brunswick accepted by England, but rejected by the U.S.
1836	Arkansas is admitted as a state
1836	Texas wins its Independence from Mexico
1836	First Oregon wagon trains organized at Independence, Missouri
1838	John C. Fremont surveys plateau between the Mississippi and Missouri Rivers
1839	Border clash between Maine militia and Canadian Lumberjacks
1840	Richard Henry Dana published a vivid description of the California coast in *Two Years Before the Mast*
1842	Webster-Ashburton Treaty settles Maine border and grants upper Minnesota to the U.S.
1844	James Polk is elected President on a "Manifest Destiny" platform
1845	John L. O'Sullivan proclaims it "the fulfillment of our manifest destiny to overspread the continent allotted by Providence for the free development of our yearly multiplying millions."
1845	The U.S. Annexes Texas officially on December 29
1846	U.S. gains sole occupation of Oregon South of 49 degrees in a Treaty with England
1846	U.S. invades Mexico in a border dispute

Time Line (cont'd)

1846	Brigham Young leads the Mormons to Utah
1848	Treaty of Guadalupe Hidalgo sets the Texas border at the Rio Grande and grants the American Southwest to the United States
1848	Gold is discovered at Sutter's Mill near Sacramento
1854	Gadsden Purchase: The U.S. purchases 54,000 square miles of what is now Southern Arizona and New Mexico

Key Terms

Manifest Destiny: The idea that it was God's will that Americans would overspread the continent bringing freedom, democracy, Christianity, and the American way wherever they went

Maine Border Dispute: Dispute between the U.S. and Great Britain over the border between Maine and New Brunswick culminating in a border clash in 1839 followed by the Webster-Ashburton Treaty.

Webster-Ashburton Treaty: Set the border between Maine and New Brunswick and awarded the U.S. upper Minnesota.

Sam Houston: Tennessean and Jacksonian Democrat that became the head of the Texas Army in the Texas Revolution and the first President of the Republic of Texas.

James Polk: Thirteenth President of the United States elected in 1844 on a Manifest Destiny platform.

Liberty Party: Antislavery party in 1844 that siphoned enough votes from Henry Clay that James Polk won both New York and the Presidency.

Election of 1844: Won by James Polk over Henry Clay on a platform of Manifest Destiny

John C. Fremont: Led several expeditions to the West in the 1840s, exploring the Oregon Trail, the Sierra Nevada, California, the Colorado River, and the Rio Grande. His well-written reports, avidly read in the East, stimulated further emigration to the West.

Stephen S. Long: Surveyed parts of the Great Plains and Rocky Mountains in 1819–1820. Long, however, described the Great Plains as the "Great American Desert,"

The Santa Fe Trail: Opened in 1821, an 800 mile trade route from Independence, Missouri to Santa Fe where Americans would trade their goods for silver at exorbitant prices.

The Oregon Trail: Opened to Wagon Trains in 1836, the route stretched from Independence Missouri to Oregon

The Oregon Dispute: Dispute between England and the United States over control of Oregon eventually settled in 1846 at the 49th parallel during the Polk Presidency

Texas Annexation: By a joint Address of Congress, Texas was officially annexed on December 29, 1845.

Chapter Review (cont'd) ▶ ▶ ▶

Key Terms (cont'd)

Texas War for Independence: Texans defeated a Mexican Army under Santa Anna at San Jacinto near Houston and won their Independence from Mexico in 1836

Sam Houston: Tennessean and Jacksonian Democrat, Commander of the Texan army during the Texas Revolution, first President of the Republic of Texas.

"Spotty Lincoln": The nickname given to Congressman Abraham Lincoln for demanding to know "the spot" where blood was shed on American soil before the American war with Mexico in 1846.

The War with Mexico: The U.S. invaded Mexico in 1846 to secure the Texas border at the Rio Grande. 13,000 Americans and 50,000 Mexicans died in the war.

Slidell Mission: John Slidell was sent to Mexico in 1846 to attempt to purchase the American Southwest from Mexico and settle the Texas border at the Rio Grande. Slidell's offer was rejected by Mexico.

Bear Flag Revolt: In 1846, a group of California settlers, aided by explorer John C. Frémont and by American naval officers, revolted against Mexican rule and raised a flag on which a grizzly bear, a red star, and the legend "Republic of California" were juxtaposed.

Nicholas Trist: Negotiated the Treaty of Guadalupe Hidalgo

Treaty of Guadalupe Hidalgo: Set the Texas border at the Rio Grande, ceded the Southwestern United States from Mexico to the U.S. and provided that the U.S. pay $18.25 million

Gadsden Purchase: The purchase of 54,000 square miles in southern Arizona and New Mexico from Mexico in 1854.

Sources Consulted

John S. D. Eisenhower, *So Far from God: The U.S. War With Mexico 1846–1848* (1989).

John Mack Faragher, *Women and Men on the Overland Trail* (1978).

Samuel W. Haynes and Christopher Morris, eds., *Manifest Destiny and Empire* (1997).

Robert W. Johannsen, *To the Halls of the Montezumas: The Mexican War in the American Imagination* (1985).

David Pletcher, *The Diplomacy of Annexation: Texas, Oregon, and the Mexican War* (1973).

John H. Schroeder, *Mr. Polk's War: American Opposition and Dissent, 1846–1848* (1973).

Joel H. Silbey, *Storm over Texas: The Annexation Controversy and the Road to Civil War* (2005).

John D. Unruh, *The Plains Across: The Overland Emigrants and the Trans-Mississippi West, 1840–1860* (1979).

Sean Wilentz, *Chants Democratic: New York City and the Rise of the American Weekly Class, 1788–1850* (2004).

9 The Nation at Mid-Century

Outline

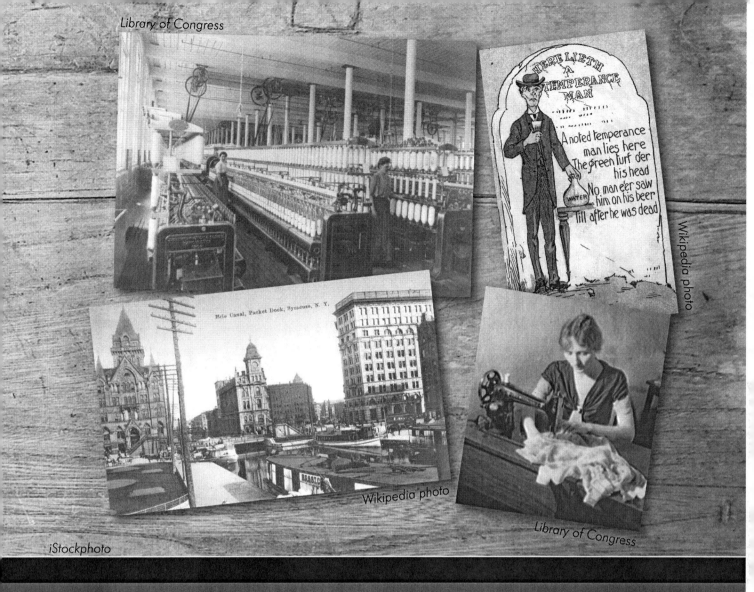

Library of Congress

Wikipedia photo

Wikipedia photo

iStockphoto

Library of Congress

A Modernizing of the Northern Region

Characteristics of Modernization

Many scholars have used the concept of "modernization" to describe and analyze the rapid change experienced by Americans in the North during the middle decades of the nineteenth century. According to this thinking—which can provide a useful way of organizing information about such a transformative period—modernization is characterized by four factors. The first is a heavy investment in "social overhead capital," or improved transportation and communication. This produces a transition from a localized subsistence economy to a regionally or nationally integrated market economy. The second factor is a rapid increase in the output per man-hour that results from technological innovation and the substitution of machines for human labor. The third factor is the evolution from decentralized handcraft manufacturing to centralized industry producing standardized, interchangeable parts. Last is the accelerated growth of the industrial sector as compared with other sectors of the economy.

Socially, modernization is marked by a growth in education, literacy, and mass communication. Furthermore, there is a transition from a static, predominantly rural populace to an urbanizing population in which farms and villages become cultural as well as economic satellites of the urban/industrial market. Politically, modernization is accompanied by the rise of nationalism and centralized authority and by increased popular participation in government. Ideologically, modernization is characterized by an outlook that emphasizes change rather than tradition. In sum, modernization is the transition from a rural, village-oriented system of traditional personal and family ties to a dynamic, urban, market-oriented system of impersonal relationships. Once again, this criteria fits the North in the mid-nineteenth century very well.

Modernization was both cause and effect of the growing differences between North and South. As a labor-intensive economic system, tying up large amounts of capital in the ownership

▶ With the movement of modernization in the United States came the substitution of technology for human labor. Slavery was on its way out as machines were used more commonly.
Wikipedia photo

of human beings, slavery inhibited technological innovation. Capital was diverted in the South from investment in factories to investment into human inventory, thus stunting technological advancement. The South feared change, while the North welcomed it and began to equate slavery and the South's conservatism as obstacles to the progress and greatness of America.

In nearly every index of modernization, this period marked the transition of America—with the partial and significant exception of the South—from a pre-modern to a modern society. In the 1850s, middle-aged Americans could look back upon unprecedented changes in their own lifetimes. Since 1815, the development of steamboats, canals, macadamized roads, and railroads had radically increased the speed and reduced the cost of inland transportation. In 1815, the average cost of shipping freight had been 40¢ per ton-mile by wagon and 6¢ by water; in 1855, it was less than 3¢ by rail and 1¢ by water. Goods sent from Cincinnati to New York in 1817 took more than fifty days to reach their destination; by the early 1850s, they required only six days. The same trip for passengers was reduced from three weeks to less than two days.

A few simple statistics will illustrate the pace of change in other indicators of modernization. While all sectors of the economy grew rapidly from 1840 to 1880, the rate of growth in the manufacturing sector was more than twice that of agriculture. The percentage of the labor force engaged in manufacturing nearly doubled during the same period, and the proportion of the population living in urban areas increased more than two and one half times. As a measure of the increased efficiency and higher standard of living produced by a modernizing economy, the per capita commodity output increased 72 percent and *per capita* income doubled during the same years.

This growth was a mixed blessing. The industrial working class did not share equally in the rising prosperity, for the real wages of blue-collar workers rose less than the income of other groups. Furthermore, no one can measure the human consequences of the transition from a craft-oriented system of manufacturing, in which skilled journeymen and apprentices worked alongside master craftsmen in small shops, to a factory system in which unskilled or semiskilled workers performed repetitive tasks at a machine. The loss of skills and of pride in craftsmanship, the growing separation of a working "class" from its employers, and the sense of relative deprivation caused by unequal distribution of increasing national wealth contributed to much of the labor unrest of this period.

In contrast with Europe, however, wages in America were high because of a relative shortage of labor. Despite rapid population growth, the supply of workers was never sufficient to meet the demand. This labor shortage in turn continued to stimulate technological innovation. New machines and new methods of production had to compensate for labor scarcity. Eli Whitney's attempt in 1798 to manufacture interchangeable rifle parts was sparked by the lack of skilled labor to make rifles in the traditional way. Although making interchangeable parts by machine was not exclusively an American development, it became known as the "American System" of manufacturing. By the 1850s, according to a team of visiting British industrialists, the American System was used for the production of a wide variety of goods—including "doors, furniture, and other woodwork; boots and shoes; ploughs and mowing machines; wood screws, files, and nails; biscuits; locks, clocks, small arms, nuts and bolts."

The Economics of Expansion

The West and the Transportation Revolution

From the beginning of human life on earth, people have lived in close association with rivers and streams. Waterways were the natural routes over which travelers moved both themselves and their goods, for rivers cut through the wilderness they could not penetrate in other ways. Therefore, when the settlers moving into the American frontier were forced to return to the most primitive conditions of living, rivers naturally became their first important means of inland transportation.

One of the great drawbacks to river transportation is that the river does not always go where the traffic needs to go. That became true in the United States as soon as the territory west of the Appalachian Mountains was opened for settlement. Rivers descended eastward from the Appalachian watersheds to the Atlantic or westward to meet the Ohio and Mississippi, but no waterway connected East and West. Thus, the great enthusiasm for building national roads during the "Turnpike Era" from 1800 to 1830 was occasioned partly by the fact that roads were needed to connect the Ohio River system with the Atlantic coastal rivers.

Transportation of goods between West and East over these road and river routes, however, was prohibitively expensive except for light and very valuable merchandise. The best outlet for the bulky western produce was not eastward but southward on flatboats down the Ohio and Mississippi Rivers to New Orleans. Any attempt, however, to try to propel flatboats back up the river against the current was still impractical. Manufactured products needed by western settlers—such as guns, ammunition, traps, axes, plows, tools, and even shoes and cloth—still had to arrive overland from the East.

America's most immediate economic problem was the need to move goods over great distances inexpensively. Thus, the new steam power developed in England in the eighteenth century was applied in America to water transportation even earlier than to industry. Beginning with John Fitch in 1786, a series of American inventors worked on the problem of driving a boat with steam, culminating with Robert Fulton's commercial success in powering his *Clermont* up the Hudson River in 1807. In the following decade steamboats were successfully tried on the Ohio and Mississippi Rivers. By 1829 there were 200 steamboats in operation on the western rivers, and by 1842 the number had reached 450. A decade later there were over 1,000. Partly because of the special needs of the West and partly because early steamboats were too fragile for ocean use (trans-Atlantic steamer service was not frequent until mid-century), more steamboats were in

▶A preserved flatboat. Flatboats were propelled southward down river to transport bulky produce. *Wikipedia photo*

MAP 9.1 Map of Territorial Growth (1840)

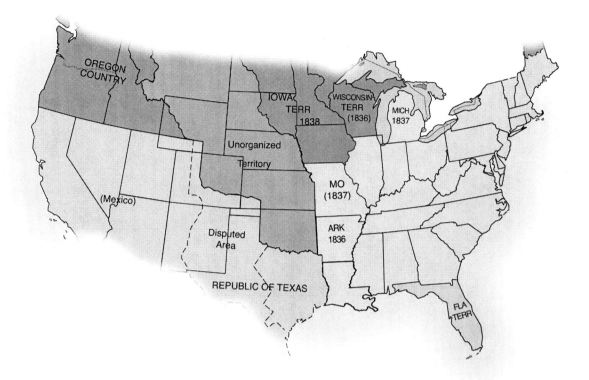

service on the Mississippi River system than anywhere else in the world. Pittsburgh, Cincinnati, and Louisville began as river towns, and New Orleans became one of America's greatest ports.

Meanwhile, in an attempt to avoid the roundabout route through New Orleans, Northerners turned their attention to canal building, which had been so successful in England in the 1760s and 1770s. The first such waterway of great importance was New York's Erie Canal, connecting the Great Lakes with the Hudson River (and therefore the port of New York). Upon its completion in 1825, freight charges from Buffalo to New York City were cut from $100 to $10 a ton, and the time of the trip was reduced from twenty days to six. Migrants began to use the canal to gain access to the West. Buffalo, Cleveland, Detroit, Chicago, and other cities began to sprout around the Great Lakes, and the area began to fill up with settlers just as the Ohio valley had earlier. As a result of the canal trade, New York City grew rapidly in wealth and population, becoming the greatest port on the Atlantic seaboard. The nation was propelled into the "Canal Era" (1825–1840), with other sections from Illinois to Massachusetts trying to imitate the success of New York.

Yet rivers and canals had their shortcomings. During winter, frozen waterways could not be used in the north. Rivers followed inconvenient courses, and canals could not be built in rough or hilly country. The development of the railroads would overcome all these limitations.

Steam-powered rail locomotives had already won success in England when the Baltimore and Ohio Railroad started the first few miles of American rail service in 1830. Soon other short lines were built elsewhere; 2,808 miles of track had been laid by 1840. Ten years later the mileage had more than tripled to 9,029 miles; by 1860 it had tripled again to 30,626 miles (as compared to industrial Britain's 10,410 miles). The railroads, which connected the Atlantic coast with Chicago and St. Louis by the 1850s, for the first time provided the West with exactly the

MAP 9.2 The Railroad Network (1850 and 1860)

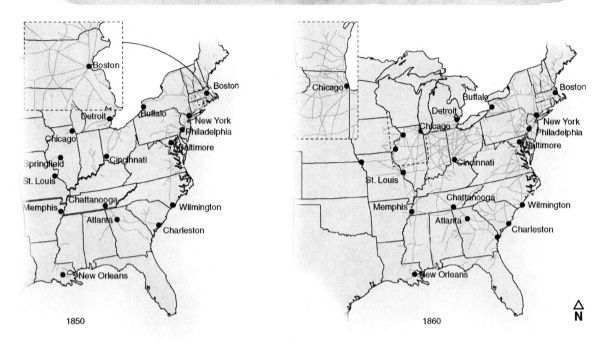

1850

1860

kind of transportation it needed. Western products, no matter what their bulk, could now be moved regardless of weather or terrain directly to eastern markets for overseas shipment. Manufactures from the East and abroad could come in freely. Traffic on the rivers and canals simultaneously declined. With the coming of the rails, the commercial and industrial Northeast and the agricultural Northwest were tied more closely together by common economic bonds.

The Northeast and Industrialization

Under the impact of continually expanding trade, each section of the country underwent a characteristic economic evolution of its own. New England, for example, the section that had achieved the lead in population in the colonial era, was the first to pass from agriculture to commerce and industry. The absence of good soil for agriculture and the abundance of good harbors adjacent to ample supplies of pine and hardwood had turned its people to shipbuilding, fishing, and overseas commerce in colonial days. It was no accident, too, that industrialism should have entered America through New England, for towns well located for commerce were also attractive for manufacturers. Mills and factories needed to be near shipping points, markets, or sources of raw materials. The Northeast provided both shipping points, with its excellent harbors, and markets, with its burgeoning population.

Other circumstances contributed to the growth of industrialism in the Northeast. In the early stages, streams were still a must for turning the water wheels that drove the machinery of mills and factories, and the Northeast was favorably endowed with waterpower. The Embargo Act and the War of 1812, in restricting overseas trade, had driven idle commercial capital into investment in domestic industry. The tremendous potentialities of trade with the West, facilitated first by the Erie Canal and then by the railroads, provided further incentive for the manufacture of industrial products. Finally, even after steam had replaced waterpower in industry, manufacturing continued to be located where capital and labor were already concentrated—in the Northeast.

The rise of industrialism in the northern United States had economic and social consequences and it revolutionized the nature of business organization, of labor, of population distribution, and of the life and welfare of all Americans.

The Corporate Revolution

The arrival of industrialism meant the beginning of the growth of large factories and large railroad networks. As the size of businesses increased, the traditional methods of organizing and financing business enterprises by means of individual ownership or partnership became inadequate. The costs of maintaining trading ships or small mills did not exceed the personal fortune of individuals, but with the coming of railroads and large-scale manufactures, the enormous costs of buildings, equipment, and stock began to run into millions of dollars. This was far beyond the financial resources of even most of the wealthiest persons, and the risks were too great to be undertaken individually. As a consequence, entrepreneurs turned increasingly to the corporate form of enterprise.

The chief disadvantage of the partnership was its "unlimited liability" for business debts. If the firm failed, creditors could force the sale of the owners' personal property, as well as their business property, to satisfy claims. The partnership, therefore, was usually comprised of a very few individuals who knew and trusted one another and who were willing to take the risks together. Moreover, the partnership had no permanence. It dissolved and the company collapsed when any single member withdrew. The corporation, on the other hand, is a separate legal entity or "person," distinct from its owners. An owner may sell his stock in the corporation without the assent of the other owners, and the corporation continues.

The most important feature of the corporation is the concept of "limited liability." If the corporation fails, the owners are liable to lose only what they paid for stock in the corpora-

▶ The Erie Canal was a bustling Western trading port during the time of the Industrial Revolution in the United States. *Wikipedia photo*

tion, and the creditors have no claim on their personal resources. Finally, by the issuance of stock, the corporation can draw on the contributions of literally thousands of investors and accumulate the large amounts of capital needed for large industry.

In spite of its advantages, the corporate form was not without its opponents in the Jacksonian period. Jackson, Jefferson before him, and even the father of free enterprise or laissez faire, the English economist Adam Smith, had attacked corporations as according "exclusive privilege" and limiting "free competition." Abraham Lincoln later warned that the power of corporations could subvert American democracy, but what they were attacking was the kind of incorporation that was known before the 1830s. Before then, corporation charters had been granted only through special legislation and only for some specific enterprise that had to be administered as a monopoly in order to be profitable. Thus, turnpikes, canals, bridges, and banks—enterprises of a semi-public character—were often conducted under charters granting exclusive privileges. Part of Jackson's hostility toward the Bank of the United States can be traced to what he viewed as its monopolistic charter. Even less clearly beneficial to all the public was the construction of industrial establishments.

Many thought that the government should have no authority over the economy. However, the wider markets in the West and the new technical processes made increased capital so necessary to industry that corporation charters were sought more and more in spite of possible public opposition. To make incorporation democratic and consonant with Jacksonian equal-rights principles, Whigs and like-minded Democrats urged "general incorporation laws" (as distinct from special legislative grants) which would make corporation charters available to all who could meet certain legal requirements. Beginning in the 1830s and continuing into the 1840s and 1850s, corporations began to propagate under the new system of general laws.

The Whig party, which generally favored business interests (as would later its successor, the Republican Party), had advocated free incorporation as a method of inaugurating a kind of "democratic" capitalism. That is, business would no longer be dependent upon rich men but could gather the combined resources of countless small investors. This multiplication of ownership, however, eventually resulted in a revolutionary change in the nature of business organization. As the number of stockholders or owners in a corporation rose into the thousands and as they were dispersed about the country, actual management or "control" of the company fell into the hands of individuals who were not dominant owners or perhaps not even stockholders at all.

Under the system of individual proprietorship or partnership, ownership and control had been in the hands of the same person. The corporate system began the process of divorcing ownership from control and of creating a vast class of investors dependent, insofar as their profits were concerned, on the actions of others—the corporate managers. The inherent danger was that the managers might not act in the interests of the owners. In former days when the owners managed their own businesses, owners who defrauded the company defrauded themselves. With the separation of ownership and control, the "insiders" or managers could systematically loot a company for their own profit.

The Rise of Industrial Populations

Before the steam engine was developed, the almost complete reliance on water power resulted in scattering manufacturing among a large number of small or medium-sized towns, for the capacity of any given dam site was limited. The first American factory, Slater's Mill, was built in Pawtucket, Rhode Island in the 1790s by British immigrant Samuel Slater, who designed his textile mill from memory based on those with which he was familiar in England. At the time, it was illegal to take a written blueprint to a textile mill out of England. By 1815, New England had over 150 textile mills producing thread and yarn from raw materials. All the mills worked on waterpower from water wheels in New England streams. This pattern would change, however, when the triumph of steam made it feasible for manufacturing to concentrate in large cities with locations off of riverbanks.

Industrial employment brought new problems not imaginable in the previous handicraft period of individual workshops. In America people did not know how to cope with the problems of health and safety in the new factories because never before had such problems existed. Congested living quarters in the growing industrial cities of New England and the mid-Atlantic states often resulted in a deplorable lack not only of sanitation, but also of the minimum requirements for decent human existence. Work hours were usually long, wages low, and schools for the children of workers inadequate. Workers could afford little for housing. The idea of public transportation had not been developed, so employees had to live within walking distance of their place of employment. All these conditions worked together to produce a type of housing for industrial workers that became slums of the worst sort.

Unlike the earlier hand industries, the new steam-driven machines did not require workers with great skill or physical strength. Increasingly, women and children were hired to perform the simple but arduous and monotonous tasks of factory work. The best-known early textile mills were in Lowell, Massachusetts, where the workers were young, unmarried New England farmwomen. By 1830, eight textile mills in Lowell employed over 5,000 women, most of whom were between sixteen and twenty-five years of age. The young women lived in company owned boarding houses with company housemothers and slept with four to six women in each bed. Company rules provided for curfews at 10:00 p.m., and prohibitions against alcohol, gambling, and unsupervised courtship. There were soon several other mills in Massachusetts and New Hampshire, so that by the 1830s there were some 40,000 women working in New England textile production. Scholars have tried to assess how much

▶At a time when it was illegal to take a building blueprint of a textile mill outside England, Samuel Slater built the first American factory from memory. Slater's Mill still stands in Pawtucket, Rhode Island. *Wikipedia photo*

This was a protest song that arose during a strike at Lowell Mills in 1836:

"Oh! isn't it a pity, such a pretty girl as I-
Should be sent to the factory to pine away and die?
Oh ! I cannot be a slave,
I will not be a slave,
For I'm so fond of liberty
That I cannot be a slave. "

Source: Harriet Hanson Robinson, *Loom and Spindle or Life Among the Early Mill Girls,* (New York: T. Y. Crowell, 1898) 83–86.

their work represented opportunity for them—for most this was their first chance to earn money—and how much it involved exploitation. What is certain is that the work day was long and arduous, the women worked in hot and humid conditions, and the power looms they tended along with all the spinning gears, and whizzing belts created an extremely noisy atmosphere. Nonetheless, the Lowell women found the energy to publish a literary magazine, the *Lowell Offering,* and when employers tried to cut wages in the 1830s, the women twice went on strike.

It has been suggested that the fact that they lived in dormitories together (so as to reassure their parents that they were being supervised) may actually have promoted solidarity among them. For most of them, after a stint in the mills, they married, having been able to put some money aside for household necessities out of their wages. Research has disclosed that they also sent money home to help educate their brothers or for other needs of their families of origin. Once Irish immigrants began to arrive in large numbers, in the 1840s, the newcomers supplanted the native-born women as textile workers.

Urban industrialism resulted not only from new production techniques and new Western markets but also from increased efficiency in agriculture: Improved farm methods and farm machinery permitted more people to be siphoned off into industrial production. In addition, many immigrants settled immediately in the cities. As a result, between 1820 and 1850 the cities grew much faster than the population as a whole. In 1820 only one person in fourteen lived in a city of 2,500 or more. By 1850 nearly one person in six lived in such a city. This meant an increase of more than fivefold in the population of cities, while the whole population had increased just over twofold during those years.

The great majority of Americans were still rural and still untouched by conditions developing in the Northeast, but those who watched the cities fill with immigrants and develop slums, vice,

MAP 9.3 Map of Distribution of United States Population (1840)

DISTRIBUTION OF POPULATION
1840
★ Center of Population

LEGEND

Under 2 inhab. to the Sq. Mile

2 - 6 " " " " "	I
6 - 18 " " " " "	II
18 - 45 " " " " "	III
45 - 90 " " " " "	IV
90 and over " " " "	V

*Cities over 8000 inhabitants in solid color
in circles proportionate to population.*

and crime were deeply disturbed. Many associated crowded cities and the factory grind with a Europe of decadence and oppression.

The Rise of Labor

Among the first to react to these unsatisfactory conditions were the workers themselves. Although workers were influential in contributing to trends toward better education, their moves in the direction of unionization were separate and distinct from most other reforms of the period.

The oldest labor organizations in America date back to the late eighteenth century when various skilled craftsmen banded together to obtain higher wages, shorter hours, and other benefits from their merchant-artisan employers. It was not until the late 1820s and the 1830s that aggressive union activity began with the establishment of strong craft unions in Philadelphia, Boston, New York, Providence, and other cities. An attempt was even made in 1834 to form a National Trades Union. Although the group held conventions for several years, the effort failed to achieve an enduring result.

The most successful of the early unions were local groups that were primarily political in their objectives. Each worked especially hard for various social reforms such as free public schools. Aided by favorable public opinion, they were able to make substantial gains by legislative action. By the middle of the nineteenth century the idea of free public education, at least through the primary grades, was pretty generally accepted.

Nowhere was the political presence of workingmen more visible than in New York City. There they organized as the short-lived New York Workingmen's Party in 1829. They again made their presence felt in the 1830s as the radical, anti-bank wing of the Democratic Party, the Loco Focos (so-called after a type of match that they struck at meetings). With so much democratic ferment taking place, there was an audience for radical lectures and a radical press. Perhaps the most colorful of the lecturers was the Scottish-born Fanny Wright. A woman who defied the taboo against women speaking in public, she then flouted it even more thoroughly by advocating a number of reforms for workers, in addition to the reform of marriage laws in the direction of more freedom, even to the extent of "free love." Sean Wilentz suggests that her advent in January 1829 marked the beginning of worker insurgency in New York City.

Beginning in the late 1840s, a number of important states began to establish the ten-hour day as the legal maximum workday. However, it was possible for workers to make a special contract with their employers to work longer, and economic necessity frequently drove them to do so, which nullified the effect of the statutory provision. Nevertheless, such laws represented a gain for labor, since they helped to establish the idea of a ten-hour limit.

Finally, in the 1850s, unions less interested in political activity than in "bread-and-butter" issues (wages, hours, and working conditions) gathered momentum. During this period, the first permanent national unions of separate trades were set up, beginning with the National Typographical Union in 1852.

The appearance of solid and enduring national unions was a sign of the end of America's industrial adolescence. Many more decades were to pass before economic conditions convinced even a substantial minority of American workers or employers that unions were a good and permanent element in industrial relations. The individualistic tradition and conditioning of both workers and employers, and an excess of labor, prevented that result sooner. National unions were here to stay, and their very existence testified to the arrival of a new period in American economic history.

Education and Innovation

A high level of literacy, an openness to change, and that intangible quality known as "Yankee ingenuity" also contributed to American technological progress. Economists consider education an investment in "human capital" that is vital to economic growth. The United States (with the exception of the South) had a higher percentage of its population in school than any other country in 1850. Literacy in the North and especially in New England was nearly universal. It was no accident that most technological advances came out of New England—the most industrialized and modernized section of the country. As one observer wrote in 1829: "From the habits of early life and the diffusion of knowledge by free schools there exists generally among the mechanics of New England a vivacity in inquiring into the first principles of the science to which they are practically devoted. They thus frequently acquire a theoretical knowledge of the processes of the useful arts, which the English laborers may commonly be found to possess only after a long apprenticeship."

Although Prussia and France were far ahead of the United States in basic science and Britain had a clear lead in engineering and machine-tool capacity, American entrepreneurs and engineers had a knack for adapting foreign technology to their own needs and improving it through dozens of incremental changes. Thus, while the basic inventions of textile machinery were British, most of the important improvements in such machinery in the 1820s and 1830s were American. "Everything new is quickly introduced here," wrote a German visitor. "There is no clinging to old ways, the moment an American hears the word 'invention' he pricks up his ears."

Technology and Agriculture

Although industrial and urban growth outpaced that of farm and village during this period, farming remained the principal occupation of Americans and the foundation of the economy. It provided most of the exports that earned foreign exchange and helped provide the capital to launch America's industrial growth. Yet in most elements of agriculture, American farmers were incomparably careless and wasteful. Crop rotation was only occasionally practiced, fallow lands were not plowed to preserve fertility, and millions of tons of manure were allowed to wash away unused each year. Not until after the Civil War did most American farmers begin to approach the careful scientific farming practiced in Europe.

The reason for such wastefulness was the existence of seemingly limitless fertile land. It was cheaper to exhaust the soil in one area and move westward than to nourish the fertility of Eastern land. The constant extension of the frontier was the main reason for the abundance of American agriculture. However, after 1830 the mechanization of farming and especially of the harvesting process became an increasingly important cause of rising productivity. Insofar as the substitution of machines for human muscles is an index of modernization, Northern agriculture (there was little mechanization in the South, due to the supply of slave labor) was at the forefront of this process before the war.

For centuries there had been little improvement in farm implements. Suspicion of "newfangled" ideas was stronger among farmers than among other groups. The same problem that stimulated innovation in manufacturing—a shortage of labor—overcame this conservatism on the expanding frontier. The first improvements came with the development of two important plows. First, in the 1810s Jethro Wood of New York modeled the iron plow. Then in the 1830s John Deere of Illinois introduced the steel plow (further improved by James Oliver of Indiana in the 1850s). Drills for faster planting of seed also came into use during the early nineteenth century. However, these implements, which increased the acreage a farmer could plow and plant, actually created the chief bottleneck of farming—the harvest. A farmer could grow no more grain than he and his family could reap.

In the 1830s, Cyrus McCormick of Virginia and Obed Hussey of Maine vastly improved the reaping process with their invention of horse-drawn reapers—the most revolutionary development in nineteenth-century agriculture. Two workers and a horse could now harvest as much grain in a day as twenty workers with sickles. Of course, even this quantum leap in productivity would have meant little if similar improvements in threshing had not come along at the same time. Here the principal invention was a combined threshing and fanning machine patented by John and Hiram Pitts of Maine in 1834. These inventions and the continued expansion of grain farming onto the prairies enabled wheat farmers to double their productivity per man-hour between 1835 and 1880 and to multiply the total wheat harvest sixfold. McCormick's reaper even made it possible for Northern farms to increase the production and export of wheat during the Civil War, despite the military enlistment of nearly a million farmers.

The Social Impact

Ready-Made Clothing

Although crude sewing machines had been developed in France and America during the 1830s, by 1846 Elias Howe of Massachusetts perfected the first patented machine with the crucial capacity to sew interlocking stitches. Howe exhibited his machine at the Quincy Hall Clothing Manufactory in Boston, where amazed visitors watched him sew 250 stitches in a minute—seven times the speed of a fast seamstress. In the next few years several other technicians made improvements in Howe's original machine. One of them, Isaac M. Singer of upstate New York,

MAP 9.4 Wheat Production

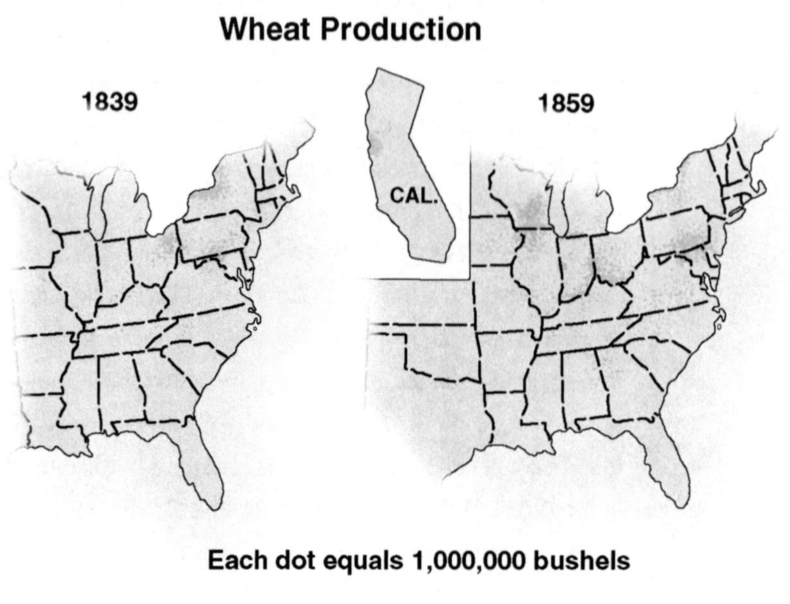

Wheat Production

1839   1859

CAL.

Each dot equals 1,000,000 bushels

began to sell sewing machines without paying Howe a royalty. Howe finally won the resulting patent suit in 1854. To avoid more patent battles several manufacturers merged in 1856 to form the "Great Sewing Machine Combination," the first monopoly in American industrial history. By the 1870s nearly a million sewing machines were manufactured each year, three-quarters of them by I. M. Singer Company, heir of the 1856 merger.

The Civil War was the catalyst for the ready-made clothing industry. The demand for millions of uniforms was a powerful spur to standardized production. When the Union government supplied manufacturers with a series of graduated measurements for soldiers, producers developed the concept of "sizing" and soon began to make clothes in regular sizes. By the end of the century, nine tenths of the men's clothing in the United States was ready-made. Although a smaller percentage of women's clothes were commercially manufactured, the development of standardized dress patterns helped standardize female fashions as well.

Technological changes and the Civil War also profoundly affected the shoemaking industry. In the 1850s, adaptation of the sewing machine to leather products hastened the trend to standardized production, although the sewing of uppers to soles remained handwork until 1862. At this time Gordon McKay, a Massachusetts entrepreneur, patented an improved sewing machine that mechanized the entire shoemaking process. This invention, and later ones, not only enabled manufacturers to fill government contracts for army boots but also laid the groundwork for a mechanized, mass-production shoe industry after the war. By the century's end, factory shoes, like ready-made clothing, dominated the market.

These developments illustrated both the positive and negative impacts of mechanization. On the one hand, they lowered the cost of clothes and shoes, improved their quality and fit

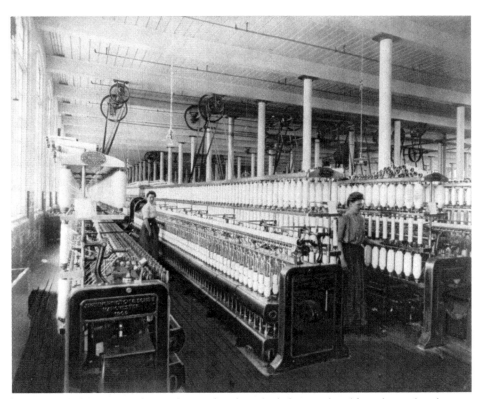

▶ By the end of the century, factory shoes and ready-made clothing produced from the textile industry dominated the market. *Library of Congress*

▶In 1856 several sewing machine manufacturers merged to form the "Great Sewing Machine Combination"—the first monopoly in American industrial history.
Library of Congress

for the lower and middle classes, and democratized a consumer product that in Europe continued to function as a symbol of class differences. The sewing machine also lightened the drudgery of housewives while providing new employment opportunities for women and children outside the home. On the other hand, sweatshops (shops or lofts where women and children worked long hours at sewing machines for piecework wages) became a byword for labor exploitation. Not until unionization in the twentieth century did garment workers begin to win decent wages and working conditions. Unfortunately, mechanization of boot and shoe production destroyed an ancient craft and provoked strikes and strife as skilled workers were replaced by machines or demoted to the status of machine tenders.

The "Balloon-Frame" House

Americans lived in a greater variety of houses a century ago than they do today. Ranging from the rickety wooden cabin of the slave or sharecropper, to the log cabin or sod hut of the pioneer farmer, to the substantial stone house of the Pennsylvania farmer and the Georgian, or to the neo-classical mansion of the rich, these structures had the virtues of variety and individuality. In an era of rapid growth, however, they also had disadvantages. Stone or brick construction was slow and required many skilled workmen. The same was true of substantial wooden houses, which for centuries had been built with thick timbers joined by mortise and tenon and then fastened by wooden pegs. The skilled carpenters necessary for this kind of construction were in short supply in the mushrooming mid-western cities of the period.

The lack of skilled workers inspired a new technique of inexpensive, speedy, standardized home construction—the "balloon-frame" house. This was the combination of machine-sawed boards (two-by-fours, two-by-sixes, etc.) nailed together as wall plates, studs, floor joists, and roof rafters to form the skeleton frame of a house. A Connecticut resident, Augustine Taylor, who in 1833 moved to Chicago—the boom town of that decade—probably invented the technique. A severe housing shortage was solved by these balloon-frame structures, so-called by skeptics who sneered that the first strong wind would blow them away. In fact they were remarkably strong. The boards were nailed together in such a way that every strain went against the grain of the wood. Such houses could be built in a fraction of the time and at a fraction of the cost of a traditional house. So successful was the "Chicago construction" that it spread to all parts of the country. By the end of the nineteenth century, at least half of all American homes were built in this fashion.

The balloon-frame house would not have been possible without a related revolution in the manufacture of nails. New England factories pioneered in the mechanization of the handcraft methods of nail making in the 1820s, cutting the price of nails by two-thirds and creating another mass-production industry.

Plumbing, Lighting, and Heating

Changes inside homes had a large impact on the way middle-class urban Americans lived. Bathing was a once-a-week occurrence, at best, when water had to be pumped by hand, heated in an open fireplace, carried to a tin tub, and drained by bailing after the bath. Before mid-century, wealthier homeowners and better hotels had installed tubs with running water heated by pipes passing through a boiler. However, such devices were rare in modest urban homes and virtually nonexistent for the majority who lived in rural areas. The same was true of toilets, which first appeared in the 1830s but made little headway at a time when relatively few cities had municipal water systems (about one hundred places had them by 1860) and even fewer had sewer systems. By the 1880s, many middle-class urban homes had hot and cold running water and "modern" bathroom equipment, but the outdoor privy and the Saturday night hand-filled bathtub remained standard for rural Americans. Even as late as 1900, Baltimore had 90,000 outdoor privies.

Improvements in lighting, cooking, and heating spread more widely than the availability of indoor plumbing. Most houses before 1860 used candles or lamps that burned one of several kinds of animal or vegetable oil for light. Whale oil was the cleanest and safest fuel, but it was expensive. Coal, oil, lard, and camphene (turpentine and alcohol) were cheaper; however, the first two were dirty and the last dangerous. Gas derived from coal had been used for lighting as early as 1806. While most cities had piped-in gas supplies by the time of the Civil War, this form of lighting was confined mainly to streets, public places, and a few wealthy homes. After the discovery of petroleum as a lighting fuel, the first commercial oil well was drilled at Titusville, Pennsylvania. In 1859, kerosene lamps became the ubiquitous source of home lighting, persisting long after Thomas A. Edison perfected the incandescent electric light bulb in 1879.

As late as 1840, food was still cooked in an open fireplace in most homes. In 1834 Philo P. Stewart—Connecticut-born abolitionist, missionary to Native Americans, founder of Oberlin College, and inveterate tinkerer—patented the first stove. With subsequent improvements it became the standard wood- or coal-burning kitchen appliance for the second half of the nineteenth century.

Another Connecticut resident, Eliphalet Nott, president of Union College, patented several improvements of the basic Franklin heating stove and invented the first stove to burn anthracite coal. By the 1840s such stoves heated many homes, and European visitors were already complaining that Americans kept their houses too warm. Central heating with hot air first made its appearance in the 1830s. The "radiator" heated by steam or hot water piped from a basement boiler became common in the last three decades of the century.

The Icebox

The use of ice to preserve food was mainly a nineteenth-century development. The icebox was such an appliance. Nothing better illustrated Yankee ingenuity and enterprise than the career of Frederic Tudor of Boston, the "Ice King." A passing remark at a party in 1805 gave him the idea of exploiting one of New England's few natural resources—the ice on its ponds. By 1825 Tudor and his Cambridge partner Nathaniel Wyeth had perfected an ice-cutting machine that mechanized the "harvesting" process, and through trial and error they had worked out the best methods for building and insulating ships to transport the ice as well as icehouses to store it. The earlier underground icehouses had suffered a minimum 60 percent seasonal loss due to melting. Inside Tudor's heavy timbered, double walls with sawdust insulation loss from melting was only 8 percent.

In 1833, Tudor sent one of his ships with 180 tons of ice from Boston to Calcutta, crossing the equator twice in a voyage of four months and arriving with the cargo intact. Although the main export markets for ice were the American South and the West Indies, Tudor shipped his product all over the world. In the 1850s Boston exported up to 150,000 tons of ice per year.

Tudor's achievements helped make possible the "icebox" (an American word), which by 1860 was a common feature of American households. These large wooden boxes on legs, lined with tin and zinc and interlined with charcoal, helped to improve the American diet and extended the season for fresh fruits and vegetables. Meat could be preserved longer without salting. Ice cream became a widely enjoyed pleasure instead of a rare luxury. Americans began to put ice in their drinks, to the consternation of European visitors. Even that abomination in British eyes, iced tea, made its appearance before the Civil War. After the war, the development of refrigerated railroad cars further improved the quality and variety of fresh fruits and vegetables available in all parts of the country. It also permitted the meatpacking industry to become centralized in Chicago and to serve a national market with its products.

The Emergence of the Modern Family

Scholars have identified a new type of family that was influenced by the impact of such rapid economic change. In the traditional family men and women both worked at home, although their chores were probably gender-specific. Industrialization removed male work from the home, except in rural areas. It also made having a large number of children less economically valuable since their work was no longer required on a farm. Furthermore, women were gaining an education. For all of these reasons, the birth rate began to drop in the early nineteenth century, and the family began to be a more democratic institution. Scholars have called this new style "the modern family."

Modernization and Reform

The Protestant Ethic and Reform

Economic growth and a rising standard of living depend not only on material factors but also on intangibles such as social values. The openness to change and the emphasis on education in Northern states have already been mentioned as important contributors to economic development. Equally important were attitudes toward work. There is universal agreement that nineteenth-century Americans (at least those in the North, and especially those in New England) were infused with the work ethic. "The national motto," wrote a British observer of the United States, "should be 'All work and no play.'"

This value system was more or less synonymous with what is generally called the Protestant Ethic—or sometimes the Puritan Ethic, since its roots originated in Puritan attitudes toward work as a glorification of God and idleness as an instrument of Satan. Emphasizing hard work, thrift, sobriety, reliability, self-discipline, self-reliance, and the postponement of immediate gratification for the sake of long-range goals, the Protestant Ethic reinforced precisely those values best suited to capitalist development. There was also a close relationship between the Protestant Ethic and many of the reform movements. These movements grew out of the evangelical enthusiasm of the Second Great Awakening (1800–1830) and the radical idealism of transcendentalism. In addition to urging Christians to stop committing such social sins as fornication, drunkenness, violation of the Sabbath, and enslavement of other human beings, reformers sought to instill in the poor, the idle, the depraved, and the intemperate "the virtues of true Protestantism—industry, sobriety, thrift and piety"—and thus enable them to reform themselves.

The voluntary associations that carried on reform activities provided another link between reform and modernization. The social network of pre-modern societies is confined mainly to kin and village. An essential element of modernization is the transcendence of these localized and prescriptive ties by local voluntary organizations formed for a specific purpose—trade unions, missionary societies, reform associations, pressure groups, and the like. This was precisely what happened in the United States. There were only a few such associations in the eighteenth century; however, by 1832, their number and variety astonished the French visitor, Alexis de Tocqueville. "Americans of all ages, all conditions, and all dispositions constantly form associations," he wrote in *Democracy in America*, "associations to give entertainments, to found seminaries, to build inns, to construct churches, to diffuse books, to send missionaries to the antipodes ... to found hospitals, prisons, and schools.... Wherever at the head of some new undertaking you see the government in France, or a man of rank in England, in the United States you will be sure to find an association."

Four of the reform movements, all related to the modernization process (though it would be too limiting simply to see them in those terms), had a crucial impact on American society after 1848: the movements for temperance, improved education, women's rights, and abolition.

Temperance

In the early nineteenth century Americans consumed an extraordinary amount of liquor. The average annual intake of spirituous and distilled alcohol per person of drinking age in the 1820s, for example, was seven to ten gallons—at least five times today's average. In addition, the average person consumed thirty gallons of some combination of hard cider, beer, and wine. The most common distilled liquor in New England and seaport cities was rum. In the rest of the country it was usually whiskey. Beer and wine were drunk everywhere, but the most popular fermented drink in those days was hard cider (about 20 proof). No social occasion, whether a corn-husking bee or the installation of a clergyman, was complete without heavy drinking. Whiskey was a form of money on the frontier, and even church subscriptions were payable in liquid coin. Wretched transportation facilities before the 1820s meant that grain could be marketed over distances only in distilled form. Liquor was cheap, untaxed in most areas, and constituted a considerable portion of people's daily calorie intake. Many men greeted each day with a gill (four fluid ounces) of grog. John Adams regularly drank a pint of hard cider before breakfast. European visitors were astonished by the "universal practice of sipping a little at a time ... [every] half an hour to a couple of hours." Rum was included in the standard daily rations for members of the American army and navy, and colleges typically served ale by the pint to students with their meals.

The temperance movement arose partly as a reaction to excessive consumption. Beginning as a local religious and moral reform led by ministers, doctors, and women, the movement had expanded by the 1830s into a well-organized national crusade. In 1826, Connecticut minister Lyman Beecher founded the American Temperance Society, dedicated to the reduction of the consumption of alcohol because of its deleterious effects on society. Beecher argued that drunkenness led to crime, unemployment, poverty, and domestic violence. Following Beecher's example, temperance lecturers rode from town to town lecturing on the damaging effects of alcohol. At the height of its power in 1836, the American Temperance Union, a federation of 8,000 local and regional societies, claimed a membership of 1.5 million; but this Union fragmented as members divided over the question of temperance versus prohibition. At first the movement had been for *moderation* in drinking, urging the elimination only of distilled spirits while endorsing temperate consumption of beer, wine, or cider. However, by the 1830s, temperance advocates became more militant, taking on the character of Christian perfectionism and moral regeneration that characterized other reform crusades of the decade. Like the abolitionists, who demanded

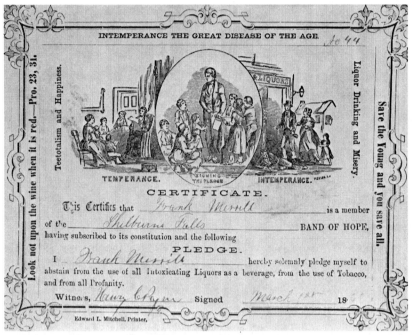

▶The Temperance Society certificate and pledge to abstain from alcohol, tobacco, and profanity, signed 1866. Many employers began requiring their employees to take a temperance pledge where employees "volunteered" to cease alcohol consumption as a condition of their employment. *Corbis Images*

universal emancipation, prohibitionists began to call for the total abolition of *all* alcoholic beverages. The requirement that members pledge total abstinence caused a dramatic drop in the membership of the American Temperance Union by 1840.

Up to this time temperance had been primarily a middle-class, Protestant movement. Its goal was to impose the values of the Protestant Ethic, especially sobriety, upon the whole society. It was here that temperance intersected with modernization. Work patterns in pre-modern society were task-oriented rather than time-oriented. Artisans typically worked in bursts of effort until a particular job was completed and then took several days off, perhaps to spend their wages in heavy drink-

▶A comic about a 'temperance man,' or one who abstained from alcohol. *Wikipedia photo*

ing. This irregularity was unsuitable to mechanized factories in which successful operation of complex and dangerous machinery required punctuality, reliability, and sobriety. Work became time-oriented rather than task-oriented.

It was no coincidence that the temperance movement in both Britain and America coincided with industrialization in those countries. As part of the effort to instill the values of reliability and self-discipline in the working classes, employers supported the temperance movement and often forbade their workers to drink on *or* off the job. Many employers began requiring their employees to take a temperance pledge where employees "volunteered" to cease alcohol consumption as a condition of their employment.

Many workers, especially Irish and German immigrants, did not take kindly to such discipline. In 1840 Protestant workingmen began to organize the Washington Temperance Societies. The first such society was founded in Baltimore by six heavy-drinking workmen who had been converted by a temperance lecture. Proudly declaring themselves "reformed drunkards," they moved with missionary zeal to organize societies all over the Northern and Western states. Native-born workers pointed to their endorsement of temperance as evidence of their superior dependability as compared to immigrant laborers.

The Washingtonian movement rejuvenated the temperance crusade. It was this period that produced an outpouring of sentimental songs with such titles as "Father, Dear Father, Come Home with Me Now" and the play *Ten Nights in a Bar Room*, which did for temperance what *Uncle Tom's Cabin* did for the antislavery movement.

The alliance of middle-class prohibitionists and Washingtonians helped push prohibition laws through fifteen state legislatures in the decade after Maine passed the first in 1846. Yet these laws had little impact on drinking habits. In a dress rehearsal for the national prohibition of the 1920s, they were widely evaded and most were eventually repealed. Whatever success the temperance cause enjoyed was the result of other factors, especially the evangelical revivals of the Second Great Awakening. In any case, the per capita consumption of alcohol appears to have declined sharply, perhaps as much as fivefold in the two decades before 1850. It never again approached the earlier level and rum and hard cider almost disappeared as American drinks.

Public Education

Traditional histories of education emphasize the great reforms inspired by Horace Mann, secretary of the Massachusetts State Board of Education from 1837 to 1849. Before then, the New

England common schools had fallen into decay, and the few public schools elsewhere were "pauper" schools to which self-respecting parents would not send their children. In addition, teachers were semiliterate, and most children outside New England grew up with scarcely any formal schooling. However, although this picture contains some truth, historians have uncovered evidence of a vigorous and growing educational system in the generation before 1837. It now appears that in New England and New York at least three-quarters of the school-age children were in school, and that in 1830 the average adult in those states had completed eight or nine years of schooling, with the typical school term only three or four months each year, however.

Elsewhere the picture was less bright. A mixture of public, private, and church schools provided some education for well over half the white population, except on the frontier and in parts of the South. If this had not been true, one would have difficulty explaining the 95 percent literacy rate for the Americans in the North.

In some respects, however, things were as bad as the reformers of the 1840s painted them. Formal teacher training was almost nonexistent. Educational standards varied widely. Schools were generally ungraded. With rare exceptions, no public school system worthy of the name existed in the Deep South. The white illiteracy rate in the slave states was above 20 percent, while the African American illiteracy rate was close to 90 percent. Pennsylvania, New Jersey, and the western states had little in the way of public school systems before 1835.

Horace Mann and his fellow New England reformers rationalized and centralized the existing patchwork pattern of public schools, professionalized the training of teachers, and spread this system through most of the North by 1860. Mann founded the first "normal" school for training teachers at Lexington, Massachusetts in 1839. During the next two decades such institutions were established in several states, and half a century later they evolved into teachers' colleges.

Massachusetts also pioneered in other reforms: a standardized graded curriculum, extension of public education to the secondary level, and the first compulsory attendance law (1852). Indeed, Mann did his work so well that some revisionist historians have criticized him for inaugurating a bureaucratic educational establishment that they regard as rigid and reactionary.

Revisionists have also condemned the school reformers for creating a system designed to impose Protestant middle-class values on all children in order to perpetuate the class structure through repression of ethnic minorities and the poor. It is true that the schools tried to teach the values of the Protestant Ethic. An essential task of education, wrote the Massachusetts superintendent of schools in 1857, was "by moral and religious instruction daily given" to "inculcate habits of regularity, punctuality, constancy and industry." *McGuffey's Readers* and the various readers and spellers of Noah Webster, which taught hundreds of millions of nineteenth-century children to read, reiterated these lessons. Most reformers of the time considered this progressive, not reactionary. The purpose of reform, after all, was not to keep the poor content in their humble station but to lift them out of poverty by equipping them with the skills and values they needed to function and hold their own in a modernizing, fluid, competitive, capitalist economy. "Nothing but Universal education can counterwork this tendency to the domination of capital and the servility of labor," wrote Horace Mann in 1848. Education "does better than to disarm the poor of their hostility toward the rich; it prevents being poor." If this was unrealistic, it nevertheless exemplifies the faith that all classes of Americans have placed in education.

▶ An early school room *Library of Congress*

Higher Education

Ever since the founding of Harvard College in 1636, higher education had been associated primarily with churches. In 1860, of the 207 colleges existing, 180 had been founded by churches. Most were established during the previous generation as population flowed westward. The Protestant denominations struggled to educate a ministry and a lay leadership that would preserve and expand the faith on the frontier.

Many of the 6,000 "academies" (with only 12,000 teachers) that provided nearly all the country's secondary education were also church-supported. In 1860 there were only 321 public high schools, nearly a third of them in Massachusetts.

After the Civil War, higher education became more secular and broadly available. By 1890 twenty-five states outside the South had followed the lead of Massachusetts and passed compulsory school-attendance laws. By 1900 there were 6,000 public high schools. The need for technical and scientific training to keep pace with rapid advances in these fields led to the founding of several schools modeled on the earlier examples of Rensselaer Polytechnic Institute (1824) and Massachusetts Institute of Technology (1865). In 1862 the Morrill Act created the land-grant colleges by setting aside public lands to support universities that emphasized "agriculture and mechanical arts." Eventually, universities would develop—such as Texas A&M and Alabama A&M—that would encapsulate the spirit of the Morrill Act in the very name of the university itself.

In the postwar decades the modern university outgrew the confines of the old Christian college. In 1869 Charles W. Eliot became the first nonclergyman president of Harvard and proceeded to liberalize the curriculum. Men that may not have had church affiliation dominated boards of regents. Students were recruited and donations were solicited from persons of all faiths. In 1868, Andrew D. White launched another university at Cornell, and in 1876, Daniel Coit Gilman started America's first true research university at Johns Hopkins.

The "Media"

Not all education took place in schools, of course. In addition to such institutions as the family, church, and voluntary associations, many channels existed for the dissemination of information and ideas. One of the most important was the public lecture. Abolitionists, temperance workers, and other reformers—including women, who won the right to appear on the lecture stage by the 1850s—found lecturing to be the most effective means of spreading their messages. Debating societies, literary associations, and the like grew up in almost every crossroads village. In 1826, Josiah Holbrook, a Massachusetts educator and friend of Horace Mann, founded the American Lyceum of Science and the Arts. The Lyceum was the first national agency for adult education, bringing lecturers on almost every conceivable subject to cities and hamlets throughout the nation. In 1838, young Abraham Lincoln spoke at the Springfield, Illinois Lyceum on "The Perpetuation of Our Political Institutions." Lyceums and debating societies fostered independent thought and new ideas, in addition to providing lecture forums for well-known thinkers such as Ralph Waldo Emerson.

Overshadowing all other means of communication, however, was the popular press. America was a newspaper culture. Technological advances in printing brought explosive growth in newspaper circulation after 1830. The expansion of the railroad network enabled urban dailies to print weekly editions for rural areas. By 1860 the weekly edition of Horace Greeley's New York *Tribune* had the unprecedented circulation of 200,000 copies. Samuel F. B. Morse's invention of the telegraph in 1844 made possible the instantaneous transmission of news over long distances and led to the formation of the Associated Press in 1848. The number of newspapers doubled between 1825 and 1840; and it doubled again by 1860, reaching a total of 3,300. Widespread literacy, the highly partisan nature of American journalism, and universal white manhood suffrage help explain the remarkable politicization of the population, an important factor in the emotion-charged controversies that led to a Civil War. Though women could not vote, the print culture gave them the opportunity to weigh in on issues related to the sectional conflict, specifically with the publication of *Uncle Tom's Cabin*, which became the outstanding (but not unique) example of this phenomenon.

Popular magazines such as *Godey's Lady's Book* (started in 1830), *Harper's Monthly* (1850), and the *New York Ledger* (1851) also enjoyed an expanding readership. Prominent features in newspapers as well as magazines were sentimental poetry and moralistic fiction. Most novels were serialized in weeklies before appearing between hard covers; and they often focused on domestic situations revolving around such themes as marriage, home, family, religion, and death. Most of the authors were women, who poured forth serialized novels year after year, reaching a vast audience—also mostly women—through the mass-circulation magazines and inexpensive books. Susan Warner's *Wide, Wide World* (1850) and Maria Susanna Cummins' *The Lamplighter* (1854) were two of the best-sellers, for example. Marion Harland's first novel, *Alone* (1854), sold half a million copies. She wrote dozens more, the last one in 1919. Mary Jane Holmes produced a book a year from 1854 to 1907.

By all odds the leader of this school was E. D. E. N. Southworth, who wrote her first novel, *Retribution* (sold 200,000 copies), in 1849 after her husband had deserted her. She followed with sixty-one more in the next four decades. Serialization of her books lifted the *Ledger's* circulation to 400,000 by 1860. Not surprisingly, given her personal history, many of her novels—such as *The Deserted Wife* (1850)—were highly critical of the gender norms of her day. Indeed, many modern critics have discerned an underlying political strain in the domestic novels, in general, because so many of them featured women trying to establish their autonomy under difficult conditions and using the moral authority of the home and the housewife to achieve this.

A particularly noteworthy work of fiction by a woman in these years was Harriet Wilson's *Our Nig* (1850), the first known novel by an African American woman. Wilson, who had been a servant, wrote a narrative that inverts many of the conventions of the domestic novel. For example, it depicts the home, not as the site of female empowerment a la *The Wide, Wide World*, but rather as the site of the oppression of a free African American servant in a northern state.

Women's Rights

The preeminence of women in popular literature was only one sign of the growing opportunities and achievements of women at mid-century. However, there was ambivalence in these achievements. Literary themes and popular culture reinforced the tenets of domesticity and the sexual double standard that tied women to home, marriage, and family while men managed affairs in the outside world. At the same time, however, economic modernization was taking many women out of the home and putting them into the wage-earning labor force. The textile and garment industries were large-scale employers of women (and children). The inventions of the telegraph (1844), typewriter (1874), and telephone (1876) created new white-collar jobs for women.

The expansion of public education and the professionalization of teaching opened a major career opportunity for women, though women were paid less than male teachers. By the 1850s the "schoolmarm" was a familiar figure, especially in the Northeast. In the decades after Oberlin opened its doors to women in 1837, several other colleges followed suit. Beginning with Vassar (1865) and Wellesley and Smith (1875), numerous women's colleges were founded after the Civil War.

The spirit generated by antebellum reform movements spurred demands for an end to women's inferior legal and political status. Female abolitionists began to speak out against sexual as well as racial slavery. In 1848 the first American women's rights convention was held at Seneca Falls, New York, and organized by Elizabeth Cady Stanton and Lucretia Mott. The movement's first priority was abolition of laws that treated unmarried women as minors and forced married women to turn over all property to their husbands.

After the war, feminist leaders decided to concentrate on winning the right to vote, believing that the ballot was the key to open other doors to sexual equality. (See *"Julia Ward Howe: Hymnist of Freedom."*) By 1890 women had won the right to vote in school-board elections in seventeen states and territories. Wyoming Territory granted women general suffrage in 1869 and, with its admission to statehood in 1890, became the first state to do so. Colorado followed in 1893, Utah and Idaho in 1896. Although no more states enfranchised women until 1910, the nineteenth century movement laid the groundwork for passage of the Nineteenth Amendment in 1920.

The Broadening Antislavery Movement

In 1831 in Boston, William Lloyd Garrison began his publication, *The Liberator,* with the uncompromising goal of immediate and complete abolition of slavery. The next year, Garrison's supporters began the New England Anti-Slavery Society, and New York and Philadelphia followed with similar groups in 1833. In the late 1830s and 1840s the antislavery movement began to reach out to—and convince—more Northerners, with 1,300 local antislavery societies comprised of some 250,000 members by 1837. Similarly, abolitionist newspapers and anti-slavery lecturers began to permeate the Northern states.

One of the key elements in this transition was the so-called "gag rule" in the House of Representatives and the battle against it by the one-term president and subsequent House member, John Quincy Adams. Antislavery advocates were circulating petitions attacking the "peculiar institution," as it existed in the District of Columbia, and sending them to Northerners in Congress. In 1836, Southerners in the House succeeded in enacting the gag rule, whereby the petitions were tabled without being officially acknowledged. Adams's battle took eight years, but he ultimately managed to get the rule overturned. During those eight years, many people began to see the antislavery effort as involving the defense of free speech as well as the opposition to slavery itself, and this broadened its appeal.

From 1839 to 1841 there was another important issue in which Adams—known as "Old Man Eloquent"—played a crucial role: the *Amistad* case. The *Amistad* was a Spanish slave ship carrying fifty-three slaves on which there had been a mutiny before it could reach its destination in Cuba. Slaves picked the lock on their hold with a nail and took over the ship. Understanding that they had sailed away from the morning sun on their way from Africa to Cuba, the slaves ordered the Spanish sailors to sail back into the morning sun. The Spanish sailors, therefore, sailed east by day but west and north by night, and zigzagging their way up the North American coast. In August 1839, some of the mutineers came ashore on Long Island, New York, with the ship remaining just offshore. Over the next two years there was a sustained legal dispute, with Spanish owners trying to get the slaves back—slaves who were in American custody. Going against the Spanish cause was the fact that the Spaniards had been engaged in the slave trade in violation of a treaty of 1817 between their country and Britain, a treaty which had prohibited the importation of slaves into Spanish colonies. The crucial evidence in the case was that none of the slaves seemed to be able to speak Spanish, although the Spaniards claimed they were all born in Cuba; and none would answer to their Spanish names. If the slaves were born in Cuba, they were legally the property of their Spanish slave owners. If they were from Africa, then they were imported to the Western Hemisphere in violation of the 1817 treaty and would be given their freedom. Adams successfully proved that the slaves were recent imports from Africa and argued for the slaves' freedom before the U.S. Supreme Court. The Spanish then tried for compensation, but to no avail.

With so much ferment going on, the antislavery movement entered politics in 1840 with the founding of the Liberty Party. The only previous antislavery organization had been the American Colonization Society, founded in 1817, by Southern planters who favored gradual individual emancipation and the return of the slaves to Africa. Even though several thousand slaves were repatriated to Liberia in the 1820s, the Colonization Society failed to take hold be-

▶ Julia Ward Howe: Hymnist of Freedom

by Holman Hamilton and Glenna Matthews

▶ Julia Ward Howe *Library of Congress*

It would be easy—but utterly misleading—to depict Julia Ward Howe (1819–1910) solely in terms of literary success. She was very successful in that way, for she wrote "The Battle Hymn of the Republic," containing the most celebrated lyrics connected with the Civil War. In her long, fruitful life, she became the most famous American woman in the eyes of many of her contemporaries.

But there is a far greater significance in the Howe story-significance not alone in terms of her own times but also as people see her today. To grasp the importance of what she did, and all she represents, it is essential to understand the status of women in the first half of the nineteenth century. Most daughters of upper-class families, sheltered from infancy on, had no active part in improving the lot of the masses of humanity and were not supposed to. They took it for granted that they were not to plunge into causes, particularly those deemed unpopular or unfashionable. It was a rare wife and mother, of courageous conviction, that chose to dedicate herself to helping African American people or to leading the fight to obtain the right to vote for the female half of the population. Such a wife and mother was Mrs. Howe.

Born in New York City, Julia Ward moved to Boston upon marrying Dr. Samuel Gridley Howe. Her choice of a husband indicated the qualities she valued, for Dr. Howe, a Massachusetts physician, devoted his career not to conventional practice but to aiding seriously handicapped children, adolescents, and adults. He gave "light" to the blind, "sound" to the deaf, and meaning to the retarded. Samuel's was a pioneering venture in medicine, psychology, and mercy. However admirable he was as physician and reformer, Dr. Howe was a domestic tyrant where his wife was concerned. Indeed, he believed that it was wrong for a married woman to engage in public life. Therefore, in becoming so well known, his wife's courage had to be deployed in defying her husband as well as on other fronts. Though the parents of six children, the Howes saw their marriage totter on the brink of divorce on more than one occasion.

Nonetheless, they also worked together in reform causes. In an era when most whites looked down on African Americans and did little or nothing on their behalf, Julia gave her best efforts to opposing slavery with her sharpest weapon—her pen. Together, Samuel and Julia edited *The Commonwealth*, an antislavery paper. Julia had a major role in the enterprise, possessing both talent as a writer and persistence as a reformer.

Nor were writing and editing the only means the Howes used in their antislavery activities. Abolitionist men and women needed a headquarters where they could gather and exchange ideas and plan the next moves in their campaigns. Julia Ward Howe provided that headquar-

Julia Ward Howe: Hymnist of Freedom (Continued)

ters in her own home not simply as hostess but as a catalytic agent for freedom's cause. As she later said, she had "the honor of pleading for the slave when he was a slave."

Most authors become famous only when they address themselves to topics in which they have deep interest. Julia Ward Howe's literary growth perfectly illustrates this fact. In 1854, at thirty-five, she published a first volume of poems. Three years later, a second book of poetry followed, as well as a play; but the latter was not a stunning triumph and the verses received little attention. The limelight where she would soon shine was reserved for a period of national upheaval. Author, subject, mind, and emotion found their inspiration in the Civil War. The accomplishment was entirely logical because now religious conviction—the Howes were Unitarian—and aggressive opposition to slavery blended with the cause of the Union, in which she also devoutly believed. Visiting the city of Washington, D.C., and the Union soldiers stationed nearby, she was inspired to write a series of stanzas to the familiar tune of "John Brown's Body."

Lyrics came to Julia one night when she could not sleep. She was scarcely able to read what she had scrawled in the dim light, and then—at last drowsy—was asleep.

When she wakened, she reviewed the words of the "Battle Hymn":

Mine eyes have seen the glory of the
     coming of the Lord

He is trampling out the vintage where
     the grapes of wrath are stored;

He hath loosed the fateful lightning of
     His terrible swift sword;
     His truth is marching on.

Although its publication brought her only four dollars in cash, the poem had a sensational impact. So stirring were her lines that almost immediately they echoed and re-echoed throughout the North. Eventually they became integral in the nationwide musical and poetic tradition.

Julia did not rest on "Battle Hymn" laurels. With African Americans freed and the Union saved, the vote for women was her next theme. This was another unpopular cause from many people's points of view, yet she adhered to it with all the enthusiasm she had earlier devoted to freeing the slaves. The Nineteenth Amendment, granting woman suffrage, would not be adopted until 1919, nine years after Julia Ward Howe's death at the age of ninety-one. However, younger women with whom she had been working carried to spectacular completion this second major reform.

By the time of her death, Julia Ward Howe was regarded as a spiritual leader as well as a literary figure.

Indeed, in her later years, she preached in Unitarian and Universalist pulpits although she had not been ordained. In 1908, just before her death, she became the first woman to be elected to the American Academy of Arts and Letters.

cause of the enormous cost of repatriation and the fact that most American slaves in the 1820s were born in the U.S. and had no affiliation with Africa.

Officially the Liberty Party stood only for the exclusion of slavery from new territories and states, for its abolition in the District of Columbia, and for prohibition of the interstate slave trade. However, some Liberty Party men insisted that the Constitution empowered the federal government to abolish slavery. In 1848, the Liberty Party was absorbed by the more broad-gauged Free Soil Party, which adopted a similar platform (omitting reference to the slave trade) but attracted many members who were more opposed to Southern political power than to slavery as such.

Genuine abolitionists watched these and subsequent developments leading to the founding of the Republican Party in 1854 with mixed feelings. While they welcomed the growth of antislavery sentiment in the North, they were well aware that it was often based on dislike of both slavery *and* African Americans. Moreover, Garrison and his adherents advocated moral suasion, rather than political parties, as the means of ending slavery. Hence, abolitionists kept their societies alive and continued to work for the equal rights and education of Northern African Americans.

Women played prominent roles in the abolition movement, forming women's auxiliaries and raising funds to support abolitionist lecturers. William Lloyd Garrison published a letter by Angelina Grimke in *The Liberator* that made her an overnight celebrity among abolitionists. Grimke and her sister, Sarah, then quickly became in-demand lecturers on the abolitionist lecture circuit. The Grimke sisters, however, also wrote and spoke about women's rights, thus sewing discord among the abolitionists themselves, although some abolitionists, such as Garrison, favored women's rights as well.

By the 1850s there was a robust antislavery discourse, fed most importantly by the publication of *Uncle Tom's Cabin* in 1852, but also by the writings and lectures of many former slaves, with Frederick Douglass being the best known. In 1845 Douglass published his *Narrative of the Life of Frederick Douglass*. He also began publishing an abolitionist newspaper, *The North Star*. Another former slave who became well known in the antebellum United States was Sojourner Truth. Born a slave in New York in 1797, Isabella van Wagenen began to call herself "Sojourner Truth" after a religious conversion. She was a familiar presence on the lecture platform in the North, and in 1850 appeared the first version of her autobiography, as dictated to Olive Gilbert.

▶ Isabella van Wagenen, who called herself "Sojourner Truth" *Library of Congress*

Finally, public opinion in the North began to be more favorable to the antislavery cause because of certain political developments, such as the Compromise of 1850 and the Kansas-Nebraska Act. The Compromise of 1850 contained as one of its key elements, a new comprehensive fugitive slave law. After its passage, as we will see in the next chapter, there were a number of notorious cases that kept the issue of slavery in the public eye.

Prejudices, Politics, and Polarization

The New Immigration

In the first forty years of the Republic, immigrants did not come in large numbers. As late as the 1820s the number of immigrants averaged less than 13,000 per year. However, rapid population growth, land shortages, and labor surpluses in Northern Europe, combined with cheap land, labor shortages, and higher wages in America, brought a quadrupling of this average in the 1830s. During the decade from 1845 through 1854, the number of immigrants averaged nearly 300,000 annually.

Although these newcomers provided much of the labor force necessary for rapid economic growth, many of them received a cold welcome in the United States. Actually, anti-immigrant sentiment (or nativism) was not directed primarily against immigrants as such, but against *Catholic* immigrants. Nearly 40 percent of the immigrants to America during these years were Irish Catholics, driven to emigrate by the potato famine after 1845. Another 12 or 13 percent were German Catholics.

Settling mainly in cities, the Irish were the most concentrated and visible of the immigrant groups. They were poor, clannish, fiercely loyal to the Roman Catholic church, hostile toward abolitionists and toward African Americans (with whom they competed for jobs), and therefore favorable toward slavery and the Democratic Party. This aroused a nativist anti-Irish movement that strongly influenced the politics of several states in the 1840s and 1850s. The movement was fueled by traditional Protestant anti-Catholicism and by temperance reformers, abolitionists, proponents of public schools, and Protestant workingmen, who saw the Irish influx as a threat to their reforms, values, or status. In the 1840s, there were numerous anti-Catholic riots and some pitched battles between Protestant and Catholic workingmen. In Philadelphia in 1844, a Catholic church was burned, thirteen people were killed, and the state militia had to be called in to restore order.

In 1843, Nativists in New York established the American Republican Party, which won 23 percent of the vote in New York City that year. The next year, the Whigs made an alliance with the Nativists, supporting their local candidates in return for American Republican support of Whig presidential candidate, Henry Clay. Though the Nativist-laden Whigs were unsuccessful in the presidential race, they won six Congressional races in New York City and Philadelphia and won the mayor's offices in New York and Boston.

Nativism reached its height in the Know-Nothing movement, whose main goal was to exclude "foreigners" from political power by lengthening the naturalization period from five to as much as twenty-one years. In 1849, a secret nativist society called the Supreme Order of the Star-Spangled Banner was organized in New York City. When questioned about the order, members would reply, "I know nothing." The Know-Nothings began to endorse political candidates; and by 1854, their strength had mushroomed to formidable proportions in several states, where under the name of the American Party they elected legislators, governors, and congressmen. In the 1850s, the Know-Nothings dominated politics in Massachusetts and received a third of the vote in New York.

Then, within two or three years, the Know-Nothing movement subsided as quickly as it had risen. This was partly because of a falling off in immigration after 1854. More important, however, was the blazing intensity of the slavery issue. Northern Nativists were absorbed into the new Republican Party, while those in the South (remnants of the Whig Party) retained the name American Party and nominated Millard Fillmore for President in 1856.

The Know-Nothing legacy persisted in Northern politics, however; and during the next forty years most Catholics voted Democratic, while evangelical Protestants usually voted Republican. Southern Whigs demanded that the Party support slavery while Northern Whigs demanded abolition. The result was the eventual dissolution of the Whigs, and the rise of the Republicans as the Northern Abolitionist Party. Local and state elections often turned on such issues as temperance, parochial schools, and the like. The animosities expressed by the Know-Nothings flared up again in the American Protective Association (APA) of the 1880s and 1890s and in continuing patterns of prejudice against Roman Catholics and immigrants.

The Know-Nothings were a party that had a brief, if significant, heyday. The other new party born in the heat of sectional conflict in these years was the Republican party.

Chapter Review ▶ ▶ ▶

Summary

America experienced rapid modernization during the middle decades of the nineteenth century, especially in the North, characterized by investment in transportation and communication, which led to a nationally integrated market economy. The invention of Robert Fulton's steamboat in 1807 aided greatly in river navigation, the completion of the Erie Canal connected the Hudson River system to the Great Lakes, and the opening of the Baltimore and Ohio Railroad in 1830 began a new era of rail transportation. All of these advancements in transportation helped create a national economy.

Simultaneously, there was an increase in the output per man-hour that results from technological innovation and mechanization, and manufacturing changed from artisanship to centralized industry utilizing Eli Whitney's system of standardized, interchangeable parts. The result was accelerated growth of the industrial sector as compared with other sectors of the economy. Income inequality, however, increased as many skilled workers found themselves replaced by machines.

Industrialization in the North also brought a corporate revolution as large amounts of capital were needed to build railroads and factories and sole proprietorships in most cases were therefore infeasible. The corporations provided the stockholders with limited liability so that bankruptcy of the corporation would cause owners to lose only what they held in stock.

Industrialization also brought population concentration to the manufacturing centers of the Northeast, beginning with the development of the textile industry in New England. Factories in manufacturing towns such as Lowell, MA employed thousands of workers and people had to live near their places of employment. The resulting concentration of population brought problems in health and sanitation in the factories, as well as worker exploitation, and led to the development of an organized labor movement and labor unions.

Meanwhile, the country experienced growth in education as Horace Mann pioneered public schools and other states followed suit. Educational opportunities expanded for women, so that by 1850, the United States had the highest percentage of persons in school in the world. Higher education also blossomed with the passage of the Morrill Act, which provided for Land Grant Universities and an explosion in college growth.

Modernization also led to advancement in agriculture with John Deere's steel plow and Cyrus McCormick's Reaper. Other technological innovations that changed the American economy and culture included ready-made clothing, balloon-frame housing, advancements in plumbing, with running water and toilets, advancement in lighting, with coal oil lamps, and in refrigeration with the Ice Box.

With the advancements came social changes, including a Temperance movement, advancements in women's rights and the beginnings of a women's suffrage movement, and the rise of an abolitionist movement. As such, modernization contributed to antagonism between North and South as Southerners attempted to retain their system of human slavery. Finally, industrialization attracted new immigrant laborers, which led to a significant nativist movement in the Unites States that was directed primarily against Catholicism and freemasonry.

Chronological Time Line

1793	Samuel Slater opens the nation's first textile mill in Pawtucket Rhode Island.
1798	Eli Whitney's interchangeable parts for rifles made by machines spawns the "American system" of manufacturing.
1807	Robert Fulton's Steamboat Clermont steams up the Hudson River.
1825	Erie Canal completed from Buffalo to New York City.
1825	Frederic Tudor begins harvesting ice
1826	Josiah Holbrook, a Massachusetts educator and friend of Horace Mann, founded the American Lyceum of Science and the Arts.
1826	Lyman Beecher founds American Temperance Society
1829	New York Workingmen's Party organizes
1830	Baltimore and Ohio Railroad begins rail service.
1833	Augustine Taylor brings balloon-frame housing structures to Chicago
1834	A combined threshing and fanning machine is patented by John and Hiram Pitts of Maine
1834	Philo P. Stewart patented a wood burning stove
1839	Horace Mann founds the first "normal" school for training teachers in Lexington, MA
1839–41	The Amistad case
1840	Liberty Party is founded
1843	Nativist American Republican Party wins 23% of the vote in New York
1846	Maine passes alcohol prohibition law
1846	Sewing machine with the crucial capacity to sew interlocking stitches is perfected by Elias Howe.
1848	The formation of the Associated Press
1849	Know Nothings founded in New York City

Chapter Review (cont'd) ▶ ▶ ▶

Time Line (cont'd)

1852	Massachusetts passes the first mandatory school attendance law
1852	National Typographical Union founded.
1854	Republican Party Founded
1856	Several manufacturers merged in 1856 to form the "Great Sewing Machine Combination," the first monopoly in American industrial history.
1859	First commercial oil well is drilled at Titusville, PA
1862	The Morrill Act created the land-grant colleges that emphasized "agriculture and mechanical arts."
1862	Gordon McKay patented an improved sewing machine that mechanized shoe manufacturing
1869	Charles Eliot becomes the first nonclergyman President of Harvard
1869	Wyoming grants women general suffrage
1876	1876 Daniel Coit Gilman started America's first true research university at Johns Hopkins.
1879	Edison perfects the incandescent light bulb

Key Terms

American System: A manufacturing system based on interchangeable parts

Turnpikes: Commercial roads from the coast to the interior

Robert Fulton: Constructed a successful commercial steam boat in 1807

Erie Canal: Commercial canal from Buffalo to New York City completed in 1825

Industrial Revolution: The great explosion of manufacturing in the nineteenth century.

Slater's Mill: The first textile mill in America at Pawtucket Rhode Island.

Lowell, Massachusetts: Location of textile mills that primarily employed women

Lowell Offering: A literary magazine published by the women working in the textile mills of Lowell, Massachusetts.

National Typographical Union: First permanent trade union in America in 1852

Fanny Wright: A woman who defied the taboo against women speaking in public and advocated reform for workers and marriage laws along with "free love" in 1829.

Key Terms (cont'd)

Jethro Wood: Invented an Iron plow in New York in the 1810s

John Deere: Invented the Steel Plow in 1837

James Oliver: Made improvements in the Steel Plow in the 1850s

McCormick's Reaper: Mechanized the harvesting of grain.

Elias Howe: Inventor of the sewing machine

Isaac Singer: Major manufacturer of the sewing machine

Balloon frame house: The now-familiar combination of machine-sawed boards (two-by-fours, two-by-sixes, etc.) nailed together as wall plates, studs, floor joists, and roof rafters to form the skeleton of a frame house.

Titusville, PA: Site of first commercial oil well.

Frederic Tudor: The "Ice King" of Boston who perfected an ice-cutting machine.

Protestant ethic: This value system's roots lay in Puritan attitudes toward work as a glorification of God, and emphasizing hard work, thrift, sobriety, reliability, self-discipline, self-reliance, and the postponement of immediate gratification for the sake of long-range goals.

Temperance: A social movement urging reduction in the consumption of alcohol

Lyman Beecher: Founder of the American Temperance Society

Horace Mann: The leading proponent of public education in Massachusetts in the 1820s and Secretary of the Massachusetts State Board of Education 1837-1849.

American Lyceum: Founded by Horace Mann, the first national agency for adult education, bringing lecturers on almost every conceivable subject to cities and hamlets throughout the nation

Samuel F. B. Morse: Inventor of the telegraph

Harriet Wilson: Author of *Our Nig* in 1850, the first known novel by an African-American woman.

William Lloyd Garrison: Leading abolitionist and founder of *The Liberator.*

The Liberator: Abolitionist Newspaper founded by William Lloyd Garrison

Amistad: Slave ship and court case that resulted in the freeing and return to Africa of 53 slaves illegally imported from Africa that had taken over a slave ship.

Angelina and Sarah Grimke: Wrote and lectured both on abolition of slavery and for women's rights.

Frederick Douglass: African-American former slave who became an abolitionist orator and writer. In 1845 Douglass published his *Narrative of the Life of Frederick Douglass.* He also began publishing an abolitionist newspaper, *The North Star.*

Sojourner Truth: A former slave who became well-known on the abolitionist lecture circuit and in 1850 appeared the first version of her autobiography, as dictated to Olive Gilbert.

Nativism: The ideological perspective that opposed immigration and anything "foreign" and favored rule by whites of English heritage.

Know Nothing Movement: An anti-Catholic movement that eventually became an anti-Catholic political party.

Chapter Review (cont'd) ▶ ▶ ▶

Sources Consulted

Tyler Anbinder, *Nativism and Politics: The Know Nothing Party in the Northern United States* (1992).

Jean Fagan Yellin, *Women & Sisters: The Antislavery Feminists in American Culture* (1989).

Lori D. Ginzberg, *Women and the Work of Benevolence: Morality, Politics, and Class in the 19th Century United States* (1990).

Steven Mintz, *Moralists and Modernizers: America's Pre-Civil War Reformers* (1995).

W. J. Rorabaugh, *The Alcoholic Republic: An American Tradition* (1979).

10 The Sectional Crisis, 1848–1861

Chapter Objectives

Wikipedia photo

Corbis Images

iStockphoto

Wikipedia photo

Wikipedia photo

E.   "The Crime Against Kansas"

F.   The Character of Franklin Pierce

V.   On the Eve of War

A.   The Election of 1856

B.   The Dred Scott Decision

C.   The Lincoln-Douglas Debates

D.   John Brown's Raid

E.   The Election of 1860

F.   The Democrats

G.   The Republican Victory

H.   Secession

I.   The Failure of Compromise

J.   Fort Sumter

K.   "Causes of the Civil War"

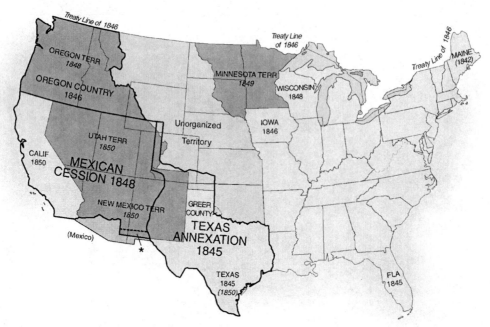

MAP 10.1 Territorial Growth (1850)

Title to Oregon Country established by treaty with Great Britain
* Disputed area: Treaty of Guadalupe-Hidalgo 1848
Western area of Texas purchased in 1850

1850

The Origins of Sectionalism

The Transcontinental Republic

Between 1846 and 1854, with the settlement of the Oregon question, the Treaty of Guadalupe Hidalgo, and the Gadsden Purchase, the United States became in the full sense a two-ocean transcontinental republic. Except for Alaska and Hawaii, the country had reached its present territorial limits. In one sense, the acquisition of the Southwest marked a fulfillment of American nationalism. No other nation on earth had grown so rapidly; and no people were more proud of their nation than the Americans, who boasted incessantly of the superiority of republican institutions. Yet, ironically, the climax of national growth also brought with it a crisis of national unity, for it precipitated a bitter rivalry between two dissimilar sections of the country—areas divided by the Mason-Dixon line and the Ohio River.

The problem of geographical rivalries was not a new one in the United States. In a country larger than all of Western Europe—with immense diversity of soil, terrain, and climate—conflicts had arisen more than once between the economic interests of one area and those of another. In fact, American history has been full of such conflicts, and divisions between East and West have often marked those conflicts. This was true, for instance, in the contest over the Bank of the United States at the time of Jackson, and later in the battle between the advocates of the coinage of silver and the defenders of the gold standard in 1896. The theme of sectional rivalry has been so persistent that historians sometimes dispute whether the deepest antago-

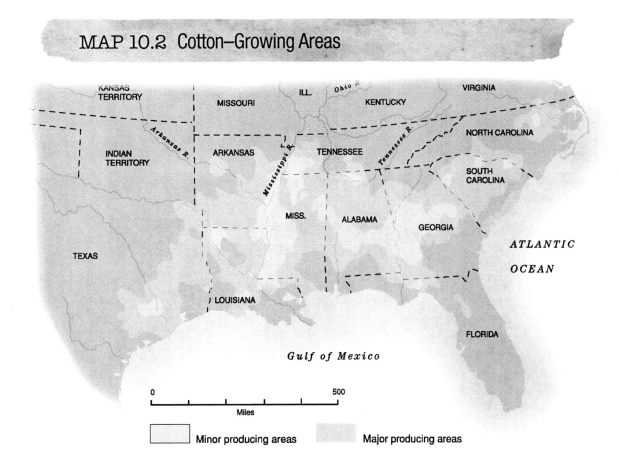

MAP 10.2 Cotton–Growing Areas

nisms in American history have been between conflicting rivalries—social classes, ethnic groups, religious denominations—or between conflicting sections.

Therefore, the sectional crisis between North and South, which approached its climax between 1848 and 1860, was in no sense unique. However, it did reach a unique pitch of intensity. Usually, competing sectional forces have sought only to gain advantage over one another within a Union which both accept, but on this occasion the South became so alienated that it made a colossal effort to withdraw from the Union.

The Southern Way of Life

Historians have never been able to agree on any one factor as the primary cause of this division, but they do agree in recognizing a cluster of contributing factors. As far back as the seventeenth century, North and South had developed along dissimilar lines. Virginia, Maryland, and the colonies to the south had based their economy on crops that were limited to latitudes of warm climate and a long growing season. Tobacco, the first of these crops to be introduced in the colonies, was followed by rice and indigo in Carolina and sugar in Louisiana. However, the most important crop was cotton, which was grown throughout the lower South after the invention of the cotton gin in 1793–94. From the cultivation of these crops the plantation had evolved as the economic unit of production. Within the plantation system the labor supply had evolved to consist primarily of slaves.

▶ A group of slaves on a South Carolina plantation. Slaves were seen as pieces of property. They could be bought, sold, mortgaged, bequeathed by will, or taken in payment for debt if their owners became bankrupt. *Library of Congress*

Actually, slave labor did not become dominant until the eighteenth century, but by the time of the American Revolution, slaves had come to outnumber free persons in many plantation districts. In 1850, 32 percent of the South's total population was held in slavery. In South Carolina and Mississippi a majority of the population consisted of slaves.

Slavery

Slavery presented a supreme paradox: while slaves were human beings, they were also considered property. The complex relationships between masters and slaves reflected this paradox. On the one hand, most white Christians recognized the slaves' humanity and believed that they had immortal souls to be saved. (Of course the idea of a better life after death could also be useful in diverting slave unrest into religious zeal.) The law viewed slaves as human beings to the extent of making them liable to punishment for serious crimes. Some masters permitted a wedding service for slave couples even though they could not legally be married. On plantations where African Americans and whites mingled closely in everyday life, relations of intimacy and affection often developed. Even the proslavery stereotype of the "happy and carefree" slave, a reflection more of the whites' wishful thinking than of reality, was an indirect way of admitting the slave's right to human happiness.

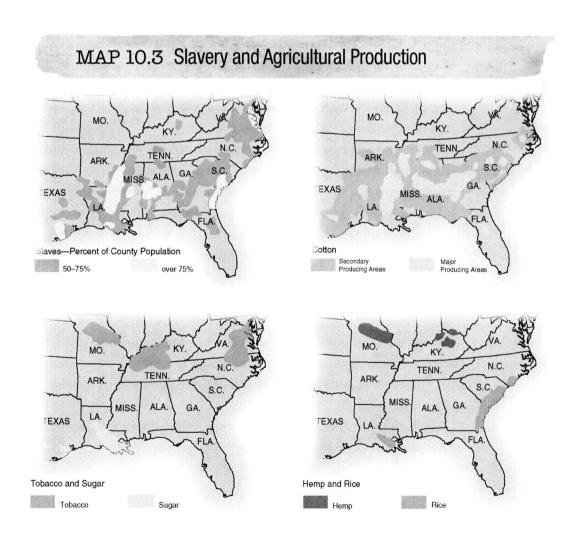

MAP 10.3 Slavery and Agricultural Production

Slaves—Percent of County Population

50–75%   over 75%

Cotton

Secondary Producing Areas   Major Producing Areas

Tobacco and Sugar

Tobacco   Sugar

Hemp and Rice

Hemp   Rice

On the other hand, slaves were chattels—pieces of property. They could be bought, sold, mortgaged, bequeathed by will, or taken in payment for debt if their owners became bankrupt. They could not legally marry, or own property, or in most states, be taught to read or write. Owners might let them have a family, earn money, and even buy their freedom; but until they were free, money, spouse, and children could be taken away at any moment.

The ills of slavery can be looked at in several ways. Many abolitionists condemned slavery primarily for its physical harshness—the flogging and branding of slaves, the separation of mothers from children at the auction block, the brutal labor conditions, especially for slaves who had been "sold down the river" to work in the sugarcane fields, and the low standard of diet, clothing, and housing. There is no doubt that slaves experienced much cruelty and hardship. However, in some instances slaves may have been kindly treated.

The worst feature of slavery may well have been its social and cultural impact on both slave and master. The slave's powerlessness tended to create a sense of dependency and to discourage self-reliance. Stable family life was difficult in a situation where parents and children might be sold away from each other. Female slaves could be sexually exploited by white men, and a slave father was legally helpless to protect his wife and children. The master's power over fellow human beings tended to create feelings of superiority and domination. The racial theories that bolstered slavery bred in most white people a belief in African American inferiority.

Of course this does not mean that all or even most slaves carried the psychological scars of dependence and inferiority. On many plantations, the African American driver, rather than the overseer, exercised authority in day-to-day operations. As a sort of labor leader as well as "boss," the driver could do much to win better working conditions for the slaves. Drivers, slave artisans, highly-skilled cooks, and other blacks with critical skills played important roles in Southern life and provided other blacks with role models of self-respect and limited power *within* a system from which few could hope to escape.

Moreover, despite repression the slaves sustained a vigorous African American culture largely independent of surrounding white institutions. Natural leaders in the slave quarters often became eloquent preachers in the "invisible institution" of the African American church, whose congregations worshipped apart from whites (sometimes secretly) in spite of laws against separate worship. Some of these preachers, especially Gabriel Prosser in 1800 and Nat Turner in 1831, plotted armed insurrections to strike for freedom. The slaves created original and moving music in antebellum America—the spirituals—that expressed their longing for freedom, as well as their resignation to sorrow, and evolved after the Civil War into the blues and eventually jazz.

Recent research suggests that while slavery made stable family life difficult—and sometimes brutal—a majority of slaves nevertheless formed strong ties of kinship and family. Thus although slavery's impact on African Americans could be repressive, the countervailing force of a positive African American culture provides an impressive example of survival in the face of adversity.

Furthermore, there were many mechanisms for resistance, some more successful than others. Some slaves—predominantly male—managed to run away. Others succeeded in being truant for a short while, though they may have faced severe punishment upon their return. Scholars have suggested that slaves may have deliberately broken farm implements or worked at a relatively slow pace by way of proving to themselves their independence from the master's interests—

or maybe even to punish the master. For women, historian Stephanie Camp suggests, the assertion of self may have taken the form of making themselves party clothes out of whatever materials they could cobble together so that they could then sneak away from the quarters at night for an unauthorized good time in their dress-up clothes. The slaves' freedom of movement was constantly at risk of being monitored by slave patrols, so the slaves had to be prudent in order to carve out time and space for either surreptitious religious services or for "frolics."

Slavery also put Southern whites on the defensive, ever fearful of slave insurrection and ever conscious that slavery was condemned throughout most of the Western world. As a result they isolated themselves more and more, imposing an "intellectual blockade" to keep out not only abolitionist ideas but also any social ideas implying freedom or change. To defend their system, they idealized their society as romantic and chivalrous. At best, they realized their ideal in the attainment of a real aristocracy, but the tradition was maintained at a high cost.

By 1850 the Southern system, with its rural life and its slave labor, had led to the development of a somewhat conservative temper, a marked stratification of social orders, and a paternalistic type of society. The power of all landowners to rule their workers on their own plantations had prevented the growth of a strong public authority. As a result, violence was frequent, and qualities of personal courage and physical prowess were especially valued. For instance, the practice of dueling, which had died out in the North, still prevailed. The taboo against women working outside the home was far stronger than in the North; and, in general, gender norms were far more conservative. Even women schoolteachers in the South were often Northerners.

The Northern Way of Life

It would be a mistake to think of the North as presenting a total contrast, for the majority of people in the free states also engaged in agriculture and lived a rural life. However, the Northern economy and culture were more diversified. In the absence of a valuable export crop such as tobacco or cotton, many New Englanders had turned early to commerce as a means of securing money to buy the imports they needed. During the Napoleonic wars, when their commerce was disrupted and the supply of imported manufactures was cut off, they had begun a manufacturing industry. As manufacturing grew, cities proliferated.

Prosperity and rapid economic growth in the North fostered a belief in progress and innovation quite different from the more traditional (or static) attitudes of the South. Although the factory system brought with it a certain amount of exploitation of labor through low wages, the fact that all men were free made for greater mobility, greater equality, more democracy, and less sharply defined social stratification than in the South. The modernizing North grew to value the commercial virtues of thrift, enterprise, and hard work—in contrast to the more traditional and military virtues, which held a priority in the South.

Such differences as these can easily be exaggerated, for a great deal of frontier Americanism prevailed in both the North and the South. Similarly, evangelical Protestantism was the dominant religion of both sections. The materialistic pursuit of wealth motivated cotton planters as well as Northern industrialists. To a European, all Americans seemed earnestly democratic. In the South the Whig Party, favored by most planter aristocrats, could not have competed against the Democratic Party at all unless it had adopted the democratic symbols of the log cabin, the coonskin hat, and the cider barrel.

The Basis of Sectional Antagonism

Regional dissimilarity, however, need not lead to conflict. In the United States today there are profound differences between the red states and the blue states, the rural and the urban regions, but few are talking about secession, let alone war. The antagonism that drove Northerners and Southerners to war in the mid-nineteenth century, therefore, needs to be explained.

Economic Causes

In one sense the antagonism was economic, for the dissimilar economic interests of the North and the South caused them to favor opposite economic policies and to clash politically. Essentially, the South, with its cotton economy, produced raw materials for a textile industry centered in Britain. Accordingly, the South sold on the world market; and in return, the South needed to buy its manufactured goods where they were cheapest, which was also in the world market, and to keep down taxes and governmental costs as much as possible.

For the more diversified Northern economy, the needs were different. Northern manufacturers and workers wanted tariffs to protect them from the competition of low-priced goods produced by cheaper labor abroad. Manufacturers and farmers alike needed improved transportation facilities ("internal improvements") in the form of roads, canals, and railroads to foster inter-regional exchanges of goods. Northern economic groups and their congressional representatives, therefore, supported state and federal appropriations to build better roads and to assist canal and railroad construction.

Some of the upper Southern states such as Kentucky and Maryland, with urban and manufacturing centers of their own, supported appropriations for these purposes; the cotton-growing South did not fit into this scheme. Most of the cotton and tobacco crop was shipped by river or by short, locally built railroads to river or coastal port cities for export abroad. Internal improvements meant only that the South would be paying part of the governmental costs of a program from which it did not benefit. Indeed, the new transportation routes diverted trade away from the South's own Mississippi River system, which drew trade southward toward New Orleans. In addition, the tariff meant that the South would be prevented from buying its manufactures from those who bought its raw materials and would be forced by law to pay a higher, tariff-supported price for its manufactures. As the Virginian, John Randolph of had angrily declared, "we shall only pay more for worse goods." Due to these economic factors, North and South tended to vote against each other on questions of tariff, internal improvements, and other extensions of the power of the central government. Their rivalry had reached a crisis at the time of the Nullification Controversy in 1833, when South Carolina was ready to defy federal law. The crisis had only been averted when other Southern states had not committed to take up arms in support of South Carolina. The South as a whole had resented fed-

eral economic policies but had never opposed them to the point of breaking up the Union—
to which most Southerners felt strong patriotic loyalty.

The Growth of the Slavery Issue

An even deeper cause of division was the institution of slavery. Until the 1770s slavery had
scarcely been regarded as a moral question at all, except by the Quakers. In one form or another
the institution had existed in other lands for thousands of years, and the slave trade had been
essential to the colonization of the Western Hemisphere. As late as 1780 there was no division
between slave states and free states; slaves were held in every state of the Union. They were less
numerous in the North only because they were less profitable there. In the late eighteenth century, however, slavery came under attack from believers in natural law, human equality, and
human rights. At the same time, emphasis in the churches shifted from a limited concern with
the personal salvation of the individual to a fuller application of Christian teaching in relation
to human society. Thus, the harsh penal code of earlier times was modified, various social reforms were adopted, and slavery came under attack.

The states from Pennsylvania northward shared in this movement against slavery. By 1804, all
of them had adopted laws for the gradual or immediate emancipation of their slaves, and after
1808 Congress had prohibited the importation of any more slaves from Africa. For a time it appeared that the South might also participate in this movement. Southern Enlightenment leaders
such as Thomas Jefferson condemned slavery in the abstract, and antislavery societies were active
in the South. Furthermore, slavery was restricted to the rice and tobacco economy, which was static
and no longer very profitable. This meant that the Southern economy as a whole did not depend
on slave labor.

▶ With the introduction of
cotton and the cotton gin,
the market for cotton grew
drastically as did the demand for slave labor. During
every decade from 1800 to
1860, the value and the volume of cotton doubled.
Corbis Images

Nevertheless, Jefferson, however, never freed more than a handful of his own slaves since his exorbitant spending habits rendered him to a state of indebtedness virtually all of his life. Slaves were his primary assets that not only could be sold at any time to pay debts but also multiplied naturally. The Southern antislavery societies devoted their efforts mainly to encouraging the emigration of free African Americans. The tenor of antislavery sentiment among Southerners, apart from the Quakers and the early Methodists, was one of anguished hand wringing over an inherited evil rather than vigorous action for its abolition.

The introduction of cotton and the cotton gin injected greater vitality into the slave system. In one generation, the cultivation of short-staple cotton spread across the lower South from middle Georgia to the banks of the Brazos in Texas. During every decade from 1800 to 1860, the value and the volume of cotton doubled. In this dynamic and expanding economy, the price of slaves rose and fell with the price of cotton. Slavery accompanied cotton as it expanded into the new areas. By 1820, both slavery and cotton were completely interwoven into the whole Southern system.

While this was happening, the humanitarian crusade against slavery in Great Britain (which abolished slavery in the West Indies in 1833), in France (which abolished it in 1848), and in the Northern states (where the abolitionists became increasingly militant in their denunciations) led the South to a defensive reaction. By 1830, Southern leaders were no longer arguing, as some had said earlier, that slavery was an evil but too deeply rooted to be abolished at once. Instead, they were beginning to assert that slavery was a positive good. They defended it with claims that it had been sanctioned in the *Bible* and that African descendants were biologically inferior to European descendants. They argued that the exploitation of African American workers by the slavery system was not as harsh as the exploitation of white workers by a wage system in which the worker received only a bare subsistence when he was working and no subsistence at all when he was not. They held that, since social divisions were inevitable, assigning leadership to one class and subordination to another was better than having an endless struggle between classes.

These clashing arguments polarized the two sections more and more with each decade after 1830. As the abolitionists became more militant in their crusade against the "sin" of slavery, the South became so defensive about criticism that it refused to tolerate any expression of antislavery opinion.

In spite of this disagreement on the ethics of slavery, several factors prevented a legal or physical clash over the question. To begin with, slavery was widely regarded as a matter for the states locally rather than for the federal government nationally (South Carolina's attempt at nullification was actually a challenge to the government's authority in this area as well as in setting tariffs). At that time, people regarded the federal system more as a loose association of states and less as a consolidated nation, and they were willing to leave many important questions to state action. Further, it was generally understood that the Constitution, in its "three-fifths" and fugitive slave clauses, protected the South's right to practice slavery. It was on the basis of such provisions that the Southern states had agreed to join the Union.

Apart from the question of legal or constitutional obligation, many Americans took the position that the harmony of the Union was simply more important than the ethics of slavery: the slave question must not be permitted to weaken the Union, and the abolitionists were wrong to keep up constant agitation on an issue that caused sectional antagonism.

The abolitionists were in the minority. They asserted that the Union was not worth saving unless it was based upon freedom.

The Mexican War and the Slavery Issue

Northern reactions to the War with Mexico were even more intense than Northern reactions to the annexation of Texas. No matter how moderate they previously had been, anti-extension Northerners began to heed the abolitionists' arguments that the South's "slave power" must be checked. According to this version of affairs, the South, having dominated the federal government since its establishment, was now afraid that population growth in the North and the proliferation of free states in the Northwest would destroy its political advantage. Hence, the South sought to strengthen itself by spreading an evil, which enlightened folk deplored. The threat would affect the Southwest (as a result of the Mexican War), the West as a whole, and Northern states as well. The "slave power," the argument continued, would try to annex every Mexican mile and Central America and the West Indies in the bargain.

At the same time, many Southerners blamed the North as the aggressor. They asserted that the pamphlets of abolitionists stirred up African Americans. Slave insurrections had resulted and would continue to result from the "senseless" agitation. As an example, Southerners pointed to the Nat Turner revolt of 1831, which Southerners blamed on Northern agitators. Most notably, David Walker, a freeborn African American man living in Boston published his *Appeal to the Coloured Citizens of the World,* which was an open invitation to all slaves to rebel. Walker's work was found in the hands of Virginia slaves, the state where Nat Turner launched his bloody revolt. Coincidentally, William Lloyd Garrison of Boston published his first issue of *The Liberator,* an abolitionist publication, the same year as Nat Turner's revolt.

▶ Depiction of Nat Turner being captured after hiding out for ten weeks. During Nat Turner's Revolt a total of fifty-seven whites were killed—including slave masters, their wives, and their children—at the hands of Turner and his followers. All of Turner's followers were eventually caught and killed, along with Turner himself.
Wikipedia photo

Nat Turner Revolt

Nat Turner was a Virginia slave who in his twenties claimed to receive the Spirit of God, appointing him a divine instrument against slavery. On August 22, 1831, Turner and six slave followers attacked their master and all of the white people on their plantation. With an axe they beheaded the slave master and his wife in front of their children. Turner and his followers proceeded to visit ten other plantations. By noon they had killed all of the white men, women, and children they encountered on each plantation. In all, fifty-seven white men, women and children were dead.

Turner's following grew to at least fifty slaves. The next day, in retaliation, the whites raised a militia and killed all of Turner's followers. Turner successfully hid out for ten weeks before being captured. He was tried, convicted, and executed. Twenty other slaves were also executed for aiding Turner in his revolt—which is recounted as the most deadly in American history.

Antislavery rhetoric had long been limited to a few Northern hotheads, but now they saw the zealotry as epidemic. Northerners had petitioned to do away with slavery in the District of Columbia and on federal property in the South. The same "intolerance" fervor had been manifested in opposition to annexing Texas. Furthermore, Southerners argued that the Northern states abysmally failed to live up to their constitutional commitments when they repeatedly refused to enforce the Fugitive Slave Law of 1793.

As the world has often seen in situations where emotion interferes with reason, there were exaggerations on both sides rather than complete departures from truth. On the one hand, there simply was no "slave power" in the abolitionist sense of the term. There was no unanimity of Southern opinion as to policies. From Jefferson's day through Jackson's to Polk's, not all Southern officeholders in high places had been of one political mind. Contrary to what was charged, there was no widespread Southern or Northern conspiracy.

In the 1840s, the issues of slavery and antislavery, expansion and containment became intermeshed. If the Civil War had never taken place, we might not now be inclined to stress North-South antipathies respecting the West. However, since the war did occur, it is evident that the relationship of the slavery question to the West involved problems loaded with political dynamite. In the North, the Mexican War sparked opposition from the young, one-term Congressman from Illinois, Abraham Lincoln, as well as from the New Englander, Henry David Thoreau—and countless others who were not destined to be so famous. The War of 1812 had triggered domestic opposition in the North on the basis of sectional self-interest. The Mexican War triggered opposition by principled opponents of slavery, and some of the arguments deployed by these opponents have inspired subsequent anti-war activists down to the twenty-first century.

The Question of Extending Slavery

This meant that as long as the institution of slavery was confined to the existing slave states, few Northerners were willing to act against it; and it was not an explosive question politically. However, when the question of extending slavery to new areas arose, the opposition was far more determined. As early as the Ordinance of 1787, the former Congress under the *Articles of Confederation* had agreed to exclude slavery from the region north of the Ohio River. Some people, motivated by sincere antislavery sentiments, were determined to "contain" slavery. Others cared nothing about the evils of slavery but wanted to reserve unsettled areas for white residents only. Furthermore, many people wanted to bring these new areas to the support of the North in the economic struggle between North and South. The South, conversely, was equally convinced that the growth of the country should not be all on the side of the North, reducing the South to a defenseless minority. This belief made Southerners unwilling to concede even the areas where there was little prospect of extending slavery.

Due to these attitudes, the acquisition of any new area, the organization of any new territory, and the admission of any new state had always involved a possible outburst over the slavery question. There had been such a crisis in 1819, when Missouri applied for admission to statehood as one of the first states to be formed out of the Louisiana Purchase. In the same way, the prospect of acquisition of territory from Mexico as a result of the Mexican War brought on a more protracted and more serious crisis beginning in 1846.

A few months after the beginning of the Mexican War, President Polk asked Congress to appropriate $2 million to be used in negotiating for land to be acquired from Mexico at the termination of the war. Many Northern Democrats were at this time angry with Polk, partly because he had vetoed the Rivers and Harbors Bill important to mid-western economic development and partly because they argued he had violated the expansionist promises on which he was elected. His platform had called for the "reoccupation" of Oregon and the "reannexation" of Texas, and for "all of Oregon or none." In fact, a Polk campaign slogan had been "Fifty-four forty or fight," suggesting that Polk would prefer to go to war with England rather than settle for a Canada/Oregon border that did not include much of what is now British Columbia, all the way to the southern tip of Alaska. This had put the question of expansion on a bisectional basis by promising Oregon, sure to be free territory, for the North and Texas, which already had slavery, for the South. After becoming president, however, Polk had compromised on Oregon, accepting the boundary at the forty-ninth parallel instead of at 54° 40′ and thus avoiding confrontation with England while pushing expansion toward the southwest to the fullest extent by waging war with Mexico.

The Wilmot Proviso

This was the state of affairs when David Wilmot, a Democrat from Pennsylvania, introduced a resolution in the House of Representatives that slavery should be prohibited in any territory acquired from Mexico with the $2 million Polk requested. This free-soil resolution passed the House where the North was stronger; but it failed to pass in the Senate, where the South had equal strength. The disagreement of Senate and House marked an impasse in Congress that lasted for four years, blocking the organization of governments for the new areas. The result was a steady increase in sectional tension.

In 1848, at the end of the Mexican War, the victorious United States acquired territory embracing the present states of Nevada, California, and Utah, most of Arizona and New Mexico, and parts of Colorado and Wyoming. Mexico also relinquished all claims to Texas above the Rio Grande. In the same year gold was discovered in California, and by 1849 the full-fledged Gold Rush was in effect.

The need for organizing the new land was urgent, and the territorial question became the foremost issue in public life. At one extreme stood Wilmot and the "free-soilers," both Whig and Democrat, who demanded the exclusion of slavery from the new areas by act of Congress. At the other extreme, most Southern Whigs and Democrats adopted the position of John C. Calhoun, who argued that the territories were owned in common by all the states (rather than by the federal government, which was only a joint agent for the states) and that all citizens had an equal right to take their property (including slaves) to the common territory. Therefore, in Calhoun's logic, Congress had no power under the Constitution to exclude slavery from any territory.

The Doctrine of Popular Sovereignty

Political leaders who wanted some kind of adjustment or middle ground were not satisfied with either Wilmot's or Calhoun's alternative—one of which conceded nothing to the South, the other nothing to the North. They sought a more "moderate" position, and some of them advocated an extension of the Missouri Compromise line of 36°30′ to the Pacific. Most of them, however, were more attracted by a proposal sponsored by Lewis Cass, senator from Michigan, for what was called "popular sovereignty" or "squatter sovereignty." Cass contended that the fairest and most democratic solution would be to let the people in the territories decide for themselves whether they would have slavery, just as the people in the states had already decided. This proposal offered an attractive means for keeping the slavery question out of federal politics, but it contained one ambiguity that Cass adroitly refused to clarify. It did not specify *when* the people in the territories should make the decision. If they could make the decision as soon as the territory was organized, free soil could be attained by popular vote as easily as by congressional vote. According to Calhoun, popular exclusion at this stage would be just as wrong as congressional exclusion, for it would mean that Congress was giving to the territory a power which Congress did not have and, therefore, could not give. If, however, the voters in a territory could decide on slavery only when they applied for statehood, this would mean that the territories would have been left open to slavery quite as much as by Calhoun's position.

MAP 10.4 Presidential Election of 1848

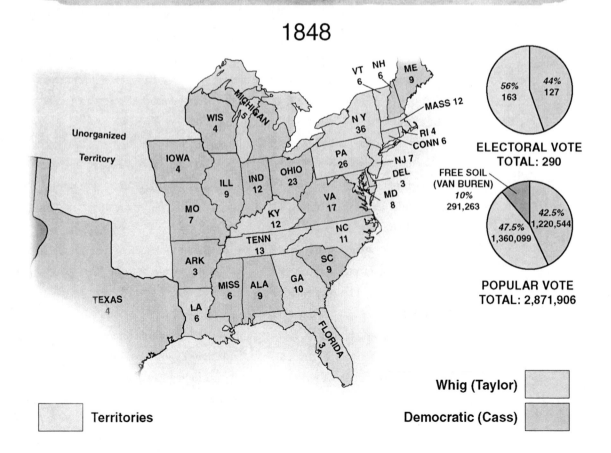

Far from reducing the amount of support for popular sovereignty, however, this ambiguity actually added to the attractiveness of the doctrine. Antislavery people argued that popular sovereignty would result in free territories, while proslavery advocates contended that it guaranteed slavery a fair chance to establish itself during the period before statehood.

The Compromise of 1850

While these various positions on the territorial extension of slavery were being developed, the impasse in Congress continued. For three entire sessions, covering most of the Polk administration, no vote could change anything for California or the Southwest. It was only after long delay that an act to organize Oregon Territory without slavery was adopted.

In 1848, when the two national parties faced this question in a presidential election, both of them evaded it. The Democrats nominated Cass, whose reputation was based on the idea

▶ Military hero Zachary Taylor won the presidential election of 1849
Wikipedia photo

of "popular sovereignty," on a platform that still did not say *when* the people of a territory could vote on slavery. The Whigs nominated a military hero, Zachary Taylor, who had never been in politics and did not have any kind of platform. Further muddying the waters was the development of the Free Soil Party, which held its inaugural convention in Buffalo. The Free Soil Party nominated former president and Jacksonian Democrat, Martin Van Buren, for president and Charles Francis Adams of the Whig Party for vice president on a platform of "Free soil, free speech, free labor, and free men." In the election campaign, the Free Soilers were successful in making slavery the main issue of the campaign, but they did not carry a single state. The main contest between Taylor and Cass, however, turned out to be a contest between forthright evasion and concealed evasion. Taylor, who owned over one hundred slaves on plantations in Mississippi and Louisiana, was triumphant; and he was inaugurated as president in 1849.

Early Secessionist Sentiment

Meanwhile, the House of Representatives had repeatedly voted in favor of Wilmot's principle of free soil by congressional action. The seeming imminence of a free-soil victory had, in turn, aroused bitter resentment in the South. For the first time many Southerners began to think of withdrawing from the Union if Congress voted to prevent them from taking their slaves into areas they had helped to win and assisted in paying the war debts. By 1848, Southerners in Congress were beginning to speak rather freely of disunion. After Taylor was elected, he sent envoys to California and New Mexico to persuade settlers in the newly acquired territories to draft constitutions and apply for admission to the Union as states, rather than as territories. The inhabitants of both territories were predominantly anti-slavery. In California, gold rushers did not want to have to compete with gangs of slave labor in gold prospecting. In New Mexico, the climate was simply too arid to grow cotton, and slave labor was not necessary on the open range. Southerners realized that, although Taylor was a Louisiana slaveholder that brought slaves with him to the White House, which he kept hidden in the White House attic, he was not going to block free-soil legislation. Therefore, they began to organize Southern resistance. Jefferson Davis of Mississippi argued, "we are about permanently to destroy the balance of power between the sections."

In October 1849 during a state convention in Mississippi, a conference of Southern state delegates was called to meet in Nashville, Tennessee, the following June to work out a united Southern position. Five Southern states officially elected delegates to such a convention, and representatives were unofficially chosen from four others.

Thus, when Taylor's first Congress met in December 1849, the need for organizing the area acquired from Mexico was urgent, and the relations between North and South were at a crisis. This crisis became more acute when Taylor announced his support for admitting California directly to statehood without going through a territorial stage, and his intention was to support the same plan for New Mexico in due course. Technically, this plan bypassed the question of congressional exclusion from the decision on slavery; however, in substance it represented a free-soil victory, for the proposed states seemed fairly certain to be free states. At this prospect Southern protests were intensified. Though historians today disagree as to whether the country was close to disunion, certainly many prominent leaders at the time feared that it was.

A separate issue threatening disunion at the time was a border dispute between the United States and the new state of Texas. According to the 1836 Treaty of Velasco under which Texas had staked its claim to independence, the southern and western border of Texas was the Rio Grande. Texans sent envoys to the upper Rio Grande Valley (present day Albuquerque) and Santa Fe to organize county governments, but the residents rebuffed them. At Santa Fe, the Texan envoys were ordered to "cease and desist at every peril" by U.S. Army General Kearney, who exercised political authority in Santa Fe in the aftermath of the War with Mexico. Nevertheless, Texans still claimed their rights to the territory, and Peter Hansborough Bell won the Texas Gubernatorial election of 1849 on a platform of retaining Santa Fe by force. Though Texas had fought for a decade to join the Union and had been an American state for less than four years, the Texans were threatening war with the U.S. over Santa Fe. However, under Texas' Articles of Annexation, a provision stated that border disputes would be settled by Congress. Northerners opposed Texas possession of Santa Fe primarily because they viewed it as an extension of slave territory into New Mexico. The Santa Fe issue would, therefore, become connected to the entire sectional debate.

The Clay Compromise Proposals

Among those leaders fearing disunion was Senator Henry Clay of Kentucky. He was an ardent spokesman of the Border States, which were always anxious to promote sectional harmony. Clay was a natural leader of compromise, one who had played a leading part in arranging the Compro-

▶ Senator Henry Clay of Kentucky proposed a compromise that would cover the slavery question in its national aspects and, ultimately, save the Union. *Corbis Images*

mises of 1820 (Missouri) and 1833 (Nullification). Although a Whig, he was at odds with President Taylor. Accordingly, Clay came forward early in the congressional session of 1850, with an elaborate compromise designed to cover the slavery question in all its national aspects. Clay's plan called for five areas of compromise. First, admit California as a free state. Secondly, organize the rest of the Mexican cession into two territories, Utah and New Mexico, which were to decide for themselves whether slavery should be permitted or abolished. Third, award New Mexico part of the area on the upper Rio Grande claimed by Texas, including Santa Fe, but compensate Texas through federal payment of the $10 million in Texas debt contracted before annexation. Fourth, abolish the sale of slaves in the District of Columbia but guaranteeing slavery itself in the District. Finally, enact an effective law to compel the return of fugitive slaves who had escaped into the free states.

Clay's proposal brought on a long, brilliant, and famous series of debates in Congress. Clay made an immensely eloquent appeal for his plan as a means of saving the Union, giving seventy speeches urging its passage. Calhoun, who did not support the compromise directly, helped it indirectly by coming into the Senate almost in a dying condition to warn solemnly of the danger to the Union and the determination of the South to maintain its rights. Daniel Webster, who was Clay's only peer as an orator, and who was generally regarded as an antislavery man, made the most important speech of the session. On the seventh of March, Webster announced his support of the compromise and made a powerful argument that slavery was naturally excluded from the West by climatic, physical, and agricultural conditions and that there was no need to bring on a crisis by adopting an antislavery law, such as the Wilmot Proviso, to accomplish what had already been settled by physical environment. "I would not re-enact a law of God," said Webster, impressively. "I would not reaffirm an ordinance of nature."

Despite great oratorical support, Clay's "omnibus bill," incorporating all his proposals in one measure, faced heavy opposition. President Taylor was waiting to veto it, and in July it was cut to pieces on the floor by a process of amendment in which Northern and Southern extremists voted together to prevent its passage. Clay—old, exhausted, and badly discouraged—went off to Newport for a rest.

The Douglas Strategy

Even before this vote was taken, the tide had turned. President Taylor died, and his successor, Millard Fillmore, favored the compromise and immediately began to exert presidential influence to support it.

Meanwhile, Stephen A. Douglas, a young and vigorous senator from Illinois, took over the management of the compromise forces in Congress. Douglas was not a great orator, but he was a supremely effective rough-and-tumble debater, a man of immense energy ("a steam engine in breeches" was the phrase) and a most perceptive political tactician. He perceived that there was not a clear majority in favor of the compromise, and it could not be passed in the form in which Clay had presented it. He did realize, however, that if Clay's proposals were considered one by one, they could be passed by a combination of those who favored the compromise as a whole and those who favored each particular measure. Douglas applied this strategy so effectively that within a few weeks Clay's entire program was enacted into law.

The adoption of the "Compromise of 1850" ended the crisis. It also broke the long stalemate and gave badly needed political organization to California and the Southwest. It was hailed as a great and final settlement that defused the slavery issue once and for all as a source of discord in the Union because it brought a great sense of relief to those who had feared for the safety of the Union. Free-Soiler Salmon Chase, however, drew the ominous conclusion that "the question of slavery in the territories has been avoided. It has not been settled." Unfortunately for the nation, Chase's conclusion would prove to be correct.

The Fugitive Slave Act

In actuality, the Compromise of 1850 resolved far less than it appeared to settle. For Utah and New Mexico the Compromise of 1850 admitted them to the Union as Territories with "popular sovereignty" to determine the status of slavery in each territory. These provisions left open the explosive question Lewis Cass had so carefully avoided: Could the citizens of the territory outlaw slavery in the territory? More importantly, while putting to rest the explosive issue of the Wilmot Proviso, it brought to life the even more explosive issue of the fugitive slave. The question of the slave in the territories was a legal and abstract question—a question of what was later called "an imaginary Negro in an impossible place." On the contrary, the question of the runaway slave was dramatic and real, involving a human creature in quest of freedom that was being hunted down by his fellow humans.

For a time, the fugitive slave question raised a terrific furor. To appreciate the uproar, one must understand that the law contained a number of very extreme features. The general idea was that when slaves successfully escaped their captors in the South and fled to territory in the North where African American persons could be free, Northerners were obligated to help the Southerners apprehend the runaway slaves and return them to their masters. Additionally, the Fugitive Slave Act denied trial by jury in the case of alleged fugitives and provided for their cases to be decided by a special federal commissioner. Those accused of being fugitives could not testify in their own defense; hence, if anyone were captured in a case of mistaken identity, he or she would not be able to say so in court. Further, it paid the commissioner a fee that was higher in cases where the alleged fugitive was returned to slavery than in cases where the fugitive was set free. Though this arrangement was defended on the ground that there was much more paper work in one case than the other, it led to severe criticism. Still further, the law stipulated that any citizen could be called upon to participate in the enforcement process, which meant that those who opposed slavery must not only permit the capture of fugitives but might possibly be made to help in their capture. Those Northern citizens who failed to assist in the capture of a slave when they were able to do so could be subject to both fines and imprisonment. The very idea that Northerners would have to assist Southern slave masters in recovering their "property" was abhorrent to Northern abolitionists, but to be jailed or fined for failing to do so was a double indignity.

Apart from these features of the law itself, the act aroused criticism because in operation it applied not only to slaves who were then running away but also to any slaves who had ever run away. There were many fugitives who had lived quietly in the North for many years and who had been quite safe from arrest under the relatively ineffectual Fugitive Slave Law of 1793. Unfortunately, under the Act of 1850, they found themselves in real danger. Some Southerners went north rounding up African Americans with little consideration of how long they had been free or, in some cases, if they, in fact, had ever been slaves. For example, in 1851 an African American man who had lived in Indiana for nineteen years was torn from his family and sent into slavery. Throughout the North, the law terrorized African Americans, for those who were not fugitives had reason to fear being kidnapped quite as much as actual runaways had reason to fear being arrested. Consequently, a wave of migration to Canada occurred, and several thousand African Americans moved to Ontario. Northern abolitionists added fuel to the fire of sectional tensions over the act by impeding the capture of fugitives even when there was no question that the person was a recent runaway.

The problems with the Fugitive Slave Act reflect the fact that the 1850 Compromise had never commanded a real majority and had been enacted only by finesse. The Southern states accepted it somewhat reluctantly; but Georgia spoke for the rest of them when its legislature voted resolutions that if the compromise were not fully enforced, Georgia would withdraw from the Union. In fact, while the Southern disunionists were agreeing not to demand secession at this time, the Southern unionists were almost forced to agree to the *principle* of secession in order to get the secessionists to agree not to exercise it at that time. Meanwhile, in the North the antislavery forces were pouring their denunciations upon the Fugitive Slave Act and upon Daniel Webster for supporting it. Perhaps never before in American politics had political invective been so bitter.

▶ Anthony Burns
Library of Congress

Resistance Against the Fugitive Slave Law

A series of fugitive slave episodes followed which kept the country at a high pitch of excitement. In Boston, leading citizens openly asserted their intention to violate the law. In October a "vigilance committee" headed by one of the foremost citizens of Boston, Reverend Theodore Parker, smuggled two undoubted slaves out of the country. Four months later a crowd, mostly African American, seized a prisoner, Shadrach, from a courtroom and took him away to Canada. Finally, in April 1851, the government succeeded in returning a slave from Boston, from which city it was boasted that no slave had ever been returned. This was accomplished only after mobs had surrounded the courthouse for several days. Only once again another slave, Anthony Burns, was returned from Boston. In his case a mob stormed the courthouse in an effort to rescue him, and a large military force was required in order to prevent his rescue.

In other cities, also, rescues and attempted rescues kept tensions high, and the fugitive slave question became, for a time, the foremost issue of the day. Yet the excitement and emotion that the issue generated made it difficult to obtain the facts about whether the escape of slaves from the South was numerically significant. On the one hand, Northern antislavery advocates boasted of their resistance to the law and claimed that they were operating a vast "underground railroad" which had helped 80,000 slaves to escape their pursuers. On the other, spokesmen of the South, indignant at the open violation of the law, complained bitterly that 100,000 slaves had been abducted over a forty-year period. (These were probably inflated figures.) The Underground Railroad was probably more extensive in legend than in reality and more important as a weapon of psychological warfare than as an escape route for slaves. It also appears that in many parts of the North the Fugitive Slave Act of 1850 had public support and was well enforced.

There is no doubt, however, that the fugitive question dramatized the issue of slavery to a spectacular degree. The human being in quest of freedom, trying to escape from bloodthirsty pursuers, was an immensely moving figure. By changing the focus of the slavery question from the legal status of an imaginary chattel in a remote territory to the human plight of an individual human being in a nearby street, the Compromise of 1850 had, perhaps, created more tension than it relieved. In the final analysis, the Fugitive Slave Act was largely an unenforceable failure as evidenced by the fact that in the decade between the passage of the Act and the Civil War, only 300 slaves were returned to their masters. Given that a major fear of many northern whites was that African Americans would leave the southern plantations and move north, one might have expected at least as many slaves to be returned to their masters during this period—even if the Act had never been passed.

▶ The dramatic scene from Harriet Beecher Stowe's *Uncle Tom's Cabin* novel in which the fugitive slave woman Eliza is crossing the icebound Ohio River with her son in her arms as a slave trader was pursuing her. *Corbis Images*

It is by no means an accident that *Uncle Tom's Cabin* (1851–1852), the classic literary protest against slavery, was published less than a year after the enactment of the fugitive law. In fact, Harriet Beecher Stowe's sister-in-law urged her to write something in response to the new law, and the novel was the result. The book's most dramatic scene was that of the fugitive slave woman, Eliza, crossing the icebound Ohio River with her son in her arms as a slave trader was pursuing her. This book, one of America's all-time best sellers, forced readers to see the humanity of the slaves and produced sympathy and tears from countless people who had never previously been moved by the abolitionists.

The Election of 1852

If the Fugitive Slave law dramatized the issue of slavery, the crisis preceding the Compromise of 1850 had dramatized the issue of Union. Many Northerners who thoroughly disapproved of slavery argued that the question of Union was more important and must have priority. Consequently, despite fugitive slave episodes, the Compromise received strong support throughout much of the country, and though there had not been a clear majority in favor of adopting it, there was certainly a clear majority in favor of maintaining it.

The firmness of public support for the Compromise of 1850 showed up clearly in the election of 1852. As it approached, Millard Fillmore, who had signed the compromise acts while serving out the term of Zachary Taylor, aspired to a term of his own. To his dismay, during the party convention Northern Whigs blocked the effort of Southern Whigs to nominate him. Instead they forced the nomination of General Winfield Scott, who had captured Mexico

MAP 10.5 Presidential Election of 1852

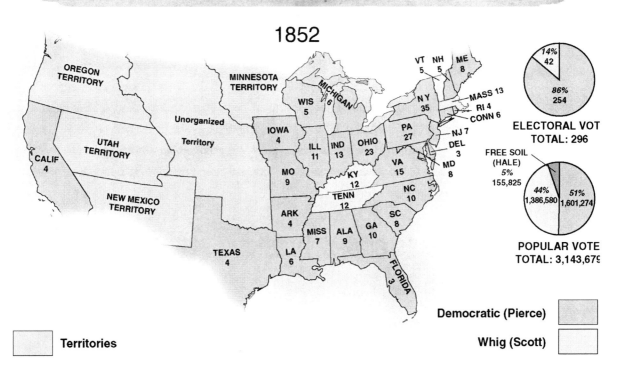

▶ Presidential candidate Franklin Pierce was expected to be a compromise for the Democrats. Though attractive as a candidate, Pierce was later found to be a reckless man and an alcoholic.
Corbis Images

City in the Mexican War. Scott was the Whigs' third military hero; they hoped that, like Harrison and Taylor, he would win the White House on his military record.

The adoption of a platform revealed a deep division among the Whigs. The majority secured the adoption of a plank accepting the Compromise of 1850, including the Fugitive Slave Act, as a final settlement; but there was strong opposition, consisting mostly of delegates who supported Scott. Scott, who was pompous and politically clumsy, tried to get out of this dilemma by saying merely, "I accept the nomination with the resolutions attached." However, it was clear that he was not an absolute supporter of the Compromise.

The Democrats settled their differences between rival candidates by agreeing on a dark horse, Franklin Pierce of New Hampshire, who had served with gallantry in the Mexican War. The position of the two parties gave the voters a fairly clear choice on the question of compromise. Pierce and his party were united on it; the Whigs were not. The voters exercised their option in a decisive way. Pierce carried all but four states—two in the North, and two in the South.

Pierce later proved a weak man with a serious alcohol addiction. Later, as president, he was arrested in Washington for recklessly trampling a woman with his horse while intoxicated. His depressed wife (Jane) was given to writing letters to their dead son. However, Pierce was an attractive candidate—handsome and pleasing in his manner—and the Democrats gave him united support on a platform that proclaimed the finality of the Compromise of 1850.

The defeat smashed the Whig Party, which was already badly divided between the "Cotton Whigs" of the South and the "Conscience Whigs" of the North. Though many important figures—including Abraham Lincoln—remained in the Whig organization somewhat longer, it was never a national party after 1852. Only one national party—the Democratic—was left. This meant that there was now only one remaining political organization in which Northern and Southern leaders were still seeking to smooth out sectional disagreements for the sake of party victory.

Kansas and Nebraska

The Douglas Bill

Pierce's campaign had promised harmony for the Union and finality for the Compromise of 1850, but his administration brought just the opposite. His first Congress had barely met in December 1853, when the territorial question arose again in a new form. Douglas wanted to organize territorial government for the region west of Iowa and Missouri. This area lay within the Louisiana Purchase; and since it was north of 36°30′, it had been closed to slavery by the Missouri Compromise of 1820. Douglas, therefore, at first introduced a bill to organize free territories.

Southern senators, however, voted against his legislation and therefore blocked it. They did this in part because they knew that Douglas wanted to promote a transcontinental railroad west from Chicago or some other Northern terminus to the Pacific. They were equally eager to run such a railroad west from New Orleans. There was simply no reason for them to give their votes to organize another free-soil territory for the purpose of facilitating a Northern railroad.

Douglas believed that he had to have their votes. In January of 1854 he was led to take the fatal step of agreeing to change his bill so that it would repeal the Missouri Compromise line and leave the status of slavery in the Kansas-Nebraska region to be settled by popular sovereignty. Douglas made the plausible argument that what he advocated was nothing new and that the legislation of 1850 had already replaced the principle of geographical division with the principle of popular sovereignty.

"Appeal of the Independent Democrats"

In a widely disseminated tract entitled "Appeal of the Independent Democrats," antislavery advocates rejected Douglas's argument with furious indignation. They insisted that the act of 1850 applied only to the Mexican cession and was thus merely supplementary to the Missouri Compromise. The South, they asserted, was violating a sacred pledge: in 1820 it had promised to recognize freedom north of 36°30′ in return for the admission of Missouri, and now it was defaulting on the agreement. To the Northerners, the territories had been free soil ever since the Missouri Compromise. Douglas' proposal was, therefore, the "reintroduction" of slavery into the territories.

The Northern arguments were not entirely accurate. To mention but one point, a majority of Southern congressmen had voted against the act of 1820 to begin with, but the act had stood for thirty-four years. Douglas was at least reckless, if not wrong, to tamper with it.

The furious blast of indignation that greeted his amended Kansas-Nebraska bill must have told him that he had made a major blunder; however, Douglas was bold, aggressive, and tenacious. After committing President Pierce to his bill, Douglas staged an all-out parliamentary battle for enactment. His own resourcefulness in debate enabled him repeatedly to throw his attackers on the defensive, and he conducted a brilliant campaign by which he succeeded in forcing the bill through both houses of Congress.

The Election of 1854

Douglas's success, however, came at a terrible price. He had correctly foreseen that the repeal of the Missouri Compromise would "raise the Hell of a storm;" but he had not predicted, as he later said, that he would be able to travel to Chicago by the light of his own burning effigies. Six months after the act was adopted, the congressional elections of 1854 took place. All over the North "anti-Nebraska" parties sprang up to capitalize on free-soil anger at the Kansas-Nebraska Act. In Wisconsin and Michigan these parties took the name "Republican," and this name soon spread to other states. In the Northeast, however, the main beneficiary of the voter uprising in 1854 was not the newborn Republican Party but rather the anti-Catholic Know-Nothings, who shared the Republicans' hostility to the extension of slavery but were even more concerned about the apparent threat of Roman Catholic immigrants. The Know-Nothings won enough votes to gain forty seats in the House of Representatives.

Whatever the name of their opponents, the Democrats suffered a stunning setback in the Northern congressional elections. The number of Northern Democrats in the House fell from ninety-one to twenty-five. From 1854 forward, the Democratic Party would function as a Southern, sectional, proslavery party.

In the long run, however, the Republicans rather than the Know-Nothings proved to be the main beneficiaries of the 1854 electoral revolution, gaining one hundred seats in the House of Representatives. Northern opposition to the expansion of slavery proved deeper and more intense than Protestant dislike of Roman Catholic immigrants. By the end of 1855, the Republican Party had emerged as the successor to the Whigs as the country's second major party. Unlike the Whigs, however, the Republicans were entirely a sectional party with no strength at all in the slave states.

MAP 10.6 The United States in 1854

Bleeding Kansas

The worst thing about the new Kansas-Nebraska Act was that, even at the price of causing the bitterest kind of sectional hostility, it did not create a real basis for stability in the new territory. Instead it merely changed the terms of the contest. Douglas and many Northern Democrats believed that popular sovereignty could make Kansas and Nebraska free territories just as well as congressional action could, while proslavery leaders, on the other hand, took the repeal of the Missouri Compromise to mean that slavery should prevail in at least one of the two new territories.

Both antislavery and proslavery groups prepared to rush supporters into Kansas to defend their respective positions. In New England, antislavery advocates organized an Emigrant Aid Society to send free-soil settlers to Kansas. In 1854 and 1855, the Society sponsored 1,240 settlers. Though the society never officially purchased weapons for these settlers, the leaders of the society bought rifles with separate funds to arm the emigrants against the proslavery groups.

From Missouri, proslavery advocates, known as Border Ruffians, traveled into Kansas on Election Day to vote and intimidate the free-soilers before riding back to Missouri. Missouri Senator David Rice Atchison publicly encouraged the election fraud. Atchison proclaimed, "There are 1,100 coming over from Platte County to vote, and if that ain't enough, we can send 5,000 to kill every God-damned abolitionist in the territory." Atchison himself led a contingent of armed men from Missouri to vote and frighten away Free Soil voters. On the other side, Senator William H. Seward of New York retorted, "Come on then, Gentlemen of the Slave States ... since there is no escaping your challenge, I accept it in behalf of the cause of freedom. We will engage in competition for the virgin soil of Kansas, and God give the victory to the side which is stronger in numbers as it is in right."

In March 1855, an election was held in Kansas to elect a territorial legislature. Of the 2,905 eligible voters, somehow 6,307 votes were cast, and Kansas quickly assembled a proslavery legislature elected through fraud primarily by proslavery zealots from Missouri. The new proslavery legislature quickly passed a law outlawing the abolition of slavery, a position that was opposed by a strong majority of the people that actually lived in Kansas.

It would have taken a strong president to keep order in Kansas, but Pierce was not strong. He appointed a succession of able governors for the territory, but he did not vigorously support them when they needed his assistance. Affairs, therefore, went from bad to worse. After the proslavery faction had stolen an election and President Pierce had given recognition to the government elected—even replacing the Kansas Governor who had objected to the election fraud—the free-soil advocates formed another government of their own. Kansas then had two governments—a proslavery one in the town of Lecompton and an antislavery one in Lawrence. The antislavery legislature not only banned slavery from the state, it also passed a measure banning all African Americans from the state, slave or free.

With President Pierce denouncing the free-soil government for its illegality, the proslavery forces secured an indictment of the free-soilers by a grand jury that was, of course, of the proslavery men's own choosing. With this indictment, a proslavery federal marshal led an armed mob, or "posse" as it called itself, and marched on the free-soil headquarters at Lawrence. There they shot cannon balls into the Free State Hotel, destroying the printing press of the free soil newspaper. They continued their havoc by burning or looting a good deal of property, both shops and private homes, and finally taking over the free soil government buildings.

Four days later, in May 1856, John Brown and six companions (four of them his sons), a free-soiler who carried his views to fanatical lengths, avenged the sacking of Lawrence and the killing of several free-soil settlers by leading a body of men to Pottawatomie Creek. There they took five unarmed proslavery settlers from their homes in the dead of night and murdered them. Brown argued that his action was just stating that "It was better that a score of bad men should die than that one man who came here to make Kansas a free state should be driven out."

These events were part of an escalation of terror and violence in "Bleeding Kansas" that followed. Both Brown and proslavery groups roamed the countryside shooting and looting for their causes. Probably two hundred people met violent deaths before a new territorial government used federal troops to restore order four months later. Brown was neither captured nor killed by the federal troops, but in October 1856 he was forced to flee Kansas and go into hiding.

Though things in Kansas were surely bad enough, exaggerated reports of the violence in the nation's newspapers made them even worse, further heightening sectional tensions. For example, one editor of a proslavery newspaper claimed that abolitionists came to Kansas "for the express purpose of stealing, running off and hiding runaway negroes from Missouri, and taking to their own bed … a stinking negro wench." Rumors circulated Missouri that 20,000 abolitionist migrants were coming to Kansas, a gross exaggeration that bore little relation with reality, but believed nonetheless. The reality was that most Kansas residents were migrants from Missouri who came to Kansas for land ownership. The vast majorities were against slavery, but in contrast, they were not for racial equality and opposed the presence of free African Americans in Kansas as well. In the words of one Kansas clergyman, "I kem to Kansas to live in a free state and I don't want niggers a—trampin' over my grave."

▶Senator Charles Sumner was an anti-slavery Republican from Massachusetts. After making a speech denouncing the Kansas-Nebraska Act, Sumner was brutally attacked by an opposing Representative, Preston Brooks, in the empty Senate chamber. *Wikipedia photo*

"The Crime Against Kansas"

Meanwhile, the intensity of sectional ill will was both illustrated and heightened by an occurrence in Washington. Charles Sumner, an antislavery senator from Massachusetts, delivered an oration entitled "The Crime against Kansas." In addition to castigating the slave power as bitterly as he could and denouncing what he termed as "murderous robbers" and "assassins," he spoke in extremely personal terms about elderly Senator Andrew P. Butler of South Carolina, accusing him of "cavorting with the harlot, slavery." He also alluded to "the loose expectoration" of the elderly Butler's speech. A nephew of Butler's in the House of Representatives, Preston Brooks, went

T he following is an excerpt from Charles Sumner's speech he made in Congress regarding the events in Kansas in 1855–56.

But the wickedness which I now begin to expose is immeasurably aggravated by the motive which prompted it. Not in any common lust for power did this uncommon tragedy have its origin. It is the rape of a virgin Territory, compelling it to the hateful embrace of Slavery; and it may be clearly traced to a depraved longing for a new slave State, the hideous offspring of such a crime, in the hope of adding to the power of slavery in the National Government. Yes, sir, when the whole world, alike Christian and Turk, is rising up to condemn this wrong, and to make it a hissing to the nations, here in our Republic, force, ay, sir, FORCE has been openly employed in compelling Kansas to this pollution, and all for the sake of political power. There is the simple fact, which you will in vain attempt to deny, but which in itself presents an essential wickedness that makes other public crimes seem like public virtues.

But, before entering upon the argument, I must say something of a general character, particularly in response to what has fallen from Senators who have raised themselves to eminence on this floor in championship of human wrongs. I mean the Senator from South Carolina (Mr. Butler), and the Senator from Illinois (Mr. Douglas), who, though unlike as Don Quixote and Sancho Panza, yet, like this couple, sally forth together in the same adventure. I regret much to miss the elder Senator from his seat; but the cause, against which he has run a tilt, with such activity of animosity, demands that the opportunity of exposing him should not be lost; and it is for the cause that I speak. The Senator from South Carolina has read many books of chivalry, and believes himself a chivalrous knight, with sentimcuts of honor and courage. Of course he has chosen a mistress to whom he has made his vows, and who, though ugly to others, is always lovely to him; though polluted in the sight of the world, is chaste in his sight I mean the harlot, Slavery. For her, his tongue is always profuse in words. Let her be impeached in character, or any proposition made to shut her out from the extension of her wantonness, and no extravagance of manner or hardihood of assertion is then too great for this Senator. The frenzy of Don Quixote, in behalf of his wench, Dulcinea del Toboso, is all surpassed. The asserted rights of Slavery, which shock equality of all kinds, are cloaked by a fantastic claim of equality. If the slave States cannot enjoy what, in mockery of the great fathers of the Republic, he misnames equality under the Constitution in other words, the full power in the National Territories to compel fellowmen to unpaid toil, to separate husband and wife, and to sell little children at the auction block then, sir, the chivalric Senator will conduct the State of South Carolina out of the Union! Heroic knight! Exalted Senator! A second Moses come for a second exodus!

Source: Charles Sumner, *The Crime against Kansas: the apologies for the crime, the true remedy speech of Hon. Charles Sumner, in the Senate of the United States, 19th and 20th May 1856* (New York: Cornell University Library, 1865).

▶John L. Magee created this lithograph *Southern Chivalry—Argument versus Club'* in 1856, depicting the attack on Charles Sumner by Preston Brooks.

to the Senate chamber when the Senate was not in session, found Sumner seated at his desk, and beat him severely with a cane. In the words of Brooks, "I gave him forty, first-rate stripes."

For several years after the assault, Sumner was incapacitated either by the blows that he received or, according to the best modern medical opinion, by his psychological reaction to the assault. The public significance of this affair, however, resided less in the attack itself than in the fact that a large part of the Northern press made a martyr of Sumner and pictured all Southerners as barbarians, while the South made a hero of Brooks and typed all Northerners as militant fanatics.

The Character of Franklin Pierce

By this time the Pierce administration was ending as a disaster because of the weakness of the President and the extent to which he let himself be dominated by Southern influence. After failing to prevent the repeal of the Missouri Compromise, Pierce might still have saved the peace of the country if he had stood firm for real popular sovereignty in Kansas. Instead, however, he had backed a proslavery regime that was obviously fraudulent, had allowed violence to go unrestrained, and had finally given his support to the idea of statehood with a proslavery government. At this point Douglas had broken with the administration and was lobbying Congress to defeat this proslavery government. Thus the political division was less between free-soil and proslavery forces than between the honest application of popular sovereignty and the perversion of it.

Indeed, Pierce had supported the South at almost every point. He had negotiated the Gadsden Purchase (1853) with Mexico, for what is now the southernmost part of Arizona and New Mexico, because the land in question was strategic for the construction of a transcontinental railroad by the southern route from New Orleans. He had permitted three of his diplomatic emissaries in Europe to meet at Ostend, Belgium, in October 1854 to propose American annexation of Cuba by purchase or, if that failed, by "wresting it from Spain." Cuba had almost 400,000 slaves and would strengthen the power of slavery. This "Ostend Manifesto," however, aroused such worldwide indignation that the administration was forced to repudiate it.

Moreover, the administration did nothing effective to prevent expeditions by adventurers, called *filibusterers*, who invaded Latin countries from American shores. One such expedition from New Orleans against Cuba failed. Another, against Nicaragua, was temporarily successful, installing American William Walker as the leader of the country. These efforts to acquire new slave territory for the United States sparked Northern anger and brought new recruits into the Republican Party. As for Pierce, he would sink even deeper into alcoholism and finally succumb to what historians believe to be cirrhosis of the liver. Pierce once explained his alcohol addiction by stating that, "After the Presidency, what is there to do but drink?"

On the Eve of War

The Election of 1856

At the end of Pierce's term even the Southern Democrats knew that he could not be reelected. The Democrats nominated James Buchanan of Pennsylvania, who as minister to England had

MAP 10.7 Presidential Election of 1856

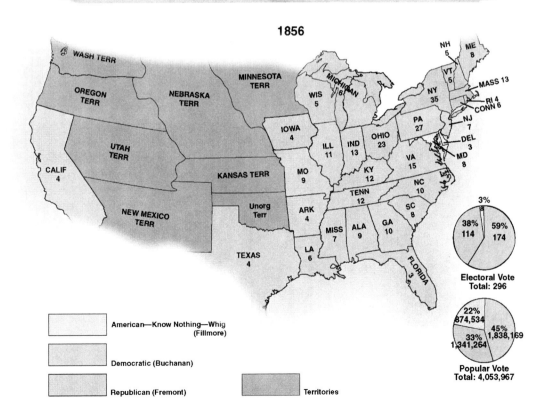

1856

American—Know Nothing—Whig (Fillmore)

Democratic (Buchanan)

Republican (Fremont)

Territories

been out of the country at the time of the Kansas-Nebraska Act. Buchanan had been secretary of state under Polk and was a veteran of American politics.

Buchanan was also a bachelor, making him a bit out of the ordinary for American presidents, and thus relied on close friends as his confidants. Buchanan's closest confidant with whom he roomed for a number of years was Alabama Senator Rufus King, whom Andrew Jackson referred to as "Miss Nancy," a common term of the era for a man with effeminate mannerisms. Clearly, Buchanan relied on King, and the two had a close enough relationship that Congressman Aaron Brown of Tennessee referred to King as Buchanan's "better half and wife" in a letter he wrote to Mrs. James Polk. In 1844 when King was appointed Ambassador to France, Buchanan wrote a friend that he was now "solitary and alone," and added, "I have gone wooing to several gentlemen, but have not succeeded with any of them." Buchanan would have even less success in keeping the country from falling apart.

To run against him, a remnant of the Know-Nothings and Southern Whigs calling themselves the American Party nominated Millard Fillmore, but the principal opposition came from the new Republican Party. The Republicans passed over their most prominent leaders to nominate the dashing but politically inexperienced young explorer of the Rocky Mountains and the west, John C. Frémont.

In the election that followed, Buchanan carried all the slave states (except Maryland, which voted for Fillmore) and four free states, consequently winning the election. The majority of the North, however, was now supporting the Republican Party, that denounced slavery as a "relic of barbarism" and which had no organization whatever throughout half the Union.

It is questionable whether, by this time, anyone could have brought the disruptive forces of sectional antagonism under control. Certainly Buchanan could not do it. Southern Democrats dominated his cabinet, as they had Pierce's. In February 1858, Buchanan forfeited his claim to impartial leadership by recommending admission of Kansas to statehood under a proslavery constitution fraudulently adopted by a convention that met at Lecompton, Kansas.

▶ Abraham Lincoln did not advocate racial equality and opposed African American suffrage, interracial marriage, African American citizenship, the repeal of the fugitive slave act, and allowing African Americans to serve on juries. Despite these opinions, Lincoln strongly believed slavery to be morally wrong.
Corbis Images

Free Soil forces, suspecting a sham, had boycotted the Lecompton constitutional convention, so conventioneers drafted a proslavery constitution without opposition and refused to allow Kansas voters to ratify the document.

Stephen Douglas and other Northern Democrats resisted the Lecompton constitution and rejected the bill to admit Kansas unless the Kansas voters could ratify the Lecompton Constitution. In January 1858, in spite of the fact that slavery advocates from Missouri again stuffed the ballot boxes, the voters of Kansas rejected the Lecompton Constitution by a two to one margin. A second referendum was held at the insistent urging of President Buchanan, and this time fewer proslavery voters were able to cross the border; the Lecompton Constitution was voted down by an even larger six to one margin. Stephen Douglas' role in opposing the Lecompton Constitution lost for him the Southern support that he had won in 1854, and the Democratic Party became deeply divided. Douglas would defeat Abraham Lincoln in 1858 to retain his Illinois Senate seat, but it would be the last victory of his political career.

The Dred Scott Decision

Meanwhile, in 1857, the Supreme Court had handed down a decision that may have been intended to restore sectional peace, but that had exactly the opposite effect. This ruling concerned a Missouri slave, Dred Scott, who had been carried by his master first to the free state of Illinois and then into Wisconsin Territory, which was within the Louisiana Purchase north of 36°30' and was therefore, under the Missouri Compromise, free territory. After he had been taken back to Missouri, Scott sued for his freedom in Missouri; and the case was eventually carried up on appeal to the Supreme Court. The justices were divided in various ways on several questions that were involved. Essentially, the five justices from slave states held that Scott was still a slave, while the four from the free states divided two and two.

The principal opinion was rendered by eighty-year-old, slaveholding Chief Justice Roger B. Taney, who stated that during colonial times African Americans had "been regarded as beings so far inferior that they had no rights that the white man was bound to respect." Following Taney, the majority of the court held that a person born a slave or the descendant of slaves was not a citizen and therefore could not bring suit in federal courts. In strict logic, therefore, the Court did not need to rule on the other questions Scott raised; however, the Court went on to state that even if Scott could have sued, he still would not have been free, for the Missouri Compromise was unconstitutional because Congress had no power to exclude slavery from the territories.

In a literal sense the Dred Scott decision added nothing new to the debate about the extension of slavery, for it merely declared void a law which had already been repealed by the Kansas-Nebraska Act three years earlier. In another sense, however, it had a shattering effect in that it strengthened a conviction in the North that an evil "slave power," bent on spreading slavery throughout the land, was in control of the government and must be checked. It justified Southerners, conversely, in believing that the free-soilers were trying to deprive them of their legal rights.

It even struck a deadly blow at the one moderate position—that of popular sovereignty—which lay between the extremes of free-soil and proslavery contentions. If, as the Court ruled,

Congress had no power to exclude slavery from a territory by its own act, certainly it could not give a power that it did not possess to the territorial legislatures; and without such power there could be no effective popular sovereignty. It made compromise by act of Congress almost impossible. Slavery, which had been illegal north of the Missouri Compromise line since 1820, was now legal everywhere unless state legislatures passed laws against it. Slaves could now be brought into northern territories such as Oregon or Minnesota.

As for African Americans, the decision was devastating. It convinced many free African Americans that they had no future in a country that denied them citizenship.

The Lincoln-Douglas Debates

The effect of the Dred Scott decision in polarizing sectional extremism showed up clearly in 1858, when Douglas ran for reelection to the Senate from Illinois and was challenged to a series of debates by his Republican opponent, Abraham Lincoln. Lincoln, a former Whig, was deeply opposed to slavery. He regarded it as morally wrong—"if slavery is not wrong then nothing is wrong"—and he insisted that the Dred Scott decision be reversed. Slavery must be kept out of the territories and placed "in the course of ultimate extinction."

MAP 10.8 Presidential Election of 1860

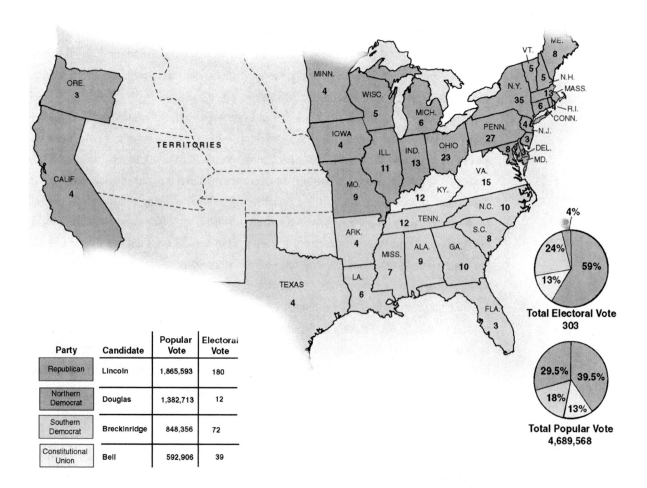

Party	Candidate	Popular Vote	Electoral Vote
Republican	Lincoln	1,865,593	180
Northern Democrat	Douglas	1,382,713	12
Southern Democrat	Breckinridge	848,356	72
Constitutional Union	Bell	592,906	39

Total Electoral Vote 303

Total Popular Vote 4,689,568

However, Lincoln was by no means an abolitionist. He did not advocate racial equality, stating clearly in the debates, "I am not, nor ever have been, in favor of bringing about the social and political equality of the white and black races." Lincoln also opposed African American suffrage, interracial marriage, African American citizenship, the repeal of the fugitive slave act, and allowing African Americans to serve on juries. Lincoln even predicted that slavery would last another hundred years, although he personally favored the repatriation of slaves to Africa.

Lincoln recognized, however, both the complexity of the slavery question and the fact that slavery was protected by constitutional guarantees which he proposed to respect—even to the enforcement of the fugitive slave law. Lincoln defined the dilemma the Dred Scott decision had created for Douglas and for all moderates. If slavery could not be legally excluded from the territories, how could the people of the territory, under popular sovereignty, exclude it? Concerning Southerners, Lincoln phrased the situation, as "they are merely what we would be in their situation."

Douglas replied at Freeport, Illinois (the "Freeport doctrine"), that unless a territory adopted positive laws to protect slavery by local police regulations, slavery could not establish itself. Accordingly, by merely refraining from legislation, lawmakers could keep a territory free. This answer was enough to gain reelection for Douglas, but it cost him what was left of his reputation as a national leader with strong bisectional support. At one time, Southerners had applauded him for repealing the slavery exclusion of the Missouri Compromise. Now they saw him as a man who was supporting the free-soilers in Kansas and who was advocating a theory that would deprive the South of rights guaranteed by a decision of the Supreme Court.

Though Lincoln lost the election for senator, he came to the attention of people throughout the country with his careful exposition of the issues raised by the Dred Scott decision. He

MAP 10.9 Territorial Growth of 1860

consolidated his growing reputation with a speech given at Cooper Union in New York City on February 27, 1860. No doubt aware of the opportunity provided by this forum, Lincoln conducted extensive research on the opinions of signers of the Constitution on the question of slavery in the territories and dazzled his audience with his logic and his erudition. Historian Harold Holzer calls it "the speech that made Abraham Lincoln president."

John Brown's Raid

If the Dred Scott decision brought to a climax the Northern belief that freedom was being dangerously threatened by a sinister conspiracy of the "slave power," John Brown's raid on Harpers Ferry created an even more intense belief below the Mason-Dixon line that abolitionist fanaticism posed an immediate danger to the social order and even to human life in the South. After the "Pottawatomie massacre" in Kansas, Brown had disappeared from the national scene. Then during the night of October 16, 1859, he suddenly descended with a band of eighteen men (including five African Americans) on the town of Harpers Ferry, Virginia, seized the federal arsenal there, and called upon the slaves to rise and claim their freedom.

Brown's plan was to arm the slaves that he expected to flock to his side for a massive revolt, after which an African American republic would be established in the Virginia mountains; and he and his supporters would wage a war against the slaveholding South. Exactly how Brown planned to have droves of slaves hear of his actions, get away from their plantations, and join his rebellion is a mystery known only to Brown. Instead, no slaves arrived to join the revolt, and within thirty-six hours Brown was captured by federal troops under the command of Robert E. Lee. Ten of Brown's men were killed in the gun battle, and Brown was charged with treason, conspiracy, and murder. Later he was tried and hanged, but not before playing the role of the perfect martyr for Northern abolitionists. Brown proclaimed, "If it is deemed necessary that I should forfeit my life for the furtherance of the ends of justice ... I say let it be done."

Brown's action had touched the South differently and at its most sensitive nerve—its fear of the kind of slave insurrection that had caused immense slaughter at Santo Domingo at the beginning of the century and had periodically threatened to erupt in the South itself. Southern alarm and resentment would perhaps have been less great if the North had denounced Brown's act—as many Northerners, including Lincoln, had done. The fact soon came out that Brown had received financial support from some of the most respected figures in Boston, and the day of his execution became one of public mourning in New England. Brown was called Saint John the Just, and Henry David Thoreau publicly spoke in support of Brown. Similarly, Ralph Waldo Emerson wrote an essay about Brown entitled, "Courage," in which Emerson argued that Brown would "make the gallows glorious like the cross."

The Election of 1860

By 1860, developments were rapidly moving toward a showdown. For more than a decade, sectional dissension had been destroying the institutions that held the American people together in national unity. In 1844 it had split the Methodist Church, and in 1845 the Baptist church

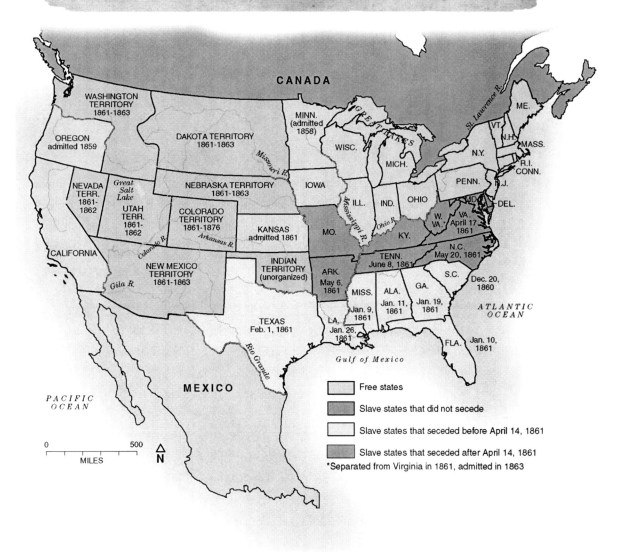

MAP 10.10 The United States on the Eve of the Civil War

Free states

Slave states that did not secede

Slave states that seceded before April 14, 1861

Slave states that seceded after April 14, 1861

*Separated from Virginia in 1861, admitted in 1863

had divided into separate Northern and Southern bodies. Between 1852 and 1856, sectionalism had split the Whig Party, and as matters now stood, the Democratic Party was the only remaining major national institution, outside of the government itself. In 1860, with another presidential election approaching, the Democratic organization, already strained by the tension between the Buchanan and the Douglas wings, also broke apart.

The Democrats

Meeting at Charleston, the Democratic Convention was divided on the question of the platform. Douglas Democrats wanted a plank that promised, in general terms, to abide by the decisions of the Supreme Court, but which avoided explicit expression of support for slavery in the territories. Southern Democrats, led by William L. Yancey, a famous orator from Alabama, wanted a categorical affirmation that slavery would be protected in the territories. When the

Douglas forces secured the adoption of their plank, Yancey and most of the delegates from the cotton states walked out of the convention.

The accusation was later made that they did this as part of a deliberate plan or conspiracy to divide the Union by splitting the Democratic Party, letting the Republicans win, and consequently creating a situation which caused the South to secede. Indeed, many of those who bolted were hoping, however, to force Northern Democrats to come to terms or to throw the election to Congress, where there was a chance that the South might have won. For weeks, desperate efforts were made to reunite the Democrats, but in the end the Northern wing of the party nominated Douglas and the Southern wing nominated John C. Breckinridge of Kentucky, vice-president under Buchanan.

Some of the conservative successors of the Whigs, now calling themselves Constitutional Unionists, nominated John Bell of Tennessee for president and Edward Everett for vice-president on a platform that said nothing about the territorial question and called only for "the Constitution, the Union, and the enforcement of the laws."

The Republican Victory

The principal opposition to Douglas came from the Republicans, whose convention was meeting at a new building called the Wigwam in Chicago. The leading candidate before the convention was Senator William H. Seward from New York, who had been the foremost Republican for some years. His talent for coining memorable phrases—"a higher law than the Constitution" and "the irrepressible conflict between freedom and slavery"—had won him a reputation for extremism. The Republicans, seeing a good chance of victory after the Democratic split, decided to move in a conservative direction in order not to jeopardize their prospects. Accordingly, they nominated Abraham Lincoln, who had made his reputation in the debates with Douglas, but who had never been militant on the slavery question. To balance this nomination they made Hannibal Hamlin, a former Democrat from Maine, their vice-presidential candidate.

To win, the Republicans needed only to hold what they had won in 1856 and to capture Pennsylvania and either Illinois or Indiana, which Buchanan had carried. As the election turned out, they won every free state except New Jersey (part of which went to Douglas), while Breckinridge won all the slave states except Virginia, Kentucky, and Tennessee (which went to Bell) and Missouri (which went to Douglas). Douglas ran a strong second in popular votes but a weak fourth in electoral votes, while Lincoln was in the curious position of winning with only 40 percent of the popular vote. His victory resulted not from the division of his opponents, however, but from the fact that his strength was strategically distributed. His victories in many of the free states were narrow, and he received no votes at all in ten Southern states. Thus the distribution of his popular votes had maximum effectiveness in winning electoral votes.

Secession

Lincoln's victory at last precipitated the sectional split which had been brewing for a long time. As we can now see in the light of later events, Lincoln was moderate-minded and would have respected the legal rights of the South even though he deplored slavery. To the South, however, fearful of Northern aggression, his victory was a signal of imminent danger. Here was a man who had said that a house divided against itself could not stand and that the Union could not continue permanently half slave and half free. To the South he denied rights in the territories that the Supreme Court had said that the South possessed. He was supported by militant antislavery men; and his victory clearly represented the imposition of a president by one section upon the other, for 99 percent of his vote had come in the free states.

Southerners had controlled the United States government most of the time since its inception. Although, as we have already seen, there was some diversity in their political opinion, especially before 1845, their prominence had been a matter of pride in the South and increasingly a matter of concern in the North. From 1789 to 1861, twenty-five of the thirty-six Presidents pro tempore of the Senate and twenty-four of the thirty-six Speakers of the House were Southerners. Twenty of the thirty-five Supreme Court justices were from the South. A Southerner was Chief Justice during all but twelve of these years, and at all times the South had a majority of justices on the Supreme Court. During forty-nine of these seventy-two years, the President of the United States was a Southerner—and a slaveholder. In addition, during twelve additional years, including most of the crucial 1850s, the presidents were Democratic from the North who were sometimes more pro-South than Southerners themselves might have dared to be.

The slaveholders regarded the 1860 election as a political revolution that foreshadowed a future dominated by the ideology and institutions of the North. To the South, this was a disaster, and a counterrevolution of independence seemed the only answer.

Proponents of secession invoked the doctrine that each state had retained its sovereignty when it joined the Union. Therefore, in the exercise of this sovereignty, each state, acting through a special convention like the conventions that had ratified the Constitution, might secede from the Union. As soon as it learned of Lincoln's election, the South Carolina legislature called a convention to take the state out of the Union. Within six weeks the six other states of

▶ The Confederates attacked Fort Sumter at dawn. Bombarded with Confederate battery, the Union fort surrendered after twenty-six hours of furious shelling. The battle of Fort Sumter marked the beginning of a war that lasted four years and was one of the greatest military conflicts the world had seen up to that time. *Wikipedia photo*

the lower South—Mississippi, Florida, Alabama, Georgia, Louisiana, and Texas—also called conventions. Delegates were elected by popular vote after short but intensive campaigns. Each convention voted by a substantial and, in most cases an overwhelming, majority to secede. By February 9, 1861, three months after Lincoln's election but almost a month before his inauguration, delegates from the seven seceded states had met in Montgomery, Alabama, to adopt a provisional Constitution for the Confederate States of America and to elect Jefferson Davis and Alexander Stephens as provisional President and Vice-President of the new republic.

The Failure of Compromise

The actual arrival of disunion, which had been dreaded for so long, evoked strenuous efforts at compromise—especially by leaders in the border slave states, where loyalty to the Union was combined with sympathy for the South. From Kentucky, Senator John J. Crittenden, heir to the compromise tradition of Henry Clay, introduced proposals in Congress to revise and extend the Missouri Compromise line by constitutional amendment. Virginia took the lead in convening a Peace Convention, with delegates from twenty-one states, which met in Washington in February. Congress actually adopted a proposed amendment that would have guaranteed slavery in the states that wanted to keep it. This amendment was submitted to the states for ratification before the war came and made it obsolete.

President Buchanan professed himself powerless to prevent the secession. Buchanan denounced the action as illegal, but as a lame duck president, did not want to commit his successor to any course of action. In the meantime, the nation waited to see if the incoming President Lincoln would attempt to preserve the Union by force or peacefully allow the secession.

Unlike Buchanan, Lincoln was unwilling to make any concessions that would compromise the basic Republican principle of excluding slavery from the territories. The Crittenden Compromise would have permitted slavery in all territories south of 36°30'. In view of the South's appetite for the acquisition of new slave territory in the Caribbean and Central America, Republicans feared that adoption of such a compromise "would amount to a perpetual covenant of war against every people, tribe, and State owning a foot of land between here and Terra del Fuego" and turn the United States into "a great slave breeding and slave extending empire." Therefore, the Crittenden Compromise was defeated. In any case, it is unlikely that adoption of this or any other compromise would have stemmed the tide of secession in the lower South, where by February 1, the Confederacy was a *fait accompli*.

Fort Sumter

When Lincoln was inaugurated on March 4, 1861, he was faced by a new Southern republic where seven states of the Union had been. This new Confederacy had seized federal post offices, customs houses, arsenals, and even federal forts, with the exception of Fort Sumter in Charleston harbor and Fort Pickens in Pensacola harbor. The federal forts in the South were by and large manned by Southerners and commanded by Southerners in the U.S. army who turned over their forts to the Confederates without a shot. In Texas alone, eighteen federal forts, along with all of their provisions, were handed to the Confederates without a fight. From North Carolina to the Rio Grande, these were the only two places where the Stars and Stripes still flew. There was great speculation at the time as to what position Lincoln would take, and there has been great dispute among historians since then as to what position he actually *did* take.

Certainly he made it absolutely clear that he denied the right of any state to secede and that he intended to preserve the Union. In his inaugural address, Lincoln denounced the secession as illegal; however, whether he intended to wage war in order to preserve it was not so clear. Lincoln also proclaimed that the North and South were not enemies, but friends. Furthermore, there were eight slave states (Virginia, North Carolina, Kentucky, Tennessee, Missouri, Arkansas, Maryland, and Delaware) still in the Union, and Lincoln was extremely eager to keep them loyal. As long as they remained in the Union, there was at least the possibility that they might help to bring the other slave states back. This split among the slave states represented a failure on the part of the secessionists to create a united South. Therefore, Lincoln had every reason to refrain from hasty action.

If he had been able to maintain the federal position at Fort Pickens and Fort Sumter, or even at one of them, he apparently would have been prepared to play a waiting game. However, less than twenty-four hours after becoming president he learned that Major Robert Anderson, commander at Fort Sumter, was running out of supplies and would soon have to surrender unless food was sent to him. Lincoln apparently gave serious consideration to the possibility of surrendering Sumter, and he might have done so if he had been able to reinforce Fort Pickens and make it the symbol of an unbroken Union. Attempts to reinforce Pickens, however, were delayed. On April 6, Lincoln sent a message to the governor of South Carolina that supplies would be sent to Sumter, but no military reinforcement would be attempted. The Southerners allowed the supplies in to the Union fort on Southern territory.

Historians have disputed whether this was a promise not to start shooting if supplies were allowed or a threat to start shooting if they were not allowed. In any event, the Confederate government decided that the supplies could not be allowed. On April 12, 1861, after Major Anderson had rejected a formal demand for surrender, Confederate batteries opened a bombardment before dawn that forced Fort Sumter to surrender without casualties after thirty-three hours of furious shelling.

On April 15, Lincoln issued a call for the loyal states to furnish 75,000 militia to suppress the Southern "insurrection." All the free states responded with alacrity and enthusiasm. The four slave states of Virginia, North Carolina, Tennessee, and Arkansas responded by seceding and joining the Confederacy as they had promised they would. The other four slave states—Maryland, Delaware, Kentucky, and Missouri—remained uneasily in the Union, though many of their men went south to fight for the Confederacy. The bombardment of Fort Sumter marked the beginning of a war that lasted four years.

"Causes of the Civil War"

Ever since 1861, writers have disputed what caused the Civil War and whether it was an "irrepressible conflict" in the sense of being inevitable. Southerners have argued that the war was fought not over slavery but over the question of states' rights. Several of the Confederate states,

▶ Hinton Rowan Helper: Antislavery Southerner

Hinton Rowan Helper was the self-proclaimed spokesman for the nonslaveholding whites who constituted three fourths of Southern white families. His book *The Impending Crisis* ranks with *Uncle Tom's Cabin* as one of the most important documents of the growing sectional conflict. It provoked a crisis in Congress and helped bring on the Civil War. In the end, however, Helper achieved little that he had hoped for and died of self-inflicted violence.

Hinton Rowan Helper was born December 27, 1829, in a section of North Carolina populated mainly by small farmers. After working as a youth on his father's farm and gaining a respectable education at a local academy, Helper went west in 1850 to seek his fortune in the newly opened goldfields of California. His unhappy failures there caused him to return east and publish in 1855 a derogatory book about California, *The Land of Gold*. The book's failure further disappointed him, and he poured some of the bitterness from this disappointment into the writing of his second and far more significant book, *The Impending Crisis*, published two years later.

Using selected statistics from the 1850 census, Helper portrayed a South stagnating in economic backwardness, while the free-labor North strode forward in seven-league boots. He contrasted the nearly universal literacy and comfortable living standard of Northern farmers and workers with the apparent ignorance and poverty of Southern "poor whites." The cause? "Slavery lies at the root of all the shame, poverty, ignorance, tyranny, and imbecility of the South," wrote Helper. Slavery monopolized the best land, degraded all labor to the level of bond labor, denied schools to workers, and impoverished all but the "lords of the lash" who "are not only absolute masters of the blacks [but] of all nonslaveholding whites, whose freedom is merely nominal, and whose unparalleled illiteracy and degradation is purposely and fiendishly perpetuated."

Although he demanded the total abolition of slavery, Helper wasted no sympathy on the slaves; he wanted them shipped back to Africa. His book was aimed at the nonslaveholders—who, like himself, disliked slavery because they disliked African Americans and resented their competition as laborers. Helper therefore assumed that the nonslaveholding whites would rally to the antislavery standard. He urged them to form state Republican parties in the South, use their votes to overthrow the slaveholders' rule, and free themselves from the curse of bondage.

Few nonslaveholding Southern whites read his message, however. No Southern printer had dared to publish the book, so Helper moved from his native North Carolina to the North to get it published in New York. *The Impending Crisis* was virtually banned in the South; some states even made it a criminal offense to possess or circulate copies of it.

Even if Southern whites had been able to read the book, however, it is unlikely that many of them would have accepted its arguments. Helper underestimated the strength of the ties that bound most whites, slaveholder and nonslaveholder alike, in a common culture. Although many residents of the South's upland and mountain regions were hostile to the plantation regime, most nonslaveholders elsewhere (who were the numerical majority of whites in the South) were loyal to the "Southern way of life," including slavery. Many were relatives of slaveholders. Others aspired to become slave-owners themselves. Even most whites who had no connection with slavery or the planters supported the "peculiar institution" as the best means of controlling African Americans and maintaining white supremacy.

The principle effect of *The Impending Crisis* in the South was to create a defensive-aggressive reaction to its popularity in the North. Republicans praised the book's economic indictment of slavery as a forceful expression of their own free-labor views. Leading Republicans raised money to print an abridged edition and distributed it as a campaign document in the Congressional elections of 1858. This angered Southerners and contributed to one of the most serious sectional impasse in the history of Congress.

Republicans had a plurality but not a majority in the House of Representatives that convened in December 1859. Because their candidate for Speaker had endorsed Helper's book, the Democrats and ex-Whig conservatives refused to vote for him. The House remained deadlocked over the election of Speaker of the House for eight weeks until a compromise candidate finally won on the forty-fourth ballot. Tempers grew short, Northern and Southern congressmen hurled insults at each other, and nearly every member came to the House armed. Many observers actually expected a shootout on the floor of Congress. When war came, a little more than a year later, the clash over Helper's book was remembered as one of the many sectional irritants that had burst the bonds of Union.

During these years Helper lived in the North and tried with indifferent success to make a living as a lecturer. Described by a contemporary as a "tall, slim, peculiar-looking person, with short black hair, whiskers and a mustache, a very bronzed complexion, and a fierce military expression," Helper had become one of the most-hated men in the country as far as slaveholders were concerned. A North Carolina senator denounced him in a scathing congressional speech. Outraged and insulted, Helper rushed to the floor of the Senate and engaged the senator in a rough-and-tumble fistfight. Sympathetic Republicans paid his fine.

In 1861 President Lincoln appointed Helper as U.S. Consul in Buenos Aires, where he served until 1866. While there he married an Argentine woman. After his return home his dislike for African Americans turned into a pathological hatred. Sensitive of his heritage as a "poor white" and plagued by a sense of failure, he made African Americans the scapegoats for the frustration and disappointments of his career. His 1867 book, *Nojoque: A Question for a Continent,* reaffirmed his earlier goal to "write the negro out of America" and expressed a desire "to write him out of existence." Another book of similar tenor, *Negroes in Negroland,* followed in 1868. Helper denounced the Republican Reconstruction program of equal rights for freed slaves. This time he received a much more sympathetic hearing in the South.

Much of the remainder of Helper's life was consumed in futile attempts to promote a trunk railroad from Canada to Argentina. During these years he made a scanty living as a lobbyist in Washington for claims against South American countries. In 1899 his wife left him. On March 8, 1909, living alone and in poverty in Washington, he took his own life.

they point out, seceded only when the others had been attacked. Economic determinists have contended that the Northern public never would support the abolitionists on any direct question (which is certainly true), that Lincoln did not even venture to issue the Emancipation Proclamation until the war had been in progress for a year and five months (which is also true), and that the conflict was really between an industrial interest which wanted one kind of future for America and an agrarian interest which wanted another. Other historians, going a step beyond this, have pictured the North and the South as two "diverse civilizations," so dissimilar in their culture and their values that union between them was artificial and unnatural.

Many historians emphasize the idea that Northerners and Southerners had formed distorted and false concepts of each other and that they went to war against these images rather than against the people they were really fighting. The war, they argued, grew out of emotions, not out of realities. Abraham Lincoln had no intention of leading a crusade against slavery in the South, but the southerners perceived that he did. That perception, unsupported by facts, became their reality.

Every one of these points of view has something to be said for it. The causes of the Civil War were certainly not simple; however, although each of the explanations points to something other than slavery, it is significant that the factor of slavery was involved in all of them. It is accurate that the South believed in the right of the states to secede whereas the North did not, but this belief would have remained an abstraction and never been acted upon if the Republican crusade against extending slavery had not impelled the South to use the secession weapon. Southerners were steadfast in their claim to states' rights, but it could be argued that the primary right that the Southern states claimed was the right to keep their slaves. At least to a degree then, the states' rights argument remained very much an argument about slavery. Evidence in support of this fact is present in the "Declaration of Causes" for secession in many Southern states, where slavery was mentioned prominently. For example, the declared "Causes" from the Secessionist Convention in Texas in 1861 included the following:

- The general government of the United States had administered the common territory so as to exclude Southern people from it (in other words, Congress had attempted to ban slavery in the Western territories).

- The Northern people had become inimical to the South and to their beneficent and patriarchal system of African slavery, preaching the debasing doctrine of the equality of all men, irrespective of race or color.

- The slaveholding states had become a minority, unable to defend themselves against northern aggression against slavery.

- The extremists of the North had elected as President and Vice-President two men whose chief claims to such high positions were the approval of the above wrongs, and these men were pledged to the final ruin of the slaveholding South.

Texans mentioned two more causes, blaming the U.S. government for the carnage in Kansas (which was, of course, also related to slavery) and for failing to defend Texans against raids from

Native Americans and Mexican banditos. Taken together, the Texans' statements suggest that the states' rights argument may have been, at least partly, Southern propaganda to aid the South in their struggle to gain European (especially British) support for their cause, while the real cause was simply slavery. England was decidedly abolitionist and could not violate its own collective moral conscience to aid the South in a war to retain slavery. Aiding the South in its struggle for "states' rights," however, was much more palatable to the English sense of morality.

Slavery was clearly important as a moral issue, but also as an economic institution that divided two different, and in many ways antagonistic, societies. Both of these societies—the modernizing, free-labor, capitalist North and the conservative, agrarian, slave labor South—were expansionist. Each believed that its social system must expand into the new territories in order to survive. Each saw the expansion of the other as a threat to its own future.

It is difficult to imagine that without slavery the general dissimilarities between North and South, even their social and cultural separateness, would have been brought into such sharp focus as to precipitate a war. It is true that in the 1850s extremist leaders came to the fore, and each section formed an emotional stereotype rather than a realistic picture of the other. (See "Hinton Rowan Helper: Antislavery Southerner.") However, this is a process that typically occurs as antagonism deepens.

Slavery furnished the emotional voltage that led to deep distrust and dislike in each section for the people of the other. In his second inaugural, Abraham Lincoln said, "All know that slavery was somehow the cause of the war." The operative word in his statement was "somehow," for the war was not in any simple sense a fight between crusaders for freedom all on one side and believers in slavery all on the other. Robert E. Lee, to name but one Southerner, did not support slavery; and many Northern soldiers who were willing to die, if need be, for the Union were deeply opposed to making slavery an issue of the war. It is also true, however, that antislavery Southerners and proslavery Northerners were caught in the web woven by the issue of slavery.

Could this issue have been settled without war? Was the crisis artificial? Was the territorial question a contest over "an imaginary Negro in an impossible place"? Was war really necessary in a situation where it seems doubtful that a majority of Southerners wanted to secede (only seven out of fifteen slave states seceded before the firing on Fort Sumter) or that a majority of Northerners wanted to make an issue of slavery? (Lincoln had only 40 percent of the popular vote, and he promised security for slavery where it was already established.) Were the American people, both North and South, so much alike in their religion (overwhelmingly evangelical Protestant), their speech (American variants of English), their ethnic descent (mostly British, Irish, and German), their democratic beliefs, their pioneer ways, their emphasis upon the values of self-reliance and hard work, their veneration for the Constitution, and even their boastful Americanism—were they so much alike that a war between them could and should have been avoided? This in turn raises the question whether disagreements are any less bitter among parties who have much in common.

What was happening in America was that the center of gravity was gradually shifting from a loosely organized agricultural society to a modern industrial society with much greater concentration of power. As this happened, the United States was being transformed from a loose association of separately powerful states to a consolidated nation in which the states would be little more than political subdivisions. In America's startling growth, the North had outstripped the South and the equilibrium that previously existed between them had been destroyed. The proposal of the victorious Republicans to confine slavery—and in this sense to exclude the South from further participation in the nation's growth—dramatized this shift in equilibrium. It seems most unlikely that the South would ever have accepted the political consequences of this basic change without a crisis, especially since Southern whites greatly feared the possibility that a preponderant North in control of the federal government might ultimately use its power to abolish slavery. Southerners well understood that if the entire frontier west of Missouri eventually came into the Union as free territory, slavery would exist only in the southeastern geographic quarter of the continent. Thus, the free soil areas would eventually have the votes in Congress to eliminate slavery democratically.

The brooding presence of race permeated this issue. Slavery was more than an institution to exploit cheap labor. It was a means of controlling a large and potentially threatening African American population and of maintaining white supremacy. Any hint of a threat to the "Southern way of life," which was based on the subordination of a group both scorned and feared, was bound to arouse deep and irrational phobias and to create a crisis. Whether this crisis had to take the form of armed conflict and whether this phase of armed force had to occur precisely when it did—or might have come a month, a year, or a decade sooner or later—would seem to be a matter for endless speculation.

Chapter Review ▶ ▶ ▶

Summary

By the mid-nineteenth century America had spread across the continent and essentially fulfilled its "Manifest Destiny" after a War with Mexico had secured the Southwestern United States and Oregon Territory was gained from England by Treaty, but the nation remained divided sectionally between North and South, each with its unique cultural features. In the South, the economy was dominated by plantation agriculture built on slave labor while in the North, though most people still engaged in agriculture, a manufacturing economy was quickly developing. The two sections had different economic interests (higher tariffs in the North to protect manufacturing and lower tariffs in the South to help boost agricultural exports) and were suspicious of each other. The 3/5 compromise gave the Southern states disproportionate strength in Congress, which caused the Northerners to oppose the extension of slavery into the Western territories in an effort to check Southern slave power.

The issue boiled over in 1854 when Illinois Senator Stephen Douglas proposed that popular sovereignty should settle the slavery question in the Territory of Kansas. Proslavery citizens from Missouri poured into Kansas and voted illegally, establishing a fraudulent proslavery government and proslavery Constitution that was eventually rejected by Kansas voters. Meanwhile, John Brown touched off a wave of violence that led to the violent death of 200 citizens after he and his followers lynched five proslavery citizens at Pottawatomie Creek.

The Supreme Court added fuel to the fire in 1857 with its ruling in the Dred Scott case, where it ruled that Dred Scott, a former slave, was property and that the part of the Missouri Compromise that prohibited slavery in the territories was unconstitutional under the 5th Amendment because Congress could not deny anyone their property.

John Brown stirred up more controversy in 1859 after he and his followers attempted to take over a federal arsenal at Harpers Ferry, Virginia in an effort to instigate a slave revolt. Abolitionists, such as Ralph Waldo Emerson praised Brown as the "perfect martyr" before Brown was sent to the gallows.

Abraham Lincoln was elected President in 1860 on the Republican Party ticket without winning any Southern States. Given that Republicans opposed the extension of slavery in the territories, Southern states, led by South Carolina, viewed his election as a threat to slavery and the "Southern way of life" and seceded from the Union. When Fort Sumter in Charleston Harbor refused to capitulate, and Lincoln gave an order to re-supply the fort, Southerners shelled the fort until it surrendered, and the Civil War had begun.

Chapter Review (cont'd)

Chronological Time Line

1804	Congress prohibits the importation of slaves from Africa
1831	Nat Turner's Revolt.
1833	Great Britain abolishes slavery in the West Indies
1848	France abolishes slavery
1848	Treaty of Guadalupe Hidalgo.
1849	Gold Rush in California
1850	Compromise of 1850 admits California as a free state and settles border dispute with Texas, but includes Fugitive Slave Act.
1851	Harriet Beecher Stowe publishes *Uncle Tom's Cabin*
1852	Franklin Pierce elected President
1854	Stephen Douglas proposes "popular sovereignty" as a solution to the slavery question in the territories in his Kansas-Nebraska Bill
1854	Gadsden Purchase.
1855	Fraudulent Election for Kansas Legislature
1856	John Brown murders five proslavery citizens in Kansas. 200 more die in "bleeding Kansas" in the 6 months that follow.
1857	*Dred Scott* Decision
1858	Kansas voters reject the Lecompton Constitution
1858	Lincoln-Douglas debates
1859	John Brown's Raid
1860	Abraham Lincoln elected President
1860	South Carolina secedes in December
1861	Seven seceded states create Confederate States of America
1861	April 12, Confederates fire first shots of the Civil War at Fort Sumter

Key Terms

Sectionalism: Antagonism between the Northern and Southern states

The Southern way of life: An agricultural export economy predicated on African slave labor

Nat Turner: Led the bloodiest slave revolt in American history in 1831

"Fifty-four forty or fight": James Polk's 1844 campaign slogan regarding the dispute with Britain over Oregon

The Wilmot Proviso: A resolution in the House of Representatives introduced by David Wilmot proposing that slavery should be prohibited in any territory acquired from Mexico. This free-soil resolution passed the House, where the North was stronger, but failed to pass in the Senate, where the South had equal strength.

Popular sovereignty: The idea that the slavery question could be settled in each territory through the popular vote of its citizens

Free Soil Party: Party that arose in 1848 in opposition to slavery in the territories

Lewis Cass: Michigan Senator who called for popular sovereignty to settle the question of slavery in the territories.

Zachary Taylor: General and hero of the war with Mexico, elected President in 1848

Compromise of 1850: California is admitted as a free state and a border dispute is settled with Texas. Includes the controversial Fugitive Slave Act.

Steven A. Douglas: Introduced the Kansas-Nebraska Bill in 1854 with a provision for popular sovereignty in the territory. Defeated Lincoln for the U.S. Senate after a famous debate in 1858.

Millard Fillmore: Became President in 1850 after Zachary Taylor died in office.

Fugitive Slave Act: Unpopular law that required that northerners help southerners capture fugitive slaves in the North and return them to enslavement in the South

Underground Railroad: System of safe houses and contacts that helped slaves flee to freedom in the North.

Franklin Pierce: Elected President of the U.S. in 1852 and known for alcoholism and his support of slavery.

Bleeding Kansas: Political unrest over slavery in Kansas in 1854 that led to the death of 200 persons

Harriet Beecher Stowe: Author of *Uncle Tom's Cabin*

Emigrant Aid Society: Organized in New England in 1854 by antislavery advocates to send free-soil settlers to Kansas.

Republican Party: Arose to replace the Whigs in 1856 in opposition to slavery in the territories.

James Buchanan: President that supported the Lecompton Constitution and took no action when South Carolina seceded.

Preston Brooks: South Carolina Congressman that beat Massachusetts Senator Charles Sumner with his cane on the floor of the Senate.

Ostend Manifesto: Three American emissaries in Ostend, Belgium, in October 1854 proposed American annexation of Cuba by purchase or, if that failed, by "wresting it from Spain."

Lecompton Constitution: A proslavery Constitution voted down by Kansas voters in 1858.

Dred Scott v. Sandford: Supreme Court decision in 1857 that struck down the power of Congress to prohibit slavery because slaves were property that could not be denied to any property owner by the 5th Amendment.

Chapter Review (cont'd)

Key Terms (cont'd)

John Brown: Antislavery fanatic that murdered five proslavery citizens in Kansas in 1856, took over a federal arsenal in 1859, and was executed for treason.

Harpers Ferry: Site of federal arsenal raided by John Brown and his followers

Emerson's "Courage": Essay by Ralph Waldo Emerson extolling John Brown as a martyr for abolition and claiming that Brown would make the gallows as glorious as the cross.

Election of 1860: Won by Republican Abraham Lincoln, but he won no Southern states.

Secession: Led by South Carolina in December, 1860 in opposition to Lincoln's election and the Republican platform that opposed slavery in the territories.

Confederate States: South Carolina and ten other Southern states that seceded from the U.S. and formed their own Confederacy.

Fort Sumter: Site of the first shots of the Civil War where Southerners fired on a Union fort that refused to turn over possession to the Confederacy.

Hinton Rowan Helper: Antislavery Southerner and author of *The Impending Crisis.*

Sources Consulted

Stephanie M. H. Camp, *Closer to Freedom: Enslaved Women and Everyday Resistance in the Plantation South* (2004).

Nicole Etcheson, *Bleeding Kansas: Contested Liberty in the Civil War Era* (2004).

Don E. Fehrenbacher, *The Dred Scott Case: Its Significance in American Law and Politics* (1978).

Don E. Fehrenbacher, *Slavery, Law, and Politics: The Dred Scott Case in Historical Perspective* (1981).

Eric Foner, *Free Soil, Free Labor, Free Men: The Ideology of the Republican Party before the Civil War* (1995).

Eugene D. Genovese, *The Political Economy of Slavery: Studies in the Economy and Society of the Slave South* (1989).

Doris Kearns Goodwin, *Team of Rivals: The Political Genius of Abraham Lincoln* (2005).

Harold Holzer, *Lincoln at Cooper Union: The Speech that Made Abraham Lincoln President* (2004).

Lawrence W. Levine, *Black Culture and Black Consciousness: Afro-American Folk Thought from Slavery to Freedom* (2008).

David M. Potter, *The Impending Crisis 1848–1861* (1976).

David S. Reynolds, *John Brown: Abolitionist* (2005).

Sources (cont'd)

Kenneth M. Stampp, America in 1857: A Nation on the Brink (1990).

Kenneth Winkle, The Young Eagle: The Rise of Abraham Lincoln (2003).

Gerald W. Wolff, *The Kansas-Nebraska Bill: Party, Section, and the Coming of the Civil War* (1977).

iStockphotos

11 The War Between the States, 1861–1865

Outline

Wikipedia photo

Wikipedia photo

Wikipedia photo

iStockphoto

Corbis Images

Bob

The Blue and The Gray

The "American" War

The War Between the States lasted four years, from April 1861 to April 1865. The war has been referred to as the American Civil War, the War of Northern Aggression, and the War Between the States. Southerners who blame northerners for the war call it the "War of Northern Aggression," but this connotes fault to northerners for the war. Northerners usually refer to the war as the Civil War but many southerners disagree with the name because a "civil war" is defined as two groups fighting for control of a national government. The southern states of the Confederacy were fighting for independence, not for control over the national government. Therefore, the most neutral term to use is the "War Between the States."

From a total of 14 million white males, 2.9 million were in uniform—2.1 million for the Union and eight hundred thousand for the Confederacy. This was over 20 percent of all white males—a higher proportion than in any other American war. The highest participation rate of any state was from Texas, where a staggering 75 percent of men between the ages of eighteen and forty-five served in the Confederate army. The Union total included 180,000 African American soldiers and perhaps twenty thousand African American sailors, nearly one tenth of the men in the Northern armed forces. Either as battle casualties or as victims of camp maladies, 618,000 men died in service (360,000 Union troops and 258,000 Confederates). More than one soldier in five lost his life—a far heavier ratio of losses than in any other war in American history. For the Confederate soldiers it was one in three.

Partly because the cost was proportionately so heavy, and partly because the war was distinctly an American war, this conflict has occupied a place in the American memory and the

MAP 11.1 Population Density (1860)

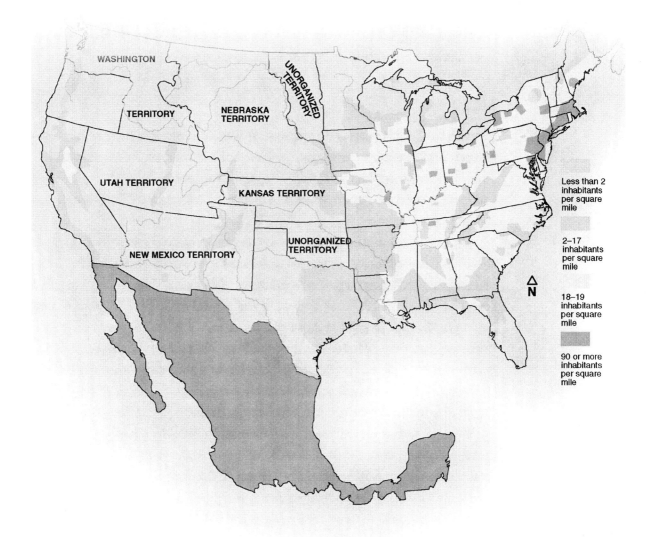

WASHINGTON

UNORGANIZED TERRITORY

TERRITORY

NEBRASKA TERRITORY

UTAH TERRITORY

KANSAS TERRITORY

NEW MEXICO TERRITORY

UNORGANIZED TERRITORY

Less than 2 inhabitants per square mile

2–17 inhabitants per square mile

18–19 inhabitants per square mile

90 or more inhabitants per square mile

N

American imagination that other wars—more recent, more destructive overall, and fought on a global scale—have never held. On both sides, men were fighting for what they deeply believed to be American values.

Southerners were convinced that their right to form a Confederacy was based on a principle of the *Declaration of Independence*—that governments derive their just powers from the consent of the governed. They were also fighting to defend their states from invasion. "All we ask is to be let alone," said Jefferson Davis in his first war message to the Confederate Congress. Early in the war some Union soldiers captured a Southern soldier, who from his tattered homespun butternut uniform was obviously not a member of the planter class. They asked him why he, a nonslaveholder, was fighting to uphold slavery. "I'm fighting because y'all are down here," was his reply.

The North was fighting to defend the flag and to prove that a democracy was not too weak to hold together. Secession was the "essence of anarchy," said Lincoln. "The central idea pervading this struggle is the necessity of proving that popular government is not an absurdity. We must settle this question now, whether in a free government the minority have the right to break up the government whenever they choose." Abolition of slavery was not a motivation for most people in the North at all at the outset of the war. Instead, the abolition of slavery became a purpose in 1863 when Abraham Lincoln believed that the North needed a greater moral purpose as motivation. Until that time, preserving the Union was the primary Northern motive, and Lincoln found it insufficient to stir the masses by the end of 1862. Thus, the greater moral purpose was added.

Lincoln

Long after these events, people who had grown up with an oversimplified image of Lincoln as a Great Emancipator became disillusioned by this record, and in the ensuing century and a half, some critics have sought to tear down his reputation, but he remains a figure of immense stature, and scholars and popular biographers continue to find nuances of his personality and achievements to explore.

Born in 1809 in a log cabin in Kentucky, Lincoln grew up on the frontier in Indiana and Illinois, doing rough work as a rail splitter and a plowboy and receiving only a meager education. Lincoln's early life was filled with tragedy as his grandfather (the senior Abraham Lincoln) bequeathed none of his 5,544 acres to Abraham's father (Thomas Lincoln) and left it all in his will to Abraham's uncle Mordecai. Thomas Lincoln was then cheated out of the land he owned in Kentucky by land speculators who paid off crooked surveyors to allow them to stake claims to his land. The family moved to Indiana in 1816 where tragedy struck again as Abraham's mother, Nancy, died of "milk sickness" after drinking milk from cows that had eaten the poisonous white snakeroot plant. Thomas remarried Sarah Bush, with whom Abe had a good relationship, but she too died in 1829.

Young Abraham spent two years on a flatboat on the Mississippi River and then managed a general store in New Salem, Illinois. When the store failed in 1834, Lincoln began his political career by becoming postmaster of New Salem. That same year, Lincoln ran and won a seat in the Illinois State legislature at age twenty-five, primarily because he needed the pay. After becoming a legislator, Lincoln realized he would benefit from studying law, so he studied law on his own and passed the bar. Later he practiced law with a partner in Springfield, and rode the circuit on horseback to follow the sessions of the court.

Lincoln's personal life of tragedy, however, continued. In 1835, Lincoln fell in love with a short, plump woman named Ann Rutledge, who tragically died of "brain fever." Lincoln, unfortunately sunk into a fit of depression and would suffer from bouts of depression for much of the rest of his adult life. Later in 1844 Lincoln stated that "I am now the most miserable man living. If what I felt were equally distributed to the whole human race, there would not be one cheerful face on earth." Lincoln refused to carry a penknife out of fear that he might become self-destructive in a fit of depression, and on numerous occasions he cleared his house of all sharp objects so as to help eliminate any self-destructive temptations. Lincoln's law partner blamed his depression on chronic constipation, but it may have also been related to the medicine he took for his depression known as "blue mass," the ingredients of which included licorice, rose water, dead rose petals, honey, sugar, and mercury. Symptoms of mercury poisoning include insomnia, tremors, and rage attacks, all suffered by Lincoln. Lincoln himself eventually made the connection and quit taking blue mass a few months into his Presidency because it made him "cross."

▶ Mary Lincoln, First Lady and wife of Abraham Lincoln, was known for being a volatile woman. On one occasion, Mary chased Abe out of the house with a butcher knife. She also spent extravagantly and racked up sizeable debt without Abe's knowledge. *Corbis Images*

After the death of Rutledge, Lincoln had another failed relationship with a woman named Mary Owens, whom Lincoln described as "pleasingly stout, weighing between 150 and 180 pounds." Owens, however, ended the relationship, stating that Lincoln was "deficient in those little links which make up the chain of a woman's happiness." After the relationship failed, Lincoln wrote to Mr. O. H. Browning that "I can never be satisfied with anyone who would be blockhead enough to have me."

In 1837, Lincoln met Mary Todd, who at age twenty-two was "just short of being an old maid." Lincoln married Mary Todd in 1842, but Mary was a Southern woman born of privilege, and Mary's sisters dropped her from their social circle because of her low social status choice for a husband. Unfortunately, Mary was also known for a bad temper, suffered from headaches, was highly emotional, terrified of storms, dogs, robbers, and prone to panic. On one occasion, Mary chased Abe out of the House with a butcher knife. On another, she struck him on the nose with a piece of firewood. Her temperament was well known, and though she was the first President's wife to be known as "First Lady," members of Lincoln's Cabinet frequently referred to her as "Hell-Cat."

While in the White House, Mary spent extravagantly, accepted gifts from office-seekers and those seeking favors, and ran up debts without Abe's knowledge. Mary sold furniture from the White House and manure from the White House stables to pay her debts. When that wasn't enough, she fired the White House Steward and kept the salary and then presented Congress with fake vouchers for nonexistent purchases. At one point, the House Judiciary Committee even investigated Mary for passing sensitive information to the South during the Civil War.

The Lincolns had four children, but Willie and Eddie died of childhood diseases. Another son, Tad, evidently suffered from a hyperactive disorder and was wholly undisciplined, unable to dress himself at age nine, and remained illiterate at the time of Lincoln's death.

The deaths of the boys along with a head injury from a fall from a carriage may have led to mental illness in Mary Lincoln by the time of her husband's death. Mary held eight séances in the White House to speak with the spirits of her deceased children, one of which was attended by the President himself. Mary reportedly once told Abe that her deceased son Willie often came to visit her at night and often, little Eddie (who died at age four) was with him! In 1875, the Lincoln's son Robert had Mary committed to a mental institution where she lived the rest of her life.

Lincoln was very much the frontiersman and except for one term in Congress, 1847–1849, Lincoln rarely went East and was relatively unknown until the debates with Douglas gained him a reputation in 1858. In many ways, it is surprising that Lincoln became the one person most

▶President Abraham Lincoln allowed the arrest of preachers that preached sermons against the war. Former Ohio Congressman Clement L. Vallandigham, who had spoken out strongly against the war, was arrested, tried and convicted, but Lincoln later commuted Vallandigham's sentence from imprisonment to banishment to the Confederacy. *Wikipedia photo*

responsible for the end of slavery. In the 1840s, Lincoln opposed the Annexation of Texas, formerly a territory of Mexico, partially because he thought of the Mexicans as "greasers." Lincoln also viewed Native Americans as a "barbarous barrier to progress" and presided over the execution of thirty-eight Indians by a military tribunal during the Civil War after the Indians had killed 350 whites because they had not been paid for their land. This was the largest mass execution in American history. Concerning the slaves, Lincoln thought African Americans to be inferior, opposed African American suffrage, African American equality, interracial marriage, African Americans on juries, and the repeal of the Fugitive Slave Act. Lincoln also favored the repatriation of African Americans to Africa as late as his debates with Stephen Douglas in 1858. In 1861, at a moment of crisis, this tall, gangling, plain-looking man, whose qualities of greatness were still unsuspected, became President.

Lincoln's relaxed and unpretentious manner masked remarkable powers of decision and qualities of leadership. Completely lacking in self-importance, he seemed humble to some observers, but he acted with the patience and forbearance of a man who was sure of what he was doing. He refused to let the abolitionists push him into an antislavery war which would antagonize Union men who did not care about slavery, and refused to let the Union men separate him from the antislavery contingent by restricting war aims too narrowly. He saw that the causes of union and emancipation must support each other instead of opposing each other, or both would be defeated.

Patiently he worked to fuse the idea of union with that of freedom and equality ("a new nation conceived in liberty and dedicated to the proposition that all men are created equal"). Thus he reaffirmed for American nationalism the idealism of freedom and gave to the ideal of freedom the strength of an undivided union. Knowing that in a democracy a man must win political success in order to gain a chance for statesmanship, he moved patiently and indirectly to his goals. His opportunism offended many abolitionists, but in the end he struck slavery the fatal blow.

Once the war started, Lincoln was very forceful in support of his goals. Lincoln closed newspapers that were too critical of his administration and arrested their editors and proprietors. He also allowed the arrest of preachers that preached sermons against the war and allowed the arrest, trial, and conviction for treason by a military tribunal of former Ohio Congressman, Clement L. Vallandigham, who had spoken out strongly against the war. Lincoln then commuted Vallandigham's sentence from imprisonment to banishment to the Confederacy.

The Resources of the North and South

In later years, after the Confederacy had gone down to defeat, men said that the Lost Cause, as Southerners called it, had been lost from the beginning and that the South had been fighting against the census returns. In many respects this seems true, for the South was completely outnumbered in almost all the factors of manpower and economic strength that make up the sinews of modern war. In 1861 the population of the Confederate states was 9 million people including 3.7 million slaves. The Union had 22.5 million people with 300,000 slaves. The Confederates were considerably outnumbered. Greater population, of course, also translated into more soldiers. At its peak, the Union army had 690,000 soldiers in 1863 as compared to 270,000 for the Confederates.

The four border states were divided, but most of their people and resources supported the Union side. Slaves strengthened the Confederate war effort in an important way, however, for they constituted a majority of the South's labor force and, thereby, enabled most white men to leave home to fight in the army.

The Union was far ahead of the Confederacy in financial and economic strength. It had a bank capital more than four times as great as that of the South. It led the South in the number of manufacturing enterprises by six and a half to one, in the number of industrial workers by twelve to one, and in the value of its manufactures by eleven to one. In railroad mileage, it led by more than two to one. The Union also had a serious naval advantage in that the South essentially possessed almost no warships at the beginning of the War. This deficiency would allow the Union to blockade the South, which was particularly damaging to the Southern economy that was dependent upon cotton exports for its revenue and upon foreign trade for its manufactured goods.

Against these ratios of strength must be placed the fact that the Union was undertaking a vastly more difficult military objective. It should be noted that virtually every advantage enjoyed by the Union during the Civil War was also enjoyed by England during the American Revolution, yet the British still lost. Much like the British during the American Revolution, the Union was seeking to occupy and subdue an area larger than all of Western Europe. This meant that armies had to be sent hundreds of miles into hostile territory and be maintained in these distant operations. This necessity involved the enormous tasks of transporting the immense volume of supplies required by an army in the field and defending long lines of supply and communication, the longest in American history, which were worthless if they were cut even at a single point. In wars prior to the War Between the States, armies had depended upon the use of wagon trains to bring supplies. As the supply lines lengthened, the horses ate up in fodder a steadily increasing proportion of the amount they could haul, until there was scarcely any margin left between what the supply lines carried and what they consumed.

During the war, for the first time in the history of warfare, railroads played a major part in the supply services. If these more efficient carriers of goods had not changed the whole nature of war, it is questionable whether invading armies could ever have marched from the Ohio to the Gulf of Mexico. Ten years earlier the United States had not possessed the railroad network that supplied the Union armies between 1861 and 1865. Therefore, at an earlier time, the defensive position of the South would have been far stronger.

Even with railroads, superior munitions, and more industrial facilities, the military tasks of the Union were most formidable. America was a profoundly civilian country. The peacetime army numbered only sixteen thousand; and few people on either side had any conception of the vast problems involved in recruiting, mobilizing, equipping, training, and maintaining large armies. It was an amateur's war on both sides, and many of its features seem inconceivable today.

Most of the troops were recruited as volunteers rather than drafted. At the outset of the war, Lincoln called for seventy-five thousand ninety-day volunteers, reflecting a bit of naivety in Lincoln's inability to foresee a protracted conflict. In defense of Lincoln, his own war experience had consisted of the Blackhawk War in 1832, where by his own admission, he survived "bloody encounters with mosquitoes and led raids on wild onion patches." Even the larger war against Mexico that Lincoln had experienced as a young Congressmen had been over in a little more than a year of actual fighting, and that war involved the invasion of a country further away and with more territory than the Confederacy.

Nevertheless, by July 1861, Lincoln's call for seventy-five thousand ninety-day volunteers had raised 186,000, and the South had simultaneously raised 112,000 volunteers. The massive recruitment effort simply overwhelmed organizational and supply capacity on both sides.

Southerners quickly began building new factories to supply their soldiers with uniforms and arms, but the Southern manufacturing and transportation capacity would never be sufficient. Although by April of 1864 Josiah Gorgas, the head of the Confederacy's Ordnance Bureau, boasted that the South was making enough guns and ammunition to meet the needs of its soldiers, at the outset there were no factories in the South that made guns, swords, shells, or powder; and the Confederate army would remain under-equipped throughout the war. Even when the production capacity of the South was sufficient, such as in food production, the products often did not make it to the troops in the field due to a lack of rail transportation.

Both the Union and the Confederacy sold war bonds, both raised taxes, and both issued paper currency to fund the war. Much like the American Revolution, however, the increased taxation and borrowing were not enough to fund the war effort; and Americans on both sides essentially paid for the War through the depletion of their savings, caused by the rapid inflation that accompanied the paper currency issues. Prices in the North increased approximately 80 percent during the War; but in the South, where the costs of the war per capita were far greater, inflation reached 9,000 percent by the end of the War.

The Confederacy enacted conscription in April 1862 and the Union in March 1863, but the real purpose of these laws was to stimulate volunteering rather than to institute a genuine draft. Both the North and the South allowed drafted men to hire substitutes until the Confederacy abolished this privilege in December 1863. The Union government also exempted a drafted man upon payment of a $300 commutation fee, until this privilege was abolished in July 1864 due to popular discontent. In the North, the $300 commutation fee gave the common people reason to denounce the War as a "Rich man's war, poor man's fight." In the South, the idea that a central authority could force anyone, anywhere, to do anything against their will was a violation of the "states' rights" principles that the South was fighting for in the first place.

Union conscription was applied only in localities that failed to meet their quotas. Thus communities were impelled to pay "bounties" to encourage men to volunteer. This resulted in the practice of "bounty-jumping." A man would enlist, collect his bounty, desert, enlist again in some other locality, collect another bounty, and desert again.

Volunteers enlisted for specified periods, normally three years. The Confederacy's draft laws compelled them to reenlist even when their enlistment terms were up. On the Union side, by contrast, volunteers could not be compelled to reenlist, and in 1864 the North had to rely on bounties and patriotic persuasion to induce more than half of its three-year volunteers to re-enlist.

Southern Strategy

Southerners believed that they would win the war because of their "just cause," superior character, and, of course, because God was on their side. With foolhardy bravado, the Southerners believed that their rugged, country outdoorsmen with their frontier mentality would easily defeat the city boys from the North, whom they viewed as soft, flabby, and unprincipled. Southerners compared their position to that of the Colonists in 1776, who triumphed against insurmountable odds over the more powerful British.

Southerners also believed that the North would collapse without Southern cotton and that without the Southern market, Northern manufacturing would collapse in overproduction with no Southerners to purchase their goods. Southerners also believed that the Europeans, especially England, would be on their side because of the need for Southern cotton. The British imported nine hundred million pounds of cotton annually, three-fourths of which came from the American South. Twenty percent of Britain's workforce was involved in the textile industry; therefore, Britain would collapse without Southern cotton and would, thereby, ensure their supply with the world's largest navy. If England could be persuaded to join the Southern cause out of their need for cotton, then victory would be assured.

Confederate President Jefferson Davis termed the Southern strategy as an "offensive-defensive" strategy. Southerners recognized that a Union victory would require that they invade, defeat, and subjugate the South on its own soil (the challenge for the British in the American Revolution), but that a Confederate victory only required that the South avoid annihilation until the North exhausted its resources and will to fight (the feat accomplished by the colonists in the American Revolution). This was the "defensive" part of the Southern strategy. The "offensive" part of the strategy called for Southern offensives, preferably into Northern territory, that would produce shocking, "decisive victories," that would break the Northern will to fight and convince the Europeans to support the Southern cause as allies. In short, the Southerners sought a Civil War version of Saratoga, where a decisive victory by the Colonists brought France into the American Revolution as an ally, and a "Yorktown," where a decisive victory by the Colonists convinced the British that the fight was too costly and induced them to negotiate peace and accept the independence of their former possession.

To combat the Union navy, the Southerners armed their merchant ships, often draping them with bales of cotton to provide protection from Union guns. These "cotton clads" seized Union merchant ships and cargo, not only disrupting Union trade, but also confiscating goods for the South. The Confederates also constructed the beginnings of a navy, purchasing ships from England.

Northern Strategy

President Lincoln's primary objective in the War was to preserve the Union, and his primary means was military subjugation of the South through a massive land invasion and naval blockade. In order to accomplish his goals, Lincoln needed to keep the war domestic and prevent European intervention on the behalf of the South. Direct European military intervention on the behalf of the South would tip the balance and secure Southern independence, so it had to be avoided at all costs. Massive economic aid from Europe to the South could perhaps tip the balance in the favor of the South as well, so Secretary of State William Seward advised a blockade on all Southern ports, which Lincoln announced on April 19, 1861. In the beginning, the blockade was really merely a paper blockade since the U.S. had fewer than 100 ships to guard 185 Southern ports and 3,500 miles of coastline. Furthermore, only forty-two of the Union's ships were considered seaworthy in 1861, and only eight were in U.S. waters at the time of the proclamation. The Union would build more ships, however, with the result that the blockade effectively crippled Southern international trade by the end of the war.

The blockade also presented a problem for the Union under international law because a "blockade" under international law was considered an act of war. Therefore, Lincoln's blockade inferred under international law that the South was an independent nation (a point disputed by the Union) and that the war was a war between two independent nations, rather than an insurrection or a domestic dispute. The rules of international law were different for wars between belligerents (two independent, warring nations) than they were for insurrections or domestic disputes. As a belligerent in a war between nations, the South could obtain loans and purchase war materials in Europe. Furthermore, European nations would have the right to trade nonmilitary goods with both warring nations, the same rights that the U.S. had claimed and fought for in the War of 1812. When Lincoln declared the blockade, he essentially inferred that the South was an independent warring nation and that the Europeans would have those rights. England immediately declared neutrality, therefore at least inferring that they were asserting their rights as neutrals to trade nonmilitary goods in Southern ports. If Lincoln interrupted this trade, he risked war with England, which would doom Union prospects in the conflict with the South.

Lincoln's other option would have been to allow the Europeans unlimited trade with the South under the premise that the South was not independent and was still part of the U.S. The advantage would be that the European powers would not be able to aid the South as an "independent country," but if the South were not independent, as England's Lord Lyons explained to Secretary of State Seward, then a blockade would not be binding because blockades under international law applied only to two nations at war. Lincoln essentially attempted to skirt international law and do both—treat the war as a domestic dispute and deny European aid to the South—while imposing a blockade (thus inferring that the South was independent) and shutting off European trade with the South. The result would be legal disputes with England over the seizure of ships at sea that would be settled after the war, but a continual risk of bringing England into the war on the side of the South over Union violations of international law.

Instead of a long protracted war of attrition and annihilation that the Civil War eventually became, Lincoln and his generals envisioned a quick strike invasion into the South that would provide a stunning and decisive victory that would quickly quell the rebellion by proving to Southerners that their rebellion had no chance in the face of Northern superiority. Given that Richmond was only one hundred miles from Washington, D.C., many Northern generals evidently believed that a quick strike on the Southern capital could produce the decisive Union victory necessary to cause the South to abandon the rebellion before it was even well-started.

Instead, it was the Union strategy that was derailed before it even began. On April 19, the 6th Massachusetts Regiment that had been mobilized for an assault on Virginia arrived in Baltimore, Maryland, a city in a slave state that had not chosen to secede. Sentiments in Maryland were divided and tensions were high. In Baltimore, the Massachusetts Regiment had to change railroad lines, forcing the soldiers to cross the city on foot. As they marched through the streets, a mob of some ten thousand Confederate sympathizers flying Confederate flags attacked them at first with rocks and then bullets. Under orders from their commander, the Union troops returned fire, and the city of Baltimore erupted into riotous violence. Twelve citizens of Baltimore and four Union soldiers were killed before the riot could be ended by military force. Secessionists cut the telegraph wires and burned the railroad bridges connecting Baltimore to both North and South, cutting off the town from the Confederacy and, also, from the rest of the Union. The destruction of the rail bridges also cut off Washington (South of Baltimore) from the rest of the Union. To prevent the nation's capital from being surrounded by hostile enemy territory, Lincoln ordered that federal forces turn Maryland into an occupied state.

In order to prevent further bloodshed, Lincoln ordered that troops be routed around Baltimore. Lincoln then suspended *habeas corpus* and ordered the arrest of Confederate sympathizers with the result that Baltimore's mayor, police chief, a judge, and nineteen Maryland state legislators were imprisoned without a trial. Chief Justice Roger Taney, who had penned the Dred Scott decision, challenged the President's action and issued a writ of habeas corpus for the release of a Southern sympathizer, John Merryman. In his opinion in *ex parte* Merryman, Taney ruled that if the public's safety was endangered, only Congress had the right to suspend the writ of habeas corpus. Lincoln, however, essentially ignored the ruling throughout the war and imprisoned, without charges or trials, whomever he saw fit.

Many Confederate sympathizers from Maryland fled the state to Virginia, formed a Confederate Maryland government in exile, and joined up with the Confederate army or simply launched guerrilla raids back into Maryland. Unionists won the Maryland state elections and gained firm control of the Maryland legislature in the fall of 1861, but Maryland would remain a battleground for invading armies throughout the war.

The situation in Missouri essentially mirrored that in Maryland. St. Louis erupted into a full scale riot and pitched battle between Unionist and Confederate militias on May 10–11, 1861, in which thirty-six people were killed. Union commander Nathaniel Lyon led his troops in a summer campaign that drove the Confederate militia, along with Missouri's governor and pro-Confederate legislators, into Arkansas where they formed a Missouri Confederate government in exile.

While in Arkansas, the Missouri Confederates recruited Arkansas comrades to help them invade back into Missouri in August. On August 10, Union commander in Missouri, Nathaniel Lyon, was killed at Wilson's Creek in southwest Missouri. The Confederates then marched northward along the Missouri River and captured a Union garrison at Lexington, Missouri, forty miles east of Kansas City, on September 20, 1861. This early victory was the South's high water-mark in Missouri and the Union would officially control the state throughout the war, but Confederate "bushwhackers" and Unionist "Jayhawkers" would launch hit-and-run raids and ambushes against each other throughout the war. Notorious postwar outlaws Jesse and Frank James, and Cole and Jim Younger rode with the Confederate bushwhackers. Throughout the war, perhaps more than any other state, Missouri suffered from a "civil war" within the Civil War.

Kentucky confederates, outnumbered approximately two to one in Kentucky, also fled to the Confederacy and formed a state government in exile, but Kentucky remained solidly in the Union. Union sentiments were also strong in the western mountain portion of Virginia west of the Shenandoah Valley where most of Virginia's delegates had voted against secession. In fact, part of the reason for placing the Southern capital in Richmond was to shore up Confederate support in the state. Western Virginia, however, was a mountainous agricultural area of small farms where family labor sufficed, and slaves were few in number. Western Virginia's economy was much more linked with Ohio and Pennsylvania than to the rest of Virginia or the South at large. Western Virginia's largest city, Wheeling, was 330 miles over rugged mountain terrain to Richmond, but only sixty miles from Pittsburgh. With the help of Union troops, who crossed the Ohio River and won several minor battles against Confederate forces in Western Virginia in the summer of 1861, the people of Western Virginia seceded from the confederacy and created the state of West Virginia, which was officially added to the Union in 1863.

The Civil War in the border states even spread into Indian territory as Confederate sympathizers manning the Union forts in the territory turned over the Union facilities to Confederates from Texas without a shot. Several Indian tribes were coaxed into signing Treaties of Alliance with the Confederacy, including the five "civilized tribes" (Cherokees, Creeks, Seminoles, Chickasaws, and Choctaws). Other Indian tribes sided with the Union, however, and aided by Union regiments from Kansas and Missouri eventually gained control of Indian Territory for the Union.

The James Boys and the Younger Brothers

▶Notable outlaws were Confederate "bushwhackers" Jesse and Frank James and Bob and Cole Younger, who together formed the James-Younger gang. Among other acts, they robbed banks and trains, and murdered. The gang gained fame throughout the 'Confederate frontier.' *Corbis Images*

The War in the Field

The Virginia Front

From the very outset of the war, attention was focused on the Virginia front. After fighting had begun at Fort Sumter and the states of the upper South had joined the Confederacy, the Confederate government moved its capital to Richmond, Virginia, about one hundred miles south of Washington. With the two seats of government so close together, the war in the East became a struggle on the part of the Union to capture Richmond and on the part of the South to defend it.

Between Washington and Richmond a number of broad rivers—the Potomac, the Rappahannock, the York, the Chickahominy, and other tributaries—flow more or less parallel with one another from the Appalachian Mountains in the west to the Chesapeake Bay in the east. This grid of rivers afforded a natural system of defense to the South and presented an obstacle course to the North. Southern armies on the defensive could lie in wait for their attackers on the south banks of these streams, as they did at Bull Run, Fredericksburg, Chancellorsville, and the Wilderness. When the Southern army was driven back after going on the offensive, it could later cross back to safety, reorganize, and recoup, as it did after Antietam (Sharpsburg) and Gettysburg.

For four years the principal army of the North, the Army of the Potomac, struggled against the principal army of the South, the Army of Northern Virginia, over this terrain. Each side placed its foremost commander here. Robert E. Lee headed the Army of Northern Virginia after Joseph E. Johnston was wounded in 1862, while Ulysses S. Grant was brought east to take overall command of Union armies in 1864 after his great successes in the West. Public attention centered primarily upon these campaigns, and they have continued to receive more than their share of attention in history.

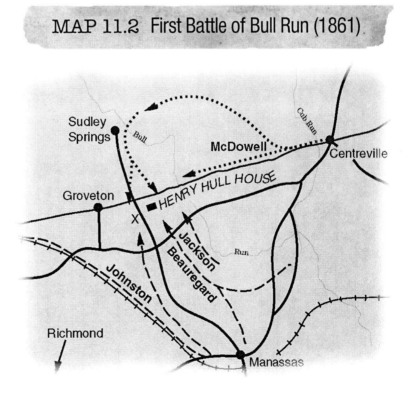

MAP 11.2 First Battle of Bull Run (1861)

The Battle of Bull Run (Manassas)

During the first half of the war, the Union met with a long succession of disappointments and defeats on the Virginia front. In July 1861, when both armies were still raw and un-seasoned, the Union sent General Irvin McDowell south with the slogan "Forward to Rich-mond" and with expectations of an easy victory (in spite of the fact that General Winfield Scott and his field commander, McDowell, both had misgivings about the ability of their green, poorly trained, ninety-day volunteers were ready to fight a real battle). In fact, Scott had argued for a cautious, long-term strategy known as the "Anaconda Plan," where the North would weaken the South gradually through blockades on land and sea until the Northern army was strong enough to move forward and crush the weakened south. The public, however, demanded bold, quick action, as did Scott's commander-in-chief, Abraham Lincoln. Thus, McDowell and his army marched into Virginia against the military judgment of its most experienced general. Twenty-five miles southwest of Washington, McDowell en-countered the Confederate armies of Generals Pierre G. T. Beauregard, a West Point class-mate of McDowell's known as the "Napoleon of the South," and Joseph E. Johnston with twenty-five thousand strong, who had been deployed at Manassas Junction to defend a key rail junction at Manassas, Virginia, from which the battle received its name from the Con-federates. In the Union, the battle was named after the creek that crossed the battlefield known as Bull Run.

On July 21, the Union army forded Bull Run, a sluggish branch of the Potomac River, and engaged the Confederate troops on the Confederate left flank, at first driving them back. By early afternoon, the Union army appeared to be on the verge of breaking the Southern lines, but a Virginia brigade commanded by Thomas J. Jackson stood their ground. A South Carolina general, seeking to inspire his own troops, pointed to Jackson and his men, standing like a

▶ The first battle of Bull Run, also known as the Bat-tle of Manassas
Wikipedia photo

"stone wall" in repelling the Union troops. Afterwards, Thomas Jackson would be referred to affectionately in the South as "Stonewall Jackson." Jackson's stand, combined with the arrival of his 2,300 fresh Confederate reinforcements from the Shenandoah Valley (who hit the battlefield with a famed "rebel yell"), drove the green Union troops into a disorganized retreat. Union troops broke ranks and fled in a panic, trampling spectators who had stupidly arrived on the battlefield with parasols and picnic baskets to witness the romantic struggle of courage. Fleeing Union soldiers abandoned their weapons and stumbled past their abandoned supply wagons on their way back to Washington.

The inexperienced Southern troops lacked the organization and supply capacity necessary to press their advantage and, therefore, failed to pursue the fleeing Union army. Casualties on both sides were light by Civil War standards (2,800 for the Union and 2,000 Confederates), but the battle boosted Southern confidence while simultaneously proving to Lincoln and the Union that victory would not be swift and a broader strategy for winning the war would be necessary. In fact, for the South the victory may have engendered overconfidence, as some Southerners mistakenly believed that the war was won. Suddenly, the Union was more realistic and Congress authorized the enlistment of up to a million three-year volunteers. Union men answered the call by the hundreds of thousands, and Lincoln and the Union settled in for a long, hard fight.

McDowell was replaced by thirty-four-year-old George Brinton McClellan, who had campaigned successfully in West Virginia. McClellan was much less the Napoleon than he appeared, however, because real resistance in West Virginia had been light and McClellan and the Union press overplayed the significance of his victories. Boldness in battle, which was the commodity Lincoln sought, would not prove to be McClellan's strongest suit.

McClellan was the child of wealthy parents in Philadelphia, educated in the best schools, and a graduate of West Point, where he finished second in his class, and then served as an army engineer. McClellan possessed real ability as an organizer, and he realized that he must make his troops into an army before he took them campaigning. McClellan was a perfectionist, however, and he refused to mount an offensive until his army was trained to his own exacting requirements. Every commander has essentially two responsibilities: to win when engaged in military conflict and to keep as many of his own men alive as possible in the process. McClellan clearly believed that latter goal to be the more important of the two and sought every means by which he could avoid unnecessary loss of life and destruction of property. McClellan even stated that he expected to win by "maneuvering rather than fighting." McClellan was averse to risk and, of course, no military conflict can be waged completely absent of risk. The President prodded McClellan to speed up the process and become more aggressive, at one point stating that, "If General McClellan does not want to use the army, I would like to borrow it." McClellan, however, was confident in his own abilities and had little respect for Lincoln, once referring to him as "the original gorilla." Consequently, there was no more major fighting on the Virginia front for almost a year.

When McClellan did at last move in April 1862, with an army of 130,000 strong, he persuaded President Lincoln to let him transport his troops by ship to Fort Monroe, a point on the Virginia coast within striking distance of Richmond. From this point he proposed to move up the peninsula between the York and the James Rivers (hence called the Peninsula Campaign) to capture the Confederate capital.

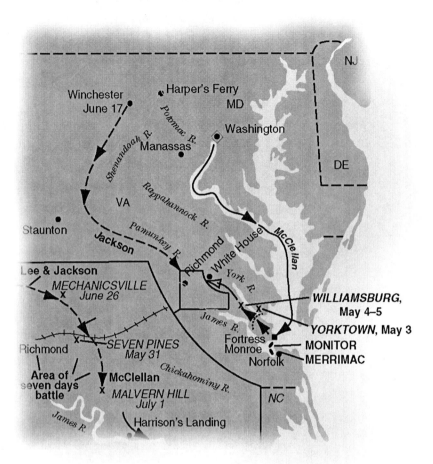

MAP 11.3 Peninsular Campaign (1862)

McClellan's plan was a brilliant solution to the difficult problem of supply, for he could now bring provisions for his army by ship without fear of Confederate raiders cutting his supply lines. The plan had one important disadvantage, however, in that it left, or appeared to leave, Washington exposed to the Confederates. Therefore, for the defense of the Capitol, President Lincoln insisted on withholding part (thirty thousand) of the troops that McClellan wanted. So although McClellan launched his invasion from Fort Monroe toward Richmond, he failed to push his offensive with the vigor the North expected. McClellan also moved with methodical precision—so methodical, in fact, that it took him over ten weeks to advance sixty-five miles. A small Confederate blocking force at Yorktown delayed McClellan for the entire month of April. McClellan insisted on bringing siege guns to the front to blast his way through an infantry that his immense army should have been able to crush on foot in a matter of days. Finally, McClellan and his men were within six miles of Richmond, close enough to hear the town's church bells.

While these developments were in progress, Confederate commander Joseph E. Johnston launched a counterattack on May 31–June 1, in what has become known as the Battle of Seven Pines. The battle was indecisive although the Confederates suffered six thousand casualties and the Union five thousand. Johnston himself, however, was badly wounded in the shoulder in the assault and was replaced by Robert E. Lee.

Lee, a Virginia aristocrat, mild of speech and gentle of manner but gifted with a daring that was terrible to his adversaries, quickly perceived that he could play upon the Union's fear that Washington was too exposed. Accordingly, he sent his brilliant subordinate, Thomas I. ("Stonewall") Jackson, on a raid up the Shenandoah Valley, appearing to threaten Washington and causing the administration to hold their defensive troops that had previously been promised to McClellan. In the month between May 4 and June 9, 1862, Stonewall Jackson's Confederates, with only seventeen thousand men, marched over 350 miles in a month and defeated three separate Union armies in four engagements. Furthermore, the number of Union troops Jackson and his men defeated were more than twice those of the Confederates.

When Jackson returned from his raid with phenomenal speed, Lee's reunited forces of eighty-five thousand took the offensive against McClellan's one hundred thousand original forces south and east of Richmond in a series of engagements known as the Seven Days' Battles (June 25–July 1, 1862). McClellan fought hard and was not decisively defeated, but he lost his nerve, moved back to a base on the James River, and sent Washington a series of frantic messages that the government had deserted him. By the time McClellan had reached the water and the safety of Union naval support, the Union had suffered sixteen thousand casualties and the South twenty thousand. Though the South had suffered greater casualties, Lee had saved Richmond, forced the Union to retreat and, at least temporarily, reversed the Union's momentum.

McClellan's retreat convinced Lincoln that the peninsula campaign would not work, and that McClellan was not the right man to lead the Union Army, so on July 11, Lincoln appointed General Henry W. Halleck, who had been the overall commander in the Western theater where the Union had experienced greater success, to be the new General in Chief.

Second Battle of Bull Run

Lincoln, who had never fully accepted the basic idea of operating by sea, through Halleck, withdrew McClellan's troops from the peninsula to northern Virginia to join a smaller force under the command of General John Pope, who had gained a reputation for aggressiveness in the West. The President hoped to launch another assault against Richmond via an overland route that he himself had preferred. As McClellan departed from the peninsula by water, Lee quickly took advantage of the opportunity that was provided him by the separation of the two Union armies and moved north with his "Army of Northern Virginia" to engage Pope's troops before McClellan could reach him. Lee sent Stonewall Jackson to attack Pope from the rear, provoking Pope to launch a counter-attack against the Confederate contingency under Stonewall Jackson. Lee then hurled the main thrust of his army against Pope's flank before McClellan and the Army of the Potomac could arrive. An exasperated Lincoln then removed Pope from command and reassigned him to Indian fighting in Minnesota. McClellan was restored to command and given a second chance.

Antietam

When Lee marched north, crossed the Potomac, and advanced into Maryland, believing that a decisive victory in Maryland could win the state for the Confederacy and influence the

Union Congressional elections in November to an anti-war stance. A decisive victory in Maryland could also perhaps bring recognition or intervention from England and thus win the war. Lee's movement into Maryland was fraught with difficulties from the start since Lee was greatly outnumbered (fifty thousand to eighty-five thousand), poorly supplied, and exhausted from the Richmond campaigns. Again Lee divided his forces, sending part of his army under Stonewall Jackson to capture Harpers Ferry, which lay amidst Lee's supply route from the Shenandoah Valley. Lee held the other part of his army on watch in the mountain passes west of Frederick, Maryland.

Union forces under McClellan had a stroke of good luck when they found a copy of Lee's battle plans wrapped in three cigars at Frederick, evidently dropped by a Southern officer. McClellan proclaimed that, "here is a paper … with which if I cannot whip Bobbie Lee, I will be willing to go home." Even with a copy of Lee's secret orders in his hands so that the Union general knew exactly what to expect, however, he still did not move quickly or decisively. Twelve thousand of McClellan's men surrendered to Stonewall Jackson's Confederates at Harper's Ferry on September 15, 1862. McClellan's delay allowed Lee the time he needed to assume a position behind Antietam Creek near Sharpsburg on September 17. McClellan threw his seventy-five thousand men at Lee's forty thousand Confederates (though McClellan, as was his nature, thought the Union was outnumbered). After a supremely hard-fought engagement at Antietam (Sharpsburg), Lee withdrew after the deadliest single-day battle of the war, bloodied, but not crushed, to the south bank of the Potomac. A total of six thousand men were killed and seventeen thousand wounded in one day. McClellan's army almost broke through the Confederate lines on a road northeast of Sharpsburg (known after as Bloody Lane), but fearing counterattacks from reserves that Lee did not have, McClelland held back twenty thousand of his troops in reserve. McClellan received reinforcements the next day and Lee did not, but McClellan did not renew his attack. The next night, the Confederates retreated back across the Potomac to Virginia.

▶ At the battle at Antietam Creek a total of six thousand men were killed and seventeen thousand wounded in one day. *Wikipedia photo*

Though the battle was a Union victory in that the Southern offensive was halted and Lee was forced to retreat, the victory was not complete because McClellan failed to press his advantage and allowed Lee's troops to return to Virginia to rebuild. Lincoln again replaced McClellan on November 7, this time with Ambrose E. Burnside. Britain and France, who had been considering intervention or recognition of the Confederacy, decided to withhold that recognition. Four days later on September 22, Lincoln issued his preliminary Emancipation Proclamation.

Fredericksburg

Ambrose E. Burnside was most certainly a more aggressive general than McClellan, but proved to be a less than brilliant battlefield tactician. In December 1862 Burnside made an unimaginative frontal attack across the Rappahannock at Fredericksburg, Virginia, against prepared Confederate defenses. Fighting the Confederates on ground of their own choosing, Burnside launched his troops on an uphill charge, where he sustained terrible losses, more than twice the casualty rate of the Confederates, and was replaced by Joseph Hooker. After Lincoln heard the bad news from the battlefield, the President reportedly groaned, "If there is a worse place than hell, I am in it." Other than his failed frontal assault at Fredericksburg, Burnside is perhaps most noteworthy for his distinctive whiskers, from which the anagram "sideburns" became part of the English language.

Morale in the Union, both among the troops and among the public, reached a new low in the winter of 1862–1863, as did Lincoln's popularity. The army was suffering from high desertion rates, and the bleak outlook is what caused Lincoln to turn to "Fighting Joe" Hooker to lead the troops. Hooker was described as ill-tempered, vindictive, and deviously in favor of a military dictator for the United States. In his letter appointing Hooker to lead the army, Lincoln acknowledges that Hooker favors a dictatorship, while he did not, but the President was appointing Hooker to lead his army in spite of this fact. Lincoln did, however, believe Hooker to be a bold general in that he cautioned him against "rashness."

Chancellorsville

Thus, Hooker seemed a man of boldness and decision and in command of 120,000 well-trained troops north of the Rappahannock River, opposite Fredericksburg. In May 1863, Hooker crossed the Rappahannock north of Fredericksburg and moved his army toward the town and the Confederate army. After executing an excellent flanking march to maneuver Lee into battle on unfavorable terms, Hooker evidently lost his poise and drew his army back to what he thought was a defensive position in a desolate area of scrub trees known as the "Wilderness." Hooker allowed Jackson's corps to roll up the Union right flank in a surprise attack that rocked the Unionists and eventually drove them back across the Rappahannock, in spite of the fact that the Confederates were outnumbered two to one. Although a great Confederate victory, the South paid a fearful price for Chancellorsville. Confederate casualties exceeded twelve thousand, and General Stonewall Jackson was accidentally wounded by his own troops and died a few days later.

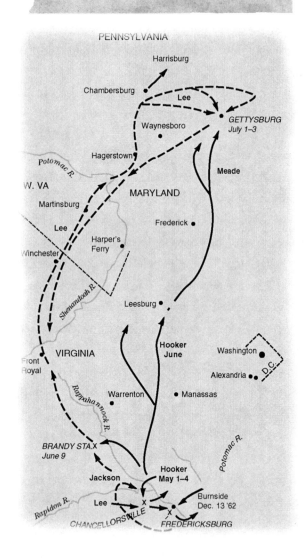

MAP 11.4 Fredricksburg to Gettysburg (1862–63)

Gettysburg

Hooker remained in command until Lee launched a second offensive against the North, this time into Pennsylvania. Lee understood that the South was losing a war of attrition, which favored the North; so he set his sights on scoring a decisive victory in the North that could break the morale of the Union and perhaps bring European intervention and recognition. When Lee escaped from Hooker with seventy-five thousand troops on the northward march, Lincoln again changed commanders, turning this time to George Gordon Meade. By late June 1863, Lee's army had fanned out across southern Pennsylvania in a fifty-mile arc from Harrisburg almost to Baltimore. Meade's army and Lee's army met at Gettysburg, though neither had planned it that way. On July 1, Confederate troops in search of shoes in the town of Gettysburg clashed with a Union cavalry unit. Both sides sent out calls for reinforcement, and the two armies converged. On the first three days of July 1863, the South made its supreme effort, and the little town in Pennsylvania became the scene of the greatest battle ever fought in North America. Confederates broke the union lines on the afternoon of July 1, driving the Union to a defensive position on Cemetery Ridge south of town. General Richard Ewell, Stonewall Jackson's successor, judged the Union position too strong to defeat and chose not to attack further as darkness fell on

July 1. The next morning, Lee and the Confederates occupied Seminary Ridge, facing Meade to the south on the high ground at Cemetery Ridge. General James Longstreet argued against a frontal assault, instead favoring a maneuver to the south toward Washington, D.C. in an attempt to get the Union to attack the Confederates when they occupied a strong defensive position. Lee, however, reportedly pointed to the Union lines and said, "the enemy is there, and I am going to attack him there." Across the valley between the two, on July 2, Lee positioned his troops against the Union positions in a series of bold attacks on the Union flanks. Having attacked the Union flanks on July 2, Lee believed that the center of the Union lines might be weak, so on July 3, Lee ordered an assault on the Union center on Cemetery Ridge, where Meade's troops were dug-in with almost a mile of clear vision. After a two-hour Confederate artillery bombardment, in an assault known as "Pickett's Charge," General George Pickett and fifteen thousand Confederates charged into Union cannon and rifle fire, but Meade's forces were too strong to be dislodged. Pickett's assault was almost successful in that it actually broke the Union lines on the afternoon of July 3, but Union reinforcements drove the Confederates back before they could secure their positions. Approximately half of Pickett's men did not survive, and Lee lost over a third of his forces at Gettysburg overall. Lee realized his mistake and was heard to state, "It's all my fault," nevertheless, Lee and his decimated army waited for more than a day to receive a counterattack that never came and then marched south. Meade did not pursue until too late, and ten days after the battle Lee recrossed the Potomac unmolested. The Army of Northern Virginia had still never been driven from a battlefield, but its great offensive power was forever broken, and Lee would be able to mount no more Northern offensives. In this, the Battle of Gettysburg is generally considered the turning point in the Civil War. The Union had survived its greatest threat, and the South was reduced to fighting defensively in a losing war of attrition.

The War in the West

While the War was raging in the East, the Union was also launching an offensive west of the Appalachians with the goal of dominating the Southern waterways and, thus, controlling Southern trade. The Confederates in the West were hindered not only by poor transportation, but also by poor communications, and inadequate supplies. For instance, many of the Confederate troops went into battle with out-of-date flintlock muskets against Union troops with repeating rifles.

The region beyond the Appalachians was far greater and more broken up geographically than the Virginia theater, and the Union campaigns in the West never had a single focus as they did in Virginia. Operations along the Mississippi were scarcely coordinated with operations in the central and eastern parts of Tennessee and Kentucky, and neither of these was synchronized with activities "west of the River" in Missouri, Arkansas, most of Louisiana, and Texas. Essentially, however, it was the objective of the Union to gain control of the Mississippi River and cut off the western wing of the Confederacy. In this way Confederate armies were deprived of reinforcements and supplies—especially of Texas cattle—which they vitally needed. A further division of the Confederacy was undertaken by driving southeast through Kentucky and Tennessee, cutting crucial Confederate rail connections at Chattanooga in eastern Tennessee and continuing thence into the heart of the Confederacy across Georgia to the sea. Such an operation cut off the Gulf Coast region from the Atlantic seaboard and left only Virginia, the Carolinas, and part of Georgia to support a hopeless cause.

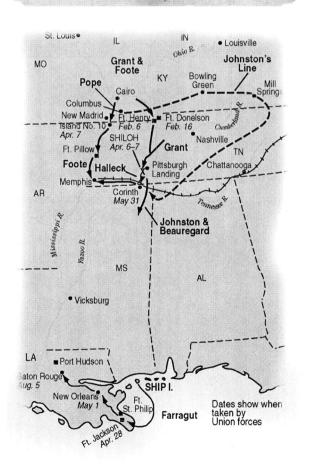

MAP 11.5 War in the West (1862)

It took three years and eight months for the Union to carry out these plans, although they had begun sooner than the great campaigns in Virginia.

Confederate Invasion of New Mexico

Some Confederates had visions of a "manifest destiny" for the Confederacy that included expanding the Confederacy across the Mexican Cession of the southwestern United States. Some Southerners even envisioned a Confederate slave empire expanding throughout all of Latin America. In furtherance of these grandiose goals and with the specific objectives of securing the upper Rio Grande Valley (Albuquerque and Santa Fe) for the Confederacy and of establishing a Confederate Pacific port on the Gulf of California at the mouth of the Colorado River, an area that through the twenty-first century remains under Mexican sovereignty, Confederate Colonel John R. Baylor on August 1, 1861, issued a proclamation establishing the "Confederate Territory of Arizona" comprised of present-day New Mexico and Arizona, south of the 43° north latitude. Baylor rode west with a Confederate force all the way to Tucson, where he captured the federal garrison there from its unenthusiastic Union defenders. Baylor established a Confederate government in Tucson, and he himself was made governor of the new Confederate territory.

In January 1862, three regiments of Confederate Texans under H. H. Sibley marched on the upper Rio Grande Valley and defeated a New Mexico militia and a group of Union army regulars at Valverde in February 1862, thus securing Albuquerque and Santa Fe for the Confederacy. The Confederate expansion was short-lived, however, as a Union regiment of Colorado miners, who had marched over the Rocky Mountains in winter, defeated the Confederate Texans at Glorieta Pass on March 26–28, forcing the Confederates to retreat all the way back to Texas. Of the thirty-seven hundred Confederates who had launched the New Mexico campaign, only two thousand made it back to Texas due not only to battlefield losses but also insufficient food supplies and the harshness of the elements.

Pea Ridge

Before the Union army could march on Tennessee, they believed they had to secure Missouri; consequently, in March 1862, Union troops under General Samuel R. Curtis advanced across Missouri into northwestern Arkansas where they engaged and defeated sixteen thousand Confederates under General Earl Van Dorn at Pea Ridge. The Confederate army included three regiments of Indians from Indian Territory who had joined up with the Confederates hoping for greater autonomy than they enjoyed in the Union. Though Curtis' campaign swept the Confederate army out of Missouri, the state remained a hotbed of guerrilla activity and violence throughout the war.

Forts Henry and Donelson

In February 1862, Ulysses S. Grant captured two Confederate forts, Henry and Donelson, in western Tennessee, which controlled the Tennessee and Cumberland Rivers. Unlike the streams of Virginia, which cut across the paths of advancing armies, each of these rivers flowed in a "U"-shaped course from the southern Appalachians southward into northern

Alabama and then reversing their courses almost due north to the Ohio River. Control of these river highways gave Grant easy entry deep into the South.

The Union's new "timberclad" gunboats, designed specifically for river warfare, took out Fort Henry without involvement by the Union infantry. At Fort Donelson, however, twenty-seven thousand Union forces under General Grant clashed with seventeen thousand Confederates. Grant famously demanded the "immediate and unconditional surrender" of thirteen thousand Confederate troops who, lacking options, surrendered on Grant's terms on February 16.

As a consequence of these victories, Union gunboats controlled the Tennessee River to Alabama and the Cumberland to Nashville. The Union army used the rivers to transport its troops, and on February 25, 1862, Nashville became the first Southern state capitol to surrender. Confederate army units withdrew from Kentucky and Tennessee to Corinth, Mississippi. From Corinth, the Confederate Western commander, Albert Sydney Johnston, planned to attack Grant's army at Pittsburg Landing just north of the Tennessee border from Mississippi.

Meanwhile, on April 26, 1862, a Union fleet under the command of David Farragut captured the port of New Orleans for the Union after running past forts south of the city. Besides securing and occupying New Orleans, Farragut proceeded to blockade the Gulf of Mexico and control traffic on the lower Mississippi. Farragut's exploits were so important to the Union that in 1866, Congress created the rank of admiral specifically for Farragut.

Shiloh

On April 6, Johnston and forty thousand Confederates attacked thirty-five thousand Union troops under General Grant near a church called Shiloh. The attack caught Grant and his men off-guard. Many of Grant's men were half-dressed, some were asleep, and others were brewing their morning coffee. Grant's army was pushed back, but held their ground by the end of the first day. The Confederates lost Johnston, who bled to death from a shot to the leg. Grant received reinforcements overnight from a Union army of twenty-five thousand under the command of General Don Carlos Buell; and the Union counterattacked the next day, driving the Confederates back to Corinth, Mississippi.

A total of thirteen thousand Union and ten thousand Confederate troops were lost at Shiloh, more deaths than in all the battles of the American Revolution, the War of 1812, and the War with Mexico combined. A full day after the battle, 90 percent of the wounded were still lying on the battlefield in a heavy rain. Many of the wounded died of exposure, but some of them actually drowned in the downpour. The massive casualty rates and gruesome battlefield proved to citizens, both North and South, that the war was not to be viewed as simply a romantic test of courage. Even Grant himself later stated that after Shiloh he "gave up all idea of saving the Union except by complete conquest." For Grant, personally, the high casualties and the fact that he was caught by surprise, plus the fact that he allowed the battered Confederate army to escape, damaged his reputation and temporarily cost him his command.

After Shiloh, however, the Union victories continued in the West. The Union armies under the general command of Henry W. Halleck expelled the Confederates from Corinth, the hub of several important railroads, by the end of May while the Union gunboat fleet wiped out the Confederate fleet at Memphis on June 6. Moving North from New Orleans, Farragut captured Baton Rouge and Natchez before meeting up with Union gunboats from the North at Vicksburg. The Union fleet, however, was unable to subdue the heavily fortified Confederate position at Vicksburg, but the series of Northern victories after Shiloh had many in the North believing that the War was won in the West by the summer of 1862. Union victories in the spring of 1862 had brought over fifty thousand square miles of Confederate territory under Union control.

The new Confederate Commander in the West, however, General Braxton Bragg, consolidated his troops in Chattanooga with plans to launch an offensive to retake Tennessee and Kentucky in the winter of 1862. Bragg and the Confederates were countered by a Union army under the command of Don Carlos Buell, and later William Rosecrans, whose goal was to capture Chattanooga. The Confederates pushed north into Kentucky and had almost reached the Ohio River by September, but they were defeated at Perryville on October 8 and forced to retreat back to Tennessee. After several months of maneuvering, the two armies clashed again on December 31, 1862, at Murfeesboro (or Stones River) where the Confederates were again forced to retreat and abandon their Tennessee offensive.

Problems for the Union in the Western theater persisted, however. Occupying and administering vast areas of territory in the South proved difficult and costly as soldiers for occupation had to be drawn from combat forces elsewhere. Furthermore, Union soldiers in the West were far from the Union infrastructure and at the end of long supply lines. The occupying Union soldiers, therefore, dangled in front of Confederate guerrillas as easy targets. During the last half of 1862, Southern cavalrymen under Nathan Bedford Forrest and John Hunt Morgan staged repeated guerrilla raids and sabotage, in which they burned bridges, blew up tunnels, destroyed railroad tracks, and stole Union supplies. The Southern guerrillas in the West very quickly reinforced the lessons learned by the British in the American Revolution: It is easier to defeat an inferior enemy in a frontal assault than to occupy and control a vast hostile country thousands of miles from home.

Vicksburg

During the winter of 1862–1863, Grant began a campaign against the Confederate stronghold at Vicksburg where towering bluffs command the Mississippi. Deep in enemy country, Vicksburg was rendered almost impregnable by vast swamps, by a succession of steep hills, and by the river itself. After making a series of unsuccessful moves against this natural fortress, Grant at last decided on the bold and unorthodox plan of moving down the west side of the river, crossing below Vicksburg, abandoning his lines of communication, and living off the country during a final drive against the Confederate defenses. In furtherance of his plan, Grant first ran his ironclad river fleet down river past the Confederate guns overlooking the river from Vicksburg. Grant's troops then marched down the Mississippi's west bank to forty miles south of Vicksburg where they were ferried across the river into Mississippi. Grant then deceptively marched his army east toward Jackson, Mississippi, instead of marching directly to Vicksburg. Grant's purpose was to scatter the Confederate forces that were concentrated at Vicksburg by making it appear that he was launching an assault on the Mississippi State capitol. Grant also sought to destroy the Southern rails so that they would be hindered in attacking him from the rear when he turned his forces toward Vicksburg. During the first three weeks of May 1863, Grant fought and won five engagements with the Confederates in Mississippi and surrounded

▶ In the battle of Vicksburg, General Ulysses S. Grant and his Union Army crossed the Mississippi River and drove the Confederate army of General John C. Pemberton into the fortress city of Vicksburg, Mississippi. Pemberton surrendered an army of about thirty thousand men—the largest that has ever been captured in North America. *Wikipedia photo*

the thirty thousand Confederate troops at Vicksburg, getting them stuck between the Union gunboats on the river and his army to their east. Grant launched assaults on the Confederate lines on May 19 and May 22, but was repulsed. Grant then settled down to lay an old fashioned siege to the city with his army that now numbered over seventy thousand. After more than a month of siege warfare, the Confederates were running out of supplies, and on July 4, 1863, the day on which Lee began his uncontested withdrawal from Gettysburg, another Confederate general, John C. Pemberton, at Vicksburg, Mississippi, surrendered an army of about thirty thousand men—the largest that has ever been captured in North America. The man to whom he surrendered was Ulysses S. Grant, and the event marked the culmination of a series of campaigns in the West which had been much more decisive in their results than the eastern campaigns. After the battle an impressed Abraham Lincoln stated, "Grant is my man, and I am his the rest of the war." After over two years of searching, Lincoln had finally found his general. Five days later, the Confederate garrison at Port Hudson, two hundred miles south of Vicksburg, also surrendered to the Union army, giving the Union the control of the entire Mississippi.

Chickamauga and Chattanooga

After the Battle of Murfeesboro (Stones River) on December 31, 1862–January 3, 1863) William Rosecrans' Union Army of the Cumberland and Braxton Bragg's Confederate Army of Tennessee maneuvered against each other for six months without major engagements. Finally, on June 24, 1863, Rosecrans launched an offensive designed to dislodge the Confederates from eastern Tennessee. Rosecrans' offensive forced the Confederates to retreat to Chattanooga. Rosecrans paused to take on supplies and then connected with another Union army commanded by Ambrose Burnside, and drove the Confederates out of Knoxville on September 2, and Chattanooga on September 9, thus severing the South's only direct east-west railway. With the capture of Chattanooga, the Union was in position to launch an invasion of Georgia.

On September 19, however, the Confederates counterattacked Rosecrans' army in the valley of Chickamauga Creek. Over the next two days of fierce fighting, the two armies suffered thirty-six thousand combined casualties, the most of any battle at that point except for Gettysburg. On September 20, Confederates under James Longstreet broke the Union lines and forced a segment of the Union army to retreat to Chattanooga.

After the battle, Lincoln replaced Rosecrans, whom Lincoln described as "confused and stunned like a duck hit on the head," with George H. Thomas, who gained the nickname "Rock of Chickamauga" for his firm stand against the Confederate assault. Lincoln then reinforced Thomas at Chattanooga with two Union armies from Virginia under "Fightin' Joe" Hooker and William Tecumseh Sherman. Lincoln also ordered General Grant to Chattanooga and appointed him to take overall command of the Union forces. By November 24, the tide had turned again in the Union's favor. On that day, Hooker's troops drove Confederates off of Lookout Mountain, and the next day, Union forces broke the Confederate Lines at Missionary Ridge in Georgia, east of Chattanooga.

Grant Takes Command

In March 1864, Lincoln brought Grant east to serve as general-in-chief and to take personal charge of the Army of the Potomac. By this time the Confederacy, outnumbered from the beginning, was disadvantaged by losses of men who could not be replaced as Union losses could. Grant, recognizing this problem, settled upon a plan of operations that was far less brilliant than his operations in the West, but no less decisive. By steadily extending his flanks, he forced the Confederacy to extend its lines, making them very thin. By continuing pressure, he gave his adversaries no rest. The Confederates no longer had the manpower to launch invasions into the North in an effort to score the decisive victory that would cause the North to quit or the Europeans to intervene, but the Southerners could still fight a guerrilla war of attrition on their own soil, as the Americans had done against the British in the American Revolution, and eventually exhaust the Union's will to sacrifice its children in the interest of saving the Union. In fact, by the summer of 1864, Lincoln's popularity may have been at an all time low; the Union Democrats nominated General George McClellan on a peace platform, and there was a strong possibility that Lincoln and the Unionists would lose the election of 1864 and Lincoln's successor would end the war to satisfy the popular will, and thus, the Union would be lost, and secession successful.

In the spring of 1864, Grant placed himself in command in Virginia and General William Tecumseh Sherman in Georgia. Grant opted for an all-out offensive on all fronts so that the South could not shift troops to where the fighting was the hottest. Lee resisted with immense skill, attacking Grant in the wilderness in early May where Union artillery and superiority in numbers were greatly mitigated. In the Battle of the Tangled Wilderness, the Confederates inflicted eighteen thousand casualties on the Union, while suffering twelve thousand them-

▶ General Ulysses S. Grant. Impressed with the General, Abraham Lincoln stated, "Grant is my man, and I am his the rest of the war." *Library of Congress*

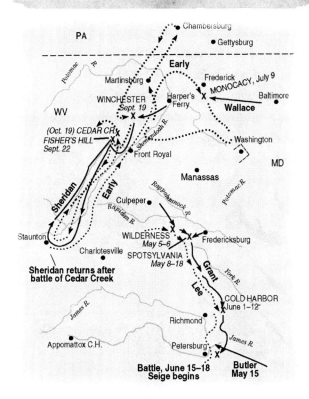

MAP 11.6 War in the East (1864)

selves. Many soldiers were burned to death by fires started by exploding shells in the dry Virginia brush.

Grant, however, simply moved his army east toward Spotsylvania Court House, ten miles closer to Richmond. Lee blocked the road junction between Grant's army and Richmond with the result that another eighteen thousand Union soldiers and twelve thousand Confederates were either killed, wounded, or captured in the twelve days between May 8 and May 19, 1864. Ahead of his time, Lee engaged in trench warfare tactics that would dominate World War I, some fifty years later.

Repulsed at Spotsylvania, Grant moved south in an effort to outflank Lee's forces, but Lee confronted him near the crossroads inn of Cold Harbor, ten miles northeast of Richmond. Grant opted for an assault on Lee's entrenched forces at Cold Harbor on June 3, only to lose seven thousand men in less than an hour. Grant again tried to outflank Lee and moved his army to the James River at Petersburg, twenty miles south of Richmond. Lee again blocked Grant's troops, and in four days of fighting on June 15–18, 1864, Grant's forces suffered another eleven thousand casualties.

Grant sacrificed men so freely in the Virginia campaign between May 5 and June 18, 1864 in the Virginia campaign that his losses (sixty-five thousand) almost equaled the total number of men in Lee's army and earned Grant the disparaging title, "Butcher Grant." During the same six weeks, the South, however, had suffered thirty-seven thousand casualties that they could ill-afford to lose. Lee was winning the battles, but Grant was winning the war.

Unable to break the Confederate lines, as he had done at Vicksburg, Grant then settled down for a siege along the Petersburg-Richmond front. With Lee no longer mobile, it was only a question of time; but Lee held on for nine long months while Richmond remained the Confederate capitol.

Meanwhile, other Union efforts in Virginia were also thwarted by Confederates. Union General Benjamin Butler attempted an attack up the James River against Richmond but was stopped by a rag-tag Confederate army under General Beauregard. A Union offensive in the Shenandoah Valley was stopped at Lynchburg by Stonewall Jackson's old troops under the command of Jubal Early. Early then led a daring raid across the Potomac almost to Washington, D.C., on July 11–12, before being driven back to Virginia.

Presidential Election and the Peace Movement

With Southerners reaching the outskirts of Washington, high casualties, and Richmond still in Southern hands, the mood of the public in the North was decidedly anti-war and anti-Lincoln.

If an election had been held in August 1864, many historians believe that Lincoln would have lost to an anti-war candidate and the fate of the United States might have been forever altered. Lincoln himself told a friend in August that "I am going to be beaten and, unless some great change takes place, badly beaten." Democrats called for Lincoln to drop the issue of emancipation and negotiate peace with the South with the understanding that slavery could continue if the South would return to the Union, but Lincoln refused.

Union casualties in three months (May–July) of 1864 had reached a staggering 110,000, double the casualty rate for any other three-month period of the war, and newspaper headlines boldly shouted to "STOP THE WAR!" Lincoln understood the public sentiments and even sent *New York Tribune* editor Horace Greeley to attempt to negotiate peace with the Confederates at Niagara Falls, with no success. In August, the Democratic Party nominated General George B. McClellan on a peace platform, and it appeared that the November election would be a referendum on Lincoln and the war and that Lincoln and his policy of continuation of the war would lose. Events in Georgia, however, would shift the mood of the public before the November election and seal the preservation of the Union.

MAP 11.7 Final Campaigns of the Civil War (1864–1865)

The Fall of Atlanta

While Grant and Lee faced each other across the trenches at Petersburg, the Confederacy was being cut to pieces from the rear. Grant had first cut it at Vicksburg on the Mississippi, and the next cut took place from eastern Tennessee into Georgia. When Grant left for Virginia, William T. Sherman, a trusted subordinate, remained to face the Confederate forces under Joseph E. Johnston in the mountains of north Georgia.

By the end of June 1864, Sherman had advanced eighty miles, suffering seventeen thousand casualties to Johnston's fourteen thousand. These losses were immense to be sure, but far less than the carnage conducted by Lee and Grant in Virginia. Johnston, a "retreating general" but a resourceful obstructionist, blocked and delayed Sherman at every step, all the way to Atlanta. At Peachtree Creek, just outside Atlanta, Jefferson Davis removed Johnston because of his unwillingness to take the offensive, and John B. Hood was put in his place. Hood made the mistake of challenging Sherman in a series of direct attacks at Peachtree Creek, Atlanta, and Ezra Church, and was so badly defeated, suffering fifteen thousand casualties to six thousand for Sherman, that he had to settle down into a purely defensive position by July 28.

After a month of stalemate, Sherman moved to attack the last rail link into Atlanta from the south at Jonesboro on August 31. On September 1, Sherman's men captured the railroad, and Confederate commander John Bell Hood abandoned Atlanta. Sherman moved his troops into the symbolic city on September 2. The news that Atlanta had fallen sent shockwaves throughout the South and waves of jubilation throughout the North. Southerners had believed that Lincoln would lose the election in November and his successor would quickly negotiate an end to the war that would result in Confederate independence with the retention of slavery. The fall of Atlanta, however, shifted the public sentiments in the North back to Lincoln and his policies of emancipation and military subjugation of the South. To most Northerners, the fall of Atlanta proved that the North had won. Similarly, the fall of Atlanta was a devastating blow to the morale of the South. Many Southerners now understood that they had lost, but they also understood that the man who had waged the irrepressible war against slavery and the South, Abraham Lincoln, would remain in the White House.

Sherman's March

General William Tecumseh Sherman believed that taking Atlanta was not enough, and he must ensure that the Southerners understood that they had lost. Of all the Civil War generals, Grant and especially Sherman had the most "modern" conception of warfare. They were pioneers in the practice of total war. Sherman had become convinced that "we are not only fighting hostile armies, but a hostile people." Defeat of the Southern armies was not enough to win this war. Sherman asserted that the railroads, farms, and factories that fed and supplied the armies must also be destroyed and the will of the civilian population that sustained the armies must be crushed. Sherman even killed the Southern livestock. "We cannot change the hearts of those

▶ General William Tecumseh Sherman led his army across Georgia, burning, killing off livestock, and leaving a carved path of destruction across the state sixty miles wide for 280 miles. *Wikipedia photo*

people of the South," said Sherman in 1864, "but we can make war so terrible … and make them so sick of war that generations would pass away before they would again appeal to it."

In order to ensure that the will of the people was crushed, Sherman believed that he must cut a path of destruction across the South so horrible that Southerners would never consider continuing the war or ever waging it again. He proposed to march his army from Atlanta to Savannah, destroying everything in his path.

After taking Atlanta on September 2, 1864, Sherman began his campaign of destruction by setting fire to the city, burning a third of the entire town, including much nonmilitary property. After assuring Lincoln and Grant, General George Thomas and his sixty thousand men were sufficient to match Hood's Confederate army in Tennessee, Sherman and sixty thousand Union troops marched out of Atlanta on November 16, beginning a march of destruction. Given that Hood's army abandoned Georgia for a campaign in Tennessee, Sherman was able to march unopposed across Georgia from Atlanta to the sea, cutting a path of charred destruction sixty miles wide for 280 miles. A Georgia woman's diary explained Sherman's impact:

There was hardly a fence left standing all the way from Sparta to Gordon. The fields were trampled down and the road was lined with carcasses of horses, hogs and cattle that the invaders, unable either to consume or to carry away with them, had wantonly shot down, to starve out the people. … The dwellings that were standing all showed signs of pillage, and on every plantation we saw … charred remains.

The march of his army from Atlanta to the sea not only destroyed Confederate resources but also functioned as a form of psychological warfare. "It is a demonstration to the world," wrote Sherman, "that we have a power which Jefferson Davis cannot resist. This may not be war but rather statesmanship."

Destruction of Hood's Army of Tennessee

Hood's attempt to retake Tennessee rather than engage Sherman in Georgia turned out little better for the Southerners than Sherman's march. On November 30, 1864, the Confederates attacked the Union army at Franklin, twenty miles South of Nashville, but were badly defeated. Hood then attempted to move on to Nashville where his army was almost wiped out by Union troops under General George Thomas. Of the fifty thousand men under his command in July, only fifteen thousand remained after the defeat at Nashville. With no real army left to lead and a record only of defeat, Hood resigned in January 1865. The South's western army, for all practical purposes, was no more.

▶ General Robert E. Lee met Lt. General Ulysses S. Grant at a farmhouse near Appomattox Court House. Upon realizing that the Union cavalry was backed up by two corps of infantry, he had no choice but to surrender the Army of Northern Virginia to Grant. *Wikipedia photo*

Sherman's March in the Carolinas

At the end of January 1865, Sherman's army of "total warriors" moved north from Savannah into South Carolina, destroying everything in their path as they had in Georgia. Sherman even left less standing in Columbia, South Carolina than he had in Atlanta. Sherman then continued his march all the way into North Carolina where he defeated a Confederate force under Joseph E. Johnston. Just as Sherman had intended, Southern morale was effectively destroyed everywhere he went. One South Carolina physician wrote, "All is gloom, despondency, and inactivity. … Our army is demoralized and the people panic stricken. To fight longer seems to be madness."

Appomattox

By 1864 the South was completely fragmented and the Confederacy's cause was hopeless. But Johnston, having returned to his command in the Southeast, held together a force that retreated across the Carolinas, with Sherman pursuing and wreaking havoc in South Carolina as he pursued. Lee, meanwhile, held against steadily increasing odds at Petersburg. By April 1865, however, the inevitable defeat could be put off no longer. Petersburg fell and Richmond was evacuated. As the Confederates fled Richmond, they set fire to all the military stores they could not carry, with the result that the fires spread out of control and destroyed more of Richmond than Sherman had destroyed of Atlanta or Columbia. Lee and his army headed west, hoping to join the remnants of Johnston's army in North Carolina; but the Union army under Philip Sheridan cut them off at Appomattox, ninety miles from Petersburg, on April 8. The next morning, Lee realized that his position against the superior Union army was hopeless. Lee stated, "There is nothing left for me to do, but to go and see General Grant, and I would rather die a thousand deaths."

Lee met Grant on April 9 at a farmhouse near Appomattox Court House, and in a moving scene surrendered the Army of Northern Virginia to Grant, who accorded generous terms and told his troops not to cheer because, he said, "the rebels are our countrymen again." Southern leaders were not arrested, Jefferson Davis was not to be "hanged from a sour apple tree" as Union newspapers had suggested. Instead, Southerners were to merely lay down their arms and go home. After Lee's surrender, General Johnston also surrendered at Greensboro, North Carolina, before the end of the month.

The War Behind the Lines

The Problems of the Confederacy

Writers on the Civil War have piled up a vast literature—one of the largest bodies of literature on any historical subject—detailing the military aspects of the war: the battles and leaders, the campaigns and maneuvers, the strategy and tactics. This military record, however, does not fully explain the outcome of the war. For, in terms of strategy and tactics, the Confederate performance equaled that of the Union and, on the Virginia front, surpassed it until the last year of the war. The final result was registered on the battlefield, but the basic factors that caused Confederate defeat lay behind the lines. Essentially, the Confederacy failed to solve the problems of organizing its society and its economy for war. It faced these problems in a particularly difficult form, and when it proved unable to solve them, it went down to defeat.

One basic disadvantage of the Confederacy resided in the fact that while the North had a balanced agricultural and industrial economy that was invigorated by war, the Southern economy was based primarily on cotton production, which was dislocated and almost paralyzed by the war. In the North, war stimulated employment, and while wages failed to keep pace with inflation, civilian morale was generally high except among the underpaid urban poor. In the South, economic conditions deteriorated so badly that what may be called economic morale declined even while fighting morale remained adequate. During the spring of 1863 "bread riots" occurred in Richmond and several other Southern cities. Historian Drew Gilpin Faust has argued that because Southern women's interests were so little represented in the way the South publicly defined the war's meaning, the women lost heart and in so doing contributed substantially to the collapse of morale.

Essentially, the Confederacy, with its rural and agricultural society, needed two things. First, it needed access to the products of European—especially British—industry. Second, it needed to stimulate production of food, of horses, and of strategic supplies within the South. Ultimately, it was unable to meet most of those needs.

In order to be able to draw on British industry, the Confederacy needed to have buying power in the European market and to be able to ship goods freely across the Atlantic. But once war broke out, Lincoln proclaimed a blockade, which meant that federal naval vessels would try to seize the merchant vessels of any neutral country bringing goods to Confederate ports.

Southerners thought that the blockade would not work, partly because there were not enough Union ships to enforce it and even more because they believed in what has been called the "King Cotton delusion." They were firmly convinced that cotton was an absolute economic necessity to Britain, because textiles were the heart of British industry. Without cotton this industry would be prostrated. Britain's factories would stand idle, and its workers would be unemployed and would starve. When this started happening, the British government would decide to intervene to acquire cotton from the Confederacy. Therefore, the British navy, which still dominated the seas, would break the blockade.

Southerners were so confident of this idea that they were quite willing to see the British supply of cotton cut off for a while. In the first months of the blockade, while it was still largely ineffective, they deliberately kept their cotton at home instead of sending a part of it abroad to be held in British warehouses for later sale to give them funds for the purchase of supplies. But the bumper crops of the previous two years had produced such a surplus that British manufacturers were able to operate without interruption for nearly a year after the war broke out.

The Importance of Sea Power

For this and other reasons, the faith in this "cotton diplomacy" idea ultimately proved to be a fallacy. Britain received increased supplies of cotton from Egypt and India. Also, British antislavery sentiment generated a strong resistance to taking steps that would help the Confederacy. And Britain was pleased that America was adopting a doctrine of international law concerning the right of blockade, which the British had always advocated and which was bound to be favorable to a nation with large naval power. But most of all, British industry was not paralyzed because Northern wartime purchases stimulated it. Britain, as a neutral, enjoyed an economic boom from supplying war materials to the Union—a boom very similar to the booms the United States later enjoyed in 1914–1917 and 1939–1941 as a neutral supplying war materials to Britain.

The British recognized Confederate naval vessels as warships, not as pirates. The British recognition of belligerency was much resented by the Union, but the real danger for the Union cause resided in the possibility of diplomatic recognition of the Confederacy, which would probably have resulted in efforts by the British to break the blockade. Such efforts would, in turn, have led to war with Britain. But this recognition, for which the Confederacy waited so anxiously, never came.

In November 1861 Confederate hopes were high when an eager Union naval officer, Charles Wilkes, stopped the British ship *Trent* on the high seas and took off two Confederate envoys to Britain, James Mason and John Slidell. Britain, at this point, actually prepared to fight, and an emergency British Cabinet meeting demanded a formal apology to the British flag, reparations, and the release of Mason and Slidell. The British then put their navy on alert and sent eleven thousand troops to Canada, who departed England with a band playing "Dixie." President Lincoln, however, wisely admitted the error and set the envoys free, thus avoiding the possibility of war with England. Meanwhile, the blockade steadily grew tighter. One Confederate port after another was sealed off. Small Confederate vessels, built for speed and based in the Bahamas, continued to delight the South by running the blockade and bringing in cargoes of goods with high value. Their volume was small and they did not in any sense provide the flow of goods that the Confederacy so vitally needed.

In addition to depending on British naval might, the Confederacy made two important efforts to establish sea power of its own. To begin with, it fitted out the first large ironclad vessel ever to put to sea. A powerful steam frigate, the U.S.S. *Merrimac*, which the federals had

▶Pictured is the USS *Monitor* versus the CSS *Virginia* in the Civil War's Battle of Hampton Roads on March 9, 1862. *Corbis Images*

scuttled in the Norfolk Navy Yard, was raised, renamed the *Virginia*, covered with armor plate, and sent out in March 1862. In its first day at sea it destroyed two large Union vessels with ease.

The entire Union navy appeared to be in acute danger, and there was panic in Northern coastal cities, but the Union had been preparing a metal-clad vessel of its own—a small craft that rested low in the water with a revolving gun turret. This *Monitor*, as it was called, challenged the *Virginia* on March 9, 1862. The battle ended in a draw, but with Monitor-type vessels the Union navy was again safe.

The Confederacy's second major endeavor at sea was to buy vessels and equipment in England. Unarmed ships built in England by private companies were then sent to the Azores Islands, outside of British Sovereignty, and outfitted with weaponry to produce fighting ships without violating Britain's neutrality. Such vessels could then raid merchant vessels flying the Union flag.

There were several of these raiders, the most famous of which was the *Alabama*. This great marauder, commanded by Admiral Raphael Semmes, roamed the seas for two years, from Newfoundland to Singapore, capturing sixty-two merchant ships (most of which were burned, after careful attention to the safety of their crews and passengers). It also sank the U.S.S. *Hatteras* in a major naval battle. It was at last cornered and sunk off Cherbourg, France, by the U.S.S. *Kearsarge*, but its career had made the American flag so unsafe on the high seas that prohibitive insurance costs caused more than seven hundred American vessels to transfer to British registry.

Prisoners of War

The issue of prisoners of war was one of the bitterest of the war, especially in the North, because the conditions in Southern prison camps were notoriously deplorable. After all, if Southern soldiers in the field had insufficient rations, what could one expect for Northern POWs in Southern prison camps. In 1862, the two sides had solved the problem by agreeing for the exchange of prisoners captured in battle, thus eliminating the need for large, long-term POW camps. This all changed, however, when the Union began enlisting former slaves in its army.

The Confederate government then announced that it would refuse to treat former slaves in Union uniforms as legitimate soldiers and would execute them when captured, along with the white Union officers for the crime of fomenting slave insurrections.

In reality, the Southerners did not implement the official policy. and Lincoln warned that he would retaliate against Confederate POWs held in the North if they did; but, Confederate troops did sometimes murder African American Union soldiers and their white commanders on the battlefield when they tried to surrender. Other captured African American soldiers were returned to slavery or put into forced labor for the Confederate army. Because of these practices, Lincoln suspended the exchange of prisoners in 1863 until the Confederates agreed to treat white and African American prisoners alike. The South, of course, refused—leading to the growth of large POW camps on both sides with squalid conditions for the POWs, especially in the South. Sixteen percent of all Union POWs held by the South died, while 12 percent of the Confederates held by the North also died.

The most notorious POW camp on either side was the Confederate's Andersonville prison commanded by Henry Wirz, the only person executed by the Union after the war. Andersonville was a stockade with no cover that held thirty-three thousand Union prisoners by the end of the war. Altogether, thirteen thousand Union soldiers died at Andersonville at a rate of one hundred per day. The Southerners lacked the manpower to tend to all of the bodies, with the result that an entire range of vermin invaded the prison. It is said that the ground essentially moved at Andersonville with all of the rats, roaches, flies, maggots, etc. that crawled amid the rotting flesh and human waste. The horrors of Andersonville would remain a symbol to the North of Southern barbarism for decades after the war.

It should be mentioned, however, that treatment of the civilian populations by the marauding armies was extremely mild by war standards. Although much Southern property was destroyed, especially in Sherman's march, rape, murder, and the general terrorizing of civilians were less common. Although Northerners had sworn that they would execute Jefferson Davis, when he was finally captured in May 1865, he was imprisoned on charges of treason and murder, but eventually released in 1867 and never brought to trial.

Economic Failures of the South

Meanwhile, on the home front, the Confederacy failed economically because it was caught between the need to stimulate production and the need to keep down prices and control inflation. The Southern government began with few financial assets other than land and slaves, neither of which could be readily transformed into negotiable currency. It faced a dilemma. It could either encourage production by buying goods in the open market at an uncontrolled price, in which case inflation would mushroom. Or it could control inflation by a system of requisitioning goods for its armies at arbitrarily fixed prices, in which case production would be discouraged rather than stimulated. Help in reducing this problem would have required a program of heavy taxation, by which the government would take back the inflationary dollars that had been spent. But the Confederacy was afraid to use its taxing power. It raised less than 5 percent of its revenue from taxes—a smaller proportion than any other nation in a modern war. Its bond drives to raise funds by borrowing also fell short of hopes.

The South's main source of money was the printing press—the most inflationary method of all. Prices rose by 9,000 percent in the four years of war. Goods grew scarcer while money grew more plentiful. It was grimly said that at the beginning of the war people took their money to market in a purse and brought their goods home in a basket, but that by the end they took the money in a basket and brought their purchases home in a purse.

In short, the Confederacy died of economic starvation—an insufficiency of goods. Its government was too weak to cope with the nearly insoluble economic problems the war had caused. President Jefferson Davis was a bureaucrat who thought in legalistic rather than in dynamic terms. He was not an innovator but a conservative miscast as a revolutionist. The state governments also competed against the Confederate government for the control of manpower and supplies. They insisted upon their sovereign status so strenuously that it has been said that the Confederacy was born of states' rights and died of states' rights.

The best chance the Confederacy ever had—and it was perhaps a fairly good one—was to win a short war before the results of economic malnutrition set in. Once that failed, the cause was hopeless. A few Confederates, such as Josiah Gorgas in the Ordinance Department, improvised brilliantly, and others did so desperately. But in a country where a vitally necessary rail line could be laid only by tearing up the rails somewhere else and re-laying them, a long war against a dynamic adversary could have but one end.

Northern Industrialism and Republican Ascendancy

The problems and limitations of the Confederacy—problems of localism and decentralization, of an agricultural economy and of small-scale economic activities—were characteristic features of the kind of folk society the Confederacy was defending, but while the South was making a last stand against the forces of the modern mechanized world, the war was rushing the North along the path toward industrial domination. Before the Southern states withdrew from the Union, they had blocked some of the governmental measures most conducive to the new industrial economy. Southern secession, however, left the new Republican Party in control. The Republicans combined a free-soil, antislavery ideology with the traditional Whig policy of using the government to stimulate economic growth. While this program was designed to promote the mutual interests of capital and free labor, Republican economic legislation in practice usually helped the former more than the latter.

Secession enabled Republicans to make major changes in policy that would not have been possible without many southern representatives leaving Congress. In February 1861, while the empty seats of the departing Southern congressmen were still warm and even before President Lincoln took office, Congress adopted the Morrill Tariff that, though not very high, was higher than the existing tariff of 1857. This was the first of many tariff increases. Meanwhile Congress repeatedly strengthened the measures by which it gave American industrial producers more exclusive control in the American market, even if this forced American consumers to pay higher prices than they would have had to pay on the world market.

The Transcontinental Railroad

In 1862 Congress broke the long deadlock that the sectional conflict had created over the building of a railroad to the Pacific. For a decade, advocates of a southern route and supporters of a northern route had blocked each other. Now, with the Southerners absent, Congress created the Union Pacific Railroad Company, incorporated with a federal charter, to build westward from Omaha and to meet another road, the Central Pacific, a California corporation, building eastward from Sacramento. To encourage this enterprise, Congress placed very large resources at the disposal of the railroads. It granted loans (not gifts) of between $16,000 and $48,000 a mile—according to the difficulty of the terrain where construction took place.

▶ The beginnings of the Union Pacific railroad, which is still operational today and remains the largest railroad network in the country. *Wikipedia photo*

The value of the lands at that time was not great, and the munificence of this largesse has often been exaggerated, but the point is that the government was paying most of the costs of construction, whereas it might well have controlled or even owned the railroad. Instead, it placed these resources in the hands of private operators, who, if they succeeded, would become owners of the world's greatest railroad, and if they lost, they would be losing the government's money rather than their own. It was "venture capitalism," as it is now called, but the government was doing most of the venturing and the private interests that constructed the road were getting most of the capital. Furthermore, the railroads committed fraud against the government by presenting fraudulent surveys that showed more mountainous terrain than actually existed (the government paid more per mile of track for mountainous terrain than for flatlands) and by needlessly zigzagging in their track construction so as to increase mileage for which the government paid.

In 1869, four years after the war ended, the Union Pacific and the Central Pacific met at Promontory Point in Utah, and a golden spike was driven to mark the event. Travelers to California no longer were obliged to go by wagon or by a lengthy sea voyage. The United States was a long step closer to being a transcontinental republic in an operative sense as well as in a purely geographical one.

The National Banking System

One other major economic measure resulting from Republican ascendancy was the creation of a new and far more centralized system of banking and money. Ever since Andrew Jackson's overthrow of the Bank of the United States in 1832, the country had had a decentralized, loose-jointed financial system period. The United States, of course, issued coins and also bills. For each bill in circulation, a corresponding value of precious metal was held in the Treasury and could be claimed by the holder of the bill. The government handled all its own transactions in such currency and was on a "hard money" basis.

This kind of money, however, was not nearly sufficient to meet the economic needs of the country for a circulating medium. The principal circulating medium, therefore, had been provided by notes issued by banks operating under charters from the various states. State laws governing the incorporation of banks naturally varied, which meant that the financial soundness of the banks was also diverse. This in turn meant that some of the notes circulated at face value, while others circulated at various degrees of discount from face value. So although the government was on a hard money basis, the economy of the country was not, and the federal government exercised little control over the principal component in the monetary system of the country.

The Legal Tender Act of 1862 and the National Banking Act of 1863 changed all this. These acts grew out of the government's need to raise the immense sums required to fight the war. The Legal Tender Act authorized the issuance of Treasury notes—the famous greenbacks—that circulated as authorized money without a backing in metal held in the Treasury.

Primarily, however, the Treasury relied upon borrowing—that is, upon selling bonds. To borrow it had to make the bonds attractive as holdings for the banks. Accordingly, the National Banking Act provided that a bank which purchased government bonds to the amount of one third of its paid-in capital might issue federally guaranteed notes, known as national bank notes, in an amount equal to 90 percent of its bond holdings.

In 1865 a tax was placed on the notes issued under state authority by state-chartered banks. The tax had the effect of making these notes unprofitable and thus driving them out of circulation. As a result of government borrowing policy the United States acquired a new, uniform, federally sanctioned circulating medium of national bank notes.

These notes became the principal form of money for the next fifty years, but they had a great defect—they made the amount of money dependent upon the volume of federal debt rather than upon the economic needs of the country. They were inflexible, and in 1913 they were largely replaced by Federal Reserve notes as a result of the establishment of the Federal Reserve System. But the principles that the United States should have a uniform currency in use throughout the nation, and that the federal government should be responsible for this currency, had come to stay.

Women and the War

Although the Civil War brought suffering and loss to hundreds of thousands of American women, the war meant progress toward independence and equality for women as a group. It meant new opportunities for employment, broadened social and political interests, and demonstrations of competence in activities previously reserved for men. Some women went to war—as nurses, spies, even as soldiers, most often masquerading as men, but the vast majority who served at home—including those who stayed in the home—did most damage to the myth of the helpless female.

It is estimated that almost four hundred women posed as men to join the Union and Confederate armies during the Civil War, and this may be an underestimate because there may be many more that were simply not discovered. So many smooth-faced and slightly built young boys joined both armies that many women could easily pass as young boys. Physical examinations on both sides were almost nonexistent, and women could merely cut their hair, bind their breasts close to their body, and show enthusiasm for the conflict. Sarah Emma Evelyn Edmonds, who joined the 2nd Michigan Volunteers as "Franklin Thompson," stated in her memoirs that her physical examination consisted only of a firm handshake. Although Edmonds' true identity was eventually discovered, she remained in service afterwards as a nurse and a spy. Many women managed to keep their true identities secret throughout the war. Albert D. J. Cashier, who served in an Illinois regiment in the Vicksburg campaign, was only discovered years later when "he" was hospitalized as a war veteran and doctors discovered that he was really Jennie Hodges. Others, such as Lyons Wakeman, who is buried at Chalmette National Cemetery in St. Bernard Parish, Louisiana, were only discovered in death. Wakeman, whose real identity was Sarah Rosetta Wakeman of Afton, New York, fought with General Nathaniel P. Banks in the Union's loss at Mansfield and also at Pleasant Hill before dying of dysentery.

▶ Sarah Emma Evelyn Edmonds joined the Second Michigan Volunteers as "Franklin Thompson." Edmonds' true identity was eventually discovered, but she remained in service afterwards as a nurse and a spy. *Wikipedia photo*

Other women accompanied their husbands as camp followers. These women not only tended to their husbands' laundry and sewing, but served as field nurses, kept weapons loaded, and carried water to cool both weapons and throats. One Rose Rooney, however, openly enlisted with the Crescent Blues Volunteers in the Confederate army at New Orleans in 1861. Her assigned duty was to serve as a cook and a laundress, but she eventually did much more than that. At the First Battle of Bull Run, she is credited with running through a field of heavy fire to tear down a rail fence so as to allow a battery of Confederate artillery to advance forward and help halt a Union charge. Rooney served in Lee's Army of Northern Virginia for virtually the entire war and remained in the ranks when Lee surrendered in 1865.

Aside from their roles on the battlefield, as in earlier wars, but in much greater numbers, women during the Civil War had to take their husbands' places as heads of households, running shops, managing farms and plantations, finding jobs to earn food for their families. In the South, many had to do housework—and field work—for the first time. Some had to face armed, hostile slaves as well as enemy soldiers. In Minnesota and elsewhere on the frontier, women had to survive Native American uprisings.

Job opportunities for women multiplied as men went off to fight or quit old occupations for better-paying ones. The war quickened the movement of women into school teaching, a profession once dominated by men. Many Northern women also went south to teach in schools for freed slaves. In both the Union and the Confederacy women also went to work for the government. By the end of the war thousands held government office jobs.

When the war began, women dominated the work force in the mills and factories of New England, while in the South female industrial workers were a small minority—another situation that favored the Union war effort. As men joined the service, women took their places in industry and helped produce military equipment and supplies. The demand for what was considered women's work also expanded: Sewing women were hired by the thousands, and brutally exploited. In self-protection, the women organized, protested, and went out on strikes.

In addition to work for pay, there was a tremendous amount of unpaid activity by women in both South and North—though there was more in the North, because women in that region had a tradition of public activism lacking in the more conservative South. Women volunteered to nurse, and some of them, above all Clara Barton, became famous. They joined aid societies and organized activities to raise funds. They wrote and spoke for the causes they believed in and even, in a few cases, comprised part of the attendance at riots, in both the North and South. Overall, many women demonstrated talents of efficiency and leadership.

In the North women took the initiative to found an organization, the United States Sanitary Commission, which did valuable work in raising money and gathering materials for wounded soldiers. Men were officially in charge; however, women supplied much of the energy. Over time, women did excellent. In an era when married women could not sign contracts (owing to the tenets of coverture), women raised hundreds of thousands of much-needed dollars for humanitarian relief.

The Civil War gave American women a chance to enter many new areas and prove themselves quite as capable as men. When the war ended, many lost their jobs to returning veterans. Some returned gratefully to domesticity, but there was no turning back the clock.

Chapter Review

Summary

The American Civil War was the bloodiest in American history with 618,000 killed and over 20 percent of all white males participating, the highest participation rate of any American war. On both sides, men were fighting for what they deeply believed to be American values.

Southerners were convinced that their right to form a Confederacy was based on a principle of the *Declaration of Independence*—that governments derive their just powers from the consent of the governed. They were also fighting because they were being invaded by the North. The North was fighting to defend the flag and to prove that a democracy was not too weak to hold together. Abolition of slavery was not a motivation for most people at the outset of the war, but became one during the War when Lincoln felt that he needed a greater moral purpose.

Lincoln was born in a Kentucky log cabin in 1809 and suffered a life of tragedy that included the loss of his mother, stepmother, romantic love, and two of his children. Lincoln struggled to make a living all of his life until he rose from nowhere politically to seize the Republican nomination in 1860 and the White House that November. The next month, South Carolina seceded, followed eventually by ten other Southern states. Lincoln tried to re-supply Union Fort Sumter, but Southerners fired on the fort and the Civil War began on April 12, 1861. Originally, both sides viewed the war as a Romantic test of courage and Lincoln called for 75,000 90-day volunteers. The First Battle of Bull Run where the Union troops were routed, however, proved that the War would not be swift and massive casualties in later battles, such as Shiloh, fairly well put to rest the notion that the War was a Romantic test of courage.

The Confederates under Robert E. Lee hoped for a decisive victory in the North that would bring recognition or intervention from Europe, but Lee's Northern invasion was repelled at Antietam in 1862. The next year, Lee would suffer a defeat at Gettysburg on July 3 from which his army would never recover and the next day, General Ulysses S. Grant took Vicksburg. Nevertheless, the South fought on and sentiments in the North turned against the War. Lincoln's approval rating in August, 1864 was sufficiently low that he was expected to lose the election in November, but Atlanta fell to the Union under General William T. Sherman on September 2, 1864, and Lincoln's political fortunes reversed as Northerners suddenly believed they had won and Southerners suddenly understood that they had lost. Sherman then reinforced that notion with a march across Georgia where he burned a sixty mile wide swath across Georgia.

Lee Surrendered April 9, 1865 at Appomattox Court House in Virginia after a bloody campaign to defend Richmond where the outnumbered Southerners fought valiantly, but finally lost the war of attrition. The Northern superiority in population, transportation, and manufacturing had eventually made the difference. Five days later, Lincoln was assassinated by John Wilkes Booth at Ford's Theater and the man that might have been "the South's best friend" because he did not favor a punitive peace, was dead.

Chapter Review (cont'd) ▶ ▶ ▶

Chronological Time Line

1809	Abraham Lincoln is born in a log cabin in Kentucky
1816	Abraham Lincoln's mother, Nancy Lincoln, dies of "milk sickness."
1829	Sarah Bush Lincoln, Abe's stepmother, dies.
1832	Lincoln fights in the Blackhawk War
1834	Abraham Lincoln is elected to the Illinois Legislature
1835	Lincoln's girlfriend, Ann Rutledge, dies.
1842	Lincoln marries Mary Todd
1846	Abraham Lincoln is elected to Congress.
1861	April 19, Lincoln announces a blockade of the South.
1861	April 19, Baltimore erupts in riots
1861	May 10–11 St. Louis erupts in riots
1861	July, Lincoln calls for 75,000 90-day volunteers
1861	July 21, First Battle of Bull Run (Manassas)
1861	August 1, Confederate Colonel John R. Baylor proclaims the "Confederate Territory of Arizona."
1861	September 20, Confederates capture a Union garrison at Lexington, MO
1862	February 6–16, General Ulysses S. Grant takes Confederate Forts Donelson and Henry in Tennessee
1862	February 21, Confederates under H.H. Sibley defeat a Union force at Valverde and take Albuquerque and Santa Fe for the Confederacy
1862	February 25, Nashville, TN is the first Southern Capitol to surrender
1862	March 8, 16,000 Confederates defeated at Pea Ridge, Arkansas
1862	March 9, battle between the Merrimac (Virginia) and the Monitor ends in a draw

Time Line (cont'd)

1862	March 28, Confederates defeated in New Mexico at Glorieta Pass and retreat back to Texas
1862	April, Confederacy institutes conscription
1862	April 6–7, 23,000 men die at Shiloh
1862	April 26, David Farragut takes New Orleans for the Union.
1862	April–July, McClellan's campaign for Richmond
1862	May 31–June 1, Confederate General Joseph E. Johnston is wounded at Seven Pines and replaced by Robert E. Lee
1862	July 11, Lincoln replaces McClellan with General Henry Halleck
1862	September 17–18, McClellan forces Lee to retreat at Antietam
1862	October 8, Confederate offensive under General Braxton Bragg is pushed back at Perryville, Kentucky
1862	December 15, Union General Ambrose E. Burnside is defeated at Fredericksburg and replaced by Joseph Hooker
1862	December 31, Confederates under Braxton Bragg are defeated at Murfeesboro and forced to abandon their offensive
1863	January 1, Lincoln issues the Emancipation Proclamation
1863	May 6, Union General Joseph Hooker is defeated at Chancellorsville.
1863	May, Union institutes conscription
1863	July 1–3, Confederate Army under Robert E. Lee is defeated at Gettysburg and forced to withdraw
1863	July 4, General Ulysses S. Grant takes Vicksburg
1863	July 13–16, Draft Riots in New York City
1863	September 20, Union is forced to retreat at Chickamauga Creek.
1864	May 5–7 Battle of the Tangled Wilderness, Virginia

Chapter Review (cont'd) ▶ ▶ ▶

Time Line (cont'd)

1864	May 8–19 Battle of Spottsylvania Courthouse, Virginia
1864	June 15–18 Battle of Cold Harbor, Virginia
1864	September 2, 1864, Atlanta falls to General William T. Sherman
1864	May 8–19 Battle of Spottsylvania Courthouse, Virginia
1864	November, Lincoln reelected.
1864	Sherman's March to the Sea, November 2-December 21
1865	April 9, Robert E. Lee surrenders at Appomattox Court House, Virginia
1865	April 14, Lincoln Assassinated.
1869	May 10, Golden Spike is driven at Promontory Summit, Utah, to complete the Transcontinental Railroad.

Key Terms

Jefferson Davis: President of the Confederacy

Border States: Slave States, Maryland, Delaware, Kentucky, and Missouri that did not secede.

Conscription: The military draft

Cotton clads: Confederate ships draped on cotton bales for protection

William Seward: Secretary of State under Abraham Lincoln

Blockade: The closing of Southern ports by the Union navy

Bushwhackers: Confederate guerrilla groups in Missouri

Jayhawkers: Union guerrilla groups in Missouri

First Battle of Bull Run: Won by the Confederates, July 21, 1861

Anaconda Plan: Union strategy where the North would weaken the South gradually through blockades on land and sea until the Northern army was strong enough to move forward and crush the weakened south.

Second Battle of Bull Run: August 28-30 1862, Confederates force a retreat by Union General John Pope

General Irvin McDowell: Union General that suffered defeat at the first battle of Bull Run

Thomas J. "Stonewall" Jackson: Confederate General who earned the name "Stonewall" for his stand at Bull Run, was accidentally shot and by his own men at Chancellorsville and later died from complications

Key Terms (cont'd)

General Robert E. Lee: Commander of the Confederate Army of Virginia

General George B. McClellan: Union General that was twice sacked by Lincoln for his lack of aggressiveness and campaigned for President on a peace platform in 1864.

Antietam: Confederate defeat on September 17, 1862, that ended General Lee's best attempt at bringing a decisive victory in a Northern Offensive

Fredericksburg: Union Army under General Ambrose E. Burnside is repulsed by Confederates under Robert E. Lee, December 11-15, 1862

General Ambrose E. Burnside: Union General that was repulsed by Confederates at Fredericksburg, also known for whiskers on the side of the face that became known as "sideburns."

General Joseph Hooker: General "Fightin Joe" Hooker favored a military dictatorship for the United States, given command by Lincoln, was defeated by Robert E. Lee and the Confederates at Chancellorsville, May 6, 1863.

Chancellorsville: Battle in May 1863 where a smaller force of Confederates under Robert E. Lee defeated a larger Union Army under General Joseph E. Hooker, but lost General Thomas "Stonewall" Jackson, who was accidentally shot by his own men.

Gettysburg: Decisive Union Victory in the North on July 1-3, 1863 normally viewed as the turning point in the Civil War

Pickett's Charge: Failed Confederate charge under General George Pickett at Gettysburg that was the turning point in the battle and therefore the war.

Pea Ridge: Confederate defeat in Arkansas on March 8, 1862 that secured Union control of Missouri

Forts Henry and Donelson: The capture of these two Confederate Forts by the Union on February 6 and February 16, 1863, gave the Union control of the Cumberland River.

Admiral David Farragut: Captured New Orleans for the Union on April 29, 1862 and rewarded with the rank of Admiral. Farragut is also remembered in popular culture for his order at the Battle of Mobile Bay on August 5, 1864, usually paraphrased: "Damn the torpedoes, full speed ahead!"

Shiloh: Major battle on April 6-7, 1862 that resulted in 23,000 combined Union and Confederate casualties and is generally credited with damaging the notion that the War was a romantic test of courage.

General Ulysses S. Grant: Conqueror of Vicksburg, the Union Commander for the duration of the War.

Vicksburg: Major Confederate port on the Mississippi River, captured by the Union under General Ulysses S. Grant, July 4, 1863.

Chickamauga and Chattanooga: September 19-20, 1863, combined casualties were 36,000, the most of any battle at that point except for Gettysburg, and the Union was forced to retreat from Chickamauga.

General William T. Sherman: Union General that captured Atlanta and marched from Atlanta to Savannah, Georgia destroying everything in his path while waging "Total War."

Chapter Review (cont'd) ▶ ▶ ▶

Key Terms (cont'd)

Battle of the Tangled Wilderness: May 5-7, 1864, Confederates inflicted 18,000 casualties on the Union, while suffering 12,000 themselves.

Spotsylvania Court House: Lee blocked the road junction between Grant's army and Richmond with the result that another 18,000 Union Soldiers and 12,000 Confederates were either killed, wounded, or captured in the twelve days between May 8-19, 1864.

Cold Harbor: One of General Grant's worst defeats, Grant lost 18,000 men between June 3 and June 18 and gained no advantage.

Sherman's March: General William Tecumseh Sherman's destructive march from Atlanta to Savanna where he destroyed a swath through Georgia 60 miles wide.

Appomattox: Court House in Virginia where Robert E. Lee surrendered to Ulysses S. Grant, April 9, 1865

Merrimac and the Monitor: The first ironclad warships that fought an historic battle to a draw on March 9, 1862

Andersonville: Notorious Confederate Prison where sanitation was poor, disease was rampant, and 13,000 prisoners died during the war.

Henry Wirz: Commander at Andersonville prison, the only Confederate soldier executed by the Union after the War

Morrill Tariff: A tariff increase in February 1861

Transcontinental Railroad: Railroad connecting East and West from Council Bluffs, Iowa to Oakland, California completed in 1869.

Greenbacks: Treasury notes that circulated as authorized money without a backing in metal held in the Treasury.

Sarah Rosetta Wakeman: Woman who fought with General Nathaniel P. Banks in the Union's loss at Mansfield and also at Pleasant Hill before dying of dysentery

Camp followers: Women who followed their husbands into battle and played support roles.

Rose Rooney: Woman who openly enlisted in the Confederate army and served in Lee's Army of Northern Virginia for virtually the entire war.

Clara Barton: Nurse who tended to Union soldiers on the battlefield and is credited with founding the American Red Cross

Sources Consulted

Jeanie Attie, *Patriotic Toil: Northern Women and the Civil War* (1998).

William C. Cooper, *Jefferson Davis, American* (2000).

David P. Crook, *The North, The South, and the Powers 1861–1865* (1974).

Faust, Drew Gilpin, *Mothers of Invention: Women of the Slaveholding South in the American Civil War* (2004).

Shelby Foote, *The Civil War: A Narrative* (1974).

Joseph T. Glatthaar, *Forged in Battle: The Civil War Alliance of Black Soldiers and White Officers* (1990).

Allen C. Guelzo, *Lincoln's Emancipation Proclamation* (2004).

Maury Klein, *Days of Defiance: Sumter, Secession, and the Coming of the Civil War* (1997).

Elizabeth D. Leonard, *All the Daring of a Soldier: Women of the Civil War Armies* (1999).

Bruce Levine, *Confederate Emancipation: Southern Plans to Free and Arm Slaves During the Civil War* (2006).

James Marten, *The Children's Civil War* (1998).

James M. McPherson, *Battle Cry of Freedom: The Civil War Era* (1988).

James M. McPherson, *For Cause and Comrades: Why Men Fought in the Civil War* (1997).

Ivan Musicant, *Divided Waters: The Naval History of the Civil War* (1995).

Mark E. Neely, Jr., *The Fate of Liberty: Abraham Lincoln and Civil Liberties* (1990).

Phillip S. Paludan, *"A People's Contest": The Union and Civil War, 1861–1865* (1988).

Phillip S. Paludan, *The Presidency of Abraham Lincoln* (1994).

George C. Rable, *Civil Wars: Women and the Crisis of Southern Nationalism* (1989).

Nina Silber, *Daughters of the Union: Northern Women Fight the Civil War* (2005).

Brooks D. Simpson, *Ulysses S. Grant* (2000).

Emory Thomas, *The Confederate Nation, 1861–1865* (1979).

Emory Thomas, *Robert E. Lee* (1995).

12 Reconstruction, 1863–1877

Outline

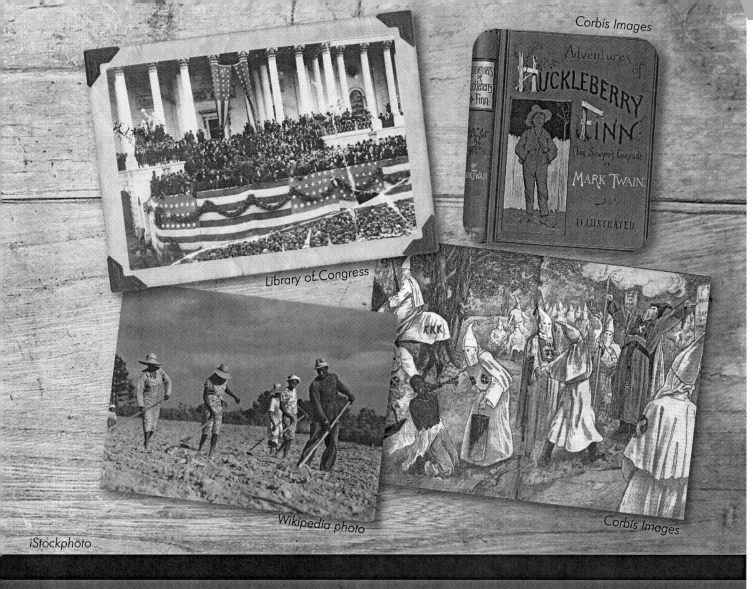

Corbis Images

Library of Congress

Wikipedia photo

Corbis Images

iStockphoto

The Road to Reunion

Wars always bring results not intended by those who fight them. The War Between the States accelerated the growth of mass production and economic centralization in the North while it destroyed much of the economic production in the South and convinced the rising generation of Southern leaders that future regional prosperity depended upon industrialization. The war also caused an increase in federal power at the expense of the states, for no government could spend the funds, organize the forces, and wield the strength the federal government did, without increasing its power. The main purpose of the war, however, was to reunite a broken union of states, and there was a question whether the abolition of slavery was necessary to the objective of reunion. Some Republicans wanted to make emancipation one of the objects of the war, simply because they deplored slavery and did not believe that a Union which had slavery in it was worth saving. Others, who were relatively indifferent to the welfare of the African Americans, believed that the slaveholding class, which they called the "slave power," was guilty of causing disunion, that to make the Union safe, this power must be destroyed, and that the way to destroy it was to abolish slavery. Still others, including many of the "War Democrats" and the Unionists in the border states, regarded the war as one against secession, having nothing to do with slavery.

Emancipation

For his part, Abraham Lincoln had stated his belief long before he became President, that the Union could not endure permanently as half-slave and half-free. He knew, however, that he could not free any slaves unless he won the war and that he could not win the war if he antagonized all the Unionists in the slave states of Delaware, Maryland, Kentucky (his own birthplace), and Missouri. As a result, he moved very slowly on the slavery question, and when two of his generals tried to move more quickly by emancipating slaves in the areas they had occupied, he countermanded their orders.

Emancipation Proclamation

Few people realize it today, but the war had raged for seventeen months and was more than a third over before Lincoln moved to free the slaves in the Confederacy. In July 1862, he made up his mind to proclaim the freedom of slaves in the insurrectionary states, but he decided to wait for a victory before doing so. The Battle of Antietam (Sharpsburg) in September was not a great victory, but it sufficed. In that month Lincoln issued a proclamation that after January 1, 1863, all slaves in areas that were at that time in rebellion should be "forever free." This still did nothing about slaves in places like New Orleans, which was occupied by federal forces, or in the border slave states because those areas were not in rebellion, therefore, the slaves in those areas were not free. The Emancipation Proclamation also did not free the slaves in areas under rebellion because those areas were obviously not under Union control and any proclamation by the President, whether concerning emancipation or otherwise, would be completely ignored. The emancipation proclamation also gave all the states of the Confederacy one hundred days during

▶ Painting depicting Abraham Lincoln presenting his first draft of the Emancipation Proclamation to his cabinet. Though the legislation did not free all slaves everywhere, it was a step in that direction.
Wikipedia photo

which they could save slavery by coming back into the Union. Clearly, the principle of the emancipation proclamation was not that one could not own slaves, but that one could not own slaves and secede from the Union.

Strongly believing in persuasion rather than force, Lincoln in December 1862 proposed a constitutional amendment for the gradual emancipation of slaves in the border states by the year 1900, with compensation to the owners, but this proposal was overtaken by events as the escalating impact of the war accelerated the destruction of slavery. On January 1, 1863, Lincoln issued the *Emancipation Proclamation* to apply in all areas under Confederate control. Although it would require Northern victory to become a reality, this proclamation announced a new Union war aim—freedom for the slaves as well as restoration of the Union. Enthusiasm for the war in the North was already on the decline in late 1862; and Lincoln sought a greater moral cause for the war than merely the preservation of the Union, which by the end of 1862 was simply insufficient cause for far too many persons North of the Mason-Dixon line. Lincoln also surmised that the emancipation cause would help prevent English intervention on the side of the South. As the self-appointed world leader of the abolition movement, England could hardly join the war on the side of slavery if the Union had made abolition one of its goals.

The caution with which Lincoln had proceeded with emancipation reflects his own scruples about the Constitution and the prudence of his own temperament, but it also reflects the fierceness of the divisions within the North and the dangers that these divisions held for the administration. On one flank, Lincoln was assailed by the Democrats. A minority of War Democrats gave him vigorous support, but a majority of the Democrats constantly called for a negotiated peace and especially assailed any move against slavery, believing that any move against slavery would force the South to fight rather than negotiate. Democratic propagandists helped convince white workingmen that they were being used in a war to free African Americans who would take their jobs away. It was this conviction that turned the "draft riots" in New York in July 1863 into mob assaults on African Americans. More than one hundred people were killed in these assaults, most of them white rioters shot down by police and troops. The riots were so tumultuous that the draft was suspended in New York City for the remainder of the war.

On the other flank, pressure was coming from many sources, including middle-class women reformers. Susan B. Anthony and Elizabeth Cady Stanton organized their fellow suffragists into the Women's National Loyal League and gathered hundreds of thousands of signatures on an antislavery petition. Further, the more militant antislavery men in the Republican Party denounced Lincoln because he did not instantly take drastic action to end slavery. These "radical Republicans" hoped to dominate the administration by forcing all moderates on the slavery question out of the cabinet, and in 1864, some of them sought to prevent Lincoln's nomination for a second term. By unrivaled political dexterity and skill, Lincoln frustrated these attacks from both directions and maintained a broad base of support among abolitionists for the war.

As late as 1864, however, the House of Representatives defeated a constitutional amendment for the abolition of slavery. The Thirteenth Amendment, abolishing slavery, was not finally voted by Congress for submission to the states until January 31, 1865. Maryland, Tennessee, and Missouri abolished slavery by state action at about this same time, but slavery was still legal in Kentucky and Delaware when the Civil War ended, and the amendment was not ratified until eight months after Lincoln's death.

African Americans as Emancipators

For African Americans, the war years were a time of elation and rejoicing, frustration and despair. African American men and women alike worked hard for the Union cause. African American intellectuals wrote and lectured, both at home and abroad. They organized their own aid and relief societies for the great numbers of freed slaves and went to them as teachers. African American women volunteered their services as nurses and hospital aids. Men by the hundreds of thousands went to war for the Union as sailors in the navy and as servants, cooks, and laborers with the army. When they were finally allowed to do so, they also went as soldiers.

For a long time, however, African Americans were not allowed to serve in the army. Not until the autumn of 1862 were African Americans officially permitted to enlist, and it was another year before the bravery of African American regiments in battle began to change the scornful attitude of whites, in and out of the service. Most instrumental in this shift was the heroic, if doomed, assault on Fort Wagner, South Carolina by a African American regiment, the Fifty-fourth Massachusetts Infantry, in July 1863. Overall, African American servicemen estab-

► Fifty-fourth Massachusetts Infantry was one of the first official African American units in the United States during the Civil War. *Wikipedia photo*

lished an admirable record, and twenty-one received the Congressional Medal of Honor. But the officers in African American regiments were mostly white men. Only a handful of African American soldiers were promoted to the rank of lieutenant or captain. Not until June 1864 was the pay of African American and white soldiers equalized.

Throughout the war, then, African Americans continued to face injustice and discrimination, despite their major contribution to the Union cause. From the beginning, their most influential spokesman, Frederick Douglass, looked on Lincoln as much too conservative, and when the President delayed taking decisive steps toward freeing the slaves, Douglass was outspoken in his criticism.

Although Lincoln had his African American supporters, including the beloved Harriet Tubman, he also gave offense by his continuing interest in some programs to move African Americans out of the country to a colony in the tropics. In fact, there were some African Americans who were so embittered that they welcomed the possibility of such separation. Martin R. Delany, who later joined with Douglass in working for African American recruitment, favored the migration of African Americans to Haiti, a project that was tried unsuccessfully early in the war. After the rejection of African American volunteers by the army, the subsequent mistreatment of African American soldiers, and attacks on both African American soldiers and civilians in several Northern cities, there were African Americans who agreed with white racists that the Civil War was indeed a white man's war in a white man's country, to which African Americans owed no allegiance.

Nevertheless, there was progress. The *Emancipation Proclamation* was finally issued. The Thirteenth Amendment was adopted. The great slave population (which, as Douglass had repeatedly pointed out, enabled the Confederacy to put so large a proportion of its whites into uniform) was finally freed. Many African Americans, Union soldiers as well as former slaves, were also freed from the bonds of illiteracy by dedicated teachers—both African American and white—and through their own efforts.

After the war, African Americans were recognized as full citizens by the federal government, and campaigns against discrimination in the law courts, the polling places, the schools, and public conveyances won victories in several states. In 1864 African American representatives from eighteen states formed the National Equal Rights League. The long, agonizingly slow march toward equality had begun.

Lincoln's Reelection and Assassination

In 1864, when the time came for a new presidential election, the Democrats nominated General McClellan to run against Lincoln. Some of the so-called Radical Republicans, who were dissatisfied with Lincoln's leniency, tried to block his renomination and put up the Secretary of the Treasury, Salmon P. Chase, in his stead. This effort failed, however, and Lincoln was renominated. In an effort to put the ticket on a broad, bipartisan basis, the party dropped the name Republican, called itself the Union party, and nominated for the vice-presidency a Southern Democrat who had stood firmly for the Union, Andrew Johnson of Tennessee.

In November 1864 Lincoln and Johnson were elected, carrying all but three Union states (New Jersey, Delaware, and Kentucky). In the following March, the new term began, and Lincoln delivered his Second Inaugural Address, calling for "malice toward none and charity for all," in order "to bind up the nation's wounds." On April 9, Lee surrendered the Army of Northern Virginia. It was clear that the work of Reconstruction must now begin in earnest.

On April 14, however, as celebrations still continued in the North in the wake of the Confederate surrender, Lincoln attended a performance at Ford's Theater, where he was shot by an assassin, John Wilkes Booth. Booth broke into Lincoln's theater box and shot the President in the back of the head with a small pistol at point blank range, then jumped to the stage with a dagger in one hand, breaking an ankle in the process, and escaped through the back door of the theater. As he left the theater, Booth shouted the Virginia state motto, "Sic simper tyrannis" (thus always to tyrants). Lincoln died the next morning, without ever recovering consciousness, and Andrew Johnson, who was also stabbed in his bed by an attempted assassin while Lincoln was being shot across town, survived the attack and became President of the United States.

Unknown to Booth, however, a Southern sympathizer who evidently killed Lincoln in a spirit of Southern revenge, he had probably just killed the South's best friend, because it does not appear that Lincoln favored any sort of punitive reconstruction and was in favor of allowing the South to manage their own affairs as much as would be possible. With Lincoln out of the way, the path was much more open for those in the North who favored a more punitive peace.

Reconstruction
Wartime Reconstruction

The process of readmission to the Union for Southern states had begun as early as 1862 when Union troops began reclaiming Southern territory. Lincoln then appointed provisional gov-

►Depiction of the assassination of Abraham Lincoln at the hand of John Wilkes Booth, a Southern sympathizer. *Corbis Images*

ernors for those parts of the Union controlled and occupied by federal troops. Although Abraham Lincoln had always opposed slavery on moral as well as political grounds, he was skeptical about the prospects for racial equality in the United States. The legacy of slavery and race prejudice, he believed, would prevent African Americans from rising to the level of whites or prevent whites from allowing African Americans to change their place in society. This was why Lincoln had supported the colonization abroad of freed slaves as a possible solution of the race problem.

By 1864, however, the President was convinced of the impracticality, if not the injustice, of this policy. The contribution of African Americans to the Union war effort and the growing strength of Northern antislavery convictions also made him more hopeful about the chances for eventual African American advancement and racial adjustment. On this question, though, Lincoln remained a moderate and a gradualist to the end of his life.

Lincoln and the Northern moderates also believed that victory in war could not really restore the Union. It could only prevent secession. After that, the Union would be restored only if the Southern people again accepted the Union and gave their loyalty to it. To bring them back, Lincoln wanted a conciliatory policy. So when in 1864 Congress adopted a measure known as the Wade-Davis Bill, imposing stringent terms for the restoration of the former Confederates and including a requirement that Southerners could only establish state governments after the majority in a state had sworn to a loyalty oath, Lincoln quickly disposed of the Wade-Davis Bill with the pocket veto. (The President did not sign the bill during the last ten days of a Congressional session, thus killing the bill through his inaction.)

When people raised technical questions about the legal status of the Confederate states (Were they still states, or conquered territories? Had they committed "state suicide"?), Lincoln was impatient about such "pernicious abstractions." All that mattered was whether the states could be brought back into their proper relationship with the Union.

By 1864, the Union had regained enough control in Louisiana, Tennessee, and Arkansas to start a process of restoring these states to the Union, and Lincoln presented generous terms on which this could be done.

▶Lincoln's tomb in Springfield, Illinois. *Wikipedia photo*

He would grant amnesty to former Confederates who took an oath of allegiance; and when as many as one-tenth of the number who had been citizens in 1860 did so; he would permit them to form a new state government. When this government accepted the abolition of slavery and repudiated the principle of secession, Lincoln would receive it back into the Union. States did not have to recognize the rights of African Americans or give a single African American the vote.

Louisiana was the first state reorganized on this basis. Despite its denial of African American suffrage, Lincoln accepted Louisiana, though he did ask the governor "whether some of the colored people may not be let in, as for instance, the very intelligent, and especially those who have fought gallantly in our ranks." In Virginia, Tennessee, and Arkansas, also, Lincoln recognized state governments that did not enfranchise African Americans.

It was clear, however, that Republicans in Congress were suspicious of these states—more because of their leniency toward the former Confederates than because of their treatment African Americans. Secondly, the Radical Republicans favored a reconstruction policy that would punish the South; and they, therefore, opposed Lincoln's plan because it was not punitive. Radical Republicans in Congress also disliked Lincoln's conciliatory "10 percent plan" because it allowed the President, rather than Congress, to establish reconstruction policy . It was also clear that Congress might deny the re-established states recognition by refusing to seat their newly elected senators and representatives.

Johnson's Policy of Reconstruction

Although a Southerner and the only Senator from a Southern state to remain loyal to the Union, Andrew Johnson was expected to be more severe in his Reconstruction policy than Lincoln. Johnson was the son of poor, illiterate parents in Raleigh, North Carolina, who could not afford to send their son to school. Instead, Johnson's mother apprenticed him to a tailor after his father died, and Johnson later worked as a tailor in Tennessee. The ambitious Johnson, who had been illiterate until his wife taught him to write, not only became a successful tailor but also accumulated a fortune in land and at one time even owned five slaves. Johnson was a man of strong emotions. As a Southerner with the roots of a common man, he hated both aristocrats, whom he blamed for secession, and secessionists in general; but when his policy developed, it turned out that he disliked abolitionists and radicals even more. In the end, Johnson proved even more lenient toward former Confederates than Lincoln had been. Johnson was a strong states' rights advocate, who as a Senator had voted against everything that smacked of increased federal power. He even once voted against a bill to pave the streets of Washington, D.C.

Johnson was a defender of slavery and accepted emancipation only grudgingly. Johnson's eventual opposition to slavery developed more out of his dislike for the planter class than out of any moral outrage against slavery or sympathy for African Americans. Johnson believed African Americans to be intellectually inferior and naturally more suited to manual labor.

On May 29, 1865, he issued a broad amnesty to all who would take an oath of allegiance, including ex-Confederate government officials and military officers, although men with property valued at more than $20,000 (in other words, planters) were required to ask for special pardon, which was freely given. In the six weeks after May 29, he appointed provisional governors in each of the remaining Southern states to reorganize governments for these states. Only men who had been voters in 1860 and who had taken the oath of allegiance could participate in these reorganizations. This meant, of course, that African Americans were excluded. When the new governments disavowed secession, accepted the abolition of slavery, and repudiated the Confederate debt, Johnson would accept them. As to what policy should be followed toward the freed men—that was to be determined by the states themselves.

The Southern states moved swiftly under this easy formula. Before the end of the year, every state except Texas, which followed soon after, had set up a new government that met the President's terms. Two conspicuous features of these governments, however, were deeply disturbing to many Republicans.

First, these Southern states had adopted a series of laws known as "Black Codes" that denied African Americans many of the rights of citizenship—including the right to vote and to serve on juries. African Americans could not testify against whites, and laws were passed against interracial marriage. Of course, African Americans were also denied the right to bear arms. Other laws were passed that excluded them from certain types of property ownership and certain occupations. In some cases, African American employment was limited to agriculture and domestic servitude. Unemployed African Americans might be arrested as vagrants and bound out to labor in a new form of involuntary servitude. African American workers truant from jobs were forced to do public service until they returned to their former employer to whom they were contractually bound.

Second, the former Confederates were in complete control. By December 1865, all former Confederate states had organized new governments, ratified the Thirteenth Amendment abolishing slavery, and elected Congressmen. Between them, the newly organized states elected to Congress no fewer than nine Confederate congressmen, seven Confederate state officials, four generals, four colonels, and Confederate Vice-President Alexander Stephens.

GRAND, NATIONAL UNION BANNER FOR 1864.
LIBERTY, UNION AND VICTORY,

Wikipedia photo

Radical Republicans

Presidential Reconstruction, as a *fait accompli*, confronted Congress when it met at the end of 1865. At this point, the Republicans were far from ready for the kind of all-out fight against Johnson that later developed, but they were not willing to accept the reorganized states. They were especially resentful because these states could now claim a larger representation in Congress with the free African American population (only three fifths of African Americans had been counted when they were slaves), without actually allowing African Americans any voice in the government. It would be ironic, indeed, if the overthrow of slavery should increase the representation of the South in Congress and if southerners should come back into the Union stronger politically than when they seceded.

For some months, the Republicans in Congress moved slowly, unwilling to face a break with a President of their own party and far from ready to make a vigorous stand for the rights of African Americans. However, they would not seat the Southern congressmen-elect, and they arranged a Joint Committee of the Senate and the House to assert their claim to a voice in the formulation of Reconstruction policy. They also passed a bill to extend the life and increase the activities of the Freedmen's Bureau—an agency created to aid African Americans in their transition from slavery to freedom. The new duties Congress wanted to grant to the Freedmen's Bureau were to expand its responsibilities to include federal protection of African Americans against white oppression in the South.

Johnson vetoed this measure as an unnecessary and unconstitutional use of the military during peacetime, and he also vetoed a Civil Rights bill that declared African Americans to be U.S. citizens and denied Southern states the ability to withhold property rights on the basis of race. Tensions increased; and in April 1866, Congress re-passed the Civil Rights Act of 1866 over Johnson's veto, the first Congressional over-ride of a Presidential Veto in American history.

The over-ride of the President's veto shifted the political upper hand to Congress, which would, henceforth, assume the lead in Reconstruction policy.

In June 1866, Congress voted a proposed Fourteenth Amendment. This Amendment clearly asserted the citizenship of African Americans by stating, "All persons born or naturalized in the U. S. are citizens", thus effectively overturning the Dred Scott decision that held that African Americans were not citizens and did not have standing to sue. It also asserted that African Americans were entitled to the "privileges and immunities of citizens," to the "equal protection of the laws," and to protection against being deprived of "life, liberty, and property without due process of law." In effect, the Fourteenth Amendment was designed to overturn the Black Codes.

Lawyers have been kept busy for more than a century determining exactly what these terms meant, but one thing was clear. The amendment did not specify a right of African American suffrage. It did, however, provide that states that disfranchised a part of their adult

▶ Portrait of Confederate Vice-President Alexander Stephens
Corbis Images

male population would have their representation in Congress proportionately reduced. It almost seemed that Congress was offering the Southerners a choice: They might disfranchise the African Americans if they were willing to pay the price of reduced representation, or they might have increased representation if they were willing to pay the price of African American suffrage. This might not help African Americans, but it was certain to help the Republicans. It would either reduce the strength of Southern white Democrats or give the Republicans African American political allies in the South.

The Fourteenth Amendment, also, provisionally excluded from federal office any person who had held any important public office before the Civil War and had then gone over to the Confederacy. This sweeping move to disqualify almost the entire leadership of the South led the Southern states to make the serious mistake of following President Johnson's advice to reject the amendment. During the last half of 1866 and the first months of 1867, ten Southern states voted not to ratify the Fourteenth Amendment. By March 1867, Tennessee was the only Southern state that had ratified the Fourteenth Amendment.

The following are excerpts from 1865 Mississippi "Black Codes" titled: An Act to Confer Rights on Freedmen and Other Purposes and An Act to Amend the Vagrant Laws of the State:

All freedmen, free negroes and mulattoes may intermarry with each other, in the same manner and under the same regulations that are provided by law for white persons: Provided, that the clerk of probate shall keep separate records of the same.

All freedmen, free negroes or mulattoes who do now and have herebefore lived and cohabited together as husband and wife shall be taken and held in law as legally married, and the issue shall be taken and held as legitimate for all purposes; and it shall not be lawful for any freedman, free negro or mulatto to intermarry with any white person; nor for any person to intermarry with any freedman, free negro or mulatto; and any person who shall so intermarry shall be deemed guilty of felony, and on conviction thereof shall be confined in the State penitentiary for life; and those shall be deemed freedmen, free negroes and mulattoes who are of pure negro blood, and those descended from a negro to the third generation, inclusive, though one ancestor in each generation may have been a white person.

All rogues and vagabonds, idle and dissipated persons, beggars, jugglers, or persons practicing unlawful games or plays, runaways, common drunkards, common night-walkers, pilferers, lewd, wanton, or lascivious persons, in speech or behavior, common railers and brawlers, persons who neglect their calling or employment, misspend what they earn, or do not provide for the support of themselves or their families, or dependents, and all other idle and disorderly persons, including all who neglect all lawful business, habitually misspend their time by frequenting houses of ill-fame, gaming-houses, or tippling shops, shall be deemed and considered vagrants, under the provisions of this act, and upon conviction thereof shall be fined not exceeding one hundred dollars, with all accruing costs, and be imprisoned, at the discretion of the court, not exceeding ten days.

All freedmen, free negroes and mulattoes in this State, over the age of eighteen years, found on the second Monday in January, 1866, or thereafter, with no lawful employment or business, or found unlawful assembling themselves together, either in the day or night time, and all white persons assembling themselves with freedmen, Free negroes or mulattoes, or usually associating with freedmen, free negroes or mulattoes, on terms of equality, or living in adultery or fornication with a freed woman, freed negro or mulatto, shall be deemed vagrants, and on conviction thereof shall be fined in a sum not exceeding, in the case of a freedman, free negro or mulatto, fifty dollars, and a white man two hundred dollars, and imprisonment at the discretion of the court, the free negro not exceeding ten days, and the white man not exceeding six months.

Source: Library of Congress, www.loc.gov.

Radical Reconstruction

Southern rejection of the Fourteenth Amendment precipitated the bitter fight that had been brewing for almost two years. Congressional elections of 1866, however, gave Radical Republicans a two thirds majority in Congress, thus solidifying their power to over-ride Presidential vetoes and take the lead in Reconstruction. Congress moved to replace the Johnson governments in the South with new governments of its own creation. Between March and July 1867, it adopted a series of Reconstruction Acts that divided ten Southern states into five military districts under five military governors. The governors were vested with "all powers necessary" to protect the civil rights of all persons, maintain order, and supervise the administration of justice. These governors were to hold elections for conventions to frame new state constitutions. In these elections adult males, including African Americans, were to vote, but many whites, disqualified by their support of the Confederacy, were not to vote. The constitutions these conventions adopted must establish universal manhood suffrage, and the governments they established must ratify the Fourteenth Amendment. Then, and only then, might they be readmitted to the Union.

Congress followed with a second Reconstruction Act that required military authorities in the South to register voters and supervise the election of the delegates to state constitutional conventions. Furthermore, new constitutions had to be ratified by a majority of voters. Two years after the war was over, when the South supposed that the postwar adjustment had been completed, the process of Reconstruction actually began.

The period that followed has been the subject of more bitter feeling and more controversy than perhaps any other period in American history, and the intensity of the bitterness has made

MAP 12.1 Reconstruction

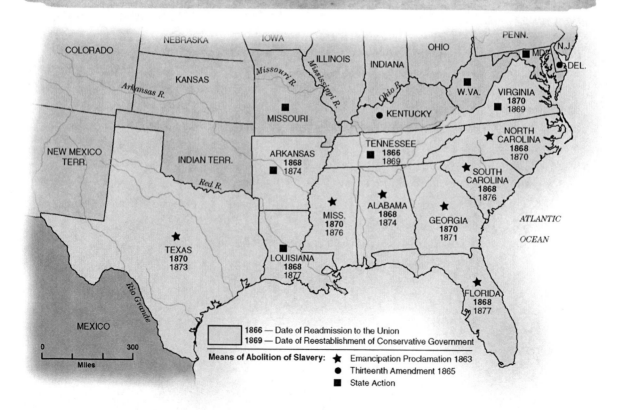

1866 — Date of Readmission to the Union
1869 — Date of Reestablishment of Conservative Government

Means of Abolition of Slavery: ★ Emancipation Proclamation 1863
● Thirteenth Amendment 1865
■ State Action

it difficult to understand what actually happened. During 1867 the military governors conducted elections, and in late 1867 and early 1868 the new constitutional conventions met in the Southern states. They complied with the terms that Congress had set down, including enfranchisement of African American men; however, many Southerners resisted. Military authorities in many places found that they could not get a majority of voters to the polls, as Congress had required. In essence, the former Confederates protested their new constitutions, which they viewed as externally imposed, by staying home and not voting. In March 1868, Congress altered the rules to allow state constitutions to be ratified by the majority of those who voted in an election. Three months later, Arkansas fulfilled the requirements necessary for readmission to the Union; and within a year after the third Reconstruction Act (of July 1867), seven states had adopted new constitutions, organized new governments, ratified the Fourteenth Amendment, and been readmitted to the Union. In Virginia, Mississippi, Georgia, and Texas, however, the process was for one reason or another not completed until 1870. In July 1870, Georgia became the last Southern state to be readmitted to the Union.

All of these new governments, except the one in Virginia, began under Republican control, with more or less African American representation in the legislatures. In one state after another, however, the Democrats, supporting a policy of white supremacy, soon gained the ascendancy. Military and "Radical" rule lasted for three years in North Carolina; four years in Tennessee (never under military government) and Georgia; six years in Texas; seven years in Alabama and Arkansas; eight years in Mississippi; and ten years in Florida, Louisiana, and South Carolina.

Historians of the past and those of the present have interpreted the experience of this so-called "carpetbag" rule (so-named in reference to a popular nineteenth-century suitcase literally made from carpet and carried by many Northerners who moved South in search of economic opportunity) in completely different terms. The earlier interpretation reflected the feelings of the Southern whites that resented this regime bitterly, seeing it as one of "military despotism" and "Negro rule." According to this version, later elaborated by a pro-Southern school of historians, the South was at the outset the victim of military occupation in which a brutal soldiery maintained bayonet rule. Then came the "carpetbaggers"—unscrupulous Northern adventurers whose only purpose was to enrich themselves by plundering the prostrate South. Southerners used the term "carpetbagger" disparagingly in reference to Northerners who moved south and became involved in Southern politics.

In the view of Southerners, in order to maintain their ascendancy, the carpetbaggers incited African Americans, who were essentially well disposed, to assert themselves in swaggering insolence. Thereupon, majorities made up of illiterate African Americans swarmed into the legislatures, where the carpetbaggers manipulated them. A carnival of riotous corruption and looting followed until at last the outraged whites, excluded from all voice in public affairs, could endure these conditions no longer and arose to drive the vandals away and to redeem their dishonored states.

This picture of Reconstruction has a very real importance because it has undoubtedly influenced subsequent Southern attitudes, but it is an extreme distortion of the realities. Historical treatments since 1950 have presented quite a different version, stressing the brief nature of the military rule and the constructive measures of the "carpetbag" governments. As for bayonet rule, the number of troops in the "Army of Occupation" was absurdly small. In

November 1869, there were 1000 federal soldiers scattered over the state of Virginia and 716 over Mississippi with hardly more than a corporal's guard in any one place.

For certain, Southern politics during Reconstruction was fraught with factionalism and corruption, and some of the blame must be placed at the feet of the "carpetbaggers." For example, Illinois native Henry Clay Warmoth was elected governor of Louisiana in 1868 with an annual salary of $8,000. Four years later, Warmoth had a net worth of over $1 million. A full 50 percent of the state budget in Louisiana during Warmoth's tenure went for the salaries and "mileage" of state representatives and their staff members. This, however, was not the only incident of overpaid public officials. One year, South Carolina's legislature voted an additional $1,000 in salary for one member who had recently lost the same amount on a horse race. Inflated and corrupt government contracts were also rampant. For example, the state of Arkansas constructed a bridge one year at a cost of $500 and then repaired the bridge the next year at a cost of $9,000. To be sure, not all of the corruption was due to "carpetbaggers" in government; but for Southerners, the transplanted Northerners made easy targets. Among the American writers who familiarized the country with the looters and scoundrels was Mark Twain, whose fictional writings presented unscrupulous characters with which Southerners became all too familiar.

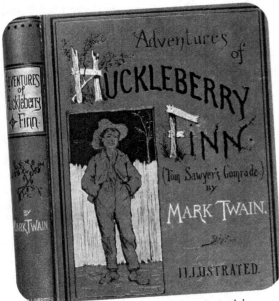

▶Among the American writers who familiarized the country with the looters and scoundrels known as carpet baggers, was Mark Twain, author of the American classic, *Huckleberry Finn. Corbis Images*

Although there were indeed looters and scoundrels among the carpetbaggers, there were also idealists that did all they could to improve conditions in the South. Many Northern women came to teach the freed slaves. Many men came to develop needed industry, which even if it enriched the Northern carpetbagger in the process, was also good for the South as a whole. Many others worked with integrity and self-sacrifice to find a constructive solution for the problems of a society devastated by war and left with a large population of former slaves to absorb and support. Many native Southerners, who joined with the "carpetbaggers" in their programs and who were therefore denounced as "scalawags," were equally public-spirited and high-minded.

As for "Negro rule," the fact is that African Americans were in a majority only at the convention and the first three legislatures of South Carolina. Elsewhere they were a minority, even in Mississippi and Louisiana where they constituted a majority of the population. In view of their illiteracy and their political inexperience, African Americans handled their new responsibilities well and they tended to choose educated men for public office. Thus many of the African American legislators, congressmen, and state officials they chose were well qualified. They were, on the whole, moderate and self-restrained in their demands; and they gave major support to certain policies of long-range value, including notably the establishment of public school systems, which the South had not had, in any broad sense, before the Civil War.

▶African Americans moved from the plantations to the state legislatures during the Reconstruction of the South. Of the conditions the Southern states had to meet in order to be readmitted into the Union, the enfranchisement of African American men was one of the most unpopular. *Library of Congress*

As for the "carnival of corruption," the post-Civil War era was marked by corruption throughout the country. All the Southern states combined did not manage to steal as much money from the public treasury as did the Tweed Ring in New York City, led by William Marcy Tweed, commonly known as "Boss Tweed." New York was also famous for fraudulent elections, and the corruption in government spearheaded by Tweed would become a major issue in national politics in the 1870s. It was true, however, that the impoverished South could ill afford dishonesty in government. Nevertheless, much that was charged to "corruption" really stemmed from increased costs necessary to provide new social services, such as public schools, and to rebuild the Southern economy damaged by war.

Finally, it should be noted that the Southern whites were never reduced to abject helplessness as is sometimes imagined. From the outset they were present in all of the Reconstruction conventions and legislatures—always vocal, frequently aggressive, and sometimes dominating the proceedings.

The Fall of Radical Reconstruction

For an average of six years, then, the regimes of Radical Republican Reconstruction continued. After that they gave way to the Democratic Redeemers—those who wanted to "redeem" the South to white rule—delaying until the twentieth century further progress toward equal rights for African Americans.

When one considers that the South had just been badly defeated in war, that Radical Reconstruction was the policy of the dominant party in Washington, and that African American and white Republicans constituted a majority of the voters in a half-dozen Southern states, it is difficult to understand why the Radical regimes were so promptly—almost easily—overthrown. Several contributing factors must be recognized.

First, the former slaves lacked experience in political participation and leadership. Largely illiterate and conditioned for many decades to defer to white people, they grasped the new opportunities with uncertain hands. Very often they seemed to wish, quite realistically, for security of land tenure and for education more than for political rights. At the same time, however, a number of articulate and able African Americans, some of them former slaves, came to the fore and might have provided effective leadership for their group if Reconstruction had not been abandoned so soon.

Second, and more importantly, one must recognize the importance of the grim resistance offered by the Southern whites. With their deep belief in the superiority of their own race, these Southerners were convinced that civilization itself was at stake. They fought with proportionate desperation, not hesitating to resort to violence and terror.

The Ku Klux Klan

On Christmas Eve 1865, six Confederate army veterans, who were simply bored and restless after the war and sought something for their own amusement, formed a half-whimsical secret society known as the Ku Klux Klan (KKK) in Tennessee. The name "Ku Klux Klan" was derived from the Greek word "Kuklos," the root of the English word "circle." Since the six founding members were of Scotch-Irish ancestry, they added the word "Klan" and then added the made-up word "Klux" to add "mystery and baffle," as well as something "secret-sounding" and "nonsensically inscrutable." With nothing sinister in mind, Jon C. Lester reportedly said to his other listless, five founding members, "Boys, let's start something to break the monotony and cheer up our mothers and girls. Let's start a club of some kind." The original purpose of the young men, evidently, was merely to play practical jokes and serenade women and had nothing to do with racism or terror.

▶The scare tactics of the Ku Klux Klan eventually escalated to extreme violence.
Wikipedia photo

In furtherance of their playful goals, however, the men donned white regalia and rode through the Tennessee countryside in search of adventure. Accidentally, the men discovered that their midnight marauding frightened the African American refugees who were aimlessly wandering the Tennessee countryside in large numbers. The accident then began to take on a more purposeful character, and the Klansmen began a campaign of scare tactics against the wandering African American refugees. An unforeseen consequence was that African Americans quickly tended to avoid the roadways in the area where Klansmen were playing their games. Word of the KKK fun and games spread across the South. People in surrounding areas contacted the Klan wanting to know how they, too, could set up KKK dens of their own for the express purpose of scaring vagrant African Americans away from the roadways. Soon every Southern state had its organization of masked and robed riders, either as part of the Klan or under some other name. Klan tactics quickly escalated from jokes and scare tactics to naked violence, contrary to the original intensions of the Klan's founders. By use of threat, horsewhip, and even rope, gun, and fire, they spread fear not only among African Americans but also, perhaps even more so, among the Republican leaders. By 1868, the Klan claimed to have five hundred thousand members, and their expressed purpose had grown from playful mischief to overt resistance to the Congressional Reconstruction Act of 1867.

Klan members were sworn to secrecy and had to swear that they were opposed to African American equality and in favor of a white man's government, including the "restoration of the civil rights to Southern White men." The Klan stated, in its bylaws, a reverence for the "majesty and supremacy of the Divine Being" and recognized the supremacy of the U.S. Constitution. The Klan claimed that it was an institution of chivalry, humanity, mercy, and patriotism that existed to protect the weak, defend the Constitution, and execute all Constitutional laws.

In 1870, KKK violence had increased to such an extent that it drew the attention of the Radical Republicans in Congress, who passed "An Act to Enforce the Provisions of the Fourteenth Amendment to the Constitution of the United States, and for Other Purposes," more generally known as the First Ku Klux Klan Act. The Act imposed heavy penalties for violations of the Fourteenth and Fifteenth Amendments and gave the state governments the authority to take whatever action they deemed necessary against the Klan. In furtherance of the execution of the Act, Union troops and state militiamen arrested Klansmen and tried them for their crimes, sending many to prison. Under this pressure from the federal and state governments, the KKK was no longer a force by the end of 1872.

The dramatic quality of the Klan has given it a prominent place in the public's mental picture of the Reconstruction. Though violence played a prominent role, the white South had other, less spectacular weapons that were no less powerful. Southern whites owned almost all of the land. Whites controlled virtually all employment, and they dominated the small supply of money and credit that was to be found in the South. Also they dominated the legal system. In unspectacular ways they could make life very hard for individuals who did not comply with

▶The Ku Klux Klan's expressed purpose had grown from playful mischief to overt resistance to the Congressional Reconstruction Act of 1867. Klan members were sworn to secrecy and had to swear that they were opposed to African American equality and in favor of a white man's government, including the "restoration of the civil rights to Southern White men." *Corbis Images*

the system. These factors, perhaps more than the acts of nightriders and violent men, made the pressure against Radical rule almost irresistible.

Another important reason for the downfall of "Radical" Reconstruction was that it was not, really, very radical. It did not confiscate the land of plantation owners and distribute that land among the freed slaves, as radicals and abolitionists such as Thaddeus Stevens and Wendell Phillips had urged. It also did not reduce the former Confederate states to the status of territories for a probationary period as many Radicals also advocated. Furthermore, it did not permanently disfranchise the South's former ruling class, nor did it permanently disqualify more than a handful of ex-Confederate leaders from holding office. It did not enact Charles Sumner's bill to require universal public education in the South and to provide federal aid for schools there; hence, the former slaves were to remain largely uneducated. These would have been genuinely radical measures; but they went beyond what a majority of Northern voters were willing to support; and perhaps these measures would have even risked the renewal of revolt in the South.

Indeed, even the limited radicalism of the Fourteenth Amendment and the Reconstruction Acts strained the convictions of most Northerners to the utmost. The North was not a racially equalitarian society. African American men did not have the right to vote in most Northern states at the time the Reconstruction Acts of 1867 enfranchised them in the South. The enactment of African American suffrage in the South was accomplished by the Radical Republicans, not because of a widespread conviction that it was right in principle but because it seemed to be the only alternative to Confederate rule.

Later, Republicans found that many Northern voters cared little about universal manhood suffrage in the South. They also found that the white South would not consent to a real reunion on this basis and that the restoration of former Confederates to political power did not threaten Northern or national interests. As a result, the Republicans let the existing forces in the South find their own resolution, which was one of white supremacy.

Yet Reconstruction was far from a total failure. It established public schools in the South that gradually brought literacy to the children of freed slaves. By 1900, illiteracy among African Americans had dropped from 90 percent after the Civil War to an estimated 48 percent by 1900. It brought abolitionists and missionaries from the North to found such colleges as Howard, Fisk, Morehouse, Talladega, and many others. These colleges trained future generations of African American leaders, who in turn led protest movements in the twentieth century. Furthermore, though Reconstruction did not confiscate and redistribute land, many freed slaves be-

▶ Sharecropping was a wage-labor system where African Americans worked the land for the white owners and paid them a percentage of their harvest. Sharecropping helped open the doors for blacks to finally achieve economic freedom. *Wikipedia photo*

came landowners through their own hard work and savings. In 1865 scarcely any African American farmers owned their farms; by 1880, one fifth of them did.

African American Sharecroppers

A full 80 percent of African American farmers, however, were not landowners, even of small plots; however, they became sharecroppers, often working on the same plantation for the same landowner that had once owned them. Sharecropping was a wage-labor system where African Americans worked the land for the white owners and paid them a percentage of their harvest (normally 25 percent of the cotton crop and one third of other crops) for the privilege of working on the owner's land. Planters generally divided their plantations into small twenty-five to thirty acre plots and signed contracts with individual African American sharecroppers to work each plot. Landowners supplied the sharecroppers with the necessary mules, seed, plows, and tools, while African Americans were responsible for their own food and necessities. A system of credit developed where local merchants would advance goods to African American sharecroppers with payment due at the time of harvest.

Sharecropping allowed African Americans the beginnings of economic freedom, and also the freedom to decide which family members would work the land, how long they would work each day, and how the labor would be divided. African Americans also typically moved out of the slave cottages and into their own dwellings. On some plantations, however, African Americans worked for wages in gangs as they had under slavery, complete with white overseers, and in some instances, even whippings.

THE FREEDMEN'S BUREAU.—DRAWN BY A. R. WAUD.—[SEE PAGE 417.]

▶ An illustration from *Harper's Weekly*, 1868; a Bureau agent stands between armed groups of Southern whites and Freedmen. The Freedmen's Bureau was created for the purpose of aiding the former slaves in their transition to freedom. *Wikipedia photo*

▶ Sojourner Truth and President Abraham Lincoln. *Wikipedia photo (left);*
Library of Congress (right)

Still, change did come with emancipation in that a full third of the African American women that had worked in the fields abandoned fieldwork either to tend to the home and child rearing or for paid domestic servitude. Indoor work, even if it consisted of cleaning and laundry, was much preferable to working in the field in the hot southern sun.

Freedmen's Bureau

Reconstruction also created the Freedmen's Bureau, which was perhaps charged with more responsibility than any federal agency in history. The Freedmen's Bureau was created for the purpose of aiding the former slaves in their transition to freedom. Though woefully undermanned and underfunded, the Freedmen's Bureau provided food, clothing, medical care, and shelter for former slaves. In the first two years after the War, the Freedmen's Bureau issued over $20 million to needy African American Americans and treated 450,000 illnesses. The Bureau also constructed forty hospitals across the South to help meet the medical needs of the former slave population.

After the Civil War, the Southern roadways were literally clogged with refugees as Southern plantation owners, who had no money with which to hire their labor, released thousands of free African Americans. With nowhere to go, thousands of African Americans wandered aimlessly across the South. Many of these refugees would be among those terrorized by the night rides of the KKK since they made easy targets without shelter on the roadways. The Freedmen's Bureau helped transport the dislocated refugees to shelter, helped African Americans find family members from whom they had become separated either before or after the War, and performed formal marriage ceremonies for the many African Americans who wanted legal sanction for the de facto marriages they had lived within under slavery. In the first two years after the war, the Freedmen's Bureau helped resettled thirty thousand displaced African Americans.

The Freedmen's Bureau also attempted to ensure fair trials for African Americans in the South, to provide for African American education, and serve as an employment agency for the thousands of unemployed African American refugees. In total, the Freedmen's Bureau constructed over 4,300 schools in the first two years following the Civil War.

Finally, Reconstruction also left as a permanent legacy the Fourteenth and Fifteenth Amendments, which formed the constitutional basis for the civil-rights movements of the post-World War II generation.

Johnson Versus the Radicals

The Republicans did not abandon their program all at once. Rather, it faded out gradually although the Radicals remained militant while Johnson remained President. Johnson had used his administrative powers to evade or modify the enforcement of some Republican Reconstruction measures. This convinced most Republicans that his removal was necessary if their policy was to be implemented in the South; and in 1868, they tried to remove him by impeachment. The immediate pretext for impeachment was Johnson's dismissal of Secretary of War Stanton in February 1868.

A year earlier Congress had passed a series of laws designed to strengthen the legislative branch at the expense of the executive. Among these laws was the Tenure of Office Act, which forbade removal of public officials who had been confirmed by the Senate without first obtaining Senate approval. Later, the Supreme Court would deem the Tenure of Office Act unconstitutional. However, at the time that Johnson removed Stanton, who was reporting to the Radicals what went on in administration councils, there had been no judicial ruling; and the

▶ The impeachment of Andrew Johnson. *Wikipedia photo*

House of Representatives voted to impeach Johnson, which meant that he must be tried by the Senate on the articles of impeachment.

The trial was conducted in a tense atmosphere and scarcely in a judicial way. Immense pressure was put on all Republican senators to vote for conviction. When a vote was finally taken on May 16, 1868, conviction failed by one vote of the two-thirds required. Seven Republicans had stood out against their Party. Johnson was permitted to serve out his term, and the balance between executive and legislative power in the American political system, which had almost been destroyed, was preserved. Johnson, however, would fail to win the Democratic Party's nomination for President at their national convention two months later.

The determination of Republicans to achieve congressional domination of the Reconstruction process also manifested itself in restrictions on the judiciary. When a Mississippi editor named Mc-Cardle appealed to the Supreme Court to rule on the constitutionality of one of the Reconstruction Acts under which he had been arrested by the military, Congress, in March 1868, passed an act changing the appellate jurisdiction of the Court so that it could not pass judgment on McCardle's case.

The End of Reconstruction
The Grant Administration

In 1868 the country faced another election, and the Republicans turned to Ulysses S. Grant as their nominee. He was elected over the Democratic candidate, Governor Horatio Seymour of New York, by a popular majority of only 310,000—a surprisingly close vote. Without the votes

▶ President Ulysses S. Grant delivering his inaugural address at the U.S. Capitol on March 4, 1873.
Library of Congress

of the newly enfranchised African Americans in the seven reconstructed Southern states, Grant might have had no edge in popular votes at all. The Radical Republicans were alarmed at their narrow margin of victory and sought to find ways to add more African American voters to the ranks. Although the Fourteenth Amendment theoretically forced African American suffrage in the South, the issue of suffrage for African Americans had been generally ignored in a number of Northern states. Between 1865 and 1869, a number of Northern states had held referendums on African American suffrage; and voters in Kansas, Ohio, Michigan, Missouri, Wisconsin, New York, and the District of Columbia voted down African American suffrage. The vote in the District of Columbia was an overwhelming 6,521 to 35 against African American suffrage. Of the Northern states that held elections on the issue, only Iowa and Minnesota passed laws granting the franchise to African Americans. To implant African American suffrage permanently in the Constitution—for the North as well as the South—Congress, in 1869, passed the Fifteenth Amendment, forbidding the states to deny any citizen his right to vote "on account of race, color, or previous condition of servitude." The Amendment was ratified in 1870; it had almost immediate impact as African American men, just five years removed from slavery, were elected to public office. Although African Americans were still severely under-represented in the 1870s, seventeen African American men served in Congress, one served in the U.S. Senate, and one African American man served as Chief Justice of the South Carolina Supreme Court. For a brief interlude, African Americans even held a majority of the seats in the South Carolina legislature.

President Grant supported the measures of the Radicals and gave his backing to their policies. Like the good military man he was, he believed that wherever violence occurred, it should be put down uncompromisingly. Accordingly, he favored the adoption of Enforcement Acts for the use of federal troops to break up the activities of the Ku Klux Klan. When these laws were passed, he did not hesitate to invoke them; and troops were sent in on a number of occasions.

Fundamentally, however, Grant was not a Radical. He wanted to see tranquility restored, and this meant reuniting North and South on any basis both would be willing to accept. Accordingly, he urged a broader extension of amnesty to all former Confederates, and he grew to resent the frequent appeals of Republican governments in the South for troops to uphold their authority. Though he realized that the tactics of the Redeemers were very bad—"bloodthirsty butchery" and "scarcely a credit to savages"—he became convinced that constant federal military intervention was worse in the long run.

Meanwhile in foreign affairs, Secretary of State Hamilton Fish was busy prompting an important settlement by which Great Britain and the United States adopted the principle of international arbitration as a means of settling American claims that had grown out of the raiding activities of the *Alabama* and other ships, which British shipyards had built for the Confederacy. Though the U.S. did not get the $2 billion in "indirect" damages it sought on the pretense that the British-built Confederate ships extended the war, it did get $15 million in damages from the British for their role in supplying the ships to the Confederacy.

The Collapse of Reconstruction

During the eight years of Grant's presidency, Republican governments were overthrown in eight of the Southern states. As Grant's second term neared its end, only three states—

Louisiana, Florida, and South Carolina—remained in the Republican ranks. The program of Radical Reconstruction still remained official policy in the Republican Party, but it had lost its steam. The country was concerned about other things.

In financial circles, there was a controversy over what to do about the greenback dollars issued during the war. Since greenbacks were not backed by gold, people had saved the more valuable gold dollars and spent the less valuable greenback dollars, thus driving gold out of circulation. The government was willing to give gold for greenbacks, even though such a policy tended to increase the value of the dollar. Debtor interests (such as farmers), who wanted a cheap dollar, fought hard against the policy of redemption; but the policy was adopted in 1875. Not only did the policy limit the growth of the money supply and therefore hinder economic recovery in a cash-short economy, the decision weakened the Republicans among farmers in the West.

Scandals Shake the Republican Party

In politics, public confidence in the Republican-led government was shaken by a series of disclosures concerning government corruption. In 1869, investors Jay Gould and Jim Fisk began purchasing gold futures for the purpose of driving up the price of gold, which skyrocketed from four dollars per ounce to twenty-five dollars per ounce. It was expected that at a certain point the U.S. Treasury Department would place U.S. gold reserves on the market in an effort to stabilize the gold market. Grant's brother-in-law in the Treasury Department struck a deal, unknown to Grant, with Gould to inform him in advance when the Treasury Department would release its gold reserves. Gould could then sell before the prices dropped. Grant's brother-in-law dutifully sent Gould a telegraph the morning that the Treasury Department released its gold to the open market, but Gould was out of the office and did not get the message. Prices quickly fell back to the pre-panic price of four dollars per ounce, and Gould's losses were $16 million.

In 1872, it was revealed that several congressmen had accepted gifts of stock in a construction company, the Crédit Mobilier, which was found to be diverting the funds of the Union Pacific Railroad—including the funds the government had granted to it—with the knowledge of the officers of the road. In 1875, Grant's private secretary was implicated in the operations of the "Whiskey Ring," which, by evading taxes, had systematically defrauded the government of millions of dollars. The following year, the Secretary of War was caught selling appointments to Native American posts. Meanwhile, in the New York City government, the Tweed Ring, headed by Tammany boss William Marcy Tweed, was exposed as guilty of graft and thefts that have seldom been equaled in size and have never surpassed in effrontery.

The epidemic of corruption inspired a revolt by reform Republicans, who bolted the party in 1872, organized the Liberal Republican party, and nominated Horace Greeley, editor of the *New York Tribune*, for President. Although the Democrats also nominated Greeley and formed a coalition with the Liberal Republicans, Grant easily won reelection because most Northern voters were not yet prepared to trust the Democrats.

In the economic orbit, the country was trying to weather the financial depression that began with the panic of 1873. With the economic problems experienced between whites in the North, the problems of Southern African Americans seemed more distant and less important to the people of the North. Moreover, the economic recession weakened the Republican Party even further. In the 1874 mid-term elections, the Democrats won control of the House of Representatives for the first time since 1856. The next year, the Democrat-controlled House threatened to withdraw any appropriations for the Justice Department or the U.S. Army that were intended for use in the South.

In a number of Southern states, white Democrats created paramilitary organizations (the White Leagues, Rifle Clubs, and Red Shirts) that unlike the Klan operated openly. In Louisiana, the Democratic paramilitary groups fought battles with Republican militias until President Grant sent the U.S. Army to restore order. Citizens on both sides of the Mason-Dixon line protested what they termed as Grant's "military rule" of Louisiana. Protests grew even louder after the U.S. Army ousted recently elected legislators in the Louisiana legislature due to electoral irregularities.

In Mississippi, in 1875, Democratic Party Rifle Clubs broke up Republican Party rallies, shooting dozens of African American Mississippi Republicans. Republican Mississippi Governor (a former Union soldier and native of Maine) called for sending federal troops to Mississippi to restore order. Grant considered sending troops, but refrained when Ohio Republicans warned him that such action

MAP 12.2 The Election of 1876

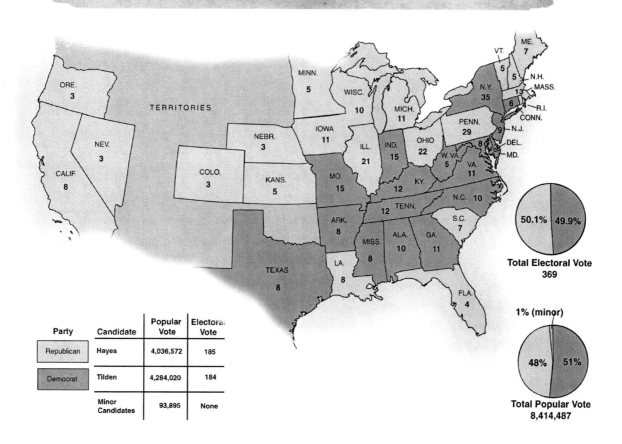

Party	Candidate	Popular Vote	Electoral Vote
Republican	Hayes	4,036,572	185
Democrat	Tilden	4,284,020	184
Minor Candidates		93,895	None

▶ Rutherford B. Hayes *Wikipedia photo*

could cost him the state of Ohio in the next election. In essence, Mississippians were left to fight out their problems among themselves. Governor Ames attempted to assemble a Republican militia to put down the unrest, but his efforts met with little success; and the Democrats won control of Mississippi in the state election of 1875.

The Courts and the End of Reconstruction

In the companion cases in 1876, *U.S. v. Reese* and *U.S. v. Cruickshank*, the Supreme Court stuck down statutes that had provided for the enforcement of the Fourteenth and Fifteenth Amendments. With these rulings, federal officials could no longer prosecute individuals for violations of the equal rights of African Americans. Instead, the protection of individual rights was left to the states and the rights of African Americans in the South were left in the hands of the white Southerners that were now in control of Southern governments.

The Hayes-Tilden Election of 1876

The election of 1876 brought to an end the program of Reconstruction, which probably would have ended soon anyway. In this election the Republicans, who were badly divided, turned to a Civil War veteran and governor of Ohio, Rutherford B. Hayes, as their nominee. Hayes was a conspicuously honest man, and so was his Democratic opponent, Samuel J. Tilden of New York, who owed his reputation to his part in breaking up the Tweed Ring.

When the votes were counted, Tilden had a popular majority (obtained partly by the suppression of African American votes in some Southern states) and was within one vote of an electoral majority. However, there were three states—Florida, Louisiana, and South Carolina—in which the result was contested; and rival officials filed two sets of returns, though Tilden had clearly won the popular vote in all three states. To count the votes in such a case, the Constitution calls for a joint session of the Congress; but the House of Representatives, with a Democratic majority, was in a position to prevent an election by refusing to go into joint session with the Senate. Congress agreed to appoint an Electoral Commission to provide an impartial judgment; but the commission divided along party lines, with eight Republicans and seven Democrats, and voted eight to seven for Hayes. As late as two days before the inauguration it was doubtful whether the Democrats in the House would accept the decision.

Many Northern Democrats were prepared to fight to the finish against what they regarded as a stolen election, but the Southern Democrats had found that one civil war was enough. Moreover, various negotiations had been in progress behind the scenes. Important groups of Southern Democrats who had been left out when the government largesse of the Union Pacific-Central Pacific was distributed hoped for a Texas and Pacific Railroad that would provide bountiful federal grants for Southern interests. They received assurances from friends of Governor Hayes that he would look with favor upon such programs of internal improvement.

▶ Electoral commission of 1877. *Wikipedia photo*

Moreover, they were assured that he would withdraw the last remaining federal troops from Louisiana and South Carolina, meaning that their Republican governments would collapse, leaving the score of states: redeemed, eleven and reconstructed, none.

With these understandings, Southern congressmen voted to let the count proceed so that Hayes was elected. Later, when they were explaining their conduct to their constituents, they thought it best to say quite a great deal about how they had ransomed South Carolina and Louisiana and very little about their hopes for the Texas and Pacific Railroad and other such enterprises. Thus a legend grew up that there had been a "compromise" by which Reconstruction had ended.

What had really happened was that Southern Democrats and Northern Republicans had discovered that there were many features of economic policy on which they were in close harmony. The slaves were emancipated, the Union was restored, and bygones were bygones. The harmony of their views made reconciliation natural and Reconstruction unnecessary. There was still the question of the African Americans, but only a few whites had ever supported African American suffrage or racial equality for its own sake. It had been an expedient; and now that the expedient was no longer needed, it could be laid aside. Such was the spirit of reconciliation.

Therefore, the country ended a period of intense friction and entered upon a long era of sectional harmony and rapid economic growth. However, this was done at the expense of leaving the question of racial relations still unattended to, even though slavery itself had, at immense cost, been removed.

Chapter Review ▶ ▶ ▶

Summary

The war had a tremendous impact on America. The war boosted manufacturing and finance in the North and the Transcontinental Railroad was finished four years after the War. African-Americans were no longer enslaved, and some even served in the War itself as did a number of women. Though Lincoln's Emancipation Proclamation had originally freed no one since it applied only to the states in rebellion, it had given the Union a greater moral purpose and helped prevent English intervention into the American conflict.

Reconstruction of the South began actually during the Civil War as the Union regained control in Southern states through military victory and began the process of restoring these states to the Union. Lincoln granted amnesty to former Confederates who took an oath of allegiance, and when as many as one tenth did so, he would permit them to form a new state government. When this government accepted the abolition of slavery and repudiated secession, Lincoln would receive it back into the Union, though States did not have to recognize the rights.

Radical Republicans opposed Lincoln's plan as too lenient, and after his tragic death, expected Andrew Johnson to be more punitive, but Johnson turned out to be perhaps even more conciliatory than Lincoln. Johnson issued a broad amnesty to all who would take an oath of allegiance, though men with property valued at more than $20,000 were required to ask for a special pardon. Johnson appointed provisional governors in each of the remaining Southern states and only men who had been voters in 1860 and had taken the oath of allegiance could participate. This meant, of course, that African Americans were excluded. When the new governments disavowed secession, accepted the abolition of slavery, and repudiated the Confederate debt, Johnson would accept them.

In April 1866, Congress passed the Civil Rights Act of 1866 declaring all persons born in the U.S. to be citizens over Johnson's veto. In November, the Radical Republicans won a veto-proof majority and in March 1867-March 1868, Congress took over Reconstruction. In essence, Congress divided the South into five military districts, required Congressional approval for new State Constitutions, required that African American men could vote and required that all Southern states ratify the Fourteenth Amendment.

Northern opportunists, labeled "carpetbaggers" by Southerners, did move South and exploited the political and economic situation. Some, such as Henry Clay Warmoth, who was elected governor of Louisiana, fleeced the taxpayers for millions. Southerners also objected to "Negro rule" as African Americans were elected to office on the state and municipal level in the South.

Many African Americans, however, became not elected officials, but sharecroppers, paying landowners for the privilege of working their land with a percentage of their harvest. The sharecroppers were among the poorest Americans in the late nineteenth century.

Whites reacted against African American freedom with the formation of the Ku Klux Klan. Though the Klan was begun as a social organization by young men seeking fun and recreation, it quickly devolved into a terror organization that targeted African Americans until it was squelched by federal authorities.

The Freedmen's Bureau was established to assist African Americans in their transition to freedom, but the Bureau was understaffed and underfunded considering the scope of the problems for the former slaves. Regardless, until the early 1870s the regimes of Radical Republican Reconstruction continued. After that they gave way to the Democratic Redeemers—those who wanted to "redeem" the South to white rule—delaying

(cont'd)

until the twentieth century further progress toward equal rights for African Americans. Radical Republicans went as far as impeaching Andrew Johnson, but the Senate failed to convict the President by one vote. General Ulysses S. Grant was elected in 1869, but his administration was fraught with scandals including the Credit Mobilier scandal in conjunction with the Transcontinental Railroad and the efforts of Jay Gould and Jim Fiske to corner the gold market in 1869.

Reconstruction would finally come to an end with the Compromise of 1877 where the Southern Democrats agreed to accept Rutherford B. Hayes, a Republican who lost the popular vote, as President in exchange for a federal withdrawal from the South. Real equality for African Americans would be an issue for future generations.

Chronological Time Line

1862   Union troops began reclaiming Southern territory. Lincoln appointed provisional governors for those areas controlled by federal troops.

1863   Lincoln outlines the 10 percent Reconstruction Plan

1864   July, Lincoln disposes of Wade-Davis Bill with Pocket Veto

1865   January, Congress passes the Thirteenth Amendment abolishing slavery.

1865   May 29, 1865, Andrew Johnson offers broad amnesty to those that will take an oath of allegiance.

1865   December, all former Confederate states had organized new governments, ratified the Thirteenth Amendment, and elected Congressmen.

1865   December 24, Ku Klux Klan forms in Tennessee

1866   April, Congress Passes Civil Rights Act of 1866 over Johnson's Veto

1866   Congress votes on the Fourteenth Amendment guaranteeing equal treatment under law and citizenship for the former slaves

1866   November, Radical Republicans gain a two-thirds majority in Congress.

1867   March, First Reconstruction Act is passed over Johnson's Veto.

1868   January-May, House of Representatives impeaches President Andrew Johnson, but the Senate fails to convict by one vote.

1868   November, Ulysses S. Grant elected President.

1869   Congress passes the Fifteenth Amendment prohibiting the denial of voting rights based on race.

Chapter Review (cont'd) ▶ ▶ ▶

Time Line (cont'd)

1869   Jay Gould and Jim Fisk attempt to corner the gold market.

1870   July, Georgia becomes last Southern state to be admitted to the Union

1870   First Ku Klux Klan Act prohibits violations of Fourteenth and Fifteenth Amendments

1872   Credit Mobilier Scandal

1872   November, President Grant reelected

1873   Financial panic plunges the economy into depression

1876   In *U.S. v. Reese* and *U.S. v. Cruickshank* the Supreme Court ruled that the Fifteenth Amendment did not confer voting rights.

1876   Rutherford B. Hayes loses the popular vote to Samuel Tilden, but wins the electoral vote in a disputed election

1877   Compromise of 1877 ends Reconstruction in the South and the South accepts Hayes as President

Key Terms

Wade-Davis Bill: Killed by Lincoln's Pocket Veto, the bill would have imposed stringent terms for the restoration of the former Confederates, including a requirement that Southerners could only establish state governments after the majority in a state had sworn to a loyalty oath.

Lincoln's 10 percent Plan: Lincoln would have allowed Southerners to restore state governments after 10 percent had taken a loyalty oath to the U.S.

Andrew Johnson: Lincoln's Vice President and seventeenth President of the United States

Johnson's Plan for Reconstruction: When the new Southern governments disavowed secession, accepted the abolition of slavery, and repudiated the Confederate debt, Johnson would accept them back into the Union. Rights for African Americans were left to the states.

"Black codes": State and municipal laws limiting African American rights.

Thirteenth Amendment: Abolished slavery.

Fourteenth Amendment: Provided citizenship, equal protection under law, and equal privileges and immunities for all persons born or naturalized in the U.S.

Freedmen's Bureau: Federal agency charged with taking care of the needs of the former slaves.

Civil Rights Act of 1866: Declared all persons born in the U.S. to be U.S. citizens. The act was passed over Andrew Johnson's veto.

Key Terms (cont'd)

Reconstruction Acts: Four acts of Congress passed between March 1867 and March 1868 that divided the South into five military districts, required Congressional approval for new State constitutions, required that African Americans could vote and required that all Southern states ratify the Fourteenth Amendment.

Carpetbaggers: Northerners that moved South after the Civil War seeking economic opportunity

William Marcy "Boss" Tweed: Head of the New York City political machine in the late nineteenth century notorious for fraud.

Ku Klux Klan: Secret society that began in the 1870s as a social organization but quickly developed into a terror organization targeting African Americans

First Ku Klux Klan Act: The act imposed heavy penalties for violations of the Fourteenth and Fifteenth Amendments and gave the State governments the authority to take whatever action they deemed necessary against the Klan.

Sharecroppers: Farmers that worked the land for landowners and paid a percentage of their harvest to the landowners

Jay Gould: Railroad tycoon and investor that attempted to corner the gold market in 1869

Jim Fisk: Partner with Jay Gould in the gold market scheme of 1869

15th Amendment: Prohibited any voter qualifications that denied voting rights based on race.

Tenure of Office Act: Forbade removals of public officials who had been confirmed by the Senate without first obtaining Senate approval.

Credit Mobilier: Construction company owned by the major stockholders of the Union Pacific Railroad that was set up to make it appear that the Union Pacific was not profiting from the construction of the Transcontinental Railroad. Credit Mobilier bribed Congressmen with shares in the company.

"Liberal" Republicans: Reform Republicans, who bolted the party in 1872 in reaction to scandals in the Grant administration, organized the Liberal Republican Party, and nominated Horace Greeley, editor of the *New York Tribune,* for President.

White Leagues, Rifle Clubs, and Red Shirts: Paramilitary groups in the South that fought battles against the Republican state militias during Reconstruction.

Election of 1876: Disputed election where Democrat Samuel Tilden won the popular vote but Republican Rutherford B. Hayes won the electoral vote when an electoral commission of eight Republicans and seven Democrats voted 8-7 to give all votes in dispute to Hayes.

U.S. v. Reese, U.S. v. Cruickshank: Supreme Court ruled that the 15th Amendment did not confer voting rights on anyone. Instead, if voting rights are denied, it cannot be on the basis of race.

Rutherford B. Hayes: Republican Elected President in the disputed election of 1876

Samuel Tilden: Democrat that won the popular vote but lost the electoral vote in the disputed election of 1876

Chapter Review (cont'd) ▶ ▶ ▶

Sources Consulted

Paul A. Cimbala and Randall Miller, eds., *The Freedmen's Bureau and Reconstruction* (1999).

Laura F. Edwards, *Gendered Strife and Confusion: The Political Culture of Reconstruction* (1997).

Eric Foner, *Reconstruction: America's Unfinished Revolution 1863–1872* (1988).

Allen C. Guelzo, *Lincoln's Emancipation Proclamation* (2004).

Mark E. Neely, Jr., *The Fate of Liberty: Abraham Lincoln and Civil Liberties* (1990).

Michael Perman, *The Road to Redemption: Southern Politics 1868–1879* (1984).

Brooks D. Simpson, *Ulysses S. Grant* (2000).

The Declaration of Independence

When in the course of human events, it becomes necessary for one people to dissolve the political bands which have connected them with another, and to assume among the Powers of the earth, the separate and equal station to which the Laws of Nature and of Nature's God entitle them, a decent respect to the opinions of mankind requires that they should declare the causes which impel them to the separation.

We hold these truths to be self-evident, that all men are created equal, that they are endowed by their Creator with certain unalienable Rights, that among these are Life, Liberty and the pursuit of Happiness. That to secure these rights, Governments are instituted among Men, deriving their just Powers from the consent of the governed, That whenever any Form of Government becomes destructive of these ends, it is the Right of the People to alter or to abolish it, and to institute new Government, laying its foundation on such principles and organizing its Powers in such form, as to them shall seem most likely to effect their Safety and Happiness. Prudence, indeed, will dictate that Governments long established should not be changed for light and transient causes; and accordingly all experience hath shewn, that mankind are more disposed to suffer, while evils are sufferable, than to right themselves by abolishing the forms to which they are accustomed. But when a long train of abuses and usurpations, pursuing invariably the same object evinces a design to reduce them under absolute Despotism, it is their right, it is their duty, to throw off such Government, and to provide new Guards for their future security. Such has been the patient sufferance of these Colonies: and such is now the necessity which constrains them to alter their former Systems of Government. The history of the present King of Great Britain is a history of repeated injuries and usurpations, all having in direct object the Establishment of an absolute Tyranny over these States. To prove this, let Facts be submitted to a candid World:

He has refused his Assent to Laws, the most wholesome and necessary for the public good.

He has forbidden his Governors to pass Laws of immediate and pressing importance, unless suspended in their operation till his Assent should be obtained; and when so suspended, he has utterly neglected to attend to them.

He has refused to pass other Laws for the accommodation of large districts of people, unless those people would relinquish the right of Representation in the Legislature, a right inestimable to them and formidable to tyrants only.

He has called together legislative bodies at places unusual, uncomfortable, and distant from the depository of their Public Records, for the sole purpose of fatiguing them into compliance with his measures.

He has dissolved Representative Houses repeatedly, for opposing with manly firmness his invasions on the rights of the people.

He has refused for a long time, after such dissolutions, to cause others to be elected; whereby the Legislative Powers, incapable of the Annihilation, have returned to the People at large for their exercise; the State remaining in the mean time exposed to all the dangers of invasion from without, and the convulsions within.

He has endeavored to prevent the population of these States; for that purpose obstructing the Laws of Naturalization of Foreigners; refusing to pass others to encourage their migrations hither, and raising the conditions of new Appropriations of Lands.

He has obstructed the Administration of justice, by refusing his Assent to Laws for establishing Judiciary Powers.

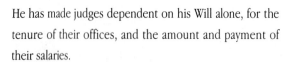

He has made judges dependent on his Will alone, for the tenure of their offices, and the amount and payment of their salaries.

He has erected a multitude of New Offices, and sent hither swarms of Officers to harass our People, and eat out their substance.

He has kept among us, in times of peace, Standing Armies, without the consent of our legislature.

He has affected to render the Military independent of and superior to the Civil Power.

He has combined with others to subject us to a jurisdiction foreign to our constitution, and unacknowledged by our laws; giving his Assent to their acts of pretended legislation—

For quartering large bodies of armed troops among us;

For protecting them, by a mock Trial, from Punishment for any Murders which they should commit on the Inhabitants of these States;

For cutting off our Trade with all parts of the world;

For imposing Taxes on us without our Consent;

For depriving us in many cases, of the benefits of Trial by Jury;

For transporting us beyond Seas to be tried for pretended offences;

For abolishing the free System of English Laws in a neighboring Province, establishing therein an Arbitrary government, and enlarging its Boundaries so as to render it at once an example and fit instrument for introducing the same absolute rule into these Colonies;

For taking away our Charters, abolishing our most valuable Laws, and altering fundamentally the Forms of our Governments;

For suspending our own Legislatures, and declaring themselves invested with Power to legislate for us in all cases whatsoever.

He has abdicated Government here, by declaring us out of his Protection, and waging War against us.

He has plundered our seas, ravaged our Coasts, burnt our towns, and destroyed the lives of our people.

He is at this time transporting large armies of foreign mercenaries to compleat the works of death, desolation and tyranny, already begun with circumstances of Cruelty & perfidy, scarcely paralleled in the most barbarous ages, and totally unworthy the Head of a civilized nation.

He has constrained our fellow Citizens taken Captive on the high Seas to bear Arms against their Country, to become the executioners of their friends and Brethren, or to fall themselves by their Hands.

He has excited domestic insurrections amongst us, and has endeavoured to bring on the inhabitants of our frontiers, the merciless Indian Savages, whose known rule of warfare, is an undistinguished destruction of all ages, sexes and conditions.

In every stage of these Oppressions We have Petitioned for Redress in the most humble terms: Our repeated Petitions have been answered only by repeated injury. A Prince, whose character is thus marked by every act which may define a Tyrant, is unfit to be the ruler of a free People.

Nor have We been wanting in attentions to our British brethren. We have warned them from time to time of attempts by their legislature to extend an unwarrantable jurisdiction over us. We have reminded them of the circumstances of our emigration and settlement here. We have appealed to their native justice and magnanimity, and we have conjured them by the ties of our common kindred to disavow these usurpations, which, would inevitably interrupt our connections and correspondence. They too have been deaf to the voice of justice and of consanguinity. We must, therefore, acquiesce in the necessity, which denounces our Separation, and hold them, as we hold the rest of mankind, Enemies in War, in Peace, Friends.

We, therefore, the Representatives of the United States of America, in General Congress, Assembled, appealing to the Supreme judge of the world for the rectitude of our intentions, do, in the Name, and by Authority of the good People of these Colonies, solemnly publish and declare, That these United Colonies are, and of Right ought to be Free and Independent States; that they are Absolved from all Allegiance to the British Crown, and that all political connection between them and the State of Great Britain, is and ought to be totally dissolved; and that, as Free and Independent States, they have full Power to levy War, conclude Peace, contract Alliances, establish Commerce, and to do all other Acts and Things which independent States may of right do. And for the support of this Declaration, with a firm reliance on the Protection of Divine Providence, we mutually pledge to each other our Lives, our Fortunes and our sacred Honor.

The Constitution of the United States

We the people of the United States, in Order to form a more perfect Union, establish justice, insure domestic Tranquility, provide for the common defense, promote the general Welfare, and secure the Blessings of Liberty to ourselves and our Posterity, do ordain and establish this Constitution for the United States of America.

Article I

Section 1. All legislative Powers herein granted shall be vested in a Congress of the United States, which shall consist of a Senate and House of Representatives.

Section 2. 1. The House of Representatives shall be composed of Members chosen every second Year by the People of the several States, and the Electors in each State shall have the Qualifications requisite for Electors of the most numerous Branch of the State Legislature.

2. No person shall be a Representative who shall not have attained to the Age of twenty-five Years, and been seven Years a Citizen of the United States, and who shall not, when elected, be an Inhabitant of that State in which he shall be chosen.

3. Representatives and direct Taxes[1] shall be apportioned among the several States which may be included within this Union, according to their respective Numbers, which shall be determined by adding to the whole Number of free Persons, including those bound to Service for a Term of Years, and excluding Indians not taxed, three fifths of all other Persons.[2] The actual Enumeration shall be made within three Years after the first Meeting of the Congress of the United States, and within every subsequent Term of ten Years, in such Manner as they shall by Law direct. The Number of Representatives shall not exceed one for every thirty Thousand, but each State shall have at Least one Representative; and until such enumeration shall be made, the State of New Hampshire shall be entitled to chuse three, Massachusetts eight, Rhode Island and Providence Plantations one, Connecticut five, New York six, New Jersey four, Pennsylvania eight, Delaware one, Maryland six, Virginia ten, North Carolina five, South Carolina five, and Georgia three.

4. When vacancies happen in the Representation from any State, the Executive Authority thereof shall issue Writs of Election to fill such Vacancies.

5. The House of Representatives shall chuse their Speaker and other officers; and shall have the sole Power of Impeachment.

Section 3. 1. The Senate of the United States shall be composed of two Senators from each State, chosen by the Legislature thereof,[3] for six Years; and each Senator shall have one Vote.

2. Immediately after they shall be assembled in Consequence of the first Election, they shall be divided as equally as may be into three Classes. The Seats of the Senators of the first Class shall be vacated at the Expiration of the second Year, of the second Class at the Expiration of the fourth Year, and of the third Class at the Expiration of the sixth Year, so that one third may be chosen every second Year; and if Vacancies happen by Resignation, or otherwise, during the Recess of the Legislature of any State, the Executive thereof may make temporary Appointments until the next Meeting of the Legislature, which shall then fill such Vacancies.[4]

---

[1] See the Sixteenth Amendment.
[2] See the Fourteenth Amendment.
[3] See the Seventeenth Amendment.
[4] See the Seventeenth Amendment.

3. No Person shall be a Senator who shall not have attained to the Age of thirty Years, and been nine Years a Citizen of the United States, and who shall not, when elected, be an Inhabitant of that State for which he shall be chosen.

4. The Vice President of the United States shall be President of the Senate, but shall have no vote, unless they be equally divided.

5. The Senate shall chuse their other Officers, and also a President pro tempore, in the absence of the Vice President, or when he shall exercise the Office of President of the United States.

6. The Senate shall have the sole Power to try all Impeachments. When sitting for that purpose, they shall be on Oath or Affirmation. When the President of the United States is tried, the Chief justice shall preside: And no person shall be convicted without the Concurrence of two thirds of the Members present.

7. Judgment in Cases of impeachment shall not extend further than to removal from Office, and disqualification to hold and enjoy any Office of honor, Trust, or Profit under the United States: but the Party convicted shall nevertheless be liable and subject to Indictment, Trial, judgment and Punishment, according to Law.

Section 4. 1. The Times, Places and Manner of holding Elections for Senators and Representatives, shall be prescribed in each state by the Legislature thereof; but the Congress may at any time by Law make or alter such Regulations, except as to the Places of Chusing Senators.

2. The Congress shall assemble at least once in every Year, and such Meeting shall be on the first Monday in December, unless they shall by Law appoint a different Day.

Section 5. 1. Each House shall be the judge of the Elections, Returns and Qualifications of its own Members, and a Majority of each shall constitute a Quorum to do Business; but a smaller number may adjourn from day to day, and may be authorized to compel the Attendance of absent Members, in such manner, and under such Penalties, as each House may provide.

2. Each House may determine the Rules of its Proceedings, punish its Members for disorderly Behavior, and, with the Concurrence of two thirds, expel a Member.

3. Each House shall keep a journal of its Proceedings, and from time to time publish the same, excepting such Parts as may in their judgment require Secrecy; and the Yeas and Nays of the Members of either House on any question shall, at the Desire of one fifth of those Present, be entered on the journal.

4. Neither House, during the Session of Congress, shall, without the Consent of the other, adjourn for more than three days, nor to any other Place than that in which the two Houses shall be sitting.

Section 6. 1. The Senators and Representatives shall receive a Compensation for their Services, to be ascertained by Law, and paid out of the Treasury of the United States. They shall in all Cases, except Treason, Felony, and Breach of the Peace, be privileged from arrest during their Attendance at the Session of their respective Houses, and in going to and returning from the same; and for any Speech or Debate in either House, they shall not be questioned in any other Place.

2. No Senator or Representative shall, during the Time for which he was elected, be appointed to any civil office under the Authority of the United States, which shall have been created, or the Emoluments whereof shall have been increased, during such time; and no Person holding any Office under the United States shall be a Member of either House during his continuance in Office.

Section 7. 1. All Bills for raising Revenue shall originate in the House of Representatives; but the Senate may propose or concur with Amendments as on other bills.

2. Every Bill which shall have passed the House of Representatives and the Senate, shall, before it become a Law, be presented to the President of the United States; If he approve he shall sign it, but if not he shall return it, with his Objections, to that House in which it shall have originated, who shall enter the Objections at large on their journal, and proceed to reconsider it. If after such Reconsideration two thirds of that House shall agree to pass the bill, it shall be sent, together with the objections, to the other House, by which it shall likewise be reconsidered, and if approved by two thirds of that House, it shall become a Law. But in all such Cases the Votes of both Houses shall be determined by Yeas and Nays, and the Names of the Persons voting for and against the Bill shall be entered on the journal of each House re-

spectively. If any Bill shall not be returned by the President within ten Days (Sundays excepted) after it shall have been presented to him, the Same shall be a Law, in like Manner as if he had signed it, unless the Congress by their Adjournment prevent its Return, in which Case it shall not be a Law.

3. Every Order, Resolution, or Vote to which the Concurrence of the Senate and House of Representatives may be necessary (except on a question of Adjournment) shall be presented to the President of the United States; and before the Same shall take Effect, shall be approved by him, or being disapproved by him, shall be repassed by two thirds of the Senate and House of Representatives, according to the Rules and Limitations prescribed in the Case of a Bill.

Section 8. The Congress shall have Power

1. To lay and collect Taxes, Duties, Imposts and Excises, to pay the Debts and provide for the common Defense and general Welfare of the United States; but all Duties, Imposts and Excises shall be uniform throughout the United States;

2. To borrow money on the credit of the United States;

3. To regulate Commerce with foreign Nations, and among the several States, and with the Indian Tribes;

4. To establish an uniform Rule of Naturalization, and uniform Laws on the subject of Bankruptcies throughout the United States;

5. To coin Money, regulate the Value thereof, and of foreign Coin, and fix the Standard of Weights and Measures;

6. To provide for the Punishment of counterfeiting the Securities and current Coin of the United States;

7. To establish Post offices and post Roads;

8. To promote the Progress of Science and useful Arts, by securing for limited Times to Authors and inventors the exclusive Right to their respective Writings and Discoveries;

9. To constitute Tribunals inferior to the Supreme Court;

10. To define and punish Piracies and Felonies committed on the high Seas, and Offences against the Law of Nations;

11. To declare War, grant Letters of Marque and Reprisal, and make Rules concerning Captures on Land and Water;

12. To raise and support Armies, but no Appropriation of Money to that Use shall be for a longer Term than two Years;

13. To provide and maintain a Navy;

14. To make Rules for the Government and Regulation of the land and naval forces;

15. To provide for calling forth the Militia to execute the Laws of the Union, suppress Insurrections and repel invasions;

16. To provide for organizing, arming, and disciplining the Militia, and for governing such Part of them as may be employed in the Service of the United States, reserving to the States respectively, the Appointment of the Officers, and the Authority of training the Militia according to the discipline prescribed by Congress;

17. To exercise exclusive Legislation in all Cases whatsoever, over such District (not exceeding ten Miles square) as may, by Cession of particular States, and the acceptance of Congress, become the Seat of Government of the United States, and to exercise like Authority over all Places purchased by the Consent of the Legislature of the State in which the Same shall be, for the Erection of Forts, Magazines, Arsenals, dock Yards, and other needful Buildings; And

18. To make all Laws which shall be necessary and proper for carrying into Execution the foregoing Powers, and all other Powers vested by this Constitution in the government of the United States, or in any Department or Officer thereof.

Section 9. 1. The Migration or Importation of such Persons as any of the States now existing shall think proper to admit, shall not be prohibited by the Congress prior to the Year one thousand eight hundred and eight, but a tax or duty may be imposed on such Importation, not exceeding ten dollars for each Person.

2. The Privilege of the Writ of Habeas Corpus shall not be suspended, unless when in Cases of Rebellion or Invasion the public Safety may require it.

3. No Bill of Attainder or ex post facto Law shall be passed.

4. No capitation, or other direct, Tax shall be laid unless in Proportion to the Census or Enumeration herein before directed to be taken.[5]

5. No Tax or Duty shall be laid on Articles exported from any State.

6. No Preference shall be given by any Regulation of commerce or Revenue to the Ports of one State over those of

---

[5] See the Sixteenth Amendment.

another: nor shall Vessels bound to, or from, one state, be obliged to enter, clear, or pay Duties in another.

7. No Money shall be drawn from the Treasury, but in Consequence of Appropriations made by Law; and a regular Statement and Account of the Receipts and Expenditures of all public Money shall be published from time to time.

8. No Title of Nobility shall be granted by the United States: And no Person holding any Office of Profit or Trust under them, shall, without the Consent of the Congress, accept of any present, Emolument, Office, or Title, of any kind whatever, from any King, Prince, or Foreign State.

Section 10. 1. No State shall enter into any Treaty, Alliance, or Confederation; grant Letters of Marque and Reprisal; coin Money; emit Bills of Credit; make any Thing but gold and silver Coin a Tender in Payment of Debts; pass any Bill of Attainder, ex post facto Law, or Law impairing the obligation of Contracts, or grant any Title of Nobility.

2. No State shall, without the Consent of the Congress, lay any Imposts or Duties on Imports or Exports, except what may be absolutely necessary for executing its inspection Laws: and the net Produce of all Duties and Imposts, laid by any State on Imports or Exports, shall be for the Use of the Treasury of the United States; and all such Laws shall be subject to the Revision and Control of the Congress.

3. No State shall, without the Consent of Congress, lay any duty of Tonnage, keep Troops, or Ships of War in time of peace, enter into any Agreement or Compact with another State, or with a foreign Power, or engage in War, unless actually invaded, or in such imminent Danger as will not admit of delay.

Article II

Section 1. 1. The executive Power shall be vested in a President of the United States of America. He shall hold his Office during the Term of four Years, and, together with the Vice President, chosen for the same Term, be elected, as follows:

2. Each State shall appoint, in such Manner as the Legislature thereof may direct, a Number of Electors, equal to the whole Number of Senators and Representatives to which the State

may be entitled in the Congress; but no Senator or Representative, or Person holding an Office of Trust or Profit under the United States, shall be appointed an Elector.

The Electors shall meet in their respective States, and vote by Ballot for two persons, of whom one at least shall not be an Inhabitant of the same State with themselves. And they shall make a List of all the Persons voted for, and of the Number of Votes for each; which List they shall sign and certify, and transmit sealed to the Seat of the Government of the United States, directed to the President of the Senate. The President of the Senate shall, in the Presence of the Senate and House of Representatives, open all the Certificates, and the Votes shall then be counted. The Person having the greatest Number of Votes shall be the President, if such Number be a Majority of the whole Number of Electors appointed; and if there be more than one who have such Majority, and have an equal Number of Votes, then the House of Representatives shall immediately chuse by Ballot one of them for President; and if no Person have a Majority, then from the five highest on the List the said House shall in like Manner chuse the President. But in chusing the President, the votes shall be taken by States, the Representation from each State having one Vote; a quorum for this Purpose shall consist of a Member or Members from two thirds of the States, and a Majority of all the States shall be necessary to a Choice. In every Case, after the Choice of the President, the Person having the greatest Number of Votes of the Electors shall be the Vice President. But if there should remain two or more who have equal votes, the Senate shall chuse from them by Ballot the Vice President.[6]

3. The Congress may determine the time of chusing the Electors, and the Day on which they shall give their Votes; which Day shall be the same throughout the United States.

4. No person except a natural born Citizen, or a Citizen of the United States, at the time of the Adoption of this Constitution, shall be eligible to the Office of President; neither shall any Person be eligible to that office who shall not have attained to the Age of thirty-five Years, and been fourteen Years a Resident within the United States.

5. In Case of the Removal of the President from Office, or

---

[6] Superseded by the Twelfth Amendment.

of his Death, Resignation, or Inability to discharge the Powers and Duties of the said Office, the same shall devolve on the Vice President, and the Congress may by Law provide for the Case of Removal, Death, Resignation, or Inability, both of the President and Vice President, declaring what Officer shall then act as President, and such Officer shall act accordingly, until the Disability be removed, or a President shall be elected.

6. The President shall, at stated Times, receive for his Services a Compensation, which shall neither be increased nor diminished during the Period for which he shall have been elected, and he shall not receive within that Period any other Emolument from the United States, or any of them.

7. Before he enter on the execution of his Office, he shall take the following Oath or Affirmation: "I do solemnly swear (or affirm) that I will faithfully execute the Office of President of the United States, and will, to the best of my Ability, preserve, protect, and defend the Constitution of the United States."

Section 2. 1. The President shall be Commander in Chief of the Army and Navy of the United States, and of the Militia of the several States, when called into the actual Service of the United States; he may require the Opinion, in writing, of the principal Officer in each of the executive Departments, upon any subject relating to the Duties of their respective Offices, and he shall have Power to Grant Reprieves and Pardons for Offences against the United States, except in Cases of Impeachment.

2. He shall have Power, by and with the Advice and Consent of the Senate, to make Treaties, provided two thirds of the Senators present concur; and he shall nominate, and by and with the Advice and Consent of the Senate, shall appoint Ambassadors, other public Ministers and Consuls, judges of the supreme Court, and all other Officers of the United States, whose Appointments are not herein otherwise provided for, and which shall be established by Law: but the Congress may by Law vest the Appointment of such inferior Officers, as they think proper, in the President alone, in the Courts of Law, or in the Heads of Departments.

3. The President shall have Power to fill up all Vacancies that may happen during the Recess of the Senate, by granting Commissions which shall expire at the End of their next Session.

Section 3. He shall from time to time give to the Congress Information of the State of the Union, and recommend to their Consideration such Measures as he shall judge necessary and expedient; he may, on extraordinary occasions, convene both Houses, or either of them, and in Case of Disagreement between them, with respect to the Time of Adjournment, he may adjourn them to such Time as he shall think proper; he shall receive Ambassadors and other public Ministers; he shall take Care that the Laws be faithfully executed, and shall Commission all the officers of the United States.

Section 4. The President, Vice President and all civil Officers of the United States, shall be removed from Office on Impeachment for, and Conviction of, Treason, Bribery, or other high Crimes and Misdemeanors.

Article III

Section 1. The judicial Power of the United States, shall be vested in one supreme Court, and in such inferior Courts as the Congress may from time to time ordain and establish. The judges, both of the supreme and inferior Courts, shall hold their Offices during good Behaviour, and shall, at stated Times, receive for their Services, a Compensation, which shall not be diminished during their Continuance in Office.

Section 2. 1. The judicial Power shall extend to all Cases, in Law and Equity, arising under this Constitution, the Laws of the United States, and treaties made, or which shall be made, under their Authority;—to all Cases affecting Ambassadors, other public ministers and consuls; to all cases of admiralty and maritime jurisdiction;—to Controversies to which the United States shall be a party;[7]—to Controversies between two or more States; between a State and citizens of another States;—between Citizens of different States;—between Citizens of the same State claiming Lands under Grants of different States, and between a State, or the Citizens thereof, and foreign States, Citizens or Subjects.

[7] See the Eleventh Amendment.

2. In all Cases affecting Ambassadors, other public Ministers and Consuls, and those in which a State shall be Party, the supreme Court shall have original Jurisdiction. In all the other Cases before mentioned, the supreme Court shall have appellate jurisdiction, both as to Law and Fact, with such Exceptions, and under such Regulations as the Congress shall make.

3. The trial of all Crimes, except in Cases of Impeachment, shall be by jury; and such Trial shall be held in the State where the said Crimes shall have been committed; but when not committed within any State, the trial shall be at such Place or Places as the Congress may by Law have directed.

Section 3. 1. Treason against the United States, shall consist only in levying War against them, or in adhering to their Enemies, giving them Aid and Comfort. No Person shall be convicted of Treason unless on the testimony of two Witnesses to the same overt Act, or on Confession in open Court.

2. The Congress shall have power to declare the Punishment of Treason, but no Attainder of Treason shall work Corruption of Blood, or Forfeiture except during the Life of the Person attainted.

Article IV

Section 1. Full Faith and Credit shall be given in each State to the public Acts, Records, and judicial Proceedings of every other State. And the Congress may by general Laws prescribe the Manner in which such Acts, Records and Proceedings shall be proved, and the Effect thereof.

Section 2. 1. The Citizens of each State shall be entitled to all Privileges and Immunities of Citizens in the several States.[8]

2. A Person charged in any State with Treason, Felony, or other Crime, who shall flee from justice, and be found in another State, shall on demand of the executive Authority of the State from which he fled, be delivered up, to be removed to the State having jurisdiction of the crime.

3. No Person held to Service or Labour in one State, under the Laws thereof, escaping into another, shall, in Consequence of any Law or Regulation therein, be discharged from such Service or Labour, but shall be delivered up on Claim of the Party to whom such Service or Labour may be due.[9]

Section 3. 1. New States may be admitted by the Congress into this Union; but no new State shall be formed or erected within the Jurisdiction of any other State, nor any State be formed by the junction of two or more States, or parts of States, without the Consent of the Legislatures of the States concerned as well as of the Congress.

2. The Congress shall have Power to dispose of and make all needful Rules and Regulations respecting the Territory or other Property belonging to the United States; and nothing in this Constitution shall be so construed as to Prejudice any Claims of the United States, or of any particular State.

Section 4. The United States shall guarantee to every State in this Union a Republican Form of Government, and shall protect each of them against Invasion; and on Application of the Legislature, or of the Executive (when the Legislature cannot be convened) against domestic Violence.

Article V

The Congress, whenever two-thirds of both Houses shall deem it necessary, shall propose Amendments to this Constitution, or, on the Application of the Legislatures of two-thirds of the several States, shall call a Convention for proposing Amendments, which, in either Case, shall be valid to all Intents and Purposes, as part of this Constitution, when ratified by the Legislatures of three-fourths of the several States, or by Conventions in three-fourths thereof, as the one or the other Mode of Ratification may be proposed by the Congress; Provided that no Amendment which may be made prior to the Year One thousand eight hundred and eight shall in any Manner affect the first and fourth Clauses in the Ninth Section of the first Article; and that no State, without its Consent, shall be deprived of its equal Suffrage in the Senate.

Article VI

1. All Debts contracted and Engagements entered into, before the Adoption of this Constitution, shall be as valid against the United States under this Constitution, as under the Confederation.[10]

---

[8] See the Fourteenth Amendment, Section 1.

[9] See the Thirteenth Amendment

[10] See the Fourteenth Amendment, Sec. 4..

2. This Constitution, and the Laws of the United States which shall be made in Pursuance thereof; and all Treaties made, or which shall be made, under the Authority of the United States, shall be the supreme Law of the Land; and the judges in every State shall be bound thereby, any Thing in the Constitution or Laws of any State to the Contrary notwithstanding.

3. The Senators and Representatives before mentioned, and the Members of the several State Legislatures and all executive and judicial Officers, both of the United States and of the several States, shall be bound by Oath or Affirmation, to support this Constitution; but no religious Test shall ever be required as a qualification to any Office or public Trust under the United States.

Article VII

The Ratification of the Conventions of nine States, shall be sufficient for the Establishment of this Constitution between the States so ratifying the same.

Done in Convention by the Unanimous Consent of the States present the Seventeenth Day of September in the Year of our Lord one thousand seven hundred and Eighty seven, and of the independence of the United States of America the Twelfth. In Witness whereof We have hereunto subscribed our Names.

[Names omitted]

* * *

Articles in addition to, and amendment of, the Constitution of the United States of America, proposed by Congress, and ratified by the legislatures of the several States, pursuant to the fifth article of the original Constitution.

Amendment I

[December 15, 1791]

Congress shall make no law respecting an establishment of religion, or prohibiting the free exercise thereof, or abridging the freedom of speech, or of the press; or the right of the people peaceably to assemble, and to petition the Government for a redress of grievances.

Amendment II

[December 15, 1791]

A well regulated Militia, being necessary to the security of a free State, the right of the people to keep and bear Arms shall not be infringed.

Amendment III

[December 15, 1791]

No Soldier shall, in time of peace, be quartered in any house, without the consent of the owner, nor in time of war, but in a manner to be prescribed by law.

Amendment IV

[December 15, 1791]

The right of the people to be secure in their persons, houses, papers, and effects, against unreasonable searches and seizures, shall not be violated, and no Warrants shall issue, but upon probable cause, supported by Oath or affirmation, and particularly describing the place to be searched, and the persons or things to be seized.

Amendment V

[December 15, 1791]

No person shall be held to answer for a capital or otherwise infamous crime, unless on a presentment or indictment of a Grand jury, except in cases arising in the land or naval forces, or in the Militia, when in actual service in time of War or public danger; nor shall any person be subject for the same offence to be twice put in jeopardy of life or limb; nor shall be compelled in any criminal case to be a witness against himself, nor be deprived of life, liberty, or property, without due process of law; nor shall private property be taken for public use, without just compensation.

Amendment VI

[December 15, 1791]

In all criminal prosecutions, the accused shall enjoy the right to a speedy and public trial, by an impartial jury of the State and district wherein the crime shall have been committed, which district shall have been previously ascertained by law, and to be informed of the nature and cause of the accusation; to be confronted with the witnesses against him; to have compulsory process for obtaining witnesses in his favor, and to have the Assistance of Counsel for his defense.

Amendment VII

[December 15, 1791]

In suits at common law, where the value in controversy shall exceed twenty dollars, the right of trial by jury shall be preserved, and no fact tried by a jury, shall be otherwise reexamined in any Court of the United States, than according to the rules of the common law.

Amendment VIII

[December 15, 1791]

Excessive bail shall not be required, nor excessive fines imposed, nor cruel and unusual punishments inflicted.

Amendment IX

[December 15, 1791]

The enumeration in the Constitution, of certain rights, shall not be construed to deny or disparage others retained by the people.

Amendment X

[December 15, 1791]

The powers not delegated to the United States by the Constitution, nor prohibited by it to the States, are reserved to the States respectively, or to the people.

Amendment XI

[January 8, 1798]

The judicial power of the United States shall not be construed to extend to any suit in law or equity, commenced or prosecuted against one of the United States by Citizens of another State, or by Citizens or Subjects of any Foreign State.

Amendment XII

[September 25, 1804]

The Electors shall meet in their respective States and vote by ballot for President and Vice-President, one of whom, at least, shall not be an inhabitant of the same State with themselves; they shall name in their ballots the person voted for as President, and in distinct ballots the person voted for as Vice-President, and they shall make distinct lists of all persons voted for as President, and of all persons voted for as Vice-President, and of the number of votes for each, which lists they shall sign and certify, and transmit sealed to the seat of the government of the United States, directed to the President of the Senate; The President of the Senate shall, in the presence of the Senate and House of Representatives, open all the certificates and the votes shall then be counted; The person having the greatest number of votes for President, shall be the President, if such number be a majority of the whole number of Electors appointed; and if no person have such majority, then from the persons having the highest numbers not exceeding three on the list of those voted for as President, the House of Representatives shall choose immediately, by ballot, the President. But in choosing the President, the votes shall be taken by states, the representation from each state having one vote; a quorum for this purpose shall consist of a member or members from two-thirds of the states, and a majority of all the states shall be necessary to a choice. And if the House of Representatives shall not choose a President whenever the right of choice shall devolve upon them, before the fourth day of March next following, then the Vice-President shall act as President, as in the case of the death or other constitutional disability of the President. The person having the greatest number of votes as Vice President, shall be the

Vice-President, if such number be a majority of the whole number of Electors appointed, and if no person have a majority, then from the two highest numbers on the list, the Senate shall choose the Vice-President; a quorum for the purpose shall consist of two-thirds of the whole number of Senators, and a majority of the whole number shall be necessary to a choice. But no person constitutionally ineligible to the office of President shall be eligible to that of Vice-President of the United States.

Amendment XIII

[December 18, 1865]

Section 1. Neither slavery nor involuntary servitude, except as a punishment for crime whereof the party shall have been duly convicted, shall exist within the United States, or any place subject to their jurisdiction.

Section 2. Congress shall have power to enforce this article by appropriate legislation.

Amendment XIV

[July 28, 1868]

Section 1. All persons born or naturalized in the United States, and subject to the jurisdiction thereof, are citizens of the United States and of the State wherein they reside. No State shall make or enforce any law which shall abridge the privileges or immunities of citizens of the United States; nor shall any State deprive any person of life, liberty, or property, without due process of law; nor deny to any person within its jurisdiction the equal protection of the laws.

Section 2. Representatives shall be apportioned among the several States according to their respective numbers, counting the whole number of persons in each State, excluding Indians not taxed. But when the right to vote at any election for the choice of electors for President and Vice-President of the United States, Representatives in Congress, the Executive and Judicial officers of a State, or the members of the Legislature thereof, is denied to any of the male inhabitants of such State, being twenty-one years of age, and citizens of the United States, or in any way abridged, except for participation in rebellion, or other crime, the basis of representation therein shall be reduced in the proportion which the number of such male citizens shall bear to the whole number of male citizens twenty-one years of age in such State.

Section 3. No person shall be a Senator or Representative in Congress, or elector of President and Vice-President, or hold any office, civil or military, under the United States, or under any State, who, having previously taken an oath, as a member of Congress, or as an officer of the United States, or as a member of any State legislature, or as an executive or judicial officer of any State, to support the Constitution of the United States, shall have engaged in insurrection or rebellion against the same, or given aid or comfort to the enemies thereof. But Congress may by a vote of two-thirds of each House, remove such disability.

Section 4. The validity of the public debt of the United States, authorized by law, including debts incurred for payment of pensions and bounties for services in suppressing insurrection or rebellion, shall not be questioned. But neither the United States nor any State shall assume or pay any debt or obligation incurred in aid of insurrection or rebellion against the United States, or any claim for the loss or emancipation of any slave; but all such debts, obligations, and claims shall be held illegal and void.

Section 5. The Congress shall have the power to enforce, by appropriate legislation, the provisions of this article.

Amendment XV

[March 30, 1870]

Section 1. The right of citizens of the United States to vote shall not be denied or abridged by the United States or by any State on account of race, color, or previous condition of servitude

Section 2. The Congress shall have power to enforce this article by appropriate legislation.

Amendment XVI

[February 25, 1913]

The Congress shall have power to lay and collect taxes on incomes, from whatever source derived, without apportionment among the several States, and without regard to any census or enumeration.

Amendment XVII

[May 31, 1913]

The Senate of the United States shall be composed of two Senators from each State, elected by the people thereof, for six years; and each Senator shall have one vote. The electors in each State shall have the qualifications requisite for electors of the most numerous branch of the State legislatures.

When vacancies happen in the representation of any State in the Senate, the executive authority of such State shall issue writs of election to fill such vacancies: Provided, That the legislature of any State may empower the executive thereof to make temporary appointments until the people fill the vacancies by election as the legislature may direct.

This amendment shall not be so construed as to affect the election or term of any Senator chosen before it becomes valid as part of the Constitution.

Amendment XVIII

[January 29, 1919]

Section 1. After one year from the ratification of this article the manufacture, sale, or transportation of intoxicating liquors within, the importation thereof into, or the exportation thereof from the United States and all territory subject to the jurisdiction thereof for beverage purposes is hereby prohibited.

Section 2. The Congress and the several States shall have concurrent power to enforce this article by appropriate legislation.

Section 3. This article shall be inoperative unless it shall have been ratified as an amendment to the Constitution by the legislatures of the several States, as provided in the Constitution, within seven years from the date of the submission hereof to the States by the Congress.

Amendment XIX

[August 26, 1920]

The right of citizens of the United States to vote shall not be denied or abridged by the United States or by any State on account of sex.

Congress shall have power to enforce this article by appropriate legislation.

Amendment XX

[January 23, 1933]

Section 1. The terms of the President and Vice-President shall end at noon on the 20th day of January, and the terms of Senators and Representatives at noon on the 3d day of January, of the years in which such terms would have ended if this article had not been ratified; and the terms of their successors shall then begin.

Section 2. The Congress shall assemble at least once in every year, and such meeting shall begin at noon on the 3rd day of January, unless they shall by law appoint a different day.

Section 3. If, at the time fixed for the beginning of the term of the President, the President elect shall have died, the Vice-President elect shall become President. If a President shall not have been chosen before the time fixed for the beginning of his term, or if the President elect shall have failed to qualify, then the Vice-President elect shall act as President until a President shall have qualified; and the Congress may by law provide for the case wherein neither a President elect nor a Vice-President elect shall have qualified, declaring who shall then act as President, or the manner in which one who is to act shall be selected, and such person shall act accordingly until a President or Vice-President shall have qualified.

Section 4. The Congress may by law provide for the case of the death of any of the persons from whom the House of Representatives may choose a President whenever the right of choice shall have devolved upon them, and for the case of the death of any of the persons from whom the Senate may choose a Vice-President whenever the right of choice shall have devolved upon them.

Section 5. Sections 1 and 2 shall take effect on the 15th day of October following the ratification of this article.

Section 6. This article shall be inoperative unless it shall have been ratified as an amendment to the Constitution by the legislatures of three-fourths of the several States within seven years from the date of its submission.

Amendment XXI

[December 5, 1933]

Section 1. The eighteenth article of amendment to the Constitution of the United States is hereby repealed.

Section 2. The transportation or importation into any State, Territory, or possession of the United States for delivery or use therein of intoxicating liquors, in violation of the laws thereof, is hereby prohibited.

Section 3. This article shall be inoperative unless it shall have been ratified as an amendment to the Constitution by conventions in the several States, as provided in the Constitution, within seven years from the date of the submission hereof to the States by the Congress.

Amendment XXII

[March 1, 1951]

Section 1. No person shall be elected to the office of the President more than twice, and no person who has held the office of President, or acted as President, for more than two years of a term to which some other person was elected President shall be elected to the office of the President more than once.

But this Article shall not apply to any person holding the office of President when this Article was proposed by the Congress, and shall not prevent any person who may be holding the office of President or acting as President, during the term within which this Article becomes operative from holding the office of President or acting as President during the remainder of such term.

Section 2. This article shall be inoperative unless it shall have been ratified as an amendment to the Constitution by the legislatures of three-fourths of the several states within seven years from the date of its submission to the states by Congress.

Amendment XXIII

[March 29, 1961]

Section 1. The District constituting the seat of Government of the United States shall appoint in such manner as the Congress may direct:

A number of electors of President and Vice President equal to the whole number of Senators and Representa-

tives in Congress to which the District would be entitled if it were a State, but in no event more than the least populous State; they shall be in addition to those appointed by the States, but they shall be considered, for the purposes of the election of President and Vice President, to be electors appointed by a State; and they shall meet in the District and perform such duties as provided by the twelfth article of amendment.

Section 2. The Congress shall have power to enforce this article by appropriate legislation.

Amendment XXIV

[January 23, 1964]

Section 1. The right of citizens of the United States to vote in any primary or other election for President or Vice President, for electors for President or Vice President, or for Senator or Representative in Congress, shall not be denied or abridged by the United States or any State by reason of failure to pay any poll tax or other tax.

Section 2. The Congress shall have the power to enforce this article by appropriate legislation.

Amendment XXV

[February 10, 1967]

Section 1. In case of the removal of the President from office or of his death or resignation, the Vice President shall become President.

Section 2. Whenever there is a vacancy in the office of the Vice President, the President shall nominate a Vice President who shall take office upon confirmation by a majority vote of both houses of Congress.

Section 3. Whenever the President transmits to the President pro tempore of the Senate and the Speaker of the House of Representatives his written declaration that he is unable to discharge the powers and duties of his office, and until he transmits to them a written declaration to the contrary, such powers and duties shall be discharged by the Vice President as Acting President.

Section 4. Whenever the Vice President and a majority of either the principal officers of the executive departments, or of such other body as Congress may by law provide, transmit to the

President pro tempore of the Senate and the Speaker of the House of Representatives their written declaration that the President is unable to discharge the powers and duties of his office, the Vice President shall immediately assume the powers and duties of the office as Acting President.

Thereafter, when the President transmits to the President pro tempore of the Senate and the Speaker of the House of Representatives his written declaration that no inability exists, he shall resume the powers and duties of his office unless the Vice President and a majority of either the principal officers of the executive departments, or of such other body as Congress may by law provide, transmit within four days to the President pro tempore of the Senate and the Speaker of the House of Representatives their written declaration that the President is unable to discharge the powers and duties of his office. Thereupon Congress shall decide the issue, assembling within forty-eight hours for that purpose if not in session. If the Congress, within twenty-one days after receipt of the latter written declaration, or, if Congress is not in session, within twenty-one days after Congress is required to assemble, determines by two-thirds vote of both houses that the President is unable to discharge the powers and duties of his

office, the Vice President shall continue to discharge the same as Acting President; otherwise, the President shall resume the powers and duties of his office.

Amendment XXVI

[June 30, 1971]

Section 1. The right of citizens of the United States, who are eighteen years of age or older, to vote shall not be denied or abridged by the United States or by any state on account of age.

Section 2. The Congress shall have power to enforce this article by appropriate legislation.

Amendment XXVII

[May 7, 1992]

No law varying the compensation for the services of the Senators and Representatives shall take effect, until an election of Representatives shall have intervened.

PRESIDENTIAL ELECTIONS

YEAR	NUMBER OF STATES	CANDIDATES	PARTY	POPULAR VOTE*	ELECTORAL VOTE**	PERCENTAGE OF POPULAR VOTE
1789	11	GEORGE WASHINGTON	No party designations		69	
		John Adams			34	
		Other Candidates			35	
1792	15	GEORGE WASHINGTON	No party designations		132	
		John Adams			77	
		George Clinton			50	
		Other Candidates			5	
1796	16	JOHN ADAMS	Federalist		71	
		Thomas Jefferson	Democratic-Republican		68	
		Thomas Pinckney	Federalist		59	
		Aaron Burr	Democratic-Republican		30	
		Other Candidates			48	
1800	16	THOMAS JEFFERSON	Democratic-Republican		73	
		Aaron Burr	Democratic-Republican		73	
		John Adams	Federalist		65	
		Charles C. Pinckney	Federalist		64	
		John Jay	Federalist			
1804	17	THOMAS JEFFERSON	Democratic-Republican		162	
		Charles C. Pinckney	Federalist		14	
1808	17	JAMES MADISON	Democratic-Republican		122	
		Charles C. Pinckney	Federalist		47	
		George Clinton	Democratic-Republican		6	
1812	18	JAMES MADISON	Democratic-Republican		128	
		DeWitt Clinton	Federalist		89	
1816	19	JAMES MONROE	Democratic-Republican		183	
		Rufus King	Federalist		34	
1820	24	JAMES MONROE	Democratic-Republican		231	
		John Quincy Adams	Independent Republican		1	
1824	24	JOHN QUINCY ADAMS		108,740	84	30.5
		Andrew Jackson		153,544	99	43.1
		William H. Crawford		46,618	41	13.1
		Henry Clay		47,136	37	13.2
1828	24	ANDREW JACKSON	Democrat	647,286	178	56.0
		John Ouincy Adams	National Republican	508,064	83	44.0
1832	24	ANDREW JACKSON	Democrat	687,502	219	55.0
		Henry Clay	National Republican	530,189	49	42.4
		William Wirt	Anti-Masonic	33,108	7	2.6
		John Floyd	National Republican		11	
1836	26	MARTIN VAN BUREN	Democrat	765,483	170	50.9
		William H. Harrison	Whig		73	
		Hugh L. White	Whig	739,795	26	49.1
		Daniel Webster	Whig		14	
		W. P. Mangum	Whig		11	
1840	26	WILLIAM H. HARRISON	Whig	1,274,624	234	53.1
		Martin Van Buren	Democrat	1,127,781	60	46.9
1844	26	JAMES K. POLK	Democrat	1,338,464	170	49.6
		Henry Clay	Whig	1,300,097	105	48.1
		James G. Birney	Liberty	62,300		2.3
1848	30	ZACHARY TAYLOR	Whig	1,360,967	163	47.4
		Lewis Cass	Democrat	1,222,342	127	42.5
		Martin Van Buren	Free Soil	291,263		10.1
1852	31	FRANKLIN PIERCE	Democrat	1,601,117	254	50.9
		Winfield Scott	Whig	1,385,453	42	44.1
		John P. Hale	Free Soil	155,825		5.0

* Percentage of popular vote given for any election year may not total 100 percent because candidates receiving less than 1 percent of the popular vote have been omitted.

** Prior to the passage of the Twelfth Amendment in 1904, the electoral college voted for two presidential candidates; the runner-up became Vice President. Data from *Historical Statistics of the United States, Colonial Times to 1957* (1961), pp. 682–883, and *The World Almanac.*

PRESIDENTIAL ELECTIONS *(continued)*

YEAR	NUMBER OF STATES	CANDIDATES	PARTY	POPULAR VOTE*	ELECTORAL VOTE**	PERCENTAGE OF POPULAR VOTE
1856	31	JAMES BUCHANAN	Democrat	1,832,955	174	45.3
		John C. Frémont	Republican	1,339,932	114	33.1
		Millard Fillmore	American	871,731	8	21.6
1860	33	ABRAHAM LINCOLN	Republican	1,865,593	180	39.8
		Stephen A. Douglas	Democrat	1,382,713	12	29.5
		John C. Breckinridge	Democrat	848,356	72	18.1
		John Bell	Constitutional Union	592,906	39	12.6
1864	36	ABRAHAM LINCOLN	Republican	2,206,938	212	55.0
		George B. McClellan	Democrat	1,803,787	21	45.0
1868	37	ULYSSES S. GRANT	Republican	3,013,421	214	52.7
		Horatio Seymour	Democrat	2,706,829	80	47.3
1872	37	ULYSSES S. GRANT	Republican	3,596,745	286	55.6
		Horace Greeley	Democrat	2,843,446	*	43.9
1876	38	RUTHERFORD B. HAYES	Republican	4,036,572	185	48.0
		Samuel J. Tilden	Democrat	4,284,020	184	51.0
1880	38	JAMES A. GARFIELD	Republican	4,453,295	214	48.5
		Winfield S. Hancock	Democrat	4,414,082	155	48.1
		James B. Weaver	Greenback-Labor	308,578		3.4
1884	38	GROVER CLEVELAND	Democrat	4,879,507	219	48.5
		James G. Blaine	Republican	4,850,293	182	48.2
		Benjamin F. Butler	Greenback-Labor	175,370		1.8
		John P. St. John	Prohibition	150,369		1.5.
1888	38	BENJAMIN HARRISON	Republican	5,447,129	233	47.9
		Grover Cleveland	Democrat	5,537,857	168	48.6
		Clinton B. Fisk	Prohibition	249,506		2.2
		Anson J. Streeter	Union Labor	146,935		1.3
1892	44	GROVER CLEVELAND	Democrat	5,555,426	277	46.1
		Benjamin Harrison	Republican	5,182,690	145	43.0
		James B. Weaver	People's	1,029,846	22	8.5
		John Bidwell	Prohibition	264,133		2.2
1896	45	WILLIAM MCKINLEY	Republican	7,102,246	271	51.1
		William J. Bryan	Democrat	6,492,559	176	47.7
1900	45	WILLIAM MCKINLEY	Republican	7,218,491	292	51.7
		William J. Bryan	Democrat; Populist	6,356,734	155	45.5
		John C. Woolley	Prohibition	208,914		1.5
1904	45	THEODORE ROOSEVELT	Republican	7,628,461	336	57.4
		Alton B. Parker	Democrat	5,084,223	140	37.6
		Eugene V. Debs	Socialist	402,283		3.0
		Silas C. Swallow	Prohibition	258,536		1.9
1908	46	WILLIAM H. TAFT	Republican	7,675,320	321	51.6
		William J. Bryan	Democrat	6,412,294	162	43.1
		Eugene V. Debs	Socialist	420,793		2.8
		Eugene W. Chafin	Prohibition	253,840		1.7
1912	48	WOODROW WILSON	Democrat	6,296,547	435	41.9
		Theodore Roosevelt	Progressive	4,118,571	88	27.4
		William H. Taft	Republican	3,486,720	8	23.2
		Eugene V. Debs	Socialist	900,672		6.0
		Eugene W. Chafin	Prohibition	206,275		1.4
1916	48	WOODROW WILSON	Democrat	9,127,695	277	49.4
		Charles E. Hughes	Republican	8,533,507	254	46.2
		A. L. Benson	Socialist	585,113		3.2
		J. Frank Hanly	Prohibition	220,506		1.2
1920	48	WARREN G. HARDING	Republican	16,143,407	404	60.4
		James M. Cox	Democrat	9,130,328	127	34.2
		Eugene V. Debs	Socialist	919,799		3.4
		P. P. Christensen	Farmer-Labor	265,411		1.0

*Because of the death of Greeley, Democratic electors scattered their votes.

PRESIDENTIAL ELECTIONS *(continued)*

YEAR	NUMBER OF STATES	CANDIDATES	PARTY	POPULAR VOTE*	ELECTORAL VOTE**	PERCENTAGE OF POPULAR VOTE
1924	48	CALVIN COOLIDGE	Republican	15,718,211	382	54.0
		John W. Davis	Democrat	8,385,283	136	28.8
		Robert M. La Follette	Progressive	4,831,289	13	16.6
1928	48	HERBERT C. HOOVER	Republican	21,391,993	444	58.2
		Alfred E. Smith	Democrat	15,016,169	87	40.9
1932	48	FRANKLIN D. ROOSEVELT	Democrat	22,809,638	472	57.4
		Herbert C. Hoover	Republican	15,758,901	59	39.7
		Norman Thomas	Socialist	881,951		2.2
1936	48	FRANKLIN D. ROOSEVELT	Democrat	27,752,869	523	60.8
		Alfred M. Landon	Republican	16,674,665	8	36.5
		William Lemke	Union	882,479		1.9
1940	48	FRANKLIN D. ROOSEVELT	Democrat	27,307,819	449	54.8
		Wendell L. Wilkie	Republican	22,321,018	82	44.8
1944	48	FRANKLIN D. ROOSEVELT	Democrat	25,606,585	432	53.5
		Thomas E. Dewey	Republican	22,014,745	99	46.0
1948	48	HARRY S. TRUMAN	Democrat	24,105,812	303	49.5
		Thomas E. Dewey	Republican	21,970,065	189	45.1
		J. Strom Thurmond	States' Rights	1,169,063	39	2.4
		Henry A. Wallace	Progressive	1,157,172		2.4
1952	48	DWIGHT D. EISENHOWER	Republican	33,936,234	442	55.1
		Adlai E. Stevenson	Democrat	27,314,992	89	44.4
1956	48	DWIGHT D. EISENHOWER	Republican	35,590,472	457*	57.6
		Adlai E. Stevenson	Democrat	26,022,752	73	42.1
1960	50	JOHN F. KENNEDY	Democrat	34,227,096	303**	49.9
		Richard M. Nixon	Republican	34,108,546	219	49.6
1964	50	LYNDON B. JOHNSON	Democrat	42,676,220	486	61.3
		Barry M. Goldwater	Republican	26,860,314	52	38.5
1968	50	RICHARD M. NIXON	Republican	31,785,480	301	43.4
		Hubert H. Humphrey	Democrat	31,275,165	191	42.7
		George C. Wallace	American Independent	9,906,473	46	13.5
1972	50	RICHARD M. NIXON***	Republican	47,165,234	520	60.6
		George S. McGovern	Democrat	29,168,110	17	37.5
1976	50	JIMMY CARTER	Democrat	40,828,929	297	50.1
		Gerald R. Ford	Republican	39,148,940	240	47.9
		Eugene McCarthy	Independent	739,256		
1980	50	RONALD REAGAN	Republican	43,201,220	489	50.9
		Jimmy Carter	Democrat	34,913,332	49	41.2
		John B. Anderson	Independent	5,581,379		
1984	50	RONALD REAGAN	Republican	53,428,357	525	59.0
		Walter F. Mondale	Democrat	36,930,923	13	41.0
1988	50	GEORGE BUSH	Republican	48,901,046	426	53.4
		Michael Dukakis	Democrat	41,809,030	111	45.6
1992	50	WILLIAM J. CLINTON	Democrat	44,909,806	370	43.0
		George Bush	Republican	39,104,550	168	37.5
		H. Ross Perot	Independent	19,742,240		18.9
		Andre Marrau	Libertarian	291,631		0.3
1996	50	WILLIAM J. CLINTON	Democrat	47,402,357	379	49.2
		Robert Dole	Republican	39,198,755	159	40.7
		H. Ross Perot	Reform	8,085,402		8.4
		Ralph Nader	Green	685,128		0.7
		Harry Browne	Libertarian	485,798		0.5

*Walter B. Jones received 1 electoral vote.
**Harry F. Byrd received 15 electoral votes.
***Resigned August 9, 1974; Vice President Gerald R. Ford became President.

Appendix

PRESIDENTIAL ELECTIONS (continued)

YEAR	NUMBER OF STATES	CANDIDATES	PARTY	POPULAR VOTE*	ELECTORAL VOTE**	PERCENTAGE OF POPULAR VOTE
2000	50	GEORGE W. BUSH	Republican	50,459,624	271	47.9
		Albert Gore, Jr.	Democrat	51,003,238	266	48.4
		Ralph Nader	Green	2,882,985		2.7
		Patrick Buchanan	Reform	449,120		0.4
		Harry Browne	Libertarian	384,440		0.4
2004	50	GEORGE W. BUSH	Republican	62,040,610	286	58.9
		John F. Kerry	Democrat	59,028,111	251	56.1
		Ralph Nader	Independent/Reform	463,653		0.0
2008	50	BARACK OBAMA	Democrat	69,456,898	365	52.9
		John McCain	Republican	59,934,814	173	45.6
		Ralph Nader	Independent	738,771		0.6
		Bob Barr	Libertarian	523,686		0.4

Index

CPSIA information can be obtained at www.ICGtesting.com
Printed in the USA
268031BV00002B/2/P